MEASURES OF WISDOM
The Cosmic Dance in Classical and Christian Antiquity

'The interpretours of Plato,' wrote Sir Thomas Elyot in *The Governour* (1531), 'do think that the wonderful and incomprehensible order of the celestial bodies, I mean sterres and planettes, and their motions harmonicall, gave to them that intensifly and by the deepe serche of raison beholde their coursis, in the sondrye diversities of numbre and tyme, a forme of imitation of a semblable motion, which they called daunsinge or saltation.'

The image of the planets and stars engaged in an ordered and measured dance is an ancient one. Plato articulated it in a passage in the *Timaeus*, where he likened the apparent motions of the planets and stars to 'choreiai' (choral dances). Through the centuries the analogy has challenged Plato's interpreters to define and elaborate the image.

Miller has examined a range of poetic and philosophical texts influenced by Platonic cosmology, and has discovered frequent comparisons of the cosmic order to 'daunsinge.' He suggests that the vision of the cosmic dance did not develop at random in Western intellectual history but originated in a specific philosophical context and passed through stages of evolution that reflect Gnostic, Christian, Stoic, and Neoplatonic responses to Plato. He argues that the historical variations of the image were often closely related to adaptation or criticisms of Plato's theories of visual perception and intellectual vision.

The dance, in conjunction with images such as the Great Chain of Being and the Lyre of the Heavens, became the dominant image of a peculiarly Late Antique world-view which Miller (after Augustine) has called the 'poetic universe': a world where metaphors, metonymies, and personifications could exist in fact as well as in word.

The result of Miller's analysis is vast in scope. The nine chapters of the book each present a thesis on a particular author, but all function together like links in a chain. Miller has been described as 'an historian of visions'; the book has been likened to Auerbach's *Mimesis*. It is a remarkable contribution to an understanding of the complex interaction of ideas and images in time.

JAMES MILLER is Faculty of Arts Professor at the University of Western Ontario. He holds a joint appointment in the Departments of English, Classical Studies, and Philosophy.

Visio: Studies in the Relations of Art and Literature 1

General Editor: John Leyerle

James Miller

MEASURES OF WISDOM

The Cosmic Dance in Classical and Christian Antiquity

UNIVERSITY OF TORONTO PRESS

Toronto Buffalo London

© University of Toronto Press 1986
Toronto Buffalo London
Printed in Canada

ISBN 0-8020-2553-6

Printed on acid-free paper

Canadian Cataloguing in Publication Data

Miller, James L., 1951-

Measures of wisdom

(VISIO)
Bibliography: p.
Includes index.
ISBN 0-8020-2553-6

1. Cosmology, Ancient.   2. Civilization, Greek.
3. Civilization, Christian.   4. Dancing (in religion,
folklore, etc.)   I. Title.

BD495.M54   1986   113   C86-093264-8

Publication of this book has been made possible by grants from
the National Endowment for the Humanities,
the Hyder E. Rollins Publication Fund of Harvard University,
and the Publications Fund of University of Toronto Press.

for
John Leyerle

Contents

9

WINDING TOGETHER
Pseudo-Dionysius: *Divine Names* IV.8–10
483

Acknowledgments

'*The voices of individuals are hidden in a chorus while the voices of all are heard, and thus a harmony emerges ...* '
MACROBIUS, *In somnium Scipionis*, preface

Such harmony as may emerge from my work, which is essentially choral in character, will inevitably hide the voices of many friends, colleagues, and scholars who contributed to it in one way or another over the last decade. If I tried to thank each of them now by name, I suspect that the chorus as a whole would fall asleep or thunderously complain that my pre-curtain roll-call was holding up the show. So to all who instructed or encouraged me in the 'noera choreia' but whose names will not be mentioned here, let me express my gratitude in the form of a solemn promise that I shall personally drink your healths one by one (over several days) during the intermission between volumes.

A bacchic salute will not do for everyone, however, for there are several participants in this volume who also deserve a sober Apollonian nod of appreciation. I have the late Douglas Bush to thank for envisioning the figure of the dance as a subject worthy of extensive historical investigation. He it was who supplied both the idea and the inspiration for this study to his student, John Leyerle, who many years later as my thesis director passed them on to me along with a graduate essay of his own on the dance of order in the English Renaissance.

If Bush was the choragus of my work, Leyerle was (and still is) its coryphaeus. Without his critical coaching and visionary impetus I would have been content to execute wobbly little caprioles over the polished floor of textual scholarship. He challenged me to make bigger leaps – bigger certainly than I would ever have attempted on my own – into fields at some distance from my home territory in English literature, fields as forbidding to a literary soul as Neopythagorean harmonics and Gnostic Christology and Pseudo-Dionysian mysticism. At the same time he curbed my tendency to float off into the Intellectual Beyond by encouraging me to think imagistically rather than ideologically. Abstractions lure me like a bad angel, I confess, and with all the Neoplatonists urging me to abandon the world of the senses I could easily have lost sight of the dancers and spectators (my true focus) in passionless attempts to contemplate the Dance as an abstract order. Thanks to Leyerle, the chorus of poets is not drowned out in this volume by the chorus of philosophers.

A procession of wise chorodidaskaloi – scholars who instructed me in various specialized subjects relevant to this study – must be thanked for keeping me on my toes in places where I could easily have fallen on my face. John Rist (in person) and John Dillon (in print) initiated me into the mysteries of Neoplatonism. Walter Jackson Bate, Morton Bloomfield, Herschel Baker, Larry Benson, and David Perkins encouraged me to contribute to the Harvard tradition of scholarship in the History of Ideas. Jaroslav Pelikan, who read my final draft with critical incisiveness, sharpened my understanding of Nicene Orthodoxy and Cappadocian mysticism. Long walks around Christ Church meadows with Rowan Williams, who drew my attention to the apocryphal Hymn of Jesus, convinced me that the Logos was more than a mere word. To Joseph Owens and Edward Synan I owe my introduction to Lady Philosophy. Lady Philology I encountered in the person of Virginia Brown, without whose uplifting lessons on the ablative absolute my fallen intellect would not have survived the Latin of Martianus Capella. And my faith in the whole enterprise has been sustained from the start by Penelope Doob, whose extraordinary nine o'clock lectures on medieval poetry first awakened my interest in allegory and iconology.

I could not have finished the present volume without the generous financial support of the Canada Council, the American Council of Learned Societies, and the Institute for Research in the Humanities at the University of Wisconsin, Madison. The Institute (located, appropriately for my cosmic subject, in an old observatory) was a veritable sanctuary for me in my last year of writing. To Robert Kingdon, Philip Harth, Madeleine Doran, and the other senior fellows who made my leave year there so pleasant and productive, I send my thanks along with a new book for their library. I am also indebted to the National Endowment for the Humanities and the Committee on Administration of the Hyder Edward Rollins Fund at Harvard University for grants that have made possible the publication of my work.

Providence – or was it Divine Prudence? – was surely behind the selection of my editors at the University of Toronto Press. Given an impossibly long manuscript on everything under and over the sun, Prudence Tracy worked miracles with the daimones who govern the mutable world of scholarly publications. Long may she intercede for the Humanities in Canada! Judy Williams worked miracles on the manuscript itself by pruning the Golden Boughs off my prose and divining with sybilline skill what I meant to say in many an obscure passage.

A bare acknowledgment cannot express the warmth of my regard for all the friends and family members who kept my spirits up during my year of blindness and other dark periods in the early eighties. My special thanks to William and Martha Nell Hardy, Patricia Eberle, Andrew Delbanco, Elizabeth McKinsey, Albert von Frank, William Alfred, Jenny Goodman, Mary Fraker, Selma Odom, William Griffiths, Mark Mitchell, Anne and David Arredondo, Richard Green, David Wilson, and Thomas C. Collins. In these pages, I am sure, my mother Jean Miller will often hear the accent of my late father's voice.

For enduring countless bedtime monologues on the Neoplatonic spirit world, and for exorcising my array of cacodemons with unfailing courage, I finally thank my wife Melissa Hardy who (if I were an Orphic bard) would certainly be hailed as Pan's 'kallistē synchoreutēs'.

James Miller
24 October 1985

MEASURES OF WISDOM

The Cosmic Dance in Classical and Christian Antiquity

Foreword

Gathered together in this volume are the great spectators of the cosmic dance in Classical and Christian Antiquity. Compared with the imaginary spectators gathered round the Dedalian chorus on the Shield of Achilles (*Iliad* XVIII.604) the historical witnesses whom I have summoned here from different centuries to express their views on cosmic order and cultural harmony do not form a very harmonious or orderly crowd. Some of them prefer to admire the whole dance at a distance. Others insist on studying its tiniest details at close range. Still others eye its evolving configurations with contempt, fearing its power over their bodies or despising the poor souls caught up in it. And several, breaking free of the crowd, try to dance their way into the Great Chorus like enraptured Bacchants. All of them will tell us (with a little prompting) what they see or at least what they are looking for, and the more religious among them will explain how their eyes adjust to the darkness of the cosmic theatre and why their minds revel when their bodies rest. There are of course a few Cynics in the crowd who will laugh at the dance with the desperate conviction that it is a disaster of mistiming and miscasting, and through their eyes the ring of restless spectators will look like a bickering rabble of pretentious pundits and crack-brained mystagogues. Most Cynics, however, simply refuse to believe that there is a dance to be seen in the theatre of worldly illusions, and so they head for the nearest exits before the show has a chance to enchant them. The Skeptics abandon the crowd too, complaining as they stalk off that too many heads are getting in the way and that nobody can be expected to make sense of the spectacle from a vantage-point as remote as theirs.

The crowd is scarcely diminished by their absence, however, for it includes representatives of all the other schools of Greek and Roman philosophy and many distinguished spokesmen for the religious sects of the early Christian era. An astronomer whom they all respect will focus our attention on the unfolding design of the dance; several mystics will tell us what moves the dancers towards their final pose; and most of the preachers will urge us to admire the craftsmanship of the dance-floor and the wisdom of the Craftsman. Among the philosophers are three Roman emperors who thought of the dance as destiny, and a destiny-despising wizard who thought of the dance as thought. Not far from them are a cluster of poets who listen for heavenly music amid the din of philosophical controversy. One of them imagines Harmonia descending from the spheres to perfect the measures of the wise, while another attunes his soul to the wise measures of Lady Philosophy and soars into the chorus of her celestial Muses.

Ask the spectators where they think the Great Chorus is dancing, and they will give a surprising variety of answers. Athenians will say a magnificent theatre or a vast telesterion. Alexandrians will say a glittering banquet hall in a cosmopolitan city or a wedding chamber full of supracosmic light. Roman Stoics and Epicureans will place it in a crowded thoroughfare where the priests of the Great Mother have just whirled past banging their tambours. Levantine Neoplatonists will argue that the best part of the dance is going on inside their heads. A bishop from Caesarea will inform an emperor that the Great Chorus revolves around his imperial throne – and God's too, let us not forget! And we shall learn from a Cappadocian monk that the basest steps in the dance are performed through a labyrinth, the noblest steps on a battlefield, the holiest steps around an altar, and the last steps in a trance. Large indeed is the crowd of ancients who contemplated the dance in light of the cosmos and the cosmos in light of the dance, and so too must be the volume that gathers their visions together.

The cosmic dance did not blaze into being with the cosmos, as the Greeks often argued, but with the Greek *idea* of the cosmos. That is to say, the Greeks first became conscious of the cosmic dance as a spectacle distinct from its spectators when they combined their novel idea of a rationally ordered world with their venerable image of a divinely harmonious chorus to produce a radiant vision of life which seemed real because it was intelligible to impartial observers. When a vision of life unites a poetic image of harmony with a philosophical idea of order in such a way that the image clarifies and enlivens the idea and the idea justifies and enlarges the image, it is bound to delight and instruct a wide variety of spectators and to last for a long time. The cosmic dance has been attracting attention in the West for over two and a half millennia, and no epoch in Western cultural history following the Greek enlightenment – not even our own shattering age – has turned away from the vision in total disbelief or despair and broken its cumulative series of variations. (As Albert Einstein remarked in 1929 with Presocratic enthusiasm: 'Human beings, vegetables, cosmic dust, we all dance to a mysterious tune, intoned in the distance by an invisible player.')[1] Ideas of order on their own tend to detach and distance us from what we normally perceive as reality. They draw us away from the ordinary whirl of phenomena to consider an extraordinary design, an unchanging pattern of changes in which our unearthly beginnings are revealed. Images of harmony have a quite different effect: they invite us to participate in a reality we normally ignore and draw us back into the primitive immediacy of sensory experience to commune with a divinity that shapes our ends. Ideas of order, since they can be tested against experience and modified in the heat of argument, tend to spark debates. Images of harmony on the other hand tend to silence debates, for they are essentially undebatable. Like prophetic dreams and flashes of insight they come to us as vivid revelations which cannot be tested against experience since they are in fact a kind of experience, and so we must either accept them for what they are or remain insensitive to what they reveal. In view of these distinctions (which point to a basic difference between philosophical and poetic modes of thought) we should expect the Great Chorus wherever it dances to transmute the debatable idea of the cosmos into something resembling a divine revelation and consequently to awaken in its spectators – even its contemptuous spectators – a desire to reconcile their limited view of its order with what they imagine is the boundless vision of life enjoyed by a soaring Bacchant. And that is just what the Great Chorus did, or was perceived to do, throughout Antiquity. A tension between intellectual detachment and imaginative participation has complicated Western visions of the cosmic dance ever since the Greeks tried to perceive its shifting configurations from a still point outside the cosmos and its internal stillness from the shifting viewpoints of the dancers.

Precisely when the dance was first regarded as an image of divine and social harmony we may never know, but according to Plato it was certainly regarded as such by the ancient Egyptians long before the Greeks invented the idea of the cosmos and resolved to prove the reality of cosmic order. The priests of Egypt were the wisest of law-makers, Plato contended, because they turned the dance into the stable foundation of their culture by outlawing changes in their choral ceremonies and identifying their ritual movements with the unchanging government of the gods.[2] The sublime wisdom of the pharaohs and their hieratic legislators may be doubted, as may the Platonic doctrine that conservatism in religious dance is inevitably a cause (rather than merely a symptom) of cultural stability. There can be no doubt, however, that the priestly rulers of the Old Kingdom observed and performed dances in honour of their gods, most of whom were heavenly rulers, and that these rites were regarded as essential to the preservation of harmony between heaven and earth. Hieroglyphic texts have survived from the third millennium BC attesting to this.[3] From such evidence we can confidently infer that the educated élite of ancient Egypt did not – as did their counterparts in classical Greece – define the dance as a paradigm of cosmic order or extol the cosmos as a paragon of choral harmony. They simply did not think in such terms. Their thoughts about the dance, as two passages of Old Kingdom poetry will serve to show, were rooted in a purely mythological conception of the heavens which seems never to have been disturbed by anything remotely like the Greek passion for ideas.

The association of ritual dancing with divine might and celestial motion is literally as old as the pyramids. Inscribed on a limestone wall in the pyramid of Pepi I, a pharaoh of the Sixth Dynasty who was buried at Saḳḳâreh in Lower Egypt around 2250 BC and promptly transformed into a star, is the text of a priestly invocation to the deceased which briefly refers to the mortuary ceremonies performed while his luminous spirit was voyaging over the ocean of the sky-goddess Nut. 'O Pepi,' the wall calls out to him across that vast gulf and to us across another,

> thou art the great star, the companion of Sȝḥ
> [another bright star, possibly Canopus],
> who traverses the sky with Sȝḥ, who voyages over
> the Dȝ.t [a watery region of the underworld]
> with Osiris.
> Thou, Pepi, ascendest to the eastern side of the sky,
> received in thy time, rejuvenated in thine hour.
> Nut has borne thee, Pepi, together with Sȝḥ;
> the year has adorned thee together with Osiris.
> Arms are given to thee, the dance comes down to thee,
> a meal is given to thee.
> (The Pyramid Texts, Utterance 466, 882a–884a)

Not one idea of order is expressed in this highly civilized utterance. It is a paid political announcement but there is no mention of the state. It is a declaration of social solidarity but there is no mention of society. Specific stars and deities are named in it but we hear nothing of cosmic harmony or natural law or divine providence. Particular times are imagined and recalled – Pepi's period in the underworld, his hour of rebirth, the anniversary of his ascent – but time itself is not hailed as a universal principle determining the sequence of movements in the pharaoh's terrestrial or celestial life. Since such a principle is inconceivable apart from the idea of the cosmos, we may assume that it could not have been conceived sixteen hundred years before the dawn of Presocratic cosmology. The divinely established, magically rejuvenated, and serenely unquestioned order of the Old Kingdom is here revealed and symbolically represented by a series of dynamic visual images: the rising of the great star on the eastern horizon; the extending of arms or hands bearing gifts for the risen king; the performance of a solemn dance in or near his burial chamber; and the presentation of a ritual meal to celebrate his rebirth as a star and his participation in the festive life of the gods.

In a literal sense the enduring order of the Old Kingdom is also represented by static pictorial signs, namely the durable hieroglyphs incised on the monument. Though we can tell from other Pyramid Texts what sort of gifts would have been offered to Pepi at his obsequies – if he was like his son and successor Merenrē', he would have expected jars of ointment, alabaster vases of perfume, luxurious garments, and a kingly quantity of bread and beer – the obdurate limestone refuses to tell us what sort of dance came down to him in his tomb or who danced it for him or where it began or whether it was inspired by the tranquil circling of S̆3ḫ across the firmament. Perhaps the dancer or dancers descended into the symbolic underworld of the tomb in imitation of Pepi's descent as a star into the marshy Osirian realm known as the D3.t, a name thought to have originally signified 'the twilight just before dawn.'[4] Perhaps in this expectant light the mourners dimly perceived the dance as part of a perpetual rite of rebirth involving their land as well as their leader, or saw as in a dream the lord Osiris guiding their procession through the shadows of the Queen of Night.

Beneath Nut's elongated arching torso the stars of the Old Kingdom drifted like ferrymen or flitted like nimble swallows or formed a military escort for pharaohs travelling over the celestial Marsh of Reeds. But did they dance when they reached the Palace of the Gods and assembled before the Throne of Osiris? Did they ever form a chorus? The limestone, eloquent as it is, does not inform us that they did. Perhaps their realm of operations was too fluid and dreamlike to have materialized into a measurable dance-floor like that pictured on the Shield of Achilles. The gods and ancestral spirits governing the Old Kingdom, however, were sometimes said to dance at 'the double doors of heaven' to cheer a dead king as he was rising into their midst.[5] The dance that came down to Pepi may not have been slow and mournful then, as we might think proper for a funeral, but lively, triumphant, and entrancing like the liminal festivities of the immortals. An inscription found in the pyramid of Pepi's son conjures up the vision of a buoyant rite of passage in which two sacred ascents, the rising of the sun-god Rē' and the resurrection of the pharaoh, were symbolically linked by the uplifting movements of their worshippers:

> Greetings to thee, Merenrē', on this thy day,
> as thou standest before Rē', as he ariseth in the east,

adorned with this thy dignity among the spirits.
The arms interlace for thee; the feet agitate for thee;
   the hands wave for thee ...
The doors are open for those in secret places.
Stand up, remove thy earth, shake off thy dust,
   raise thyself up,
voyage thou with the spirits.
Thy wings are those of a falcon; thy brightness
   is that of a star.

(*The Pyramid Texts*, Utterance 419,
743a–743d, 747a–748b)

Could we but open the doors of their secret places and cross the long-buried threshold of prephilosophical thought we might know again through our tactile and kinetic senses – senses not of the head but of the arms, the hands, the feet – what the dancers in the pyramids knew of the interlacing of all living and dying things under the sun. We might feel our pulse quicken as Merenrē' stands up again, shakes off the dust of mortality, recovers his royal dignity among the spirits, and soars off to heaven on the falcon wings of Horus – actions perhaps imitated by those who agitated their feet and waved their hands in his honour long ago in Sakkâreh. We might even experience harmony again as a stream of unanalysed intuitions and unquestioned images, enjoying its magical benefits as the pharaoh and his worshippers did without the slightest idea of what it was or the slightest doubt that it existed everywhere. But the Greeks have made the process of thinking without ideas, abstractions, and logical distinctions extremely difficult for educated spectators of the dance. With their startling idea of the cosmos (which destroyed the primitive intimacy of gods and men) came doubt and detachment and inevitably a closing of old doors.

In the Pyramid Texts images of the dance are associated exclusively with myths of departure, resurrection, and apotheosis, which is hardly surprising since the pyramid-building pharaohs and their priests were more inclined to look forward to the starry ending of life at the court of Rē' than to cast their thoughts back to the gloomy abyss of Nut's forefather Nun from which their splendid world arose.[6] We must look outside the Old Kingdom to discover early poetic associations of the dance with myths of emergence and creation. The earliest I have found is recorded in the *Enûma elish*, the Babylonian Genesis. Certain myths in this epic fantasy of creation are thought to have existed in some form before the reign of King Agum ii in the fifteenth century BC, though its oldest fragments survive on clay tablets dating from around the turn of the first millennium – three or four hundred years before Hesiod sang to the Greeks of the emergence of the gods from

Chaos. The Babylonian counterparts of Chaos were Apsû, the father of fresh waters, and Ti'āmat, the mother of salt waters, from whose boundless gulf all things in heaven and earth sprang forth at the command of the sun-god Marduk. In this gulf the fresh and salt waters mingled before creation but did not form currents or waves. No storms angered its peaceful surface. So inert were Apsû and Ti'āmat by nature that their only unprovoked action was to beget five children. No new parents have ever been as naïve as they, or as disappointed, for after their mighty efforts at procreation they expected to sink back into their old silent abyss and sleep forever in its darkness. Needless to say, their offspring kept them awake at night (or at all hours, rather, since night had not yet been distinguished from day) with little regard for their wishes, the most restless of all being the sky-god Anu who fathered a boisterous and bellicose wizard named Enki. War erupted between the old and the new gods when Enki and his playfellows enraged Apsû by dancing inside Ti'āmat's oceanic belly with such wild energy that Anu's sky almost collapsed into the primordial abyss. 'The divine brethren met to-gether,' chanted the priests of Marduk whose duty it was to recite the *Enûma elish* twice through during their New Year's festival,

> *and nimbly stepping toward one another*
> *they roiled Ti'āmat,*
> *roiled Ti'āmat's belly.*
> *By dancing they had the heart*
> *of heaven's foundation worried.*
> *Apsû could not subdue their clamor,*
> *and Ti'āmat kept silent before them.*
> (Tablet I, 21–6)[7]

This titanic movement cannot be called a cosmic dance for the simple reason that no cosmos existed in Ti'āmat's stagnant womb (or in the Babylonian poet's lively imagination) for Enki to measure or control or beautify with his nimble steps. What his dance amounts to – if it can be called a dance at all – is the frantic rebellion of potential energy against the massive force of inertia. It is movement purely for its own sake, mere activity without artistic motivation, and the unbearable din arising from it that not even Apsû with all his powers could silence is a far cry indeed from the music of the spheres.

No wonder Ti'āmat kept silent before the peace-breakers: she was struck dumb by the fatal violence born within her and by the painful prospect of having to fight it till her death. Considering what follows from Enki's momentous revelry – the birth of Marduk, the defeat of the old gods, and the formation of the temporal world from their dismembered bodies – one might be tempted to call it a 'theogonic' or perhaps even a 'cosmogonic' dance and to perceive it as a necessary transitional phase between the comatose passivity of primal chaos and the dynamic order of an emergent or primitive cosmos. But these are Greek terms with Greek implications of poetic design and organic development rooted in Greek perceptions of stasis and motion, chaos and cosmos, cause and effect. Are such subtle terms applicable to an event as crudely and profoundly violent as the roiling of Ti'āmat's belly – an event oddly reminiscent of that random riot which modern physicists (those at least who are deaf to Einstein's 'mysterious tune') are calling, without a shudder, the Big Bang? I would be inclined to regard Enki's explosion of energy as a cosmogonic dance if the world-order instituted by Marduk were a cosmos of sorts, or had the makings of one. But it is not even a primitive cosmos. Like the empire of Rē' the Babylonian world of wheeling constellations and inexorable destinies is essentially an arbitrary order imposed on the whirl of phenomena by a militant theocratic régime and sustained by the predictable but ultimately unintelligible motions of the sun-god. Basic to any cosmos are an artistic rationale and a unifying system of causes, and Marduk's world has neither. To create it he must kill, and to sustain it he must kill again. In its stormy atmosphere a ceaseless battle rages between the forces of light and darkness while below on its blood-soaked desert plains giant locusts swarm and scorpion-tailed monsters writhe and scuttle to the thunderous beat of Anu. No entrancing choragus crowned with reason's rays, no gentle musician with a golden lyre, channels the energy unleashed by Enki's dance into the invincible revolutions of the stars: the prime mover here is a merciless conqueror born in a dark dream of omnipotence who marches on and on and forever on, scourging demons, subduing oceans, suppressing the ungodly. The world of Marduk the Almighty has the coherence of a recurrent nightmare.

Among the haunting and prophetic images of the dance preserved in the literature and on the monuments of the ancient civilizations of the Near East I have yet to discern even the faintest glimmer of the Great Chorus, and I suspect that even if such a glimmer were discernible in the D3.t-like gloom preceding the dawn of Greek philosophy it would not lead us to any recognizably Western vision of the cosmic dance. I use the strategic term 'Western' here with some regret: it is a confession of my cultural limitations. Had I the languages to light my way into the East, I would gladly move on from Sakkâreh and Babylon to whirl with the Dervishes and leap into Shiva's fiery circle and lose all consciousness of East and West in the pulsing flow of Taoist meditation. The gravity of ignorance holds me back, however, even as it oppresses the many meditative people in the West today who regard the cosmic dance as an exclusively Eastern vision of life. Ignorance is never bliss, but it is sometimes a blessing. Without its kindly restraints I would undoubtedly have drifted into oceans vaster than Ti'āmat and expanded this already voluminous volume to chaotic dimensions.

I therefore use 'Western' as a purely descriptive term with a certain sense of relief, for it serves to indicate the historical and geographical limits of my field of inquiry. All the poetic, philosophical, theological, and homiletic texts presented in this volume as evidence of the continuity of the vision of the cosmic dance in the West date from the relatively short span of Antiquity between the founding of Plato's Academy in the early fourth century BC and the dissolution of Proclus' Neoplatonic Academy in the early sixth century AD – the Academic Millennium, as it might be called, during which Attic Greek was the pre-eminent language of philosophical and rhetorical culture in the Mediterranean world. Western civilization is commonly and rightly thought to have come ito its own during this momentous period, and though its momentum may owe more than we realize to the civilizing currents of the Nile, the Tigris, and the Euphrates, the Greeks who started it dancing were from the start conscious of their physical and spiritual remoteness from the valley civilizations of the Near East. Their religious and theatrical dances came to express (like all their other arts) the wonder of their cultural autonomy and the wisdom of their critical spirit. It was no accident then that the first Greeks to perceive their civilization as a reflection of the cosmos and to defend its distinctive ideals of order and harmony on cosmological grounds were also the first authors in the West to record their perceptions of the cosmic dance.

In the Academic Millennium the spectators of the dance become a restless and obtrusive part of the spectacle. They demand attention. They insist on altering viewpoints – their own or those of prejudiced and unenlightened viewers – in the belief that there is always a clearer, broader, truer vision of the dance to be had by anyone who strives to transcend the limits of his or her present visual field. Their philosophical demand for critical objectivity inevitably clashes with their poetic desire for mystical involvement and compels them to resolve the tension between detachment and participation which is characteristic of their Western outlook. No such tension seems to have bothered the silent and unobtrusive spectators of the dances mentioned in the Pyramid Texts. As a corpse Pepi could not have worried much about observing or joining the movement of his mourners, while as a spirit he was able to look down on them with divine detachment without having to interrupt his perpetual journey across the heavens. In the Babylonian Genesis Apsû and Ti'āmat were shocked into awareness of a primeval conflict between inertia and the vitality of the dance, but this was quite different from the tension latent in Greek visions of the Great Chorus. For Ti'āmat there was no possibility of detachment from Enki's dance since it took place inside her. For Apsû there was no possibility of participation since the dance was the very antithesis of his entropic state of being. Its energy eventually destroyed him. Ancient Egyptians and Babylonians, I suspect, would have had great difficulty understanding the ambition of the Greeks to study the design of the dance as impartial observers while experiencing the fullness of its harmony as enraptured initiates. The fulfilment of that ambition will remain a blessed possibility in the West as long as the viewers of the Great Chorus strive to resolve the tension between their philosophical and poetic modes of thought.

The source of the tension lies (as I suggested earlier) not in the diversity of the viewers but in the complexity of the vision, which is both an idea of order and an image of harmony or rather a dynamic synthesis of idea and image. One way to eliminate the tension at its source is simply to ignore the theoretical status of the cosmos. We shall encounter a fair number of spectators who take the reality of the cosmos for granted and interpret its revolutions as revelations, convinced that no view of the Great Chorus is valid but their own. They usually part company with the philosophers in the crowd to become prophets or proselytes in the dance. A second way – simpler than the first but less satisfying since it effectively eliminates the vision – is to reduce the Great Chorus to a mere figure of speech by ignoring the theatrical éclat and epiphanic brilliance of the dance as a visual representation of life. Sophists tend to do this, as we shall see, and if their wits are sharp enough to reduce all theories of world-harmony to absurdity they are likely to regard the Great Chorus only as a quaint philosophical fancy and to end up doubting its existence. They break away from the philosophers too, but move in the opposite direction intellectually – towards the alienated ranks of the Skeptics. (Since the Skeptics as a dogmatic sect prided themselves on having no dogmas or visions to speak of, we shall be leaving most of them severely alone.) A great many spectators strive to reconcile the viewpoints of the critics and the initiates through action rather than contemplation and push their way into the dance as political reformers, ascetic reactionaries, pagan revivalists, Christian martyrs, satiric poets, or philanthropic sorcerers, each driven by an impetuous desire to alter the direction or organization of the Great Chorus. A few are crowned in heaven for their revolutionary efforts. Most end up in the dust. The wisest and most companionable spectators I have found in the crowd are those who probe the foundations of their belief in the vision and revise or recreate it by discovering new metaphoric links between chorus and cosmos which strengthen its credibility and save it from dullness, absurdity, triviality, and extinction. They are the great visionaries of the Academic Millennium, the philosophers and poets who look for proofs of cosmic order in the transient beauty of choral harmony and find significance for choral harmony in the eternal source of cosmic order. They will try to convince us with their lives as well as their words that intellectual detachment from the physical attractions and partnerships in the dance is the only sure route to participation in the spiritual joy and unity of the dancers. Plato is the common mentor of these dispassionate sages and for many the only master, though not a few are moved by the wisdom of one who piped to them in the marketplace.

The responsiveness of this restless crowd to the major political and cultural crises in the unacademic life of the Academic Millennium was not at all apparent to me when I first entered the ancient precincts of the cosmic dance with the aim of studying it from the viewpoint of an intellectual historian. This remote and serenely impersonal viewpoint naturally inclined me to think that the dance of the stars (which was the only movement of the Great Chorus I perceived at the time) had very little to do with the lives and feelings of people immersed in the blood-drenched tide of history; that the significance of this heavenly vision was unaffected by the mutability of earthly life and by the diversity of human responses to misfortune; and that the vision itself was a quaint pantomime of ideas – uncommon, otherwordly ideas – flitting noiselessly through the minds of cosmologists and metaphysicians into the consciousness of an educated élite who dared to distinguish their sublime philosophical knowledge from the wordly wisdom of the folk. That such an élite did exist in Athenian society in the classical period Plato has left us vivid proof in his dialogues. Socrates himself was on its fringes and enjoyed making fun of it even as he taught its members to take him seriously. From him I learned that what I was setting out to study was not an idea or a stream of ideas removed from the world of the senses but a vision of life shared with varying degrees of comprehension by a whole society keenly sensitive to the visible beauty of that world. His and Plato's influential perceptions of the world of the dance, as I soon discovered, were definitely not cut off from the tragic wisdom of the dance-loving and sometimes dance-crazed society from which they sprang. As they saw it, the Great Chorus included the common narthex-carriers who danced out their fears and looked for grace along the public road to Demeter's temple as well as the rare philosophical mystagogues who measured their wisdom by lofty Socratic standards back in Athena's city.

A Greek of Plato's era did not have to be an intellectual to regard the stars as his 'synchoreutai,' his 'fellow-dancers.' The prephilosophical image of the harmonious chorus of immortals – be they Muses dancing to Apollo's lyre, Dryads skipping to the pipes of Pan, Graces and Horae circling with Aphrodite to soft Lydian airs, or Satyrs and Maenads leaping with Dionysus to the thunder of Corybantic drums – expressed the religious, social, political, and artistic ideals of harmony familiar to everyone in the Greek world and valued above all by the citizens of Athens, and even after this profoundly popular image had been refined and universalized by the founder of the Old Academy it remained so closely identified with the culture of the Greek people that Plato's indomitable spokesman for intellectual élitism, the Athenian Stranger, was prompted to remark offhandedly – as if back where he came from it was perfectly obvious to everyone, even the dullest menial – that 'a person is without culture who is without the dance.'

'Apaideutos achoreutos' is how he put it in his own language, and it is an epigram worth thinking about for its meaning is expansive and complex and by no means obvious now. As a dogmatic social reformer and irrepressible pundit the Athenian Stranger naturally had his own rather limited notion of what his epigram meant, which Plato has him explain with daunting vigour in the second book of the *Laws* (654a ff). For now, however, let us freely unfold its implications apart from him as if it were a proverb rather than an epigram – an expression of Athenian folk-wisdom – which is what he suggests it was before he folded it up neatly and squeezed it into his tightly argued oration on the social and political benefits of choral education. Let us pry apart the two negative adjectives which are its interlocking halves and examine each on its own with the aim of reconstructing the proverb in positive terms and recovering its vast significance.

To be 'apaideutos' was to be ignorant, boorish, uneducated, uncultured, uncritical, undisciplined, unsocialized, intellectually unformed, morally disordered, deprived of consoling religious and artistic traditions, pitifully unaware of the perfecting (if not exactly perfect) design of the cosmos, and thus wholly outside the perfectible sphere of classical Greek civilization. Only an utter barbarian from the wilds beyond the Black Sea could bear to have this insulting adjective hurled in his direction without feeling intensely ashamed and alienated from all that was good and beautiful in life – without indeed feeling on the verge of chaos – for it would mean that he lacked all that originally adhered, and that Werner Jaeger has recently given back, to the noble noun 'paideia.' The meaning of the adjective 'achoreutos' was no less insulting. If a person was not trained in the fine and public art of 'choreia,' which blended the arts of poetry and song with the visible rhythms of the dance, he was bound to be out of step with society and incapable of graduating into responsible adulthood. 'The chorus,' as Jaeger remarked in the offhanded manner of the Athenian Stranger, 'was the high school of early Greece, long before there were teachers of poetry; and its influence always went far deeper than merely learning the meaning of the words to be sung. It was not for nothing that the institution of *chorodidaskalia* preserved in its name the word which means "instruction." '[8] Far deeper indeed: its influence ultimately sprang from the heavens ruled by Apollo and Dionysus, the supreme 'chorodidaskaloi' or 'dance-instructors' of the Olympian universe. A drop-out from their high school (which with the Muses and the stars on its immortal faculty was as high a school as could be imagined in those days) was doomed to be a wretched and presumptuous mortal, a truant from life's sacred festival, a soul perilously out of tune with the harmonious powers governing the cycles of nature. Such a person was inevitably ungodly because he was unable to imitate the gods. He could not move like them or with them or be moved by what moved them, and as everyone knew from Homer and Hesiod there was no god or goddess on Olympus who was not an accomplished dancer except poor Hephaestus, who was a cripple. But even the lame god delighted in the spectacle of the dance and became a kind of dancemaker, as his portrait of the chorus and their admiring spectators on the Shield of Achilles plainly indicated. If a danceless man was ungodly then he was surely also godless and joyless and lifeless. And if he could bear to be all these, and nothing could induce him to improve his life by learning the sacred arts of the chorus, then he was obviously not a Greek. He was obviously – there was no other word to describe him – 'apaideutos.'

If this volume were compressed into a single sentence, it would read 'ton de pepaideumenon hikanōs kechoreukota theteon': 'To be considered cultured one must be fully trained in the dance.' That was how the Athenian Stranger restated his negative dictum 'apaideutos achoreutos' in positive terms.[9]

Like him I would have the accent fall on the adverb 'fully.' No dancer, however graceful his poses, and no spectator, however practised his eye, can be considered 'cultured' in the classical sense of the term until he has perceived his involvement in the dance from a cosmic perspective and his involvement in the cosmos from a choral perspective. A complete education in the arts of the chorus entails a full and deep understanding of the connections between choral harmony, cultural integrity, and cosmic order. The argument of this volume (which is *my* positive restatement of 'apaideutos achoreutos') has a triangular structure. It connects three ancient Greek concepts

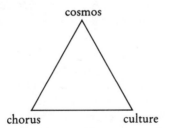

with ancient Greek correspondences based on visual analogy, metonymic symbolism, formal causality, numerological parallelism, and mystical assimilation. While an historian of ideas would be mainly concerned with the conceptual apexes of the triangle as discrete points of reference, an historian of visions (if I may coin a phrase) would be inclined to focus his attention on the visual and visionary lines of correspondence between them and to contemplate the bounded figure. The Platonic vision of the choral cosmos, I believe, was what sustained the old metaphoric connection between chorus and culture (which as Jaeger observed certainly existed long before there were professional teachers of Greek poetry and philosophy) in the Hellenistic, Greco-Roman, and Late Antique phases of the Academic Millennium, for then as in the heyday of classical Athens the 'true cosmos' set in motion by the Demiurge was perceived by educated spectators as both the dynamic archetype of Greek choral dance and the divine cause of Greek cultural supremacy.

The Athenian Stranger's equation of choreia and paideia raises a number of intriguing questions which pertain to the sides rather than the apexes of my triangle and which I have endeavoured to answer in this volume as an historian of visions. The connections between chorus, cosmos, and culture were regarded by the Athenian Stranger as strong, obvious, reasonable, and divinely ordained. The gods themselves had bounded the figure, and he was simply the seer who discovered the bonds. But what if any or all of the sides of the triangle should weaken or appear arbitrary? What would happen to the world of the dance and the dance of the world if classical Greek culture should be transformed or superseded by a rival paideia? Conversely, what would happen to classical Greek culture if the noble forms of dance expressing and epitomizing its ideals should evolve into outlandish new forms or degenerate into lewd and ignoble posturing or be eclipsed by the choreia of a god not of Greek origin? What would become of the link between choreia and paideia if the design of the cosmos were radically revised, or if the stable centre of the Great Chorus were suddenly shifted to an invisible point beyond the cosmos, or if the visible signs of cosmic harmony in the heavens were clouded by the Devil and all his works and lost in a haze of superluminous abstractions? To what extent has the tradition of classical Greek culture been reflected in the continuity of the cosmic dance as an optimistic vision of life? How was the vision affected by the emergence of Christendom from the pagan Roman Empire and by the Church Fathers' pessimistic view of the World and the Flesh? How and why did the vision survive the traumatic change from a predominantly cosmological to a severely eschatological outlook on life in the early Christian centuries? These are all questions of an historical character. They pertain to continuities and variations perceived over a measurable stretch of time and documented in datable records which time has not rendered incomprehensible. They draw our attention to causal sequences of various kinds such as emergence and diffusion, revolution and reaction, conflict and resolution, decadence and reformation, and so on, which have long been of interest to historians. And finally they are questions answerable in historical terms, because, as we shall see, the cosmic dance became after Plato a comprehensive vision of time itself and hence of human history, a vision which reflected and gave meaning to the rise and fall of empires, the growth of sects and countercultures, the reconciliation of the individual with society, the revival of sophistic education, the confrontation of Church and State, and the transmission of Late Antique intellectual culture to post-classical Europe.

From the perspective of the whole (as Plotinus would say) my visionary history might be regarded as a diachronic extension and dynamic elaboration of Jaeger's study of the ideals of classical Greek culture. For several presumptuous years I seriously considered calling my work *Choreia*, and I cannot deny that I hoped this title would steal some of the Olympian thunder of *Paideia*. Great was my dismay when I discovered in the *Oxford English Dictionary* that the word I fancied for my title, or rather its Latin form 'chorea,' exists in modern English as a medical term signifying 'a convulsive disorder, usually occurring in early life, and characterized by irregular involuntary contractions of the muscles, especially of the face and arms; also affecting horses.' This was quite the opposite of what I was attempting to contemplate on a cosmic scale! The tragic fate of my noble Greek word forced me to question my naïve assumption that the mighty themes of order and harmony could be conveyed through the centuries on a verbal vehicle so frail and easily overturned. I had to abandon the assumption along with my Jaegeresque title.[10] My debt to Jaeger remains intact, however, and I doubt that it will ever be diminished by the vagaries of semantic change.

The organization of this volume reflects my conception of the cosmic dance as a continuous series of historically connected movements – I sometimes call them 'phases' or 'variations' or 'episodes' – in the evolution of the Platonic vision of culture as a choral imitation of the cosmos. I have distinguished nine such movements in Antiquity and to each have devoted a chapter. How to chart an orderly course through the shifting and disputatious crowd drawn to the Great Chorus over the centuries without imposing for my own convenience a simplistic or prejudicial design on the diverse viewpoints of the spectators and the intricate configurations of the spectacle was the most perplexing problem I had to face in organizing my nine chapters, and I would certainly have been defeated by it if a solution had not been suggested to me by the ingenious design of Erich Auerbach's *Mimesis*. Like Auerbach I have let my argument emerge out of a series of remarkable and revealing works by ancient authors studied in chronological order, and have allowed myself the bacchic freedom of looking backwards and sideways as I marched forwards with the procession of history. Each chapter opens with a longish quotation from one of these works, followed by an explication of its difficult points and an analysis of its significance in the history of the vision. The ancients thus have a chance to speak for themselves, and the moderns to judge by their own standards the wisdom of the spectators, before I offer my assistance in making sense of the spectacle. For purposes of contrast and comparison I often introduce into my discussion of the principal author and principal quotation in a chapter secondary quotations from other works by the same author or by authors related to him. The introductory excerpts sometimes serve as entrances into the social and intellectual worlds of my principal authors and sometimes as fixed points around which my contemplations of the chorus and the crowd temporarily spiral. The literary works studied by Auerbach were by his own admission selected at random so that they would not be otherwise connected than by his critical commentary.[11] My sources (which for this volume are predominantly philosophical) were already linked by history before I thought of fashioning them into a chain. Why I chose Plato's *Timaeus*, Philo's *On the Creation*, and the seven other works listed in my table of contents as the focal points of my study will be explained in detail chapter by chapter, author by author. My choices, I trust, will not appear arbitrary to a reader who follows my sequence of steps through the restless crowd.

1

Chorus and Cosmos

The Craftsman fashioned the stars mainly out of fire so that their divine race would be most luminous and beautiful to behold, and he made them perfectly spherical like the cosmic sphere and distributed them round about the whole heaven which was to be a true cosmos embroidered with them everywhere. Setting them to follow closely the direction of the Supreme Circle, he gave each star two motions: a uniform rotation about the same point, since each star always thinks the same thoughts about the same things; and a forward revolution, since each is subject to the circling of the Same and Uniform. But by the other five motions they were to be unaffected so that they should most certainly attain the highest possible excellence. And for this reason the fixed stars were created: to be living creatures divine and eternal, always remaining the same and uniformly revolving in the same position relative to each other. The creation of the stars that reverse their motion and wander about in other ways has been described in a previous passage [on the planets]. As for the earth our nurse which winds about the pole extended through the universe, he fashioned it to be the guardian and craftsman of night and day, and the first and eldest of the gods born within the heavens. To describe the choral dances of these same gods [choreias de toutōn autōn], their juxtapositions and their retrogradations and their progressions, or to say which of these gods meet in conjunction and which in opposition, and how at times they hide each other from us, disappearing and appearing again, sending terrors and warnings about future events to those who cannot calculate their motions – to tell all this without visual models would be labour spent in vain.

PLATO, *Timaeus* 40a–d[1]

The Wellspring of Fair Dances

Two concentric rings of neatly hewn stone lie in the outer courtyard of the ruined Sanctuary of Demeter at Eleusis, a village thirteen miles west of Athens. The craftsmen who laid them there in the late sixth century BC would hardly recognize the courtyard now: its broken slabs of pavement, shattered columns, leaning parapets, and lizard-haunted stairwells look more like the world Demeter devastated in her grief for Persephone than the northern entrance to her great temple and the gateway to Elysium. But the two rings seem to have defied change. The four stones of the inner circle still rise step-like above the eight outer stones, their clean edges marred by only a few weathered cracks, while the hallowed chamber that once enclosed and protected them has fallen to the elements. Neither the slow erosion of the ages nor the shock of barbarian battering-rams (Alaric's hordes razed the Sanctuary in 394 AD) has damaged the clamps embedded in the tightly fitted structure, and so the ancient circles continue to surround the mouth of a sacred well known in Antiquity as the Kallichoron or 'Wellspring of Fair Dances.'

Once, when the world was still mourning the loss of Persephone, the daughters of the Eleusinian queen Metaneira discovered a poor old woman resting by this well. They took the stranger home with them, little realizing that she was Demeter, and their mother kindly offered her shelter in the palace and employment as nurse to her infant son Demophon. In the dead of night the goddess secretly fed Demophon ambrosia and bathed him in the flames of the palace hearth in an effort to immortalize him. When Metaneira discovered this, she was duly horrified and begged the nurse to stop her strange rites. Demeter angrily revealed her true identity, denounced mankind for interfering in divine affairs, and refused to continue the prince's deification. Recalling the hospitality of the Eleusinians, however, the goddess regained her composure and promised the trembling queen that an annual feast would be held in Demophon's honour. 'Come now,' she commanded,

> *let all the people build me a great temple*
> *And an altar under it, beneath the city and its high wall,*
> *Above the Wellspring of Fair Dances, upon a rising hill.*
> (*Hymn to Demeter* 270–2)

Metaneira dutifully obeyed, and thus the Wellspring of Fair Dances became an important landmark in the area set aside for Demeter's temple on the southeastern slope of the Eleusinian acropolis.

Precisely when the well gained its evocative name is not known, though

Figure 1

This Eleusinian wellhead dating from the late sixth century BC is believed to be the Kallichoron described by Pausanius as the place where 'the women of Eleusis first danced and sang in honour of the Goddess' (*Description of Greece* 1.38.6). That it was also the well named in the *Hymn to Demeter* has been disputed by George Mylonas (*Eleusis*, pp 45–7). Its outer ring is 2.85 metres in diameter.

the mention of the Kallichoron in the *Hymn to Demeter* (which probably dates from the seventh century BC) indicates that the poetic epithet was almost certainly in use long before the construction of the circular wellhead. Perhaps, as the poet of the Hymn implies, the association of the well with fair dances antedates the cult itself, which was founded probably in late Mycenaean times. By the turn of the fourth century BC, when Plato was embarking on his career as a philosopher, statesman, and critic of popular religion, the Eleusinian Mysteries had been in existence for about a millennium: time enough for the cult to have evolved from an annual feast in honour of Demeter and Demophon into a seasonal cycle of lesser and greater ceremonies, private initiation rites, public festivals, processions, fasts, vigils, sacrifices. The boisterous revelry of the worshippers eventually took on a divine existence of its own and was given the name Iacchus, which pilgrims shouted at the stars along the well-trodden route from Athens to the courtyard of the Kallichoron. Inevitably the Athenians confused the shadowy figure of Iacchus with their beloved Dionysus, the playful, intoxicating god of revelry and ecstatic dance, who thereby came to preside with Demeter and her daughter over the fortunes of the cult members.

What did the dances around or beside the Kallichoron symbolize in the mythical context of the Mysteries as a whole? In what rites were they performed? Were they imitations of astral movements? Who was permitted to perform or observe them? These are mysteries (in a modern sense) which may never be solved by the excavators of the Sanctuary. The initiates and their hierophants might have celebrated Persephone's ascent from Hades by circling round the holy waters which rose up like the goddess from the darkness of the underworld. They might have perceived their dance as an imitation of the seasonal cycle or beheld the bereavement of Demeter enacted by the priestesses in the temple chorus. Whether their dancing was imitative or purely ecstatic we have no way of knowing now. The throngs of torch-bearing revellers and sleepless initiates who regularly marched from Athens to Eleusis seeking assurances of a blessed afterlife faithfully kept their vow not to divulge what they had seen or heard in the precincts of the temple.[2]

On the southern slope of the Athenian acropolis was a less mysterious but no less religious setting for the vanished art of the Greek chorus: the Theatre of Dionysus with its circular dance-floor or orchestra (from the verb 'orcheisthai,' 'to dance'). Around a permanent altar which stood in the centre of the orchestra and often served as a stage-property the Athenian 'tragikoi choroi' wove drama, song, and dance together into a single art during the spring festival of the City Dionysia. A white marble throne in the front row of the amphitheatre was reserved for the high priest of Dionysus, who presided over the city's annual competitions in comedy, tragedy, and dithyramb. (Dithyrambic performances typically consisted of a round-

dance or 'kyklios choros' accompanied by lyrical hymns in praise of Iacchus.)
At this theatre Plato would have seen the final flowering of classical Greek
tragedy in the poetic dramas of his elderly contemporaries Euripides and
Sophocles. He would have seen the mad dance of Dionysus – 'hē manikē
choreia' – transformed by Euripides into the choral artistry of the *Bacchae*
and parodied by Aristophanes in the dance of Eleusinian initiates in the
Frogs. In these two settings, the private many-chambered temple of the
mysteries with its sacred wellspring and the open-air theatre of the city with
its public stage, the poets and philosophers of Antiquity saw the choruses
that inspired their visions of the cosmic dance.[3]

Though there is no way of knowing when the Greeks began to perceive
analogies between choral dancing and cosmic order, we can be certain that
Plato was not the first author in the Greek world to praise the motions of
the world-chorus. Considering the brevity and simplicity of his reference
to the dances of the stars in the *Timaeus* we may assume that the metaphor
was familiar enough to his earliest readers to require no explanation or
defence and that he considered its philosophical implications self-evident.
In its Platonic context the metaphor certainly *seems* clear and uncomplicated
– at least at first glance. But are its philosophical implications as easy to pin
down as Plato leads us to suppose? Surely the meaning of his metaphor
depends to some extent on the sort of stars he observed in his heavens and
the sort of dances he pictured them performing. But he does not tell us
whether his stars were the sort to dance like initiates in the temple of the
mysteries or like choruses in the public theatre. He leaves us wondering
whether their motions were manic in a religious sense or rational in a philosophical sense. Perhaps they were both at once. As we might expect, the
metaphor grows more complicated the moment we pause over it long enough
to consider what it might have meant and might still mean. The suspicion
dawns on us that as a symbolic image of order the dance is perhaps just as
mysterious as the cosmos it was once supposed to resemble and clarify.

Images of dancing gods and dancing stars were borne into the light of
classical Athens on currents of mythopoetic thought that sprang like the
waters of the Kallichoron from prehistoric sources hidden in 'the dark backward and abysm of time.' At some remote period the Greeks may have
imitated the diurnal revolutions of the stars in their religious ceremonies
and felt all of nature dancing with them in their choral festivals. Those who
contrasted the harshness of mortal life with the concord and freedom of the
immortals may have seen in the heavens a reflection of the joyous dance of
Apollo and his Muses and aspired to participate in it by studying the measures of the astral chorus. Perhaps their wise men developed the concept of
the cosmos in isolation from the art of the chorus and fused chorus and
cosmos into a metaphor of world-harmony long after they had ceased to

dance with the stars like primitive shamans.[4] In his two epics Homer often
refers to the dances of mortals and at least twice to the dances of immortals
('the chorus of Artemis,' *Iliad* XVI.183; 'the lovely chorus of Graces,' *Odyssey* XVIII.194); but he never speaks of the heavenly bodies as dancing in
chorus with men or gods, or of human dancers imitating the revolutions of
the stars. He seems to have envisioned the dance as a metonymic figure for
all the pleasures and benefits of peaceful society threatened by the heroic
enterprise of war.

In his minutely detailed description of the great shield made for Achilles
by the divine craftsman Hephaestus we can find scenes of the dance of peace
set within a world at once broader and narrower than the plains of Troy.
The shield displays an image of the Homeric universe in miniature, an image
so ingeniously wrought that its many figures seem to move with the vitality
of nature itself. On it are depicted

> *The untiring sun and the full moon*
> *And therein all the constellations crowning heaven,*
> *The Pleiades and the Hyades and the mighty Orion,*
> *And the Bear, also called the Wain,*
> *Which turns in its own place and watches Orion,*
> *And alone has no share in the baths of Ocean.*
>
> (*Iliad* XVIII.484–9)

Homeric stars do not dance, but they are animated in other respects,
appearing as maidens or hunters or animals, crowning heaven with their
untiring revolutions, dipping into the baths of Ocean, watching each other
and the world below. It was in such animistic skies as these, essentially
poetic skies, that the dance would first make sense as an image of cosmic
order. (Only 'living creatures divine and eternal,' as Plato would call the
stars centuries later, would dance in the Craftsman's heavens.) After
surveying the celestial images on the shield Homer turns his attention to
the details of earthly life fashioned within its glittering rim. Townsfolk
are glimpsed at a wedding feast. Elders preside at a trial. Warriors clash.
Farmers reap. The dateless scenes of early Greek civilization are presented
in a series of brief tableaux. The final scene is a choral dance of youths
and maidens:

> *And therein the famous lamed god skilfully fashioned*
> *A dance-floor [choron], like that which Dedalus once wrought*
> *In broad Cnossus for the fair-tressed Ariadne.*
> *Youths and maidens worth the price of many cattle were there*
> *Dancing [orcheunt'], holding their hands on each other's wrists.*

Of these the maidens were dressed in fine linen, while the
                                                        youths
Wore well-woven tunics softly glistening with oil;
And the maidens had beautiful garlands, and the youths
Had daggers of gold hanging from silver belts.
At one moment they ran round with skilful footwork,
As when a potter sits by his wheel fitted between his hands
And tests it to see whether it will run;
And at another moment they ran in rows towards each other.
And a large crowd stood round the lovely choral dance
                                                        [choron],
Delighting themselves; and two tumblers leading the dance
Twirled round through the midst of them.

(Iliad XVIII.590–606)

One might be tempted to see in the configurations of 'the lovely choral dance' a reflection of the astral movements encompassing the crowded portrait of earthly life. The circular movement of the dancers' first figure, suggested by the simile of the potter's wheel, might recall the revolutions of the 'constellations crowning heaven'; the opposing lines of their second figure, together with the labyrinthine complexity of their 'skilful footwork' (hinted at in the comparison of their dance-floor to the orchestra built by Dedalus at Cnossus where Theseus and the Athenian youths and maidens saved from the Minotaur performed a serpentine dance imitating their escape from the Labyrinth), might represent the oppositions, conjunctions, and winding processions of the planets along the zodiac; and the two whirling soloists rise to prominence in the dance like 'the untiring sun and the full moon.' (See figure 2.)

If Homer meant this final scene on the shield to symbolize man's harmonious participation in the order of the heavens, he certainly was not explicit about it. One cannot even say that the dance clearly symbolizes anything: it is simply a visual image juxtaposed beside many other curiously wrought designs or 'daidala' (XVIII.482) on the Shield of Achilles. What the large crowd who stood around the dance-floor saw in the delightful spectacle is as enigmatic as everything else in their metallic world. Did the lovely choral dance (which is a remote ancestor of the public choruses in the Theatre of Dionysus) appear to them as a vision of order opposed to the tumult of the battle scenes depicted elsewhere on the cosmic shield? Did its dynamic craftsmanship remind them of the unbroken rounds of the heavenly bodies or the joyful play of the gods in the halls of Olympus? Homer does not say. Hephaestus created images rich in potential symbolic meaning, figures which can never fully be explained or fixed like rigid metal forms within a circumscribed plane.

Figure 2

On the top band of side B of the François Vase (p 26) is depicted a choral chain of
youths and maidens, their interlocking hands presenting an elementary image of
'harmonia' (detail, p 27). Their dance has traditionally been identified as the 'Geranos'
led by Theseus on Delos after the rescue of the Athenian hostages from the Labyrinth,
but this has been recently questioned. An alternate setting might be the Dedalian
'choros' built for Ariadne on Crete. The vase (now in the Museo Archeologico,
Florence) was painted by Kleitias around 570 BC.

Plato may have had Homer's cosmic shield in mind when he devised his own mythical vision of choral dances in the 'true cosmos' of the *Timaeus*, a world fashioned by a new and mathematically minded Hephaestus whom he called simply the Demiurge or 'Craftsman.' Tales of the birth of gods, the creation of the heavens, and the origins of mankind had been told all over the Aegean world for as long as anyone could remember – certainly long before Athenian philosophers and their predecessors in sixth-century Ionia opened up these subjects to systematic investigation. The Myth of the Craftsman may be read as Plato's answer to such folk tales, an expression not only of religious wonder and poetic delight at the mysteries of nature but also of intellectual confidence that human reason (with a little help from the Muses) may penetrate those mysteries and ultimately answer every question the universe poses its observers. The *Timaeus* is full of poetic echoes. It is a critical retelling rather than a polemical rejection of popular cosmogonic legends. Plato's description of the earth as 'the first and eldest of gods born within the heavens,' for example, is a barely concealed allusion to the mythical genesis of the gods set forth by the poet second only to Homer in his influence on Greek philosophers, the Boeotian shepherd Hesiod (fl c 700 BC), who had declared in his *Theogony* (116–18) that the first gods to spring from the womb of Chaos were the 'broad-breasted Earth' and her two primordial brothers, Eros and Tartarus. Hesiod might have begun his genealogy of the gods with a description of the disorder prevailing before their birth, the terrifying limitlessness and aimless commotion of Chaos. But he chose instead to begin his poem with a vision of his divine source of inspiration, the chorus of the Muses, whom he pictured as dancing around a sacred wellspring:

> *Let us begin our song with the Heliconian Muses,*
> *Who dwell on the great and sacred mount of Helicon,*
> *And dance [orcheuntai] with delicate feet around*
> *The purple fountain and around the altar of mighty Zeus;*
> *And when they have washed their soft skin in Permessus*
> *Or in the Horse's Spring or in Olmeius they perform*
> *On Helicon's sacred summit choral dances [chorous],*
> *Both lovely and delightful, with swift motions of their feet.*
> *From there they arise, veiled in dense mist, and go out*
> *At night to utter their song with very beautiful voices,*
> *Hymning Zeus, the aegis-bearer, and queenly Hera,*
> *The Argive goddess who walks on golden sandals,*
> *And Zeus' aegis-bearing daughter, the bright-eyed Athena,*
> *And Phoebus Apollo, and Artemis the shooter of arrows,*
> *And Poseidon the earth-bearer, the earth-shaker,*

And venerable Themis, and quick-glancing Aphrodite,
And gold-crowned Hebe, and beautiful Dione,
Leto, Iapetus, and Cronus the wily counsellor,
Dawn and the great Sun and the shining Moon,
Earth and the great Ocean and the dark Night,
And the holy race of all the other gods who exist forever.

(Theogony 1–21)

The purple fountain of Helicon represented (as did, perhaps, the Kallichoron at Eleusis) the mysterious source of inspiration for both poetry and the dance – arts all but inseparable in the ancient Greek conception of 'mousikē.' 'Music' for Hesiod and for Plato signified all the gifts bestowed by the Muses on man and on nature, including visual harmony, aural concord, rhythmic grace, creative spontaneity, and profound insight into the origin of the visible and invisible gods; hence, though the magical encircling movement of Hesiod's Muses cannot be called a cosmic dance in any explicitly mimetic sense, it is unmistakably resonant with cosmic implications and would be recollected by Plato as an image of the archetypal harmony reflected in the choral rounds of the stars. Just as the Craftsman gave us the gift of sight so that

we might behold the revolution of Reason in the heavens and make use of this spectacle for controlling the revolutions of the rational faculty that is within us,

so the Muses, according to Plato, bestowed their artistic gifts on deserving individuals for the same therapeutic purpose:

For harmony, which has motions akin to the revolutions of the soul within us, has been given by the Muses to him who makes use of the Muses intelligently, not for the sake of irrational pleasure (as they now seem to be used) but as an auxiliary to the revolution of the soul within us, when it has lost its harmony, to restore it to its proper order and concord. And rhythm, in turn, was granted to us by the same goddesses and for the same reasons, to restore the measure and grace that are lacking in most of us.

(Timaeus 47c–e)

In their nocturnal hymn, the Hesiodic Muses praised not only the fabled gods of Olympus but also cosmic deities such as Earth, Sun, Moon, Ocean, Night, and 'the holy race of all the other gods' (including, no doubt, the stars), which indicates that if their choral dance was not exactly an imitation of cosmic order it was at least a vehicle for worshipping the awesome forces of nature that antedated the Olympian pantheon. Zeus had placed the heav-

ens under his sovereignty after wresting power from his father, the wily
Cronus, who had himself seized command of the universe by deposing and
savagely castrating his own father Uranus. Under Zeus, whose children
included the divine patrons of the arts and of all intellectual pursuits, Apollo
and Athena, together with the goddesses of choral dance and poetry and
aesthetic refinement, the Muses and the Graces, the universe ceased to be a
barbaric battleground of death-dealing primitive gods. It became a sacred
theatre of civilization, the dancing-floor of the Olympians and their mortal
worshippers. The Muses circled not only round the purple fountain whose
waters rose up from Earth and from Earth's dark chaotic source, but also
round the altar of aegis-bearing Zeus, the father and defender of a world
governed according to divine law, illuminated with Athena's wisdom, and
made lovely by Apollo's 'mousikē.'

Choral dance epitomized for the Greeks all that was most beautiful and
most fragile about the society of the new gods, the divine gift of harmony
which they bestowed as best they could on the primeval face of nature and
the tragic struggling life of man. Under the spell of Apollo's lyre, as an
unknown poet of the sixth century BC sang in a paean to the founder of the
Delphic oracle, the gods left off their petty wranglings, grasped each other's
wrists to form a chain (a detail of choral dancing also mentioned by Homer),
and celebrated the wonder and nobility of their privileged existence:

> All the Muses together, voice answering lovely voice,
> Now hymn the immortal gifts of the gods and the miseries of
> men,
> Who, enduring so much at the hands of the undying gods,
> Live recklessly and helplessly and cannot find for themselves
> A cure for death and a defence against old age.
> And the fair-haired Graces, the cheerful Hours,
> Harmonia, Hebe, and the daughter of Zeus, Aphrodite,
> Are dancing [orcheunt'], holding their hands on each other's
> wrists;
> And with them dances one neither ugly nor little
> But great to behold and wondrous in form –
> Artemis, shooter of arrows, raised with Apollo.
> Among them play Ares and Hermes, the keen-sighted slayer of
> Argus;
> And Phoebus Apollo plays the lyre among them,
> Striding high and nobly, and around him shines a radiance
> From his flashing feet and finely woven tunic.
>
> (Hymn to Pythian Apollo 11–25)

Plato would also see the gods as dancing in perpetual harmony beyond the miseries and terrors of the human condition; but in borrowing this poetic image for his philosophical myth of creation he would alter the implications of the divine chorus in three respects. First the goddess Harmonia who danced in the company of the Pythian Apollo would be translated into a cosmological principle of harmony inherent in the Craftsman's mathematical design. A 'harmony' (from the verb 'harmozein,' 'to join') literally meant the fastening together of lumber or stones or any material things, and figuratively, the blending or sequential arrangement of musical tones. When the Olympian chorus formed a chain or a circle by holding each other's wrists, they produced a harmony with their bodies just as Apollo produced a harmony with his lyre. The Craftsman fitted the body of his cosmos together with sequences of simple ratios which, according to Timaeus, were the pervasive and inviolable bonding agents in all cosmic harmonies. Since the human composite of body and soul – like all else constructed by the Craftsman – was a harmonious structure bound together by the invisible powers of number, man too could hope to participate in the choral dance of the gods. Not permanently, of course, for the human body was destined to disintegrate at death. But even if the human race were as vulnerable and oppressed by the immortals as the poet of the Homeric Hymn pessimistically assumed, at least certain mortals, illuminated by philosophy, could master the rhythmic rules governing the divine chorus and learn to imitate Apollo's serenely rational motions in both body and soul. This optimistic qualification was the second change Plato made in the poetic image of the dance of the gods. The third was simply this: the choral dances of Timaeus' gods, the stars, were not merely imagined in a flight of poetic fancy or a fit of religious enthusiasm. They could be seen with the naked eye.

Choragus of the Fire-Breathing Stars

The earliest poetic references to the dance of the stars in Western literature are to be found in the choral odes of Greek tragedy, where, as one might expect, the cosmic chorus dances more often to the ominous thunder of Dionysian drums than to the soothing measures of Apollo's lyre. In the *Antigone* of Sophocles, for instance, after Tiresias has pronounced his dire prophecy of Creon's death and the king has hastened from Thebes in a mood of desperate but futile repentance to prevent the deaths of Antigone and Haemon, the chorus of Theban elders sing a solemn hymn to Dionysus in which they beg the god to save their ill-fated city from the plague and political strife that will follow Creon's downfall. Dionysus is first invoked as the patron of Thebes and then as a cosmic deity who by ruling the stars can lead his worshippers through their dark night of violence:

O Choragus of the fire-breathing stars [chorag' astrōn],

Leader of the voices of the night, visit us!
Son begotten of Zeus, Ruler,
Appear before us with your attendant Bacchants
Who all night long in frenzy dance [choreuousi] with you,
The Giver of Gifts, Iacchus!

(*Antigone* 1146–1151)

The function of the choragus was literally 'to lead a chorus' (choron agein) in the dual capacity of principal dancer and conductor of the chant. In Athens, however, the title was also given to the wealthy citizen who generously volunteered, or was assigned by municipal officials, to defray the cost of costuming and training a chorus for the City Dionysia. In describing Dionysus as a choragus, Sophocles no doubt had both senses of the word in mind. As 'Leader of the voices of the night,' Dionysus was believed to appear in person among his ecstatic adorants and to conduct their torchlit processions and dizzying rounds beneath the fire-breathing stars; and as Iacchus, 'Giver of Gifts,' he was the divine patron of the performing arts who furnished his chorus with health and prosperity. Like his mountain dance, the 'oreibasia,' which ended in the savage rending of a sacrificial victim and in a heightened consciousness of the divine presence in nature, tragedy was for the Greeks both a confrontation with all that was agonizing and destructive and amoral in the human condition, and also a consolation for human suffering through the mystic awareness of an all-encompassing moral order behind the catastrophic spectacle of human destiny. This was why the Theban elders hailed their god as the choral leader of Fate's primeval agents, the stars, for if Dionysus could turn the inexorable revolutions of the heavenly bodies into a dance such as he led on earth then out of the madness and havoc wrought by their fatal influences would spring a serene assurance that humanity had not been abandoned by the gods in a wilderness of unspeakable terrors, and with that wisdom, a restored sense of harmony between human society and the powers of nature.

The psychological paradoxes of the Dionysian dance – its wisdom-in-madness and serenity-in-agony, which are also paradoxes at the heart of tragedy – were expressed by Euripides in the great choral odes of the *Bacchae*. The leader of the cosmic chorus is not merely invoked in this dark perplexing play. He appears on stage, in his own theatre, to combat the tyranny of his human adversary Pentheus. Into the Thebes which Pentheus has peacefully if oppressively ruled following the retirement of his grandfather Cadmus rushes a band of wild-haired Asian Bacchants led by a golden-haired youth who claims (and later proves) to be Cadmus' other grandson, Dionysus, child of the Theban princess Semele. In their first thrilling chant the Bacchants urge the Thebans to join their 'manikē choreia':

O Thebes, nurse of Semele,
Crown yourself with ivy!
Burst forth, burst forth with the lovely fruit
Of pale-green bryony,
And dance in ecstatic frenzy [katabacchiousthe]
With wands of oak and pine!
Wind round yourself garments
Of dappled fawn-skin, of fleecy white wool;
Purify yourself by waving the wanton wands!
Now all the earth will dance [choreusei]:
Bromius is he who guides the revelling throngs.
To the mountains, to the mountains!
There remains the band of women
Driven from their weaving and from their loom-combs,
Driven mad by Dionysus!

(*Bacchae* 105–19)

The fawn-skins, phallic wands, and other emblems of Dionysus in his role as Bromius, 'the Clamourer,' betray his original identity as a god of instinctive sexuality and of the fertility of nature. Bromius is he who causes the pines to flourish on the mountain-sides, the bryony to bear fruit, and the deer and sheep to procreate in the springtime. Disorderly as their convulsive leaps and turns might appear to the eye, the Bacchants claim to participate in a divinely incited dance which is inseparable from the cyclical order of nature. All the earth, the wild earth, will revel with them when they follow the Clamourer. He will restore the sympathy between man and nature that the dictators of urban civilization have deadened or striven to replace with purely human allegiances. Yet the Dionysus who had taught mankind the techniques of viniculture and the arts of music, poetry, drama, and religious dance could not be considered an enemy of civilized life. Joining in his frenzied dance, the 'baccheia,' was a means of purging the unhealthy effects of civilization from one's soul and of relaxing the customary restrictions of society (at least temporarily) so that the inherently oppressive order of urban life would never grow unbearable. Hence the institution of the City Dionysia: at regular intervals the clamorous population of Athens strove to dance itself back into harmony with the Eleusinian cosmos.

Peculiarly Athenian are the attitudes towards social and cosmic harmony expressed by the chorus of Creusa's handmaidens in the *Ion* of Euripides. Creusa, daughter of the legendary Athenian king Erechtheus, plots to poison her husband's new-found heir Ion (who is in fact her unrecognized son by Apollo) before he can be returned to Athens from Delphi where he has been serving as a priest of his divine father. Her handmaidens, fearing that Ion will depose his royal patron and disrupt the mystic communion of the Athenian people with the gods of Eleusis, express their approval of the queen's murderous plans in the following strophe:

> I would be ashamed before the oft-hymned God,
> If on the twentieth day a stranger stood
> Beside the Wellspring of Fair Dances [kallichoroisi pagais]
> And saw, sleepless at night, the torch and holy envoy,
> When Zeus' star-eyed sky
> Has begun its choral dance [anechoreusen].
> And the moon is dancing [choreuei],
> And the fifty Nereid maidens
> Who dwell beneath the sea,
> Beneath the whirlpools of the everflowing streams,
> Are hymning in their choral dance [choreuomenai]
> The gold-crowned maid Persephone
> And her majestic mother Demeter.
> There Ion hopes to rule,
> Rushing in upon the work of other men,
> That vagabond son of Phoebus!

(*Ion* 1074–1089)

The 'oft-hymned God' is Bacchus, Bromius, Iacchus, Dionysus – the cosmic choragus whose many names were shouted into the night by pilgrims to Eleusis; perhaps, as their torches leaped and flickered in the long procession to the temple, and afterwards, on the 'eikas' or 'twentieth day' of the month and the sixth day of the Mysteries, the torches were lit again for some secret nocturnal ceremony around the Wellspring of Fair Dances, the pilgrims were reminded of the moving lights in 'Zeus' star-eyed sky' and the image of the cosmic dance was born, or reborn, in their mind's eye. Creusa's xenophobic handmaidens portray the cosmic dance as both an enduring and a curiously fragile vision of world-harmony. The 'theōros' or holy envoy (literally 'spectator') who was sent from Athens to present offerings at the temple would observe and participate in choral movements which, when projected outward from the Mysteries to all the domains of the mythical universe, to Heaven and Ocean, to Earth and Underworld, bound man and his myriad gods in a sympathetic union as inviolate as that between the dancing moon and the Nereids' flowing tides. Yet somehow this peculiarly Athenian vision of the world-chorus, at once poetic and philosophical, with man both a participant and a spectator at the dance of the gods, could be shattered by the intrusion of a single foreigner – a bastard son of Apollo who was out of sympathy with the cult and the culture of Dionysus.

In some sense Apollo and his offspring did invade the cosmic theatre of Dionysus, transforming the satyr-choruses and manic revels of pre-classical Attic culture into the tragedies and dithyrambic dances of the City Dionysia. Thus, despite the fears of Creusa's handmaidens, the creative and mysterious and irrational energies of the oft-hymned God were not suppressed by the cultivation of Apollonian rationality. They were disciplined, civilized, harnessed for artistic ends. When the Bacchants of the theatre leaped in ecstatic possession, tossing their heads back in the air and waving their wanton wands, they were imitating the savage dance on the mountain-tops rather than actually surrendering to it. The frenzied chorus had become, paradoxically, a subordinate episode in an intricate poetic design. In his celebrated choral ode on old age in the *Heracles*, Euripides declared that Phoebus with his seven-stringed lyre, as well as Bromius with his wine, had inspired the art of tragic poetry. As an old man the poet would still sing the praises of the leader of the Muses –

> *Just as the maids of Delos sing a paean*
> *Circling in their dance round the temple gates*
> *In honour of Leto's fair son,*
> *Apollo the beautiful dancer [kallichoron] ...*
> (*Heracles* 687–91)

The choral dance of the classical Greek theatre, like the poetry accompanying it, was neither purely Dionysian nor purely Apollonian in spirit. Somehow in the evolution of a transient culture into an enduring civilization the antagonistic characters of these two dancing gods were harmonized or at least temporarily reconciled, and the measure, the grace, the geometrical order of the circling Muses were wedded to the freedom, passion, and mystical rapture of the soaring Bacchants.

Not all the choral odes in Euripidean tragedy presuppose a harmony between chorus and cosmos as clearly as the chant of the Bacchants or the hymn of Creusa's handmaidens: most, in fact, make no mention whatever of the movements of the heavenly bodies or the mystical sympathy between man, nature, and the gods established in the sacred dance. In general the choral ode functioned simply as a lyrical interlude or as a moral commentary on the human events unfolding in the drama. Yet in the prosodic structure of many tragic odes, which probably grew out of the patterns of choral movement around and in front of the altar of Dionysus, might still be detected the imitative design of a cosmic dance. That was the theory of at least one commentator on Greek tragedy in Antiquity – an anonymous scholiast on Euripides' *Hecuba*. Though choral passages in Greek tragedy reveal an enormous variety of highly complicated metrical and stanzaic forms, they are typically composed of a series of strophes (literally 'turns') balanced by antistrophes ('counterturns'). These divisions, sometimes though not always in contrasting metres, were occasionally followed by a brief lyric known as the epode ('after-song'). The scholiast explained the significance of these three terms in the following note:

One ought to know, moreover, that the choral dancers [hoi choreutai] would sing the strophe as they moved to the right, and the antistrophe as they moved to the left, and the epode as they stood still. The strophe, as they say, signified the movement of the heavens from east to west, the antistrophe the movement of the planets from west to east, and the epode the immobility of the earth, for then the choral dancers sang while standing still.[5]

Unfortunately, the vagueness of the directions 'left' and 'right' renders this ancient gloss all but useless for historians of the Greek theatre. Did the scholiast intend his directions to be understood from the audience's or the chorus's viewpoint? Do they refer to linear movements across the dance-floor or revolutions and counterrevolutions around the altar? If circular movements are meant, then might not the scholiast be referring to the 'kyklios choros' of dithyramb rather than the choruses of tragedy?

Tragic choruses, originally consisting of twelve dancers but later of fifteen, typically made their entrance by marching in from the right of the audience in a dense rectangular formation, either three dancers by four or three by five. They did not leave the stage until their exit at the conclusion of the play. During the performance their dances seem to have varied considerably in configuration, tempo, and mood, depending on the characters imperson-ated by the chorus and on the dramatic episodes inspiring their movement. For instance, the chorus of Furies in Aeschylus' *Eumenides* (307–96) prob-ably danced in a ring as they sang their hellish incantation about 'binding round' the soul of Orestes, perhaps imitating in the entwining turns of a circular chain-dance or with rotatory gesticulations of their hands the spin-ning out of the protagonist's destiny and of all-encompassing Fate.

If other odes in Greek tragedy were similarly chanted while the chorus danced in a circle, then the scholiast's second and less perplexing generali-zation, that choral movements and pauses corresponded to the revolutions of the heavenly bodies and the motionlessness of the earth, may have had some historical validity in the interpretation of both tragic and dithyrambic dances. When Euripides has his chorus of Argive countrywomen in the *Electra* condemn Clytemnestra's murder of Agamemnon by reviewing the king's glorious exploits in the Trojan War and recalling, in an echo of Homer's description of the cosmic Shield of Achilles, how

In the shield's centre shone

The sun's blazing circle,
Drawn up by winged horses,
And the ethereal choral dances of stars
[astrōn t' aitherioi choroi],
The Pleiades and the Hyades,
Terrifying in the eyes of Hector ...
(*Electra* 465–9)

his momentary analogy between choral dancing and the fateful wheeling of
the constellations (a visual metaphor implied by Homer, perhaps, but not
expressed in the *Iliad*) may have been much more than a passing reference
to cosmic designs displayed in the strophic and antistrophic movements of
the tragic chorus. Despite his vagueness with respect to theatrical practice,
the Euripidean scholiast had a very clear theoretical notion of cosmic order
as a natural model for choral dance – or of choral dance as a visual image
of cosmic order – which links his otherwise obscure and isolated remarks
with the mainstream of ancient Greek cosmology. Plato too would assume
that a natural analogy existed between earthly and celestial choruses. But
unlike the chorus of Euripidean stars whose ominous strophes and antistrophes struck terror in the hearts of all mortals, the stars in Plato's musical
heavens were terrifying only to 'those who cannot calculate their motions.'

Strophe and Antistrophe

The astronomer Timaeus whom Socrates introduces to his colleagues as a
distinguished citizen of the Italian town of Locris and whom many Platonists
in Antiquity believed to be a member of the school of Pythagorean philosophers residing in southern Italy in the late fifth and early fourth centuries
BC narrates the Myth of the Craftsman without once referring to a doctrine
which posterity would regard as a hallmark of Pythagorean cosmology: the
music of the spheres. Sometime in the early fifth century BC, a hundred or
so years before Timaeus is supposed to have delivered his lecture in Athens,
Pythagoras reputedly discovered that the relation between the tones and
semitones in the musical scale could be expressed by simple numerical ratios.
The exciting discovery that sounds as well as the movements of the stars
seemed to be governed by numbers prompted the followers of Pythagoras
to interpret the design of the cosmos musically. They wondered, for instance,
whether the distances between the planets might correspond proportionally
to the measured intervals of a lyre-string, or whether the planets as they
were whirling through the ethereal realms might each emit a note in con-
sonance with the heavenly melodies of the Muses. If the celestial notes made
up the same scale measured on the strings of earthly lyres, then heaven and
earth would indeed be joined harmoniously. Those who interpreted cosmic

order as a musical 'harmony' still understood this term in its original sense of 'interlocking structure,' but with one theoretical modification. The components of their universal structure were held together by eternal mathematical laws rather than by impermanent material bonds. These divine laws of number were so complex and awesome that Pythagoras supposedly restricted knowledge of the celestial music to a select brotherhood of initiated disciples who believed in it as a matter of faith and endured rigorously ascetic lives in the hope of hearing its ineffable concords. Enchanting as the idea of celestial music would always be, the sound of the planetary chorus unfortunately escaped most human ears; as a result most cosmologists in Antiquity relegated it to the realm of pure mathematical theory or mystical contemplation. More a physicist than a pure mathematician or mystic, Timaeus never claimed to have heard the music of the spheres and nowhere in his lecture described the astral chorus as a choir. Seeing the design of the heavens as a choral dance was not the same as hearing it, or hoping to hear it, as a melody.[6]

The only character in all of Plato to have heard the song of the heavens – and his strange story, recounted by Socrates in the tenth and final book of the *Republic* (614b–621b), includes the earliest extant reference to cosmic music in Greek philosophy – was not, oddly enough, a Pythagorean initiate or a musician with extrasensory perception but a valiant Pamphylian soldier by the name of Er. His enemies having struck him down in battle one day, Er fell unconscious among the heaps of slain soldiers on the field and was mistaken for dead by those who survived the combat. His body was placed upon a pyre to await cremation on the twelfth day after the battle, but just before the pyre was lit, not a moment too soon, he revived, and to the astonishment of his comrades recalled all his experiences in the realm of the Dead. He had journeyed to a mysterious region between heaven and earth where the souls of the just were separated from those of the wicked, and there he had seen a curious mechanism which he called 'the spindle of Necessity.' This device consisted of a long adamant staff around which spun eight concentric whorls, each placed one inside another like a set of mixing bowls. The bottom of the staff rested on the knees of the goddess Necessity, who spun it to the musical accompaniment of her divine attendants. The whorls represented the planets and the fixed stars, and on the rotating rim of each sat a Siren who uttered a single note in perfect harmony with the notes of her sisters. In traditional Greek mythology the Sirens resided not on the heavenly bodies but on a rocky Mediterranean island where they lured mariners to their deaths by singing an irresistible melody; in the Myth of Er, however, the music of the celestal Sirens was not perceived as evil, though it retained its enchanting and irresistible quality. According to Er, this fateful music within nature was echoed and completed by a fateful music beyond nature. Seated on thrones outside the cosmic spindle were three other singers, the Fates, who accompanied the Sirens' song by chanting of the things that were and the things that are and the things that are to come. Unlike the free-soaring chorus of Hesiod's Muses, who celebrated the harmony of heaven and earth in dance as well as song, the stern goddesses in Er's deterministic vision performed their endless chant without leaving their stations around or within the mechanism of destiny.

The Myth of Er serves both as a visionary conclusion to the discussions of virtue, justice, and political order in the *Republic* and also as a link between this dialogue and the lecture on cosmic order in the *Timaeus*. The two dialogues form a 'harmony' in other ways as well. Timaeus supposedly delivers his lecture on the day after Socrates narrates the Myth of Er, and in the conversation preceding the Myth of the Craftsman Socrates summarizes the main points in his argument of the day before (without, however, mentioning the vision of the planetary Sirens). Plato therefore invites his readers to interpret the *Timaeus* as a cosmological extension of the political and moral theories expounded in the *Republic*. He will show how the visible world would appear to the eyes of a philosopher who had made the contemplative ascent from the cave of the senses, glimpsed the eternal World of Being, and returned with transcendent insights into the World of Becoming. In tacit contrast to Er's fantastic tale, however, Timaeus presents what he calls a 'likely story' (29d) of the formation of the cosmos and the disposition of its harmonious parts. His independent interpretation of the world of temporal change is expressed in symbolic images very different from those in the Myth of Er. The music of the Fates and Sirens is not heard at the dances of the stars. No music is heard at all. The image of the dance will not imply a whirling deterministic mechanism but a living sky full of living stars, and the stability of the Craftsman's cosmos will not depend on external forces (like the hand of Necessity) continually applied to insensitive matter but on a purely psychological impulse to imitate a divine paradigm of order. While the music of the celestial Sirens was a cosmic design normally beyond the range of mortal perception, the dance of the stars could be seen by anyone who gazed at the night sky.

The technical details of cosmology, as Timaeus himself admitted (40d), are difficult to explain 'aneu diopsēos toutōn autōn mimētatōn,' that is, without astronomical diagrams and other visual models (literally, 'without a close look at imitations of these matters'). One important model in classical astronomy was the armillary sphere, a globe of metal rings corresponding to the diurnal and annual revolutions of the heavenly bodies, at the centre of which, speared by a wire pole, was a small solid ball representing the earth. Lacking such a teaching device for his Athenian lecture, though spheres of this sort almost certainly existed by the fourth century BC, Timaeus avoids the obscure technicalities of astronomy by conveying a vivid picture of the Craftsman's cosmos in verbal images anyone might understand. His visual models are implicit in his metaphors: the stars are an embroidery on the fabric of the cosmic sphere; the earth is a nurse, a guardian, a craftsman; the heavenly bodies perform choral dances of wondrous intricacy. In the geometrical configurations of choral dancing Timaeus saw a moving image of his sidereal system. As a theatrical art involving imitative gestures choreia presupposed the relation between a model and its artistic image; as a physical skill requiring mental discipline it coordinated the external motions of the body with the internal operations of the soul; and as a harmonious round or chain linking diverse individuals it entailed a general sameness or con-formity of movement within which soloists could perform idiosyncratic steps like those of the two tumblers on the Shield of Achilles. These three pairs of concepts – model and image, body and soul, sameness and difference – are the recurrent analytical distinctions in Platonic cosmology. In the as-tronomer's cursory reference to the cosmic dance one might sense, even without expert knowledge of the geometry of the armillary sphere, the fundamental assumptions of his world-view.

The word 'cosmos' (from the verb 'kosmein,' 'to marshal' or 'to adorn') originally signified either an orderly arrangement of things or a decorative artefact. The Craftsman therefore created a 'true cosmos' because he arranged the elements of earth, water, air, and fire in a fitting sequence, and also because he fashioned a beautifully symmetrical object out of their diverse mixtures. The true cosmos, like a chorus, was more than just a strict mar-shalling of moving bodies: it was a dynamic design intended to please the eye. Unlike the aesthetically pleasing but wholly artificial cosmos on the Shield of Achilles the true cosmos was obviously not modelled on the visible world, for it *was* the visible world.

Timaeus accordingly assumed that the Craftsman made the cosmic sphere in the image of an eternal, divine, and living Model antedating space and time and existing far beyond the range of the senses (exactly where he does not say – for that would be the subject for an altogether different lecture). By endlessly repeating the relation of image and model within the visible world, the Craftsman supplied clues to his whole design in the structure of its parts. He formed each star as a miniature replica of the celestial globe and modelled each stellar revolution on the pattern of a master-orbit which Timaeus called 'the Supreme Circle' or 'the Circle of the Same.' This was represented by the largest ring on an armillary sphere, the celestial equator. As the imaginary projection of the earth's equator onto the celestial globe, the Circle of the Same was not a material object like its metal model but an abstract configuration such as a dancer in a 'kyklios choros' might run over in his mind before tracing with his feet. No matter where the stars were set within the cosmic sphere they followed the rotation of the celestial equator from east to west in concentric orbits diminishing in circumference to the fixed points of the pole-stars.

Anyone who gazed for only a few hours at the night sky would notice that the fixed stars (so called because their positions relative to each other in the chorus never changed) revolved slowly but continuously around the axis linking the centre of the earth with the motionless star at the pole. If the Craftsman had not fashioned their bodies mostly out of fire, Timaeus reasoned, the circular configuration of the astral chorus would never have been visible to mortal eyes; and if he had not also created intelligent souls to control their luminous bodies the stars would never have danced their rounds so consistently and for so many ages. Timaeus' inference that an unseen inner presence, a rational soul, guided each star in its diurnal revolution and maintained its course unchanged according to a Divine Plan was affirmed as a philosophical conclusion of the utmost wisdom by the principal speaker of another Platonic dialogue, the Athenian of the *Epinomis*:

And as proof that the stars and the whole moving system of the heavens possess intelligence, mankind ought to consider the fact that the stars always do the same things and have done so for an amazingly long time. Because they are carrying out what was planned long ago, they do not alter their plans now this way, now that, sometimes doing one thing and sometimes another, wandering and changing their orbits. Many of us have thought just the opposite – that because they do the same things in the same way they do not possess soul. Most people have followed the lead of fools, imagining that whereas the human race is intelligent and living because it can move about, the divine race is unintelligent because it keeps to the same orbits. Yet man might have accepted the fairer, better, more favourable interpretation. He might have concluded that that which always does the same things in the same way and for the same reason must for this very reason be considered intelligent. And thus the nature of the stars is the fairest to behold, for they dance the fairest and most magnificent procession and choral dance of all the choruses in the world [poreian de kai choreian pantōn chorōn kallistēn kai megaloprepestatēn choreuonta] and accomplish whatever is needed for all living creatures.

(*Epinomis* 982d–e)

Though Plato's authorship of this brief treatise on the value of mathematics and astronomy in the education of a wise citizen has often been questioned in recent times, its canonical status as a genuine Platonic dialogue was rarely doubted in Antiquity. Its rhetorical and ideological affinities with Plato's late works, particularly the *Timaeus* and the *Laws* (the principal speaker in the latter being also an unnamed Athenian), are so pronounced that if Plato was not its author then whoever was must have been either a talented imitator or a wholly unoriginal disciple of the Master in the early days of the Old Academy. Like Timaeus, the Athenian commends the vision of the astral chorus for being just that – a vision in its literal sense, of all dances 'the fairest to behold' (idein men kallistēn). To them both, moreover, the 'kallistē choreia' of the stars offered compelling evidence that a mind of superhuman powers resided within each heavenly body and indeed within the cosmic sphere as a whole. Turning this elementary inference into a premise of his cosmology, Timaeus argued that the ultimate source of rationality in the cosmos must be the transcendent intellect or 'nous' of the Craftsman. Endowed with an intellect surpassed only by its Creator, the cosmos would not require divine movers in the Beyond to initiate its uniform daily rotation. It would simply move itself. The World-Soul, like the soul in a human dancer, would impel and regulate its movements from within.

In accordance with his psychological theory of celestial motion, Timaeus interpreted the Circle of the Same as a never-ending cycle of thought in the World-Soul, a continuous process of thinking the same thoughts about the same things. A human 'nous' could imitate the flow of thoughts in the World-Soul by considering the various steps a dancer requires to whirl his body round in a complete turn and then in another and in yet another. The Circle of the Same represented the continuity and uniformity of this train of thought on a universal scale. Timaeus referred to the Supreme Circle as 'the Same and Uniform' to signify the kind of reasoning inherent in the cosmic soul as inferred from the sameness and uniformity of the visible rotation of the cosmic body. The intelligence symbolized by the Circle of the Same would never impress the foolish masses (as the Athenian had admitted) with its sparkling originality or creative spontaneity: its chief virtue was an ideal stable-mindedness. Its untiring concentration on the Divine Plan ensured that the stars were maintained in their perpetual rounds and the cosmic body kept under firm control. By analogy with the World-Soul the souls of the stars also thought the same thoughts about the same things in order to keep their bodies moving in harmony with each other and with the rotation of the cosmic sphere. This stable coordination, at an individual as well as a general level, prevented the fairest and most magnificent choral dance from degenerating into chaos.

The 'kallistē choreia' of the fixed stars was the most harmonious (in its old sense) but by no means the only movement visible in the celestial theatre. Against the revolving background of the astral chorus, the sun, moon, and other planets performed a complicated series of periodic motions distinct from the revolutions governed exclusively by the Supreme Circle. The sun was the leader of this wandering troupe of soloists and also the crucial intermediary betwen their inner chorus and the outer circles of the stars. Like the latter the sun appeared to revolve daily around the earth from east to west; but in the course of a year the position of the sun relative to the fixed stars gradually shifted in the opposite direction until it had traced out a great circular path through the constellations. Timaeus called this path 'the Circle of the Different.' It was different from the Circle of the Same not only in its counterrevolution from west to east but in its distinctive position on the celestial globe. According to his Divine Plan the Craftsman tilted the sun's annual orbit at an acute angle to the celestial equator with the result that the Circle of the Different intersected the Circle of the Same at two points, dividing it into two equal arcs (see figure 3). In the modern solar system the earth is endowed with two main motions: a daily rotation about its axis, and an annual revolution around the sun. The first accounts for the apparent daily revolution of the fixed stars, and the second for the sun's apparent revolution along the Circle of the Different. To see how ancient astronomers were tricked into adding the Circle of the Different to their visual models of the cosmos, consider a star-gazer with such powerful eyes that he can pierce the veil of daylight to observe the starry background behind the sun. As the earth gradually completed its annual revolution the spectator would see a continually changing cluster of stars in the sun's apparent vicinity. If he assumed that the earth was at rest he would naturally conclude that each year the sun moved in a broad circle within a fixed band of constellations. The band would appear fixed because the plane of the earth's orbit does not vary appreciably from year to year. Ancient astron- omers, unable of course to pierce the daytime glare, were nonetheless able to determine the position of the Circle of the Different by recording the various constellations appearing on the horizon at the points where the sun rose and set. The apparent tilt of the Different results from the 23 1/2-degree slant of the earth's equatorial plane relative to its heliocentric orbital plane. Because solar eclipses may occur only when the moon crosses the slanted circuit astronomers now refer to the Circle of the Different as the 'ecliptic.'

The Circle of the Different was easy to spot on an armillary sphere because the conspicuous slanted ring representing it was typically broadened into a band marked with the constellations (or the astrological symbols of the constellations) along which the sun appeared to pass. These sun-signs are the familiar twelve constellations of the zodiac. Though the ecliptic could be understood simply as a circle projected onto the celestial globe, Timaeus adapted it to the design of his living cosmos by endowing the Different with a psychological significance beyond its original geometrical definition. If the Circle of the Same could represent a mental process in the World-Soul, the uniform cycle of thoughts governing the uniform revolutions of the fixed stars, then by analogy the Circle of the Different might represent the in-

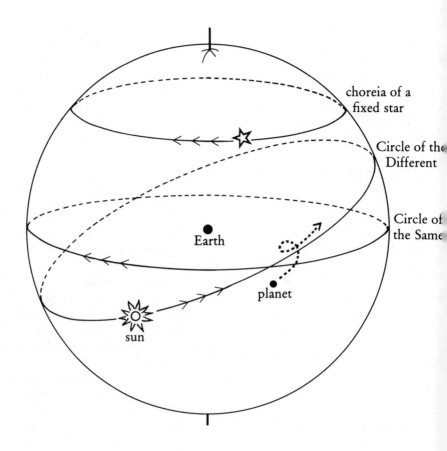

Figure 3

The Platonic cosmos, or World of Becoming, was a composite of body and soul patterned on a spherical Model existing in the eternal World of Being. Each day the cosmic body made one complete turn from east to west, bearing with it the fixed stars and planets. Each year the sun completed an additional revolution from west to east, tracing out its own orbital path through the zodiac. The other planets completed similar counterturns over different periods. Plato referred to the cycle of thoughts within the World-Soul corresponding to the 'kyklios choros' of fixed stars around the celestial equator as the Circle of the Same. The Circle of the Different was his term for the cosmic thought-processes giving rise to the dances of the planets.

tellectual operations behind the diverse motions of the wandering stars. This ingenious inference was supported by a striking observation: in their apparent wanderings the planets crossed and recrossed the ecliptic but never moved beyond the narrow band of the zodiac. Their mazy motions seemed to be governed by the Different just as the astral rounds were governed by the Same.

All along the zodiac the planets added their idiosyncratic movements to the cosmic dance. Mars would advance from west to east and then loop backwards a few degrees before carrying on in its original direction. Venus would appear beside the sun in the evenings, disappear, and then rise beside the sun in the mornings. And the moon, as it crossed the slanted circuit, would periodically eclipse the sun.

The Circle of the Different was thus aptly named on account of the different planetary choreiai visible near the ecliptic. Though Timaeus failed to explain these motions in rigorous technical detail, he proudly distinguished himself from superstitious folk who were unable to calculate the changing positions of the planets and were consequently terrified by their deviations from the circular norm of the astral choreiai. Solar eclipses and other spectacular episodes in the cosmic dance were not dreadful portents, he calmly argued. From the viewpoint of a rational man – and who was more rational than he? – they were simply puzzles to be solved mathematically or artistic variations to be admired amid the splendid uniformity of the cosmic design. His firm belief that the maze of planetary motions might be plotted as clearly as the circling of the fixed stars encouraged Platonic cosmologists in later ages to assume that the orbits of the planets were no less regular than the stellar circles. The fearfully irregular wanderings of the planets seem neither fearful nor irregular when perceived as choreiai. A quick glance at an armillary sphere would assure anyone that the Craftsman had firmly linked the Circle of the Different to the Circle of the Same. Seeing their harmony, who could doubt that an assuringly stable design encompassed the frightening diversity of the cosmos? Far from disrupting the uniform order of the cosmic dance, the Circle of the Different graced it with new and varied figures – linear, looping, labyrinthine.

The Athenian Spectator

A few isolated references to the cosmic dance may be found in the fragments of Presocratic philosophy. Though most of these were preserved by doxographers and commentators who lived many centuries after Plato, they may shed light not only on the various characteristics of the Craftsman's cosmos implicit in Plato's vision of the world-chorus (its rationality, divinity, harmony, visual symmetry, numerical regulation, and psychological dynamics) but also on that intervening stage in the history of the image when it flowed away from the mythological wellsprings of Greek poetry and drama into the currents of analytical, teleological, and empirical thought that became Greek philosophy.

An early and rather obscure Pythagorean named Petron (fl c500 BC) is reported to have taught

that there were one hundred and eighty-three worlds arranged in the form of a triangle, each side of which had sixty worlds. The three remaining worlds were each situated at one of the corners. These were all joined to each other in succession and moved around gently as in a choral dance [hōsper en choreiai].

(Diels and Kranz 1, fr 16 [6])

Since Petron's bizarre theory of cosmic geometry has come down to us in a treatise by Plutarch of Chaeronea, a Platonist of the early second century AD, there is no telling whether the phrase 'hōsper en choreiai' was originally Petron's. Chances are that it was not, for Plutarch undoubtedly coloured his paraphrase of Petron's teachings with rhetorical formulas familiar from Plato. Still, if this fragment preserves anything of Petron's original vision of world-harmony, it might point at least to the highly theoretical yet visually imaginative context in which the image of the cosmic chorus found its way into philosophical writings before Plato. Petron evidently regarded the cosmos as so neatly measured in its motions, so schematic in its visual design, that anyone skilled in the geometry of the triangle – a disciple of Pythagoras, for instance – could easily calculate and predict all the motions of the heavenly bodies. Numbers in Pythagorean cosmology did not function as do numbers in modern astrophysics. Far from being purely analytical concepts formulated by the human mind they were eternal principles of world-harmony antedating the visible world and actively binding it together. Divine in origin, they provided a limit and a shape for the dynamic design of the cosmos. The heavenly bodies in Petron's universe (and in the Craftsman's true cosmos) did not perform their gently flowing choral dance on the dark stage of infinity, in a limitless, unintelligible, and terrifying void, for even the outermost movements of the stars had been measured by divine numbers and could therefore be understood by every educated spectator.[7]

Numerical measure was also of central importance in a vision of the cosmic dance attributed to Philolaus of Croton, a Pythagorean who flourished in the second half of the fifth century BC. At the centre of his cosmos, as on the altar of an immense temple, burnt a sacred fire from which the binding energies of nature radiated. Here the Creator had placed the mysterious ruling principle or 'metron' of the universe. 'Philolaus places fire in the middle of the universe,' testified Aetius, a scholarly summarizer of philosophical doctrines who lived sometime in the second century AD,

and he calls it 'the Hearth of the Universe,' 'the house of Zeus,' 'the Mother of the Gods,' 'the Altar, Binding-Force, and Measure of Nature.' Then again there is another fire, which envelops the universe around its outermost regions, but the central fire was the first to be kindled. Around it ten divine bodies dance in chorus [choreuein]: first the sphere of the fixed stars, then the five planets, next the sun, the moon, the earth, and the counter-earth. Finally the fire of the 'Hearth' keeps its station in the centre.

(Diels and Kranz I, 44 [32] A fr 16)

Again, given the second-hand testimony, one cannot determine whether Philolaus actually spoke of the heavenly bodies as dancing around the central fire or whether Aetius was simply echoing the rhetoric of Timaeus in his paraphrase; but if the doxographer *was* faithful to his Presocratic source – and his direct quotation of several of Philolaus' metaphorical epithets for the central fire lends support to this hypothesis – then the fragment may be taken as further evidence that the figure of the dance was a visual model of world-harmony in Pythagorean cosmology before Plato.

The Pythagoreans were supposed to have revered the number ten because as the sum of the first four integers it was thought to embrace the fundamental powers of number and thus to be an especially important principle in binding the multiplicity of nature into a unity. If the sacred Decad is indeed what Philolaus meant by the 'Binding-Force' residing in the central fire, then that might explain why exactly ten divine bodies dance around the magical centre like votaries around the altar of Zeus. To end up with a measure of ten for his cosmic chorus Philolaus had to make certain theoretical adjustments to the visible spectacle of celestial motion – adjustments which Timaeus would not make, and which Petron had no need to make since his system of world-order belonged completely to the realm of pure mathematical theory. First Philolaus perceived the multitude of fixed stars as a single member of the sacred chorus, which was not difficult to accept since all of them moved in the same circular configuration as if motivated by a single will. Next, contrary to all visual evidence, he shifted the earth away from the centre of the dance and transformed it from a static or rotating sphere into a revolving body. Most daring of all was his addition of a tenth heavenly body, Antichthon ('counter-earth'), which lay between us and the central fire but which was never visible because the earth always held its face away from the altar of the universe towards the sun and the fixed stars.

Though a cosmic chorus implied a cosmic choragus, no clamorous Dionysus or lyre-strumming Apollo materialized in the universe of the early

Pythagoreans to lead the fire-breathing stars around the orchestra of heaven. Petron and Philolaus might have argued that such gods were simply not needed in a numerically regulated cosmos, that the 'chorēgia' or office of the choragus had been taken over by divine numbers, silent, efficient, impersonal purveyors of unity and concord.

In contrast to the Pythagoreans, Milesian cosmologists like Diogenes of Apollonia (fl c440–30 BC) believed that a single material principle determined all the orderly phenomena of nature and that any physicist who understood its properties fully could explain the workings of the cosmos without resorting to superstitious fantasies about the Olympians or mystical theories about the sacred Decad. Like his predecessor Anaximines, Diogenes was convinced that the single material principle was the element air. He identified air in its most rarefied state with life, soul, intelligence, and divinity, and in varying degrees of condensation with fire, water, and earth. Air became his Dionysus and his Apollo, at once the thunderous whirler of the stars and the divine intellect guiding their choral rounds. According to the Peripatetic commentator Alexander of Aphrodisias, whose summaries of the doctrines of Presocratic physicists were preserved in the sixth century AD by the Neoplatonist Simplicius, Diogenes taught that the heavenly bodies were originally set in motion by convection currents in the upper atmosphere and that air was therefore the choragus of the cosmic dance. 'For after the sea was established around the earth,' he is said to have concluded,

then part of the moist element was evaporated by the sun. From this arose 'breaths' or currents of air which gave rise to the courses of the sun and the moon. Since those heavenly bodies follow their courses as a result of the same current of risen vapours, they have the same choragus whose function [hē tautēs autois chorēgia] is to make them revolve.

(Diels and Kranz II, 64 [51] A fr 17)

The influence of Diogenes and Anaximines on Athenian philosophers in the generation immediately preceding Plato is evident in the fragmentary cosmological poem of Critias of Athens, who, perhaps echoing Diogenes directly, also described the revolution of the heavenly bodies as a dance arising from a primeval galactic whirlwind. A contemporary of Euripides, Critias is now acknowledged to be the author of a reverent invocation to the Creator which is so reminiscent of the tragedian's style that it was once thought to be an excerpt from a lost Euripidean tragedy. The dynamic imagery of the invocation –

*You, the Self-Made One, who have woven
The nature of all things in the ethereal whirl,*

Round whom light and dark shimmering night
And the scattered throng of stars
Perpetually dance [amphichoreuei] . . .
                    (Diels and Kranz II, 88 [81] B fr 19)

– certainly recalls prototypes in the choral odes written for the Athenian stage. Though the cosmic dance seems to have assumed a variety of configurations in the visual imagination of Presocratic philosophers, from a rigid equilateral triangle to a mystical sequence of concentric circles to a freely flowing ethereal whirl, the image of the world-chorus invariably expressed a philosophical assumption common to all these early thinkers, which was, in sum, that behind the shimmering diversity of lights and shadows and ever-evolving appearances of the world lay a single, permanent, measurable design. They were assured that the universe was not the frightening womb of Chaos and Old Night or the tragic Fury-haunted plain of inscrutable Necessity. Timaeus echoed their assurance by adapting their visual model of order to the stable design of the Craftsman's cosmos. The figure of the dance exactly suited the astronomer's vision of a universe rationally measured, divinely created, and vibrantly alive.

In the Athens of Plato's youth mythic images of order brought to life in the Theatre of Dionysus were fused with philosophical ideas of order current in the schools of the Sophists. That this unique interpenetration of drama and philosophy occurred in the writings of professional playwrights as well as professional pedagogues is nowhere more evident than in the comedies of Aristophanes, particularly the *Clouds*, which was first staged in 423 BC at the City Dionysia. In this incisive satire of contemporary 'scientific' education (which to his bitter disappointment won only third prize) Aristophanes literally reduced the air-is-all philosophy of Diogenes and his disciples to a puff of rank vapour in a whirlwind of nonsense by mischievously placing its ethereal tenets in the mouth of Socrates – even though the historical Socrates was intensely skeptical of all high-flown materialistic cosmologies. The Aristophanic Socrates is the very opposite of a Skeptic. Having suspended himself in a basket from the ceiling of his house so that he might be free of dull earth-bound thoughts and at one with the primal intelligence of the ether, the deluded philosopher initiates his boorish neighbour Strepsiades into the mysteries of air by summoning up a chorus of ethereal goddesses, the Clouds, who inspire the one with celestial wisdom and the other with intestinal gas. In their first ode, accompanied by rumblings of atmospheric and abdominal thunder, the Clouds inform Strepsiades that they have arisen from the tumultuous depths of Ocean at the command of their High Priest. How they danced their grand entrance can only be imagined now, but if the male chorus swept on stage in the diaphanous robes of winged nymphs and pretended to be blown around the orchestra on primeval convection currents, the effect would no doubt have been ludicrous.

The cosmic dance was not above the laughter of the Athenians. With characteristic irreverence Aristophanes twisted the venerable dance of order into a vortex of elemental and intellectual chaos, into the universal Whirlwind that Socrates in his madness worships as a force greater than aegis-bearing Zeus. The Whirlwind alone exists for the philosopher. Unable to distinguish anything beyond the dense mist of his sophistries and the hollow thunderclaps of his rhetoric, he startles Strepsiades by denying the existence of all gods save Chaos, the Clouds, and the Tongue. A conservative in religious matters, the country-born neighbour ultimately refuses to believe the philosopher's blasphemous revelation and ironically emerges from his initiation a wiser man than his initiator. The impieties of Socrates are not even countenanced by the Clouds, the supposed genii of his school. In their second ode they call into the Whirlwind the great Olympian deities (along with their divine father, Ether, of course) in the earnest hope that Athens will regain her former piety:

> First, then, I call
> Into the choral dance [eis choron]
>   Great Zeus ruling on high, King of the gods;
> Next Poseidon, mighty wielder
>   Of the trident,
> Fierce upheaver of the earth
>   And salt sea;
> And our father of glorious name,
>   Ether, most majestic sustainer
>   Of all living things;
> And Helios the charioteer, who fills
>   With his exceedingly bright beams the plains
> Of earth, great among the gods
>   And among mortals also.
>   (Clouds 563–74)

Despite these lofty invocations, which are as serious (in their own way) as the invocations sung by the tragic chorus of Theban elders before the death of Antigone, the immortal choragoi of heaven, ocean, air, and fire do *not* descend from the cosmic to the comic stage to lead the sophist-maddened city back into harmony with the divine chorus. Socrates bursts in upon the Clouds exclaiming 'By Chaos!' and their ode is cut short.

No steps are taken to rescue Athens from the chaos into which the Sophists have hurled her until the final moments in the play, and even then order is not restored through the creative intervention of a divine choragus but by the destructive act of an outraged clown. Convinced that the subversive doctrines of the Sophists are undermining everything he cherishes – his economic prosperity, his religious certainties, his mental health, his whole universe – Strepsiades hoists himself onto the roof of Socrates' little house and sets it on fire. The Clouds scatter in the smoke, the High Priest of Chaos is heard shrieking for help, and on that unresolved discord the comedy ends.

In the face of such violent conservative opposition to philosophical free-thinking – which eventually led to the arrest and execution of Socrates for impiety in 399 BC – Plato was understandably anxious to portray his mentor as an essentially ethical and religious thinker whose view of the physical world depended on the mysterious revelations of his tutelary daimone, and to cast him as the leader of a circle of learned friends whose dedication to the cause of intellectual enlightenment did not undermine their deep respect for the Olympian gods. Ironically, not unlike Aristophanes, the Platonic Socrates presents himself as an enemy of the professional philosophers of his day and as an educator whose sole aim is to clear the clouded vision of the spectators in the cosmic theatre. Such is also the aim of Timaeus, who prefaces his lecture with a prayer to Athena for divine illumination and is very careful not to exclude the 'invisible gods' from the chorus of the Crafts-man's heavens. To the Presocratic versions of the image of the world-chorus Timaeus made one simple but crucial modification: the two circular config-urations in the dance of his gods, the Same and the Different, had been determined by astronomical observation rather than by mathematical theory, numerological inference, or poetical fancy. In the Myth of the Craftsman choreia became a truly visible – as well as visual – model for world-har-mony.

Intelligible as the cosmic triangle might have seemed to mathematicians like Petron, the scattered population of stars and planets that greeted the eyes of astronomers like Timaeus clearly numbered more than one hundred and eighty-three worlds and moved in a multitude of concentric revolutions rather than along three neatly coterminous lines. Though Philolaus had preceived this circular pattern in the dance, he too seemed to have dreamed up its structure instead of looking for it in the heavens. Who had ever set eyes on Antichthon? As for his startling claim that the earth was also orbiting in the dance, what could be more preposterous? Anyone could plainly see that the earth resided at the centre of the cosmic sphere and like a nurse provided man with nourishment and a secure foothold in the whirl of life. The only continuous movement Timaeus attributed to the earth was a mys-terious winding motion about the pole extended through the universe. Per-haps what he meant by this was an axial rotation running counter to the uniform spin of the celestial globe and exactly offsetting its effect, for if the earth did not perform this antistrophic movement it would simply be borne round with the cosmic sphere and the circling stars would then appear motionless relative to a human observer.[8] With religious enthusiasm Critias had imagined the universe dancing around its self-made Creator, and no doubt, as Timaeus instructed, a supreme Craftsman was responsible for the beauty and rationality displayed by the fairest of all dances. But in Timaeus' view the earth belonged at the centre of the dance, not the mythical Craftsman, though the earth could be considered a craftsman in its own right since its stable position relative to the sun's annual course helped to create the regular alternations of day and night and the predictable timing of the equinoxes.

Plato's two astronomers, Timaeus and the Athenian, being both of a pedagogical turn of mind, were especially impressed by the never-ending lesson in mathematics that the dance of the visible gods provided humanity. It was a spectacle intended to educate as well as to delight its spectators, they concluded, for the Craftsman had set the world in motion so that man might learn the numbers one and two by observing the binary sequence of day and night, and the relations between whole, half, and quarter by studying the changing faces of the moon, and the rudiments of geometry by plotting the Circles of the Same and the Different (*Timaeus* 47c–d; *Epinomis* 978d–e).

In Plato's longest and probably last dialogue, the *Laws*, the Athenian went so far as to equate choreia with paideia, arguing that the art of choral dance could not be mastered without a full understanding of the mathematical principles of music, the structure of the human body, the dynamics of the human soul, the celestial models for earthly dance, the political benefits of training a society to move together and to obey the commands of a choragus, the divine origins of harmony, in short, everything that might be learned in a comprehensive philosophical education. 'In our view,' he remarked sententiously to his companion Clinias,

the art of choral dance as a whole [choreia] is identical with education as a whole [paideia]; and the part of it pertaining to the voice consists of rhythms and harmonies... And the part pertaining to bodily motion has, in common with vocal motion, rhythm; but it has as its peculiar attribute gesture, just as the movement of the voice has melody.

(*Laws* II 672e)

Substantiating his theory that the unchanging choral dance of the stars revealed their divine rationality were two pertinent observations drawn from earthly experience: first, that a rigorous training in choral dance promoted emotional stability and reasonableness in children; and second, that the preservation of choral songs and dances by the Egyptians over many centuries resulted in the extraordinary stability of their society. With evidence such as this the Athenian strove to persuade his interlocutors that the harmony of his cosmological and pedagogical principles was not some pleasant fiction concocted by a Muse-maddened poet, or worse, some cloudy delusion mistaken for the truth by a deranged Aristophanic Sophist, but a reality, an enduring, demonstrable, and indeed obvious reality.

Gaze through the clouds and behold the sun, Timaeus or the Athenian only needed to say in defence of their interlocking doctrines. See the harmonious society of the gods in spectacular action. See how the Craftsman brought his principles of measure to light and expressed his formal ideas in visible images. Eyesight was the most valuable of all the senses, they insisted, because it alone revealed the geometry of the great circles and the rhythms of time and was thus responsible for inciting man's insatiable curiosity about the universe and its divine origin. Without sight man would never have taken his first upward steps out of the cave towards philosophical enlightenment, which in classical Platonism began with the mastery of the arts of number. Without sight he would never have learned that only seven basic motions accounted for all the steps in the cosmic dance – forwards and backwards, up and down, to and fro, and uniform rotation in the same spot – or that these had been tidily arranged by the Craftsman in a cumulative distribution throughout the cosmos. The celestial globe turned with a single uniform rotation about the celestial pole; the fixed stars combined uniform rotation with a forward movement along the concentric orbits governed by the Supreme Circle; and the planets, subject (like man) to all seven types of motion, orbited the earth at intervals carefully fixed by the Craftsman according to regular geometrical ratios. The visible design of the world-chorus was ultimately stabilized by the fixed angle at the intersections of the Same and the Different.

The same mathematical principles imposing limit, shape, rhythmic periodicity on the dances of the stars also seemed to govern the intelligent processes of human thought. After creating the two great circles, Timaeus revealed, the Craftsman went on to reproduce their geometrical pattern within the human soul; as a result all motions arising from the exercise of human reason – most notably choreiai – would reflect the stable system of motions visible in the heavens. Assuming an innate correspondence between the external movements of the stars and the internal operations of his soul Timaeus could cast his eyes over the length and breadth of the universe with the optimistic assurance that his calculations were determined by the absolute and invariable rules governing the superhuman intelligence of the stars. That man was able to calculate the timing of the sequences in the dance was a clear indication that the Craftsman had implanted a miniature Same and

Different within the human mind. The eternal system of numbers actively restrained the moving parts of the universe just as the regular beats of a drum entered the minds of the chorus and kept the individual dancers in step with their choragus. Echoing Timaeus' assertion that the Muses bestowed their gifts of harmony and rhythm on mankind so that human intelligence might be raised to a divine level, the Athenian attributed the beauty of earthly choreia (in both its vocal and corporeal aspects) to divine numbers underlying the unearthly concord of the Muses:

Between six and twelve come two means: nine, which is one-and-a-half times larger than six; and eight, which is larger than six by one-and-a-third. Since nine has as far to turn back to reach six as it has to turn forward to reach twelve [i.e. 6 + 3 = 9; 9 + 3 = 12], it provides men with concord and symmetry for use in their rhythmic and harmonious pastimes, and has been given to the blessed choral dance of the Muses [eudaimoni choreiai Mousōn].
(*Epinomis* 991a–b)

A model of Apollonian order, their blessed chorus was associated with the number nine because the Muses were traditionally nine in number; the association of their names with nine different arts, as in the following little poem –

> *Calliope discovered the art of heroic song;*
> *Clio, the honey-sweet music of the cithara accompanying the*
> *fair dance [kallichorou];*
> *Euterpe, the sonorous voice of the tragic chorus [tragikoio*
> *chorou];*
> *Melpomene found for mortals the many-stringed barbitos,*
> *a delight for the mind;*
> *Graceful Terpsichore furnished us with the artful flute;*
> *Erato invented delightful hymns to the gods;*
> *Polymnia, wise in all things, discovered the joys of the dance*
> *[terpsias orchēthmoio];*
> *Urania discovered the pole and the choral dance of the stars*
> *in heaven [ouraniōn choron astrōn];*
> *Thalia invented the plots and sage moral teachings of comedy.*
> (Anon, *Greek Anthology* IX 504)

– was a Late Antique elaboration of the classical image of the Muses, whose original function, as imagined by Hesiod, was to preside over all the choral arts as an ensemble. The Athenian also suggested a second and rather more Pythagorean explanation for the ninefold harmony of the Muses' chorus. As the arithmetical mean between six and twelve, nine was a convenient symbol for the immutable mathematical intermediaries binding the parts of the universal design together: no matter what changes might occur in the World of Becoming, nine would always be three more than six and three less than twelve. Platonic cosmologists respected such mathematical relations as the key to understanding the wondrous and apparently invariable constraints that linked the great bodies of the heavens to the tiny bodies of humanity in the dance of time. Nine was also, of course, the number of visible spheres in the cosmic chorus: earth, sun, moon, Mercury, Venus, Mars, Jupiter, Saturn, and the Aplanes or sphere of the fixed stars. It was to be the distinctive and prevailing assumption of the Athenian's long line of successors – and defenders, elaborators, practitioners, expositors, and critics of his theory of paideia have arisen in every major period in Western intellectual history from 348 BC (the year of Plato's death) to the present day – that by slow measured steps, leading from the rhythmic and harmonious pastimes of the body to the mind's ascent through mathematics and astronomy, a spectator educated in the theatre of the stars would ultimately become a dancer, an ecstatic participant, in the choreia of the gods.

The 'eudaimōn choreia' of Muses circling round the Heliconian spring had its visible counterpart (as Urania's poets would never tire of singing) in the 'kallistē choreia' of stars circling round the broad-breasted earth. What were the constant and most consoling rhythms in human experience – the daily transformation of light into dark shimmering night, the monthly cycle of the moon's changing faces, the yearly progress of the sun through the zodiac – but a sign that the heavenly bodies were divine beings of Muse-like grace and beauty? Who else but 'living creatures divine and eternal' would have the intelligence to impose rhythmical order on their bodily motions and to keep their glowing bodies in step day after day, month after month, year after year? Time, as Timaeus defined it, was more than the mere measurement of celestial motion: it was a moving image of the immortal order the early Greeks had dreamed of in their myths. Lifted from the shadows of the cave, the successors of the Athenian would cast their eyes over the Craftsman's cosmos and behold a spectacle of order as fair as the dances round the Eleusinian Kallichoron, as radiant as the measures on the polished orchestra of Olympus. As Plato's greatest pupil and severest critic, Aristotle, remarked in his early treatise *On Philosophy* (fr12b), which he probably composed while still a student at the Old Academy, philosophy was born when

those who first looked up to the heavens and saw the sun running its courses from its rising to its setting and the well-ordered choral dances of the stars [asterōn de eutaktous tinas choreias] sought after the Craftsman of this very beautiful design and conjectured that it came about not by chance but by the agency of some mightier and incorruptible nature, which was God.

2

The Leap of the Corybant

As I have stated, Moses says that man was brought into existence after all the other creatures and was created in the image of God and after his likeness. He is quite right in saying so, for nothing earthborn is more like God than man. But one should not imagine the likeness to be a corporeal image since God is not human in appearance and the human body is not godlike. No, the likeness meant by Moses pertains to the mind as ruler of the soul, for the one archetypal Mind of the universe was the model after which the mind in every individual was patterned. He who reveres the mind as a divine image may in some sense consider it a god, for just as the Great Ruler controls the whole world so the human mind seems to control man. The mind is unseen but sees all things itself, and while it reveals the essences of all other things, it keeps its own essence hidden. By arts and sciences it opens up roads branching in many directions, all of them great thoroughfares, and comes through land and sea examining what is in each element. After it has been raised on the wing and has observed the air and all its properties, it is borne still higher to the ether and to the revolutions of the heavens and is whirled round with the choral dances of the planets and the fixed stars [planētōn te kai aplanōn choreiais] in accordance with the laws of perfect music, following the love of wisdom which guides its footsteps. Having transcended all substance discernible by the senses it soon yearns for the intelligible world; and beholding the very beautiful sights in that world, namely the patterns and original forms of sensible things, it is seized by a sober intoxication just as those who perform the rites of the Corybants are possessed by ecstatic frenzy. Yet it is filled with a longing other than theirs: a nobler desire. Drawn by this to the topmost arch of the things discernible by the intellect, it seems to advance

towards the Great King himself; but as it strives to see him, multitudinous
rays of pure unmixed light stream forth like a torrent so that the mind's eye
is dazzled by the blinding beams. Not every image closely resembles its model
and pattern. Many indeed are unlike it. On this account Moses further in-
dicated his meaning by adding 'after his likeness' to the phrase 'in his image'
[Genesis 1:26]. He was thus referring to an accurate cast producing a clear
replica.

PHILO JUDAEUS, *On the Creation* 69–71

The Alexandrian Spectator

The astral chorus delighted Plato's successors with its visible confirmation
of three fundamental hypotheses of their cosmology: first, that the stability
and uniformity of the patterns of motion detected in the heavens revealed
the existence of an archetypal Mind governing both the psychological and
physical dynamics of the temporal cosmos; second, that the radiant bodies
of the stars were controlled from within by sublimely intelligent souls responsive to the immutable laws of mathematics; and third, that a predictable
cycle of changes, itself unchanging, always emerged out of the welter of
conflicting elements in nature to console mankind with visions of Apollonian
harmony in the midst of Bacchic dissolution.

The assurance of Pythagoras and his Presocratic disciples that the rules
of world-harmony could be deduced from the geometry of the celestial dance
and from the simple ratios determining musical intervals nourished in Plato's
two most Pythagorean spokesmen, Timaeus and the Athenian, a hope that
through rigorous philosophical training the human intellect might discern
the eternal order beyond the Aplanes and be raised to an ecstatic awareness
of the archetypal Mind. Providing the West with its first great manifesto of
intellectual optimism, Timaeus had shown how a single educated spectator
in the cosmic theatre could explain every entrance and exit and configuration
in the unfolding spectacle of the astral dance by understanding its unchanging
principles of organization. Then the Athenian had incorporated the astronomer's insights into a systematic theory of education, concluding that even
as amazement at the cosmic dance had turned primitive naïfs into philosophical spectators, so philosophy, if brought to perfection, could transform
mere spectators into fully engaged participants in the chorus of the gods.
So firmly interlocked were the concepts of choreia and paideia in the teachings
of the school of Plato that the diffusion of Athenian education throughout
the Greek-speaking world in the Hellenistic period ensured that Timaeus'
half-mythical, half-scientific picture of the cosmic dance was deeply im-
printed on the visual memory of the West.

No Platonist of the Greco-Roman era observed the chorus of the stars with greater delight than Philo Judaeus, a wealthy Alexandrian (born c 13 BC) who received in his youth the general education or 'enkyklios paideia' characteristic of the ruling class of his day. Socially destined for an active career in politics and imperial diplomacy, he was temperamentally inclined towards a life of scholarly contemplation. His youthful efforts to master Greek rhetoric, music, mathematics, and astronomy were directed towards the lofty goal of philosophical enlightenment, and his extensive knowledge of Greek philosophy – principally that of Pythagoras, Plato, and the Stoics – was applied in later life to the exposition of the Pentateuch. Though a Greek by culture, and a Roman by necessity, he was by faith and family and national allegiance a Jew. Around 40 AD he journeyed to Rome as the senior member of a special delegation hoping to persuade Caligula to release the Jews from the offensive obligations of emperor worship and to ensure their right to live according to the sacred laws of Moses. Aside from this diplomatic mission, which took place within ten years of his death, little else is known of Philo's life in its external details. Though he occasionally complained that politics robbed him of the time and energy for philosophical reflection, his huge corpus of biblical commentaries, apologetical works, and cosmological treatises bears witness to the breadth and richness of his contemplative life. His writings also attest to the survival of Greek intellectual optimism in an age commonly associated with Roman pessimism and insanity, though some of them clearly point ahead to the broodingly mystical and introspective mentality of the Platonists of Late Antiquity.

His influential treatise *On the Creation* reveals as clearly as any of his works the subtle fusion of Greek and Jewish elements in his world-view, for in it he combined an enthusiastic exposition of Platonic cosmology with a pious commentary on the first three chapters of Genesis. Like Plato, he assumed that the range of human vision was potentially much broader than most people supposed. Since God had endowed the human soul with a restless intellect which (though itself unseen) was able to see everything around it, nothing in the world of the senses was too far from man to be detected or too complex to be understood. Even the distant multitudes of the stars were comprehensible: they were simply decorations in an old banquet-chamber or competitors in a civic stadium or dancers in a theatre displaying the munificence and rationality of their Creator. 'Just as the hosts of a banquet do not issue invitations to supper until everything for the feast has been prepared,' he explained,

and just as the sponsors of gymnastic and theatrical contests, before gathering the spectators into the theatre or stadium, have in readiness a number of contestants pleasing to spectators and auditors, in the same way the Ruler of all things, like some provider of contests or host of a banquet, when he was about to call man to a feast and a spectacle, prepared the material for both well in advance. His preparations were made so that on entering the cosmos man might find at once a banquet and a most sacred spectacle. The one was full of all things that earth and rivers and sea and air produce for use and enjoyment; the other comprised all sorts of displays most astonishing in their substance and qualities, extraordinarily wondrous movements and choral dances [thaumasiōtatas de tas kinēseis kai choreias], in configurations linked together according to the proportions of numbers and the concord of revolutions.

(*On the Creation* 78)

The intricacy of the cosmic dance having long been applauded, Philo could look upon its most sacred spectacle as a prelude to the far grander vision of the Great King himself and assume (with a certain aristocratic complacency) that the industrious designers of armillary spheres would eventually solve every minor technical problem in astronomy. For him, as for Timaeus, such details as the unpredictable appearance of comets or the apparent retrogradations of the planets were of little concern: the quest for wisdom in its absolute Platonic sense, for knowledge of the transcendent World of Being, was what chiefly occupied his thoughts. Like an eager spectator who was not content merely to watch the celestial orchestra but wished to rise out of the audience and join the chorus, Philo sought to experience the dance of life from the viewpoint of its divine participants.

Two types of vision – the one rooted in the body and turned outward to the flickering shadows of time, the other latent in the mind and directed inward to reminiscences of eternity – guided Philo's ascending steps through the cave of the sensory world towards the sunlit throne-room of the Creator.[1] In the first stage of the ascent his physical eyes surveyed the expanse of the cave-world by following the light of the sun and stars across the heavens. What he observed was a cosmos composed of the four traditional Empedoclean elements, earth, water, air, and fire, with the addition of a fifth substance, ether, which Plato had defined as the purest form of air (*Timaeus* 58d) and located between the cloudy sublunary atmosphere and the regions of celestial fire (*Epinomis* 924c). Aristotle had defined ether as an element in its own right, a 'wonderful and divine essence' which constituted the heavens and was entirely separate from the base materials of the sublunary world (*On the Heavens* I.iii, 270b 17–25). A mixture of Platonic and Aristotelian ether seems to have pervaded Philo's upper atmosphere, for in his buoyant description of the dance of the human mind through the World of Becoming (*On the Creation* 70) he located the ethereal zone beyond the cloudy reaches of the air but did not clearly distinguish its properties from those of air or its motions from those of celestial fire.

Like Plato, Philo valued eyesight above all the other senses and attributed to it and to the divine gift of light the momentous discovery of the cosmic dance which led to man's escape from the sorrows of the cave. 'Light,' he explained,

became the source of many other benefits for mankind but especially of the greatest blessing, philosophy. For eyesight, led upwards by light, observed the nature of the heavenly bodies and their harmonious movement; it discerned the well-ordered revolutions of the fixed stars which travelled around all alike in the same courses and of the planets which sped round idiosyncratically in two circuits opposing each other; and it perceived how the concordant choral dances of all these [choreias te pantōn emmeleis] were ordered according to the laws of perfect music. This produced in the soul an indescribable joy and pleasure.

(*On the Creation* 54)

The theory that philosophy was closely linked to visual sensation and the pleasure afforded by the dance of the stars was frequently affirmed by Philo, even in works which were not specifically concerned with cosmology. In his enormous commentary on the Ten Commandments, for instance, he paused from his discussion of the laws of the Jews to clarify the relation between philosophy and eyesight:

Now let us describe how eyesight acted as a guide to philosophy. The eye looked up to the region of the ether and beheld the sun and moon and the planets and fixed stars, the most sacred host of the heavens, a cosmos within a cosmos; then it saw their risings and settings, their harmonious choral dances [choreias emmeleis], their conjunctions at periodic intervals, their eclipses, their reappearances ...

(*The Special Laws* III 187–8)

The love of wisdom was a divine gift implanted in the human soul by God, Philo believed, but without eyesight to draw man's attention upwards to the heavens and to serve as a kind of intermediary between man and his unseen Maker philosophical speculation would never have been stimulated. The natural and indeed inevitable consequence of this ascending line of vision was a curiosity about the divine origins of the spectacle and a rudimentary awareness of the Creator. The dance of the stars not only assured Philo that God existed. It provided him with dramatic visual evidence that God exerted a profoundly civilizing influence over the citizens of the world.

The Philonic cosmos was in many ways a magnification of the civilized urban environment of Alexandria, with its cosmopolitan diversity, teeming population, artistic wonders, and distant imperial rulers. 'Is it not therefore likely, or indeed necessary,' he insisted,

that he who comes to the truly great city, the cosmos, and beholds hill and
plain laden with animals and plants, the currents of rivers that rise in the
country and those that are swollen with winter snow, the expanses of the
seas, the temperateness of the air, the transition of the yearly seasons, then
the sun and moon ruling day and night, and the other heavenly bodies,
planets and fixed stars, and the revolutions and choral dances [choreias] of
the whole heaven, must gain an understanding of the Maker and Father and
Ruler also?

(The Special Laws 1 34)

But philosophy could not be brought to perfection until man ceased to gaze
like a spellbound visitor on the wonders of the cosmic city and employed
his second sense of sight, the eye of his mind, to interpret its harmonious
architecture and orchestrated movement as reflections of the rationality of
its eternal Ruler. Insight followed and transcended eyesight. By concentrating his thoughts on the order of the heavenly bodies an aspiring philosopher could imagine himself whirled round with the momentum of the
cosmic dance and magically transported to the dizzying summit of the Aplanes.
Entranced by the unceasing revolutions of the stars he could begin to form
in his mind a picture of the surpassing loveliness and formal perfection of
the timeless Model copied by the Craftsman. As his inner vision took leave
of the visible world, his mind would seem to divorce itself from the gravity-
bound body and float up into a dimension of the Platonic universe which
Timaeus had assumed but left unexplored in his lecture.

Philo did not merely accept the astronomer's assumptions and hypotheses.
He restlessly examined them. Was the Myth of the Craftsman no more than
a finely woven tissue of opinions, metaphors, calculations, and educated
guesses easily punctured by Aristotelian skepticism? Was it just another
'likely story' passed on from one dreamer to another in the cave? Though
religiously predisposed to accept Timaeus' theory that a single Divine Mind
was responsible for creating the order of the cosmos and that the intellect
of a rational man imitated the stable thought processes in the Divine Mind,
Philo did not always experience this ideal stable-mindedness in practice. The
intellect of an aspiring philosopher was not necessarily content to think the
same thoughts about the same things, as he discovered, for driven by an
insatiable desire for wisdom his own thoughts often led straight up to supracosmic heights of contemplation where his inner eye was blinded and
his dancing intellect suffered a kind of mystical vertigo.

Timaeus had recommended star-gazing as a method for attaining mental
stability. By following the astronomer's steps Philo ironically experienced
the reverse – a curious sensation of teetering on the brink between sensory
and extrasensory knowledge. Faithfully he had raised his eyes from the
spectacle of earthly mutability to contemplate the unchanging patterns of

celestial motion, duly distinguishing the uniform revolutions governed by the Circle of the Same from the diverse orbits governed by the Circle of the Different. Then his intellectual eye perceived the numerical principles determining the geometry of the two great circles and the rhythmic sequences of time. In full accord with Timaeus Philo concluded that the Craftsman's numbers organized human thoughts as well as heavenly motions. Recalling how the Craftsman had reproduced the geometry of the celestial circles within each man's mind, he surmised that the intellect of a wise man had a kind of regular and unwavering motion analogous to the revolutions of the stars. This non-spatial movement, the steps of a mind seeking virtue and theological insight, was also a phase of the cosmic dance. 'For God wished to picture the soul of the sage,' he explained,

as a close imitation of the heavens, or rather, if we may say so, as an image transcending it. The soul of the sage was to be a heaven on earth, having within it, as the ether has, pure natures, ordered motions, harmonious choral dances [choreias emmeleis], divine revolutions, most star-like and dazzling rays of virtues. And if it is beyond our powers to count the stars discernible by the senses, how much more truly can that be said of the stars discernible by the intellect!

(Who Is the Heir 88–9)

To understand the harmony of the external world a philosopher only needed to match a geometric image in his mind with the corresponding configurations in nature. He could deduce the order of stellar movements from the systematic sequences of his own thoughts.

Philo's extreme confidence in deductive reasoning seemed justified by the success of armillary geometry in the analysis of celestial motion, but like all successful scientific theories this triumph of human ingenuity stirred minds to further inquiry rather than setting them to rest. Unresolved questions disturbed Philo's thoughts whenever he contemplated the stars. Who was the mysterious Craftsman who had designed the fairest of all dances? How were the diverse members of the cosmic chorus linked in a unified design? Where was the visionary Model whose beauty was reflected in the visible heavens? Philo could not satisfy his curiosity by following the steps of thought laid down by Timaeus. Before his vision of cosmic order would be complete he had to see the Craftsman face to face.

Since physical vision failed to reveal the designer of the dance or its eternal paradigm, Philo focused the eye of his understanding on the problematical nature of their existence. Perhaps such subjects of thought could be said to exist in the same way that numbers existed. Though no one had ever laid eyes on one, two, or three, the properties of these numbers were universally understood by all rational men. That one and two added up to three seemed to be absolutely true no matter where or when or why a human mind should contemplate the sum. If the invisible laws of number existed, why could the same not be said of concepts such as absolute Beauty or the First Cause? Philo accommodated their existence within his system of beliefs by accepting Plato's deduction that all such subjects of thought belonged to an eternal realm, the 'intelligible world,' so called because it was perceptible only to insight unaided by eyesight. Aspiring philosophers have often found Plato's World of the Forms somewhat less than intelligible. It certainly daunted Philo. Having transcended the things perceptible by the senses, his intellect could rest only for a precarious instant on the topmost arch of the eternal world before it fell dazed and spinning at the thought that numbers, aesthetic ideals, and the exemplars of all visible things did not originate as concepts within the human mind but actually existed apart from it in an unchanging World of Being beyond the World of Becoming. So fervent was his desire for wisdom that he adventurously explored every area of thought, even one as remote as the Platonic intelligible world, in his quest to understand the supernatural origins of the cosmos and to reconcile the science of the Greeks with the religion of the Jews.

Looking back on man's intellectual progress from primitive Chaldean astrology and star-worship to Presocratic physics and Platonic cosmology, Philo was confident that the human intellect was gaining an ever-clearer understanding of the divine laws governing the great city of the universe. The long centuries in which man had simply gazed in wonder at the stars had resulted in the philosophical insight that the fleeting images in the temporal world did indeed fit together into a harmonious whole. Among the great intellectual achievements of the Greeks (in his opinion) was their definition of the crowded field of physical vision as a single unified cosmos. 'In one sense the word 'cosmos' signifies the system of the heavens and the stars including the earth and the plants and animals on it,' noted Philo didactically, 'and in another sense it denotes the heavens only.' Lest this old familiar concept be taken for granted by his sophisticated Alexandrian readers, he recounted the following anecdote from the life of the Presocratic philosopher Anaxagoras to prove that the definition of 'cosmos' had not been formulated by the Greeks without considerable mental and even physical exertion:

Anaxagoras had been gazing on the heavens when someone asked him why he endured hardship by spending the night under the open sky. He answered that he did it 'in order to contemplate the cosmos,' meaning by 'cosmos' the choral dances and revolutions of the stars [tas choreias kai periphoras tōn asterōn].

(*The Eternity of the World* 4)

Reaching the intelligible world, however, required a purely mental kind of stamina very different from that which Anaxagoras had displayed in his nocturnal vigil. It demanded a concentrated effort to block off the distractions of the visible world and to focus on the patterns and original forms of sensible things. A philosopher could reach the World of the Forms only when the firm ground of sensory experience had fallen away beneath his dancing intellect. He had to leave the cosmic theatre and retire to the solitary temple of his mind.

Like a spectator at Eleusis who could not see beyond the torchlit throngs in the courtyard of the Kallichoron but did not doubt the reality of the mysteries unfolded in the inner chambers of the Sanctuary, Philo was entirely certain that beyond the astral chorus lay the brilliant reality of the intelligible world. He believed that it was in fact *more* real than the unstable world of the senses, the imperfect copy of the Craftsman's design. He had more than Plato's word to assure him that the Creator and his ideal world waited to be seen beyond the dance of the stars. He had the word of the Creator himself. As a devout Jew he was convinced that God had spoken to his chosen people through the sacred writings of their prophet Moses.

The Prophet's Graces

Philo regarded Moses not only as the heroic deliverer of the laws of the Jews but also as an exemplary philosopher who had raised his mind from visible to invisible things and through divine grace had succeeded in contemplating the Forms. The glorious precedent of Moses prevented Philo from losing his intellectual high spirits, for the writings of the prophet assured him that the intelligible world had truly been intelligible to at least one mortal intellect. In contrast to Timaeus, who for all his wisdom was merely a fictional (or semi-fictional) character with a likely story of creation, Moses had been the wisest of all seers and the historical ruler to whom God had entrusted the destiny of Israel and revealed the secrets of the Divine Plan.

In his two encomiastic books *On the Life of Moses* Philo described the prophet's preparation for the Jewish priesthood as if it were a training in Platonic philosophy. First Moses enriched his mind with the admirable truths of ethics, politics, mathematics, and astronomy (I 23, II 66); consequently he was possessed by a heaven-sent rapture during which he contemplated the immaterial forms of material things (II 67); next he conversed with God on the holy Mountain (II 70); and finally he imitated the Craftsman by creating the Jewish tabernacle as a miniature cosmos (II 76 ff). Having brough the 'divine revolutions' and 'dazzling rays of virtues' within his soul into harmony with the macrocosm, Moses was able to perfect the qualities of leadership, justice, piety, and foresight required for his four divinely ordained roles in Jewish history – as philosopher-king, law-giver, high priest, and inspired prophet. 'Beautiful and wholly harmonious is the union of these four intellectual powers,' Philo explained,

for intertwined and clinging to each other they dance together [synchoreuousi], receiving and repaying favours, and imitating the virgin Graces whom an immutable law of nature prevents from being separated.

(*Moses* II 7)

The Graces were a chorus of immortal virgins whose traditional role in Greek mythology was to preside with Aphrodite over the freshness and sexual vitality of youth, and whom painters and sculptors in Antiquity sometimes depicted as dancing naked in a graceful circular knot formed by their clasped hands and intertwining arms. Philo's rather daring comparison between their interlocking dance and the harmony of the virtues in the soul of Moses is an allegorical variation of the Platonic analogy between the choral dances of the natural world and the non-spatial movements of the human soul, though he probably derived the specifically ethical interpretation of the Graces from Aristotle, who noted in the *Nichomachean Ethics* (v. v 1133a 3) that the shrine of the Graces was placed in a prominent position in Athens to remind men to requite each other's kindnesses, or possibly from the Stoics, who interpreted the goddesses' Greek name 'Charites' to mean 'graces' either in its aesthetic sense (the graceful features and movements of a beautiful maiden) or in its ethical sense (the gracious giving and receiving of favours).² Philo hints at both meanings in his metaphor, but explicitly the latter, with its further implication that the harmonious soul of Moses is both a result and an image of the supreme grace of God manifested in the 'immutable law of nature.' The law-giver of Israel was thus a microcosmic image of the law-giver of the universe.

In his role as high priest Moses had ensured that Israel worshipped the God of nature rather than nature itself. He had saved the Jews from the religious errors of the Chaldeans, whose astrological superstitions and star worship prevented them from attaining the highest favour of the Lord. The Jews were a more enlightened race than the Chaldeans, Philo argued, because they had been taught by Moses to prefer the intellectual vision of God to the spectacle in the cosmic theatre:

Now to see the best of things is the lot of Israel, the best of races, for Israel means 'the act of seeing God.' The race that strives for second place sees the second best, namely the heavens perceptible by the senses and in it the harmonious order of the stars and the choral dance moving as truly as possible to the universal music [pammouson hōs alēthōs choreian].

(*The Preliminary Studies* 51)

The Chaldeans had discovered the universal music but failed to respond to its supracosmic source. They had not truly participated in the cosmic dance, therefore, because their minds had failed to make the all-important leap from temporal to eternal objects of contemplation. The superiority of Jewish monotheism to Chaldean pantheism was a theme Philo never tired of elaborating. 'Moses differs from the opinion of the Chaldeans concerning God,' he noted proudly,

since he believes that neither the cosmos nor the soul of the cosmos is the primal God, and that the stars and their choral dances [choreias] are not the ultimate causes of the things that happen to man. On the contrary, he teaches that the universe is held together by invisible powers which the Craftsman made to reach from the ends of the earth to the farthest limits of the heavens. For the Craftsman took care that what was well bound should not be broken apart; for the powers of the universe are chains that cannot be sundered.
(On the Migration of Abraham 181)

The human intellect alone was free to soar beyond the choral dances of the stars, to break through the causal chains of time which imprisoned the body. The freedom to return to God through contemplative rapture and ultimately through the ascent of the soul into Heaven after death was the mark of the Lord's special favour for mankind, and particularly for Israel, whose impulse to see God was its defining characteristic as a race. But the Greeks had also sought to participate in a higher phase of the cosmic dance than the spectacle of the astral chorus. They too had sensed the presence of a supreme Craftsman beyond the stars and attributed the harmony of creation to his invisible powers. To Plato as well as to Moses Philo could turn for philosophical confirmation that the human intellect was fashioned after an eternal model and that it could be raised like a bird 'on the wing' – an image Philo borrowed from the impassioned oration of Socrates on the ascent of the soul in *Phaedrus* 249e – into the perpetual sunlight of the Promised Land.

Moses, to whose inspired authorship Philo piously (though erroneously) attributed the Book of Genesis, seemed on many points to agree with the cosmology of Plato. Both Genesis and the Myth of the Craftsman recounted the primordial deeds of a supreme Creator who set time in motion and produced a material image of a divine paradigm. In Genesis 1:26, for example, Moses taught that God had created man 'in his image' and 'after his likeness.' To a learned Alexandrian such as Philo, whose education had been dominated by Greek philosophy, the mention of 'image' and 'likeness' in a cosmological context inevitably implied the basic assumptions of Timaeus. The relation between image and exemplar was an essential structural principle in Platonic cosmology. The body and soul of the cosmos were copies of a timeless model existing in the intelligible world; the model was imitated at a second remove by the stars, whose bodies were perfectly spherical like the cosmic body and whose souls were divinely rational like the cosmic soul. Man himself reflected the eternal model at another remove by corresponding in body and soul to the heavens. The human head was (roughly) spherical like the celestial globe, for instance, and within it thoughts seemed to pass in orderly logical sequences like the predictable steps in the cosmic dance.

The eye of Philo's understanding was so dazzled by the correspondences between Genesis and the Myth of the Craftsman that he failed to notice their significant differences. He saw no disparity between the Platonic Craftsman, whose powers were restricted by the raw materials at his disposal, and the omnipotent God of Moses, who had created matter out of nothing. While he accepted the Platonic theory that the stars were divine beings, he nevertheless revered the God of Moses as the one true God and chose to ignore (if he was conscious of them at all) the latent contradictions in his synthesis of a montheistic religion with an animistic cosmology. Having studied Genesis in a Greek translation, Philo was inclined to read Platonic meanings into the Hebrew concept of 'image' simply because it was translated as 'eikōn.' This was the word Plato had used to describe the temporal world in relation to its eternal model (*Timaeus* 29b). The occurrence of 'eikōn' in Genesis 1:26 was enough to bring the entire design of the Craftsman's cosmos, with its endless analogies between model and image, dancing into Philo's mind as he pondered the cosmology of the prophet.

Philo took care to explain the scriptural usage of the term because some images, as he observed, were considerably closer to their originals than others. If an image conveyed a clear impression of its model, he called it a 'typos' or 'replica.' Man could be called an 'eikōn' of God because the human mind was a 'tranos typos' or 'clear replica' of its divine Creator. Like God the mind was unseen and all-seeing; it kept order in the body just as God kept order in the cosmos; and it reflected the perfect rationality of God by comprehending the numerical order of the heavens. Since the Craftsman formed the true cosmos by making miniatures of its greatest parts, the close analogy between God and man was an inherent condition of the divine design. Their likeness existed not just in word but in fact – in the actual scheme of things as well as in the Book of Genesis. But the Creator and his image were not identical, of course, for the divine original was completely immaterial while its human copy was partly mixed with matter. Only in the purely spiritual part of man could the Creator produce a clear replica of himself. So close was the likeness, in fact, that philosophers who revered the human intellect as a divine image could also regard it as a god in its own right. Moses himself seemed to stress the close correspondence between God and man in the phrase 'after his likeness,' which clarified the scriptural meaning of 'eikōn' and supported Philo's Platonic interpretation of the passage.

'Not every image,' he noted in *On the Creation* 71, 'closely corresponds to its model and pattern.' The contrast between the Creator and any bodily image or 'somatos charactēr,' for example, was so striking that comparison between them was barely admissible. Not even the human body, which of all earthly things seemed most worthy of comparison with God, could convey an accurate impression of the Creator's wholly incorporeal essence. One could consider close likenesses as existing only between two material things or between two divine beings: comparisons between a divine being and a material object could reveal only faint resemblances. Since the Craftsman had skilfully copied all temporal things from divine forms existing in the intelligible world, imperfect images abounded in the Philonic (as in the Platonic) universe. Even the luminous bodies of the stars, which were the most beautiful sights in the physical cosmos, were imperfect images of the single inexpressibly beautiful Form after which they had all been patterned. The disparity between the visionary Form and its visible images was not the Craftsman's fault. He had done his best to recreate the formal perfection of his Model in the raw materials at hand; but the purest fire he might find in the chaotic mixture of elements existing before creation failed to radiate the 'multitudinous rays of pure unmixed light' perceptible only to the eye of the understanding. As an artistic 'eikōn' the world of the senses was an illustrious failure admired only for its faint resemblances to the intelligible world.

Philo's distinction between clear replicas and faint copies might apply not only to natural but also to verbal images. The metaphors in his commentary on Genesis 1:26 all imply a comparison between two terms: a primary subject of reference, drawn from the immense range of things surveyed by his physical eyes or by the eye of his intellect; and a secondary image, by which he interprets his perceptions and communicates them to his reader. Many of Philo's metaphors imply a high degree of similarity between the rhetorical image and its visual or visionary reference. By recognizing the essential features of the image the reader may also know the significant properties, or structure, or purpose of what it is said to resemble. Analogies of this sort might be said to depend on 'affirmative' imagery because they are meant to convey a great deal of positive information about the philosopher's subject of thought. Certain metaphors in Philo's commentary suggest only faint resemblances between the terms of the comparison. The reader is faced with a paradoxical analogy: though some similarity is meant to exist between the image and its reference, their extreme differences seem far more significant to the philosopher than their faint resemblances. The metaphor might thus imply what its subject does *not* resemble rather than what it is actually like. A comparison of this kind, because it conveys more negative information than positive, might be said to depend on 'negative' symbolism. A negative symbol is meant to convey a slight impression of its reference but the impression is so qualified that the reader immediately understands it as somehow faulty, tentative, and inaccurate. Since its rhetorical function is to emphasize the utter disparity between the visible world familiar through common human experience and the visionary world discerned by the contemplative intellect, a negative symbol is like a 'somatos charactēr' of God.

An affirmative image, on the other hand, is like a 'tranos typos.' Its rhetorical effect is to present a conceptual replica by which the reader may visualize some aspect of the philosopher's universe clearly and accurately. In his comentary on Genesis 1:26 Philo marks his ascent from the visible to the visionary world by an abrupt change from affirmative imagery to negative symbolism. At the Great Dividing-Line between time and eternity the cosmic dance changes from a spectacular showpiece in the theatre of the stars to the whirling of an ecstatic intellect around the Wellspring of Light.

Whirling to Perfect Music

Philo consistently interpreted choreia as an affirmative image for the order of the visible cosmos. Celestial motions seemed to him so much like a choral dance that the image and its reference were all but identical, their differences being merely those of degree rather than of kind. The dance of the stars was older, nobler, grander, more intricate, more beautiful than any human dance, but the two activities were essentially the same. In one basic respect choral dance could represent the order of the Philonic cosmos more accurately than the most accurate armillary sphere: it was an animate rather than mechanical model. Whereas the static rings of an armillary sphere could not reflect the interaction of psychological forces impelling the living cosmos in all its parts, a chorus in motion conveyed a very clear image of an organic whole composed of sympathetically attuned members. It could imitate the flow of time, turn with the revolving seasons, impose shape and meaning on what might otherwise be perceived as a stream of random changes, evanescent sensations, and unintelligible memories. Only the moving pattern of life presented in the dance could project undistorted reflections of 'the moving image of eternity,' which was for Philo, as for Plato, the definition of time.

Just as the Olympians dancing in eternity had followed the music of Apollo's lyre, so the stars dancing in time obeyed what Philo called 'mousikēs teleias nomoi' or 'the laws of perfect music.' These laws, the eternal principles of mathematics, were conceived by the Hellenistic revivers of Pythagoreanism as divine powers existing in (or just below) the World of the Forms and exerting their influences on all things caught in the flow of time. Numbers in Philo's cosmos possessed unitive properties which served to connect the great world of the heavens with the little world of man, and long stretches of *On the Creation* are accordingly devoted to the exposition of numerological correspondences between the macrocosm and the microcosm. The number seven, for example, was observed to link the order of the planets with the design of musical instruments and the components of human speech:

For the seven-stringed lyre, which is analogous to the choral dance of the planets [tēi tōn planētōn choreiai], produces the harmonies which are held in high esteem, and I dare say that the manufacture of all musical instruments is based on the prototypic design of the lyre. And among the elements of grammar there are seven letters properly called vowels, since they apparently can be sounded by themselves and can produce articulate sounds when combined with the other letters.

(*On the Creation* 126)

Philo also observed that the art of dancing was a perfect 'tranos typos' of macrocosmic order because it displayed the same number of potential movements as the planetary chorus:

For it happens that there are seven movements: upwards and downwards; to the right and to the left; forwards and backwards; and in a circle. These are most clearly displayed by those who perform pantomimic dancing [tēn orchēsin].

(*On the Creation* 122–3)

This is precisely the same number of motions that Plato counted in the heavens (*Timaeus* 40a–d). From correspondences such as these Philo concluded that the number seven exerted a powerful influence over the motions of stars and men, uniting words and worlds in the same rhythmic imitation of eternity.

If this conclusion strikes us today as rather absurd, that it because we have all but lost the knack of interpreting metaphors in highly literal terms. Like choral dancers the planets in Philo's heavens were able to respond voluntarily to a predetermined numerical order because they were living creatures endowed with minds. Their perfect music, which was not a fanciful touch to the metaphor of the cosmic dance, had all the practical functions of the music accompanying the dances of men. It served to unite the wandering stars in a single movement by providing a sequence of rhythmic measures perceptible to all who participated in the chorus. The musical accompaniment to the cosmic dance was 'perfect' in an aesthetic sense, as the most exquisite harmony imaginable to the human intellect; and in a mathematical sense, as the exact measurements determining the complete sequence of tones within an octave; and in a metaphysical sense, as the eternal archetype of the fleeting melodies heard on earth. To a mind convinced that such music actually resounded through the heavens (inaudible though it might be to most human ears) the theory that numbers had an active influence over the souls in the cosmic chorus would have seemed entirely reasonable.

By numerical 'influence' (dynamis) Philo did not mean deterministic compulsion. No Sirens sit on Philo's planets to hypnotize the heavens with the song of the Fates. The perfect music of the planetary chorus functioned exactly like a law: without necessitating the actions of individuals who willingly submitted to its ruling, it constantly kept their society in step with a divinely prescribed order. A dance naturally calls for music. A cosmic dance naturally calls for cosmic music. Once the reality of the cosmic dance had been seen, one could easily believe in the Pythagorean dream of cosmic music.

As an expert in the laws of perfect music, Moses had organized the religious and political life of the Jews so that they might always be attuned to the order of the macrocosm and to the moral law of the Great King. The cosmic dance was integrated into their daily lives and into the cultural life of their race through the ritual movements and symbolic objects instituted by their high priest in his cosmic tabernacle. The Menorah, for instance, was interpreted by Philo as a symbol of world-harmony:

The holy candlestick and the seven candle-bearers are an imitation of the choral dance of the seven planets through the heavens [tōn hepta planētōn choreias mimēma]. 'Why?' one might ask. Because, we shall answer, each of the planets brings light like the candle-bearers. For they are extremely bright and transmit their supremely lustrous rays to earth, especially the planet central among the seven – the sun.

(Who Is the Heir 221–2)

As the sun was among the wandering stars, so Moses was among the Jews – the source of their enlightenment, the guardian of their laws, the leader of their sacred dance in honour of the Great King. Through the grace of God, the prophet's intellectual Graces had been extended to Israel as a whole, with the result that the Jewish religion had evolved (so Philo believed) into an ideal synthesis of divine revelation and Platonic rationalism. In this synthesis the laws of cosmic harmony became one and the same as the moral laws brought down from Sinai by the prophet. To participate in the one was to obey the other.

In a striking passage from his treatise *On the Virtues*, Philo imagined the final moments in the life of Moses as a dramatic consummation of the union of the laws of nature and nation. With his dying breath the great hierophant sings a song of farewell and praise and warning to the universe, and his song becomes the perfect music accompanying the cosmic dance:

He gathered together in a divine assembly the elements of the universe and the most productive parts of the cosmos, earth the home of mortals and heaven the home of immortals, and he sang with full harmony and sweet concord so that men and ministering angels would hearken to his hymns. His fellow men, on the one hand, were to listen so that they might learn a thankfulness of heart similar to his own; and the angels, on the other hand, were to be guardians watching over man and judging according to their skill in music whether his song had any unmelodious note. At the same time they were to have confidence that man, even though inhabiting a perishable body, could have trained his soul in the ways of the Muses, following the example of the sun and moon and the wholly sacred chorus of the other stars [tōi tōn allōn asterōn panierōi chorōi], and attuning himself to the divine instrument, the heavens and the whole cosmos. From his place among the choral dancers [choreutais] who are arranged throughout the ether, the hierophant blended with his thankful hymns to God his just feelings of kindness towards his nation. ...

Like the dancing intellect whose course through the heavens Philo depicted in his commentary on Genesis 1:26, Moses seems to have soared beyond the sublunary realm during the chanting of his hymn and to reside, like Helios or an apotheosized Orpheus, amid the astral chorus. But this was only a temporary station, for his time had come to leave the cosmic theatre forever:

Having concluded the choral dances which had been woven together as it were out of his piety and human kindness [tas choreias hosiotēti kai philan-thrōpiai tropon tina synyphasmenas], he began to change from mortal to immortal life and therefore gradually experienced the disunity of those mixed elements which composed his nature.

(On the Virtues 72–6)

This remarkable episode foreshadows two developments in the Late Antique interpretation of choreia as an image of world-harmony. First Philo has made the choragus of the dance a holy man who has revealed the word of God to mankind and who has the supernatural power to unite all levels of creation, from angels to elements, in a single movement of piety and human kindness in response to God. The motivation of the Platonic choreia, by contrast, was the rationality of the all-pervasive but nebulous World-Soul, and the revolutions of the stars had expressed the unending operation of Reason throughout the cosmic body. The Mosaic choreia is more than a display of universal rationality. It is essentially a religious movement, a 'panieros choros' or 'wholly sacred chorus' expressing the love felt by man and nature for the transcendent Ruler of the universe. Second, Philo focuses his attention not on the unbroken continuity and uniformity of the astral dance but on a climactic image of disunity, the disintegration of the elements composing the earthly Moses and the ascent of the prophet's soul into Heaven. The dance of time (from the viewpoint of the individual at least) was ever moving towards this destructive end. As a man of strong religious convictions, Philo refused to interpret death as a mere extinction of the human soul. The ending of his cosmic dance was a liberation of the soul from the coils of time, a metamorphosis of the just man into an immortal spirit.

Sober Bacchants

Philo could perceive the image of the dance from many different angles without turning the cosmic choreia into a fantastic conceit beyond his reader's credulity; but the moment he extended his metaphor to express the order of the intelligible world or of the afterlife, the closeness of the comparison inevitably disappeared. The visibility, the motion, the bodies, and the rhythmic timing of an earthly dance could never correspond to the unearthly order of a world which by philosophical definition and prophetic revelation was known to be invisible, motionless, incorporeal, and timeless. Ultimately his experience of cosmic order was transformed from the pleasures of a spectator into the raptures of a dancer. The experience of losing all sense of time and space, the momentous rush towards divine union, the enthusiastic initiation into the highest mysteries of Platonic and Mosaic wisdom – these found their closest analogue in the baccheia of the Corybants.

Contemplative participation in the astral chorus led the soaring intellect of the holy man into a superior phase of the cosmic dance, an impassioned leaping of the spirit which transcended the continuous revolutions characteristic of choreia. This climactic rite of passage was not a rational imitation of nature but a suprarational union with the God of nature. It was an initiation into the brilliant world outside the candlelit sanctuary of the cosmic tabernacle. It was an impulse to let go of time, to abandon the theatre of the stars. Astronomy, music, mathematics, and all the branches of philosophy were not ends in themselves, Philo stressed, but simply preparations for leading the life of virtue and piety which allowed the human spirit to leap into the Kingdom of Heaven.

Moses had implied this in all his arguments against the Chaldeans, and before him Abraham had learned the lesson from God himself. Commenting on God's speech to Abraham in Genesis 17:2–16, Philo imagined the Lord as a Socratic teacher whose probing questions inspired the Father of the Jews to love wisdom only for the sake of virtue. 'For what purpose,' asks God,

> do you investigate the choral dances and revolutions of the stars [choreias kai periodous asterōn]? Why have you leapt from earth up to the region of the ether? Is your purpose merely to busy yourself idly with what is there? And what great advantage may be gained from all that idle labour? How does it serve to purge pleasure, to overthrow lust, to suppress grief and fear? What surgery has it for passions which rock and confound the soul? For just as trees are useless if they bear no fruit, so also is the study of nature useless if it does not lead to the acquisition of virtue.
>
> (On the Change of Names 72–3)

The virtues acquired by Abraham and Moses in their contemplation of the heavens were the same self-control, sobriety, and freedom from disruptive passions that the Athenian sought to inculcate in the citizens of his utopian society through the study of astronomy, music, and choral dancing.

Yet the Jewish seers, through the grace of God, had harvested spiritual virtues more sublime than the fruits of moderation and philosophical imperturbability. So deeply had they drunk from the overflowing cup of God's goodness that their sanity had become a kind of divine madness, a heightened state of consciousness in which the visionary plane of eternity had been revealed to them. Only a mind, as Philo taught,

> which has become an initiate in the divine mysteries and has travelled with the choral dances of the heavens [tais tōn ouraniōn choreias] ...
>
> (On Rewards and Punishments 121)

would be blessed with the supreme virtue of piety and raised to an ecstatic communion with God. On passing beyond the chorus of the heavens the dancing intellect did not cease to dance. It merely ceased to be a remote spectator of the divine chorus and became an active participant in the mysteries of the intelligible world. Converting its contemplative movement from a virtuous imitation of the divine in nature to a mystic initiation into the secrets of divinity beyond nature, the mind of the seer could abandon the peaceful disciplined chorus of Apollo for the spiritual freedom, the manic leaping, the mountain revels of Dionysus.

The Revel-King numbered among his miscellaneous entourage a band of

Phrygian priests known as the Corybants, whose mythological fame rested on their invention of the raucous timbrels or hide-drums originally used in the worship of the mother-goddess Rhea.[3] When Rhea, fearing the murderous intentions of Cronus, hid the infant Zeus in the cave of the Corybants, they protected the child by beating on their drums so loudly that his cries could not be heard. Philo might have read how their celebrated invention passed into the service of Dionysus, becoming, like the ivy-tipped thyrsus, emblematic of the ecstasies induced by bacchic dancing, in the third antistrophe of the first ode sung by the Bacchants of Euripides. They invoke the sacred haunts

> *Where the Corybants with triple plume*
> *Invented in their caverns*
> *The drum with stretched skin*
> *Which we beat,*
> *And blended its wild bacchic revels [bacchia]*
> *With the intense sweet-sounding voice*
> *Of Phrygian flutes,*
> *And put the din of its bacchic shout*
> *In the hand of Mother Rhea;*
> *But the frenzied satyrs*
> *Obtained it from the divine Mother,*
> *And wedded it to the choral dances [eis de choreumata]*
> *Of the triennial festivals*
> *Which delight Dionysus.*

(*Bacchae* 123–34)

Like the Mevlevi dervishes of Turkey the Phrygian priests initiated new members into their cult by whirling themselves out of their senses until their souls were seized by an exhilarating mania similar to bacchic intoxication. Plato described their mental agitation as a state of divine possession or 'enthousiasmos,' implying that in their sacred rage the Corybants were genuinely in contact with the divine powers controlling nature (*Symposium* 215e); but his final spokesman, the Athenian, diagnosing their hallucinations, ravings, and muscular spasms as the symptoms of a mental illness, recommended rhythmic bodily exercise as a treatment for 'Corybantic troubles' (*Laws* VII 790d). Though the image of a religious lunatic who has exhausted his body with relentless gyrations and stupefied his soul with delirious fantasies would hardly seem comparable to the elated mind of a seer who has attained the pinnacle of Platonic wisdom, such is the bizarre comparison Philo drew in his commentary on Genesis 1:26. He likened the 'enthousiasmos' of the dancing intellect to the mindless frenzy of 'those who perform the rites of the Corybants' – 'hoi corybantiōntes.' Both experiences were dizzying. Both were initiatory. Both produced visions of the world beyond the senses. For an instant, at least, one might be tempted to think that contemplative rapture had much in common with the exhilaration of total Dionysian release.

The jarring contrasts between orgiastic dance and intellectual ecstasy soon shatter the slight foundations of this analogy. Any detail Philo adduces to support their correspondence is either negated in the same sentence or undermined by subsequent qualifications. To express the inexpressible he is driven to paradoxes and contradictions. The experience of exalted insight is like an 'intoxication' (methē) provided that this is understood to be utterly 'sober' (nēphalia). Like the Corybants the dancing intellect may desire liberation from earthly cares, knowledge of the spiritual world, and union with the Almighty; but its yearning is 'other' (heterou himerou) and its desire 'nobler' (pothou beltionos) than the manic impulses of Dionysian revellers.

The noble goal of Moses and Abraham was to see the Great King himself and to lead their people away from physical stimulants, orgiastic rituals, and bloody sacrifices. When a drunken Corybant went out of his senses he merely stunned his body with severe physical exertion; when a true mystic went out of his senses he expended the greatest mental effort to transcend the imperfections of his life in the material world. To distinguish the true insights of a philosopher from the illusory visions of a Dionysian initiate Plato sometimes described philosophical meditation as if it were an exalted form of bacchic madness. Men who affected a love of wisdom but never allowed it to guide their footsteps towards virtue reminded him of Dionysian revellers who carried the emblematic thyrsus of the god without participating in the sacred rage induced by wine and the dance. True philosophers were like the true 'bacchoi,' fully initiated participants who gained wisdom by a strenuous effort to separate soul from body during the mystical transports of Dionysian intoxication (*Phaedo* 69d). The language of baccheia was more than just figurative in this context: it was playful and ironic, with a distinct tone of superiority. How better to distinguish the wisdom of the philosophical élite from the mania of the popular mystery cults than by juxtaposing them momentarily in a half-serious metaphor?

In the same ironic spirit Philo imagined the human intellect entering the rounds of the stars as a disciplined choral dancer and emerging as a raving Corybant. This rhetorical volte-face makes little sense if bacchic revelry, like choral dance, is interpreted as an affirmative image for the visible order of the heavens. Platonists did not believe that the universe at its highest levels became a whirling bacchanal. Such was their optimistic vision of world-harmony that the universe became more rational, more stable, more orderly the closer it was examined by the eyes of the body and the deeper it was penetrated by the eye of the mind. Sober intoxication, contemplative madness, pious revelry were Philo's most characteristic negative symbols for the philosophical vision of the intelligible world and the mystical experience of divine union.[4]

Interested always in the spiritual and moral applications of philosophy rather than in the accumulation of knowledge for its own sake, Philo found a striking example of the true 'bacchoi' in the sect of the Therapeutae, or 'Devotees,' a Jewish religious community living in his day near Alexandria. In his treatise *On the Contemplative Life*, from which all that is now known of the sect's ascetic practices and solemn rituals derives, Philo praised the Therapeutae for having renounced the vanities of the world and for choosing to live in simple huts where they could fast, study the scriptures, and contemplate the divine order of Creation. He found in their rigorously pious life a perfect synthesis of Platonic and Mosaic wisdom, a society of seers in harmony with the cosmic laws discovered by the Greeks and the moral laws revealed to Israel.

Though open to both men and women the sect was strictly celibate, and the aim of its protomonastic rule was to purge pleasure, overthrow lust, and heal the disorderly passions which rocked and confounded the soul in its quest to see God. By withdrawing from the corrupting influences of Alexandria the Therapeutae had become true citizens of the great city of the cosmos. They were admirable spectators of the dance of time, praising God for what their eyes beheld in the theatre of the stars and timing their daily prayers to coincide with the rising and setting of the sun; but their love of wisdom always urged them to leap beyond the dark dome of the heavens and to initiate their minds in eternal mysteries. 'Since the Therapeutae are a people always trained from the start to use their eyesight,' Philo explained,

> they are inevitably led to desire the vision of Being and to soar over the sun of the senses and never to leave this orderly company which leads them to perfect happiness. And those who enter this service not just out of custom or because others have recommended or requested it, but because they have been seized by a heavenly love, are divinely inspired like the Bacchants and Corybants [hoi baccheumenoi kai corybantiōntes] until they see the object of their desire.

> (*On the Contemplative Life* 11–12)

What they desired to see, as lovers yearning to behold their beloved, was the otherworldly light of the Divine Presence which the Corybantic intellect in *On the Creation* glimpsed for an instant before falling back to the visible world. Unlike the Gnostic and Christian mystics who would succeed them, the Therapeutae did not close their eyes to achieve intellectual vision but valued eyesight as the surest access to the spiralling route of contemplation which lifted the soul into Heaven. Seers in both a physical and spiritual sense, they observed the Divine Plan in the dynamic order of bodies as in the virgin Graces of the soul.

When they joined in the cosmic dance they actually danced. Their muscles obeyed the laws of perfect music no less than their minds. Every fifty days, Philo relates, the Therapeutae would gather together for a communal feast which was followed by a night-long ceremony of singing and dancing:

After the supper they hold their sacred night-festival which is conducted in the following way. They all rise up together, and standing in the middle of the dining room form themselves into two choruses [choroi], one of men and the other of women. The leader who is chosen for each chorus is the most honourable among them and the most gifted in music. They then sing hymns to God composed of many metres and melodies, sometimes singing together and sometimes chanting harmonies antiphonally.

Then, having set their souls in rhythm with the cosmic music, they expressed their inner concord in the visual harmony of a dance:

With their hands they perform rhythmic gestures [epicheironomountes] and to their music they dance [eporchoumenoi]. Sometimes they are inspired by the metres of their procession and sometimes perform the pauses, turns, and counterturns characteristic of a choral dance [tas en choreiai]. Then when each of the choruses has separately done its part in the festivities and has drunk of the pure wine of divine love just as in the bacchic rites [en tais baccheiais], they mix together and out of both groups is formed a single chorus in imitation of the chorus formed long ago beside the Red Sea in honour of the marvels wrought in that place.

(On the Contemplative Life 83–5)

Most religious dances are vaguely celestial in reference, if only because they are intended to place their participants in communion with the star-gods or with the spirits governing destiny or with the Almighty.[5] But the nocturnal dance of the Therapeutae seems to reflect the order of the cosmos in a specifically Platonic sense, as a visual imitation of the heavens leading to an intellectual vision of eternity.

In their movements, which recall the rituals Philo imagined to have taken place in the cosmic tabernacle designed by Moses, one might discern the complex configurations of the astral dance. Their two choruses might have represented the two great rounds of the Platonic cosmos, the Circles of the Same and the Different; their strophes and antistrophes symbolized, perhaps, the revolution of the fixed stars from east to west and the counterrevolution of the planets from west to east; and their pauses, the stillness of the earth or the apparent immobility of a planet between its apogee and perigee. The final movement in their dance, the merging of the two choruses in a triumphant revel, would correspond to the baccheia of the Corybantic intellect after it had whirled round with the dances of the planets and the fixed stars and leapt into the Empyrean. Having transcended the multiplicity of movements in the visible dance, the initiates in the mysteries would join in a single movement expressing their desire for union with God. If this fusion of the male and female choruses was a foreshadowing of the heavenly union of the Platonic lover with his divine object of desire, it was also a reenactment of the victory dance led by Miriam on the shore of the Red Sea following the deliverance of the Israelites from Pharaoh's armies (Exodus 15:20). The exodus of the contemplative soul from the visible world was thus allegorically associated by Philo with the exodus of Moses and his people from their bondage in Egypt. Interpreted either in a philosophical or a scriptural light the cosmic dance of the Therapeutae symbolized the liberation of the human soul from the bondage of the corruptible body: it was simultaneously a communal ascent into the intelligible world and a joyous rite of passage into the threshold of the Promised Land.

The ceremony ended at dawn with a salute to the rising sun, a gesture which recalls the turning of the Corybantic intellect towards the rays of pure unmixed light streaming from the Divine Presence. 'Beautiful are their thoughts and words!' exclaimed Philo at the end of his treatise, much moved by the spirit of otherworldly love displayed in their nocturnal festival,

Holy are the choral dancers [hoi choreutai]! The ultimate aim of the thoughts and words and choral dancers is piety. Thus they celebrate until dawn, drunk with the same honourable intoxication, not drowsy or with their eyes closed, but more wakeful than when they came to the banquet. They stand with their faces and their whole body turned to the east, and when they see the sun rise they stretch out their hands towards the heavens and pray for prosperous days and knowledge of the truth and the sharp-sightedness of reason.
(*On the Contemplative Life* 88–9)

Though the sect of the Therapeutae apparently died out in the first century AD, their impulse to reconcile the rational order of choreia with the ecstatic release of baccheia would continue to stir contemplative lives throughout Late Antiquity. Drawn by the mixed light of Athens and Alexandria, the devotees of new religious sects and new schools of mystical philosophy – Gnostics, Christians, Neoplatonists – would stretch out their hands towards the same rising sun and feel the same desire to alter the dominant movement in the dance (if this might be expressed in biblical terms) from genesis to exodus. The inebriation of the sober Bacchants was a physical and spiritual reality for Philo which could not be expressed except through the imaginative synthesis of metaphor. It defied logical analysis. It meant both an opening of the eyes to the sinfulness of life in the body and an opening of the mind to the purifying light beyond the cave of the senses. If Philo had rewritten the Myth of the Cave to foreshadow the intellectual history of Late Antiquity, he would have kept the escaped cave-dweller dancing in the sun-drenched upper world and not have insisted (as did Plato) that the philosopher return to the captive masses in the gloomy shadows underground.

3

Chorus and Charis

Before he was seized by the lawless Jews who were governed by the lawless Serpent, Jesus gathered all of us together and said: 'Before I am given over to them, let us sing a hymn to the Father and then go forth to what lies ahead.' Then he bid us hold each other's hands and form a circle with him in the middle. 'Answer me with Amen,' he said. Then he began to sing a hymn, saying,

> *Glory be to you, Father.*

And going round in a circle we answered him:

> *Amen.*
> *Glory be to you, Logos.*
> *Glory be to you, Grace.*
> *Amen.*
> *Glory be to you, Spirit.*
> *Glory be to you, Holy One.*
> *Glory be to your glory.*
> *Amen.*
> *We praise you, Father.*
> *We give thanks to you, Light*
> *in which no darkness dwells.*
> *Amen.*
> *Now I shall say why we give thanks.*
> *I wish to be saved and I wish to save.*
> *Amen.*

I wish to be freed and I wish to free.
    Amen.
I wish to be wounded and I wish to wound.
    Amen.
I wish to be born and I wish to beget.
    Amen.
I wish to eat and I wish to be eaten.
    Amen.
I wish to hear and I wish to be heard.
    Amen.
I wish to be known, I who am wholly mind.
    Amen.
I wish to be washed and I wish to wash.
    Amen.
Grace is dancing.
[Hē charis choreuei.]
I wish to pipe.
Dance all of you.
[Orchēsasthe pantes.]
    Amen.
I wish to mourn.
Mourn all of you.
    Amen.
One ogdoad sings together with us.
[Ogdoas mia hēmin sympsallei.]
    Amen.
Twelve is the number dancing on high.
[Ho dōdekatos arithmos anō choreuei.]
    Amen.
Ah, it is possible for the whole world to dance!
[Tōi de holōn ō choreuein hyparchei!]
    Amen.
He who dances not knows not what comes to pass.
[Ho mē choreuōn to ginomenon agnoei.]
    Amen.
I wish to flee and I wish to remain.
    Amen.
I wish to create order and I wish to be ordered.
    Amen.
I wish to be understood and I wish to understand.
    Amen.
I have no temple and I have temples.
    Amen.
A light am I for you who behold me.
    Amen.

A mirror am I for you who perceive me.
  Amen.
A door am I for you who are a wayfarer.
Listen, and respond to my choral dance.
[Hypakouō de mou tēi choreiai.]
Behold yourself in me as I speak, and seeing what I do, keep
                    silent about my mysteries.
You who are dancing, know that this human suffering which I
                    am about to bear is yours.
[Ho choreuōn noei ho prassō, hoti son estin touto tou
                    anthrōpou pathos ho mellō paschein.]
For you could not have fully understood what you suffer, had I
          not been sent to you as the Logos from the Father.
When you saw what I endured, you saw me as a sufferer, and
    seeing this you did not stand firm but were wholly moved.
You who have been moved to become wise have me as a bed.
Rest upon me.
You will know who I am when I have departed.
I am not he who I am seen to be.
You will see when you come.
If you had known how to suffer, you would not have had the
                    power to suffer.
Acknowledge suffering and you will have no suffering.
I myself shall teach you what you do not know.
I am your God, not the God of the betrayer.
I wish to set holy souls in rhythm with me.
[Rhythmizesthai thelō psychais hagiais ep' eme.]
Understand the word of wisdom.
Again say to me:
Glory be to you, Father.
Glory be to you, Logos.
Glory be to you, Holy Spirit.
If you wish to know what concerns me, know this.
All I have said, I uttered playfully, and I was by no means
                    ashamed.
I leapt.
[Egō eskirtēsa.]
Now, on your part, understand the Whole.
And having understood it, say:
Glory be to you, Father.
  Amen.

Thus, my beloved ones, having danced with us [choreusas meth' hēmōn] the Lord went away, and like wanderers or rather like men dazed with sleep,

*we fled this way and that. Then, when I saw him suffer, I did not remain
by him in his agony, but fled to the Mount of Olives and wept at what had
happened. And when he was crucified, darkness fell upon the whole earth
at the sixth hour. Then the Lord stood in the midst of the cave, enlightening
it, and said: 'John, before the multitude down in Jerusalem I am being
crucified and pierced with lances and reeds and given vinegar and water to
drink. But here I am speaking with you. Hear what I have to say. I put it
into your mind to come up to this mountain so that you might hear what a
disciple should hear from his teacher and a man from his God.'*
ANONYMOUS, The Acts of John 94–7[1]

A Time to Mourn and a Time to Dance

To turn from the splendid classical façades, the brightly lit thoroughfares,
and the law-abiding choruses in Philo's Alexandrian cosmos to the dark,
perilous, crime-ridden Jerusalem of the Acts of John – the capital of the
'lawless Jews' in the empire of the 'lawless Serpent' – is to sense a sudden
chill in the religious atmosphere. Something demonic has eclipsed the glowing Platonic sun of the Therapeutae. Someone divine has disrupted the order
of the Mosaic chorus. Somehow we have fallen back into a cavernous darkness where our eyes fail us, and our ears are disturbed by echoes of a strange
hymn sung by a strange Jesus. To hear his disciples chanting 'Amen' as they
circle him in an hypnotic choreia which is suddenly interrupted (as if a spell
were broken) by his departure for Calvary is to sense an interruption of
another order – a break with the high culture of the Hellenistic past.

Philo lived some four hundred years after Plato, and yet (if intellectual
affinities could be measured in calendar time) scarcely a generation seems
to separate the Athenian master from his Alexandrian disciple. Conversely,
a great gulf of time seems to separate Philo from the unknown author of
the Hymn of Jesus – an epoch of momentous revelations and conversions
– though in calendar years probably no more than a century elapsed between
the death of Philo (c 50 AD) and the inclusion of the Hymn in the apocryphal
Acts of John (c 150 AD). The Jerusalem from which the disciples fled 'like
wanderers or rather like men dazed with sleep' was in fact contemporaneous
with the Alexandria from which the Therapeutae retired to live in contemplative seclusion and to imitate the heavenly dance with body and soul 'not
drowsy,' as Philo had noted in his treatise *On the Contemplative Life* (88),
'but more wakeful than when they came to the banquet.'

Yet the first Christians, at least those represented in the Acts of John,
seem, to have been as ignorant of the mystic symposium of the Therapeutae
as the Therapeutae apparently were of the Last Supper. The gulf between
their respective cities and cultures is reflected in the rhetoric of the works
commemorating their religious vocations. Absent from the apocryphal Acts

are the mythological topoi of classical Platonism, the subtle terminology of Stoicism, the figures of Hellenistic oratory, and the allegorical word play of Philonic exegesis. In their place we find the haunting incantations of an obscure plebeian mystagogue and the starkly laconic narration of his beloved disciple John – once a mere fisherman, now a divinely chosen fisher of men – who is recollecting for his intimate circle of converts the miraculous events that befell him at the time of the Crucifixion.

His cultural remoteness from Philo and the Therapeutae is further marked by the conspicuous absence of any affirmative reference in the Hymn to laws or to the Law. If one single purpose can be said to have dominated Philo's contemplative life, it was to reconcile the four interlocking systems of law that governed his life in the world: the religious customs of the Jews; the political statutes of the Romans; the harmonic principles of the stars; and the moral commandments of the God of Moses. That these diverse laws did not always accord with one another Philo the diplomat knew only too well; yet Philo the moralist never lost hope that an ideal union of earthly and heavenly laws could be achieved on a grand scale through the exercise of 'piety and human kindness,' the two virtues woven together by Moses in the theme of his cosmic hymn and made visible in the interweaving motions of the Jews, the stars, and the angels. Philo the political theorist had seen his ideal realized in the harmonious society of the Therapeutae, and Philo the mystic in the evolving patterns of their symbolic dance, which after an initial sequence of turns and counterturns performed by separate choruses always ended in an ecstatic procession of all the dancers expressing before God, their attentive and critical spectator, the community's unanimous hope for a safe passage into Heaven in return for their strict adherence to the universal laws of harmony and the special laws of Israel.

No such hope inspires the dancers in the Acts of John: they join hands against a mob, a city, an empire, a world where laws that should have promoted piety and human kindness are superseded by the cruel dictates of the lawless Serpent or twisted by his malevolent agents so that the guilty thrive and the innocent suffer. In such a world, irremediably fallen, inherently discordant, Philo's triumphant synthesis of the laws of nature and nation can have little meaning. Communal salvation through obedience to the Law does not even figure in the religious expectations of the twelve disciples. Salvation is for them an entirely personal affair, dependent on the power of their personal Redeemer and on their knowledge of his supernatural identity. They dance because Jesus calls upon them in person, on a unique occasion, to prepare for the public drama of his Passion in a private ceremony of divine praise and thanksgiving. They are not moved to do so as were the Therapeutae from a sense of historical continuity, social duty, or religious obligation.

To dance with Jesus is to break away from the law-abiding past, to break out of the lawless society of the present, and to break up the monotonous round of seasons and seasonable activities that the world-weary Preacher in Ecclesiastes had seen as the vain pattern of the law-bound future. The Preacher's calm but comfortless lines assigning a season to everything and a time for every purpose under heaven,

> A time to kill, and a time to heal; a time to break down,
> and a time to build up;
> A time to weep, and a time to laugh; a time to mourn,
> and a time to dance ...
> (Ecclesiastes 3:3–4)

are echoed in the alternating declarations and imperatives of Jesus in the Hymn,

> I wish to pipe.
> Dance all of you.
> Amen.
> I wish to mourn.
> Mourn all of you ...

but without the Old Testament note of sombre resignation. The times and actions distinguished by the Preacher merge in the mystic round of Jesus and lose distinctness. The disciples dance while they are mourning, and mourn while they are dancing. Their dance must break down so that their faith may be built up. The choragus must be killed (or appear to be killed) so that the chorus may gain eternal life.

At the centre of this paradoxical revolution is a law-breaker instead of a law-giver, a plebeian opponent of the Pharisees who is destined to be arrested as a political traitor and handed over to the Roman governor for trial and execution; but beneath this lowly human guise is a divine ruler whose wish (as expressed in the Hymn) is 'to be freed' from the trials of the World and 'to free' his dancers from their imprisonment in the Flesh, and whose power over the World and the Flesh is so great that he can appear in two places at once, writhing on the cross before his deluded tormentors and hovering in an otherworldly aureole in a cave on the Mount of Olives. His bilocation provides John – and is meant to provide his converts – with proof that their Redeemer can break the laws of an unyielding and remorseless universe.

How preposterous would this choragus have seemed to Philo, and how chaotic the ending of this dance! Instead of merging into a single concordant chorus with the sun and the other stars, instead of contemplating the immutable laws of God in auroral serenity, instead of reaching out towards

Heaven in the light of a new day, the disciples emerge from their round as bewildered wanderers, as men driven to action rather than contemplation. They scatter in all directions, reel at the spontaneous grace of Jesus, flee into a day grown unnaturally dark or into a cave grown unnaturally bright. The disquieting aftermath of their dance seems to reverse or upset all that the Therapeutae had achieved at the quiet finale of their festival. In the Acts of John one perceives as a violent lurch forward, a headlong rush into mystical darkness, what in the canonical Gospel of John (particularly 1:17: 'For the law was given through Moses; grace and truth came through Jesus Christ') had been presented, some fifty or so years before the composition of the apocryphal text, as a gradual unfolding of the Divine Plan into the light of human history – the transition from the Age of the Law to the Age of Grace.

If the Acts of John were the only early Christian document attesting to the continuity of the cosmic choreia, we might suppose, judging from the sharp contrast between the Philonic and Johannine visions of the dance, that the second century had almost nothing in common intellectually or spiritually with the first; that the pale ghostly shape of a supernatural redeemer flitted through Plato's cave where once the bright rays of philosophy had shone; and that the torch-bearers of Athenian paideia (with which the astral choreia as an educating spectacle was intimately associated) had for some mysterious reason been stopped dead in their tracks. But they had not been stopped, of course. Platonic cosmology still illuminated the captives in the cave. The Empire's second century can be said to coincide with the second century of the Christian era only in retrospect, for at the time, especially during the reigns of Trajan (98–117), Hadrian (117–38), and Antoninus Pius (138–61), no era in Roman history would have seemed more self-confidently pagan or more self-consciously Hellenized – at least to the governing classes. The Empire as they saw it was succeeding not only as a mammoth political organization, then at its greatest territorial extent, its borders remaining virtually unchallenged until the last years in the autumnal reign of Marcus Aurelius (161–80), but also as a cherished cultural ideal, a civilizing synthesis of Roman government and Greek education which peoples as diverse as the Britons and the Armenians had been taught to respect, and which gods as ancient as Jupiter and as recent as Augustus, the philanthropic overseers of Rome's imperial destiny, had evidently decided to perpetuate for the benefit of all mankind.

The late summer of classical paganism produced its fair share of philosophical dialogues, treatises, and orations testifying to the continuity of the Platonic vision of choreia – enough, certainly, to correct any exaggerated impression of a breach in Late Antique intellectual history that might arise from a simple juxtaposition of the dances of the Therapeutae and the Apostles, a breach following the emergence, or as it might seem the eruption, of primitive Christianity.

Listen, for example, to the serene recapitulation of Plato's myths of world-harmony in the following speech from an urbane and leisurely dialogue on love by Plutarch of Chaeronea, a pagan rhetorician who achieved literary eminence under the patronage of Trajan and Hadrian:

> *For the true lover, when he has reached the heavenly realm and has consorted with the beautiful beings there in the customary holy manner, grows wings and joins in the mystic celebrations, dancing around his god and moving with him in the chorus on high [peri ton autou theon anō choreuōn kai symperipolōn], until the time comes for him to go back again to the meadows of the Moon and of Aphrodite, and to fall asleep before he begins another existence in this world.*

(*Erōtikos* or *Amatorius, Moralia* 766b–c; Loeb vol IX)

Not a false note is sounded in this imitation of the famous set speech of Socrates in the *Phaedrus* (247b–c) concerning the participation of the human soul in the chorus of the gods, a speech also blatantly imitated by Philo in his account of the soaring dance of the Corybantic intellect. Plutarch has captured the rhapsodic tone of Socrates with accomplished ease, transposing the language of the popular mysteries into the lofty key of Platonic eroticism and subtly amplifying its cosmological implications with echoes of the Myth of Er and the lecture of Timaeus.

But when the same mystic language – including the phrase 'anō choreuein,' 'to dance on high' – is transposed into the unsettling minor key of the Hymn of Jesus, recurring in such purely incantatory verses as

> *Twelve is the number dancing on high.*
> *Amen.*
> *Ah, it is possible for the whole world to dance!*
> *Amen ...*

it seems at once to lose its erudite Platonic overtones and to recover the deep indefinable resonance of folk poetry. Proud as they were of their philosophical and literary sophistication, the pagan rhetoricians (or 'Sophists' as they were still called in the second century) were not wholly insensitive to the primitive rhythms of the cosmic mystery dance celebrated in the popular Dionysian and Apollonian cults of their day. Plutarch, for one, served as a priest in the temple of Apollo at Delphi and must have chanted hymns to the choragus of the planetary Muses as unphilosophical in tone and cultish in spirit as the Hymn of Jesus.

Nevertheless, when the Sophists tried to convey in poetic diction an impression of the religious awe, the aesthetic rapture, which they imagined their primitive ancestors to have felt on first beholding the dance of the stars, they invariably sounded like pedantic aesthetes rather than prophetic bards. They were incapable of perceiving the cosmos except through a veil of literary allusions. 'If you agree with Plato,' wrote Apuleius of Madaura, who imported the extravagantly allusive style of the Greek Sophists into the Latin literature of the mid-second century,

you will also place the other stars in the same category of visible gods,

> *Arcturus, the rain-bringing Hyades, and the twin Chariots,*

and the other radiant deities, too, whose celestial chorus [caeli chorum] we have seen adorned and crowned when the weather is clear and the nights are embellished with an austere grace and a savage impetuous beauty. Lifting our eyes towards this perfect 'necklace of the world,' as Ennius says, we admire its variegated bas-reliefs glittering with marvellous fires.

(*De deo Socratis* I.120–1)

Ironically, though Apuleius seems to have been impressed more by the wild barbaric splendour of the cosmos than by the stable, placid, civilizing order imposed on its discordant elements by the Divine Mind, he described nature's 'savage impetuous beauty' in the most refined and civilized terms, recalling delicate phrases from Virgil and Ennius to evoke the sparkling ornamentation of the night sky and transmuting the stars' impetuous chorus into a precious objet d'art, a decorative frieze in a sumptuous cosmic villa.

And what if the planets seemed to disrupt this universal still-life with their individual counterrevolutions? No problem. Apuleius was always ready to adapt the old metaphor of the chorus to minimize apparent discrepancies between cosmological theory and astronomical observation. 'But, notwithstanding the diverse movements of the planets,' he insisted,

the world as a whole has but one rotary movement in which it periodically returns to its point of departure, one concord, and one choral dance of stars arising from their diverse risings and settings [unus stellarum chorus ex diversis occasibus ortibusque]. The Greek language assigns the very appropriate word 'cosmos' to this necklace-like ornament. For just as in choruses [ut in choris], when the leader chants the first part of a hymn, the troupe of male and female choristers respond with one resounding harmony by mixing low voices with high, so the Divine Mind, following the model of a single unified concert, alleviates the various discords in the world.

(*De mundo* XXIX.335)

When the living cosmos stiffens into a lifeless academic monument or fades into a concert of abstract principles conducted by the Divine Mind, the dance which is the natural image of its visible and dynamic harmony inevitably loses vitality too. Where Philo had seen animated fires whirling through the ether, Apuleius imagines constellated gods and nymphs frozen in a celestial bas-relief; where the Therapeutae had imitated cosmic harmony in both song and dance, Apuleius simply defines it – and reduces what he defines –by likening celestial concord to the fusion of voices in a stationary choir. The image has lost its dramatic immediacy, its visual interest, its mystery for him: it has become a mere topos, a stock theme for rhetorical embellishment and exposition but not for lively philosophical or religious consideration. Why did the Platonic image of the dance fail to stimulate his visual imagination? Not because his imagination was feeble, surely: Apuleius the Platonist is also believed to have written the exuberantly fanciful poetic romance known as *The Golden Ass*. No, the reason for his dull academic response to the image probably lies in the rhetorical bias of his education. At the heart of the Second Sophistic Movement (the First having been in full swing during Plato's lifetime) was a sometimes flippant, sometimes profound contempt for the whole enterprise of philosophy – its rival schools, its obscure terminology, its unresolved questions, its fractured visions of life – an attitude which would doubtless have shocked the conservative exponents of paideia in Philo's day.

This contempt underlay the urbane skepticism prevalent among the educated élite of the second century and reinforced their belief that philosophy was distinctly inferior to rhetoric, that what one thought was ultimately less important than how one expressed it. The image of the world-chorus was rejuvenated in the second century – as opposed to merely revived or repeated as a classical topos – by the relatively uneducated spectators in the cosmic theatre, the speakers of 'koinē,' who by setting it once again within the framework of a mythological drama imparted to its mundane revolutions a sense of mystical rapture, of dramatic urgency, of impending agony, of 'austere grace.' What makes the dance of Jesus so alive, so vibrant, in comparison with Plutarch's languid cycles of reincarnation and Apuleius' monotonous astral rounds is its spontaneity: it goes against the predictable course of things, establishes a tragic tension between humanity and the powers of destiny, and drives its participants towards joyous transcendance rather than apathetic acceptance of 'the various discords in the world.'

A glance at one other Sophist's remarks on the harmony of the world-chorus will reveal, by way of a brief digression, how strikingly *out* of harmony the dance of Jesus was with the universal movements approved by the intelligentsia in the palmy days of imperial paganism, and also, incidentally, how a truly gifted orator could invest the old topos of choreia with new life, when the occasion called for it, by adapting its political significance (which Plato had conceived in terms of the closely knit society in a Greek city-state) to the expansive new conditions of the Roman Empire.

Around 101 AD the citizens of the Bithynian city of Prusa were treated to an oration in elegant Attic Greek by their most famous native son, Dio Chrysostom, a professional rhetorician and man of the world who was a close friend of the Emperor Trajan. What Dio delivered in fact was an oration within an oration: a report of the speech he had given several years before in Borysthenes, a Milesian colony north of the Black Sea, at a time when he was out of favour with Trajan's brutal predecessor Domitian. Outraged by Dio's adverse criticism of his régime, Domitian had banished the Sophist from Italy and Bithynia in 82 AD. For fourteen long years, until the accession of Nerva in 96 AD, he had been forced to wander as an exile through remote provinces of the Empire, at times living in penury as a Cynic, at other times enjoying the hospitality of culture-starved provincial governors. During his exile he chanced to visit Borysthenes, where to his great surprise – for civility was hardly to be expected in a settlement on the edge of nowhere – he was warmly received by a tribe of fair-haired unshaven barbarians. Their heroic mien and noble manners amazed him. He was sure that he had stumbled upon the descendants of that golden race of bearded Greek warriors immortalized in the epics of Homer. Barbarians in appearance only, the Borysthenians turned out to know their Homer as well as anyone in Athens or Rome and to be such fervent admirers of Achilles that they had built a temple in his honour on the outskirts of their town.

They had also acquired a remarkably civilized taste for the burnished rhetoric of the Sophists, an aureate alloy of poetic allusions, archaic idioms, academic quips, political anecdotes, and witty elaborations of philosophical clichés. Delighted to have a Master Sophist in their midst, the Borysthenian elders escorted Chrysostom (the 'golden-tongued') to their council-house where they begged him to deliver an impromptu speech on the laws of cosmic harmony and the definition of a truly law-abiding city. This is part of what he told them:

Perhaps, then, someone might ask whether a community whose rulers and leaders being provident and wise govern the rest of the populace in accordance with their judgment, lawfully and sanely, may accordingly be called sane and law-abiding and a 'city' in the full sense of the term because of those who govern it – just as we might perhaps say that a chorus is 'musical' [choron isos phaiēmen an mousikon] if its leader is musical and if its members follow his lead and utter no deficient and indistinct sounds contrary to his melody.

However, no one knows of a good city composed entirely of good citizens,
that is, of mortal men, as having existed in the past – or thinks it worthwhile
speculating that such a city will arise in the future – unless it be a city of the
blessed gods in the heavens, who, far from being motionless or idle, are
exceedingly active and progressive, and whose divine guides and leaders know
neither discord nor defeat. For it is impious to suppose that gods quarrel
discordantly among themselves, since they are friends, or that they suffer
defeat at the hands of beings more powerful than themselves: on the contrary,
one must think of them as performing their actions without hindrance and
always in a spirit of total friendship which is shared by all. The most con-
spicuous of them pursue an independent course – I do not mean wandering
aimlessly and senselessly, but rather dancing a joyous dance in accordance
with their intelligence and supreme wisdom [choreian eudaimona choreuon-
tōn meta te nou kai phronēseōs tēs akras] – while the rest of the celestial host
are drawn along by the general movement, the whole heaven being governed
by one single purpose and impulse.

(*The Thirty-Sixth Discourse* 21–2)

The Sophists were, like Dio's stars, 'exceedingly active and progressive' in
the political life of the expanding Empire: they toured the great Mediterranean cities as guests of the most powerful men of their age, journeyed
from the provinces to Rome as spokesmen for special interest groups, sped
back from Rome to the provinces as apologists for the Emperor, wandered
as restless exiles along the frontiers of the civilized world, and sometimes,
as pioneers in the field of cultural anthropology, ventured beyond those
frontiers to study the customs of barbarian tribes at close hand and to reflect
upon the glorious potential of their own culture from an objective critical
distance. Thanks to this adventurous legion of literati, who considered themselves the leading exponents of 'pure' classical culture and the arbiters of
'pure' classical taste, Athenian paideia was more widely diffused during the
first two centuries of the Empire than at any other period in Roman history.
And wherever the torch of paideia was carried, even to the forbidding plains
beyond the Black Sea, new lights were lit in the ancient theatre of the cosmos
and new spectators drawn in to admire the 'choreia eudaimōn' of the gods.

While the Prusans no doubt understood these gods to be the deified stars
of Plato and detected in Dio's encomium of their dance echoes of *Timaeus*
40d, *Laws* II 653c, *Phaedrus* 247b, and *Epinomis* 991b (where the words
'choreia' and 'eudaimōn' occur together in a cosmological context), the
Borysthenians for the most part would have heard such phrases as 'choros
mousikos' and 'choreia eudaimōn' not as literary echoes or academic commonplaces but as fresh, perhaps still rather mysterious evocations of a civilizing world-order. Dio borrowed Plato's myths and metaphors to instruct,

to enlighten, indeed to convert the Borysthenians. He took it upon himself to initiate a quaintly Homeric but culturally backward and isolated tribe into the communal ideals of a divinely ordained world-culture, a brave new empire from which he could not in spirit be exiled. Hence his glum Stoic contrast between the imperfectly governed cities of men and the perfectly peaceful city of the gods is balanced and tempered by an idealistic Platonic analogy between the human and the divine chorus, and this analogy, with its emphasis on the sanity and public-mindedness of the chorus, the single purpose governing the dancers' multifarious motions, the undefeated spirit of their independent leaders, and the joyous concord achieved and perpetuated by their willing submission to a common set of laws, may be read as an implicit manifesto of Roman imperialism as it ought to be – and would be, Dio maintained, if malevolent despots like Domitian were prevented from ruling the Empire.

Though the Borysthenians responded to this vision of the imperial universe with ingenuous enthusiasm, Dio could not have expected the same uncritical response from his sophisticated Prusan audience. Yet that is probably why he chose to repeat his Borysthenitic oration in his native city: to restore confidence – or rather (imperial politics being inseparable from imperial religion) to revive faith – in the philanthropic ideals of Roman rule which the unhappy era of Domitian had no doubt gravely undermined.

The optimistic message of his political homily, which is essentially a restatement of the myths of the Craftsman and the Chariot heralding (like Virgil's fourth eclogue) the dawn of a new age of peace on earth and the reconstruction of human society on the pattern of the divine chorus, would certainly not have been unanimously applauded by the barely literate but intellectually vigorous substratum of imperial society, the once inarticulate masses. The cities of the Eastern Empire were thronging with articulate speakers of demotic Greek – slaves, women, fishermen, ropemakers, soldiers, tax-collectors – who had little faith in the power of dead or distant emperors to restore the peace of the Golden Age and who therefore refused to be pacified by the mythology of imperial concord. Many among them felt trampled upon rather than divinely guided by the chorus of the Empire, and many desperately yearned for release from the ignorance, drudgery, poverty, and anonymity of their earthly lives.

For such an audience the Acts of John was written. They are the Levantine crowds to whom John preaches on the liberation of Christian believers from the demonic government of the World, and the 'beloved ones' who gather round him like children when he recounts the parable-like incident of the dance of Jesus. Did they imagine this ruptured and rupturing dance against the slowly turning background of the Roman heavens, against the panorama of the uninterrupted choral round praised by the Sophists? Were they struck by the sharp contrast between this new movement and the old? Joyous the dance of Jesus was not, at least not in a worldly sense. Nor was it victorious, or public-spirited, or serenely rational, or perpetually unified, or in any way reminiscent of Dio's 'choreia eudaimōn.' But it promised them liberty. It foreshadowed a counterrevolution of the lowly and the powerless against the powers that turned the Roman world, against the stars, against the emperors, against the judges, against the legions, against all the agents of the Devil. Deep within the pagan Empire, while Trajan and his successors were occupied with the fortification of its far-flung boundaries and Dio and his colleagues were busy bringing civilization to the barbarian hinterlands, another empire was slowly, unsuspectedly forming, another chorus amassing itself and beginning to turn like the Circle of the Different against the Circle of the Same, though its divine ruler, its choragus, had insisted that his kingdom was not of this world and that his dance was only for holy souls bound for the world beyond.

Like the fresco of the Dionysian dance in the Villa of the Mysteries at Pompeii, which in its private setting and introspective mood seems remote from (if not deliberately opposed to) the grandiose but rather impersonal public spectacle of the divine dance conceived by Greco-Roman Sophists, the poignantly intimate scene of the mystic round in the Acts of John still miraculously evokes the physical excitement and spiritual aspirations of the many ordinary people who flocked to the various mystery cults revived or founded in the heyday of the pagan Empire. Though like Pompeii the Acts of John is a monument of popular, and for the most part, unsophisticated culture, having been preserved by chance a little beyond the main thorough-fares of intellectual history and only recently brought to light (again like Pompeii, in the late nineteenth century) after the people, the rooms, the fears, the mysteries suspended in it had fallen into complete obscurity, this anonymous 'eyewitness' narrative, with its unintellectual and perhaps de-fiantly anti-intellectual Hymn of Jesus, deserves for three reasons to be considered in the foreground of second-century intellectual life: first, be-cause it testifies to the traumatic incursion of supracosmic powers into the psychological confines, and if John and other witnesses are to be believed, the physical confines of Late Antique society; second, because it reveals how this incursion caused jagged fissures to appear on the smooth marble surface of classical culture and startling new mythologies to pour forth from the wellsprings of the mysteries; and third, because it turns a standard classical model for cosmic harmony and philosophical education, choral dance, into a striking emblem of the era's revolutionary new idea, conver-sion, which was in fact an old idea newly conceived in terms of the inner life of the common man. The dance of Jesus represents the genesis of a new paideia, with the choragus assuming the role of teacher as in the old choreia

Figure 4

A time to dance follows a time to mourn in this fresco of an initiation ceremony (painted c50 AD) in the Villa of the Mysteries, Pompeii. The spirited dancer seems ready to spring into heaven without bodily shame.

of the philosophers. But the new teacher wishes to release his disciples from the coils of time rather than unite them with the revolutions of the World-Soul, and his disturbingly simple promise

I myself shall teach you what you do not know

anticipates a sudden preternatural influx of wisdom rather than a gradual progress from ignorance to enlightenment. In sharp contrast to Timaeus, Jesus turns the eyes of his disciples inward towards a numinous centre instead of outward – the direction of Platonic education – towards a luminous horizon.

We Have Piped unto You

Conversion is conceived today mainly as a psychological change affecting a person's religious beliefs or moral standards, an experience so private that even after it has drastically altered the convert's perceptions of the world the effects of the change may be quite hidden from the world's eyes. Once the opposite was true: conversions mainly occurred outside the mind and were as easy to see as the sky. If asked to point out a conversion, Cicero or Virgil would most likely have looked up to the heavens, for the Latin noun 'conversio' (which literally meant a 'turning together' of people or things in a single unifying motion) usually denoted the diurnal revolution of the fixed stars. By the second century of our era the word had acquired its metaphoric reference to turns of thought or changes in belief and was beginning to refer, in particular, to changes in religious belief. The Greek noun for 'convert,' 'proselytos,' underwent a similar semantic development. Originally it signified 'someone who has moved over from one place to another,' but in the second century it was used by Christian authors to mean 'someone who has moved over to a new faith by changing his religious position.' The second century was an age when conversion and proselytizing were, as the root senses of these words imply, dynamic processes in a widespread revolution in thought which was moving people away from old points of view and driving them towards new interpretations of the Divine Plan. The turning together of the disciples in the Acts of John seems to reflect the transition from physical to psychological movement implicit in the developing senses of 'conversio' and 'proselytos.' While their round-dance is a conversion of bodies like the round-dance of the stars, it also symbolizes a movement in the inner lives of the dancers, a turning of their souls towards a goal outside of time and space.

The cosmic theatre in which Philo and Dio had viewed the joyous chorus of the stars lost a small but noticeable part of its second-century audience to the Universal Church – or rather to the various churches, each claiming that title, which were springing up here and there mainly in the eastern cities of the Empire and vociferously (though not with one voice) challenging the philosophical assumption that man could most readily penetrate the mysteries of the Divine Mind by observing the manifestly rational design of the cosmos. Clement of Alexandria, an early Christian apologist (c150–c215) who received as thorough an education in Platonic cosmology as Philo and occasionally consulted Philo's commentaries on Genesis, was no longer persuaded by the Platonic dictum – which was philosophy's oldest advertisement – that inside the cosmic theatre was the fairest of all sights and the model for all virtuous behaviour. For Clement, the fairest sight was the face of God and the model for virtue was the life of Christ.

While Philo had confidently asserted that the light of the temporal world led man upwards to the Great King, he had also confessed that the mysterious rays streaming from the Great King blinded the eye of his understanding. The proponents of various dualistic cosmologies and myths of personal salvation which, for convenience, may be labelled 'Gnostic' as distinct from 'Christian' (though the distinction was certainly not clear, or even important, to everyone who became a proselyte in the second century) also questioned the Platonic assumption that physical vision automatically stimulated intellectual vision. Though the Christians of Clement's circle would have disagreed with the Gnostics on many fundamental issues, such as whether the material world was inherently evil and whether the knowledge of salvation was tantamount to salvation itself, together they were yearning to see what the Greek philosophers, the Jewish prophets, and the Roman moralists had failed to show them: the chorus of eternal spirits encircling the wellspring of life.

By rejecting the intuitive analogy between physical and intellectual vision that underlay the Platonic theory of knowledge, the Gnostics literally closed their eyes to the critical problem of why philosophical enlightenment ironically resulted in mental blindness. While they could agree with Philo that beyond the world of the senses was a Heaven of Light where the source of all truth and wisdom resided, they did not search the sky for signs of the benevolent operations of the Divine Mind. Wisdom, they claimed, had come to their privileged souls through the communications of inner voices and through the teachings of divinely inspired seers. The same antivisual bias was shared by certain converts who, though they would have called themselves Christians, promoted doctrines of the Incarnation and Resurrection which were essentially Gnostic in character. The author of the Acts of John was one of these.

The central episode in his narrative of the miracles, perilous journeys, public orations, and last days in the life of Christ's beloved disciple concerns a glorious proselytizing mission John supposedly undertook to Ephesus, a city on the southwest coast of Asia Minor, where he had the good fortune to convert the praetor Andronicus and his virtuous wife Drusiana. Andronicus and Drusiana are the beloved friends to whom he tells his behind-the-scenes story of the Crucifixion, including the episode of the dance; the Hymn of Jesus is thus contained in an historical flashback which serves not only to reveal John's special role in the secret drama of the Passion but also to teach his converts the 'true' meaning of Christian discipleship and salvation.

The singer of the Hymn is not exactly the Jesus of the Gospels or the Christ worshipped by Clement of Alexandria. Though the apocryphal Redeemer is given the name Jesus, honoured as the Logos, recognized as the Son of God, and crucified by the Jews, he describes himself in the Hymn as a purely spiritual being ('I who am wholly mind') and as such cannot be identified with the Incarnate Word proclaimed by John the Evangelist. He resembles, rather, the otherworldly messengers of salvation who communicated telepathically with the élite members of Gnostic sects during the early Christian centuries. His ambiguous identity makes the purpose of his dance equally ambiguous, for as its central figure he is literally the focus of its inner meaning. Perhaps his dance is meant to reflect the harmony of Creation and to celebrate a universal order attuned to the New Song; or perhaps it is intended to release the dancers from the oppressive order of astral fate, and by eventually overpowering its compulsive movement, to thrust them beyond the evil powers controlling the material world.

The Four Evangelists make no mention of a dance of Jesus, though Matthew and Mark (but not John, oddly enough) do refer to a hymn sung by the Lord and his disciples just after they had eaten the bread and drunk the wine at the First Eucharist:

And when they had sung an hymn, they went out into the Mount of Olives.
(Matthew 26:30; Mark 14:26)

The author of the apocryphal Acts expands this tiny incident into a lengthy episode by reporting not only the words of the Hymn but also the dramatic circumstances under which it was chanted. A eucharistic context for the Hymn is suggested by such verses as

I wish to eat and I wish to be eaten,

which seems to echo Christ's command 'Take, eat; this is my body' (Matthew 26:26), and

I wish to be washed and I wish to wash,

which may refer to Christ's ritual washing of the disciples at the start of the Last Supper (John 13:4–12). But many verses in the Hymn have no clear antecedents in the Gospels. Indeed, a few, such as

I wish to be known, I who am wholly mind,

and the ominous

I am not he who I am seen to be,

seem to contradict what the Evangelists, especially John, have to say about the fully human nature of Christ and about his fully human agony and death upon the cross.

Perturbed by the unorthodox implications of such lines ('unorthodox' in retrospect, of course, since the boundaries of Christian orthodoxy were only just beginning to be defined at the period when the Acts of John was composed), St Augustine denounced the Hymn as uncanonical in a letter to a certain bishop Ceretius. No true Christian could read the Hymn with pleasure, he insisted, because it mocked the sacred doctrines of the true Church and presented Christ not as a sage and serious teacher – as John the Evangelist had portrayed him – but as a jesting minstrel, a piping fool 'who made sport of all things.' In the same letter Augustine stated that the Hymn was customarily to be found 'in apocryphal scriptures,' which indicates that by the late fourth century all or part of it had been excerpted from the Acts of John and inserted by various fringe sects into their collections of sacred literature. One such sect, the Spanish Priscillianists, were said to have held the Hymn in high regard because it contained secret wisdom which could be understood only by their divinely illumined souls and not by the corrupted souls of 'carnal men.'[2]

Seeing that anyone who disparaged the Hymn would appear unenlightened and unredeemed and, worse still, vulgar in the eyes of its unorthodox defenders, Augustine knew that he could not convince them of their folly (via Ceretius) merely by complaining about its offensive tone. Ever resourceful in these minor skirmishes in the wars of truth, he tried to refute their evidently Gnostic interpretation of the Hymn by demystifying its prophetic verses, by showing that its supposedly secret wisdom was expressed quite openly and clearly in the Gospels. For instance, the singer's command 'Dance all of you' reminded him of what Jesus said to the skeptical disciples of John the Baptist when they rather petulantly asked him, during his Galilean ministry, whether he was the great Messiah whom they had been told to follow. 'But whereunto shall I liken this generation?' Jesus retorted,

It is like unto children sitting in the markets, and calling unto their fellows, and saying,

> *We have piped unto you, and ye have not danced;*
> *We have mourned unto you, and ye have not lamented.*
>
> (Matthew 11:16–17; also Luke 7:31–2)

Though his contention that the Hymn was a mere extension of this parable may be discounted as polemical overstatement, Augustine was no doubt right in assuming that the parable was in some sense 'behind' the Hymn, that the analogies established in the former were played out in the piping, dancing, and mourning mentioned in the latter. The children sitting in the marketplace, those who wish to play the game of 'weddings' and 'funerals' in imitation of their parents, represent (with disarming humour) Christ and his disciples; their fellows, the recalcitrant children who do not wish to play the game, stand for the disciples of John the Baptist in particular but also for the many Jews of their generation who failed to respond to the Word of God and then for everyone who in subsequent generations would resist the call to conversion and repentance. Piping symbolizes the preaching of Christ in particular but also the spreading of the Good News through the proselytizing missions of the Apostles and ultimately through the charitable offices of the Church; dancing typifies the joyous response of the convert when his soul is wedded to Christ and his body is moved by the rhythms of the New Song.

Conversion is not a wedding game only, however, for it also entails a burial of the unconverted self amid wails of repentance and a dying of the new self to the sins of the Fallen World. All these analogies have been carried over from the New Testament to the Acts of John, the dominant theme of which is the interplay of conversion and repentance, except that the negatives in the canonical parable are removed from the apocryphal Hymn. Christ has piped unto the disciples and they have danced. He has wailed unto them and they have lamented. The 'paides' ('children') have learned the rudiments of the new paideia – or of a new paideia, one should say, since the doctrines passed on from John to Andronicus and Drusiana were to fall well outside the bounds of what would in Augustine's day be considered orthodox Christology. Clever as his polemical tactics were, Augustine could not reduce the Hymn to a poetic paraphrase of the parable of the children's games or convert its mystic enigmas into plain expressions of orthodox Catholic dogma. Too many verses in it supported the contention of his sectarian opponents that the singer of the Hymn did not intend his revelations to be piped to everyone in the marketplace or understood by the carnal multitude represented by the lawless Jews. Excerpts from the Acts of John, including the Hymn, were read out at the Second Council of Nicaea in 787 and denounced in no uncertain terms. 'These writings are ludicrous!' declared a patriarch named Tarasius. Finding them less risible than blasphemous, Theodosius bishop of Catania is reported to have exclaimed at the Council: 'Behold a book which destroyed the beauty of Christ's holy Church!'³ And with such indictments the Hymn of Jesus was relegated to oblivion.

Though its impact on the development of Christian doctrine was negligible in comparison with that of wholly pagan works such as the *Timaeus*, the Acts of John might still be read as a significant document in Western intellectual history because it is symptomatic of a major tendency in second-century thought, the dissociation of physical from intellectual vision, which would have a profound influence on the cosmological imagination of Christian apologists and pagan philosophers in the centuries to come. It also provides a rare opportunity to see the cosmic dance from the viewpoint of an early Christian convert and to participate (even at several removes) in the excitement of what was for him not just a personal but a cosmic conversion. The full meaning of the Hymn can be recaptured only in the context of the three apocryphal stories recording the early stages of this conversion: the parable of the dance at the Last Supper; the secret history of the Crucifixion and the epiphany on the Mount of Olives; and the encompassing tale of John's proselytizing mission to the Ephesians. Isolated from these interlocking stories the Hymn has nothing but the vaguest meaning, a haunting and magical obscurity, as if it were not meant to be understood so much as muttered to oneself as a spell.

Similarly, if the disciples' dance is isolated from the narrative flow of the Acts of John and imagined as an allegorical fresco or as a theatrical tableau vivant designed for spectators who must stand apart from it in order to interpret its imitative configurations, then its inner meaning will be as elusive as the mysteries inspiring it. We must assume the inner viewpoint of the convert, adapt our eyes to his new way of seeing, in order to make sense of his vision of the dance of Grace. And to prove that this is necessary, let us adopt for a moment the old way of seeing, the way of Philo and Dio Chrysostom, who like the earliest Greek philosophers saw the cosmic dance first with their eyes and then with their intellect and assumed that a mystical understanding of its eternal design would naturally follow from an analysis of its temporal appearances.

To the eyes of a pagan Sophist the first movement in the dance of Jesus would present a clear picture of 'harmonia' in its radical sense of 'a fastening together': at the command of their choragus the disciples fasten their circle together by joining hands. The same physical impression of harmony was created in the same timeless way by the round of choral dancers who first linked themselves in chain formation on the Shield of Achilles. Like ancient Greek choristers the disciples perform a strophic movement to the regular rhythmic patterns established by their lead singer and accented by their choral responses to his song. Their initial configuration, a circle turning around a fixed central point, immediately recalls the principal figure in the choral cosmos, the Supreme Circle, with its myriad imitations in the rounds upon rounds of fixed stars turning about the fixed central point of earth. This gives way, just as in the antistrophic episodes in the dance of the Therapeutae, to a sequence in which the disciples apparently demonstrate their command of astronomical geometry by imitating the diverse motions of the planets. Their uniform revolution breaks down into different individual movements, and in case any spectator should fail to see in this a dynamic representation of the Circle of the Different, the dancers are explicitly described as 'planēthentes' ('wanderers'). Since their wandering 'this way and that' must still reflect the order of the material world, which may appear discordant and unpredictable at times but is always governed by the laws of perfect music, their choreia clearly shows us – if our old way of seeing is not leading us astray – that the little world of humanity was designed by the Craftsman to turn with, and indeed to imitate, the great world of the heavens. The choragus seems to confirm this basic tenet of the old paideia by teaching his chorus to regard itself as a miniature cosmos:

> *One ogdoad sings together with us.*

If his resonant phrase 'ogdoas mia' is taken to mean 'one group of eight,' it might refer to the group of eight concentric spheres of the material universe, extending from the Aplanes with its countless stars down through the seven inner heavens governed by the planets. Their song, of course, would be the music of the spheres, the diverse tones of which comprised another group of eight – the diapason or perfect octave. The same phrase might also be translated 'the number eight as one in a series' and interpreted as a reference to the Aplanes, the one and only Eighth Sphere where the celestial gods danced in fixed circles patterned on the Circle of the Same.

Having attuned the souls of his disciples to the celestial music and set their bodies moving in imitation of the Supreme Circle, the singer of the Hymn immediately draws their attention to another important cosmic number implying another great cosmic circle:

> *Twelve is the number dancing on high.*

As any imperial astrologer would have noted, twelve is the number of zodiacal constellations dancing with the sun in its daily revolution around the earth and against the sun in its annual counterrevolution along the Different. Since Judas Iscariot was apparently present at the Last Supper (according to Matthew and Mark) when Christ sang his hymn, twelve would also have been the number of disciples in his chorus. Now, if Philo had been a secret spectator at their dance, he would not have regarded this numerical correspondence as a mere coincidence but as a fundamental principle uniting stars and men in a perpetually harmonious 'conversion.' The integration of choral and cosmic order (as he saw it) depended on the unitive power of the numbers governing the cycles of time, the laws of perfect music that the angels had revealed to Moses and the stars had taught the Greek philosophers. Is it not to the divine mathematics of the Craftsman that the singer of the Hymn refers in his lessons on the ogdoad and the number twelve? And when he exclaims

Ah, it is possible for the whole world to dance!

is this not the optimistic assertion of a cosmologist who has deduced from his observation that the design of the astral choreia encompasses everything moved or moving within the cosmos the general truth that rational order is indeed universal? So the singer's exclamation might be read by unconverted eyes in the light of the old paideia. Had Dio Chrysostom cast his unconverted eyes over the Hymn (which is highly unlikely since its earliest extant version appeared some thirty years after his death) he might have assumed that the choral round of the disciples was intended to reflect the benevolence and concord of the gods presiding over the destiny of earthly governments. When the singer declares

I wish to create order and I wish to be ordered ...

is he not, like Plato's Athenian, proposing a grand scheme for transforming the imprudently governed cities of men into true reflections of the ideal city of the gods? Yet unlike the Athenian, who had no delusions of grandeur, the singer of the Hymn speaks of himself as a divine mind desiring 'to create order' (kosmein) throughout the world – as if he were a second Craftsman about to create a new cosmos! Surely he must be speaking in metaphors. No sane citizen of the Empire, not even the Emperor, would have boasted that his mind was indistinguishable from that of the Creator. Unless he is mad, the singer of the Hymn must mean that the human mind which can create a choral dance is a miniature replica of the Divine Mind which created the archetypal dance in the theatre of the stars.

We have only to read a few lines of the Hymn from Philo's or Dio's viewpoint to realize that the mystery unfolded in the dance of Grace eludes philosophical analysis. To peer at the dance from the detached perspective of a Platonic or Stoical spectator is to obtain a very distorted impression of the disciples' conversion and to suffer the blinkering effects of what modern psychologists would call a 'mental set.' For centuries philosophers assumed that the orbits of the planets had to be perfect circles or combinations of perfect circles simply because the fixed stars were perceived to move in perfect circles: their minds (like the minds imagined by Plato to pilot the stars) were conditioned to think the same thoughts about the same things and to instil certain time-honoured cosmological assumptions in the minds of their students. As Philo's commentary on Genesis has illustrated, the old way of seeing was a mental set of the most powerful and enduring sort. It had conditioned his visual imagination to perceive the heavens as a living sky full of dancing stars and then to project the Greek design of the choral cosmos onto the universe of Moses. His education in Greek cosmology had formed his mind in the image of all the countless earlier minds that had perceived circular dances among the stars. The new paideia transmitted in the dance of Grace disrupts this old intellectual vision in a thoroughly dramatic way. The impulse of the divine mystagogue is to counteract the visual bias of the philosophers by altering the implications of their cherished image of world-harmony, choreia. Only by focusing perversely on a few scattered words in the Hymn – 'kosmein,' 'ogdoas,' 'anō choreuei' – can one read the old cosmic dance into the conversion around Jesus. And to do so is to ignore the implicit command of the Word himself: do not trust your eyes.

The great moment of revelation during the dance is an emphatic denial of visual evidence. 'I am not he,' the Redeemer insists, 'who I am seen to be.' Nor is his dance, any more than its maker, what it is seen to be. Despite its external appearance as an imitative choral dance designed to convey information outwards to a spectator looking in, it conveys no information at all to anyone outside the circle of disciples. The Last Supper had no spectators. Even if onlookers had been present at the dance, they would not have understood what the disciples' participation in the movement truly meant. Its symbolic meaning is a secret shared only by the dancers, who must (as their choragus bids them) keep silent about its mysteries. Their knowledge of the Redeemer depends entirely on the psychological experience of being saved, on the redeeming process itself, which by its very nature cannot be communicated to detached observers. So Jesus informs them, simply and straightforwardly, during the Hymn:

He who dances not knows not what comes to pass.

Subjective experience, not objective analysis, is the sole basis of knowledge for his disciples. Each individual must be caught up in the dance before he can begin to understand how the dance-maker has altered his perception of the world. Though the disciples enact their shared experience of conversion by turning together around Jesus, the emphasis in their communal ritual is still on the individual: each 'you' in the Hymn is a singular pronoun in Greek. Like a Dionysian rite the dance of Grace is fully understood only by its individual participants, for only they are in a position to hear the Hymn and to discover the inner meaning of their movements; and this, as the configuration of the dance suggests, depends on the secret nature of the Logos at the innermost point of the round. Their circle effectively excludes disinterested spectators, cuts off the chosen listeners from the rest of the world, marks the boundary between those who are ignorant of the Logos and those who eventually understand his true nature by responding to the Hymn. Denied access through the eye, knowledge of the Logos must enter the disciples' minds through the ear.

Unlike a spectator, a dancer senses the design of his dance primarly through aural perceptions. Since the rhythm of his musical accompaniment provides his cues and times his paces, he must 'pick up the beat' before his body can move in harmony with the music and with the other bodies in the dance. His ear will also tell him when the tempo of the dance is accelerating to a climax, when its mood is to be joyful or solemn, and when the performance is soon to end. From a vantage-point within the dance an individual dancer may never see the general visual design of which he is a part. The geometric configurations which seem so striking at a distance may be completely lost on a participant at close hand, for his mind is usually taken up with sensations that are not visual: the touch of a partner's hand; the dizziness after spinning; the exhilarating spring in his muscles; and always the rhythm sounding in his ears, linking him to his fellow dancers by a shared aural perception, and joining all participants to the choragus who commands the beat.

John could have been entirely blind as he wheeled around Jesus, and still he would have sensed the divine presence controlling the dance. The revolutionary implications of the Redeemer's demand

I wish to hear and I wish to be heard ...

following his crucial order

Listen, and respond to my choral dance ...

(with its imperative verb 'hypakouō' which in New Testament Greek denoted the consecutive actions of listening carefully and responding obediently to a divine command) may be sensed by contrasting the aural rhythms of the Hymn with the rhetoric of vision, discernment, illumination, and blindness which characterized Philo's descriptions of the cosmic dance and betrayed his essentially objective and analytic approach to cosmology. Even after his mind had supposedly relinquished its viewpoint as a spectator and assumed the guise of a leaping Corybant, Philo continued to describe his mystical participation in the invisible world primarily as a visual experience. Jesus turns his disciples into participants, full participants, right away. They have no preliminary stage of spectatorship and no metaphoric rise to participation. They respond to the divine order as an integral part of it, submitting to its harmonious motion, uniting themselves with its rhythm, for the Creator of the dance has ceased to be an inaccessible being beyond the visible cosmos. He has descended into their very midst. He has become their intimate companion, someone they can understand, a leader who can unite their bodies in an earthly dance and their souls in a movement towards Heaven. If intellectual history were imagined as a ceremonial progression of enlightenments and altered perceptions, much like the initiatory rites in an ancient mystery religion, the Hymn of Jesus would be the song of initiation into a new phase of the collective consciousness, a new mental set, which from the second century onwards conditioned Western perceptions of cosmic order as pervasively as the visual bias of Timaeus.

Cosmic order, which had been for Greek philosophers primarily a descriptive concept, the orderliness everywhere apparent in the architecture and dynamics of the temporal world, acquired for second-century Gnostics and Christians the force of a divine prescription. Timaeus had merely described the dances of stars and men. Jesus orders them to be performed around him. Timaeus had merely contemplated the orderly stages of creation. Jesus acts to create order in the midst of demonic confusion. One might say, then, that the disciples of Timaeus experienced order from the outside in: they admired the visible dances of the stars, deduced mathematical principles governing the geometric design of the cosmos, and then projected the same visual design inward onto their own rational thought processes (the invisible choreiai believed to exist within the souls of educated spectators). This long-established sequence of observation and deduction was completely reversed by the disciples of the Redeemer. They understood order from the inside out: first they felt the presence of the Logos deep within their souls or heard inner voices commanding them to escape the bondage of the Devil; then, in response to their personal encounter with the numinous, they adjusted their view of the outside world and redirected their lives towards the threshold of Heaven. Cosmic order was an ecstatic seizure for them, not an exalted spectacle. It was within them, driving them to act. Gnostics awoke from the charmed sleep of earthly life and separated their souls from the common mass of carnal men. Christians charmed restless souls with the New Song of the Gospels and spread the hope of eternal life to all classes of people. If the compelling power of the new order, including all the revelations and interior commands and 'supernatural solicitings' that initiated the proselytizing movements in the early Christian centuries, might be concentrated in one symbolic image, it would not be an image at all, at least not in a visual sense, for it would have to be a sound: the rhythm of a piper.

Since the Logos through whom the Father's saving grace is transmitted to mankind commands the dance even though he does not actually take part in its movement, the piper's simple assertion of purpose

I wish to set holy souls in rhythm with me ...

acquires in its narrative context the force of a divine decree. By setting the pace of the dance and playing upon the darkest anxieties of his dancers, the piper, like Dionysus of old, moves his chorus emotionally as well as physically towards wisdom, drives them towards a serene state of knowledge in which they may rest their souls without fear of the Serpent's sting. So Jesus assures them with these 'comfortable words':

You who have been moved to become wise have me as a bed.
Rest upon me.

Unlike the frenzied Corybants who danced with Dionysus, the disciples do not have to leap towards Heaven for wisdom. Wisdom has come down to them from its heavenly source. The piper's promise of ultimate stability through wisdom, of psychological security through dissociation of the self from the mob-world of the Serpent, is expressed dramatically by his physical relation to the chorus. While his isolation from the Twelve anticipates his imminent separation from their earthly company, his position within the dance, at the still centre of the circle, foreshadows his stable presence as their unseen heavenly choragus.

His saving powers will always be transmitted to them like the rhythm of his piping, invisibly but with miraculous effects, as John himself discovers in Ephesus when he is granted the power to raise Drusiana from the dead. Thus the souls made holy by the dance of Grace will not cease to be in rhythm with Jesus after his departure from this life. Echoes of his music will be heard as long as the imperatives of the Logos are preached to the few who are willing to mourn during the dance.

The Converted Spectator

A clue to the secret wisdom conveyed in the Hymn is contained in the Redeemer's lyrical dictum 'Grace is dancing' with its epigrammatical pun on the noun 'charis' and the verb 'choreuei.' Like a Buddhist koan, this cryptic line may have challenged the converts to abandon reason in their quest for wisdom and to fathom its meaning by exercising their native powers of intuition. How the second-century readers of the Hymn understood the line is difficult for an uninitiated modern reader to determine either by reason or by intuition, especially since the term 'grace' has come to mean so many things in the intervening centuries that its early implications are all but lost in a labyrinth of patristic definitions, medieval expansions of those definitions, and protestant formulations of its supposedly primitive meaning.

Still, if intuition leads us to believe that the line is a key to unlocking the mystical subtext of the Hymn, reason can at least distinguish the various second-century contexts of belief – Stoic, Christian, Gnostic – in which the collocation of 'charis' and 'choreuei' might have made sense. A Roman Sophist with Stoical leanings would probably have interpreted the line as an ethical maxim, though his interpretation would have required a slight alteration in the original wording of the Hymn. Instead of 'Grace is dancing' (or '*The* Grace is dancing,' as the line literally reads in the Greek) he would have preferred 'The Graces are dancing' – for the three Charites or Gratiae of classical mythology, Aphrodite's handmaids, never danced except in each other's company and were usually depicted with hands joined or arms intertwined. One Grace on her own was unthinkable. The ethical and ultimately cosmological significance of their dance depended entirely on the continuity of the circular chain formed by all three sisters. So the great Roman Stoic Seneca (a contemporary of Philo) had taught in his treatise on the conferring of benefits in a just society:

Why do the Graces, hand linked to hand, dance a choral round which returns upon itself [in se redeuntium chorus]? For this reason: a benefit that passes in an orderly succession from hand to hand nevertheless returns to the giver of the benefit. If the orderly succession is interrupted at any point, the beauty of the whole is destroyed. The whole is most beautiful if it is continuous and maintains its orderly cycle of changes.

(*De beneficiis* I.iii.4)

To a Stoic of the Senecan mould, the dance of Grace would have seemed utterly graceless – a travesty of the choral round of the Charites – for though the disciples formed a circular chain by linking hands their movement was essentially unworldly in spirit and emphatically opposed to the demonic political world that had conferred its benefits on Judas. The beauty of their round was destroyed by the evil presence of a 'betrayer' who would not accept the benefits conferred by the Redeemer or pass them on to other souls outside the original circle; it was imperfect, therefore, because it was discontinuous. Graces did not flow out from the giver, Jesus, to circulate among his companions and then return to him. Jesus offered the gift of everlasting life without asking for anything in return, save obedience, and his reward ironically was the kiss of death.

Who is this solitary goddess invoked in his Hymn, then, this Grace whose mystic dance seems far removed from the vernal revels of Aphrodite and from the circular flow of benefits in the cosmic city of the Stoics? Would a philosophically educated Christian have regarded her as a mythical representation or personification of the grace of God? Clement of Alexandria, for one, would certainly never have thought of grace as a divine being in its own right but rather as the gift of knowing God and the power of becoming divine which Man had received from God through the Logos. Yet Clement would not have been offended by the transformation of a pagan image like the dance of the Graces into a Christian image of the transmission and reception of divine grace, for a favorite proselytizing tactic of his was to compose sacred parodies of the pagan myths by purging them of their ancient religious or philosophical meanings and translating what remained into allegories of 'the Truth,' that is, the new paideia of the Logos. This was an effective way of expressing the newness, the strangeness, the exhilarating shock of the Christian message in terms which could still be understood by pagans who were hearing the Good News for the first time.

In the startling first chapter of his *Exhortation to the Pagans*, for example, Clement ushers Christ into the cosmic theatre in two pagan guises, first as Orpheus, the human musician whose lyre overcame the harshness of Death, and then as Apollo, the divine musician whose lyre inspired the dance of the planetary Muses and resounded in the whole symphony of creation. And in the even more startling conclusion to the same work he ushers Christ out of the cosmic theatre as the new Dionysus – choragus of the fire-breathing stars, like his pagan counterpart, but also of the angels and the prophets and all the saved souls who will outlive the tuneful heavens by dancing around the Logos and receiving the grace of the Father. 'For I wish,' declares this Dionysian Christ, turning unexpectedly from his chorus of initiates to address any and every pagan who might be listening to the hymn of the Saved,

I wish to share with you this grace [tēs charitos] and to confer [chorēgōn] the perfect benefit upon you: immortality. I freely offer you the Logos, the knowledge of God – I grace you [charizomai] with my perfect self. That is what I am, that is what God wishes, that is the symphony, that is the harmony of the Father, that is the Son, that is Christ, that is the Logos of God, the arm of the Lord, the power of the universe, the will of the Father!

(Exhortation XII.120.3–4)

This public exhortation is the last sort of speech an initiate in the pagan mysteries would have expected from a hierophant at the ecstatic climax of his choral rite: instead of whispering his revelations to a private congregation of initiates, Clement's Christ proclaims the mysteries of grace to the world at large; instead of demanding payment for his spiritual consolations, he freely bestows immortality on all who dance to his music; instead of alienating his chorus from the material world by focusing their minds on a purely spiritual centre, on a divine power within them, he brings humanity back into harmony with the symphony of creation and extends to all who seek salvation 'the arm of the Lord,' a human arm, his own, so that by joining hands with the Logos they might enter into the dance of grace and come to know 'the power of the universe,' the divine power beyond them.

In the language of his mysteries the verb 'chorēgein,' which originally meant 'to lead a choral dance' and also 'to defray the costs of training and costuming a chorus' in return for social prestige and political favours, has become synonymous with the verb 'charizesthai,' 'to offer freely,' literally 'to grace,' for in his dual role as human and divine choragus Christ has given up all he has, his life, his body, his blood, to provide for the salvation of his followers, and yet seeks no earthly favours in return, needing nothing to complete his 'perfect self,' having from his heavenly Father an inexhaustible supply of 'charis' to share with his chorus.

Certainly something of Clement's full-blown allegory of conversion, something of his expansive view of grace as both the means by which Christ teaches his chorus to dance around the Truth and also the end, the state of grace, towards which his dancers direct all their physical and intellectual energies, can be read between the lines of the Hymn of Jesus. The revolution of the Twelve is like the first ring that forms around a stone dropped into a pool of water: it must be seen in its narrative context as the beginning of a wider movement. The dynamic process of transmitting and receiving 'charis' in the sense of 'divine knowledge,' a process which for heretical as well as mainstream Christians implied an historical interplay between God and Man, is suggested not only by the line 'Grace is dancing' but also by Christ's subsequent command, 'Dance all of you.' Together, even in their grammatical sequence of indicative and imperative, these lines anticipate the rhythm of events in the history of the Apostolic missions – the self-perpetuating rhythm of conversion which is a dominant theme in the Acts of John. Just as Jesus revealed the signs of God's favour to his disciples and then commanded them to initiate new dancers into the circle of grace, so John (in his homilies and healing miracles) reveals the same signs to Andronicus and Drusiana and commands them to dedicate their lives to the conversion of Ephesus. As more and more Ephesians, and Corinthians, and Romans, and Alexandrians convert to Christ, the signs of divine grace in operation throughout the Fallen World become more and more apparent to the unconverted, and this in turn inspires new conversions, which lead to new manifestations of grace, which inspire more new conversions, and so on and on until the ring expands in the pool of Christian history to its divinely ordained limits.

Yet there is another way of reading 'Grace is dancing' which removes the line entirely from the historical context of the Apostolic missions and translates it from an allegorical into a mythological statement – the equivalent, say, of 'Venus is dancing' rather than 'Faith is dancing' – referring vaguely, evocatively, to an eternal world outside the bounds of Clement's Heaven and to a pantheon which Clement's polemical Logos would have condemned as a fiction, a mirage, a demonic lie. If 'Grace is dancing' were the only line in the Hymn that contained the word 'charis,' then one might be content to read Clement's doctrine of grace (and the implications of his play on the words 'chorēgein' and 'charizesthai') into the dictum of the apocryphal Redeemer, and to leave the line at that, having 'solved' its mysteries through allegorical exegesis in the Alexandrian style. But the word also appears in the third verse of the eight-line doxology at the start of the Hymn – 'Glory be to you, Grace' – where it evidently functions as the proper name of a divine being in the company of the Father, the Logos, the Spirit, the Holy One, and the Light. Assuming that this Grace is the same as *the* Grace who a few lines later is said to be dancing, one is faced with two new mysteries to solve. First, in whose pantheon did this unclassical Grace appear? And second, what might her dance have signified to the singer of the Hymn?

An answer to the first question is provided by St Irenaeus in the first book of his *Adversus haereses*, a vitriolic attack on second-century heretics which was written in Greek a few decades after the composition of the Acts of John and translated into Latin around the turn of the third century. The disciples of a prominent Gnostic teacher named Valentinus, noted Irenaeus,

say that there exists in the invisible and ineffable heights a certain perfect preexistent Aeon. They call him First Cause, First Father, and Profundity, and describe him as being invisible and incomprehensible. Everlasting and unbegotten, he has remained in great serenity and rest for countless ages. And with him existed Thought, whom they also call Grace [Charis] and Silence.

(*Adversus haereses* I.1.1)

Whereas for Clement the grace of God was expressed in a crescendo of sounds – the music of the spheres, the hymn of the Saved, the exhortations of the Logos – for Valentinus the grace of the first Aeon or 'everlasting being' was identical with silence, the utter silence of pre-verbal, pre-logical, and even (if this can be imagined) pre-mental thought in the unfathomable depths of eternity.

A Valentinian initiate did not, then, 'receive' grace or 'share in' grace like a Christian. He hoped to penetrate it, strove to imitate it, worshipped it in the silence of his own thoughts. Since it, or rather she ('Grace,' 'Thought,' and 'Silence' all being feminine nouns in Greek) had coexisted with the First Father through innumerable ages, the Valentinians also considered Grace an Aeon in her own right. In their elaborate theogonic myths she figured as the female consort of the First Father, the primordial female principle, from whose womb sprang two further Aeons: a male deity called Mind and his female consort Truth. This pair in turn generated Logos and his sister Life, who subsequently begot Anthropos or the Primal Man and his sister Ecclesia or the eternal Church. These first eight Aeons were known collectively ('known' in a very vague sense, of course, since their sublime natures and activities surpassed anything that a human mind might hope to comprehend) as the spiritual Ogdoad, the inner circle of a perfectly stable and luminous sphere of existence which the Valentinians called the Fullness or Pleroma.

The Pleroma was filled with various groups of lesser Aeons after the formation of the spiritual Ogdoad (see figure 5). Logos and Life generated five pairs of male and female spirits known as the Decad, a group no doubt meant to recall the archetypal Ten of Pythagorean cosmology; Anthropos and Ecclesia produced six more pairs, the Dodecad, of which the youngest female member was given the name Wisdom or Sophia; and then the First Father and Mind, their union being both incestuous and homosexual, begot Christ and the Holy Spirit. 'They tell us' snorted Irenaeus, much offended by the shameless fecundity of the Gnostic pantheon,

that when everything was established in this way and brought into a state of perfect repose, these beings sang a hymn with great joy to the First Father, who shared in their abounding cheer.

And from this multiplicity in repose, this eternal chorus, sprang a god representing the perfect unity of all the Aeons:

Then, in response to the great beneficence of the Father, who approved of their conduct, and with the consent of Christ and the Spirit, the whole Pleroma of the Aeons with one desire and resolve brought together and contributed whatever was most beautiful and flourishing in each of them. These they blended harmoniously into a concordant whole, producing to the honour and glory of the Profound One a being of perfect beauty, the very star and perfect fruit of the Pleroma, namely Jesus, whom they also call

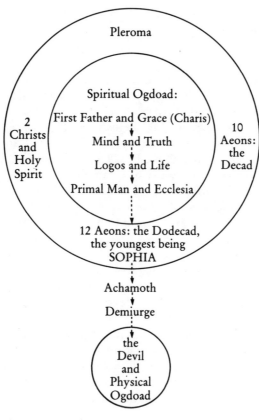

Figure 5

The hierarchical design of the Valentinian universe reflected (and was ultimately inseparable from) the genealogical table of the divine beings inhabiting it. Thirty-three eternal beings or Aeons filled the highest abode, the Pleroma, with their radiance and concord. Below them in a dark middle abode dwelt Achamoth, the female shadow of the Aeon Sophia, and her son the Demiurge. Together – she providing the raw materials, he the creative energy – they generated the eight celestial spheres of the physical Ogdoad in memory of the eight primary spirits in the Pleroma. They also created the Devil to govern the physical world. Two Christs figured in the Valentinian myth of redemption. The first, son of the First Father and Mind, remained eternally hidden in the Pleroma; the second, offspring of all the Aeons, descended to Achamoth's world to lead her and certain 'spiritual men' (ie Gnostic initiates) back to the presence of the Father. Lines in the Hymn of Jesus which seem to refer to the physical heavens – eg 'One ogdoad sings together with us' – might in fact refer to the spiritual heavens, to the *other* Ogdoad in the Pleroma.

*Saviour and Christ and Logos (his patronymic title) and the Whole, because
he was formed from them all.*

(Adversus haereses 1.2.6)

Though the Valentinians identified the 'star of the Pleroma' with the Jesus
of the New Testament, their second Christ was not (as one might suppose)
the human or historical counterpart of the divine Christ who dwelt apart
from mankind in the company of the Holy Spirit. Both Christs were revered
as wholly spiritual beings. Both participated in the choral rites of the Aeons
and shared in the knowledge of the First Father. They differed then not so
much in nature – though Christ two, combining in one being all that was
virtuous or beautiful in the natures of all the other Aeons, evidently ranked
higher on the Gnostic scale of perfection than his older namesake – as in
function, in the role each was ordained to play in the drama of the fall and
redemption of Sophia.

Shortly after the genesis of Christ two the peace of the Pleroma, a state
of sublime intellectual repose arising from the Aeons' inborn knowledge of
the existence of the First Father and their calm acceptance of the incom-
prehensibility of his nature, was momentarily disturbed by the passionate
desire of Sophia to know what she was incapable of knowing: the essence
of the First Cause. The product of her futile contemplations was a stillborn
idea of God, a vague, inchoate, immature notion which turned out to be a
projection of her own wavering female nature rather than a reflection of the
Father's motionless and unfathomable being. Assuming a bizarre half-ex-
istence of its own, her aborted brainchild was given the name Achamoth (a
corrupted form of a Hebrew word for 'wisdom') and expelled from the
Pleroma into the darkness of the Void. Sophia, then, did not fall in the same
sense that Satan or Eve fell. A shadowy image of her fell away into nothingness, while she, the Gnostic Athena, retained her position in the chorus
of the Aeons and recovered her original peace of mind.

Achamoth, meanwhile, drifted insensibly through the darkness and
loneliness of vacant space, until Christ one, the companion of the Spirit,
pitying her hapless condition, extended his luminous influence over the
boundary of the Pleroma and imparted three things to her: a female form;
a consciousness of the agony of her fall; and a desire to return to the bliss
of the Pleroma. He left her more wretched than before, however, for now
she was aware of her loss, terrified of the darkness surrounding her, and
ignorant of what had inspired her to seek the Light. At the request of the
elder Christ (who still felt pity for the daughter of Sophia but was unwilling
to endure a second visit to her gloomy abode) the younger Christ leapt
across the Great Dividing-Line, dispelled Achamoth's ignorance of her divine origins, and healed her violent passions by partially separating them
from her mind. Her joyous encounter with the Saviour, an archetypal Gnos-

tic conversion, was brief but momentous. It left her with the profound conviction that she would eventually return to the Pleroma and be reunited with her unfallen other self, and this transformation of her inner life resulted in a burst of creative energy which thoroughly transformed the Void.

Her conversion had cosmogonic consequences. The griefs, terrors, and perplexities she had suffered after her fall condensed into earth, water, air, and fire, the inherently restless elements of the physical Ogdoad. The joy she had experienced during spiritual intercourse with Jesus engendered a new male god, the Demiurge, who subsequently created the living stars, the plants and animals of earth, and the ruler of all temporal life-processes, the Devil. (Unlike the rebellious Satan in Christian accounts of the Fall of the Angels, the Valentinian Devil did not suffer a fall from the pinnacle of divine favour. As the Cosmocrator or governor of the stars and planets, he came into being with the temporal world and had no direct knowledge of the spiritual Ogdoad.) Finally, from Achamoth's desire to return to the peace and security of the Pleroma sprang the supracosmic soul of the Demiurge and the World-Soul and the souls of all the life-forms, corporeal and incorporeal, that the tyrannous Cosmocrator held captive within the sphere of astral fate.[4]

Though the Acts of John is not known to have circulated among the Valentinians (who according to Irenaeus were particularly attracted to the Fourth Evangelist because of his mystical doctrine of the Logos), the universe evoked by the pseudo-Apostle in his homily on the Crucifixion nevertheless bears a strong family resemblance to the fractured world of Sophia and Achamoth and may in fact have been a variation of the Valentinian world-system. In the penultimate sentence of his homily John salutes the God who is older and mightier than 'all Aeons' (104), a phrase which recalls the hierarchical organization of the Valentinian Pleroma. Moreover, the phantom Christ who appears in the cave on the Mount of Olives shows John 'a cross of light' (98) which is set high above the vile wooden cross of Calvary and separates 'the things that are from the things that are below' (99). In the Valentinian universe the Great Dividing-Line between Pleroma and Void was known as the Stauros or Cross because it bore up and supported the Heaven of Light and prevented the chorus of Aeons from mixing with the carnal multitudes in the physical Ogdoad. Valentinus, who was familiar with Platonic cosmology, might have derived his supernal boundary-cross from the image of the two bands of soul-stuff that the Craftsman, in *Timaeus* 36b–c, was said to have joined cross-wise when he was constructing the circles of the Same and the Different. Valentinus' Stauros and John's cross of light, if they indeed mark the same metaphysical dividing-line, might therefore be considered visionary prototypes of the cross formed by the intersecting arcs of the ecliptic and the celestial equator.[5]

In light of these tantalizing connections several lines in the Hymn of Jesus take on distinctly Gnostic and perhaps specifically Valentinian meanings. If the grace saluted in the doxology is none other than the Thought or Silence of the Profound One, then 'Grace is dancing' might refer either to the coupling of this Aeon with the First Father, the erotic dance of primal goddess with primal god in which the spiritual Ogdoad was generated, or to the participation of Grace in the choral ceremony of the Aeons preceding the emanation of the second Christ. Was the consort of the First Father perhaps thought to lead the immortal chorus in their hymn of praise? If so, then Grace would have been an appropriate Aeon for a Gnostic Jesus to invoke in his doxology and for his disciples to imitate in their choral round. Were the disciples by imitating the dance of Grace brought into harmony with the inner circle of the Pleroma? If so, then the line 'One ogdoad sings together with us' would have resounded in their ears with the concord of the spiritual Ogdoad, the other group of eight, not with the music of the eight heavens. And were the Twelve by singing with the Eight sympathetically linked to another Twelve, a Twelve beyond the Stauros? If so, then Jesus was referring not to be constellations of the zodiac but to the Dodecad of the Pleroma, including the unfallen Sophia, when he sang 'Twelve is the number dancing on high.'

The sequence Father-Grace-Ogdoad-Dodecad suggests the flow of divine beings out from the wellspring of life, the expansion of the spirit population to the limits of the Pleroma, and the final or 'perfect' term in this sequence was the Saviour, the second Christ, whom the Valentinians also called 'the Whole' because he was formed from all the Aeons and expressed their choral unity in his composite yet concordant nature. Might the singer of the Hymn not be pointing to himself, then, to his own luminous, invincible, otherworldly identity as opposed to the world of shadows enclosed by the Aplanes, when he whispers 'Now, on your part, understand the Whole'?

Irenaeus does not mention the Acts of John in his condemnation of the Valentinians or in any of his other extant writings, which may indicate that the Hymn of Jesus and its accompanying narrative were unknown in the Western Empire in the second century; but the other great opponent of the Gnostics at that time, namely Clement of Alexandria, does allude to the Acts of John – and with the disapproval one would expect from an early exponent of the Johannine doctrine of the Incarnate Logos.

In his commentary on the canonical First Epistle of John, Clement cites the pseudo-Apostle's testimony that at various times before the Crucifixion he had reached out to touch Christ's body only to find a ghostly immaterial form through which his hands could pass without resistance (Acts of John 93). But Christ must have been with us in the flesh, Clement argued, for otherwise he could not have taken upon himself the guilt of Adam and triumphed over Satan by rising from the dead.[6] In the angel-guarded universe of Clement and Irenaeus, as in Philo's star-guarded cosmic city, souls were harmoniously united to bodies by a benevolent Creator whose laws were designed to sustain the harmony of matter and spirit until the end of time. A phantom Christ could not, and did not, fit into such a world. He belonged instead to a disjointed universe where souls were intensely hostile to bodies, where spirit was intrinsically opposed to matter, and where the benevolent God of Heaven was distinguished from his fallen counterpart, the Demiurge, and his satanic opposite, the Cosmocrator. In certain Gnostic myths (other than those of the Valentinians) the Demiurge was conflated with the Cosmocrator and identified with the rebel angel who was expelled from the Heaven of Light for challenging the authority of the First Father. As a result of his own fall the Gnostic Lucifer caused the scattering of other luminous spirits into the darkness of the material world, some of whom were incarcerated in the stars and others in human bodies. Eventually all the dispersed particles of light, among which the Gnostics tended to include their own spiritual natures, would rise to the summit of the physical Ogdoad where they would escape the oppressive cycle of birth, death, and rebirth that had trapped them inside mortal bodies.

Their liberation typically began with the descent from the Pleroma of a divine teacher, who by transmitting to his disciples a special kind of knowledge or 'gnōsis' (hence the term 'Gnosticism') awakened them to the otherworldly origins of their inner or spiritual selves and alienated them from the ignorant multitudes sunk in the abyss of matter. The phantom Jesus of the Acts of John is such a teacher, the central figure in a Gnostic drama of redemption. When at the height of the dance he utters the prophetic command 'ton logon gnōthi,' which may mean both 'Understand the word of wisdom' and 'Gain insight into the Logos,' and afterwards, in the dark privacy of the cave, when he bids John listen to 'what a disciple should hear from his teacher and a man from his God,' we are allowed, like Andronicus and Drusiana, to overhear for a few tantalizing moments the communication of gnosis from a divine to a human mind, to eavesdrop on the intimate process of Gnostic redemption.

Gnosis was a more specialized and subjective kind of knowledge than the psychological lore Dio would have found in the Myth of the Craftsman or the theological wisdom Philo sought in the writings of Moses. It concerned the fate of individual souls rather than the operations of the human psyche in general, and was received as a personal rather than tribal revelation of the Divine Plan. From his divine teacher a Gnostic initiate would acquire the essential information that would allow his little spark of light to find its way back to 'the Light in which no darkness dwells,' back to the Pleroma, and this was all he really cared to know. Nothing else mattered. Whereas a mainstream Christian would distinguish his knowledge of salvation from the saving power of divine grace, a Gnostic, even if he called his saviour Jesus, generally would not make such a distinction. His knowledge was the secret mark of his superiority, his plan of escape, and his power to rise beyond the stars.

Since Gnosticism spawned many quite different teachers who claimed to be the instruments of divine grace, it never developed a rigid system of orthodox doctrines or became a unified religious movement with a clearly defined revelation. Each teacher interpreted the main characters in the Gnostic myths of creation and redemption according to his own inclinations or divine promptings. The unknown author of the second-century *Apocryphon of John*, for instance, regarded the Demiurge as an utterly evil being, an 'Abortion of Darkness,' who had created a cosmos as dark and perverted as his own nature; on the other hand, the Gnostic seer who wrote the *Poimandres*, a mystical treatise included among the works of the fictitious Egyptian wizard Hermes Trismegistus, spoke of the Demiurge as a divine 'intellect' who was inferior to the Supreme Mind of the Pleroma but not especially wicked, although the seven Archons or Administrators whom he had stationed on the planets were regarded as wicked because they afflicted each man with his characteristic vices and kept his spiritual self imprisoned within a succession of mortal bodies.[7] Though the inferior or evil Creator is not mentioned in the Hymn of Jesus, he might lurk behind Christ's enigmatic reference to 'the God of the betrayer,' who might otherwise be simply identified as Satan. Perhaps both are meant. In any case, the opposition between a lower god associated with evil and a supreme God identified as pure light is a recurrent theme in the Acts of John which might as easily imply a Gnostic dualism as a Christian Fall.[8]

The dualistic impulse underlying the new paideia of the Gnostic seers split the physical and intellectual revolutions of the old Platonic choreia into two distinct movements. First, rising under the influence of gnosis through the seven planetary spheres, the Gnostic initiate was admitted after death into the dance of the stars around the dark centre of the physical Ogdoad; then, miraculously transported into the Pleroma, he would be empowered by his understanding of 'the Whole' to circle with the Aeons around the source of perpetual Light. His rite of passage between the two orders was the momentous turning of his soul in the Eighth Sphere, simultaneously his farewell tour of the material world and his début in the world beyond.

These two dances were clearly distinguished by the author of the Acts of Thomas (a third-century apocryphal text belonging to the same genre as the Acts of John) in a justly celebrated lyrical passage known as the Hymn of Sophia:

The maiden is the daughter of light, in whom the bright

effulgence of kings is inseparably infused;
And the sight of her is delightful for she shines in joyous
beauty.
Her garments are like the flowers of spring, and from them a
sweet fragrance is wafted.
And on the crown of her head is seated the King, who
nourishes with ambrosia those who have him as their
foundation.
In her head lies truth, and with her feet she reveals joy.
And her mouth is open, which suits her well.
Thirty and two are they who sing praises to her.
Her tongue is like the veil over a door, which waves to and fro
for those who enter in.
Her neck is stretched out like a stairway which the first
Demiurge has fashioned.
And her two hands make signs and trace a pattern, heralding
the dance of the happy Aeons [ton choron tōn eudaimōn
aiōnōn kērussontes], while her fingers indicate the gates of
the City.
Her bridal chamber is luminous, breathing forth the scent of
balsam and all spices and the sweet smell of myrrh and leaf.
And within it myrtles are strewn and wreaths of many sweet-
smelling flowers, and the doorways are adorned with reeds.
And her bridal retainers, who are seven in number and whom
she has herself chosen, surround her and maintain her.
Her bridesmaids are seven, and they dance in chorus
[choreuousin] before her.
And twelve in number are those who serve before her and are
her subjects.
Towards the bridegroom they direct their gaze and attention,
so that they might be illuminated by the sight of him.
(Acts of Thomas 6)

This psalm, oracular in tone, apocalyptic in reference, is sung by a Hebrew cup-bearer at a royal wedding attended by Thomas during his mission to Andrapolis, 'the City of Man.' Though Sophia is not mentioned by name in the hymn, the divine maiden who is the subject of the psalmist's praises has all the attributes of a Gnostic goddess of wisdom: she is descended from the majestic light of an eternal kingdom; she now abides in a mysterious mansion somewhere below the realm of the Aeons and above the City of Man; she preserves within her head the truth, that is, an idea or memory of the Pleroma; she stands beneath a divine king, who is probably Christ

the elder; and she leads a dance before her divine bridegroom, who is probably Christ the younger. All these details suggest that the maiden of light
is none other than Achamoth, the fallen Sophia, who is destined to be
reunited with the divine wisdom of the Pleroma through the grace of Jesus.
The 'thirty and two' who sing praises to her must be the whole chorus of
Aeons, minus one, of course, the thirty-third and final Aeon being the
bridegroom himself, and on this occasion only, because it marks the return
of Achamoth to the City of God, the noble inhabitants of that city have
deigned to sing in harmony with the lowly servants of the bride. The seven
bridesmaids who dance in chorus around her luminous chamber almost
certainly represent the planets, and the seven retainers accompanying them
the planetary Archons. The constellations of the zodiac are symbolically
present at the dance in the guise of twelve servants, though their number,
like the twelve dancing on high in the Hymn of Jesus, points beyond the
cosmic wedding chamber to the Dodecad in the Heaven of Light.

During the dance of time the maiden assumes the role of a pantomimic
soloist, tracing the pattern of the eternal dance with her hands and pointing
with her fingers towards the gates of the City of God. Her symbolic gestures
can be seen and understood only by the Gnostic illuminati, the wise men
of Andrapolis, who like the Hebrew cup-bearer may seem lowly and powerless during this life but who will share in the next the majesty and power
of the risen Sophia. By marrying Sophia, Jesus will temporarily unite the
dances of time and eternity and allow his disciples to leap from the material
world back into the Pleroma.

The dance in the Acts of John seems to be a similar interlude between a
purely physical and a purely spiritual conversion. As a ring of bodies revolving around a central body, the disciples' chorus recalls the cyclical motion of time and the revolution of the stars in the Eighth Sphere; and as a
conversion of enlightened souls around a divine mind it seems to anticipate
their ultimate participation in the chorus of the Aeons. The dance of Jesus
might be regarded as a psychological preparation for the ultimate movement
in the dance of Gnostic initiation, the sudden departure of the illuminati
from temporal to eternal life. It is a private rehearsal for an exclusive rite
of passage. While the starry sphere is still over their heads, the future bridegroom runs his twelve servants through their paces before departing for the
wedding chamber of Sophia. Possessing the secret gnosis learned only by
divine union (which in the Hymn of Sophia was symbolized both by the
dance and by the marriage), John and his fellow dancers will eventually pass
far beyond the starry sphere and escape the tyranny of the Demiurge.

Sophia's tongue – a metonymy for the language of Gnostic revelations –
is 'like the veil over a door': it hides the entrance into Heaven from the
unenlightened multitude while it 'waves to and fro for those who enter in,'

for the chosen few who will receive gnosis and exit with Christ from the celestial wedding chamber. The language of the Hymn of Jesus might be considered a symbolic veil also, simultaneously concealing and revealing 'the door' (as Jesus calls himself) through which the wayfaring disciples will enter into the Pleroma. The message that he veils in the enigmas of the Hymn and unveils to John in the cave on the Mount of Olives accords with the heretical teachings of a second-century Gnostic sect, the Docetists, who came under fire from Clement of Alexandria for wilfully subverting the fundamental doctrine of the Incarnation.[9] The Docetists taught that Christ only seemed to have a body and therefore only seemed to suffer and die upon the cross. They simply refused to believe that an Aeon would have sullied his divine nature with the dust of Adam or suffered the indignity of a criminal's death. Since he did not occupy physical space during his earthly ministry the Docetic Christ was able to perform certain miraculous feats (such as walking across soft earth without leaving footprints) which alerted the Twelve to his superhuman nature. John mentions this particular miracle in an anecdotal preface to the Hymn (Acts of John 93) so that Andronicus and Drusiana, like the original disciples, will be amazed by the Redeemer's mysterious nature and eager to have it explained. What they will learn from the prophecies of the piper and from the vision of his cross of light is that the Incarnation was an illusion, the Crucifixion a cleverly staged hoax, and the Resurrection a magical sound-and-light show in the darkness of the sixth hour.

On this heretical interpretation of the main events in the life of Christ hangs the inner meaning of his Gnostic round, the motions of which are a symbolic expression of his Docetic nature. Both the visible configuration of the dance and the visible figure of Jesus are deceptive appearances which conceal a truth at their centre. The dance appears to end when the circle of bodies is disrupted by the violence of the Crucifixion, and the choragus appears to die when his body is broken on the cross. But neither the movement nor its leader in fact suffers. Since the unity of the round depended on a shared intellectual response to the inviolable concord of Grace, its spiritual order remains unaffected by the calamities of fate; similarly, since the nature of the Docetic Jesus is purely intellectual and incorporeal, his true self, his luminous essence, cannot be harmed by the powers of darkness controlling the Crucifixion. The dancers enact his imminent suffering on the cross, an agony which proves to be no more painful to him – and to them – than a wedding dance or a game of weddings and funerals such as children play in the marketplace. By becoming sufferers in ritual play the disciples learn by experience that Christ is no sufferer but an immortal spirit sent down to them from the Aeons whom they salute at the start of the Hymn.

A doxology similar to theirs is chanted at the end of the *Poimandres* by a Gnostic sage who awakens from a prophetic dream in which his soul has conversed with the Divine Mind:

> *Holy is God, Father of the Universe, who existed before the*
> *beginning;*
> *Holy is God, whose wish is fulfilled by his Powers;*
> *Holy is God, who wishes to be known and is known by those*
> *who are his own;*
> *Holy are you, who by your Logos have constructed all that is;*
> *Holy are you, whom nature has not obscured;*
> *Holy are you, of whom all nature is an image;*
> *Holy are you, who are stronger than all sovereignty;*
> *Holy are you, who are greater than all eminence;*
> *Holy are you, who are above all praises.*
>
> (*Corpus Hermeticum, Libellus* I 31)

This prayer echoes the hymn of praise to be chanted by his soul in the Eighth Sphere, when he will awake from another dream, his mortal existence, and hear the harmonious praises of the unfallen spirits in the Heaven of Light.[10] The disciples of the Docetic Christ also anticipate the experiences of their afterlife. Not only do the revolutions of their dance foreshadow the circling of their souls in the Eighth Sphere, but their vocal participation in the Hymn must be part of their rehearsal as well, a preparation for the responses they will chant as a password into Heaven. The ending of their dance prefigures the Redeemer's release from the material world, and through it, their own release. That is why Christ presents himself to them as 'a mirror' in which they may behold themselves and recognize what is in store for them after death.

Like its central figure the choral round serves as a magic mirror for their souls – a glass through which they may see the face of God not darkly but clearly and foresee the Docetic Crucifixion, the Gnostic ascent of the soul, and the mystic revolutions of the Aeons around the First Father. The episode of the dance also casts prophetic reflections within the context of John's homiletic narrative, functioning as a preliminary parable of perception to condition Andronicus and Drusiana, and with them the reader, to distrust whatever their eyes tell them. By rejecting what the dance is seen to be, they will also be inclined to reject what its leader is seen to be. The Hymn of Jesus is a perfect prelude to John's Docetic revelations, for Docetism is based on the assumption that eyesight is the perception of mere 'seeming' (dokein) while insight, illuminated by a supernatural power, offers an altogether separate vision of reality.[11]

Whereas Plato's cave symbolized the natural limits of the visual field and the narrow-mindedness of the unphilosophical masses who equate reality with visible appearances, John's cave represents the supernatural extension of the visionary field and the expanded consciousness of the Gnostic initiate who has severed the old Platonic correspondence between visual and mystical perception. As a character in his own narrative, John learns the truth about the Crucifixion only after his eyes have ceased to gaze on the cross. As a proselytizing narrator, he subsequently turns his visionary experience into a parabolic illustration of the convert's new way of seeing. To see the order of the Whole the convert must close his eyes to the deceptive appearances of the material world and retreat deep within his soul. ('The closing of my eyes,' declared the Gnostic dreamer in the *Poimandres*, Lib 1 31, 'is true vision.') Then, in the dark recesses of his consciousness, he will receive the Gnostic illumination that will assure him of his spiritual safety and guide his steps out of the darkness of mortality.

John's movement into the cave is prefigured by his entrance into the dance: both motions represent a turning away from the betrayals of the external world, a turning inwards to a purely intellectual centre, and a turning upwards to the soul's release into Heaven. Similarly, his departure from the cave is prefigured by his ecstatic emergence from the dance. Having turned his eyes inwards to the Redeemer's light, he must move out into the world to behold its persecutions and suffer its agonies without ceasing to dance in the spirit with the holy souls who have heard the piper's rhythm. All references to sight in the Hymn must therefore be read in the context of John's radical dissociation of visual and visionary perception. When Christ says 'Behold yourself in me,' he does not mean 'Observe my exterior form with your eyes, and note how your humanity is reflected in it.' Indeed, the disciples are commanded to see through Christ's human disguise, to understand the Aeon moving them at their centre, and to recognize in his insouciance to pain a pattern for their own souls. Once again the round functions as a magic mirror, reflecting to those who see themselves inside it an image of their inner natures. The Gnostic disciples must see themselves inwardly as invisible spirits, like the Docetic Christ; they must feel enclosed by the cycles of the material world, as Christ is enclosed by the circle of bodies; they must acknowledge the agony of their mortal condition, symbolized by the breaking of the circle; but above all they must picture themselves as invulnerable to its evil order, like the god moving them at their centre.

By playing out the Docetic Crucifixion as a dance they are literally 'moved to become wise,' for they learn directly from this experience that the agonies of the cross are no less a game for Christ than his piping to the round. If they see his 'suffering' in its Docetic sense, as a mere appearance, of course they 'will have no suffering' when their own turn comes to suffer death and follow their leader into Heaven. 'You will see when you come' is Christ's oracular assurance that their eyes will see him as a suffering victim when they come to Calvary, but their minds, despite all external signs to the contrary, will see him as a victor when they come to the cave of contemplation. Once this initial divergence of insight and eyesight has occurred, they will continue to isolate the two modes of vision until eyesight is ultimately abandoned with their mortal bodies. They will 'see,' that is understand, Christ's mysterious nature only after they have become spirits themselves, and have joined the dance of Grace and the other Aeons encircling the First Father. This supreme vision, reserved solely for the eye of their understanding, will conclude the separation of insight from eyesight that was initiated by the dance at the Last Supper. A spectator would see the dance as twelve bodies breaking their round and dispersing outwards from the centre. A participant would envision the same movement as twelve souls uniting themselves with God and converging in one central identity.

Revels of the Logos

The communal identity of initiates in the dance of Grace was patterned on, derived from, in essence formed by the Logos, though who or what the Logos was – his sacred uniqueness – could not easily be defined in the profane language of the City of Man. Whereas the City of Man, the human social order, had been the usual focus of attention in philosophical visions of the cosmic dance before the second century, the focus shifted in Gnostic and Christian revisions of the image to a bridegroom or choragus from the City of God: hence the gaze of Sophia's twelve servants is directed away from the multitude of dancing lights in the cosmic wedding chamber towards a source of Divine Light, the descending Christ, 'so that they might be illuminated by the sight of him.' This new focal point in the dance was a charismatic teacher whose humanity was a matter of debate, whose ministry alienated holy souls from the City of Man, and whose audacious claim to be the Logos or a kinsman of the Logos or a spokesman for the Logos shocked skeptics into fervent belief and drew fervent believers away from Judaism or the pagan mystery cults. 'For you could not have fully understood what you suffer,' Jesus informs his disciples during the dance, 'had I not been sent to you as the Logos from the Father.'

But what kind of Logos does he mean? Surely not the Logos or 'Word' of the Fourth Gospel: though the Docetic Christ might be identified with the Word which 'was with God' and 'was God' (John 1:1), he cannot also be the Word which 'was made flesh' (John 1:14). Moreover, if the Docetic Christ were the one and only Logos, why would he salute himself in the doxology at the start of the Hymn? Would this not imply that another Logos existed above him, an intermediary Aeon between the Father and the Son like the offspring of Mind and Truth in the spiritual Ogdoad of the Valentinians? The precise relation between the Logos and the singer of the Hymn must remain a mystery in its modern as well as ancient sense, a secret passed over in silence by the author of the Acts of John. Nevertheless, like Andronicus and Drusiana, we are meant to assume that John not only learned this secret during his private tutorial in the cave but also communed with the living presence of the Logos during the dance and beheld on earth what Philo's Corybantic intellect had tried to see in Heaven – 'the Light in which no darkness dwells.'

To Philo may be traced both the theological concept of the Logos as a divine intermediary linking God to his creatures and also the mystical vision of the Logos as the leader of the cosmic dance. Originally signifying either 'the verbal expression of an inward thought' or 'the inward thought itself,' the term 'logos' was used by Presocratic philosophers such as Heraclitus to denote the harmonious union of divine, natural, and human order observable in the cosmos. The ambiguity between spoken and unspoken logos was carried over into its cosmological senses, with the result that it could signify either the outward expression of reason in the design of the cosmos or the inner meaning of the cosmic spectacle – the hidden principle of unity and prevailing pattern of life which true philosophers had the gift of perceiving but which most mortals, like sleepwalkers, failed to notice in the mutable worldscapes passing before their eyes. Though he usually employed the term in these philosophical senses, Philo occasionally spoke of a divine Logos who served as the executor of the Great Architect's designs and the caretaker of the material world. In a treatise on the immutability of the divine nature Philo contemplated the endless rise and fall of empires and concluded that a stable pattern could be discerned in the apparently unstable course of human history. This pattern, a cyclical redistribution of goods and powers among mankind, was an effect of the same Logos that guided the stars in their cyclical dance:

For the divine Logos dances [choreuei] in a circle, which most men call fortune; and so it always flows along, turning from city to city, people to people, land to land, and distributing to some what belonged to others, and to all what belonged to all.

(The Unchangeableness of God 176)

Since most men saw only an isolated episode here and there in the continuous circling of the Logos, they assumed from their partial vision of the flow of life that it was governed purely by fortune and must in the end amount to no more than a violent succession of meaningless changes; but the wise man, the 'logical' man, perceived causal connections between these seemingly random events which assured him that a just and benevolent power constantly channelled the turbulent energies of the material world into the predictable steps of a dance. The round-dance of the Philonic Logos was the cosmic equivalent of the circular flow of social and political benefits symbolized by Seneca's Graces.

The early Christian apologists and Gnostic heresiarchs who were Philo's direct intellectual heirs rarely praised the chorus of the stars in their exhortations to the unconverted because they feared (not without cause) that potential proselytes would follow the example of the ancient Chaldeans and Egyptians and worship the stars instead of the Logos and the First Father. 'Concerning the spectacle of the heavens,' Clement preached in the *Exhortation* (II 26.1), 'some men were deceived from the first: trusting solely in eyesight they observed the heavenly bodies and in their amazement deified the stars.' Though he still believed in the divinity of the stars, the Gnostic sage of the *Poimandres* would have agreed with Clement that profound insight into the Divine Plan was not a natural or inevitable consequence of eyesight but an entirely separate vision akin to dreaming and achieved only when the eyes were closed to the deceptive light of the Fallen World. Man no longer needed complex astronomical calculations or subtle philosophical arguments to understand the Whole, he insisted, because the First Father had sent a divine teacher to illumine the human soul from within and to initiate the inward-turning movements of conversion. Both Clement and the Gnostic sage referred to their respective illuminators as the Logos, which, in a simple sense, was an appropriate title for the divine messenger who delivered God's 'word' on the subject of human destiny.

Its significance was complicated, however, by the ancient Greek association of speech and reasoning: the bringer of God's word could also be related to the rational principle underlying the providential plan of creation. Whereas 'logos' had been a purely descriptive term in Greek cosmology, it quickly acquired a prescriptive force in the vocabulary of Christian and Gnostic proselytizers, especially those who drew heavily on the rhetoric of Genesis and the Fourth Gospel. Since the universe as revealed in Genesis had come into being through the verbal commands of God, the Word of God could be understood as the expression of his moral law in the harmonious structure of the material world and in the cycles of human history. The Johannine Logos could then be interpreted as the Word of God in both its descriptive and prescriptive senses. Like the Philonic Logos Christ entered into the flow of history, fitted into the conservative design of creation, and played an active role in the fortunes of mankind; yet within the old order of the Fallen World this new Logos, the messenger of the Father's grace and truth instead of his law, set out to create a new moral order and to teach a new interpretation of the Divine Plan by drawing his disciples back into the loving embrace of their once distant, threatening, implacable God.

Hence the twofold aim of the Logos expressed in the Hymn of Jesus: 'I wish to create order and I wish to be ordered.' The first wish implies the prescriptive force of the Word in the formation of the disciples' dance and in the eventual formation of their Church, while the second, which might also be translated 'I wish to be set in order' or perhaps even 'I wish to be adorned,' either anticipates the return of the Word and his followers to the glory of Heaven or commemorates his historic entrance into the inglorious order of the Fallen World.

The creation of a new order within the harmonious sphere of the old Hellenistic cosmos, not beyond it or in place of it, was, as we have seen, the manifest intention and miraculous achievement of Clement's Apollonian Logos, whose New Song blended in with – but did not drown out – the tremendous diapason of the eight heavens. In his enthusiastic acceptance of the Logos as the Son of God and Saviour of Man, Clement by no means rejected the basic tenets and organizing metaphors of Platonic cosmology: he was still willing to argue that the Muse-like concord of the astral chorus (even without the triumphant descant of the New Song) was sufficient to assure man of the benevolence and rationality of God. Except for the Star of Bethlehem, however, the stars were not very important in the drama of what concerned him most – his salvation. Having room in his universe for one God only, Clement condemned as idolatrous the Platonic doctrine that the stars were 'living creatures divine and eternal' and insisted that they were merely useful instruments for measuring time. Thus the animate order of the Platonic cosmos, which like a theatrical chorus depended on the co-operation of countless rational beings under the leadership of the World-Soul, gave way very early in patristic cosmology to the mechanistic concept of the heavens as an admirably constructed but ultimately disposable timepiece.

The principal theme of the New Song was not that the great world of the heavens was saved from chaos by dancing to the numbers of time but that the little world of man would be saved from Hell by dancing with the Logos in eternity. If the stars measured time to the enchanting rhythm of the Logos, their conversions were largely incidental to the primary purpose of that rhythm, which was to lure sinners away from the World, the Flesh, and the Devil. Any repentant sinner – shepherd or king, Hebrew or Hellene – could hear the heavenly reverberations of the New Song. That was why it was new.

For the Gnostic disciples of Hermes Trismegistus, however, the harmony of the heavens represented the fateful means by which the Devil bound mankind in the oppressive cycle of reincarnation which was the World and in the bottomless mire of vice which was the Flesh. The old song of the goddess Necessity still reverberated through their cosmos like the ravishing air of the Sirens, but it had become a siren-song in a bad sense, a nightmarish incantation which drove wayfaring souls to madness and dragged them down into the abyss of matter. The powerful counter-magic that was needed to break the spell, to reverse the downward spiral of metempsychosis, was taught to the lucky few by 'thrice-greatest' Hermes, who received it, heaven be praised, straight from the Logos. 'Human souls,' avowed the arch-magus,

change into daimones when they have reached the first stage in their ascent to immortality; then they proceed at once to the choral dance of the gods [eis ton tōn theōn choron], in which there are two choruses – one of planets and the other of fixed stars. And that is the supreme glory of the soul.

(*Corpus Hermeticum* Lib x 7)

The ascent to immortality was also the theme of Poimandres, the luminous apparition of the Logos who conversed with the Gnostic dreamer in the first book of the Hermetic canon. This dream-tutor assured the anxious sage that if he shut his ears to the music of Necessity and concentrated all his attention on the words of wisdom pouring down to him from the Divine Mind, his soul after death would be released from 'all that had been inflicted on it by the harmony of the heavens': it would rise through the chiming spheres, leaving behind on the seven planets the particular vices associated with each of the planetary Archons, until completely purged of mortality it would leap beyond the physical Ogdoad and experience the joy of divine union. Poimandres prophesied that the dreamer would ultimately be 'in God' – 'en theōi' – at the climax of his star-defying ascent (Lib I 26a). This union of the Gnostic soul with God recalls the free-soaring experience of Dionysian dancers, who also strove to be 'full of God' – 'entheoi' – at the climax of their nocturnal revels. It also recalls, of course, Plato's half-serious comparison of philosophical contemplation to bacchic ecstasy and Philo's elaboration of that conceit in his vision of the philosophical Corybant leaping into eternity. But with one arresting difference: what had simply been a metaphor for the supreme experience in the contemplative life of a Platonist, the mystic leap from the human to the divine chorus, is treated as an actual event in the afterlife of a Gnostic sage.

Not to be outdone by his Gnostic rivals, Clement also converted the negative symbolism of sober intoxication and intellectual bacchantism (which Philo had exploited to the full in his encomium of the Therapeutae) into affirmative imagery designed to convey an immediate, unqualified impression of the ecstatic momentum of conversion – not just its spiritual raptures, the leaping of contemplative souls at the prospect of salvation, but also its physical exuberance, the rushing of multitudes towards the pipers in the marketplace and the interlocking of countless hands in the expansive chorus of the Church – a momentum which lifted body as well as soul into the loving embrace of the Logos, swept both into the Church's by no means allegorical battle against the legions of the Devil, and carried both, the flesh rejoining the spirit on the Last Day, into the triumphant procession of the Saved.

According to classical standards of sanity the faith Clement advocated was indeed a kind of communal madness, an enthusiastic disruption of old patterns of social and intellectual conformity, and its appeal to the disaffected public was not unlike that of primitive bacchic revelry. In the language of the pagan mysteries a 'paraplēx' (madman) was one who had danced in the revels of Dionysus and achieved the blessed state of divine possession; but in the rhetoric of Christian conversion a madman was one who ignored the wisdom of the Logos and refused to participate in the new moral order of the Church. Clement plays on both senses of 'paraplēx' in the following passage from the finale of his oration to the pagans, a parody of the impassioned rhetoric of the *Bacchae*:

Come, o madman, but not with your thyrsus supporting you or with an ivy crown. Throw away your headdress, throw away your fawn-skin, come to your senses. I will show you the Logos and the mysteries of the Logos, explaining it according to your own images. This is the mountain beloved of God: but unlike Cithaeron, it is not the subject of tragedies. Rather, it is consecrated to the dramas of the Truth. It is the Mountain of Sobriety, thickly shaded with the Forests of Purity. On it revel [baccheuousi] not the sisters of Semele 'the Thunderstruck,' not the Maenads, not those women who are initiated in the unholy ritual of distributing flesh, but the Daughters of God, the beautiful lambs who reveal the holy rites of the Logos and gather together a sober chorus [choron ageirousai sōphrona]. The chorus are the Righteous, the song is the hymn of the King of the Universe. The maidens strike the lyre, the angels praise God's glory, the prophets speak, the sound of music bursts forth, they pursue the band of revellers as in a race, the Elect make haste in their great desire to receive the Father.

(*Exhortation* XII 119.1)

After condemning Dionysian rites as a false religion, Clement suddenly reverses his rhetorical strategy by claiming in a highly positive manner, that is without ironic qualifications and paradoxical retractions, that Christ offered everything Dionysus had to offer in his mysteries – and one thing more, the Truth. The Christian Bacchant then summons the pagans to the dramas of the Truth with this exultant cry:

These are the bacchic rites of my mysteries [emōn mystēriōn ta baccheumata]! Be initiated if you wish, and you too shall dance [choreuseis] with the angels around the unbegotten and imperishable and only true God!

(*Exhortation* XII 120.1)

The new religion surpassed (rather than simply opposed) the old in every respect: it embraced the full range of experiences associated with Dionysian revelry – liberation from the mortal body, illumination of the enraptured soul, union with the divine chorus – while heightening the emotional trans-ports of the dancers with revelations of the 'only true God' and purging their rites of the frenzied blood-lust which had possessed the Euripidean Maenads in their 'unholy ritual of distributing flesh.' Christianity enhanced the spiritual delights of bacchic ecstasy by eliminating the brutality and physical pain of bacchic sacrifice. The Logos did not eliminate sacrifices from his mystery dance, however, as Clement explains in the following character sketch of an ideal Christian contemplative:

His whole life is a holy festival: his sacrifices, for example, are prayers, and praises, and readings from the Scriptures before meals, and psalms and hymns during dinner and before bed, and prayers again during the night. By these he unites himself to the divine chorus [tōi theiōi chorōi], having been enrolled in it for the purpose of everlasting contemplation in consequence of his un-ceasing recollection of Heaven.

(*Stromateis* VII.49)

Clement audaciously referred to this full initiate in the Christian mysteries as a 'true Gnostic,' wresting this potent term from his religious rivals (just as Plato had stolen the phrase 'true Bacchant' from the Eleusinian myst-agogues) in order to redefine it at their intellectual expense. The true Gnostic, he taught, was a divinely inspired seer who set himself apart from the common flock of believers by concentrating all his thoughts on the mysteries of the Incarnate Logos and by dedicating his every waking moment to the cultivation of piety in himself and in his fellow man. Yet this special position in the holy chorus did not turn him into a silent recluse or an intellectual snob. Quite the reverse:

He, then, who has gained a clear understanding of what pertains to God from the mystic chorus of the Truth itself [pros autēs tēs alētheias chorou mystikou], uses the language of exhortation, revealing the greatness of virtue according to its inherent worth and exhibiting the consequences of virtue. Such a man is associated as closely as possible – is united 'gnostically' – with intellectual and spiritual things through the uplifting inspiration of prayer.

(*Stromateis* VII.45)

Participation in the mystic rites of the angels began for the true Gnostic in the unmystical Here and Now, in the exercise of his moral and intellectual virtues for the benefit of all mankind. He had no desire, like his heretical or pagan counterpart, to keep silent about the mysteries of grace or to confide his special gnosis in only a few carefully chosen disciples. Like the Logos himself he was to be a public teacher of the new paideia, a charismatic orator who drew skeptical spectators to the drama of the Truth and transformed them into zealous members of the chorus of the Righteous. The revels of Clement's Logos included much more than an apocalyptic race up the holy mountain from the valley of death to the summit of everlasting life: the first steps in his dance were taken slowly, deliberately, communally, through virtuous conduct and private prayer and public worship before the hour of death. Making full use of 'the language of exhortation' – the 'logos protrepōn' – to draw sinners away from Cithaeron towards the Mountain of Sobriety was an essential part of the role of a true Gnostic in the mystic chorus of the Truth.[12]

Ironically, in his zeal to dispel the superstitious awe with which pagans venerated the objects employed in their mysteries, Clement recorded many details about the mystery cults which time and secrecy would otherwise have obscured. His intimate knowledge of the cults indicates that he may have undergone certain stages of initiation himself before his conversion to Christianity. He was certainly acquainted with the whole inventory of sacred objects revealed to the worshippers of Dionysus during their initiation, among which, as he testifies in the *Exhortation* (II 18.1), were mirrors. As they looked into the mirror of Dionysus, revellers were perhaps meant to see themselves in the god, to merge their separate souls into a single divine identity; to their minds the god would reflect prophetic knowledge during the ecstatic convulsions of the dance. An outsider to the Dionysian mysteries might examine the sacred mirror and see a reflection in its material surface; but this would not be the reflection seen by the worshipper, for only an initiate who had undergone ritual inebriation and perceived the god's mirror in his mind would know the secret meaning invested in the material mirror. The Gnostic round-dance in the Acts of John, which is also the mirror of a god, is similarly endowed with meaning perceptible only to its participants. It also casts a double reflection. If it is seen from the external viewpoint of a spectator, the dance appears to be an Apollonian choreia. Yet if this objective and analytical stance is abandoned and one assumes instead the inner viewpoint of an ecstatic initiate, then the image of the dance is radically altered. Behind the chanting of the Logos can still be heard the pipes and tabors, the hissing snakes and star-binding spells, of a baccheia. The Maenads' piercing cry 'Euoi, Euoi!' is echoed by the disciples' deep 'Amen.'

'That suffering I showed you and the others in the dance,' the Logos murmurs to John in the cave (Acts of John 101), 'I wish it to be called a mystery.'

While the piper's rhythm is still ringing in his ears, the Gnostic disciple is thus commanded to review his experience of the cosmic mystery dance and to interpret it as a prelude to his vision of the cross of light. Jesus goes on to explain that he 'contrived all things symbolically' (102), and with this knowledge John must look back on the dance not only as a physical response to the explicit utterances and exhortations of the Logos as teacher, but also as a mystical symbol for the implicit significance, the unutterable spiritual identity, of the Logos as god. The movement of the dance from ritual drama to sacrificial agony to prophetic illumination repeats the classical pattern of experiences in Dionysian revelry, which was called a 'mystērion' because its participants were entrusted to keep silent or 'close-mouthed' (mystēs) about the wisdom bestowed on them by the god. The word 'mystery' is also related etymologically to the Greek verb 'muein,' meaning 'to close the lips' or 'to shut the eyes,' which suggests that participation in a religious mystery originally entailed not only silence and secrecy but also a blacking out of physical vision in preparation for spiritual enlightenment.

Like the revels of Dionysus, the 'mystērion' of Jesus temporarily releases its participants from the inhibitions and anxieties of adult life by returning them to a state of childhood innocence and insouciance to death. The defiant playfulness of their dance expresses the attitude of mockery that only a Docetic Christ, quite certain that the unstable world below the Eighth Sphere can do nothing to harm him, could adopt at the prospect of his imminent 'death.' He can well afford to pipe and play. Though the world of the lawless Serpent were a thousand times more vile and oppressive than it is, he could still escape its evil order. His lightheartedness at the end of the Hymn in no way cancels the serious tone of his mysterious revelations, but rather reinforces it, confirming his complete nonchalance in the face of tragic adversity. All his gloomy remarks about suffering were in fact 'uttered playfully' and he 'was by no means ashamed.' The New Dionysus has come like his predecessor to wash his dancers of the vices inflicted on them by the stars and to save their souls from the shame of mortal corruptibility. Their purification, enacted ritually as an earthly dance, is a necessary condition for their entry into the heavenly dance. As mirror images of their choragus the disciples experience Christ's shamelessness and innocent freedom during the dancing out of his mystery. They too may defy the repressive order of the lawless Serpent and feel no embarrassment in their rapturous abandon.

The disciples first understand the liberating operation of grace as a game of stimulus and response, an interplay between Christ's insistent rhythm and their answers to it in body and voice; but the rules of the game are set up only for a temporary activity and do not bind the player after they have served their purpose. In fact they are quickly broken. Jesus opens the Hymn with the formal rhythmic pattern of the doxology; this gives way to a new rhythm in the verses modelled on 'I wish to save and I wish to be saved'; this pattern in turn yields to another and another and another, until the freely shifting rhythms of the Hymn lack any strict metrical or syntactic pattern and can best be evoked in translation by the irregular lineation of free verse. The regular sequence of verse and choral response similarly breaks down halfway through the Hymn, only to be resumed for a single verse at the end. By this time the formal restrictions of the dance are suddenly released, the inhibiting chain of hands falls away, and the round falls apart into random motion. Behind this movement from formal restrictions to looseness and randomness lies the old Dionysian impulse to break through the inhibitions of a culturally imposed order. Revellers flee tyranny. The mad women of Thebes fled the political rule of Pentheus, the religious rule of their temples, and the domestic rule of their houses for the wild spaces of mountain and meadow. Their rebellion against human rule was also a submission to a divine command superior to the impositions of civilization.

The singer of the Hymn also wishes 'to flee,' inciting his dancers to escape the bounds of earthly civilization, and of earthly life itself, symbolized architecturally by the houses or 'temples' which he claims not to possess; at the same time he wishes 'to remain,' assuring his circle that his power will not disappear after the Crucifixion, but will reside in the inspired souls of his followers. They will be the sacred buildings he claims to possess, for in them grace shall live, be worshipped, and find a ground from which to extend the movement of conversion. Their voluntary submission to the divine rule of the Logos, which drives them away from their homeland to turn new souls from spectators into participants, is only a temporary imposition like the rules of the dance. After death the Light shall lead them dancing through the cosmic cycles to their breakthrough into Heaven.

In second-century hymns Dionysus was sometimes invoked as Lysios, 'the Loosener,' an epithet the Logos in the Acts of John might have adopted with little incongruity.[13] By liberating his disciples from the bondage of the flesh, he fulfilled his role in the game of redemption and was himself freed from responsibility. His loosening of the circle, his fleeing to Calvary, and his escape into Heaven are a supremely Dionysian coda to the Hymn at the Last Supper. Simultaneously a flight towards suffering and a flight away from it, Christ's final actions are as paradoxical as the finale of a baccheia. Both movements led to violence and destruction, but at the same time to rest and rebirth. Stimulated by the irresistible rhythm of pipe and tabor, revellers rushed headlong towards death, first in playful leaps and bounds, but soon with a feverish pace in response to the mounting excitement of the music, until their movement changed from a dance into a wild pursuit, a chase into a seizure, a catch into a killing. Its fierce climax, like the suffering at the end of Christ's round, was the suffering of a sacrificial victim; its gentle aftermath, like the peace Christ promises his disciples, was a sensation of extreme tranquility, as if all the torments of the world had disappeared.

The New Dionysus reiterates the paradoxical promise of his predecessor, that through strenuous motion his dancers will achieve psychological repose. This essentially bacchic theme underlies Christ's prophecy (uttered, oddly enough, in the past tense as if the fateful events had already occurred) that after seeing their leader in agony the disciples 'did not stand firm but were wholly moved,' and that having been moved they could rest in the knowledge of Christ's invulnerability. As their mirror the god of the dance offered his followers a respite from the anguish and insecurity of earthly life by reflecting to their souls a consoling image of themselves as free spirits divorced from the sufferings below the Eighth Sphere.

The alternation of strenuous movement and serenity, exertion and relaxation, was shown by Euripides to be the dominant rhythm of Dionysian experience, the Messenger in the *Bacchae* attesting that the Theban Bacchants always fell into a state of complete exhaustion after their rampages and rested peacefully on the ground until Dionysus incited them once again to tear through the glades of Cithaeron. Perhaps this bacchic pattern of repose and arousal underlies the peculiar alternation of passive and active verb forms repeated rhythmically through several lines in the Hymn.

The Dionysian resonances of one such line – 'I wish to be wounded and I wish to wound' – are particularly striking. Christ offers himself as the sacrifice in the drama of the disciples' redemption, the victim who must be wounded (or appear to be wounded) at the climax of their orgiastic dance; but as the divine initiator of the dance he will also wound his bestial adversary, the lawless Serpent, by leaping onto the cross and triumphing over death. Among the magic properties ascribed to bacchic dancers in ecstatic communion with Dionysus was an invulnerability to the bite of serpents. The Messenger in the *Bacchae* (767–8) observed that the Theban women were able to charm snakes and wreathe them in their hair, and that the tamed snakes licked clean the Bacchants' blood-stained cheeks after the rending of the sacrificial victim. Clement, who also bears witness to the importance of snakes as a sacred emblem in bacchic rituals (*Exhortation* II 12.2), associated the Maenads' snakes with the serpent of Eden in order to draw yet another inverse correspondence between the demonic mysteries of Dionysus and the holy revels of the Logos. Whereas the Old Dionysus had protected the bodies of his dancers from the sting of merely earthly snakes, the New Dionysus could save their souls from the everlasting pain inflicted by the arch-serpent Satan.

The Maenads' characteristic movement, the leap, compressed into a single step the psychological rhythm of the Dionysian rite as a whole, which would rise in excitement to a moment of climactic intensity and then suddenly subside, lose its compulsive momentum, leaving the band of revellers dispersed about the ground in a state of euphoric lethargy. The Dionysian impetus behind conversion is suggested by the only verb Jesus uses in the Hymn to describe his own motion, 'skirtān,' meaning 'to leap' or 'to frisk like a young animal,' which was the same verb chosen by Plato to describe the playful motions of young children untrained in choral dancing (*Laws* 653e) and by Euripides to denote the energetic capering of Maenads and Corybants (*Bacchae* 446). The image of a leaping, frisking Christ, his spirits youthful, his steps nimble and ebullient like a colt's, might strike modern Christians (who know the proper Jesus to be a sombre dance-hating moralist or a meek-eyed pastor draped in the heavy blankets worn only by biblical characters in Sunday School pamphlets) as distinctly ludicrous or even sacrilegious. Early Christians seem to have responded as much to the playfulness as to the piety of the Redeemer, who was free to leap into time and out again with all the passionate vitality of a Dionysian dancer. Hippolytus of Rome, a Christian apologist contemporary with Clement, identified Christ with the joyful man who 'cometh leaping upon the mountains, skipping over the hills' (Song of Songs 2:8), explaining in his commentary on this passage that the leaping of the Logos symbolized the four major events in the drama of Christian redemption – the Incarnation, the Crucifixion, the Descent into Hell, and the Resurrection:

O these great mysteries! What is meant by this leaping? The Logos leapt from Heaven into the womb of the Virgin, he leapt from the womb of his mother onto the cross, from the cross into Hades and from Hades once more back to earth.

(*Eis to asma* XI)[14]

Though the Docetic Logos by leaping from God to Man without becoming human altered the purpose of his leap onto the cross, cancelled his harrowing leap into Hell, and speeded up his leap from Man back to God, he nevertheless exhibited to his Gnostic disciples in the Acts of John an unrestrained exuberance in the enactment of his mystery comparable to that of the Incarnate Logos worshipped by Clement and Hippolytus.

His bacchic movement should not be understood as a metaphoric leap, however, like the leap of contemplation imagined by Plato and Philo or the leap of faith contemplated by modern agnostics. The New Dionysus capered for mysterious reasons across vast distances that defied human understanding, but his dramatic leaps were historical facts in the annals of the converted. He had sprung down from Heaven to be among them, and that was as real a motion in their new cosmic dance as the uniform revolution of a trillion stars was for the spectators of the old Platonic choreia. The indicative mood of Christ's verb 'eskirtēsa' ('I leapt') implies that his leaping was as much a part of an actual historical dance as the circling of the Twelve; its tense, the aorist or simple past, suggests that the action occurred before the dance at the Last Supper and was perhaps the cause of that dance, the initial movement in conversion which permitted the disciples to understand the Whole and ultimately to make their own leaps in the revels of the Logos. In the Greek New Testament (Luke 1:14 and 6:23) the verb 'skirtān' was used to denote the initial movement in the new cosmic dance, the leaping of a child in his mother's womb, and also its culminating movement, the joyful leaping of the Saved on the Day of Judgment.

The dance of the New Dionysus was as deeply charged with eroticism as the mountain revels of his pagan prototype, an eroticism heightened by the identification of Christ with the energetic lover in the Song of Songs who comes leaping upon the mountains and skipping over the hills to summon his beloved to their wedding. By sympathizing with his joyfulness, spontaneity, and rapturous desire for union, the chorus of the Logos understood the moving force behind their dance to be love, not reason, and not a rarefied, otherworldly, dispassionate sort of love like the Platonists' love of wisdom but an overwhelming tenderness, an instinctive, impregnating desire to be wedded forever to a specific person. As a release for erotic passions Dionysian revelry was recommended with disarming frankness by the throngs of lascivious satyrs who pursued wild-haired Maenads, panting and half-naked, through the nocturnal glades on ancient Greek vases, their mad dance resembling sexual intercourse in its compulsive rhythm of chase and capture, mounting excitement and climactic release, exertion and repose. As wanderers at the end of the Hymn the disciples are not consciously imitating the motions of the wandering stars but staggering in an ecstatic daze like Bacchants who have just had intercourse with a god. 'I wish to beget,' announces the god in his Hymn, and what he begets in the wedding of himself to his disciples is a passionate intimacy between God and Man that would have startled even the Therapeutae. The dancers learn by intuition rather than reason that the chorus of the Logos will expand from a miniscule round into the ever-widening circles of a cosmic and then a supracosmic dance, with them nearest its creative centre, not remote from it as the

Figure 6

Side A of Attic red-figure pelike from Nola (Louvre G 433, late fifth century BC; Beazley vol II, p 1342; *Corpus Vasorum* Louvre III 1 d pl 43, 7–11 and 4). The swelling body of this vase enhances the bacchic sense of tipsy imbalance and whirling erotic energy conveyed by the 'manikē choreia' of Dionysus, Maenads, and Satyrs depicted on it.

philosophers assumed, and that the stars and planets, which once seemed so close to God, were in fact very distant from the Light in which no darkness dwells. The disciples do not dance and sing in imitation of the heavens: the eight spheres sing together with *them*. While men in the Apollonian cosmos of the philosophers imitated the dance of divine and rational stars, stars in the Dionysian cosmos of the Logos danced in erotic sympathy with divinely inspired men.

'By night in my bed,' lamented the maiden in the Song of Songs (3:1), 'I sought him whom my soul loveth: I sought him, but I found him not.' Her plaintive verse, which would echo through the patristic period as the cry of the repentant soul for Christ or as the prayer of the maiden Ecclesia to her immortal bridegroom, is answered by the Logos in the Acts of John: 'You who have been moved to become wise have me as a bed.' The implications of this line, the most erotic in the Hymn, are consonant with the emphasis on love rather than reason in the cosmic mystery dance of the Logos. Like the maiden, John must lament for a while in solitude before finding the faithful lover for whom his soul has searched; then, in the darkness of the cave, he is reunited with the begetter of his faith and ever after will fall back upon Christ's loving spirit, unseen in the dark night of the Fallen World, as onto a bed where his fears of suffering and death and demonic entrapment are put to rest by the knowledge that he will soon be rising into the Light. Jesus wished not only to beget a new paideia in his dance but also 'to be born' within it, to generate images of himself by recreating his loving spirit among the converted. If his love was akin to erotic desire in its impulse to reach out and embrace the beloved disciple and to engender in him a new self-image, it was also far superior to sexual love in its intensity, constancy, selflessness, and consummate repose. Second-century converts, having turned their eyes away from the stars, could look back on the old mountain where Dionysus had leapt with the Bacchants of Thebes, and see in its place a new Cithaeron where the Logos was leading the angels and the Blessed in a love-dance before the Father.

The apologists for Gnosticism and Christianity voiced their protest against Greek cosmology by reversing its cherished metaphors of order in startling and audacious ways. As the New Song burst upon second-century ears, the inherent correspondences between choral dance and cosmic order were boldly ruptured: either the chorus of humanity sought to escape the evil order of the stars, or the cosmos and its stars ceased to live, move, reason like a human chorus. In the rhetoric of conversion inaudible music was made audible and invisible dances were visualized. Bacchic revelry was converted from a highly negative to an increasingly positive image for the initiation of human souls into the eternal order of Heaven. For the initiated the cosmic dance was no longer a primarily visual image implying the presence of an analytical spectator. It became a visionary experience demanding the believer's total involvement, whether he participated in the dance through his muscles, by performing religious rituals, or through his mind, by contemplating the mystic chorus of the Truth. Before the proselyte could see the order governing his life, he first had to participate in it. In the revels of the Logos he would turn with the cosmic revolution, surrender to its immortal choragus, and abandon the multiple viewpoints of the philosophers for the communal insights of the Saved.

4

Holding the Pose

Since the celestial revolution is sustained not by chance but by reason, by the logos that bears the stars along in their courses and operates throughout the Living Being, a harmony must therefore exist between what acts and what is acted upon, and a certain orderly design must link each thing to every other thing in such a way that when the heavenly bodies alter their configuration the parts of the cosmos lying beneath the celestial revolution have to adjust themselves from one arrangement to another. They are like the performers in an intricately woven choral dance, the many who create a single pantomimic dance-play [hoion mian orchēsin en poikilēi choreiai poiountōn].

In our pantomimes we may distinguish certain activities external to the dance itself which nevertheless contribute to it during its variously changing movements: for example, flute-playing, singing, and other accompaniments. Why bother discussing these aspects of the performance? Is their significance not obvious? But the parts of the dancer cannot be described in the same way – that is, as external accompaniments to the dance. By necessity the dancer conforms to each pose [schēma] and follows along with the dance by bending the limbs of his body. In the course of striking different poses he may lower one limb, raise another, put one limb in motion, keep another at rest. The will of the dancer, however, looks to an end other than changing from pose to pose. His body, not his will, is what suffers these changes. His limbs follow the sequence of the dance, assisting the performance and helping to complete all of it. Consequently anyone with expert knowledge of pantomimic dancing may explain why in a particular pose one limb of the body is raised high, another bent, one hidden from sight, another lowered. The pantomimic dancer [orchēstou] does not choose to perform the dance in any other way, but in the dancing of his whole body, holds this pose because it is necessitated by the design, and performs it in that part of his body which furthers the dance-play towards its conclusion [tēn orchēsin diaperainontos].

Now this is the way the heavenly bodies must be said to act when they cause or indicate things; better yet, one might say that the whole Living Being activates its own universal life, always moving its greatest parts within itself and causing them to change positions. It coordinates the configurations of its limbs relative to each other and to the whole, and organizes its diverse positions and their consequences. Acting as a single living creature in motion, it holds its limbs in a manner similar to the poses and posturings and configurations of the dancer. Its activities correspond to these in several respects. The parts forming the poses are not the causal agents creating the gestures, but simply things acted upon, limbs put into place; the active cause is the being who wills the poses into existence. He acts upon corporeal parts which are to a certain extent distinguishable from himself; yet these are parts of his own body and so cannot be different from him. The Living Being is everything that comes into existence. Up there, among the stars, are its poses; down here, round about the cosmos, are the necessary consequences of these poses. Thus moving as a unit, it is so constituted that by its nature it has inevitably combined into itself both that which is acted upon and that which acts, both object and subject of its activities.

PLOTINUS, *Ennead* 4.4.33

The Tortoise and the Chorus

The serenely unpolemical tone of this passage from Plotinus' second treatise 'On the Soul' is not what one might expect from the pagan philosopher now regarded as the first great intellectual opponent of the new paideia. From what his pupil and biographer Porphyry has to say about his oral teachings – namely, that between 243 AD when he started teaching philosophy in Rome, and 270 when he died at the age of sixty-five, Plotinus often lectured against 'the many Christians in his time' and attacked with particular vigour the Gnostic sectarians 'who had abandoned the old philosophy' (*Vita Plotini* 16) – one would expect to find in his writings strong traces of reactionary contempt for the cult of the Nazarene mixed with nostalgic praise for the golden age of Plato and Pythagoras. His posture ought to be defensive. His philosophy ought to be boldly controversial. And his voice should be raised against the countercultural sophistry that Clement of Alexandria had proudly called 'the language of exhortation.'[1]

Plotinus is rarely preachy, however, and his voice typically sounds like that of a relaxed seminar leader who is used to discussing a wide variety of questions with the greatest possible intellectual freedom among a close circle of urbane professional acquaintances. His exhortations are few, and would not have carried far in the marketplaces of the third century. His debating style, even by pagan Roman standards, would hardly have seemed dogmatic.

Where then is his brave manifesto against the enemies of the old philosophy? Where in his fifty-four treatises does he exhort his loyal pagan disciples (as Porphyry suggests he did) to resist the ground swell of conversion and to follow his lead in refuting the outrageously new and therefore erroneous doctrines of the converted? Not once in all his extant writings does he mention Christ or refer to the Christians or denounce any particular Christian author. True, he did write one explicitly polemical treatise 'Against the Gnostics' (*Enneads* 2.9); but this turns out to be a general refutation of dualistic doctrines prevalent in many Near Eastern religions popular in the third century and not a specific attack on any clearly identifiable Gnostic or Christian sect. It is in fact an editorial creation: originally it was simply a long digressive section of an unpolemical treatise on the relation of the temporal cosmos to its eternal model.[2]

His usual authorial tone (which prevails in his magisterial treatises 'On the Soul') bespeaks a calm indifference to the rhetoric of conversion that was filling the air of the third century with exultant promises of everlasting life and thunderous exhortations to martyrdom. If Plotinus had not stood out among his contemporaries for the originality of his thought, he would have done so for the tranquillity of his voice. In contrast to Clement, whose pupils he perhaps encountered in Alexandria when he began his study of philosophy there around 232, Plotinus was content to assume that men of outstanding virtue and wisdom (such as his own Alexandrian mentor Ammonius) could participate in the mystic chorus of the Truth without the aid of an Incarnate Logos. He would look for his incarnate god and his divine principle of reason in the living cosmos of the Platonists. Following the example of Timaeus whose cosmology he knew intimately and whose rhetoric he frequently echoed, Plotinus still held the intellectual pose of an ancient Greek astronomer: head raised in wonder towards the heavens, eyes fixed on the interweaving dances of the stars, mind enraptured by the mathematical order of the spectacle.

He most clearly presents himself as a follower of Timaeus in his treatises on astral causation and psychology, which Porphyry, whom he appointed as his editor, brought together in the second and fourth *Enneads* respectively. Porphyry divided the works of Plotinus into six groups, each containing nine treatises loosely related to one general area of philosophical interest; the collection as a whole he called the *Enneads*, which simply means 'Groups of Nine.' It was first published, with the *Vita Plotini* as its preface, sometime between 301 and 305.

In the thirty-third section of the fourth treatise of the fourth Group of

Nine – that is to say, in *Ennead* 4.4.33 – Plotinus turned his attention away from abstruse questions such as whether the stars can remember the events they influence and whether their souls are endowed with the faculty of volition to the crucial problem of reconciling his doctrine of individual free will with his belief in astral causation. Underlying his argument in this passage are the cosmological inferences and assumptions established in the Myth of the Craftsman – an old foundation of belief from which his thoughts often rose into realms far beyond the Circle of the Same.

The Plotinian cosmos, like its Platonic ancestor, was a vast animate sphere endowed with a rational soul which activated and regulated its multitudinous physical processes. Because the 'Living Being' was motivated by consistent and uniform processes of thought, a systematic sequence of causes and effects determined the prevailing physical motions of the stars and planets, and because the stars and planets were rotated by the spherical body of the All, their dances inevitably reflected and were influenced by the cyclical dynamism of the World-Soul. Seeing no reason to doubt Plato's doctrine that the heavenly bodies were living creatures divine and eternal, Plotinus was prompted in *Ennead* 2.9.8 – and implicitly here in 4.4.33 – to refute the Gnostic argument that the stars were evil spirits wheeling in fated circles or at best insensitive lumps of matter pushed along by the spinning of the outermost sphere. Their conspicuously beautiful choreia proved beyond a shadow of a doubt, at least to him, that the astral gods were benignly rational creatures who chose to cooperate with the artistic plan of the cosmos as a whole. From their viewpoint they acted freely. From the viewpoint of the Living Being, who saw them as limbs in his gigantic body, their actions were to some extent determined by a numerical design imposed on them from above by his creative will. What was freely willed and what was providentially fated in the dance of life became simply a matter of perspective – a distinction hinging on the differing viewpoints of the part and the whole.

Under the guidance of the cosmic soul or rather of the rational power activated within it, its logos, the movement of the whole directly affected the movement of each of its parts. For example, the rotation of the cosmic body led to the daily revolution of the sun and moon which led in turn to the rhythmic ebb and flow of the tides. Convinced by evidence such as this that the network of astral influences was more than an astrological superstition, Plotinus was willing to admit that many other earthly events – natural calamities, sudden financial gains, the formation of an individual's character at birth – might also be affected or at least indicated by the motions of the heavenly bodies. The Plotinian cosmos was like a finely branched, delicately integrated nervous system, the lower, weaker, duller parts of which were sympathetically in touch with parts which were higher, stronger, more sensitive to the will of the whole, so that even the tiniest fleshly limbs in the dark extremities of life were connected to the cosmic soul by a harmonious chain of causality. Yet in sharp contrast to the Archon-fearing Valentinians, the Hermetic mages, and the ubiquitous astrologers of his age who conceived this metaphorical chain as if it were indeed a series of material links, a rigid concatenation of souls to bodies and bodies to other bodies all locked within an inflexible cycle of fated events, Plotinus insisted that the harmonious activities of the Living Being depended more on the cooperation than the coercion of its diverse members, their forms, fortunes, partnerships, and conflicts being at every moment woven into the seamless star-embroidered fabric of the cosmos.

Life in his world, however, was not passive and neatly patterned as this textile metaphor might imply. Like the fluid interplay of muscles in a dancer's body or of dancers in a choral ensemble, it was an intensely active and free-flowing process of adjustment to new circumstances. Plotinus found these images of cosmic order – the decorated fabric and the choral dance – side by side in *Timaeus* 40a–d, where Plato had described the firmament as 'pepoikilmenon' or 'embroidered' with stars and adorned with choreiai too complicated to be explained without an armillary sphere. Both images are combined by Plotinus in the single phrase 'poikilēi choreiai' (4.4.33), which alters the implications of Plato's words even as it echoes them.

Whereas Plato had merely suggested the beauty and rational design of the heavens through these visual images, inviting his readers to make of them what they would, Plotinus subordinated the static image of the embroidered cloth to the dynamic image of the chorus and analysed the intricate self-adjusting order of the dance from the dual perspective of the part and the whole. He then brought his analysis of the dance to bear upon specific philosophical problems (such as astral causality) which tended to confuse the sense-bound human intellect and to burden it with needless anxieties. In contrast to Timaeus, who had focused his eyes on the bewildering variety of choral movements in the heavens, Plotinus saw one single dance and broadened his vision of it to include all the subordinate parts of the cosmos. His was a prospect of the world-chorus at once more diversified in its members and more unified in its motives than the visual design of the astronomer.

With the cool scorn of a professional academic who, on discerning the rapid spread of certain prejudices and superstitions from the ignorant masses (where they are endemic) to his friends in high social positions and, worse yet, to his learned colleagues, enters into debate with the mystagogues of his age without much hope of bringing them to their senses, Plotinus criticized the Gnostics for failing to see the unifying artistic motive behind the diversity of cosmic motions, and then for claiming, which is what truly appalled him, that they alone had been entrusted with the true vision of the

Divine Plan. 'If the Gnostics should claim that they alone have the power to see,' he warned his students in 2.9.18, 'indeed, merely by making this claim, they would not be any the nearer to vision.' It was not their intellectual élitism, bizarre mythology, or intense loathing of the human body that profoundly disturbed Plotinus: it was their stubborn refusal to see what danced before their eyes. They simply would not behold the resplendent symmetries of the chorus in the celestial theatre, would not share the age-old wonder of the Greeks who gathered round the Dedalian dance-floor on the Shield of Achilles, would not even hold the pose of an admiring spectator while their minds were straining to behold the chorus of the Aeons. Their anxious obsession with astral determinism and their irrational fear that the whole world was turning against them were the psychological consequences of one elementary mistake: they had severed what to Plotinus seemed the natural connection between seeing and knowing.

If their antivisual bias had resulted in the blindness of primitive ignorance, a state of mind for which Platonists had always had a curious respect, the Gnostics could easily have been cured by a few lessons in astronomy; but it had afflicted them instead with a kind of intellectual double vision which seemed to be exacerbated rather than cured by education, and which grossly distorted their world-view by transforming distinctions into dualisms. Light did not penetrate their darkness. It opposed it. Spirit did not animate matter. It abhorred it. The active enslaved the passive. The free escaped the fated. All sense of the smooth flow of life was lost. Plotinus also criticized the Gnostics for blurring the one distinction they ought to have kept clear in their minds, the crucial difference in cosmology between the whole and the part:

Now the constitution of the universe differs from that of the individuals living within it. In the universe, one might say, soul runs over everything ordering the parts to keep their places; in the individual, however, the parts are bound fast to their proper places by a second bond, as if they were trying to escape from the orderly design. But the parts of the universe have no place to which they may flee. Therefore soul does not have to hold them together within or press hard upon them from without and force them inwards; its nature remains where it wished to be from the beginning. Suppose, however, that the parts of the universe are moved somewhere in the natural course of things. Those parts which move in opposition to that natural course will suffer, but those which are borne along as parts of the whole will fare beautifully. The former will be destroyed because they are unable to endure the order of the whole. Consider this analogy: a tortoise was caught in the midst of a great company of dancers as they were moving in an orderly advance [chorou megalou en taxei pheromenou], and was trampled upon because it

could not escape the orderly movement of the chorus [tēn taxin tou chorou].
Yet if it had fitted itself into that movement, it too would have suffered no
harm from them.

(*Ennead* 2.9.7)

The Gnostics despised 'the natural course of things,' the inexorable advance of the Great Chorus, for two reasons. First, they felt that all the souls caught up in the cosmic whirl including the World-Soul were compelled by the overwhelming pressure of the advancing multitude and by the dictates of the dance-plan itself, a plan not of their own choosing, to hold their respective bodies together and to keep their rebellious limbs in their proper places, which meant that no soul on its own was ever free to contemplate its supracosmic origins and ultimately to escape the monotonous cycles of time. It was doomed to do what it did not want to do, what was not in fact 'natural' for a purely spiritual essence to do. Second, they complained that however orderly, creative, or beautiful the macrocosm might at any moment appear, its pitiless revolution inevitably led to suffering and death for the weaker members trapped within it. Even a minor change in the configuration of the stars might have dire consequences for sublunary creatures, not only for the heroic few who dared to oppose the natural course of things but also for the submissive throngs who drifted peaceably along with the current.

Plotinus answered their first objection by arguing that what was true of the parts was not necessarily true of the whole. While each soul within the cosmos had to maintain the formal coherence of its body and to govern the body's often refractory limbs, the World-Soul had only the first task to perform, its 'limbs' being all internal. Moreover, since its vast body could move nowhere outside itself and therefore had to stay in its proper place by simple necessity, the World-Soul was free to remain 'where it wished to be from the beginning,' that is, in ecstatic communion with the supracosmic gods.

The Gnostics' second objection usually elicited from academic philosophers a long and ponderous justification of the presence of inescapable evils and irresolvable discords in the best of all possible worlds, but Plotinus chose to answer it with brevity and a touch of wry humour, compressing his theodicy into the rather bathetic anecdote of the chorus and the squashed tortoise. The tortoise crawls into the debate rather unexpectedly, with little regard for the agonizing seriousness of the Gnostic view of the human condition; it even seems to mock at Plotinus' own high-minded discussion of the contemplative freedom of the World-Soul. But perhaps that is why the little tale, which has the vivid particularity of a personal reminiscence, was interjected into the polemic – to bring the Gnostics back to earth for an instant, to diffuse their cosmological angst (which seemed to grow more intense the more abstruse the discussion became) by reducing the problem of suffering and death to its proper sublunary proportions. The death of a particularly careless tortoise would hardly seem worthy of philosophical comment, and yet something about the creature's foolish disregard for its immediate environment, something about its natural slowness in the face of imminent danger, and something about the peculiarity of dying at the hands (or rather the feet) of a chorus of dancers who were no doubt as oblivious to its presence as it was to theirs must have caught the philosopher's eye and set him thinking about the ultimate insignificance of all earthly suffering relative to the triumphal march of the life-affirming, life-engendering stars.

What might be called the 'choral consciousness' of Plotinus, his strong Platonic sense of physical and intellectual participation in the harmonious motions of a living cosmos, has translated the simple visual memory of the collision of chorus and tortoise into a fable with quite complex implications, a fable illustrating not only the rationality of conforming to the natural course of things but also the practical advantages of seeing life from the perspective of the whole instead of the part. The tortoise saw life only from the perspective of the part, and suffered the consequences; it could have prevented its death at the last moment simply by changing directions, but chose to pursue its own independent course, to exercise free will (which even lumbering reptiles seem to possess in some measure) without advantage to itself or to its unwitting adversaries. Had it only moved with the chorus, its life would have been improved as well as saved. It would have 'fared beautifully,' contributing what it could to the aesthetic enhancement of the spectacle and sharing in the benefits of its harmonious order. So the Gnostics must learn that free will is not excluded from the sublunary realm; that self-survival depends to some extent on voluntary conformity to the cosmic design; that such conformity is tantamount to self-improvement; and that mortals can prevent or alleviate a great deal of suffering by choosing to act in harmony with nature.

Why despise the dance merely because of a squashed tortoise? Why despise the cosmic dance merely because of occasional mishaps at ground level, mishaps that may offend the eyes of a few easily distracted spectators but matter little to those who can see the dance from the perspective of the whole? The latter appreciate the beauty of the emerging design, know the reason for each new gesture or configuration as it appears at the appointed time, and never blame the Great Chorus for failing to notice stray individuals when it must concentrate, as one being, on a communal activity which is meant to benefit everyone, which exercises the dancers' limbs, disciplines their minds, delights and educates their spectators.

But who in the fable best represents those who see life from the perspective of the whole – the dancer so caught up in his performance that he fails to notice the tortoise in his path, or the philosophical spectator who sees both from a distance but cannot know the full force of the dancer's ecstatic impulse or prevent the chorus from crushing the non-conformist? As Plotinus suggested in 4.4.33, the spectator's knowledge of the dance need not be radically different from what the participant knew or felt about his performance. Someone with expert knowledge of dance could observe at a distance how each posture and step fitted into a single unfolding design, and would not be distracted by things external to the dance or accidental movements contributing nothing to its enactment. Moreover someone within the dance might still admire the intricate coordination of the parts within the whole even if he could not see the general movement very clearly from his shifting vantage-point, for if he were moved to ecstasy by the whirling of the Great Chorus his inward eye might glimpse another whole, an eternal design beyond the general movement yet somehow united with it through his ecstatic vision. 'The will of the dancer,' observed Plotinus, 'looks to an end other than changing from pose to pose'; looks, in other words, to a period of rest at the culmination of the dance; looks to a distant point of stasis towards which all his movements and the movements of all his fellow dancers have been directed.

The advance of the Great Chorus would not cast the dancer (as did the Gnostic Round of Jesus) into a sleepwalker's trance during which he would see the true order behind the diabolical illusions of the visible world. He would always see the choral round as a true order, an epitome of Plato's 'true cosmos,' no matter how transcendent his thoughts became in the course of the dance. At the same time, the Dionysian experience of straining upwards to God, of losing all sense of time and space in a Corybantic frenzy, of communing with a divine presence at the wellspring of life, was not to be denied the Plotinian spectator: he too could enter into sympathy with the highest initiates in the cosmic mystery dance and feel their common impulse driving his soul back to its divine progenitor. The viewpoints of the spectator and the dancer ideally complemented each other. Together their separate visions merged into the perspective of the whole, the natural and only perspective of the Living Being.

If the authorial voice of Plotinus, with its characteristic tone of benign intellectual detachment, seems far removed from the Roman lecture room where he originally aired his views against the Gnostics and resolutely confronted anyone, disciple or detractor, who wished to dispute any aspect of his all-embracing philosophical system, the same cannot be said of the metaphorical images with which he strove to elucidate that system, to distance it from the nightmarish worldscapes of the sectarians, to set it firmly on the time-hallowed ground of the old paideia: these are manifestly polemical in function, and none more so than his recurrent image of the cosmic dance.

He did not simply see the world as a 'poikilē choreia.' He wanted his stubborn opponents to see it that way – to see it that way again.

That Gnostics of the third and fourth centuries did indeed lose sight of the Great Chorus, either because they refused to perceive the sphere of darkness as an admirable artistic order or because they focused their attention exclusively on the spiritual harmony of the Pleroma, is attested by the absence of any reference to the cosmic dance in the numerous apocalypses and cosmogonic treatises of Valentinian, Sethian, Hermetic, Zoroastrian, and Gnostic-Christian provenance which were unearthed in 1945 near the Egyptian village of Nag Hammadi; this total blackout of the image, so to speak, can be sensed most keenly in certain narrative and descriptive contexts – such as flights of the soul through the heavens and meditations on the divinity of the stars – where choral imagery had traditionally appeared. For instance:

But we bent our knees, I and Peter, and gave thanks and sent our hearts upward to heaven. We heard with our ears, and saw with our eyes, the noise of wars and a trumpet blare and a great turmoil.

And when we had passed beyond that place, we sent our minds farther upward and saw with our eyes and heard with our ears hymns and angelic benedictions and angelic rejoicing. And heavenly majesties were singing praises and we too rejoiced.

(*The Apocryphon of James* 1.2.15)

This disturbingly matter-of-fact account of a mystical ascent into Heaven supposedly experienced by the apostles James and Peter after a ghostly visitation from Christ is typical of many visionary passages in the Nag Hammadi Library, which offers, one might way, the ultimate in 'escape literature.' Their escape is not the gradual ascent from a lesser concord (that of the planets) to a greater (that of the stars) to the greatest (that of the intelligible world) which Philo's Corybantic intellect undertook in learned and leisurely Platonic style in the first century; it is a breathless sprint from utter discord to utter concord, with trumpet blasts ringing in their ears at one moment and angelic harmonies at the next. Instead of the peaceful hymn of creation, they hear only 'the noise of wars': instead of a great chorus dancing to the laws of perfect music, they see only 'a great turmoil.'

No wonder, then, that a tough-minded defender of Platonic cosmology like Plotinus, who built up his own systematic interpretation of the order of the Living Being on the foundation of scholarly commentaries produced by second-century Platonists such as Severus, Gaius, and Atticus, and Neopythagoreans such as Cronius and Numenius, should be irritated by the upstart Gnostics' claim to 'true vision' after reading the obscurantist twaddle that passed in their circles for visionary literature. And that he did read works of the same esoteric character as the *Apocryphon of James* (though not that particular work) is attested by Porphyry in the *Vita Plotini* 16. In fact, at least two sectarian treatises mentioned by Porphyry as having provoked the polemical spirit of Plotinus – the secret books of revelations attributed to Allogenes and Zostrianus – have turned up in the codices of the Nag Hammadi Library.[3] Praising the cosmic chorus had been little more than a rhetorical reflex for most scholarly commentators on Plato in the second century, but for their successors in the third it became a defensive, pointedly philosophical response to the antivisual bias of world-contemning sectarian pedagogues. Merely by asserting that the order of the Living Being, life as seen from the perspective of the whole, was an inviolably beautiful choreia, Plotinus was also asserting the natural – which was as much as to say unquestionable – validity of the old paideia. But he would do more than repeat old praises of the fairest of all dances. He would analyse the image from new viewpoints, expand the boundaries of its reference, adjust its focus to correct the aberrant vision of his opponents, and at the same time, for his visual imagination worked in tandem with his pedagogical instincts, redefine the benefits and emphases and mystical goals of Platonic education.

Plotinus drew explicitly cosmological and ethical morals from the fable of the tortoise and the chorus, but if its polemical context is borne in mind along with the enduring symbolic association of choral dance with the astral origin, mathematical basis, and conservative rationale of Platonic education, the implicit moral of the fable, its satiric point, is surely pedagogical. The orderly advance of the Great Chorus represents not only the celestial revolution but also the intellectual movement corresponding to it, the 'natural' revolution in human thought which the Greeks called philosophy, and – if the metaphor is stretched to its limit – the whole philosophical movement, the long triumphant culturally unifying progress of Greek intellectual history from the age of Pythagoras and Plato through Hellenistic times to the Roman present. Seen from the perspective of *this* whole, the Gnostics were like the renegade tortoise: witless, obstinate, absurdly self-centred, momentarily distracting, but in the long run utterly unimportant to the prevailing representatives of the collective intellectual life of the West – the educated spectator and the ecstatic dancer. The Gnostics had crawled unexpectedly onto the philosophical scene. They had chosen to ignore the spectacle in the cosmic theatre and the imposing weight of eight hundred years of systematic speculation about it. They had followed their own quirky lines of thought towards their own preposterous apocalyptic goals. Now they were colliding with the academic establishment, Plotinus covertly warns, and if they refused to fit themselves into the communal advance of all rational creatures towards enlightenment their independent movement would surely be stamped out of existence by the indifferent tread of the Great Chorus.

Plotinus' insistence on the immanent unity of life on the intellectual as well as physical plane is often considered the hallmark of his philosophy, the distinctly personal note in his affirmation of Platonic cosmology. But he did not speak for himself alone when he insisted in 'Against the Gnostics' that all rational creatures must sense the unity of the Living Being and seek to see life from the unifying perspective of the whole. He spoke for his revered teacher Ammonius, for his own school at Rome, for the pagan intellectuals throughout the Roman world, indeed for a whole academic culture which was losing its authority along with its sense of coherence and facing what to it must have seemed the suicidal madness of those who had abandoned the old philosophy.

Despisers of the Dance

While the harmonic cosmology, erotic psychology, and idealistic ontology of Plato were the doctrinal bases of Plotinus' vision of world-order, the old philosophy to which he remained (as Porphyry was proud to report) uncompromisingly loyal also encompassed the musical mathematics of Pythagoras and certain Aristotelian doctrines of causality, motion, intellection, and actuality traditionally regarded as consonant with classical Platonism. Of course Plotinus was not so fanciful in his perception of intellectual history or so inattentive to developments in Hellenistic philosophy ever to have supposed that the choral dance of teachers and disciples around the truths of the old philosophy had gone on for generations without a false step here and there and a discordant note now and again, or that the two hallowed assumptions on which the old philosophy was based, namely that the natural world was manifestly harmonious and that its harmony sprang from a purely intellectual source exisiting outside the physical sphere, had never been criticized, qualified, or rejected before the advent of the Gnostics. The Great Chorus had met with more than tortoises along the way from Athens to Alexandria to Rome. It had had to contend with three major groups of dissidents – the Epicureans, the Stoics, and the Cynics – who had emerged within its ranks during the early Hellenistic period to challenge one or both of the assumptions sustaining the choral consciousness of its educated spectators and ecstatic dancers.[4] Each of these groups came to despise the dance for reasons of its own, and each tended to divert the spectator's attention away from the chorus of the stars. All three eliminated the ecstatic motivation and the otherworldly leap of the cosmic dancer. None could let go of the image entirely. Their protests against the old philosophy can be read in the different ways they twisted the Platonic analogy between chorus and cosmos to suit their ethical preoccupations and to reflect their very un-Platonic cosmologies. Plotinus' response to their protests was usually hostile, sometimes sympathetic, but always very serious, and it left its mark – an even deeper mark than his reaction against the Gnostics – on his own polemical revision of the roles of spectator and dancer in the design of the Great Chorus.

The Epicurean Spectator

Epicurus founded his controversial and much vilified school of philosophy in his garden in a suburb of Athens around the turn of the third century BC. He was fond of dispensing wisdom to his followers in the form of eminently quotable and slyly dogmatic aphorisms, many of which have survived in collections dating from several centuries after his death. Among them is this quasi-religious declaration –

Love dances in a circle around the world [perichoreuei tēn oikoumenēn], calling upon us all to awaken to the praises of the happy life.
(Vatican Fragment LII)

– which might almost pass for a fragment from the secret hymns of initiation chanted at Eleusis or a poetical pronouncement by a disciple of Empedocles on the miraculous integration of life according to a principle of cosmic love. What possible meaning could a statement like this have outside the mental boundaries of the choral cosmos? It seems to bind man and the cosmos together like a spell, to proclaim the erotic sympathy of all living things, to echo the age-old applause of the Greeks for the circular harmony of the divine design.

But its cosmological reference vanishes as soon as the aphorism is walled up in the garden of Epicurus and read only in the context of his other words of wisdom. Its metaphorical language, particularly in translation, proves deceptive. The world round which Love is said to dance is not the old macrocosmic theatre bounded by the Circle of the Same but simply 'hē oikoumenē,' 'the inhabited world,' which for Epicurus did not extend much beyond the boundaries of Alexander's empire; and the love, 'hē philia,' which he imagines as a herald proclaiming to all mankind the praises in store for those who achieve happiness through his philosophy is not a principle of cosmic concord like the Philia of Empedocles or a primordial cosmic deity like the Eros of Hesiod. It is a quite down-to-earth sort of friendship, the bond of kindly affection and mutual understanding uniting an Epicurean sage with his circle of disciples and linking all the members of the Garden, circle after circle, into a chain of sympathetic souls enjoying the same happy life in the healthy pursuit of pleasure and the honourable avoidance of pain. To a Platonist this chain of friends would have seemed a poor substitute for the all-embracing harmony of the Great Chorus, which alone could awaken humanity to the happy life of the gods, and the aphorism on friendship no more than a weakened version of the Athenian Stranger's witty definition of paideia as choreia.

Yet this purely human bond was the only harmony that an Epicurean could count on in this life, could consider real, and since he prided himself on having calmly abandoned all notions of a spiritual or physical afterlife the pleasures of true friendship assumed the highest value in his worldly code of ethics. He also calmly abandoned belief in the divinely crafted and divinely supervised harmony of nature. No soul, star, or god had ever danced round the circumference of the Epicurean universe and brought it within the bounds of human understanding by determining its mathematical constants, for it had no circumference, no boundaries of any sort, nothing that could be called the constant measure or shape of the Whole. It was mostly empty space, a dark lifeless indifferent void stretching away from the Garden on all sides and reducing even the great empire of Alexander to ludicrous insignificance. No Craftsman could have created it, no World-Soul pervaded it, no Mind controlled it. Whether it could even be said to exist at all was a debatable point. Still, something did exist within it: an infinite number of tiny indivisible particles of matter which were discovered – invented, a Platonist would say – by the Presocratic physicist Democritus while he was observing the movement of dust particles in a shaft of light. Motes are sometimes said to 'dance' in a sunbeam, but the atoms of Democritus were not pictured by Epicurus as dancing in the void. They simply fell through it like hail, now and then bumping into each other, here sticking together to form temporary clusters, there colliding with harder or larger clusters so that stones or stars dissolved, and formed again, and dissolved again, their atoms all the while moving at random, without purpose, mindlessly, inartistically. Minds exposed to this atomic hubbub were not likely to entertain visions of the dance of life. Nor were they inclined to perceive dances in the heavens, for Epicurus had taught them that all visible motions great or small were ultimately derived from millions of random atomic collisions. In fact all mental processes were derived from the same indeterminate motion, for Epicurean minds were content to define themselves as jostling aggregates of very thin and easily dispersed atoms.[5]

Lucretius, who preached the gospel of Epicurus to the Romans in the first century BC, devoted the second book of his mammoth cosmological poem *De rerum natura* ('On the Nature of Things') to a systematic account of the unsystematic motions of his material principles, revelling in sonorous descriptions of the 'blind blows,' the 'war waged from infinity,' the 'everlasting conflict' of atom against atom.[6] In this section of the poem is also to be found his only reminiscence of the cosmic mystery dance, which is pictured, or perhaps simply heard, as through the tumult of his atomic consciousness:

> *Taut drums, palm-beaten, thunder, and concave cymbals*
> *Clash all around; threatening horns sing a raucous song;*
> *Hollowed fifes excite the mind with a Phrygian cadence,*
> *And spears borne in front display signs of violent fury,*
> *Filling the ungrateful minds and impious hearts*
> *Of the crowd with fear of the majestic Goddess.*
> *Therefore, as soon as she passes through great cities*
> *And generously bestows on mortals her silent blessings,*
> *They strew the whole length of her route with copper and*
> *silver,*
> *Enriching it with a bountiful offering, and cover the Mother*
> *And her military escort in a snowy shower of rose petals.*
> *Here an armed troop – Phrygian Curetes the Greeks call them,*
> *Perhaps because they sport with arms amongst themselves*
> *And leap up rhythmically, stained with blood,*
> *Shaking their terrifying crests with a nod of the head –*
> *Recall the Dictaean Curetes, who are said long ago*
> *To have concealed the wailing of infant Jove on Crete,*
> *When, as boys encircling a boy in swift choral dance,*
> *[cum pueri circum puerum pernice chorea,]*
> *Armour-clad they rhythmically clashed bronze shield*
> *Against bronze shield, lest Saturn, catching Jove, should eat*
> *him*
> *And give his mother's heart an everlasting wound.*
>
> (*De rerum natura* II 618–39)

One might suppose from this stirring evocation of the revels of the Corybants, or 'Phrygian Curetes,' whose ecstatic dance around Rhea is here (as usual) associated with the cacophonous pyrrhic dance performed by the 'Dictaean' or Cretan Curetes around Rhea's infant son, Jove, that Lucretius was an enthusiastic participant in the cult of the Great Mother. But this impression is instantly dispelled by the following brusque disclaimer:

> *These lines may be well expressed, excellently set forth,*
> *But they are nevertheless far removed from true reasoning.*
> *For by their intrinsic nature all the gods*
> *Must enjoy everlasting life in supreme peace,*
> *Separated by a great distance from our troubles.*
> *For divinity is free from pain, free from danger,*

Powerful through its own resources, wholly independent of us,
Neither impressed by our merits nor touched by anger.
If anyone here decides to call the sea Neptune
And the fruits of the earth Ceres, and to refer to wine
Not with the proper word but with the inappropriate name
*   Bacchus,*
That is all right with us – let him even call the round earth
Mother of the Gods – provided that he forbears
In reality to infect his mind with base superstition.

(*De rerum natura* II 644–57)

The cosmic significance of the rites of the Great Mother was not ignored by Lucretius, though he did his best to downplay it by expressing his scorn for 'base superstition.' To the superstitious masses the majestic figure of Rhea represented not just the bounty of the earth but the earth itself, including the mighty cities through which her procession passed as well as the wild domains of Neptune, Ceres, and Bacchus, and her appearance on a lion-drawn chariot taught the crowd that 'the great globe is poised in the spacious air' and that 'the earth cannot rest upon earth' (II 602–3). The Corybants dancing round her chariot must have symbolized the heavenly bodies, then, and their ritual combat the conflict of planet against planet or planets against fixed stars within the general harmony of the living cosmos.

Like the revolutions of the stars their 'pernix chorea' was a threatening display of power, a death-dealing commotion, but it also protected the divine life-force at its centre and was thus essential to the creative order of the Goddess. Why did Lucretius bother to interrupt his exposition of Epicurean atomism with this vibrant scene of mystic revelry? Was he merely intent on purging his (and his reader's) mind of atavistic notions of a divinity inherent in the cosmos and of a cosmos instinct with divinity? Two completely different spirits seem to have warred in him for possession of his pen: the myth-enraptured spirit of a poet who imagines himself in the midst of Rhea's ecstatic procession hymning the ancient order of the gods; and the myth-disdaining spirit of a philosopher who sets himself apart from Rhea's deluded worshippers and in his heart despises the primitive rhythms, the frenzied leaping, the terror, the conflict, the impetuous life of the dance.

Whenever the Phrygian cadences of the mysteries threatened to excite his poetic spirit and disturb his inner calm, he promptly liberated his mind from the terrors of pain and death and primeval gods (which gave rise to base superstition) by reciting the sober, sensible, entirely unmystical religious dogmas of Epicurus. The gods have nothing to do with man. They know nothing of our emotions. They are composed of atoms thinner and subtler than those of human souls. They dwell in the peaceful vacant lots between the innumerable worlds forming and dissolving in the void. Thus the philosophical Lucretius invariably won out, tranquillizing his poetic spirit with dismal homilies on the true nature of things; but if the poetic Lucretius had only been allowed to sing at length, as his religious digression in book two indicates, the rhythms of the cosmic mystery dance might not have been drowned out so easily in his poem by the atonal din of atomic hail striking the walls of the Garden.

Plotinus refuted the natural philosophy of the Epicureans by defending the old philosophical doctrine that the universe is orderly through and through, that whatever appears disorderly in nature must simply be an order not clearly observed or not properly understood. Hence his emphasis in 2.9.7 on the orderly advance of the Great Chorus, and in 4.4.33 on the rational principle governing every movement in the dance of the Living Being: such passages serve not only to correct the Gnostic vision of astral determinism but also to counter the Epicurean theory of atomic randomness. His every reference to the cosmic dance is, in a sense, a statement against the Epicurean world-view. Sometimes the statement is quite explicit. 'Let us recall, if we may,' he concluded in 4.4.35,

that the cosmos we are discussing is a living creature, that it must therefore also be sympathetically attuned to itself, that the ongoing process of its life is governed by reason and is wholly harmonious within itself, that there is no randomness in its life but only harmony and order, that its configurations are formed according to reason, and that every single part of the living creature is dancing in chorus [choreuonta] under the guidance of numbers.

Plotinus could sound like a Pythagorean when circumstances called for it, and so he does here, defining cosmic order as a dance conducted 'under the guidance of numbers' in order to gainsay the three basic doctrines of Epicurean physics: the immeasurableness of space; the indeterminacy of motion; and the derivation of reality solely from material principles. What exactly these cosmic numbers *were* does not seem to have interested him much. Porphyry, who was more inclined to dabble in the mystical numerology of the Pythagoreans than his mentor, admitted that while Plotinus did study the rules of astronomy he did not penetrate very far into the subject 'on the mathematical side' (*Vita Plotini* 15). The general rule that numbers regulated the motions of the Living Being was all that really mattered to him, and if any doctrine of the old paideia had stood the test of time it was the mathematical regularity of the cosmic design. The fault therefore lay with the spectator – not with the chorus – if the cosmic dance seemed to vanish into an incomprehensible void, to shrink from an all-embracing reality into a mere metaphor for the happy life, to lose its mystical impetus with the relegation of the ancient gods to the realms of popular superstition.

In the Plotinian vision of the true nature of things the dance does not vanish. The void does. And the dance does not shrink. It encompasses every single part of the temporal world and expands (as we shall see) into the circles of eternity. And finally the dance does not lose its mystical impetus. New gods will emerge to lead the Great Chorus towards the eternal source of all the numbers guiding its movements through time, towards the one number Plotinus cared to contemplate with all his powers of concentration – One.

The Stoical Spectator

The essential oneness of the natural world as a living creature 'sympathet-ically attuned to itself' was a key concept in Plotinian physics, the roots of which may be traced to the cosmology of Timaeus and to the Athenian Stranger's pedagogical maxim that life must be seen from the perspective of the whole (Laws x 903b-d). After Plato, however, the concept was refined and championed for many centuries by the only school of dissident Hel-lenistic philosophers with whom Plotinus had any intellectual affinity: the Stoics. A clear mark of Stoical influence on the cosmology of Plotinus is his frequent use of the term 'sympathy' to denote the organic or biological (as distinct from mechanical or mathematical) integration of parts within the cosmic whole. The term itself is absent from his discussion of the dance in 4.4.33, but strong traces of the doctrine of cosmic sympathy may be detected in almost every sentence of this passage. It is implicit, for example, in his assertion that 'the whole Living Being activates its own universal life, always moving its greatest parts within itself and causing them to change positions'; and in 4.4.34, which continues this Stoic line of thought with a brief analysis of how the vital powers of the Whole are distributed throughout its greatest parts, the image of the dance is explicitly associated with the doctrine of sympathy:

Well then, a twofold power, the power to create and also to indicate, may in many instances be attributed both to the particular celestial configuration and to particular stars within that configuration. Sometimes, however, only the power to indicate is present. Thus we may reasonably argue that power resides both in the configurations and in the parts forming the configurations. Consider those who dance pantomimes [tōn orchoumenōn]: first each hand or other limb has a certain power; second, the patterns formed by the limbs have a great power; third, there is the power of the concomitant parts, the accessories brought to the dance [eis tēn orchēsin] by the performers, and other parts such as the fingers of a hand pressed together and sinews and veins responding in sympathy.

In the sympathetic universe the dance of life gains a certain visceral energy, a vein-and-sinew physicality, which it did not have in the ethereal heights of the Platonic cosmos. Plato tended to look through the outward spectacle of the world-chorus in order to analyse the mental processes of the dancing stars. Plotinus will consider this inner dance too; but first he lets his eye play over the physical surfaces of the dance and then, stripping away layer after layer of living tissue with the penetrating gaze of a surgeon, anatomizes every limb of the cosmic dancer to find the dance going on even there, beneath the skin, unseen, unsuspected, yet responsive to the slightest shift in the configurations of the stars.

The Stoic with whom Plotinus has most often been linked, Posidonius of Apamea (c 135–50 BC), was so deeply committed to the doctrine of cosmic sympathy – which taken to its logical extreme implies both the necessary connection of all events in the universe and the predictability of all events – that he was prepared to defend the scientific validity of astrology and divination. So too was Plotinus; his analysis of the twofold power of the stars 'to create' (by shaping or causing events) and 'to indicate' (by fore-shadowing events without influencing their sequence or outcome) is certainly Posidonian in spirit though not necessarily in origin.[7] If Posidonius did not actually shape Plotinus' vision of the web of events in the sympathetic universe as 'an intricately woven choral dance,' he can at least be seen, in the following fragment from his lost treatise on astronomy or meteorology, to have foreshadowed the Plotinian association of astral teleology with the image of the dancing cosmos:

Now it is not at all the task of an astronomer to understand why nature is calm and why it has motions of a certain kind. His task, rather, is to make observations and to propose hypotheses concerning stationary and moving objects and then to make celestial phenomena follow from his hypothesis. He must accept the fact that the simple and even and regular motions of the stars are principal causes of things in the natural world. Concerning these motions he will demonstrate that the choral dance [tēn choreian] of all the whirling bodies in the world, both those revolving in parallel orbits and those in slanting orbits, is circular.

(Fr 18; apud Simplicium, *In Physica* 11.2 193b23)

These remarks on the difference between the intellectual goals of an astron-omer and a natural philosopher were prompted by the audacious hypothesis of Heracleides Ponticus (who lived three centuries before Posidonius) that the appearance of the irregular motions of Mercury and Venus near the sun and of the regular revolutions of the fixed stars around the earth could be easily explained away if one assumed that the earth rotated daily on its own axis and revolved annually along with Mercury and Venus around a central stationary sun. Posidonius did not object to this hypothesis as an hypothesis. Astronomers were supposed to 'save the appearances' by making what they saw in the sky follow from what they drew with their compasses, even if that meant halting with one ingenious stroke the eternal choral dance of all the fixed stars and suspending the vital movement of the great sun itself. But no diagram could actually stop the dance, of course, and no astronomer could tell from his latest clever arrangement of cycles and epicycles why nature consistently revealed certain motions and not others. Saving the appearances was one thing, perceiving the true causes of things quite another. And for the Stoics the ultimate cause of everything was a divine life-force endowed with reason and sustained by its own self-generated creative energy, which they called God, Zeus, Craftsman, Necessity, Providence, and most commonly, Nature.

Cosmic sympathy was the direct result of Nature's two primary functions: holding the world together in a shimmering organic voidless continuum, and making all earthly things, including stones, grow at their appointed times under the influences of the stars. Stoic physics, as a blend of pantheism, vitalism, and what might be called 'cosmic physiology,' was still fairly compatible (far more so, indeed, than Epicurean physics) with the old philosophical vision of the world-chorus. It was close enough to Platonic cosmology to sustain the choral consciousness of an analytical spectator like Posidonius, for one, and he was by no means the only Stoic to echo the rhetoric of Timaeus unapologetically. A Platonist would find nothing objectionable in the orthodox Stoic view that it was the business of the astronomer to search for Nature's design in the intersection of circles but the delight of the philosopher to find it in the interinanimation of the dance.

Plotinus parted company with the Stoics over their theory of the autonomy of material existence and their rejection of the Platonic intelligible world. While they believed in a cosmos sympathetically attuned to itself and only to itself because nothing existed outside itself (except perhaps the Void),he based his entire philosophy on the doctrine that the cosmos was a living rational whole *only* because it attuned itself, freely, in the dance, to spiritual principles of life, reason, and unity abiding beyond the Circle of the Same.

In Stoicism the universe was equivalent to the cosmic body. Everything in existence was either a body or a part of a body, including souls, moral qualities, even God himself, entities which in the old philosophy were generally defined as incorporeal. Since the Stoics defied both Plato and Aristotle in identifying God with Nature, they were forced to argue not only that the material world was infused with divinity but also that God was somehow mixed with matter, that his essence penetrated the whole material world and was ultimately inseparable from it. A systematic confusion of ancient distinctions shrouded in Heraclitean obscurity – so Stoicism must have seemed to the puzzled Athenian crowds who first heard the founder of the school, Zeno of Citium, defending his doctrines beside the Painted Porch or Stoa (whence the name of his school) in the great public square near the Acropolis around 300 BC; but defend it he did, as would his imediate successors Cleanthes and Chrysippus, by wedding physics to ethics with such logical coherence that their philosophy of personal submission to the impersonal law of Nature would appeal to generations of Greco-Roman intellectuals, literati, public officials, military leaders, and world-weary emperors down to the time of Plotinus.

But how could God be a body subject to material change? How could matter enjoy divine autonomy? The fusion of old categories of being in Stoicism was accomplished, paradoxically, by a profusion of subtle conceptual distinctions. Matter, for instance, was carefully distinguished from body with respect to form and from God with respect to function. From Aristotle the early Stoics borrowed the concept of a formless material substrate underlying all corporeal existence and bearing the same relation to it as a lump of raw clay to a beautifully turned, painted, and fired amphora. Matter in its primal state was strictly indefinable since it had no formal characteristics, no properties of its own, only the potential to be endowed with shape, colour, hardness, and so on through an imposition of form which was equivalent in Aristotelian and Stoic terms to an act of creation. The end product of creative activity was something definable, a three-dimensional object with its own set of characteristics and its own unique boundaries, in other words a body. Primal matter had no function of its own other than to exist in a perpetual state of readiness. It was entirely passive. It simply awaited formation and endured transformation. God, or Nature, could therefore be differentiated from matter as the active force in creation shaping all things as it moves according to its rational inclinations and causing the cyclical dance of all the whirling bodies in the world. But for God 'to exist' in Stoic terms divinity had to be corporeal, and so Zeno defined the active principle in life as 'an artistic fire proceeding on its way to create.'[8] This definition, which was not metaphorical, also implied that God was inseparable from primal matter since his fiery nature emerged out of the material substrate and pervaded the cosmic body from end to end. Matter and divinity both became aspects of body in Stoicism. They could be distinguished in thought and speech, but in reality the active principle did not exist apart from the passive or the material apart from the divine. All merged into one continuous self-governing flow of life.

Plotinus was both repelled and fascinated by the paradoxical materialism of the Stoics. 'If matter needs nothing external to itself,' he reflected in 6.1.27,

and if it can become all things merely by shaping itself into various config-urations and assuming various poses, just like a pantomimic dancer who shapes himself into everything [hōsper ho tei orchēsei panta hauton poiōn], then it would no longer be subject to the actions of beings above and beyond it. Rather, it would be all things itself.

Appalled by this conclusion, he pressed the analogy further to see where it would lead him:

For just as the pantomimic dancer [ho orchēstēs] is not acted upon by the poses he strikes or by the characters he mimes – these are, rather, his acts – then what they call 'matter' will not be acted upon, either. It will not be subject to anything at all; on the contrary, all other things (if this were true) would be derived from it. Moreover, if matter were indeed to subsume all other things in the same way that a pantomimic dancer possesses a repertoire of poses and characters [hōs pōs exōn ho orchoumenos ta schēmata], then all other things will cease in any full sense to exist.

The twists and turns of his argument in this passage, which may be read as an extension of his thoughts on the activity and passivity of the cosmic 'orchēstēs' in 4.4.33, are difficult to follow if one assumes that Plotinus is thinking out his refutation of Stoic physics logically or systematically and then articulating his views in tidy sophistic analogies. Rather, he seems to argue directly from his analogies – to think imagistically – in order to break through the circular logic of Stoic hypotheses and deductions and strategic definitions.

The image of a pantomimic dancer shaping his body into a protean series of dramatic characters and poses is conceptually divisible into 'orchēsis' and 'orchēstēs,' yet the dance and the dancer are in this particular style of solo performance visually continuous, the boundaries of the one being identical with those of the other. When they tried to see life from the perspective of the whole, the Stoics could not tell the dancer from the dance: the cosmic 'orchēstēs' was visually continuous with the shifting contours of the great body of matter animated and shaped in the course of the cosmic 'orchēsis.' The identity of the Stoic cosmos, in other words, was simply the sum of its innumerable material parts moving in harmony according to the law of Nature. While the Epicureans envisioned no dance at all in the dynamics of their material principles, the atoms, the Stoics conceived the dynamics of material existence as the whole dance and all there was to the dance. Like the pantomimic soloist the mixture of primal matter and artistic fire which was the Stoic universe needed nothing outside itself to assume every possible shape in existence, to become all characters in the unfolding drama of time, to impose form and order and meaning upon the inchoate substrate. Yet the image of the 'one single pantomimic dance-play' (as interpreted in 4.4.33) might also imply that at least one part of the dancer, his will, was unaffected by the particular shapes and configurations imposed upon his limbs, that this part of him at least was not material, that it perhaps followed a logic of its own which an educated spectator might follow too and read back into the cosmos from which the dancer and the dance were ultimately inseparable.

Plotinus formulates, thinks through, in a sense discovers his argument against Stoic physics by analysing the teleology of the dance and reconstructing it on a cosmic scale. His vision of 'that which acts' and 'that which is acted upon' in the cosmic 'orchēstēs' is not a consequence of his refutation of the Stoics; his argument in 4.4.33 and 6.1.27 follows rather from his contemplation of the cosmic 'orchēsis' as a psychological as well as physical activity, the image functioning both as a stimulus and a vehicle for his own meditations on the creative force shaping matter into living art. That force, he believed, had to be external to the dance itself – 'external' either in a teleological or a metaphysical sense. The will of the dancer was external to the dance because it was not acted upon by the veins, sinews, hands, legs, or other material parts moved about in the performance, even though it existed within the boundaries of the dancer's individual self and was causally related to the movements of his body; the singers and flute-players accompanying the dancer were also external causal agents contributing to the order of the performance, but their transcendence of that order was even greater than that of the dancer's will since they existed as separate individuals outside the peripheries of his soul and body.

If the creative force or forces motivating the cosmic pantomime were not external to it in one or both of these senses, Plotinus contended, two absurd conclusions would have to be drawn about the nature of things: first that the cosmic dance could never have begun, since all things would be subsumed by matter, and matter was, by definition, entirely passive; and second that the cosmic dancer could not in any full sense have existed, since true being implied formal permanence and eternal life and divine rationality and inviolable unity, none of which could inhere in a volatile and ultimately self-destructive mixture of primal matter and artistic fire. But the dance obviously had begun and the dancer obviously did exist. Therefore something – and not the Void – had to exist in the fullest possible sense outside the material confines of the cosmos, something that urged the analytical spectator to tell the dancer from the dance and permitted the ecstatic dancer to distinguish his true self from his repertoire of poses.

The poses one struck in the face of adversity, the movements one performed in the pursuit of happiness, the roles one enacted in the administration of society – these all added up to 'character' in the Stoic sense, that is, to moral character; and if those poses, movements, and roles were always in harmony with one's natural instincts, and were always chosen to accord with the fixed plan of Nature as seen from the perspective of the whole, and were at every moment adapted to the changing circumstances of Nature as seen from the perspective of the part, then the resulting character was perfectly virtuous: it was the character of an ideal Stoic sage.

'Our limbs appear to have been fashioned for a certain purpose,' observed Marcus Cato, Cicero's spokesman for Stoic ethics in his dialogue on the goals of the philosophical life,

in order that we should conform to a certain reasonable way of living, similarly, the soul's appetitive instinct (which the Greeks call 'hormē') has been given to us not that we might lead any sort of life we choose but that we might incline towards a particular way of life. And the same is true of reason and perfected reason. For just as a specific role – not just any role – is assigned to an actor, and just as a specific movement – not just any movement – is assigned to a dancer [saltatori], so life must be conducted in a certain fixed way and not in any way we choose. This way of life we describe as 'compliant' and 'concordant.' We do not think that wisdom, the art of living wisely, is like seamanship or medicine but rather like the aforementioned arts of acting and dancing [saltatione]: its goal, the actual exercise of the art, exists within the art itself and should not be sought as something extraneous to it. Still, in another respect, there is a dissimilarity between wisdom and these same arts. In acting or dancing, movements that are correctly executed nevertheless do not involve all the roles, gestures, or motions which constitute those arts; but in the art of living wisely, what we may call, if you will, 'right actions' or 'rightly performed actions' (or as these are called by the Stoics, 'katorthōmata') embrace all the categories of virtue. For wisdom alone is entirely self-contained, entirely turned in upon itself, which cannot be said of the other arts.

(*De finibus* III 23–4)

Cato's definition of wisdom as the art of living wisely, a creative activity which generates its own reward, virtue, and justifies its own end, moral integrity, is just similar enough to Plotinus' description of the artistic activity of the Living Being in 4.4.33 to highlight the Stoic nuances in his worldview.

The Stoic art of wisdom was like the art of dancing in that it demanded conformity to a 'ratio vivendi,' a certain fixed reasonable methodical way of governing one's body and establishing one's relations with others and conducting one's every movement in life; but it surpassed the intermittent activity of a 'saltator' in that it brought into play at every moment all the virtues of the artist, particulary prudence, temperance, justice, and fortitude, which were conceived not as latent qualities of the Stoical sage but as well-integrated and constantly exercised powers of his rational soul and hence, in retrospect, accomplishments or demonstrable effects of his morally creative life. These accomplishments fitted in with what was produced all around him by the physically creative life of Nature, and thus his character was shaped, perfected, fixed in imitation of the divine life-force from which he derived his natural instincts for virtuous conduct. Stoic ethics had its snags and dilemmas, not the least of which was the apparent incompatibility of Nature's fixed way of life with Man's freedom as a moral agent, but it was ideally supposed to form a coherent logical system in harmony with, and deducible from, the principles of Stoic physics. That is why Cato proudly observed that the art of living wisely was 'entirely self-contained': it needed nothing outside itself to enable the wise man to distinguish right from wrong and to perform the right action at the opportune moment, the rectitude and integrity of his character being a reflection of the self-contained system of Nature.

The objective order of Nature provided the Stoical sage with an inspiring example of virtue to follow in his day-to-day interactions with society – and he was by instinct a public-spirited man – so that the long sequence of right decisions and right actions which made up his 'compliant' life could be seen in the end, from the perspective of the whole, as a brilliantly executed solo performance within the cosmic 'saltatio,' It was the performance of a divinely inspired virtuoso, rarely appreciated, more rarely attempted, most rarely accomplished.

Plotinus seems to be considering just such a dance, or just such a dancer, in his portrait of the cosmic 'orchēstēs.' Certain remarks in 4.4.33, such as

By necessity the dancer conforms to each pose and follows along with the dance by bending the limbs of his body ...

and

The pantomimic dancer does not choose to perform the dance in any other way, but in the dancing of his whole body, holds the pose because it is necessitated by the design ...

which seem purely descriptive on a first reading have a clear Stoic ring to them and gain a distinctly prescriptive force when read next to Cato's definition of wisdom.⁹ They are ethical exhortations doubling as statements of fact in a ostensibly objective cosmological argument. Like the fable of the tortoise and the chorus, which would no doubt have appealed to Cato as an exhortation to conformity, all the statements in 4.4.33 touching on the dancer's voluntary submission of his limbs to the poses necessitated by the design of the dance have as their primary reference the order of the whole but are also meant to be read as advice and consolation for the philosophical spectator who sadly contemplates the perfectible yet easily downtrodden and too often erratic parts.

But as usual, just when Plotinus seems to be drawing very near the Painted Porch, he takes a giant step away from it and beckons us to follow. In contrast to Cato he does not speak of the dance – or the poised artistic life it epitomized – as an end in itself, as its own end, as the ultimate end of personal conformity to the grand design of Nature. The dance may from the outside appear entirely self-contained, but the dancer who must be distinguished from it as the psychological agent of its physical actions looks to another end (pros allo) which transcends the temporal goal of fitting limbs into prescribed postures and exists in its own right beyond the confines of his physical movement. What that end might be is not revealed in 4.4.33, but it is sufficient by virtue of its isolation from the cosmic pantomime to prevent the dancer from turning wholly inward upon himself.

Cato's discussion of the art of living wisely is typical of the ethical contexts in which the Stoics seem to have been most inclined to compare life to a dance. So rarely, in fact, does the cosmological version of the analogy turn up in extant Stoic writings that one might hastily conclude that the philosophers of the Porch were inclined to contemplate the dance of life solely within the sphere of ethics. That the vision as a result seems to lose its classical depth of field, to become egocentric, to narrow, may be simply an effect of the strongly ethical bias of the late (that is post-Posidonian) Stoics and Stoicizing men-of-letters, Cicero, Seneca, Epictetus, and Marcus Aurelius, whose treatises comprise the great bulk of extant writings representing the cumulative wisdom of their long-influential school. Zeno and Chrysippus are known to have written a prodigious number of works on physics and psychology as well as ethics, in which no doubt the figure of the dance occasionally appeared, but not one complete treatise by them or by any representative of the Early and Middle Stoa has survived.

If this great lost corpus should by some archeological miracle come to light like the Nag Hammadi Library, two hypotheses which must for now remain likely but unprovable might pass into the realm of certainty: first, that the early Stoics preserved the Platonic vision of the cosmic dance by associating it with the logos manifested in *all* of Nature's cycles, elemental, seasonal, biological, historical as well as celestial, an association which undoubtedly lurks behind Philo's un-Platonic assertion that 'the divine Logos dances in a circle' (see above, page 125) and Plotinus' insistence, two centuries later, that the dance of life was sustained not by chance but 'by the logos that bears the stars along in their courses' (4.4.33); and second, that some early and highly innovative Stoic – perhaps Chrysippus or his immediate successor as head of the Stoa, Diogenes of Babylon, from whom Cicero probably derived most of the ethical doctrines propounded by Marcus Cato in the *De finibus* – was the first philosopher in the West to make the imaginative leap from 'poikilē choreia' to 'mia orchēsis,' to fuse the diverse movements of the diverse bodies in the heavens' intricate choral rounds into the one single movement of the one single body in Nature's protean pantomime.

If this fusion did indeed occur in the Stoic imagination, then one would have to say that the original thinkers of the Porch expanded rather than narrowed the old cosmological vision of the dance, leaving its ethical implications to be worked out by later members of the school who could add little to the ingeniously contrived, and closed, system of Stoic physics.

The style of dramatic solo performance that the word 'orchēsis' (and its Latin equivalent 'saltatio') came to designate in the Hellenistic period was visually more suggestive of the dynamics of the self-contained and self-shaping body the Stoics called Nature than the massed choral movements signified by the Platonic term 'choreia,' though the one image could easily be reconciled with the other by associating 'choreia' with the perspective of the part and 'orchēsis' with the perspective of the whole (as Plotinus does in 4.4.33). Whoever first reconstructed the vehicle of the old metaphor in this way inevitably modified its philosophical tenor, bringing unity into prominence as the essential virtue of the living cosmos and the ultimate cause of its rationality, divinity, and creative vitality. By the mid-first century BC, when Cicero composed the discourse of Cato, the image of the unique 'orchēstēs' emerging out of Nature's myriad 'choreutai' had probably long been a commonplace in the literature of Stoic exhortation, epitomizing the self-control, moral expertise, indivisible nexus of virtues, adaptability to life's changing circumstances, and indomitable allegiance to a fixed standard of conduct which were the hallmarks of the Stoical Sage.

Because it lent intellectual support to their native moral earnestness, sustained their faith in the providential design of history, and justified their ambition to unite humanity under one government analogous to the divine administration of Nature, Stoicism was bound to make a deep impression on educated Romans in the first three centuries of the Empire. But the Romans, in turn, were to leave their own mark on the Painted Porch. They scaled the Olympian ideal of the Stoical Sage down to human size, softened its austere edges, made it accessible to any virtue-loving citizen who wished to order his daily life in accordance with natural law and to enhance the sympathetic order of the Empire as a whole. 'For,' as Hierocles, an early second-century expositor of Stoic ethics observed,

that which profits the choral dancer in his role as choral dancer [tōi choreutēi hōs choreutēi] would also be profitable to the whole chorus [tōi holōi chorōi].
(apud Stobaeum, *Anthologii* lib III p 733)

So inclined were the Roman Stoics to free the art of living wisely from the tangled technicalities of physics and logic that it ceased to be an elaborate conceptual system understood only by a few Levantine intellectuals and became something close to a popular monotheistic religion offering consolation to the hostages of Fortune, sensible advice to the favourites of Zeus, and dignity even to the weakest member of the Great Chorus.

It is perhaps no accident, therefore, that the two greatest Stoics in the century preceding Plotinus were from opposite ends of the social scale – one a manumitted slave, the other a meditative emperor. Here is how the slave, Epictetus, calmed a man who was anxious to see life from the perspective of the whole yet unable to fathom the complexities of physics:

'What do I care,' says Epictetus, 'whether existing things are composed of atoms, or of indivisibles, or of fire and earth? For is it not enough to learn the essential nature of good and evil, the limits of desires and aversions and also of impulses and undertakings, and by employing these as rules, to order the affairs of our life, and to consider as unimportant the things that are beyond us? Perhaps these things may not be grasped by the human mind. Yet even if one were to assume that they are perfectly comprehensible, what profit may be gained from comprehending them? Should one not say, rather, that those men who think it necessary to assign all this to the philosopher's system of thought are labouring in vain? But surely that does not mean that the precept at Delphi – "Know thyself" – is beside the point?'

'Indeed no,' answers the man, 'that is not what it means.'

'What, then, is its meaning? If one were to order a choral dancer [choreutēi] "to know himself," would he not heed the command by turning his thoughts towards his fellow dancers in the chorus [tōn synchoreutōn] and also towards their mutual concord?'

'Of course.'

'Is the same not true of a sailor or a soldier? Does it seem to you, then, that man has been created to live for himself alone or for society?'

'For society.'

'By whom?'

'By Nature.'

'What Nature is, and how she organizes the universe, and whether she really exists or not – these are questions about which we need not trouble ourselves.'

(Fragment 1)

The Late Stoics could dispense with all the dogmas of the physicists associated with their own or with any other philosophical school. They could banish from their thoughts the vainly optimistic assumption that human minds were capable of understanding the organization of Nature. They could even abandon the concept of Nature as something other than a mere concept, as a fiery breath actually existing and constantly manifesting itself in the dynamics of the material world. But they clung with an almost religious tenacity to the belief that ethics was an exact science providing absolute standards for judging the essential nature of good and evil and incontrovertible rules for bringing order into man's brief uncertain life, and to the corollary doctrine that self-knowledge was desirable and indeed attainable in a universe that was largely unknowable, so that even on the brink of utter uncertainty about the objective world – the howling brink towards which, question by Socratic question, Epictetus drew the man who was perplexed by the conflicting definitions of the word 'existence' – they did not lose their choral consciousness of order or cast the ordering image of the dance into the inner void of skepticism.

Epictetus was not a skeptic so much as a pragmatist. He was less interested in proving that all questions concerning the reality of Nature were unanswerable (for skepticism must ultimately turn back upon itself and undermine the certainty of ignorance) than in persuading his perplexed interlocutor that such questions were not worth fussing over, that even if answers to them lay within the bounds of human understanding the deepest insight into the secrets of Nature would be of no practical advantage to a man striving for self-knowledge and the advancement of society. Self-knowledge was for Epictetus equivalent to social awareness, and if it was not the great lawmaking Zeus or Nature or Providence that determined the role one had to play through life and the steps one had to take to endure it, then the commanding force was society – the collective pressure of the human chorus – which in practical terms was as hard to resist as the spinning of the cosmic body.

The Stoical 'choreutēs' obeyed the Delphic oracle not as his Platonic counterpart would, by searching his soul for rational movements corresponding to the revolutions of the stars, but by looking outside himself, by turning his thoughts towards the steps and poses and configurations of his 'synchoreutai': he only knew who he was by discovering his proper social role; he only knew what he ought to do by following the orderly movement of his fellow dancers; and he only knew why he ought to do it by studying the exact science of Stoic ethics which was designed to promote the political concord of society as well as the psychological concord of the individual. Thus, at the brink of skepticism, the philosophical vision of the world-chorus tended to narrow into a metonymic image for social unity.

Three types of unified bodies were distinguished by the Stoics of the second century: organic unities (hēnōmena) such as plants and animals; inorganic or artificially conjoined unities (synaptomena) such as ropes and turrets; and composite or social unities made up of discrete individuals (synkeimena) such as armies and flocks. This classification implied a descending scale of integration, the highest degree of unity being that of the 'hēnōmena' and the lowest that of the 'synkeimena.'[10] Epictetus evidently had the latter category in mind when he spoke of the 'mutual concord' of a chorus as similar to that of a troop of soldiers or a crew of sailors. That the Early Stoics also saw the chorus as exemplifying multiplicity-in-unity may be inferred from a doctrine of Chrysippus cited by Plutarch – 'Here on earth we can often find a single body composed of separate bodies, such as a legislative assembly, an army, and a chorus, each member of which happens to be capable of living, thinking, and learning, as Chrysippus believes …' – a doctrine which may be traced at least as far back as the fourth century BC, to Xenophon, who described choruses and armies as specimens of the same type of strictly marshalled but easily confused and potentially chaotic social body.[11] When a Stoic compared human society or the sidereal system or life as a whole to a chorus, then, the image would have implied potential disorder and ultimate disintegration as well as apparent order, harmony, unity and so on. This disquieting vision of the world-chorus would not have been out of line with the Stoic doctrine of 'ekpyrōsis' or cosmic conflagration. In contrast to Plato, the physicists of the Porch typically maintained that the cosmic body was periodically destroyed by its own fire, that it was then reborn phoenix-like from its ashes, and that 'Zeus' was therefore a collective name for an infinite succession of divine but not immortal cosmocrators.

As a Platonist Plotinus could not have been much in sympathy with the Stoic definition of unity as an attribute of mortal bodies only, or with the Stoic assumption that organic unities were necessarily higher on the scale of integration, and hence perfection, than social unities. The unity of a Plotinian chorus transcended corporeality: it was a cause rather than a consequence of the juxtaposition, concatenation, or marshalling of a multiplicity of bodies; it was a cause also of the psychological or intellectual sympathy of the individuals participating in choral harmony; it was something divine, something imperishable, something inherent in the World of Being rather than Becoming.

'In what sense, then, might one call each thing that exists a unity?' inquired Plotinus in 6.2.10. He immediately answers this question by recalling and challenging the Stoic classification of corporeal unities:

Listen! One something is not 'one' in an absolute sense: in so far as it is 'one' and 'thing' it is already a multiplicity. As for species, each is a unity only in an equivocal sense. Since each species includes a multiplicity of individuals here in the world of the senses, its unity is that of an army or a chorus [choros]. The unity up there, in the intelligible world, is not the unity of species, and so one should not identify the unity of particular beings with the unity of Being.

The Stoics tended to define unity with reference to the agent or agents resonsible for producing the unified structure of a particular body or imposing a unified design on a multiplicity of bodies, that is, in terms of efficient causality; hence, their distinction between organic, artificial, and social unities implies a hierarchy of efficient causes – the great artisan Nature producing 'hēnōmena,' lesser human artisans 'synaptomena,' and a host of individuals and their leaders 'synkeimena.' Plotinus, by contrast, typically defined unity in terms of formal causality, relating the degree of unity in each existing thing to an eternal paradigm of oneness (or wholeness) entirely isolated from the hierarchy of efficient causes existing within the sphere of Nature. His classification of unified beings is accordingly very different from the Stoic classification of unified bodies, though it too is threefold and hierarchical. Lowest on his scale is the unity of the individual in the World of Becoming; above that, the unity of the species to which the individual belongs by virtue of certain shared formal characteristics; and highest of all (save for the First Cause of all oneness), the unity of the gods in the World of Being to whom the formal distinction between individual and species does not apply because they subsume the eternal forms of all temporal species.

The Stoic scale of integration and perfection collapses in the Plotinian universe because all things, including organic unities, are perceived as multiplicities in comparison with the isolated First Cause which is absolutely and essentially one, whole, indivisible, and self-sufficient. Even the unique Living Being, which was the supreme example of wholeness and self-sufficiency in Stoic cosmology, becomes in Plotinian terms a multiplicity simply because it is 'one something': its nature may be broken down into two parts, its existence as a thing and its accidental property of wholeness, though, of course, its degree of wholeness is far greater than that of any individual thing dancing within it. Even so, the Plotinian cosmos could not be called essentially 'whole' or completely 'self-sufficient' since it depended on divine causes outside itself for both its unity and its existence.

This departure from Stoicism had a striking effect on the significance of the chorus as an image of universal order. Having carried over from the Porch the definition of the chorus as a multiplicity living, thinking, and learning as a unity, Plotinus would associate the image not only with physical or corporeal multiplicities participating in a unifying artistic movement (groups of dancing bodies) but also the metaphysical or incorporeal multiplicities participating in a unified scheme of existence (temporal species, intellects in contemplative harmony, the design of intelligible reality). The Great Chorus would therefore spread its ordered ranks all the way up the scale of being from the basest material parts of the cosmos to the highest circle of the stars and from there across the Great Dividing-Line to the highest, stillest, simplest multiplicity encircling the wellspring of all unity.

Corybantic leaps into the distant reaches of metaphysics were neither applauded nor advised by Epictetus, whose scorn for the vain efforts of philosophers to understand 'the things that are beyond us' was matched only by his contempt for the indifference, cowardice, impatience, and resentment displayed by the many unphilosophical fault-finding spectators at the dance of life. From his viewpoint the Great Chorus stopped at the borders of the material world. It had to, for there was nothing living, thinking, or learning outside of Nature, nothing multiplied or unified, nothing intelligible, nothing divine, nothing at all. Philosophers who thought something did exist out there and spent all their time dreaming of immortality seemed to him not only pretentious but irresponsible. They foolishly ignored the harsh facts of the human condition, paid no heed to the Delphic oracle, failed to prepare their disciples to die in the manner of a Stoical Sage – quietly, gratefully, with a clear understanding of the rightness and timeliness and finality of death.

The purpose of philosophy, as Epictetus conceived it, was essentially therapeutic. It was to calm nerves and cure passions, to purge bitterness and reconcile all who despised the dance to their divinely ordained roles in it. Asked Epictetus of one fault-finding spectator:

As what did God bring you into the world? Was it not as a mortal? Was it not as one destined to live on earth with a small share of pitiful flesh, to be for a short while a spectator of his government, to follow him in his procession, and to celebrate his festival with him? Do you not wish therefore to be a spectator of his pageant and his festival for the whole of the time allotted you, and then, when he leads you forth, to go, having made your obeisance and expressed your gratitude for what you have heard and seen?

'No,' you may say, 'I wanted to continue celebrating the festival.'

Well then, you are like the initiates in the mysteries who want to go on with their initiation, or perhaps even like the crowds at Olympia who want to see other athletes. But the festival has an end. Leave. Depart as a grateful and modest spectator. Make room for others. Others must be born, even as you were born, and once born they must have land, houses, the necessaries of life. If the first-comers do not gradually withdraw, what is left for their successors? Why are you insatiable? Why dissatisfied? Why do you crowd the cosmos?

'All right,' you concede, 'but I want my children and my wife to be with me.'

Are they yours? Do they not belong to the Giver? To him who made you? Will you not therefore give up what belongs to another? Will you not yield to your superior?

'Why then did he bring me into the world on these conditions?'

If the world does not suit you, leave. God has no use for a fault-finding spectator. He needs those who join in celebrating the festival, who dance together in chorus [tōn synchoreuontōn], so that they may applaud rather, and invoke the gods, and sing hymns in praise of the festival. As for the indifferent and the cowardly, God will not be annoyed to see them left out of the festival; for when they were present they did not celebrate as at a festival, nor did they fill the proper role. They were miserable, found fault with God, with Fate, and with their fellow men.

(Discourses IV 104–9)

The dance envisioned here has a distinctly religious character which sets it apart from the geometrical choreiai to which Posidonius compared the astral revolutions and the histrionic 'saltatio' to which Marcus Cato likened the moral life of the Stoical Sage. Yet it is not distinct from these in meaning: cosmic order merges with ethical order so subtly and persuasively in the religious vision of Epictetus that conceptual distinctions between dancer and dance, spectator and spectacle, even dancer and spectator, are soon lost in the flow of Socratic questions which overwhelm the fault-finder, humble him, strike him with the quick vibrant energy of the dance itself.

The festival has a measure of pageantry and a milling crowd of applauding and jeering spectators, though it is not primarily a dance-spectacle; it has a fixed number of roles and a multitude of people to fill them, though it is not simply a dance-drama. Epictetus clearly had in mind some sort of popular dance-ritual in which a large chorus of initiates accompanied by their friends and families processed behind a divine choragus or a mystagogue representing the god or a chariot bearing the garlanded statue of the god, perhaps specifically the festive march from Athens to Eleusis preceding the Greater Mysteries (which were still being celebrated in the second century). It is also reminiscent of the mystic dance to which Socrates referred in his rhapsodic oration on the Forms glimpsed at the beginning of time by the unfallen souls of men destined to become philosophers:

At one time these men saw Beauty in all its radiance. That was when they were with the blessed chorus [syn eudaimoni chorōi], while we were following in the train of Zeus and others were in the company of some other god. Then did they see the blessed sight and spectacle; then were they initiated into what is rightly called the most blessed of mysteries.

(*Phaedrus* 250b–c)

Epictetus has removed the basic images from this seminal passage – Zeus leading the cosmic chorus, his train of human worshippers, the blessed spectacle applauded by the initiates – from their primeval context in Platonic mythology and recomposed them within the framework of the Stoic universe to form a picture of the enduring Here and Now. The Socratic vision has been thoroughly Stoicized. Zeus changes from a mythical sky-ruler and archetypal percipient of intelligible reality into an omnipresent natural force, the provident administrator of the living cosmos, God in Nature and God as Nature; his train of worshippers expands from a tiny chorus of enlightened philosophical souls into the common mass of humanity, into everyone 'destined to live on earth with a small share of pitiful flesh'; and the blessed spectacle glimpsed and applauded by most of these frail mortals is not the blinding radiance of Primal Beauty – for no such light existed in the Stoic scheme of things – but the familiar pageantry of the celestial revolutions and the consoling rejuvenation of social order generation after generation and all the other signs of Zeus' cosmic government.

Whereas Socrates looked down on the popular celebrations of the cosmic mystery dance because he considered philosophy a superior sort of initiation into divine knowledge, and Lucretius looked askance at them because he sharply distinguished the true vision of divinity provided by Epicurus from the utterly false impression of the gods conveyed by the mystagogues, the discontented spectator whom Epictetus introduces into the picture looks at the choral festival from the viewpoint of the common man – anxiously, uncertainly, as part of the crowd pressed into worshipping a god whose justice he cannot understand. He has no philosophical standpoint from which to criticize the spectacle, no dogmas on which to lean, only simple heartfelt protests against fate and mortality and the oppressiveness of the Great Chorus which were the hardest objections for a dogmatic philosopher of any school to answer. Why must he die in the dance of life? Why must he forsake his wife and children? Why did God even bother to create him? His questions strike at the central nerve of Stoic ethics, the sensitive issue of how individuals can possess moral freedom in a deterministic universe, which forces Epictetus to express the subtleties of Stoic theodicy in simple undogmatic terms. He does so, as Plotinus would later do, by drawing ethical inferences from the image of the dance. The fault-finding spectator is placed in an awkward position at the mystic rites: either he must dance along with the crowd as the procession passes by, and therefore cease to be merely a spectator; or he must leave the scene of the dance altogether, which (since the dance represented the whole of life) meant committing suicide.

Intolerable as the jostling crowded festival might become, the individual always had the option of taking his own life. God would of course prefer him to leave the dance as a 'grateful and modest spectator' who had entered into the festivities enthusiastically; but if conformity was not to the individual's liking, then he was encouraged to die by his own hand rather than crowd the cosmos and disrupt the progress of the 'synchoreuontoi.' Though the Roman Stoics reserved their highest praise for those who endured the private agonies of the dance without losing sight of its communal benefits and creative purpose, they also condoned suicide if it was committed dispassionately at an opportune moment as the last resort, the last free act, of a virtuous man. Their pragmatic take-it-or-leave-it attitude towards life was not mirthless or grim or 'stoical' in a popular sense, but it did imply that the cosmic dance was certainly nothing to get ecstatic about. Literally so: ecstasy, the Platonic experience of 'standing outside' the cave of the body and beholding the fullness of existence in the light of an eternal sun, was denied the Stoical 'choreutēs' – was an impossibility in his self-contained universe – because there was no outside for his soul to stand in and no eternal sun to light it. Bodies alone existed for him, the small shares of pitiful flesh called men within the vast rippling pulsating gesticulating body of Nature; even at death his soul could not stand outside the body since it was a corporeal entity itself and simply melted back into the great self-shaping All along with the arms and legs and organs it once controlled. Epictetus does not promise ecstasy for the 'synchoreuontoi' in his cosmic mystery dance – only existence. And existence was for a Stoic wholly dependent on participation in the artistic activity of God, even if the mode of participation was largely unconscious or subservient.

In sum, all beings in the Stoic universe were beings by virtue of God's formative presence within them. Or as this might be restated in ethical terms: all beings were beings by virtue of their acceptance and performance of divinely ordained roles in the cosmic dance. Plotinus would disagree:

All beings are beings by virtue of the One. This holds true for things that are beings in a primal sense and for things that are said in any other sense to belong to the class of beings. For what thing would exist if it were not a unity? Separated from the One, it ceases to be that which is said to be. For an army or a chorus [choros] or a flock has no existence unless it exists as a unity.

(*Ennead* 6.9.1)

By 'the One' Plotinus meant the formal cause of unity which stood outside the Great Chorus in a metaphysical sense, being absolutely indivisible, immovable, independent, inscrutable, and indispensable to the unified order of existence. The One was not a dynamic choragus like the God of Epictetus. It did not create or lead or inform the world-chorus. Yet it could be called a choragus in the special sense that it supplied the vast population of temporal and eternal beings with an immutable model of unity which allowed them to form a single chorus and dance in imitation of its transcendent presence.

Because of the One, moreover, existence became a state of ecstasy (for eternal beings) or a movement towards ecstasy (for their temporal inferiors) since every Plotinian dancer was straining to see beyond the boundaries of the dance, to reach the perfect stillness at the end of things. The function of philosophy as Plotinus conceived it was not to calm nerves but to stimulate vision. By a creative act of the visual imagination he would fuse the Stoic vision of the sympathetic chorus with the Socratic vision of the ecstatic chorus in order to turn spectators who might easily despise the dance and dancers who might simply endure it into true 'bacchoi.'

Not every Roman Stoic would agree with Epictetus the slave that spectators who chose to remain in the cosmic festival had to applaud the dance because it would inevitably engulf and overpower them, and to respect God because his power over their lives and the lives of their families was that of a benevolent governor over the destiny of an enslaved populace. One who looked down at life from the throne of Caesar refused to be overpowered by the spectacle, and offered this advice to others who wished to avoid enslavement:

If you were to analyse a melody into its various notes and in each case ask yourself whether you are inferior to it, you would surely recoil from admitting that it overpowered you. Consequently you will regard the delightful art of song with contempt. The same holds true of the art of dancing [orchēseōs]. Were you to analyse each movement and pose, you would feel superior to the dance and so despise it. So too with the art of wrestling. In sum, except for virtue and those things that spring from virtue, remember to run over the component parts of things in your mind and by analysis come to despise them. Consider song, dance, wrestling as metaphors for life as a whole, and bring the same analytic process to bear on life also.

(*Meditations* XI.2)

After the flood of chatty cajoling questions by which Epictetus expressed his resolutely optimistic theodicy, the terse statements of the Stoical emperor Marcus Aurelius come like splashes of icy rainwater: at first they startle: then they invigorate: at length they numb.

The terseness of his prose style is not in itself startling, since his meditations were probably jotted down hastily at odd moments between 172 and

180 AD, when the emperor was busy defending the northern boundaries of the Empire, touring the eastern provinces with his ailing wife Faustina, and securing the succession of his ne'er-do-well son Commodus. He was also laconic by choice, having rejected the florid Attic eloquence of the Sophists in favour of the plain expository style of the Stoics when he was about twenty-five years of age. At this turning-point in his intellectual life (c146–7) he was 'converted' from rhetoric to philosophy by a circle of eminent Roman Stoics including his law-tutor Rusticus who introduced him to the *Discourses* of Epictetus. These became his Bible. They provided a foundation for his own not particularly original though often arrestingly candid reflections on the vanity of human wishes, the transitoriness of earthly life, and the supremacy of the Divine Will, and few would be the soliloquies he later penned as an aging war-weary emperor between battles on the shores of the Danube that did not echo the pragmatic consolations of the Phrygian slave.

That is just what is startling about his meditations: despite their often religious tone and the omnipresent influence of Epictetus they are not very consoling. Epictetus can be sobering to read, but he is rarely glum. Marcus, however, will talk himself into a state of morbid melancholy or complete contempt for the world without knowing how to cure himself, without assuming that a cure exists. Inclined to see life more as a wrestling-match than a triumphal march, he constantly tried to gain the upper hand in a struggle against his passions and vices, and against the perversity of human nature itself, which he knew was as futile as his struggle against the northern barbarians. He set himself impossible goals to which no ordinary Stoic would have aspired: to be completely unworldly as supreme ruler of the civilized world and to achieve otherworldliness without believing in an afterlife or a reality beyond the World of Becoming. Had Epictetus been alive during Marcus' reign, he would no doubt have been moved (either to tears or to laughter) to see his noble disciple striving in vain to become a Platonic philosopher-king within the intellectually constricting mould of a Stoical Sage.

The mould inevitably cracked, though it did not break, and Marcus here and there in his meditations diverges from Stoic orthodoxy without ever abandoning wisdom's public portico for the private hinterlands of despair. His divergent perspective is clearly marked for instance in the unusual way he compares life as a whole to the arts of song, dance, and wrestling in XI.2. Epictetus and the Stoics before him, as we have seen, employed such comparisons to reconcile the fault-finding spectator with the complex and easily misunderstood spectacle of social and cosmic change, to assure him that life had its rules and that its rules were just and that the justness of the cosmic administration was a reflection of Zeus the All-Powerful. Marcus sounds very much like them in his analysis of the power of the individual parts within an artistic whole and his recommendation of 'virtue and those things that spring from virtue'; but the whole point of his comparison, the unorthodox point, is that one should become an expert spectator of life in order to feel superior to the spectacle and 'so despise it.'

The emperor justified his contempt for the dance (and the corporeal vice-tainted life it represented) on the rather dubious grounds that expert knowledge of 'orchēsis' inevitably endowed the critical observer with a certain power over the 'orchēstēs' – the power to remain unaffected, unmoved, by displays of sensuous beauty or physical strength. Apathy rather than ecstasy was his goal as a spectator. In order to achieve this special 'unfeelingness,' an ascetic invulnerability to disruptive passions which was the moral opposite of its native virtues, and so no art but the art of wisdom was ultimately of any value or concern to the Stoical Sage. Music and dance, once the Olym-his aesthetic and tragic sensibilities. Pleasure, pity, terror, or any other emotional reaction to the cosmic pantomime could only distract the philosophical soul from its proper enterprise, which was to perfect the harmony of its native virtues, and so no art but the art of wisdom was ultimately of any value or concern to the Stoical Sage. Music and dance, once the Olympian arts of harmony, fell into the same category of 'art' in its unexalted technical sense as the brutal sport of the pancratium, a combination of wrestling and boxing; as a metaphor for life the pancratium obviously implied a violent power struggle underlying the superficial regulation of move and countermove. But so too, in a different way, did the arts of harmony: for anyone intent on achieving Stoic apathy, listening to a song or watching a dance became a test of virtue and a clash of wills.

The Stoical Spectator pitted his will against the will of the artist. He was trained to attack what the artist presented to his senses with all his analytical powers, to tear it apart note by note or pose by pose in order to prove its fragility. His aggressively intellectual approach to musical or visual harmonies was essentially defensive, for he dreaded the prospect of surrendering himself to the potentially corrupting influence of the melody or the dance before he could bring himself to despise them. The distinction drawn by Marcus Cato between the performing arts and 'the art of living wisely' broadens into a dichotomy in the Stoicism of Marcus Aurelius, even as 'the art of living wisely' dwindles into the sombre business of learning how to die with Socratic impassivity. 'One's readiness to die must be calculated and dignified,' he reflected in XI.3, 'and should have nothing tragic or theatrical about it if it is to persuade others.' Life as a whole might be no more than role-playing in the social theatre, an inconsequential pantomime, but death was the one pose that every man, emperor or slave, would strike in earnest.

Though the philosopher-king earnestly steeled himself during the long years of his Danube campaigns to die an exemplary Stoic death without the religious certainty that dying was a mystic passage into a new life, he had himself and Commodus initiated at Eleusis in 176 – he took no chances – after founding chairs of philosophy for each of the major schools, Stoic, Epicurean, Academic, and Peripatetic, at the University of Athens.

Though Plotinus evidently read and cited the *Discourses* of Epictetus, his familiarity with the soliloquies of Marcus Aurelius is difficult to establish. He may not have known of their existence. Still, in 4.4.33, he momentarily observes the dance in precisely the way Marcus advised, assuming the viewpoint of a critical expert who can explain why one limb is raised in a particular pose while another is lowered and why the dancer 'does not choose to perform the dance in any other way.' Like Marcus he breaks the flow of the performance down into a sequence of discrete steps and poses, demands that each movement further the dance-play towards its conclusion, and brings the same analytical process to bear on life as a whole. But does this process turn Plotinus into an apathetic spectator whose only concern is his readiness for death and the enhancement of his personal integrity? Is contempt for the harmony of life his immediate philosophical goal? Analytical observation most certainly does not lead him (as it led Marcus) to despise the dance *in itself*; on the contrary, it deepens his appreciation of the delicate interaction of parts within the artistic whole and stimulates his interest in the inner life, the contemplative yearnings, of the dancer. If he had any disdain for the dance and other visual arts, it was for the following reason:

As arts of imitation, painting, sculpture, pantomimic dancing and hand-gesturing [orchēsis te kai cheironomia] are all closely tied to the world of the senses. They use models found in that world, imitate shapes and movements, and reproduce visible symmetries.

But since the visual arts were not necessarily confined to the lower order of existence they were not always contemptible. They could be turned into arts of true vision, intellectual vision, if the artist chose to imitate the transcendent causes of beauty and harmony and if the spectator strove to comprehend the guiding visionary instinct – the logos – behind the artist's choice of forms, movements, symmetries. For, as Plotinus went on to explain,

if it were not for the rational principle in man, these arts probably would not be led up to that other world – the intelligible realm. If one were to turn from the symmetry of individual living things and observe the condition of life as a whole, one would gain some of the power which up there, in the intelligible realm, observes and contemplates the symmetry reigning among all things.

(*Ennead* 5.9.11)

Of course not all dancers were inclined to contemplate the World of Being or to enhance the visionary powers of their spectators, but the cosmic 'orchēstēs' was – indeed had to be – since the only external models the Living Being could imitate existed in the order of intelligible reality.

Analysing the poses in the pantomime became an anagogic experience for the Plotinian spectator: his intellect was inevitably 'led up to that other world' in the process of understanding the dancer's mystical motivations. Thus, where Marcus had scrutinized the pantomime for fear of losing his powers of detachment, Plotinus observed it with rapt and appreciative attention in the hope of gaining superhuman powers of vision through total sympathy with the will of the dancer. Only when he contrasted the Many bound together in the dance with the isolated motionless One, whose state of perfect repose and indivisibility was the conclusion towards which every movement of the Living Being was directed, would Plotinus allow himself to regard the harmony of life with sagacious (but never priggish) contempt.

The Cynical Spectator

Porphyry reports that Plotinus did not always make the logical coherence of his thoughts absolutely clear during his lectures and did not care to simplify his complex responses to the arguments of his professional rivals, adding in his mentor's defence that he was 'completely free of the theatricality and long-winded rant of the Sophists' (*Vita Plotini* 18). This remark is evidently meant to prepare the discriminating reader for the jolt of Plotinus' prose style, which is indeed rather awkward and conversational in comparison with the gilded Attic periods of the imperial orators; but it may also be taken as a commendatory reference to the originality and seriousness of the sage's teachings. Plotinus must not be mistaken for a mouther of philosophical clichés or a mocker of the old philosophy. He actually respected the intellectual optimism of the ancients and had something new and positive to say about the unity of everything under the sun, or rather under the One, something that no histrionic orator could have invented since it was revealed to his exceptionally penetrating intellect (Porphyry claimed) through divine inspiration. Nevertheless, those who were unable to follow his inspired thoughts and envied his just reputation for sagacity had the nerve to call him 'a great babbler' – the usual insult hurled at all academic philosophers by the arch-debunkers of the ancient world, the Cynics, and by the Greco-Roman Sophists who helped to revive Cynicism as a mock-serious philosophical response to chaos in the cosmic theatre.

Diogenes of Sinope, the reputed founder of the Cynic sect, left little behind him after his death (c320 BC) save the memory of his eccentric vagabondish personality, which would become the model of the establishment-spurning Cynical Sage, and perhaps also a number of tragedies and dialogues on ethical themes which have since been lost. The few fragments remaining of the works of his follower Bion of Borysthenes indicate that the serious common-sense tone of Diogenes the moralist and tragedian was sustained in the Cynic literature of the early third century BC. Bion compared life to a festival which men must be prepared to leave, an athletic contest in which they must struggle for survival, and a drama for which they must learn many roles.[12] These Cynic metaphors would reappear in the writings of the Roman Stoics, particularly Epictetus, sometimes in combination with the image of the cosmic dance. No evidence has survived to indicate that Bion himself compared life specifically to a dance rather than a drama, but that he did so, given his dynamic vision of celebration and conflict in the theatre of the world, is not unlikely.

Bion's contemporary, Menippus of Gadara, seems to have been the first Cynic to popularize the sharply critical yet bemused and sad-clownish attitude towards life that is still implicit in the non-technical sense of the word 'cynical.' He combined 'spoudaia' with 'geloia' – 'serious writings' with 'jests' – to produce the sect's characteristic literary form: the mock-serious diatribe or 'spoudaiogeloion.' All but the titles of most works in the Menippean corpus are now lost, though their contents can be reconstructed in part from scattered allusions and quotations in the works of Greco-Roman Sophists. Many of his 'spoudaiogeloia' seem to have been parodies of Platonic dialogues, and one can only suppose that he also debunked Plato's optimistic myths of enlightenment and metaphors of cosmic order. A stray comment in the encyclopaedic dialogue of the rhetorician Athenaeus (fl200 AD) indicates how Menippus might have reduced the image of the cosmic dance to absurdity:

In his 'Symposium' Menippus the Cynic calls to mind another dance called 'The Conflagration of the World' [allē orchēsis kosmou ekpyrōsis].
(*Deipnosophistae* XIV.629)

Why he called this dance to mind is not entirely clear. Athenaeus assumed that he was referring to an actual Greek folk-dance called 'kosmou ekpyrōsis,' which is not all that strange a title for a dance in light of some of the other vaguely cosmological titles (for example, 'stoicheia,' 'The Elements') listed in the same section of Athenaeus' rambling survey of the performing arts. But 'ekpyrōsis' was a technical term in Stoic physics, signifying the periodic destruction of Nature by the very fire which normally gave it life, shaped its body, provided its energy. Might the theory of world-conflagration have been the subject of Menippus' discourse rather than the naming of Greek folk-dances? Could he have been poking fun at the Stoics by pointing out the ironies in their vision of the best of all possible worlds? If as a jest some (no doubt drunken) speaker at the Cynic's symposium had compared the conflagration of the world to a dance, he would have totally reversed the usual cosmological implications of the image – turning cosmos into chaos, creative metamorphosis into cataclysm. The Cynics were notorious in Antiquity for jeering at philosophers who babbled about the beginning and end of the universe but ignored the basic Socratic questions of what virtue was and how man could train himself to attain it.

No Sophist in the era of Marcus Aurelius took greater delight in ridiculing the great babblers in all the philosophical schools than Lucian of Samosata, who discovered the satires of 'the mocker of mankind' (as Marcus called Menippus in *Meditations* VI.47) while studying philosophy in Athens around 156 AD. Lucian never became an out-and-out Cynic like his predecessor Dio Chrysostom, but he modelled many of his satiric diatribes on the 'spoudaiogeloia' of Menippus and recommended the Cynic's lively wit to his Roman audiences as an antidote to the deadly earnestness of the dogmatic philosophers. He also introduced Menippus into several of his best-known dialogues as a commentator on the vices of civilization, and so, despite the regrettable loss of the Menippean corpus, something of the historical Cynic's laughter may still be heard in the maliciously witty speeches of his literary avatar.

In the following speech Menippus tells a friend how, having flown up to the heavens on Icarus-wings amputated from an eagle and a vulture, he suddenly acquired aquiline powers of sight which allowed him to look down on the comic theatre of earth and observe the farcical performance of the human chorus:

You can imagine how jumbled the earth looked with all those activities going on at the same time! It was as if someone had put on the stage a great many choral dancers and singers or rather a great many choruses [pollous choreutas, mallon de pollous chorous], and then ordered each of the singers to abandon harmony and to sing a melody of his own. Now, with each one competing for honour and performing his own song and striving to sing louder than his neighbour, what, by god, do you suppose the song would be like?

His friend replies that it would seem utterly ludicrous and confused. Lucian has Menippus push the metaphor further:

Well, my friend, such are all the choristers on earth [hoi epi gēs choreutai] and of such discord is the life of man composed! Not only do they sing discordant tunes, but they also strike different poses in the dance [ta schēmata]

*and move at cross-purposes and agree on nothing until the choragus drives
each of them off the stage, saying that he has no further use for them. After
that, however, they are all alike, all silent, no longer singing that disorderly
medley of theirs. But everything that took place in the theatre itself, with its
varied and ever-shifting scenes, was truly laughable!*

(*Icaromenippus* 17)

The mockery here is not vapid persiflage. It is cutting, severe, relentless –
the booing and hissing of a Socrates gone mad in a universe of fools.

As a parody of the Platonic-Stoic topos of the perfectly harmonious and
happily governed chorus, the passage seems at first to be pure 'geloion': if
anything in life's shifting scenes was guaranteed to make the Cynical Spectator laugh, it was the sight of men competing for 'timē' – 'honour' – the
worthless praise bestowed by society on those who perpetuated its vice-
ridden institutions and willingly conformed to the roles assigned them. As
an elaboration of the Cynic topos of the world-theatre, however, the speech
turns out to be rather more 'spoudaion' than one might have expected.
Instead of placidly reflecting (in the manner of Bion) on the necessity for
each man to sing many different notes and strike many different poses
skilfully during life, Menippus contemplates the stillness and silence of death
and the futility of all social actions, honourable or dishonourable, skilfully
executed or stupidly fumbled, in a world tyrannized by Fate. As the imperious choragus who drives the dancers out of the theatre when they can
no longer serve his mysterious, and apparently not very artistic, purpose,
Fate casts a dark shadow across the comic stage. Only in death, ironically,
are the choristers fated to achieve the concordant unity their chorus was
supposed to represent in life. Death comes as an aesthetic relief – or so it
seems to the Cynical Spectator – after the cacophony and commotion of the
dance.

Menippus can laugh at the disorderly medley of life and appreciate the
austere aesthetics of death because he has acquired the two virtues held in
highest esteem by the Cynics: 'autarkeia,' a combination of self-sufficiency,
independence of spirit, and ascetic renunciation of the values and comforts
of civilization, which is vividly represented in Lucian's fable by the astronomical distance separating the Cynical Spectator from the chorus of world-
lings; and 'apatheia,' its complement, an insensitivity to the blows of Fate
which resulted not from intellectual analysis of the poses and melodies of
the world-chorus (like the apathy esteemed by the Stoics) but from emotional
and physical resistance to the pressures of social conformity. The Cynical
Spectator looked down on the dance for reasons quite different from those
of his Stoical and Epicurean counterparts. Whereas Marcus Aurelius felt
superior to it because as an artistic whole it could be reduced to a predictable

and thus rather boring sequence of minute corporeal movements which, taken individually, posed no threat to the harmony of his inner life, Icaromenippus (as Lucian calls his winged satiric persona) wastes no time trying to discern a system of intelligible 'schēmata' in what appears to him, from his lofty vantage-point, to be a spectacularly inartistic muddle.

The Cynical Spectator sees no dance at all from the perspective of the whole – merely the pretence of a dance. Earthly life is a jumble of many different choruses moving at cross-purposes and many different choristers subverting whatever unity might once have existed in human society. To the deluded multitude down below who see life only from the perspective of the part yet fondly believe, as they compete for honour, that their miserable self-centred little lives all fit into some grand imperial, cosmic, and divine order, the metaphor of the chorus might still have meaning. But not to the Cynical Spectator: Icaromenippus uses his eagle eyes to perceive the bleak truth behind the theatrical illusions of order which the Greeks, and then the Romans, had mistaken for reality. And when those same unblinking eyes are turned on the exalted order of the gods, it too proves a sham. In contrast to Lucretius, who despised the dance as a religious rite because it conveyed a false impression of the transcendent serenity and stability of the gods, the Cynical Spectator perceives the divine chorus as an absurd projection, a grotesque counterpart, of the rabble in the sublunary theatre. Emblematic of the society of the gods as seen through Cynical eyes is the last dance Icaromenippus glimpses in Zeus' banquet hall before swooping down to earth on his unmeltable wings. At the climax of the banquet Silenus performs the 'kordax' – the wildly indecorous phallus-flaunting dance of the Old Comedy.[13]

Lucian's Menippean diatribes leave one with a strong impression that the Cynics had lost all faith in philosophical education as a means of promoting social harmony and inevitably recoiled from comparing their intensely individualistic style of ethical training to the training of a competitive urban chorus. This view is not without historical support. Since many members of the sect, especially in Lucian's day, led mendicant lives in imitation of Diogenes, they were disinclined to organize themselves into a philosophical 'school' comparable to the Academy, the Porch, and the Garden, or to organize their doctrines into a coherent system of physics, logic, and ethics. (Physics and logic they usually dismissed as superfluous to the welfare of the individual.) The literary Cynicism of Lucian, however, must be distinguished from the historical protest movement of the same name. Lucian's attitude towards education and the cultural pretensions of imperial society was far closer to sterile pessimism than to the ascetic philosophy of Diogenes and his disciples, which was originally motivated by an urgent – and positive – desire for social reform, and by an ardent belief that such reform could be effected if individuals were to return to a simple unfettered way of life. Diogenes may have disliked the Greek city-states, but he chose to live and teach in their public squares.

A distinctively Cynic version of the analogy between paideia and choreia is preserved in one of the many didactic epigrams attributed to him by his biographer and namesake Diogenes Laertius, a contemporary of Plotinus:

Diogenes used to say that he imitated the trainers of choruses [tous chorod-idaskalous]: for they too pitch their note too high so that the rest may hit the right note.

(Lives VI.35)

This saying is probably apocryphal, but it 'hits the right note' as the sort of remark any serious proponent of Cynicism might have made in defence of the shameless incivility, theatrical contrariness, and other pedagogical tactics of the Cynical Sage. Diogenes did not expect or desire his chorus, the crowds in the marketplace, to model their lives exactly on his; he did not order the Athenian public to abandon harmony in the name of anarchy and to dance to their own music without paying attention to the performance of their neighbours. That was what they were already doing, after all, in their vain competition for honour and renown in the social theatre. True social harmony might only be achieved, ironically, if they were all to behave a little less like socially acceptable choristers and a little more like self-sufficient individuals. In contrast to the Stoical Sage, who, detesting the-atricality, strove to blend his harmonious and compliant character into a greater harmony, society, and into the greatest harmony, Nature, so that his art of living wisely and dying calmly might recommend itself to the rest of the human chorus, the Cynical Sage deliberately exaggerated his abrasive individuality, made a public spectacle of himself wherever he wandered, and proclaimed with raucous insistence that he was a citizen of no city but Cosmopolis – the City of the World.

In his outward life, at least, Plotinus assumed the role of a Stoic rather than a Cynic. He was anything but a social misfit or a spurner of civilization or a cosmopolitan beggar. While Cynics from Diogenes down to the exiled Dio Chrysostom typically treated all political leaders (especially emperors) with contempt, Plotinus welcomed members of the Roman Senate to his lectures and had an admiring friend in the Emperor Gallienus. As a teacher he was assertive but untheatrical, and as a friend critical but kind-hearted. Though the Roman Stoics found the antic behaviour and tattered appearance of the mendicant Cynic offensive, they tended to admire the self-sufficiency and inner freedom which were the rewards of Cynic asceticism. The ideal

Stoic, preached Epictetus, was a true Cynic in his inner life.[14] And in his inner life Plotinus was to renounce the vices of this world with the asperity, and to endure his exile from 'that other world' with the apathy, of a true Cynic.

That he should betray in his own pages a certain sympathy for the individualistic bias of the Cynical 'chorodidaskalos' is not surprising, therefore, in view of his strong intellectual ties with the Roman Stoics. 'Choral dancers,' he observed in 3.6.2,

dance and sing in harmony with each other [choreutai choreuontes kai synaidontes allēlois] even if the same ones do not always do the singing and one sometimes sings while the others are silent. Each one sings in his own way. For not only is it necessary that they sing together but also that each one sing his own part beautifully according to his own personal skill in music. Similarly, there is a harmony in the soul when each part is doing what befits it. Yes, indeed; but this same harmony must depend on something that precedes it, the virtue of each part of the soul.

Choral harmony, as he perceived it, was a unity that presupposed and subsumed – but did not annihilate – diversity. It grew out of the individuality of the choristers, was an effect of their varied skills and artistic virtues, and was a voluntary response to something beyond them all rather than an inevitable condition of existence imposed on them by society or the gods or Fate. Wherever such harmony prevailed, in a human chorus, in a virtuous soul, in a band of living stars, each contributor to its unrepressive order recognized the uniqueness of 'his own part' and performed it 'in his own way.'

Two conditions had to be met, however, before choral harmony could flow from such independent sources. First, the choristers had to agree that they would sing and dance together as one chorus; and second, they all had to be moved by instinct, by reason, or by inspiration to perform as beautifully as their personal skills in the arts of harmony permitted. These were precisely the two conditions that were not met in the Menippean world-theatre. Icaromenippus saw a mob of choristers trying to be soloists, each striving to sing louder than his neighbour, and a mayhem of independent actions motivated not by a communal sense of beauty but by a divisive craving for honour. Plotinus was too much of a Stoic to be that pessimistic about society, and too much of a Platonist to be that insensitive to beauty and the love awakened by beauty as primary motivations in the dance of life. His defence of the dance in 3.6.2 followed from his unshakable belief that choral harmony prevails in this world because each chorister is divinely moved 'to extract vice if it exists in his soul, and to instil virtue, and to set his soul in order by producing beauty in it where previously there had been ugliness.'

The Pantomime of Eros

Images of cosmic order, like scientific models, are no more than approximations of the true nature of things. To see nature as a chain, a mirror, a lyre, or a dance is inevitably to reduce an enormous blur of particles and people and planets to the sharp outlines of a few familiar forms, but those forms of course are not to be equated with the unimaginable diversity of things they represent. If they were so equated, they would become unimaginable too and would simply vanish into the blur, losing with their visual definition their usefulness as stimuli of perception and comprehension. Such images may, however, be identified – very loosely or very closely, as the viewer of the blur pleases – with whatever is out there whirling before his eyes, with nature as a whole or in part, so that the diverse elements and activities in the blur seem to conform to some readily intelligible design or to fall into place within a coherent structure definable in mathematical terms. The links in the chain of being may be numbered from the First Cause down through the multiplicity of its effects; the reflections in the mirror of creation may be arranged with the strictest regard for symmetry; the lyre of the eight heavens may be tuned according to simple Pythagorean ratios; and the configurations of the dancing stars may be drawn with a set of compasses. Like scientific models, images of cosmic order undergo continuous revision and refinement. The pictures of time and space they present to the viewer's inner eye may be drastically modified to suit new theories of the physical world and may even be subject to empirical investigation.

However, while scientific models are happily forgotten when new models are devised which can explain a wider range of phenomena in fewer and simpler terms than their predecessors, images of cosmic order are passed on from generation to generation in the expectation of their eternal validity. The chain of being, the mirror of creation, the music of the spheres, and the dance of life may all fade for a time from scientific consciousness, but some trace of them always lingers on the poetic and philosophical palimpsest of our culture which prevents their disappearance into the void of skepticism. Like mirages these images may be only illusions, easily seen through, but they have long assured us that behind their alluring sheen lies a permanent basis for our visions of order and an end to the bleak deserts of scientific uncertainty. The dance of the stars was an optical illusion of this sort: a trompe-l'oeil concealing perhaps a true vision of world-harmony. Knowing now (or thinking that we know) that the sun and stars do not revolve around the earth, we can easily dismiss the image of the cosmic dance as a vain fantasy. Now, though our eyes were for many centuries fooled by the very light which stimulates our vision, we are all Heracleides Ponticus and can all see straight through the mirage. But the planets still move, the stars still move, the human mind in its own way still moves. Perhaps still in harmony. Long after the scientific model of the armillary universe was discarded in favour of new paradigms, the image of the cosmic dance continued to inspire poets and philosophers with its optimistic prospects of order within and beyond the blur.

Though images of cosmic order can be consciously transmitted from one culture to another, as was the vision of the cosmic chorus by the missionaries of Greek education, they need not be and in certain instances cannot have been diffused in this manner. They seem to share with the paradigms of Jungian dream psychology a remarkable tendency to surface in the religious and philosophical thought of widely divergent cultures without any sign of pedagogical transmission. Jung hypothesized that every human being in-herits from his ancestors certain primordial symbolic images or 'archetypes' which serve as the raw materials in the unconscious creative processes in his psyche, and which might be detected in the recurrent motifs of Eastern and Western mythologies and in the patterns of dream symbols common to primitive and civilized men. These archetypes of the Collective Unconscious, he contended, reflect the persistent substructure of human consciousness but reveal nothing at all about the objective world of stones and stars. They are always current in the wellspring of the imagination, at the source of dreams, and so escape the rigidity and obsolescence that seem to befall scientific models of the universe. Might all the visions of the cosmic dance behind and before us be variations on a single archetypal theme of order latent in the depths of humanity's ever-primitive tribal soul?

An absurd and unanswerable question this may be, but it is not a question to be begged. There *is* a persistently mystical – and mysterious – side (or centre?) to the image which cannot be explained away as an effect of vague unscientific thinking, and which certainly sets it apart from any scientific model of objective reality, such as Ptolemy's concentric spheres, with which it happens at any moment in its history to be associated. One can construct and analyse and test the accuracy of an armillary sphere, but one cannot participate in it. It is always distinct from the spectators of the cosmos, even as the circles of the heavens are distinct from it. But the cosmic dance impels, uplifts, illuminates, terrifies, calms, inspires, involves its spectators, for as in a dream they can be both watching its unfolding design from an objective distance and participating subjectively in its symbolic action.

The names Jung bestowed upon his archetypes – Anima, Animus, Earth-Mother, Shadow – sound very much like epithets of the gods and goddesses worshipped in Late Antique mystery religions, which is perhaps not sur-prising in view of Jung's own avowal that he borrowed the term 'archetype' from pagan authors of the second and third centuries AD.[15] To the shadowy pantheon of the Collective Unconscious one might be tempted to add Eros and his twin sister Orchesis, the apotheosis of the dance. The archetypal character of the latter was the subject of the following magniloquent eulogy by (of all Late Antique pagans) Lucian of Samosata:

Now, those who most truthfully record the genealogy of Orchesis will tell you that she sprang up at the same moment that the universe came into being, blazing into sight with that primeval love, Eros. Indeed, the choral dance of the stars [choreia tōn asterōn], the interweaving of the planets with the fixed stars, their rhythmic partnership and well-ordered harmony – these are signs proving the illustrious birth of Orchesis. Having grown up little by little, always improving with each new addition, she would now seem to have reached the height of perfection, and to have become a richly diversified, wholly harmonious, and multi-talented delight.

(*The Pantomime* 7)

Away with the mask of Menippus! Proteus-like, Lucian assumes for his dialogue *The Pantomime* (sometimes given the misleadingly general title *The Dance*) the role of a connoisseur of theatrical dancing named Lycinus whose idealistic vision of world-harmony is the exact opposite of the Cynic's, and hence, in its own way, just as absurd. Lycinus is prompted to deliver a compendious lecture in praise of the pseudo-Hesiodic goddess Orchesis by his rather priggish friend Crato, who has been scolding him for wasting so much time in the theatre. His speech on the divine genealogy of Orchesis opens the lecture on a note of exaggerated reverence and enthusiasm, and he proceeds from there to heap extravagant praises on the unpraiseworthy (a typical rhetorical exercise of the Sophists) by reeling off a long list of Olympian and Asiatic deities who have contributed to the development of his favourite art.

Instead of viewing the cosmic dance in a Platonic light as a sign of the Craftsman's rationality, Lycinus sees it as the expression of a primitive physical instinct latent in the cosmos, an instinct older than reason and spontaneous rather than systematic in its operations: 'that primeval love, Eros.' The Eros he has in mind is not the mischievous arrow-shooting child of Aphrodite but the august pre-Olympian deity whom Hesiod celebrated in the *Theogony* (116–22) as the eldest of the gods and the principle of union in nature. While the dance born with Eros produced the 'rhythmic part-nership' of the stars and planets and the 'well-ordered harmony' of the sublunary realm, its unitive energies sprang from Love's dark unfathomable father, Chaos, whose creative urges were sudden and inexplicable and whose primordial act was not to think in orderly numbered steps like Plato's Crafts- man but to overflow and generate. The pantomime of Eros cannot be re- garded as simply a cosmic dance. It was in the beginning and remains essentially a cosmogonic movement. It is the push and struggle of life coming into being as well as the harmonious disposition of living creatures already in existence. Though its dazzling first episode was the formation of the astral chorus, it is no longer simply a circular dance periodically ending where it began and beginning again without varying its configurations. The goddess Orchesis delights her spectators by the surprising variety of her steps, her unexpected metamorphoses, her inventiveness. She represents a progressive movement within Nature's invariable cycles – the gradual sophistication of dancing as a human art. Having grown up little by little and improved herself as she matured, Orchesis has at last realized all her potential for aesthetic refinement in the mythological dance-plays of the Greco-Roman stage.

If a modern balletomane were to claim that all celestial movements from time immemorial anticipated and culminated in the ballet season at his local theatre, his view of the world would be no less absurdly distorted by his passion for the dance than that of his second-century counterpart Lycinus. Lucian has trivialized the Platonic analogy between dancing and cosmic order by exaggerating their similarity and reversing the terms of the comparison. Cosmic order has become a metaphorical image expressing the artistic com- plexity and divine mystery of the dance – rather than the other way round! The relative values of image and reference have also been reversed in this sophistic conceit. While a serious Platonic spectator would have regarded theatrical dancing as an imperfect imitation of the celestial rounds, Lycinus presumptuously perceives the interweaving of the stars and planets as a primitive stage in the development of the erotic pantomime.

Crato is Lucian's caricature of the moralizing Stoical Spectator. Dismayed that his once studious friend should be 'oblivious to Plato and Chrysippus and Aristotle' and drawn towards effeminate male dancers pranked up like 'love-lorn trollops,' he complains in his first speech that the decent and comely choral dances of the ancient Greeks have given way to the salacious writhings of the Roman mimes and that this change in fashion proves that the art of dancing has declined since its inception rather than improved (as Lycinus claimed) 'little by little.' The dancer Lycinus saw as the supreme product of Greek philosophical education Crato portrays as a vulgar artiste whose popularity depended on his ability to combine the low talents of a contortionist, a story-teller, a buffoon, a female impersonator, and a male prostitute. Orchesis was no goddess in his opinion. She was a strumpet. And if her command of the stage in their day reflected anything about the world, it was the disorder into which imperial society was surely slipping through its disrespect for the high ideals of classical culture and its tolerance of the very lowest kinds of erotic entertainment.

The debate between Lycinus and Crato is sparked by the comic challenge of persuading a dance-despising Stoic to worship the Dance – a challenge roughly equivalent in difficulty to convincing a Puritan of the spiritual benefits of pornography. Lycinus' rhapsody on the cosmic manifestations of Eros and Orchesis must be read within the satiric framework of the debate as a momentarily bathetic rebuttal of Crato's harrumphing remarks on the degeneration of civilized society and not as a sublime variation on an archetypal theme of order reflecting the world-view of Lucian or his audience. Still, *within* that debate, Lycinus manages to defend his vision of Orchesis with such fervour and with such a profusion of learned arguments that when Crato admits in the end that his opponent might well have a point, the reader too, if he is inclined to be a Crato, might be inclined to agree that the erotic pantomime does indeed awaken in the souls of its spectators an archetypal vision of world-harmony implanted there by the eldest of the gods.

If the recurrence of similar mythological figures and symbols in the iconography of completely independent or adjacent but insular cultures may be taken as a sign that humanity is united psychically by a common ground of unconscious subjective experience and that sunk deep in that ground is a collective dream-glimpsed treasury of archetypal images, as Jung contended, then perhaps the image of the cosmic dancer – call him Eros or Nature or Shiva – belongs to this atavistic treasury and flickers through the consciousness of the captives in the cave not because of what they once saw in the sun but because of what they once buried in the darkness. Though a Skeptic might easily halt this Jungian train of thought by inquiring how anyone could consciously prove anything about what is by definition unconscious, he would be hard pressed to deny that visions of Eros and Orchesis have (in one form or another) surfaced in cultures both Eastern and Western and figured in literatures both ancient and modern. The Indians, as Lycinus points out to Crato,

face the sunrise and salute the sun with a pantomimic dance [orchēsei], posing themselves in silence and imitating the choral dance of the god [tēn choreian tou theou].

(The Pantomime 17)

Praising the pious Indians for participating in the ritual play of their deity, Lycinus notes a similarity between their exotic custom and religious dances in his own culture and concludes that all men have certain ritualistic and artistic inclinations in common. Dance, he instructs Crato, is the art that most clearly illustrates the universality of those inclinations. It calls into play man's most elementary artistic medium, his own body, and expresses through its silent poses his inborn desire for participation in the rhythmic life of the cosmos.

The Indian counterpart of Lycinus' cosmic 'orchēstēs,' Shiva, was given the title 'Nataraja' or 'Lord of the Dance' when he brought the creative and destructive forces of the universe into harmonious balance by dancing on the golden summit of Mount Meru at the world's centre, surrounded by an aureole of flames. The crescent moon shone as an ornament in his headdress, and the stars were the sparkles scattered by his jewelled and braided locks as he twirled them in his violent dance, the 'tandava,' their cascades shimmering down to earth as the purifying waters of the Ganges. A stanza from a Sanskrit poem of benediction (anthologized in the late eleventh century AD but probably written several centuries earlier) evokes the tempestuous rhythms of Shiva's mountain-revel:

> May the god of tangled locks protect you,
> at whose dance of madness in the fullmoon twilight
> the golden mountain sways with leaping woods,
> as sway the sun and moon, to the rhythmic motion;
> as if the earth, of head resplendent,
> with hair and earrings flying,
> did nod in admiration.
> (Vidyākara's *Subhāṣitaratnakoṣa*, sec 4, st 52)

Another stanza from the same anthology conveys an even more dazzling impression of the cosmic 'tandava':

> May the graceful dance of the moon-crested god protect you,
> who whirls about by the wind of his ever circling arms
> a firewheel made of fierce-rayed stars;
> a dance at which the earth sinks, fire flames, and all the
> mountains leap,
> his headdress shakes, the moon within it flashes,
> out shoots his eye-flame and the Ganges stream
> thunders in steep cascade.
> (sec 4, st 58)[16]

The Hindu poets' conception of Shiva's elemental dance of whirlwinds, firestorms, waterfalls, and earthquakes may have originated in pre-Aryan shamanistic rituals conducted in cemeteries and crematoria where some primitive death-god among the Nataraja's remote ancestors stamped his feet and whirled his terrifying arms in a nocturnal revel accompanied by capering demons.

These ecstatic movements were long afterwards incorporated into a graceful and restrained ritual, the 'nadanta' dance, performed by Shiva's worshippers in the golden hall of the temple of Chidambaram in southern India. There sculptors depicted him in his most famous guise: a four-armed dancer balancing himself on one leg while raising the other, bent at knee and ankle, before his serenely vertical torso. The five extended limbs each represented one of his divine activities. One hand held a drum symbolizing his role as the creator of rhythmic order in the material world. In the palm of another hand sprang a tongue of flame suggesting his opposite role, the destroyer, and recalling his midnight revelry over graves and burning-grounds. A third hand signified his activity as protector and preserver of the balance of nature, and a fourth, usually depicted pointing downwards to his extended foot, indicated that Shiva had veiled in illusion the base world of the senses and trapped man in the toils of cosmic causality. Salvation was the fifth of Shiva's activities: the ascending motion of his left foot represented the release of man from the Hindu cycle of reincarnation and the rise of the human soul to eternal bliss. The upturned foot therefore served to balance the lowered arm just as the hand with the drum counteracted the hand with the flame. His right foot trampled on a demon who symbolized all the evil forces hindering the soul's release. By resting this foot in the centre of the material world so that his body became the axis of that world, the Nataraja was able to maintain his buoyantly vertical poise and preserve the exquisite balance of his activities.

Shiva's dance was paradoxical in two respects. At once orderly and disorderly, it resulted in the activation of all cyclical patterns in nature yet also in the struggle of his worshippers to burst through the repressive order of his circle of fire. It was, to use Western words, a peculiar fusion of choreia and baccheia. Moreover, though the cosmic dancer seemed to those who were still bound within the world of illusions to be in perpetual motion, his dance was not really a movement at all. It was a sculptured pose. If any limb were out of place, if the left foot were not raised to meet the descending right hand, if the drum were not held far away from the fire, his dance would no longer exist as a balanced whole within the 'firewheel of fierce-rayed stars,' and the stars for all their fierceness would be extinguished on the pyre of the universe. Like primeval Eros, or like Stoic Nature with its inborn creative fire, Shiva was the binding force in all that danced out of the darkness of Chaos. No eye can peer for long at a sculpture of the Nataraja without being drawn towards the lithely erotic yet firm and immovable torso at the centre of the wheel of fire, for it is there that the pose is held and there that the god's diverse limbs with their diverse activities are bound together into a single resplendent form. [17]

Figure 7

A single dancer became the entire dance in Hinduism as in Stoicism. Cast in the
tenth century AD, this bronze from Madras (now in the Victoria and Albert Museum)
represents Shiva Nataraja triumphing over evil.

Lucian was by no means an expert in Hindu mysticism, and if he had anything more than a dim perception of the cult of the Nataraja or a superficial interest in the religious dances of the Indians he does not show it in *The Pantomime*. Still, his (or rather Lycinus') eclectic vision of Orchesis is tinged with a certain oriental exoticism that distinguishes it, as Crato rightly observed, from what the ancient Greeks saw in their theatres or in their heavens. That the Indian perception of the dance as a tumultuous release of divine energy, destroying and dispersing as well as shaping and uniting, should impinge on the choral consciousness of a Hellenized Syrian like Lucian was perhaps not extraordinary in the cosmopolitan second century, when the boundaries of the Empire stretched for a time all the way to the Persian Gulf and the memory of Alexander's foray into India was kept alive by the Sophists.

Lucian could not have read the classical Indian treatise on the dance, Bharata Muni's *Nātyaśhāstra* (written c200–100 BC), but if Sanskrit had presented no barrier to him and this remarkable text had circulated in the West in his day he would not doubt have been struck by the many similarities between Indian and Greco-Roman pantomimic technique. Bharata and Lucian both perceive the pantomime as a sequence of stylized poses in which legs and arms are symmetrically balanced, and both prescribe a rigorous literary training for the dancer who, like an actor, was required to learn a wide range of mythological roles. Bharata lists sixty-seven gestures for the hands alone and ascribes symbolic meanings to each pose.[18] In *The Pantomime* (64) Lucian recounts an anecdote from the life of the first-century Cynic Demetrius to illustrate the fascination such hand-dancing (the Greek word for which was 'cheironomia') could exert on even the most contemptuous spectators. On seeing an unaccompanied dancer mime the whole story of Aphrodite's lust for Ares, Demetrius was supposed to have called out to him at the top of his voice: 'You seem to be talking with your very hands!'

With his aversion to the flippant philosophizing and showy eloquence of the Sophists, Plotinus would not have been much inclined to read works like *The Pantomime* and is in fact not known to have read any Lucianic dialogue. Nevertheless, having been formed in the same cosmopolitan pagan cultural milieu from which Lucian drew the contrasting attitudes of Lycinus and Crato, Plotinus' attitude to 'orchēsis' as a human art (which inevitably coloured his vision of 'orchēsis' as a cosmic activity) might be conveniently summed up as falling between the unqualified approval of the idealistic spectator and the critical disdain of the moralistic spectator. His balanced view of the erotic pantomime is apparent in the following argument from his treatise 'On Providence,' which also illustrates his balanced view of Eros as a universal instinct:

Erotic lovers often destroy what they love (if the objects of their desire are mortal) in the pursuit of what they consider good, and the instinctive yearning of the part to cast itself towards or to reach out for the Whole causes it to draw to itself whatever it can. And so there are good men and wicked men, just as there are opposing characters portrayed by a pantomimic dancer [orchoumenou] in the course of his performance – characters created according to the dictates of a single art. We shall call one part of his act 'virtuous' and another part 'villainous,' and in this way his performance is held to be successful.

(*Ennead* 3.2.17)

The Eros motivating the Plotinian pantomime was something more than the 'primeval love' hymned by Hesiod and extolled by Lycinus as the principle of harmonious union in nature. It was also a principle of vision, interior vision, combined with the desire to generate images of the beauty which blazed within the cosmic dancer's soul and which inspired the procreative motions of the Living Being.

Plotinus delighted in drawing analogies between the gods of ancient Greek mythology and the gods descending from his First Cause, the One. Following Hesiod, he drew a distinction between two Aphrodites on the basis of priority and parentage. Aphrodite the elder, daughter of Cronus, he identified with a deity in the World of Being whom he regarded as the supracosmic archetype of the World-Soul and thus of every other soul, astral or human, within the cosmos, and whom he usually called Psyche. Aphrodite the younger, daughter of Zeus and Dione, he identified with the soul of the Living Being. For, he reasoned in 3.5.2, just as the second goddess of beauty could be considered morally inferior to the first because of her carnal liaison with Ares, so the World-Soul could be considered ontologically inferior to Psyche because of her union with the cosmic body. Each goddess gave birth to a son whose name, Eros, he derived from the noun 'horasis' ('an act of seeing'): an etymology which, though philologically spurious, is philosophically significant as a definition of the Plotinian concept of primeval love. The higher Eros, son of Aphrodite the elder, represented Psyche's introspective vision of the Divine Mind and her desire for mystic union with the One. The lower Eros, son of the carnal Aphrodite, symbolized the inner vision of the Living Being, its act of seeing and desiring the ideal order beyond it which resulted in a constant aspiration on its part to imitate the purely spiritual nature of Psyche. This aspiration led in turn to the constant rotation of the cosmic body, the constant revolution of the fixed stars, and the constant yearning of each member of the cosmic chorus 'to cast itself towards or to reach out for the Whole.' Thus was Orchesis born with Eros in the Plotinian universe: Lucian's genealogy of the dance would not have seemed fanciful or ludicrous to the defender of the old philosophy.

Since the Eros motivating the World-Soul was akin to the higher Eros motivating Psyche, all the lovers in the cosmic pantomime were driven by an essentially virtuous impulse which tended to lift their souls up towards immortal objects of desire. Only incidentally, in its physical manifestations, was Eros 'erotic' in a sexual or carnal sense, and only when it was completely perverted from its true nature did this low kind of love become reprehensible as a base craving for purely material objects of desire. When the Living Being imitated the constant turning of Psyche towards the One – when, in other words, the cosmic 'orchēstēs' enacted the roles of the higher Eros and the supracosmic Aphrodite – which was always, as the constant turning of all the fixed stars made clear to the Plotinian spectator, it was expressing and participating in a beauty superior to the visible world: it was not enacting a lewd and ignoble story like the bawdy tale that the human 'orchēstēs,' pranked up like the other Aphrodite, mimed for Demetrius the Cynic in Lucian's anecdote. Observed through Plotinian eyes, which were not the eyes of a Cynical Spectator, the pantomime of Eros was an undeniably successful performance – its virtuous and villainous parts being all worthy of applause when considered from the perspective of the whole.

Attracted by the harmony of the whole design, the Plotinian spectator would reawaken his inborn knowledge of the archetypal beauty of Psyche and experience a strong erotic urge to participate in its transcendent order; as a result he would begin to moderate his daily life according to the universal standard of virtue exemplified by the Living Being. His external vision of order would be gradually translated into an internal act of seeing, an understanding of moral excellence and a desire to make his soul as virtuous as possible. By shaping his life into a beautiful image of the macrocosm, the Plotinian Spectator would contribute all his energy to the vital play of the artistic universe. He would enter into the cosmic dance by falling in love with, and by falling in with the love of, the cosmic dancer.

Participation in the dance of life meant more to Plotinus than a purely contemplative act. It was not restricted to the extraordinary experiences of a few lofty souls who could waft away from earth and whirl with the choral dances of the stars. Dancing with the Living Being brought the body into play as well as the mind and encompassed all the practical actions required of a virtuous man within society. It meant the moderation of physical instincts and violent passions, for example, and the maintenance of harmonious relations with other people; it inspired a serenity of mind in the face of personal calamities and a courage to withstand the collapse of empires. The sage employed the metaphor of the dance sometimes to sweeten and sometimes to purge the bitterness of man's earthly life. On the one hand he could interpret the malicious deeds of the least valuable members of society as the creative enactment of a beautiful and rational design. Robbers, he remarks with Stoical impassivity in 3.4.15–16, seem to disrupt the orderly flow of human affairs by depriving the innocent of their worldly possessions; yet if the victims of theft were only to see that 'the activity of life is not a random movement,' they would not lament their losses but instead rejoice in their good fortune. The robbers had rid them of material things which were by nature transitory and which would only have distracted their souls from their rightful occupation, contemplating the One.

On the other hand, instead of exalting mundane misfortunes as the ultimately joyful movements in a cosmic play, he could reduce the woefullest realities of human life – unheroic wars, fatal illnesses, crimes of passion – to minor episodes in an inconsequential drama at which the soul wiled away its time before returning to its permanent home outside the starry theatre. 'But a great life-force exists in the universe,' he would still maintain,

and it makes all things and fashions in its life-process an intricately embroidered cosmic design and never stops creating beautiful well-shaped living toys. Men battling against each other with their weapons, men doomed to die yet elegantly marshalled in their ranks as if enacting their pyrrhic dances [pyrrichais] and playing games – these show us that all human troubles are but play, that even death is nothing terrible.

(Ennead 3.2.15)

The great life-force animating the Plotinian universe might be conceived most simply as erotic energy channelled downward towards physical multiplicity, its effects being the generation of new dancers for the 'poikilē choreia' and the growth of new limbs for the 'mia orchēsis.' As such it was distinct from the lower Eros, which, like its higher counterpart, was an upward-straining desire for union with the Whole. The great life-force was an effect of Eros: an image-forming impulse stemming immediately from the love kindled in the World-Soul by the sight of Psyche and ultimately from the love kindled in Psyche by the sight of the Divine Mind. It was what we might call today the 'genetic capacity' of living things to pass on their various kinds of intelligence as well as their various physical characteristics to their descendants.

Plotinus called it on that account the logos, carefully distinguishing it in his treatise 'On Providence' from the supracosmic gods in his vision of the drama of the universe and also from the fiery logos animating the Stoic dance of life:

Let us explain again, and more clearly, what the logos is, and assert that it is what it is for a good reason. The logos, then, is – let us dare to define it! Perhaps we might even succeed! This logos, then, is not Nous, not pure or

*absolute intellect. It does not even belong to the same class as Psyche, pure
soul, though it depends on pure soul and is a kind of radiation outward from
both Nous and Psyche. Nous and Psyche (that is, pure soul under the steady
influence of pure intellect) generated this logos as a life-force calmly harbouring a certain rationality. All life, even paltry life, is activity – but not
the random sort of activity manifested by fire. The activity of life, even where
there is no perception, is a movement which is not random. For if a thing in
any way participates in life, even when it has life without perception, it is
immediately endowed with logos – that is, formed – since the activity characteristic of life has the power to shape things and moves in such a way that
it shapes them. Thus the activity of life is artistic, like the movement of one
who dances a pantomime [ho orchoumenos]. For the pantomimic dancer
[orchēstēs] is like life, the life which is artistic by shaping as it moves, and
his art moves him, and moves him in such a way that his artistic movement
is similar to that of life itself.*

(Ennead 3.2.16)

While Stoic Nature simply shaped itself as it moved, the Plotinian Living
Being moved itself by shaping artistic images of Psyche and Nous and by
miming their archetypal responses (erotic and intellectual) to the solitary
presence of the One. The cosmic dancer could be criticized, of course, for
failing to reproduce the eternal beauty of his models in temporary poses;
but his artistic goal was noble, and to sympathetic spectators who understood
the sublime nature of the models he was trying to imitate, inspiring, and so
however short of realizing that goal his actual performance fell it could never
seem utterly despicable to Plotinus – even when he was perceiving it through
a glare of Stoic terminology, as in 3.2.16 and 4.4.33. If the Plotinian spectator
was ever tempted to regard the pantomime of the lower Eros as mere 'ka-
tagelasta pragmata,' 'most ridiculous goings-on,' as Crato spoke of it in his
first speech to Lycinus, it was not because he despised the show as a hollow
illusion or an immoral distraction or a pointless display of metamorphoses,
but because, once having glimpsed what the dancer aspired to be and what
the dancer loved in his soul, the Plotinian spectator could be a spectator no
longer but had to become an aspirer, a lover, in the chorus of the higher
Eros.

Like Shiva, the Plotinian 'orchēstēs' was a posed figure representing the
steady balance of creative and destructive forces in life and also a protean
mime enacting the struggle of the virtuous soul to rise above the world of
cyclical change. A coincidental similarity? Or does Plotinus deserve his
reputation as the most Eastern of all Western philosophers for having acquired at some point in his education a detailed knowledge of Hindu mys-

ticism? In perhaps his most tantalizing and least informative chapter, Porphyry asserts that Plotinus, during his formative eleven years as a student of the mysterious Ammonius, developed a strong interest in the philosophies of the East and was particularly eager to investigate 'the system of thought successfully established among the Indians' (*Vita Plotini* 3). To what extent he succeeded in realizing this long-standing dream of Greek philosophers his biographer fails to record. His own writings indicate that if his thoughts ever strayed far from the concerns and controversies of the Academy, the Lyceum, the Garden, and the Painted Porch, the direction they took was upward towards the wellspring of fair dances in the ethereal temple of Psyche rather than eastward towards the Ganges and the sculpted temples of the Nataraja.

Who can tell whether a Jungian archetype does or does not underlie man's varying dreams of the cosmic dancer? Jung seems to have brought the Platonic World of the Forms (or perhaps the Gnostic Pleroma with all its Aeons) down from the Empyrean and calmly relocated it deep within the human psyche, where, ironically, except to initiates in the mysteries of the Collective Unconscious, its eternal bournes seem as vague and impenetrable as ever. Lycinus persuaded Crato that the dance was a universal image of order because it reflected the enduring patterns not of an imperceptible psychic domain but of the world perceived and in a sense recreated by our eyes: the goddess Orchesis came into being with the universe by 'blazing into sight.' The primeval source of the image might not lie in a Collective Unconscious, then, but in certain visual perceptions common to the whole human race, perceptions which may be coloured and distorted and narrowed – but are not determined – by the cultural conditioning of the spectators.

Like rainbows, images of cosmic order are not visible to everyone at once and are not appreciated in the same way or for the same reasons by all who are in a position to make out their familiar forms against the sky. Their beauty is very much in the eye of the beholder, and the origin of their variations in the visual imagination of the conscious individual. They might be called 'Archetypes of Collective Consciousness.'[19] Transmitted through the poetic, philosophical, religious, and artistic heritage of a culture, and in that sense collective, they are constantly subject to reinterpretation by individual poets, philosophers, mystics, and artists, and for this reason evolve as conscious and often highly systematic responses both to the prospect of eternity and to particular moments in intellectual and cultural history. Besides the blurry dimensions of time and space, the dance and other images of cosmic order join together the extremes in man's imaginative responses to reality. They are his perennial compromise between the lucid but transient models of the scientist and the vague but enduring symbols of the dreamer.

Procession and Return

All lines of thought in the *Enneads* converge on the problem of knowing the solitary presence outside the circumference of knowable reality. Proceed with Plotinus into the dense thickets of ethics and psychology or over the airy plateau of physics or up the vertiginous slopes of metaphysics, and sooner or later he will lead you towards the same vanishing point on the horizon of rational inquiry. Return with him to the paradox of that absent presence, the One, and before you know it he has you heading off again across the broad terrain of Greek philosophy seeking to confirm his intuition that if the One were identical with the Good it could be seen in a positive light as the never-vanishing point at the centre of the dance.

The Great Chorus had had many different centres before Plotinus centred it on the One. Timaeus chose to arrange the circles of his dancing stars around 'the earth our nurse' at the midpoint of the line of imaginary centres forming the celestial pole, its focal position having been determined as much by the geometrical dictates of the armillary sphere as by the Hesiodic dictum that the goddess Earth was (along with her brothers Eros and Tartarus) 'the first and eldest of the gods born within the heavens.' Venerable as this ancient deity was, Timaeus was more interested in the dynamic circularity of the astral dance than in its divine centre. He did not single the earth out for special consideration as the only stable point in all the spinning globe. His earth, in fact, moved in the dance along with everything else, always 'winding about the pole extended through the universe' in its role as guardian of night and day.

To the astronomer's choral rounds Philo added the centrifugal dance of the souls from the Myth of the Chariot. The Philonic Moses was more inclined to forsake than to venerate the earth our nurse, and though he stood at the hour of his death in the centre of creation uniting the motions of the Jews, the stars, and the angels, his soul had often practised its escape into Heaven by dancing contemplatively through the circles of the stars and leaping for a moment into the luminous waters above the firmament. No mortal, however favoured by the Great King, could be the stable centre of the dance. In his final hymn the holy choragus had taught the Jews that the true and everlasting centre for their chorus must lie beyond the Circle of the Same.

With the rise of Gnosticism and Christianity the visual emphasis of the cosmic dance shifted from movement to stasis, from circling bodies and spiralling souls to the inviolable peace and stability of an unearthly centre. Converts to the various movements within the ground swell of the new paideia were in fact returning to a very old religious design for the dance: a chain of worshippers encircling an altar, idol, wellspring, shaman, or some other medium through which messages could be carried to and from the gods.[20] Into the sacred centre as into a pool of light shielded from diabolical darkness by the dancers' protective ring stepped the phantom Logos in the Acts of John and the Incarnate Logos in Clement of Alexandria's vision of the New Cithaeron. In his various epiphanies the Logos focused the attention of his dancers on his unique identity as the choragus-pedagogus of their movement, and through his focal presence, on the uniqueness of his transcendent Father. From the Logos came the inspiration for their choral ritual and the revelation that it was in harmony with the revolutions of the stars and the angels. He was the charismatic begetter of their new lives in the spirit and the temple in which their spirits would be purged of mortality. His music was the power that would bind their movement together through history. (The religious symbolism of the centre as a procreative origin, a source of harmony, a holy of holies, and a locus of prophecy was doubtless already ancient in the fifth century BC when Philolaus the Pythagorean hailed the fiery nucleus of his dancing universe as the 'House of Zeus,' the 'Mother of Gods,' and the 'Binding Force.' The Gnostic-Christian Logos retained the mystique of the cosmic centre but insisted that his light and harmony flowed from a supracosmic source.) Though the chorus of conversion expanded to embrace souls outside the original circle of the Logos, its psychological thrust was intensely centripetal. The eyes of the dancers were directed inwards to the centre, as if drawn there by a bright light reflected in a looking-glass.

Following this introspective gesture their minds were also drawn inwards to perceive the Logos as a divine mirror through which revelations and prophecies and glimmers of the Empyrean were conveyed to their souls. The theocentric round inspired egocentric meditations. Each dancer looked into the divine mirror to see himself, to gain self-knowledge, for he wished to find out who he really was and why his soul had received grace and where his fortunate spirit was going. By turning away from the external world of the senses he could concentrate on the Word of God and contemplate the nature of his redeemed identity. The simple routine of the dance, like the repetitive chanting still practised today by many religious initiates especially in the East, released the mind from bodily concerns and set it moving towards the goal of self-awareness. Uplifted in a daze, the dancer would ultimately lose consciousness of himself as an individual and be united with the divine powers drawing him back to Heaven. In the mirror of the Logos the individual dancers all saw the same image of themselves as children of God confined for a while within the Circle of the Same but soon to be liberated through the supernatural agency of grace. Under the spell of the New Dionysus their separate identities fused into a single communal self which was then assimilated into the divine nature at their centre. Their hands interlocked. Their ears heard the same piping. Their chorus circled with the Aeons in the Pleroma or with the angels on the Mount of Truth.

The history of choreia is not without its ironies. One might have expected Plotinus as a defender of the old philosophy to have resisted the inward gravitation of the new paideia by turning the eyes of the cosmic dancer outward towards the heavens, and as a critic of Gnostic cosmology to have demystified the centre of the dance by focusing the attention of the astral chorus downward on the earth our nurse. Yet quite the opposite happened. As he would envision it from *his* perspective of the whole – which reduced the Stoic perspective of the whole to that of a minor part – the Great Chorus did not lose its unearthly centre or its inward gravitation or its ecstatic impetus: all the essential characteristics of the Gnostic round (minus, of course, the Logos in human form) were projected by Plotinus onto the Platonic image of the astral chorus and magnified to infinity. When his cosmos danced around two centres, the distance between its earthly and unearthly focal points was more clearly defined than ever before. When his dancers were moved to introspection, their intellectual activity had no proselytizing motive and was therefore more intensely centred on the relation of the self to God than the meditations of any dancer in the Acts of John. When his own soul was lifted to ecstasy, it did not stagger like a drunken Corybant but held the pose of a humble adorant gazing into a divine centre that could not be separated from the expanding circles of existence. Plotinus was to give the Gnostic round a centre which could never depart, never lose contact with the souls of the dancers, never break the orderly chain of bodies. Membership in his theocentric chorus would be the very opposite of exclusive, depending neither on the private invitation of a Redeemer nor on the initiation rites of a secret brotherhood. To be endowed with logos, to be formed into a living creature under the influences of the stars, to function as a tiny limb on the self-shaping body of Nature was somehow, even without knowing it, to be engaged in the contemplative response of the Living Being to the absent presence of the One.

In his treatise 'On the Circular Motion of the Heavens' Plotinus distinguished two senses of the term 'meson' ('centre' or 'middle') which are relevant to his expansive conception of the world-chorus. When he used the term in reference to bodies, it signified a spatial centre such as the midpoint of a line, the focal point of a circle, or the interior point equidistant from all points on the surface of a sphere; when he used it in reference to souls it designated 'the source from which another nature is derived' (2.2.2.), in other words a causal centre or generative origin assumed to be of a higher and more unified nature than any of its offspring. One can easily see by drawing a circle with a compass how the second concept of centre might be derived from the first. Without a fixed point upon which to set one arm of the compass, no circumference can be drawn; the centre is therefore the starting-point that determines and in a sense generates the relative positions of all the other points in the configuration.

As a composite of body and soul the Plotinian cosmos had two distinct centres, one spatial and physical, and the other causal and psychological. The first was the intersection point of the celestial axis and all the diameters of the celestial equator, which was located at the earth's core as in the Platonic cosmos. Since the centres of all the concentric rounds in the dance of the stars lay along the celestial axis, and since the spatial centre of the earth coincided with the midpoint of this line of centres, the earth's core could be conceived as a centre-of-centres. The proximity of the human race to the earthly centre-of-centres did not fill Plotinus with a glowing sense of the dignity of Man, as one might suppose, but with just the opposite feeling: a keen sense of personal and racial shame at having to live within a vulnerable body (he was to die of a kind of leprosy) at the diseased heart of the material world. The earth was by far the least desirable spot in his universe, a dark inner city with dingy tenements and twisting alleys far inferior to the spacious estates and brilliant concourses of the stars. Still, like a traveller to Rome who wanders for a few hours among its ancient slums and admires its local colour and popular entertainments without being too upset by the disparity between his own standard of living and that of the Romans, Plotinus was willing to defend the earth and its inhabitants from their detractors, the Gnostics, who hated to set foot in such filthy surroundings and blamed the stars for imprisoning them in the ghetto of all evil.

Whatever shone out amid the gloom of earthly life as pure or whole or noble or in any respect worth living for – and the melancholy third century had enough that was corrupt and crumbling and inglorious about it to drive Porphyry to the brink of suicide – sprang, Plotinus taught consolingly, from the world's other centre, from the permanent focus of all the thoughts of all the stars as they danced in their permanent rounds. A dancer who knows his role well is free to contemplate whatever he wishes during his performance, to lose all sense of himself as an individual in the communal meditations of the chorus. 'This is what the stars experience in performing their rounds,' he reasoned in 4.4.8,

They are occupied with their own affairs and do not move merely for the sake of moving along the courses they actually traverse. They are not concerned with the spectacle of the things that appear along the way, or with the act of passing from one point to another, or with the accidental circumstances of the journey itself. Their minds are set on other goals, greater goals. They always travel through the same circles, and so make no reckoning of the time they spend in any given part of the journey, even if time-divisions were possible from their point of view. If this is granted, they need have no memory of either the places or the times through which they pass. They all lead the same life, a life wherein movement from place to place is always directed around the same point; hence, their spatial movement does not really involve a change of place at all. Yet it must be a motion full of life. It must be the motion of a single living creature whose vital functions are activated within itself, an organism apparently at rest if it were observed from the outside. It moves because of the life inside itself, its eternal existence. And so the motion of the stars admits comparison to a choral dance [choreia].

If human dancers could learn a simple ring-dance with little effort, with how much less strain must the stars with their superhuman intellects have mastered the same figure on a cosmic scale! Their physical motion must have ceased to concern them very soon after their dance began; now, untold revolutions later, they must move totally by reflex, their chief activity being (as Timaeus realized long ago) not moving but thinking – 'always thinking the same thoughts about the same things.'

Plotinus has in this passage embarked on an extraordinary thought-experiment, the aim of which is to see what the cosmic dance is like, to remember what it must have been like, to anticipate what it will always be like from the communal viewpoint of the stars. He has attempted to analyse the choral consciousness of the visible gods. Other philosophical spectators – Platonic, Epicurean, Stoical, Cynical – were markedly anthropocentric in their perceptions of the Great Chorus, even, as in Lucian's fantasy of the heavenly flight of Menippus, when their vantage-points were celestial. Plotinus could be so too, of course, especially when he was in a Stoical mood. But here his thought-experiment has yielded perceptions of the cosmic dance quite unlike anything recorded in the extant writings of his pagan predecessors. Freed from spatial and temporal concerns by the monotonous routine of their dance, the Plotinian stars could turn their attention towards other goals – 'greater goals,' Plotinus added emphatically – namely the contemplation and imitation of the life of the gods abiding beyond the Circle of the Same. The stellar intellects would be inclined to ponder the challenging question of their origin, and, like the earliest Greek philosophers who followed them in such meditations, to conclude that their harmonious existence reflected the formal perfection of an eternal model and the rationality of a creative god. Plotinian stars would not stop there. Next they would consider who was the creator of their creator, and from what god sprang the previous two, and what was the ultimate source of all sources and the source without a source.

Answers to such questions might come easily to the exalted intellect of a star, but they are difficult for merely human intellects to follow (let alone express) without the aid of analogies drawn from the sphere of physical space. Ever conscious of the disparity between the intelligence of his pupils and his gods, Plotinus obligingly described the psychological focus of the Living Being and the fountainhead of everything in his universe as the causal 'centre-of-centres' (6.9.8) corresponding to the spatial centre-of-centres at the earth's core. Few metaphors have ever stretched a substellar imagination farther than this: the terms of the comparison are more than poles apart, literally, and therefore less like potential analogues or even distant ontological relatives than absolute opposites. How could the utter darkness of the earthly centre have anything in common with the unearthly source of all light, virtue, beauty, reason, and unity? Any Gnostic bold enough to have attended the lectures of Plotinus might well have asked himself how a philosopher who posited so severe a contrast between the worlds of Being and Becoming could possibly have considered himself an enemy of Gnosticism.

Plotinus would be the first to admit that the difference between his two centres was undeniably extreme; yet he would still insist that no matter how widely he separated them for the sake of argument their incalculable disparity never reached the limit of absolute dualism. By no stretch of his imagination would he snap the basic assumption of his cosmology that each part of the universe must be linked to every other part, which meant that the highest spiritual cause had to have some connection, however tenuous, with the basest material product. To preserve the bond uniting the physical and psychological centres of his universe he would rebut any opposing argument, extend any metaphor, twist any myth, dispute even Plato's authority.

According to Plato, the Craftsman was not responsible for creating the elemental medium upon which he imposed the spherical form of the cosmic body. Like a goldsmith modelling geometric designs, he had impressed order on pre-existing raw materials, or rather on physical space itself, which Timaeus called the 'Receptacle' (50a) because it could receive the appearance of fire, air, water, and earth. These he conceived not as material elements but as fleeting qualities bestowed upon physical space like reflections in a mirror. Plotinus eliminated the Receptacle from his theory of the procession of the Many from the One. It might have fitted into the Platonic metaphor of a craftsman, a model, and a workable medium, but it did not suit the metaphors of cosmogony that most appealed to Plotinus. In general the sage did not imagine the genesis of the Living Being as a technological achievement on the part of an Hephaestus. He tended to avoid the metaphor of craftsmanship and rarely spoke of a divine Craftsman in the Platonic sense, preferring instead to picture the procession of the Many from the One as a spontaneous overflowing or miraculous birth or perpetual dance because such images suggested that the union between cause and effect persisted long after the essential structure of reality had been completed. The water drops were still affected by the outward thrust of the wellspring. The children were still related by blood to their common progenitor. The dancers were still yearning for the stillness out of which their dance had arisen.

To imagine the procession of the Many without the One would be like using a compass to draw concentric circles without first resting one of its ends on a predetermined point. The starting-point in the circular design is a given. It is located rather than drawn by the wielder of the compass. In 4.4.16 Plotinus compared his psychological centre-of-centres to a dimensionless point round which the circular design of existence was formed and from which the circling dancers perpetuating that design descended. Nous, the archetypal intellect, was the first being to issue from the One, and since Nous participated in the absolute stasis of the First Cause by fixing its attention on its centre and never deviating to lower objects of thought, just as later in the procession the stars would be totally absorbed in introspection and oblivious to the effects of their rational motion on the multitudes beneath them, Plotinus pictured its intellectual activity as a 'kyklos akinētos' or 'motionless circle.' Nous subsequently brought the archetypal soul Psyche into existence, the act of thinking being tantamount in Plotinian terms not only to imitating the stillness of the One in the inner life of the mind but also to generating an image of its virtues external to the thinking self. Nous and Psyche were both hypostases of the One: that is, they came into being by 'standing or settling under' the First Cause (hyphistamai) and forming what Plotinus understood to be the intelligible world.

To mark the inferiority of Psyche to Nous – for an effect was always conceived as inferior to its cause in the procession – he likened the archetypal soul to the locus of a rotation, a 'kyklos kinētos' or 'moving circle' (see figure 8). Like all the souls generated in its likeness, Psyche not only thought but desired and willed and remembered and hoped, and since it was more diversified in its mental operations than Nous it was also further removed from the absolute stasis of the One. Striving nevertheless, like Nous, to imitate the One as far as its nature permitted, Psyche experienced a continual aspiration – an 'ephesis' or 'hurling' of itself – towards the goal of knowing the Good, which is to say the One conceived as Final Cause of all the motions in the dance of life. With this aspiration was born the dynamism of the dance, as Plotinus indicates in 1.8.2:

The Good stays still within himself, but Nous is active around him even as it lives around him. And Psyche, dancing around Nous on the outside [exōthen peri touton choreuousa], gazes towards it and by contemplating its interior sees God through it.

The inward gravitation of Psyche had the paradoxical effect of generating a

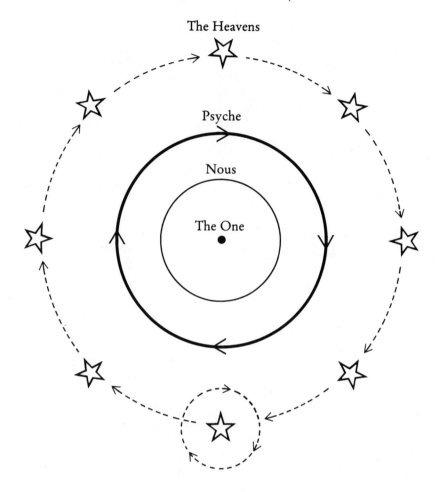

The Heavens

Psyche

Nous

The One

Figure 8

The procession of the Many from the One was conceived by Plotinus as a centrifugal movement from perfect unity and repose through increasing degrees of individuation and mutability. The two inner circles in the diagram (described in *Ennead* 4.4.16) represent the mental activity of Nous and the incorporeal life of Psyche. Though it did not actually move in the dance, Nous was part of the Great Chorus by virtue of a duality between thinker and object of thought which set it apart ever so slightly – and ever so far – from the One. The dynamism of the dance originated in the desire of Psyche to see the Good reflected in the Divine Mind, a mystical aspiration which at a later stage in the procession was expressed in the visible choreiai of the stars and the erotic 'orchēsis' of the Living Being.

tremendous centrifugal force which expanded the bright ring of existence around the One by vastly multiplying the forms of life, and as these forms became less and less like the hypostatic gods in the World of Being their cyclical chorus gave rise to the fleeting illusory condition of Becoming.

At a critical moment in this later stage of the procession, life-forms that were purely psychological must have generated life-forms that were composites of body and soul. But how? To explain this difficult transition Plotinus drew the following analogy between the design of the material world conceived by the World-Soul and the design of a pantomimic dance with a multitude of roles to which the dancer, despite the difference between his own nature and the natures of what he represents, must adapt himself if the design is to be successfully executed:

For what is there to prevent the power of the World-Soul (since she is the rational principle in the universe) from drawing a preliminary pattern before the psychic powers issue from her? And what prevents this pattern from casting preliminary rays of light into primal matter? The souls that execute the design have only to follow the traces of the pattern and to articulate its parts one by one. Each soul adapts its form to the part which it approaches, just as a pantomimic dancer [ton en orchēsei] shapes himself to suit a dramatic role which has been given to him.

(Ennead 6.7.7)

This simile was doubtless derived from the Stoics; but where Marcus Cato and Epictetus had used it in ethical contexts to commend the wisdom of those who adapt themselves to life's unhappily changing circumstances, Plotinus ingeniously fitted it into a cosmological argument to excuse the World-Soul and her psychic assistants for having lowered themselves to create horses and oxen and countless other inferior life-forms out of matter. To take the procession as far as it would go, the cosmogonic dancers had to move in the direction of darkness and evil and mortality towards the extreme condition of formlessness which was primal matter.

So long as a single ray of light could be cast into the material substrate, so long as a single perishable body could be formed out of its near-nothingness, even it, the farthest anything could be from the One, had some faint existence in the procession (though it was an utterly passive existence, as Plotinus argued in 6.1.27). Despite this ultimate diminution in the quality of existence, the procession generated a simultaneous countermovement, a contemplative return of the Many to the One, by which each creature endowed with logos, following the example of Psyche, aspired to see the Good reflected in the Divine Mind and by imitating these superior causes to enhance the unity of the Great Chorus.

With the design of the two centres and the dynamics of procession and return, Plotinus initiated a new intellectual movement on the old foundations of Hellenistic philosophy, a movement known today (though the label would have surprised him) as 'Neoplatonism.' In the Neoplatonic theatre no one could be a spectator only: even someone who obstinately shut his eyes to the spectacle had to be a participant in the processional sequence of the dance – simply by existing as 'one something.' Only the degree of participation could vary from member to member in the Great Chorus. One who analysed the visible evidence of the procession would be drawn into the returning sequence of the dance to a much greater extent than a dull inattentive spectator who was content merely to watch the luminous surfaces of Nature without pondering why each pose was struck, each figure composed, each circle formed in imitation of a divine archetype. Neoplatonic participation in the fullest sense presupposed a gradual transition from the analytical perceptions of a viewer who knew the parts to the choral consciousness of a visionary who perceived the whole. Before a viewer could perfect his own proper role in the chorus he first had to observe how the Living Being was responding to the aspirations of Psyche, and to learn his steps from ecstatic contemplatives like the stars who had danced to the same harmony since the world began.

Plotinus conceived this preliminary stage in the return as a delicate adjustment in vision. To see the whole dance through Plotinian eyes, therefore, requires more than an adjustment in our astronomical beliefs: we must also suppress modern notions of visual perception and consider the peculiar way in which Plotinus understood the mechanics of sight.

The Neoplatonic Spectator

Porphyry's recollection that Plotinus rarely revised the first drafts of his treatises 'because his eyesight was too weak to bear the strain of correcting them' and the further testimony of his friend Eustochius that the sage's final illness aggravated 'the blurriness of his vision' (*Vita Plotini* 8 and 3) impart to the many passages in which he praises that sense above all others or commends 'the symmetry, proportion, and orderly arrangement of things presented to the eyes' (2.9.16) an undertone of melancholic irony. His vague references to the symmetry of the celestial revolutions seem quite primitive beside the Dedalian diagrams and calculations set forth by Ptolemy in the *Almagest*, which was written in Alexandria some sixty or seventy years before Plotinus went there in search of a teacher. Perhaps his disinclination to pursue the study of astronomy on the mathematical side was a consequence of his weak eyesight: even if he had wanted to chart the configurations of the astral dance with Ptolemaic precision he may not have been able, at least not in later life, to trust what his eyes beheld in the cosmic theatre or to resolve the blur into Ptolemaic epicycles, eccentrics, and equants.

Plotinus the star-gazer was little more than a rhetorical pose he adopted for his confrontations with the Gnostics. He repeated the Athenian Stranger's encomium of the visible beauty of the heavens in defence of the old philosophy, and meant every word of it; but astronomy was only of interest to him when it confirmed or corroborated his metaphysical speculations concerning Psyche, Nous, and the One. That he was inclined to consider the psychology of visual and visionary perception might also have been due, in part, to the poor condition of his eyes. If his thought ever verged on scientific empiricism, it was when he turned away from the visible design of Nature to consider the nature of his senses, particulary sight, and to wonder how light stimulated his eyes, why distant objects appeared smaller than they really were, and whether vision was possible without a transparent medium linking the beholder to the beheld. Then he was able to test the hypotheses of his predecessors against his own observations and to present what seems at times like experimental evidence to support his own theories of vision. How we see was more important in his philosophy than what we see; more important still was when and why we ought to close our eyes.

When we look at objects other than our own bodies, we are usually conscious of a gulf separating them from us – either a distance which can be quantitatively measured or a difference between their sizes, shapes, colours, and movements, and our own. This gulf instantly narrows when we look at one of our own limbs or at our eyes in a mirror, and it seems to disappear when we shut our eyes and peer into the recesses of our consciousness. In states of intense introspection, as Plotinus observed in 6.9.11, the beholder becomes 'one with the beheld.' If physical vision is necessarily accompanied by a perception of the twoness of beholder and beheld, then one could argue that it is not in fact a fitting analogue for the purely subjective processes by which a soul becomes its own object of perception and gains knowledge of its uniqueness as a self and its unity as a descendant of the One.

Plotinus defended the old Platonic analogy between physical vision and philosophical enlightenment in a rather idiosyncratic way: not by arguing (as Philo had) that since philosophy began with the study of the objective design of the astral chorus intellectual vision was originally an effect and therefore inherently an analogue of physical vision; but by contending that physical vision was in essence a kind of introspection, though most beholders failed to recognize themselves in the beheld. 'For though Nature is like an artisan creating a multitude of beautiful things,' he explained in 5.8.2,

its own origin lies in a Beauty which existed long before it. We are not accustomed to look inwards, however, and so we know nothing of its origin. We pursue external goals, not knowing that the inner vision is our motivation. We are like a man who sees a reflection of himself and not knowing whence it came chases after it.

Whereas a Stoical Spectator looked to Nature for what he believed were objective standards of beauty, harmony, order, rationality, and so on, Plotinus insisted that true objectivity was only to be gained by those who perceived the transcendent model of nature's artistry in the Beauty contemplated by Psyche. What the Neoplatonic Spectator saw in the celestial revolutions was a reflection of his own mental processes, an image of his inner life; what he saw in his inner life was a distant reflection of Psyche's dance around the static circle of Nous – that is to say, a restless desire (a desire shared and passed on to him by all the dancing stars) to behold the source of intelligible Beauty and to become one with the beheld. Those who failed to perceive the essential subjectivity of physical vision reminded him of a man who on seeing his own reflection failed to recognize it as an image of himself and consequently mistook the illusion for the actual presence of another person.

Since the motivation to look outwards at the stars came from within our souls, Plotinus reasoned, our external vision of Nature must be causally connected with our latent understanding of intelligible reality; and since all the spectators of the astral chorus and the chorus itself sprang from a common divine forefather, a sympathetic union must have been established between beholder and beheld long before we became conscious of a gulf separating us from them. The Plotinian distinction between inner and outer vision therefore does not imply a dichotomy between subjective and objective perception, though the terms 'inner' and 'outer' seem at first to suggest such an opposition. They simply indicate differences in the high degree of unity Plotinus always assumed to exist between the beholder and the beheld. Thus, without contradicting himself, the same Plotinus who advised the Gnostics to open their eyes in 2.9.16 could in 1.6.8 offer precisely the opposite advice:

You must abandon all the world of sense and refuse to see. Having shut your eyes, you must exchange one kind of seeing for another and awaken this other vision which all men possess but few tend to use.

This exhortation may sound similar to the enigmatic dictum 'The closing of my eyes is true vision' whispered by the Gnostic dreamer at the end of the *Poimandres*, but its implications are entirely different. The Gnostic dreamer shut his eyes to alienate the beholder from the beheld. The Neoplatonic spectator shut his to perfect their union.

Plotinus developed his highly subjective theory of sight from three prem-
ises concerning the mechanism of the eye: first, that physical vision depended
on the sympathetic operations of all physical organs within the Living Being;
second, that the visible object had to be in some way analogous to the eye
before vision could take place; and third, that the eye played an active role
in the formation of visual images and was not a passive receptor of images
formed in the transparent medium separating the viewer from the visual
field.

'Sensation,' explained the sage in 4.5.8, 'seems to occur for some such
reason as this: that the Living Being, this entire cosmos, is sympathetically
attuned to itself.' It may seem odd to begin an analysis of how man senses
his physical environment by considering the organization of the entire cosmos rather than the structure of the human sense organs, but Plotinus had
his reasons for doing so, and as usual they were bound up with his preoccupation with unity. By resting his general theory of sensation on the broad
foundation of the Stoic doctrine of cosmic sympathy he could assume from
the start, as he worked out his particular theory of sight, that the beholder
and the beheld were physically united even before their interaction in the
visual process and that the divisive presence of the transparent medium was
not essential to the formation of visual images.

As a result, the Neoplatonic Spectator tended to perceive every object in
his visual field – even a distant object like the sun – as if it were touching
or indeed merging with his body. In a sense it was. He could see the object
with little or no awareness of an airy gulf between them because both he
and it were parts of the living body of the cosmos and were thus sensitive
to (though not necessarily conscious of) each other's movements and functions. By moving its celestial limbs in the dance the Living Being not only
generated its own internal spectators but also stimulated their eyes so that
they opened to its light and beheld its harmonious motions. It had no need
for eyes itself, of course, since there was nothing corporeal for it to see
outside the cosmic body; it was by necessity supremely introspective. When
his weak eyes grew weaker during his final illness, Plotinus was perhaps
consoled by his increasing resemblance to the Living Being, which in its
eternal blindness, its eternal indifference to the distracting multiplicity of
beautiful forms created within it, surpassed all sighted creatures in the power
of its intellectual concentration and the clarity of its mystical insights.

The second premiss underlying the Plotinian theory of vision, the doctrine
that the eye responds only to objects analogous to its own nature, probably
originated in the medical lore of the ancient Pythagoreans. Plotinus most
likely accepted it on the authority of Plato, whose brief but influential
discussion of the structure of the human eye in *Timaeus* 45b–d includes a
physiological justification of the principle of 'like sees like.' While modern

physiologists liken the eye to a camera and the pupil to an aperture through which light is admitted, Plato pictured the one as a delicately crafted lantern containing its own source of pure fire and the other as a filter of finely woven fabric through which the fire was emitted in a thin ray or 'visual current.' The existence of ocular fire was proven by such common observations as the gleam in a cat's eye (a phenomenon now explained as the reflection of light off the inner lining of feline retinas) and the flashing colours and sparkling pinpoints of light which usually appear when the eye is pressed (now explained as a result of prolonged stimulation of the optic nerve). Observing that ocular fire gave off no smoke, Plato concluded that it must be the same as the pure fire of the sun and stars, and that the visual current must differ from rays of celestial light only in origin and intensity.

Vision was thought to occur when the visual current mingled and coalesced with kindred fire in the viewer's environment and to be clearest during the day because then the ocular ray encountered the direct light of the sun or sunbeams reflected off objects in the visual field. At night vision was necessarily reduced because the visual current either encountered no kindred fire when it issued into the air or found only the faint gleam of the moon and stars with which to coalesce. Plato's conception of the beholder as a lantern-bearer actively exploring the cosmos and making himself sunlike or starlike every time his ocular fire united with the fire of heaven inevitably appealed to Plotinus because it paralleled his conception of the introspective sage as an explorer of the visionary world of Psyche, a seeker after unity, a seer who became sunlike or starlike in a psychological sense.

By directing his visual current at the celestial dance, the Neoplatonic Spectator would instantly begin to unite himself with its divine participants; the merging of his internal fire with their external fire would enkindle in his soul a vision of concentric revolutions corresponding to the mathematical pattern implanted in his memory at the birth of time, when, as Timaeus had revealed (41c–42b), his undescended soul had been placed upon a star and shown the harmonious design of the Living Being from the perspective of the whole. If any passion or vice disrupted the smooth flow of his reminiscences, his soul would lose its likeness to the unbroken round of the heavens and his understanding of its eternal archetype would consequently be reduced. The doctrine that 'like knows like' followed logically from the doctrine that 'like sees like,' as Plotinus concluded in his treatise on the relation between visual and visionary beauty: 'For never did eye see the sun unless it became sunlike, and never may the soul know Beauty unless it become beautiful' (1.6.9). The Living Being proved that its soul was beautiful by imitating the Primal Beauty, the higher Aphrodite, in the erotic movements of its pantomime.

In *The Pantomime* Lycinus observed that a dancer gains most praise from his audience 'when each spectator recognizes his own traits or rather beholds himself in the dancer as in a mirror, observing there his customary feelings and actions' (81). Having established this bond of sympathy, the dancer is able to reshape the self-images of his spectators by altering his own image, and if he mirrors the beauty of the gods or the virtues of the ancient heroes in his performance he will be able to improve the moral condition of his audience. The goddess Orchesis offers mankind more than a pretty picture of harmony: she 'sets in rhythm the souls of the beholders and exercises them in what is beautiful to behold' (6), thus turning mere spectators of her divine order into full participants. Lycinus' remarks on the psychological identification of the spectator with the spectacle anticipate the Plotinian and subsequent Neoplatonic theme that the truly attentive spectator, the enthusiast with expert knowledge of pantomimic dancing, is always ready to dissolve his own identity into the spectacle and to discover the true, noble, and permanent identity of the cosmic dancer. Like the goddess Orchesis, the Plotinian cosmos was a consummate shape-shifter, forever dissolving one form into another, recreating the fluidity of water and the flickering of fire, moving its greatest parts within itself and causing all material things to change position. Yet for all its protean transformations it never altered its essential identity as a god meditating on the origin of its own rationality, and in this inner unchanging self the Neoplatonic Spectator recognized his own introspective character.

In a commentary on the *Timaeus* written sometime between 145 and 165 AD (now lost save for a few fragments preserved in a polemical treatise by the sixth-century Christian theologian John Philoponus), an obscure Platonist by the name of Calvenus Taurus argued that while the cosmos was ever-changing like Proteus it was also, like a pantomimic dancer, constant in its underlying identity:

The cosmos is said to have 'come into being' because it is always in the process of generation, even as Proteus changes into manifold forms. Now, with regard to the cosmos, the earth and all things up to the moon change from one form into another, while all things above the moon scarcely change from one form into another, and are more or less the same with respect to their underlying nature. They change in their visible configurations, just as a pantomimic dancer [orchēstēs] changes into many forms by means of certain gesticulations but remains one and the same in his underlying self.

(*De aeternitate mundi* VI. 8)

Plotinus probed this 'underlying self' more deeply than any of his predecessors, and what he perceived to be the constant identity of the cosmic 'orchēstēs' became the prototype of the serene and passionless mentality of the Neoplatonic Spectator who had achieved contemplative union with the One.

Seeing the cosmos through Plotinian eyes was like reaching out from the audience to touch the dancer, to feel through the closest possible contact between perceiver and perceived how the dancer aspired to imitate the archetypal order of the Hypostases. Plotinus reached his startling conclusion that 'the process of seeing will be very much like that of touch' in a treatise on the psychology of visual perception (4.5.4) appended to his two treatises on the problems of the soul, 4.3 and 4.4, the latter containing his analysis of the poses in the cosmic pantomime and his defence of the doctrine of cosmic sympathy. He begins 4.5 in aporematic style by proposing to determine whether sight can or cannot occur without the presence of a transparent medium between the beholder and the beheld; then with grave impartiality reviews the established arguments on both sides of the debate; and finally, showing his true polemical colours, advances his own theory to counter the conclusions reached by his illustrious predecessors. Despite its rather Aristotelian tone and organization, the first Neoplatonic treatise 'On Sight' was written – ironically – as a refutation of almost everything Aristotle had to say about the structure and function of the eye.

Aristotle assumed that vision was not an essentially active process, the voluntary emission of ocular rays towards their kindred fire, but a passive reception of visual images impressed on the eye by an external medium such as air or water. His concept of sight as a series of impressions, of minute physical alterations in the surfaces of the eye, effectively reversed the Platonic theory and foreshadowed modern explanations of vision. Light is now known to be focused by the ocular lens onto photosensitive cells in the lining of the retina which in turn stimulate the optic nerve, causing sensory messages to be relayed to the visual centres in the brain.

Plato and Aristotle were both unaware of the optic nerve and its function, and bequeathed to Plotinus their physiological misconceptions as well as their philosophical speculations about vision. Aristotle located the sensitive area of the eye on its outer surface, noting, however, that vision was immediately obscured whenever a coloured object was placed directly in front of the eye. This simple experiment (recorded in *De anima* 419a 10–20) convinced him that colour on its own could not produce visual sensations without the presence of a continuous transparent medium linking the viewer to the visible object. Today we can scarcely think of colour apart from light, for the perceptible differences in the visible spectrum are attributed to differences in the frequency of light waves reflected off opaque surfaces or refracted through prisms. We speak of different colours of light, and even of invisible colours such as infrared and ultraviolet which are frequencies beyond the range of human perception. Aristotle, by contrast, sharply distinguished colour from light, defining the former (in *De anima* 418a 30) as the power latent in visible objects to set in motion the transparent medium in their immediate vicinity. Aristotelian colour was a kind of potential energy. Light, which we would define today as a kind of energy and which Plato simply equated with fire, Aristotle understood to be the actual state of transparency or the end result of the process of becoming transparent. We tend to think of air or water as transparent even when no light happens to be shining through them. Aristotle would say that only under illumination could these substances become transparent; otherwise they were only potentially so. The illumination of the medium activated the power of colour in the visible object, which in turn caused a series of visual images to stream off the object and pass through the medium to the eye. At the moment of impact the sight-wave would produce a tiny qualitative change in the surface of the organ. Just as wax may take on the impress of a signet ring without turning into metal, so the Aristotelian eye would receive an imprint of the formal qualities of the object, minus its matter. The force of the impression would then activate the sensitive faculty of the viewer's soul, and the final effect of this chain reaction would be a visual sensation.

Plotinus was willing to admit that transparent substances might have some small role to play in the visual process, but he refused to regard the presence of the illuminated medium as a necessary condition for vision because it seemed to drive a material wedge between the eye and the object which not only prevented the coalescence of their kindred fires but also prohibited the beholder from comprehending the beheld. The duality of viewer and visible object was indeed an inevitable condition of external vision, he conceded in 4.6.1; but the divine rationale for sight (as he understood it) was to break down that twoness as far as possible. The intervention of the medium seemed to annihilate as well as aggravate the duality of subject and object – a horrifying paradox – for, if the viewer never came into close physical contact with the object he hoped to see but only with a secondary or vestigial image of it, he would never truly see or know the object *in itself*. The object would effectively be deleted from his visual field. The spectator would have no need to look outward beyond himself to the dances of the stars because the stars would long ago have impressed their images on his eyes and on the sensitive faculty of his soul. Seeing with Aristotelian eyes would be like trying to read in the dark, he complained, for the viewer's most vivid sensations could be no better than dim shadowy images which the mind's eye would have to strain to see. How could the vastness of the heavens ever impress an image of itself on something as tiny as the eye? How could the beholder ever take his first steps in the returning sequence of the dance if his vision of cosmic order were a submissive and largely involuntary reception of haphazard impressions? Repelled by the passivity of the Aristotelian spectator, Plotinus defined the process of seeing in 4.6.1 with verbs denoting strenuous action. When we look through Plotinian eyes we 'grasp' (lambanontes) and 'attack' (metaballomen) the visual field.

The goddess Nature, whom Plotinus understood to be the lowest phase of the World-Soul and as such the divine agent maintaining the sympathetic bonds between all physical organs in the Living Being, emerges in 3.8.4 as a model for the Neoplatonic Spectator. Nature's visual experience is imagined as exactly the opposite of Aristotelian passivity. Instead of receiving visual images, Nature actively brings them into being and shapes them while she sees. 'My visual faculty creates visible things,' Plotinus imagines her saying to herself, 'even as geometricians draw diagrams of the things they see; but I draw nothing; I gaze, and the configurations of bodies, the material forms they draw with their pens, settle into existence as if falling out of my vision.' Since all the objects in the field of external vision were contained and created within the sphere of Nature, her vision was by necessity inward-turning or contemplative and at the same time image-forming or creative.

What Plotinus defined as the visual faculty of Nature is what a psychologist today would call 'the visual imagination' and associate with certain areas of the human brain rather than with the world at large; but wherever this image-forming centre is located, the artistic (or in a general sense, poetic) mode of thinking born of it was what the Neoplatonic Spectator strove to nurture in himself through participation in the cosmic dance. His vision of the dance would transcend that of the geometricians, the Ptolemaic astronomers, for while they were busy drawing diagrams of what Nature created as she gazed, he was trying to sense how Nature gazed as she created and to shape his inner and outer life into a beautiful image of the Beauty she looked towards in her meditations. The distinctive mode of Neoplatonic vision is further defined in 4.5.4, a passage in which Plotinus is struggling to refute the Aristotelian theory of the transparent medium:

For if the coalesced light becomes ensouled, that is, if the soul travels through it and permeates it, just as in interior vision, then in grasping or laying hold of the exterior object – which is what seeing truly is – the light in the intervening medium would not be a necessary condition for sight: the process of seeing will be very much like that of touch.

In these loose, tentative clauses can be discerned a strange new development in the theory of coalescent light. Whereas Plato described the visual current as a purely material ray, a beam of ocular fire, Plotinus speculated that its nature might be a mixture of fire and soul. In directing his eye-beams at the astral dance, then, the Neoplatonic Spectator would also be sending into the heavens a delicate filament of his own soul like a finger or antenna capable of infinite extension. This ensouled light would range over the visual field with absolutely no dependence on the illuminated medium and search the sky for composites of fire and soul, the stars, analogous to its own nature and therefore capable of being seen through the fusion of like with like. Strange as this hypothesis seems, it was a simple extrapolation from what Plotinus considered a basic fact of psychology: the source of the eye's internal fire had to be joined to the viewer's soul at all times since everything inside the human body was supervised and permeated by the soul's lowest phase, its faculties of growth and sensation. The visual current did not radically change on leaving the eye, he reasoned. Its light retained its ensouled quality and bestowed this on the coalesced light resulting from the union of ocular and celestial fire.

The lowest phase of the Neoplatonic Spectator's soul (corresponding to Nature in the World-Soul) had fallen so far from the One in the procession of the Many that it had mingled with the material substrate to form a human body, and because of this original contact with matter it could permeate the body of the cosmos with little difficulty during the visual process. However, the physical union it established between the beholder and the beheld was always spoiled by some degree of separation. Their inevitable dissociation was due to the existence of another phase of the soul, its highest intellectual faculty, which (as Plotinus argued in 4.3.12) had in fact *never* descended from the intelligible world during the procession of the Many. The intellective soul was like a foreign correspondent in a remote land, always remaining in communication with the spectator's earthbound soul but keeping away from its temporal sphere of interest by concentrating on the eternal occupation of contemplating the One.

The activity of the intellective soul was thus quite distinct from our usual kind of thinking, the analytical or discursive processes of thought by which we draw inferences from sense data, conceive theories about the cosmic design, and criticize the opinions of our philosophical adversaries. That kind of thought Plotinus relegated to a middle phase of the human soul. Since analytical reasoning did not seem to require external physical organs, it could be considered somewhat removed from material things; yet it was also partially mingled with them, for its objects of thought existed within the world of the senses. The highest phase of the Neoplatonic soul might be conceived as thought at its most sublimely abstract level or perhaps even as subconscious intuition, and, though all men were supposed to have such an elevated faculty of understanding, only a very few were ever conscious of its existence or anxious to awaken its vision of archetypal reality. These rare individuals, Plotinus believed, were philosophers of exceptional mental concentration and outstanding moral probity. A perfect fusion of the beholder and the beheld was only possible when the Neoplatonic Spectator shut his eyes to the pantomime of the lower Eros and looked for the dance of the higher Eros in the nonspatial movements of his intellective soul. His return to the static circle of Nous was the response of his unfallen self to the commands of Psyche: be virtuous, be beautiful, be secure, be solitary.

The Neoplatonic Spectator faced the world of fate like a Stoic and refused to shut his eyes when its order seemed repressive or unjust. Yet nothing could persuade him to despise his external vision of the dance. Secure in his knowledge of the psychological centre-of-centres, he could look on the stars without terror, assuring himself that the Great Chorus was not conspiring minute by minute to trap his precious spark of supercelestial light in the doomed centre of their magic circles, and that if any conspiracy existed at all among their blessed troupe its motive was rather to uplift his soul beyond mortal cares and to delight it with a vision of its highest phase, a joyful surprise of which it had too long been unconscious, the knowledge that a part of itself had never fallen from eternity. The anxieties of the Gnostic dreamer did not disturb the Neoplatonic Sage, nor did the suspense of the Last Judgment trouble his serene consciousness that his intellective soul had no need of a Redeemer to lead it to the heavenly dance. It was already there, and had been from the beginning.

The Neoplatonic Sage could appreciate his external vision of cosmic order as a spectacle of divine beauty witnessed ages before in the infancy of his soul, his only complaints against eyesight being that its fusion of like with like was imperfect and that its focus was on the minute particularities of the spectacle rather than on the whole. He depended on his visual imagination to perfect the coalescence of subject and object initiated by his eyes. 'Let us imagine a double light,' mused Plotinus in 5.6.1, 'a weaker corresponding to the soul itself and a purer to its object of thought; if now we assume that the beholder's light is equal to the light which is beheld, then we cannot distinguish between them: the two will be fused into one.' Analytical thinking could be compared to the coalescence of a weaker with a stronger light (that is, the visual ray with the pure rays of the sun and stars) because it always resulted in an imperfect fusion of like with like: the analytical thinker achieved only a partial understanding of his divine object of thought and thus only partially assimilated himself to its exalted nature. Mystical thinking, the intensely introspective process by which the fallen soul regained consciousness of what its unfallen intuitive self experienced in blissful communion with the hypostatic gods, had to be imagined as somewhat different from the visual process: Plotinus accordingly describes it not simply as a coalescence of lights but as an intensification and purification of the weaker light *before* coalescence so that the two lights are virtually identical at the moment of fusion.

The Neoplatonic Spectator achieved a mystical understanding of the stars by first imagining the cosmic dance from their outward and inward viewpoints, and then by recreating their choral consciousness within his own soul, and finally by raising his mind to their superhuman level of intelligence. But turning himself (mentally) into a star was just the beginning: he could not rest in his contemplative reversal of procession until he had achieved mystical union with the Living Being, with Psyche, with Nous, and with – but there was, of course, a limit. 'All that we see as a spectacle,' urged the sage in 5.8.10, 'we see with external vision: the time has come to transfer this vision into ourselves, to see it as one and to see it as our very selves, just as a man filled with a divine spirit, by Apollo or one of the Muses, may create the vision of the god within himself, since within himself he has the power to behold the deity.'

Encircling the Mystic Wellspring

The rhetorical design of the *Enneads* as a whole is so poetic and figurative in comparison with the tough, gritty, and unpoetical stretches of Plotinian prose within it that one might suppose Apollo to have left the philosopher's daunting genius severely alone and to have inspired instead the humbler editorial soul of Porphyry. Porphyry did not simply edit the *Enneads*. In a formal sense he created them – or it, rather –by joining many works into a single Apollonian composition which might be interpreted from the perspective of the whole as a verbal image of the Plotinian cosmos.

Like the limbs of the Living Being, the diverse treatises in the edition seem sympathetically attuned to each other even though the coherence of paragraphs in a single treatise or of treatises in a single Group of Nine might be hard to discern. Beneath the multiplicity of topics and disputations can be sensed the constant presence of a single eccentric master-mind, a tireless debater struggling to direct his intellectual energies away from temporary academic controversies towards an absolute and undebatable knowledge of eternity. His terms, nowhere defined systematically, gather meaning by reference to an indefinable point (the One) and an unattainable goal (the Good), so that each sentence in the *Enneads* implies the underlying network of assumptions, inferences, and intuitions about the spiritual centre of the Great Chorus implicit in every other sentence. Porphyry's numerical orchestration of the treatises reflects the mathematical order that Plotinus believed must regulate and harmonize the Great Chorus. The scheme of six groups of nine treatises was no doubt chosen because six and nine, being both multiples of three, symbolized the multiplicity of temporal beings generated from the eternal triad Psyche-Nous-One. Porphyry was particularly inspired in his choice of a final treatise for this Apollonian edition, a relatively early work (chronologically the ninth) entitled 'On the Good or the One,' in which the dominant themes of Plotinian philosophy seem to draw together after many pages of inventive variations and to resolve into an ecstatic hymn of praise around an eternal Kallichoron.

In this most visionary of his metaphysical works Plotinus unveils, as a preview of what we might expect to perceive as initiates in the Neoplatonic mysteries, a prospect of choreia from the wholly internal viewpoint of the intellective soul. 'We are always before the One,' he declares in 6.9.8, referring to his peculiar doctrine that the most rational part of the human soul remains above in the presence of God,

but we do not look towards Him. So a chanting chorus [choros exaidōn] encircles its choral leader and may turn towards the outside of the spectacle while still holding its pose around him. But let the chorus only turn back towards him, and it chants beautifully and keeps its place because it is around him. Thus we are always around Him, but when we are not turned towards Him we will be totally destroyed and will no longer exist. Yet we do not always turn towards Him. When we look to Him we reach our moment of completion, our fulfilment, and we achieve repose. Then we do not sing out of tune, and in a state of divine possession we truly dance around Him an ecstatic choral dance [choreuousin ontōs peri auto choreian entheon].

Losing in the dance of life all sense of 'the outside of the spectacle,' all bodily feelings, all egocentric desires, all analytical thoughts, all twinges of self-consciousness, might seem like suspending the animation of the Great Chorus in a mental void. The living dancers fade into blank abstractions. The theatre and the spectators disappear. The circles stop.

Against such a negative view of mystical contemplation we must set the fullness of the experience itself, the sage goes on to insist in 6.9.9; we must interpret these apparent losses as a miraculous strengthening of our hold on reality and an infinite expansion of our mental horizon. The moment will come when we can peer directly into the centre at the mystic wellspring:

In this choral dance [en de tautēi tēi choreiai] one beholds the Wellspring of Life, the Source of Intellect, the First Principle of Being, the Cause of Good, the Root of Soul. These do not lessen Him as they pour forth from Him, for He is not a corporeal mass. If He were such, His offspring would be perishable. But they are eternal because their Origin remains the same. He remains whole by having not divided Himself among them. And that is why they remain. As long as the sun continues to shine, there will be light. For we have not been cut away or separated from Him even though the nature of the body has crept in and dragged us to itself. But we breathe and save ourselves because He does not give and then withdraw from us but always provides for us like a choragus [aei chorēgountos] so long as He remains what He is. Surely, now, we are bending forward towards Him and towards our prosperity! To be distant from Him is to be alone and less than we were. Here, beyond the reach of evils, the soul reposes itself and ascends to a region untainted by evils. Here it gains understanding, and here it is insensible to suffering. Here is the true life: there, life as experienced at the present moment, apart from God, is but a faint trace of life, a mimicry of that life. Life in the world beyond is an activity of the intellect. And this activity, in the tranquil touching of the intellect and its source, engenders gods, engenders beauty, engenders justice, engenders moral excellence. For the soul is pregnant with all these when it has been filled with God, and this state is its beginning and its end. This is its beginning because it originated in God; and this is its end because the Good lies here. Having come into existence here, it finds its true self and the very one it was. For life there, in the world of the senses, is a falling off in these virtues, and an exile, and a shedding of feathers. The soul's inborn love is an indication that the Good lies here; hence Eros was coupled with the Psyches in pictures and stories. Though the soul is different from God its originates in Him and so, by necessity, loves Him. So long as it exists here, it embraces the heavenly Eros; but if it turns there, its love turns into the vulgar Eros. Here is the heavenly Aphrodite; there Aphrodite has been mated and is debased.

In the enthusiastic rush of this great religious passage, which conveys with its short urgent sentences a far better sense of the mystical rapture inspired by the heavenly Eros than all the effusions of the Sophists on the same Platonic theme, Plotinus shows how the Neoplatonic Spectator creates the vision of God within himself by an instinctive exercise of the visual imagination, transmuting the base and ever-shifting elements of the temporal world into the golden prospect of life in Psyche's timeless telesterion.

No image of cosmic order furnished by the old philosophy was more brilliantly refined by the alchemy of Neoplatonism than choreia: the choral dances of the stars which the lower Eros diversified and wove together to the music of time, the Neoplatonic Spectator simplifies and unweaves in his imagination so that the dynamic becomes static, the vulgar transcendent, the incomplete perfect, and the divided whole. The image he fashions is of a single circle of dancers drawn inward by the heavenly Eros towards their eternal choragus, who is both their director and their provider. This vision of the universal mystery dance differs from earlier pagan versions of the same image in that the initiated spectator looks wholly inward to God and holds (or tries to hold) his introspective pose because the dancing stars and everything else on the outside of the spectacle have ceased to have any real existence for him. Here Plotinus leaves the controversies of the Hellenistic schools far behind; here, one might also say, he leave the Hellenistic era itself behind, and steps over the border, or withdraws into the sanctuary, or ushers in the mystic sensibility, of Late Antiquity.

The peculiarly Late Antique quality of his vision of the ecstatic chorus can perhaps best be sensed by comparing 6.9.8–9 with the following sophistic elaboration of the topos of 'choreia entheos' from a discourse by Dio Chrysostom delivered at Olympia in 97 AD:

So our idea of God must have originated in an experience very similar to that of a Greek or a barbarian who has been brought for initiation into the innermost chamber of an extraordinarily beautiful and spacious temple, where he would see many mystic sights and hear many mystic voices, where darkness and light would alternately appear to him, and where countless other things would occur. If the circumstances under which our first conception of God was formed were anything like the rite called 'enthronement' – during which the priests conducting the initiation ceremony are accustomed to place the novices on seats and to dance around them in a circle [kyklōs perichoreuein] – would it be likely that the initiate would feel absolutely nothing in his soul and would have not the slightest suspicion that what was taking place was the result of a very wise intention and preparation? Would it be likely that someone possessing a human soul could be unmoved by all this, even if he belonged to the most remote and nameless tribe of barbarians and had no guide and interpreter by his side? No, it would be impossible! Similarly, can one suppose that the whole human race, which is participating in the complete and truly perfect ceremony of mystic initiation, not in the small temple prepared for the reception of a small company by the Athenians, but in this cosmos, this delicately adorned and cunningly crafted cosmos, where countless marvels appear at every moment and where the mystic rites are being conducted not by mere mortals who are of the same nature as the initiates, but by the immortal gods, who night and day both in sunlight and in starlight are – if it is proper to say so – truly dancing in chorus forever [atechnōs perichoreuontōn aei] around mortal men in order to initiate them, can one suppose, I repeat, that the human race could have sensed nothing of all this?

(*The Twelfth Discourse* 33–4)

The Eleusinian trappings of this scene from the crowded echoey theatre of the sophistic imagination, the many-chambered temple, the ancient telesterion, the thrones set up for the initiates, the circle of divinely inspired priests, the chanting of unseen choirs, flashes of light, deep darkness, more flashes, deeper darkness, and above all this in the deepest darkness the innumerable stars dancing forever within the spacious temple of the cosmos and teaching mankind to worship the Stoic God, Zeus the Omnipotent, who was knowable through the senses because he existed in the Here and Now, are absent – banished, stripped away – from the starkly conceived (because inconceivable) and simply described (because indescribable) communion of Plotinian souls around the utterly unknowable One.

Dio's Hellenistic common sense demanded a philosophical demystification of God, and so he projected the 'many mystic sights' and 'many mystic voices' of an Eleusinian initiation rite familiar to his audience onto the daunting blur of the Everywhere and Always, making it seem, ironically, quite unmysterious, quite within the range of human experience and understanding – something, good heavens, even a barbarian might sense on his own and comprehend with a little help from the Greek interpreter by his side! Dio's initiated spectators sat enthroned like gods at the centre of everything and from there looked outward, only outward, at the other divine presences in the choral rites of Nature and consequently (Nature and God being only distinguishable *in verbo*) at the Divine Presence itself.[21]

By eliminating all the tangible paraphernalia of the mysteries from his vision of the ecstatic chorus, Plotinus defied Hellenistic common sense and made the whole prospect of God mysterious again. His Late Antique sensibility – introspective, otherworldly, ascetic – called for a philosophical redefinition (for Plato had defined it before him in the myths of the Craftsman, the Chariot, and the Cave) of the unfathomable otherness of God. All that remains of Eleusis in 6.9.9 is the sacred wellspring, but it has become the least tangible and the least accessible object in the mystic rites, for the We who are always before the One can see it only indirectly through the flood of its effects and the force of that titanic emanation drives many of us back to our divided selves and to the darkness outside the sanctuary.

All the circles in the Plotinian universe seem to coalesce in the bright ring of dancers encircling the mystic wellspring and to contribute their various symbolic meanings to the meaning of this final vision – 'final' both in a causal sense as the goal of the sage's contemplative life and in a rhetorical sense as the retrospective summary and introspective conclusion of all the arguments in the *Enneads*. The ecstatic chorus represents and subsumes the virtuous inner life of the Great Chorus (2.9.7), the eternal paradigm of all the astral rounds (4.8.8), the concentric circles of Psyche and Nous (4.4.16), the cyclical dynamics of procession and return (1.6.9), and the intellectual concord of Plotinus and his disciples as they concentrated on the mystic truths of the old philosophy.

It might also be identified with the 'eudaimōn choros' or 'blessed chorus' of stars, gods, and human souls imagined by Socrates in the Myth of the Chariot (*Phaedrus* 250b–c) and interpreted as the archetype of the cycle of rational thoughts in the World-Soul, the 'kyklos exōthen' or 'circle on the outside,' which the Craftsman united with the cosmic body to ensure that its axial rotation would be rationally controlled (*Timaeus* 36e). Plotinus tended to interpret the Platonic analogy between the Craftsman's Model and its cosmic image in the light of an Aristotelian distinction which allowed him to extend the reference of the term 'choreia' from visible and temporal manifestations of order to the visionary order of the intelligible world, namely the distinction between potentiality and actuality.

Potential movements were those that had yet to begin or were still in progress and had some way to go before reaching their appointed end; actualized movements were those that had reached their appointed end, leaving the mover and objects moved in a stable relation to each other. Though an archetype or model can certainly be conceived apart from any images reflecting its formal characteristics, an actualized movement always presupposes a phase of potentiality and so cannot be conceived in total isolation from the events or stages of development leading up to it. By imagining the dance of life as both a potential and an actualized movement, Plotinus was able to distinguish the temporal chorus of stars encircling the earth from the eternal chorus of intellects encircling the One without wrenching the two choruses apart into a Gnostic dualism of matter and spirit.

The pantomime of the Living Being was a dance still in progress, a potential movement, for the limbs of the dancer continued to move from point to point; the ecstatic circling of intellects around the One was a dance (in fact the same dance) on the verge of completion or actualization; and the static circle of Nous was the 'choreia entheos' in its actualized state. 'If the chorus of the stars should at some time come to a stand-still,' he reflected in 4.4.8,

> the whole dance ['hē pasa' sc 'choreia'] would be perfected or executed from beginning to end or indeed endless, complete in each part. If their round might be compared to such a dance as this, it would exist forever and be forever complete.

To conceive the dance of the stars as a movement 'executed from beginning to end,' that is, in its actualized state, one might imagine the slow diurnal revolution of a single star accelerated to an infinite speed: as the star whirled round the earth faster and faster like the bright tip of a rapidly rotating pinwheel, it would no longer seem to pass from point to point but to be on all points of the circumference at once. The resulting visual image would not be of a moving point of light but of an unbroken circle, timeless because it is motionless, and it would represent not a diminution in the star's existence but rather the sum of all its moments of life seen simultaneously. Such a circle is the Plotinian 'choreia entheos,' except that the We who participate in it include all the stars and all the rational creatures subordinate to the stars and all the primal beings subordinate to the One. In such a ring the 'archē' or beginning of the dance of life cannot be distinguished from the 'telos,' its consummation or final pose.

Jung has interpreted the circular design of mandalas, the diagrams drawn by Hindu mystics for use in ritual meditation, as archetypal images of the self withdrawing from the world of the senses and contemplating its role in the cyclical patterns of the cosmos.[22] If the endless choral round in 6.9.8–9 were conceived as a kind of mandala, then its circular configuration would appear to symbolize the defensive boundary of the self and thus to divide subject from object, participant from spectator, the life-forces of the soul from the forces of destruction lurking outside it. In this light the design of the dance might also be read as an archetypal image of the introverted personality, which Jung associated with such tendencies as absent-mindedness, withdrawal from social contact, preoccupation with purely subjective interests, and obsessive self-analysis. Yet this is *not* how Plotinus (who with his many social interests was hardly an introvert, despite his powers of intense concentration and his periods of self-absorption) would have us perceive his mystic circle. If we try to imagine it with internal vision – 'to see it as one and to see it as our very selves' – it ceases to be a dividing-line at all. It is an emblem of the first person plural, the united We, not of the first person singular, the isolated I. The ring cannot be observed by a single detached spectator, for everyone and everything generated in the dance of life must to some extent participate in the virtues flowing out from the central 'archē,' though only a few human souls (Plotinus regretted to say) also perceive the undiminishable unity of that centre to be their spiritual 'telos.' They alone could realize their potential as dancers in the contemplative return of the Many to the One, and foremost among them (Porphyry rejoiced to announce) was the author of the *Enneads*.

Like the chorus of Gnostic disciples in the Acts of John, the chorus of Neoplatonic spectators in 'On the Good or the One' enact in ritual play the paradoxes peculiar to their unitive centre. Since their centre overflows with creative energy their round-dance must represent the artistic activity of all living creatures guided by the logos; yet since their centre remains utterly immobile their movement in the round has been reduced to an absolute minimum. The dancers strive only to hold their positions and to chant beautifully. Gone from their dance are the leaping and turning of the Redeemer's ring and the continual shifting of limbs in the pantomime of the Living Being. In fact the only movement disturbing the serenity of their circle is a purely psychological vacillation, a turning outward and a turning inward, representing, respectively, the impulse of the fallen soul to abandon itself to the world of the senses and the contrary desire of the soaring contemplative intellect to unite itself with God.

The Plotinian 'choreia entheos' is hardly a dance at all yet it is the whole dance at the moment of its perfection. It is supposedly an initiation into divine mysteries yet what it reveals to its initiates is the infinite mystery of their unknowable centre. It binds its dancers forever in a cycle of thoughts more inhibitive than the fateful circling of the World-Soul yet it releases their intellects from the divisive concerns of the body and of the self in an ecstasy more exhilarating than the rush of the Revel-King. To analyse the parts of this coalescent image is to be teased out of thought by a circle whose centre is nowhere and whose circumference is everywhere. In it all contraries meet. It is a movement in stasis, a beginning in an ending, a rational order leading to divine mania, a Gnostic round with an absolutely secret centre yet with no secret knowledge of salvation. The coalescent image can be glimpsed only for an instant before the multiple details of the cosmic pantomime, the lines, the colours, the bright limbs raised and lowered, crowd back into view and force the initiate to see once again in the mode of separation, dividing the beholder from the beheld.

The disparity between the One and its first offspring was felt by Plotinus to be so much greater than any difference between Nous and its innumerable descendants that everything in the mirroring worlds of Being and Becoming tended to coalesce into a single category of existence (multiplicity-in-unity) beneath the autonomous presence of the One, which lay, as the sage remarked rather cryptically in 5.5.6, 'beyond Being.' The distinction between the musical director and the chorus in 6.9.8 corresponds to the ontological distinction between the One beyond Being and the Many who come into being because of the One; the same contrast might now be seen to underlie the distinction Plotinus insisted upon drawing between music and dance in his description of the cosmic pantomime in 4.4.33. The flute-playing, singing, and other accompaniments, and by implication the musical director, contributed to the pantomime but were nonetheless 'external to the dancing itself:' so too was the One external to the dance and yet essential to its artistic perfection. Out of the One in an immutable sequence flowed two, three, four, and all the numbers underlying the harmony of the Apollonian cosmos, a sequence imitated in the generation of Nous, Psyche, the World-Soul, and the multiplicity of the visible world, and then reversed in their contemplative return to the unity of their Origin.

As Lycinus informed Crato in *The Pantomime* (69), the most skilful pantomimic dancers were said to be 'cheirosophoi' or 'hand-wise' because they could express through an elaborate system of symbolic and imitative hand-gestures abstruse Pythagorean and Platonic doctrines concerning the divine origin of numbers, the mathematical basis of cosmic sympathy, and the formal perfection of intelligible reality. These were the very doctrines that the Living Being, the wisest of all pantomimic dancers, communicated to the Neoplatonic Spectator through the subtle arrangement and rearrangement of its many limbs. Pantomimic dancing was an art not only of changing and forming but also of holding poses: the dancer moved, and froze, and moved, and froze, constantly punctuating the flow of his performance with set poses (known technically as 'scheseis' or 'schēmata') which displayed his supple limbs in various symmetrical configurations. These static moments are described by Lycinus (36) and Plotinus (4.4.33) as a distinctive aspect of pantomimic technique, and might be conceived as the culmination of the dynamic sequences leading up to them, or in Aristotelian terms, the actualization of individual movements within the dance. As Plotinus indicates in 4.4.33, the spectators fixed their attention not so much on the dynamism of the dance as on its static poses, which they would read one by one like words in a sentence or glyphs in an inscription. By knowing the sign-language of the dance the spectators could tell how each pose helped to advance the dancer's mythological or philosophical theme and why at any given moment in the performance such and such a pose, and no other, was required to express the deed or emotion or concept appropriate to the dancer's subject. The dancer was thus always striving to reach an end – in the short run the momentary pause at the end of each dynamic sequence, and in the long run the concluding moment when his theme was fully expressed and his performance could be contemplated as an artistic whole. The end towards which the Living Being was dancing, the 'telos' of all its temporal movements, was the stillness of the ecstatic intellects in the circular 'schēma' of eternity.

Whatever his role in the selection of 'On the Good or the One' as the final text in the orchestrated edition of the sage's writings, Apollo was certainly responsible for providing Porphyry with a fitting text to end his homiletic account of the sage's life: namely, an oracle on the death and apotheosis of Plotinus which was sung by the choragus of the Muses amid the tuneful spheres and then delivered to Porphyry via his friend and fellow disciple Amelius. The gushing Homeric verses of this oracle fill the twenty-second section of the *Vita Plotini* with consoling images of the Apollonian harmony of superlunary life, the timely release of the sage from the body of which he had been ashamed, the swift ascent of his soul through the celestial circles, and finally his entrance into the eternal chorus of heroes and philosophers in the Empyrean, a climactic vision which neatly parallels the vision of the ecstatic choral dance at the end of the *Enneads*. As Apollo reveals in his opening verses, the glory of Plotinus will be no less than that of Achilles:

> *I strike my lyre and raise my voice in an immortal song*
> *About a gentle friend, weaving it out of honey-sweet tones*

Of the tuneful cithara struck by the golden plectrum.
And I call upon the Muses to raise their voices with me
In revel-cries spanning all the notes, in floods of
universal harmony,
As when they set their dance in motion [stēsai choron]
And glorified Aeacides in Homer's divinely inspired verses.
Come, sacred chorus of Muses, let us sing with one voice,
Breathing forth the greatest and loveliest of all songs,
While I, Phoebus of the thick hair, sing in your midst.

Having set the dance in motion, the divine poet proceeds to welcome the
spirit of Plotinus into the eternal chorus by reviewing the three stages in
the philosopher's contemplative return to Heaven. The first stage, purgation
of the sins of the fleshly life, he compares to the shipwrecked Odysseus'
victorious struggle against the ocean waves (*Odyssey* v.399):

Spirit, once a man! Now you are nearing the diviner lot
Of a spirit, for the bond of human necessity has been loosened
For you! From the loud-roaring surge of the fleshly life
To the shore of the full-flowing stream, swiftly, vigorously
You swam, aloof from the crowd of the sinful,
There to get a firm footing on the curved path of the pure soul,
Where the radiance of God shines round you, where
divine laws
Abide in purity far away from lawless sinfulness.
Then, too, when you were striving to escape the bitter wave
Of this blood-gorged life, from its loathesome whirlpools,
In the midst of its billows and unexpected surges,
Often the Blessed Ones showed you the nearness of the goal.

The second stage, illumination of the soul by the astral gods, Apollo predictably describes as a strengthening of the sage's powers of vision:

Often when your mind was venturing out impulsively
Upon crooked paths, the Immortals raised you by a
straight path
To the celestial circles and lifted you up to the divine road,
Sending down to you an intense ray of light
So that your eyes might see out of the mournful gloom.
Never were your eyelids closed by sweet sleep;
Rather, while you were borne in the whirl, you dispelled
The heavy cloud that would have closed your eyes and saw

Many graceful sights which may not easily be seen
By men, not even by those who search for wisdom.

Union with the gods, the third stage, is the reward of purgation and the
result of illumination:

But now that you have been freed from the stage,
Have left the tomb of your godlike soul, you go at once
To the company of the gods! There blow the winds of delight;
There, in Heaven, one sees affection and soft desire
Full of pure felicity, forever brimming with ambrosial streams
From the gods whence flow the allurements
Of the Loves, and a sweet breeze, and a tranquil sky;
There dwell Minos and Rhadamanthus, brothers of the
                                                    golden race
Of great Zeus; there dwell Aeacus the just,
And Plato the sacred power, and Pythagoras the virtuous,
And all who have established the dance of immortal Eros
[hossoi te choron stērixan erōtos athanatou]
And deserved to share a common bond of kinship
With spirits most blessed, where the heart delights
Forever in joyful festivities. How many trials, o blessed one,
Have you endured! Now among holy spirits
Do you move, bearing a crown of vigorous life.

Like Plotinus in the conclusion of 'On the Good or the One,' Apollo echoes
in these climactic verses of his oracle the ardent rhetoric of Plato's *Symposium*, particularly the speeches of Pausanius, Agathon, and Socrates; his
reference to 'the dance of immortal Eros,' for instance, is probably a direct
allusion to Agathon's encomiastic remark that 'at festivals, at choral dances
[en chorois], at sacrifices Eros becomes our leader' (197d). What Agathon
meant by this was quite simply that the conviviality of men and women on
such social and religious occasions was due to a natural instinct, prevalent
throughout the cosmos, for creatures of the same species to enjoy each
other's company and to prefer amity to discord. In typical Neoplatonic
fashion Porphyry's Apollo transmutes this visual image of earthly conviviality into a visionary image of heavenly unity, spiritual kinship, and sanc-
tification through desire for the Good.

Plotinus' participation in the dance of immortal Eros symbolized his union
with the gods in two respects: first, intellectually, through his exalted understanding of their virtues and perfect sympathy with their desire to remain
near the fountainhead of eternal life; and second, ontologically, through the

complete assimilation of his once-fallen nature to their unfallen state of harmony. Thus metamorphosed into a 'sacred power' like Plato and Pythagoras, the defender of the old philosophy joins ranks with the old philosophers to perpetuate the analogy between choreia and paideia in Heaven as they once did on earth.

To their everlasting dance the choral harmony of Apollo and the Muses has been a consoling prelude, though the prelude itself must have an ending:

> Let us stay our song and the gracefully turning circle of
> our dance
> [Stēsomen molpēn te chorou t' eudinea kyklon]
> In honour of Plotinus the happy, o Muses! This much
> Has my golden lyre to tell of his blessed fortune!
> (Vita Plotini 22.13–63)

As if the revelations in the oracle were not proof enough of the sage's sanctity, Porphyry goes on to claim that Plotinus achieved union with the One 'in ineffable actuality and not just in potentiality' no less than four times *before* his death, and that he, Porphyry, had done so at least once before the end of his sixty-eighth year (*Vita Plotini* 23). The first apologist for Neoplatonism was also Late Antiquity's first great anti-Christian polemicist, and he was proud of such mystical statistics because they proved that pagans who refused to listen to the exhortations of Christian proselytizers could participate in the heavenly chorus through their own intellectual efforts and win their crowns of eternal life without the agony of martyrdom, the offices of Ecclesia, and the grace of a crucified Redeemer.

'He who would speak precisely,' concluded Plotinus in 6.9.3, 'must not call the One a 'this' or a 'that': we can but circle round it on the outside, wishing to put into words our experience of these things, sometimes revolving near the One, sometimes falling away because of the perplexities surrounding it.' By creating a verbal image of the cosmos, the Neoplatonic Sage could in a practical sense overcome this failure of language: he could structure his writings in such a way that the artistic plan implicit in the circling world of time would also be implicit in the circling words through which his perplexing vision of the One was at least partially clarified. If his readers could be rhetorically induced to participate in the circular contemplations of the Living Being, then they too might share the same inner vision as the sage and so the need for strictly analytical language ('this' distinguished from 'that') would disappear.

The notion that the grammatical and especially the poetical ordering of language might reflect the order of the cosmic dance was expressed five centuries before Plotinus and Porphyry by the Sanskrit grammarian Patañjali. In his *Mahābhāṣya* Patañjali related that Shiva Nataraja had appeared in person to the first great Indian linguist Panini (c 400 BC) and communicated to him the fourteen principal phonemes of Sanskrit by beating fourteen times on his drum. Panini promptly recorded his divine revelation in fourteen sutras or aphorisms which established the Sanskrit alphabet and formed the basis for all subsequent rules of phonology, syntax, word-formation, and prosody in that language. Reviewing these primary linguistic rules, which are still known as the Shivasutras, Patañjali remarked that the traditional alphabet of Sanskrit 'is eternal like the moon and stars,' and that by studying its order one could acquire knowledge of its divine source and salvation for the soul.[23] The full implications of the theory that words as well as stars could dance under the rule of number were not to be realized in the West until the Neoplatonic vision of choreia had entered the poetry of Late Antique philosophers and emerged in the philosophy of late medieval poets.

5

Chorus in Chaos

*Plato says that the earth is 'the guardian and craftsman of day and night'
for the following reasons: day is created when the sun is brought near the
earth and illuminates the regions lying beneath it; and the dark veil of night
arises because the earth faces the curving courses of the sun and is cast partly
in the shade. He also expressly called earth 'the guardian' of night and day
because it is immobile. For night is not born when day has perished, nor does
day arise at the loss of night. It never fails that each follows the other
unharmed, and this is so because the earth always remains in its own place
as a spectator (I think one might say) of all that takes place before its sight.
Hence it deserves to be called their guardian. I believe that he also calls it
'the first and eldest of the gods' for perhaps two reasons. First, it is a place
capable of supporting living creatures, and by necessity a place will be conceived as older than the things existing in it. Second, it possesses the essential
characteristics of a point, and a point as our minds innately conceive it
is older than all magnitudes and quantities. As Hesiod says ['Theogony'
116–18]:*

> *Indeed Chaos existed first; but thereafter arose
> Broad-breasted Earth, the stable foundation of all
> Who live forever. ...*

*The poet teaches that after Chaos, which the Greeks call 'hylē' and we call
'silva,' the earth was established as a fixed and immobile foundation in the
middle of the universal revolution. Our minds naturally perceive things at
rest before things in motion, and every motion of course begins after a period
of rest.*

The wandering stars are famous for their measured and harmonious com-motion, which Plato calls a choral dance [choream]. We can see their artistic activities most clearly in their progressions and revolutions (as when they appear to advance quite far with a very rapid motion or stand still for a long time in one and the same spot or are thought to be borne backwards); then in their conjunctions, illuminations, eclipses at dawn or sunset, periodic re-turns, equinoxes, and all their changes in size and shape; and lastly in the waning and waxing of their light and other changes of this sort. In case anyone should wish to dispute these matters, Plato says that the labour of arguing over them would be wearisome and unavailing, and excuses himself from doing so on the grounds that such a discussion would pertain more to astronomy than to natural philosophy.

CALCIDIUS, *Commentary on the Timaeus* CXXIII–CXXIV[1]

Excusing the Commotion

The Apollonian oracle with which Porphyry drew his life of Plotinus to a triumphant close assured pagan intellectuals that if they raised their minds above the bitter tides of 'this blood-gorged life' they too, like Plotinus, would hear the supracosmic harmony of the Muses and dance through the heavens into the exalted company of Plato and Pythagoras. Besides this peculiarly academic apotheosis the oracle also heralded the confluence of poetry and philosophy in the turbulent intellectual life of the fourth and fifth centuries. Though few Christian intellectuals at the time of Porphyry's death (c 305 AD) would have been inclined to enter into the 'gracefully turning circle' of the Neoplatonic Muses, many of them were as anxious as their pagan counterparts to see the dance of time from the perspective of the whole and to circle nearer and nearer in the spirit to the eternal wellspring of light and life.

So persistent was the afterglow of the Second Sophistic Movement that Platonists of all religious tempers – those fiercely opposing Christianity, those agonizing over conversion, those marching gladly in the ranks of the Church Militant – would perceive the menacing 'agitatio' or commotion of the planets through an aura of nostalgic metaphors of universal peace and stability, and the more agitated grew the bitter tides of life in this era of clashing creeds, fractious synods, protracted schisms, and imperial aposta-sies, the more fervently were contemplative souls in the midst of the tumult to utter the ancient consolations of choreia. Order had always reigned among the errant stars, they assured themselves, and it would ultimately reign among their risen spirits even if at the present no order seemed to prevail among the colliding choruses on the earthly stage. Like allegorical poets they tended to veil their cosmological arguments in subtle webs of mythological or biblical imagery and to view nature not as an enigmatic series of phenomena to be measured and demystified but as an oracular hymn celebrating the power of the Divine Poet who had translated chaos into choral harmony.

Of all the Late Antique philosophers who blurred Plato's distinction between poetic fiction and philosophical truth, and whose philosophical fictions and poetic truths would stimulate the visual imagination of the great cosmological poets of the Latin Middle Ages, perhaps the least poetic as a writer (though not necessarily as a thinker) was Calcidius. Just who Calcidius was and what career he may have pursued under what emperor are still disputed questions, but what sort of writer he was *not* may be easily ascertained by a quick glance at even a small stretch of his prose. He was not a master of Latin rhetoric like Augustine or an exuberantly fanciful allegorist like Martianus Capella or a subtle prosodist like Boethius. He may not even have been a native speaker of Latin. One could hardly have predicted from his prose style alone, which is gnarled with Greek constructions and pestered with forbidding technical terms, that his only surviving work – an incomplete Latin translation of the *Timaeus* (17a–53c) accompanied by an unfinished commentary in two books – would be directly linked to a prodigious series of medieval cosmological poems. Yet such was its odd destiny: when Greek scholarship declined to the point of extinction in the Latin West after Constantine's removal of the imperial court from Rome to Byzantium, the only Platonic dialogue that would survive the barbarian invasions to have a significant impact on the intellectual and literary history of medieval Europe was the *Timaeus* – Calcidius' *Timaeus*. From the mighty current of Hellenistic and Late Antique Platonism that had sprung directly from the fountainhead of Plato's complete oeuvre, only a trickle would ever reach medieval Chartres, Paris, and Florence, and much of that would be channelled through the Stygian Latin of this obscure self-effacing scholar.

Drab and sluggish as it is, his prose can at odd moments catch the retrospective eye with unexpected glints of poetry. A stray term or definition can suddenly evoke the mythical cosmos of the Chartrian poets who looked for signs of the Christian Heaven in the dances of Platonic stars, and here and there an old image of cosmic order, its oracular implications barely noticed by the unimaginative commentator, can reflect the distant glory of the carollers in Dante's Heaven of the Sun. This oddly poetical cast to Calcidius' thought – if indeed his 'average intellect' (as he aptly described it in section IV of his commentary) ever produced anything that might be identified as *his* thought – is of course partly an effect of reading him with his celebrated medieval readers in mind: his notions of world-order have inevitably acquired a certain poetic lustre because they were inherited and polished up by Bernardus Silvestris in the mid-twelfth century, Alanus de

Insulis in the late twelfth and early thirteenth, and Dante in the early four-teenth. Bernardus would turn the Calcidian term 'silva' (literally 'lumber') into the name of a primordial goddess representing the formless material substrate of all temporal existence; Alanus would transform the 'measured and harmonious commotion' of Calcidian planets into a 'chorea' of gems on the crown of his heroine Natura; and Dante would have his beloved mentor Beatrice discourse on the origins of the human soul according to 'Timeo' (that is, according to Calcidius) in the Heaven of the Moon.[2]

Yet, quite apart from their literary transmutation of elements in the Cal-cidian world-picture, something intrinsically poetic might be discerned in those raw elements – the figurative terms, the imagistic definitions, the mythological doctrines accepted by the comentator – to which these alle-gorical poets responded in sympathy and were instinctively drawn. Certainly the best that can be said of Calcidius as a thinker in his own right is that his work would not be out of place in a minor but respectable philosophical journal, and for that very reason, because it offers such a prosy matter-of-fact description of a cosmos now felt to be little more than a quaint literary invention, his commentary is a striking indication that at one time the poetic universe was conceived as neither a poet's fiction nor a humanist's daydream. Calcidius wrote about dancing planets, musical stars, choruses of daimones, astral souls, and ocular fire as unrhapsodically as someone today might write about the random collisions of subatomic particles.

When he rhapsodized at all it was over Plato's accomplishments as a teacher and rhetorician. Where other philosophers had blocked the flow of intellectual illumination with their matter-moulded language, Plato had mi-raculously communicated the loftiest secrets of the Divine Plan in words that everyone (with a little help) might understand. The Latin West would see the *Timaeus* through Calcidian eyes as Plato's 'inexpressible outpouring of abundant blessedness' (iv) – a phrase indicating that Calcidius wished the dialogue to be read not as a piece of speculative prose but as the sublime effusion of a divinely inspired poet. Plato was thus elevated to the ranks of Homer and Hesiod and distinguished from the contentious rabble of pe-dantic academics who called themselves philosophers in the Late Antique schools. Conceiving his translation as a humble extension of Plato's inex-pressible outpouring, a channel by which those who knew too little Greek to fathom the Myth of the Craftsman on their own might gain access to the abundant benefits of a Platonic education, Calcidius added to it his copious commentary mainly to dispel the notorious and what he considered merely apparent obscurities in the Myth. But his commentary was written for a second purpose, a polemical purpose, which was to counteract the academic élitism of certain learned contemporaries of his who wished to dam up Plato's effusion of wisdom and shower its blessings on a private circle of students initiated in the mysteries of Attic Greek. (Who precisely these academic adversaries were he declined to say: perhaps they belonged to some Platonizing Gnostic sect or to the mystical coteries of the second and third generation of Neoplatonists.) Their intellectual snobbery appalled him because it ran counter to what he felt was the original public-spiritedness of Platonic education, and thus seriously threatened the continuity of the old philosophy.

His earnest desire to be as generous with his own knowledge as he believed Plato to have been with his is reflected in the expansive structure of his commentary, which opens up into a series of encyclopaedic treatises on psychology, arithmetic, geometry, harmony, astronomy, and physics loosely arranged according to the sequence of topics in the first half of the Myth and containing far more information than a simple annotation of Plato's text would require. Like most Late Antique Platonists he assumed that the poets of ancient Greece could be cited as oracular authorities to substantiate the conclusions Plato had drawn from 'proofs appropriate to his questions' (1), and so for pedagogical corroboration as well as rhetorical variety he wove into his commentary a generous number of poetic excerpts – six from Homer, six from Empedocles, two from Euripides, and one each from Hesiod and the author of the so-called 'Golden Poem' whom he supposed to be none other than the fabled Pythagoras – all translated with fair accuracy into passable Latin verse. The Muses may not have filled Calcidius with heavenly inspiration or welcomed his average intellect into the Chorus of Immortal Eros, but they did not entirely desert him. In his own plodding bookish way he manifests as strong an intellectual attraction to poetry as Porphyry or Augustine or Boethius.

For instance, in his treatise 'On the Four Kinds of Living Creatures' which begins the second part of his commentary, he draws attention to the poetic source of Plato's dictum that the earth was 'the first and eldest of the gods born within the heavens' (*Timaeus* 40d), namely Hesiod's revelation that broad-breasted Gaia or Earth was the first deity, along with Tartarus and Eros, to come into being after Chaos (*Theogony* 116–18). Twentieth-century comentators on the dialogue such as A.E. Taylor and F.M. Cornford agree with Calcidius that Plato was indeed echoing Hesiod in this passage, but where Taylor and Cornford simply note the allusion Calcidius cites the relevant verses from the poet in order to validate the philosopher's pronouncement and to unfold its implications.[3] Identifying Plato's literary sources is of minor interest to him: his prevailing aim is to demonstrate the undying truth of Platonic cosmology by translating its mythological fictions into encyclopaedic facts. Hence Plato's quasi-poetic description of the earth as a divine craftsman and steadfast guardian becomes in its Calcidian paraphrase an astronomical exposition of the earth's role in the measurement of time and a geometrical account of its position in the celestial sphere. Hesiod's quasi-philosophical passage on the birth of Gaia is paraphrased in a similar manner: first Calcidius translates it into the diction of Latin cosmological poetry and then into the technical language of Hellenistic physics. The Greek noun 'chaos,' which Hesiod used as a divine name, is rendered by the Lucretian term 'caligo' (misty darkness) and then defined as synonymous with the Stoic term 'hylē' and its Ciceronian equivalent 'silva' (primal matter). These paraphrases serve not only to demonstrate that Hesiod and Plato reached the same conclusion regarding the antiquity and divinity of the earth but also to verify the literal significance of their figurative language. Calcidius is determined to prove that what was known to the poet through divine inspiration and to the philosopher through rational inquiry must be true knowledge (and not mere opinion) since it is based on certain fixed conceptions of cosmic order latent in every human mind.

His tendency to interpret Plato's cosmological metaphors not as metaphors at all but as momentarily enigmatic or paradoxical expressions of prophetic wisdom which prove upon careful consideration to be literally true – in effect, as oracles – is further illustrated in his discussion of the perplexing 'agitatio' of the planets 'which Plato calls a choral dance' (CXXXIV). Plato did not in fact speak of the 'commotion' or 'violent tossing' of the planets in his summary of the four kinds of living creatures, nor did he compare such tumultuous motion to the harmonious revolution of a chorus. A glance back at *Timaeus* 40d will confirm that he used the noun 'choreia' (which Calcidius passed on to the Middle Ages in its transliterated Latin form 'chorea') solely in reference to the diversified motions of the heavenly bodies – motions that appeared violent or threatening only to spectators ignorant of mathematics and astronomy. In his paraphrase of the passage Calcidius turns the metaphor of the dance into an oxymoron or rhetorical contradiction by defining the motion of the planetary chorus as an 'agitatio' which is nevertheless 'modulata' ('measured' or 'rhythmical') and 'consonans' ('harmonious' or 'accordant'). In its original context the metaphor served to reinforce Timaeus' optimistic suggestion that an artistic plan determined and united the diverse motions of the planets, though of course it did not prove this hypothesis.

Neglecting for once to provide a 'proof appropriate to his question,' Plato simply dismissed the problem of determining the laws of planetary motion on the rhetorical grounds that the subject would be difficult for Timaeus to explain without an armillary sphere and wearisome for an audience unacquainted with the technicalities of astronomy. These excuses (for what amounts to a blatant instance of Platonic question-begging) Calcidius accepts without a blink, though he must have suspected that his more skeptical readers would notice the hiatus in the argument and cast doubt on the Great Oracle's authority, for, springing to Plato's defence, he offers yet another excuse for the omission of the proof. Since Plato in his abundant wisdom was always careful to argue in terms appropriate to the discipline under consideration, and since he would therefore have expressed the solution to a complex astronomical problem in the technical language of an astronomer, and not in the terms, say, of a musician or logician, his remarks on the planetary 'chorea' must pertain not to astronomy (at least not primarily) but to that science which sets forth the general causes of cosmic order, namely 'physiologia' or 'natural philosophy.' Having chosen to write in the terms of a natural philosopher, Plato was not obliged to lose his readers in the maze of astronomical diagrams and calculations required to prove the hypothesis implicit in his metaphor.

Despite these excuses, the awkward question remained: where were the diagrams and calculations to prove that the wanderings of the planets were truly integrated into the circular design of the cosmic dance? If Calcidius could not supply these in his commentary, then his oxymoronic phrase 'measured and harmonious commotion' would cease to be merely a rhetorical contradiction. It would point to an unresolved paradox at the core of Platonic cosmology, a clash between Plato's optimistic conviction that cosmic harmony was essentially a visual phenomenon and his unquestioned assumption that irrationality, disorder, randomness, and inconstancy were excluded from the nature of the highest temporal life-forms, the celestial gods. Excusing Plato for skipping a few steps in his all-encompassing argument was far easier than excusing the planets for the perpetual commotion they seemed to cause in the midst of the universal revolution, and Calcidius must be given credit for braving the complexities of Hellenistic astronomy in order to guard Plato's 'physiological' vision of cosmic order fom Skeptical attack, and for realizing that the credibility of that vision, and hence its continuity, depended largely on his supplying the mathematical proofs that would resolve the paradox.

This he attempted to do by translating or closely paraphrasing several long excerpts from a Greek manual on mathematical astronomy and celestial harmonics (probably Theon of Smyrna's *Expositio*, written in the early second century AD) which he incorporated without acknowledgement into his commentary whenever he needed an impressive technical explanation to back up Plato's pronouncements about celestial order.[4] His detailed discussion of the planets in LXIX–CXVIII proves to be hardly less tangled and perplexing than their idiosyncratic motions along the Circle of the Different. Though Theon's synopsis of epicyclical astronomy provided him with rudimentary theoretical explanations of such planetary phenomena as retrograde motion and eclipses, he could offer his reader no constant harmonic formula or comprehensive geometrical schema to account for all the planetary deviations, either individually or sequentially. His valiant efforts to resolve the paradox mathematically merely obfuscate the problems Plato had so craftily evaded, and the imposing façade of macrocosmic diagrams and harmonic ratios behind which he hoped to enshrine the metaphoric tenets of Platonic cosmology fails to conceal the glaring inconsistencies in his argument. In one breath he could assert that all the vicissitudes of sublunary life were the direct result of the unpredictable behaviour of the planets (LXXVI), and in the next insist that 'there is no inconsistency in divine acts' (LXXVII) and that the divine chorus of the planets must therefore circle 'with an equal and orderly pace' (LXXVII) and chant 'musical measures in their whirling' (XCV).

A paradox may be resolved in at least two ways: either by denying the truth of one or other of its contradictory propositions; or by redefining the terms in one or both of the propositions to eliminate the contradiction *in facto* (though it may of course remain *in verbo* as an oxymoron). Calcidius, more by trial and error than by logical deliberation, tested out both ways in his attempt to reconcile his ocular perception of the planetary 'agitatio' with Plato's oracular vision of the planetary 'chorea.' If he was to integrate the planets into the astral chorus, he had to lose confidence in the power of the human eye to discern the true order of the heavens, which was tantamount to denying the Platonic assumption that cosmic order was primarily a visual phenomenon. Yet if he was to defend the validity of the Platonic world-view, he had to make certain refinements in Plato's theory of eyesight in order to redefine the circumstances – the ideal circumstances – under which the human eye might make out the configurations of a dance in the commotion along the zodiac.

That is not to say that Calcidius was ever tempted to reject the Platonic explanation of the mechanics of sight (which would survive, after all, in the portion of the dialogue he chose to translate) or to doubt the distinctively Platonic assumption that vision, being the first sense bestowed on man by the Craftsman, was the most useful and most trustworthy of all the senses. On the contrary, intent on championing the opinion that without eyes man could never have made any progress along the high road to philosophical enlightenment, he went so far as to claim that the Peripatetic and Epicurean theories of sight, which were based on Aristotle's hypothesis that visual images were impressed on the outer surface of the eye, were merely distortions of the authoritative account of vision presented in the Myth of the Craftsman. What were Aristotle and Epicurus, he complained, but jealous heirs who had squandered the rich legacy of Platonic wisdom by breaking it up 'into small mutilated opinions' (CCXLVI)? How better then could he serve the cause of education, which had been so severely damaged by the Hellenistic criticism of Platonic cosmology, than by acting as a kind of intellectual trustee whose duty was to preserve at least part of the legacy for future generations and perhaps even to add to its incomparable treasury of knowledge in some small measure?

In this conservative spirit the commentator ventured to adduce in CCXLVI what he believed was an important piece of anatomical evidence in support of Plato's doctrine of the coalescence of fires during physical vision – the existence of a two-branched channel linking the eyes to the brain. This channel, the optic nerve, had obviously been designed by the Craftsman as a means of conveying ocular fire from the organ of thought to the organs of sight so that the light generated within man's little world might merge with the kindred light of the great world's eye, the sun.

All the time-worn Platonic arguments relating the gift of sight to the genesis of philosophy were preserved for the cosmological poets of medieval Europe in the encomiastic conclusion to Calcidius' treatise 'On Vision' (CCXXXVI–CCXLVI), which is similar in both tone and content to the many passages in praise of seeing scattered throughout the exegetical works of Philo. Like Philo, Calcidius supposed that intellectual history began when those who first observed the revolutions in the cosmic theatre perceived the rhythms of time, discovered the timeless truths of mathematics, and glimpsed through the shadows of Becoming the radiance of God. 'For no one,' he declares in CCXLVI, 'would have searched for God or aspired to piety, which is the proper aim of theology, or even considered whether we ought to do what we are doing, had not the heavens and stars first been seen and a love of knowing the causes and origins of temporal things been fostered.' In spite of his vague reference to piety and theology, which was intended perhaps to assuage any Christian readers who might take offence at his assumption that human reason was alone sufficient to comprehend eternal realities, it is the creed of the old philosophy – the much-challenged belief that intellectual vision depends on physical vision – that he rattles off so zealously here, so defensively, like a lecturer of the Old School speaking to an empty room.

If his *De visu* consisted of nothing more than the encomiastic platitudes in CCXLIV–CCXLVI, one would be tempted to conclude that Calcidius accepted the divine gift of sight as cheerfully and thankfully as Philo; but since much of the *De visu* is given over to a discussion of the many potential defects of the human eye and the many ways it may be tricked by appearances, the treatise reflects the commentator's highly cautious (though not utterly skeptical) attitude to the Platonic doctrine of knowledge as an extension of physical vision. In CCXLIII, for instance, he noted that certain men were born with double vision and that others went blind on account of a 'dense humour' which congealed over the iris and prevented the emission of ocular fire. These were exceptional cases, of course, but as he knew from his study of optics the emission of ocular fire could be easily disturbed even when the viewer's eyes were of normal construction and in perfect health. Whenever a clear-sighted person directed his gaze at a concave mirror, his ocular rays were forced to bend and leap in such a way that false images of reality were conveyed to his soul: his face would appear elongated and contorted or would suddenly seem to jump from the lower rim of the mirror to the higher. Calcidius called this type of optical illusion a 'prava intuitio' or 'distorted reflection' (CCXLI) to distinguish it from a 'tuitio' or 'simple and unobstructed visual sensation,' which was supposed to occur when the ocular ray was neither bent nor fractured during coalescence with the light emanating from the visible object (CCXXXIX). Looking at the heavens with this crucial distinction in mind he could excuse the alarming commotion of the planets on the grounds that, whereas the spectacle of the fixed stars circling forever around the earth was the grandest 'tuitio' in human experience, the apparent disorder of the planetary chorus was undeniably the most spectacular and the most deceptive of 'pravae intuitiones.'

Even though the Calcidian eye was constructed out of the purest fire and water, it was still a material organ and as such was susceptible to the imperfectibility of matter as a whole. The imperfection of the best of senses was evident in the innate incapacity of the eye to perceive objects correctly within a curved field of vision, and such a field (Calcidius explained in LXXIV) was the inner surface of the celestial globe. Like a vast concave mirror the dome of the heavens had tricked many eyes – particularly the eyes of the uneducated and the superstitious – into seeing irregularities in the planetary dance which could not exist in reality because of the divine and therefore consistently rational nature of the dancers. Just as our eyes may soon detect the falseness of reflections in a concave mirror, so may our minds see through the appearance of planetary disharmony to the unchanging circular courses that the planets follow under the guidance of their choragus, the sun. We must imagine how 'they are borne through the higher curve of the zodiac according to an orderly plan which gives rise to motion both consistent and uniform, even though this seems preposterous to the eyes of men' (LXXVII). Calcidius also surmised that the appearance of disorder in the heavens might be due in part to the earth's turbulent atmosphere, which like a dense humour clouding over a diseased eye distorted and restricted our vision of the planetary chorus. The deviations of the planets 'seem from our point of view to happen, but they do not in truth happen as they seem; indeed our mistaken impression that the planets travel through the outer sphere, when in fact they travel through their own proper circles within the sphere of the fixed stars, is caused by the body of air which from our earthly vantage-point obstructs our vision of the zodiac' (LXXIV).

Given the natural weakness of the human eye, the distorting effect of a curved visual field, the constraint of an earthly vantage-point, and the shifting veils of the atmosphere, Calcidius could perceive the dance of the planets *only* in his imagination. It was no longer the grand public ceremony that Philo had seen as the visible proof of the Great King's power to unite, govern, and adorn the City of the Universe; it was not even the ludicrous little pantomime that Plotinus had looked down upon from the portals of the temple of Psyche, the rather too visible – and all too distracting – performance of a protean cosmos struggling to imitate in bodily gestures the bodiless union of intellects around the One. Seeing the dance as a whole, understanding its design, and joining its mystical movement towards God had been for Philo and Plotinus the natural steps the human intellect might take to reach the threshold of eternity, and if those steps had seemed almost effortless to their upwardly mobile intellects, that was because their intellects, made starlike by the Craftsman and more starlike by Platonic education, had perceived little distance separating the educated spectators in the cosmic theatre from their long-familiar educators, the dancing stars.

From the viewpoint of Calcidius the cosmic dance seems to take place far away – almost beyond the range of an average man's physical and intellectual vision. He has heard of its concordant motions from Plato, and from Philo (whom he cites as an authority on cosmology in CCLXXVIII), and he has even caught a partial glimpse of it himself in the revolutions of the fixed stars, which are clearly as regular and harmonious as his ancient authorities claimed. But, like a humble citizen who is too poor and insignificant to attend the noble entertainments at the palace of his emperor, he is constrained to sit in his terrestrial tenement and muse upon the remote glory of the spectacle. Occasionally he catches sight of the sun's jewelled courtiers whirling out of the East and rising along the Different, but they pass by him on their exalted way with little regard for his inferior station or his speculations about life in high circles. He does not resent their indifference. They perform the duties required of their class, and he performs those of his.

As an apologist for the celestial status quo he gladly recounts to anyone unfamiliar with the nobility their various names, ancient titles, social connections, distant relations around the globe, and proper places in the ball of the Great World:

The celestial sphere turns around eternally stationary poles and around an axis connecting those poles, the midpoint of which corresponds to the middle of the earth. All the stars accompany the whirling of the celestial sphere, and their population includes the constellations which embroider their circles about the axis and measure their orbits uniformly according to their own particular revolution. The multitude of their circles defies enumeration. Nevertheless a few of them are famous because of their noble name, and these are useful to know for the spectacle of the celestial dance [ad spectaculum caelestis choreae].

He then supplies a 'noble name' for each of the major configurations in the dance, observing the whole spectacle from an imaginary vantage-point outside the celestial sphere:

Near the superior pole which is visible and known to us is the celestial arctic circle, and it is called 'Septentrionalis' because the constellation of the seven plough-oxen containing the North Star 'Septentrio' is clustered near it. Opposite and equal to this is the celestial antarctic circle or 'Antarcticus,' which is near the hidden submerged pole and is itself hidden. Greatest of all is the middle circle which divides the sphere in two. It is called the celestial equator or 'Isemerinon' (as the Greeks say) because it causes all nights and all days to be of equal duration in those regions of the earth lying beneath it. Nevertheless, to those regions which see the sun rise and set but do not lie directly beneath this circle, it will mete out equal hours of day and night whenever the sun comes into contact with it.

(*Commentary* LXV on *Timaeus* 37–8)

Since the rhythmic interplay of the sun and the fixed stars, unlike that of the sun and the planets, invariably presented to the naked eye an orderly 'spectaculum' (theatrical show) of circular motions, Calcidius could here safely omit from his description of the cosmic dance such oxymoronic phrases as 'harmonious commotion' and 'discordant concord.'

Among the sun's more spectacular steps in the dance were its biennial traversings of the celestial equator which appeared to cause the vernal and autumnal equinoxes in those areas of the earth that saw the sun rise and set each day of the year and lay north or south of the terrestrial equator (see figure 9). If to a lowly earth-bound spectator whose eyes could never take in more than a small portion of the whole show the timing of the equinoxes offered dramatic evidence that the show was grandly ordered in all its parts, how much grander would the order of the 'caelestis chorea' seem to an educated spectator whose visual imagination could extend the arcs of the stellar revolutions visible to him on earth into full circles, then twin them by the laws of symmetry with circles in the celestial hemisphere hidden from his eyes, and thereby fashion from a supracosmic viewpoint a complete picture of the Stellatum rotating on its axis! Against this serene background of unchanging circles, how else could an educated spectator view the commotion of the planets but as a preposterous illusion of mutability?

Little wonder, then, that Calcidius stressed the usefulness of learning the noble names of the great circles of the Stellatum: 'the fairest and most magnificent procession and choral dance of all the choruses in the world' (as the Athenian Stranger had described the revolutions of the fixed stars in *Epinomis* 982e) was to Calcidius' eye the only celestial motion that still appeared fair, the only 'spectacular' evidence left to sustain his belief in the artistic design of the heavens. To name the principal figures in the dance was to be assured of the actual existence of an all-encompassing design behind the motions in the cosmic theatre. Naming brought the distant spectacle

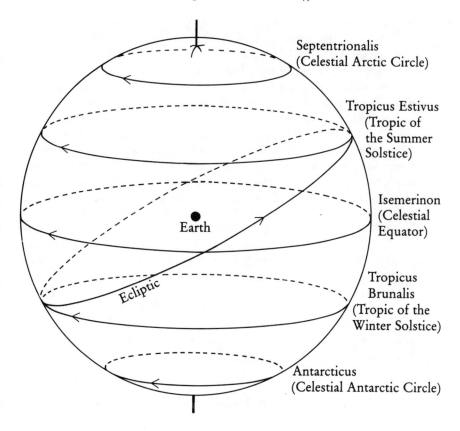

Figure 9

The principal circles traced by the fixed stars in the 'spectaculum caelestis choreae' provided Calcidius with his only visual evidence for the providential order of celestial motion. The motions visible along the ecliptic (with the exception of the sun's annual revolution) were perceived by him as a distorted reflection of the perfectly circular dance of the planets. This diagram is a modification of the *Descriptio Aplanes* ('Representation of the Sphere of the Fixed Stars') reproduced by J.H. Waszink in his edition of Calcidius' commentary, section LXVII, p 114.

intellectually nearer to the namer. In CXXVII Calcidius cited the *Epinomis* – known to him as the *Philosophus* – in order to prove that Plato had not accepted the cosmological doctrines of Orpheus and other ancient poets (doctrines often expressed in the divine names the poets gave to the parts of their mythical universe) on faith alone, but had insisted on demonstrating the truth of their oracular revelations through logical arguments.

Ironically, when his attempt to verify the Athenian Stranger's hypothesis that the harmonic laws of planetary motion could be deduced from visual evidence alone fell short of resolving a commotion into a choral dance, the literal-minded commentator had no intellectual recourse but to turn the philosopher's argument back into a poetic revelation. To reject Plato's inexpressible outpouring as plainly untrue in many particulars was quite unthinkable to him, and his credulity resulted in the intellectual equivalent of myopia. His world-view was blurriest when he tried to focus on distant objects like the planets and sharpest when he considered what was closest to his eyes – namely, words, the hallowed words of Homer, Hesiod, Euripides, Pythagoras, Plato. Without their noble names for all the 'choruses of divine powers' (CLXXXIX) that kept the tumultuous world of matter under the harmonious rule of Providence, the fragile structure of his imaginary universe would have dissolved before his eyes, leaving only a dark nameless confusion more frightening than the primitive Chaos from which had arisen, broad-breasted, the poets' immortal Earth.

The Middle Platonic Spectator

Though Calcidius' links to Platonic commentators who lived several centuries before him (like Theon of Smyrna) or several centuries after him (like Thierry of Chartres) are clear enough, his relation to the Platonists of his own era is singularly obscure. Attempts to fit his small indistinct voice into this or that section of the large dissonant chorus of those who sang the praises of the old philosophy in the fourth century have been frustrated by his virtual anonymity, his vagueness concerning the identity of his pedagogical adversaries, his ambivalent attitude to Christianity, and his apparent failure to make the least impression on any pagan or Christian author in Late Antiquity. Was he a pagan from the Levant who defied the Western ecclesiastical establishment by advertising in Latin the benefits of Platonic education? Or a Christian in the wake of a difficult conversion who struggled to reconcile the wisdom of the Greeks with that of the Hebrews? Or an old-fashioned Alexandrian Platonist whose eclectic interest in Pythagorean harmonics and Stoic physics was comparable to Philo's? Or an avant-garde Neoplatonist whose ambition was to popularize not only Plato's but also Porphyry's doctrines of world-harmony? The need to pin labels on Calcidius would not be urgent if his translation and commentary were not such prominent links in the chain of works by which Platonic cosmology was transmitted to the philosophers of post-classical Europe, and until his position in the 'chorus philosophorum' has been assessed (even if it cannot be conclusively determined) one cannot begin to define the peculiar strain of Late Antique Platonism that echoed in the cloisters of medieval Chartres and awakened the 'chorus poetarum' at the portals of the poetic universe.

The most recent editor of Calcidius, J.H. Waszink, has called attention to certain passages in the commentary which he insists show unmistakable signs of Neoplatonic, specifically Porphyrian, influence.[5] In one such passage from his treatise 'On the Four Kinds of Living Creatures' (CLXXVI–CLXXVII) Calcidius briefly distinguished three supracosmic deities: a Supreme God identified with the Good, who was 'beyond all substance and all nature'; a Divine Mind identified with Providence, 'whom the Greeks call Nous'; and a second Divine Mind identified with the World-Soul, who sustained the cosmic dance by introducing into the material world 'the harmony of divine intelligence' (known here below as the law of Fate). Though this triad does bear a certain resemblance to the Neoplatonic triad of the One, Nous, and Psyche, Calcidius did not identify his Supreme God with the One or ever mention a 'One' in his commentary, which seems a rather strange omission for an initiate in the Neoplatonic mysteries.

Disputing Waszink's interpretation of this passage, John Dillon has pointed out that the theory of a supreme principle above Nous had been suggested before Plotinus by Neopythagoreans in the second century AD, and indeed by Plato himself in his cryptic statement that the Good existed 'above Being' (*Republic* VI 509b). While Calcidius certainly knew and consulted the works of at least two second-century Platonists with Neopythagorean leanings, Theon and Numenius, and was certainly familiar with at least the main myths and arguments of the *Republic*, which he cites at several points in the commentary (for example, V, XCV, CCCXLIX), he shows no clear sign of having read or even heard of Plotinus and Porphyry, whose names do not appear in his extant writings. If he was indeed a convert to their way of thinking, he evidently chose not to reveal his Neoplatonic sympathies in his commentary – perhaps because their mystical extrapolations from Platonic cosmology were too abstruse or controversial for the kind of elementary textbook he intended to write. Dillon has concluded that Calcidius was probably not a Neoplatonist but a rather late and isolated exponent of doctrines derived from certain academic commentators on Platonic and Pythagorean cosmology who flourished mainly in the first and second centuries AD, that is, between Philo and Plotinus, and who may be conveniently labelled 'Middle Platonists' to distinguish them from the heirs of Plotinus dominant in pagan intellectual circles after the death of Porphyry.[6]

Calcidius' view of the cosmic dance as a strictly temporal spectacle is so like that of several Middle Platonists – and so unlike the Neoplatonists' distinctive vision of the dance of eternal intellects around the One – that the two passages in which he discusses the world-chorus (CXXIV and LXV) may be taken as evidence to support Dillon's reading of the commentary as a late Middle Platonic encyclopaedia. (True to his second-century roots, Calcidius spoke of the invisible activity of Nous in CLXXVI as a 'conversio' but not as a 'chorea'.) What has survived of the heterogeneous writings of the Middle Platonists in the way of doxographical quotations and para-phrases and the occasional complete treatise indicates that they were gen-erally systematic thinkers who enjoyed tying together the many loose ends in Plato's arguments, sharpening the definitions of his recurrent terms, ex-plaining away the discrepancies between the world-views of Socrates and Timaeus, and suggesting ingenious solutions to minute philosophical prob-lems without challenging the Master's comprehensive answers to the major riddles of existence. On the whole they were as modest in their intellectual attainments and aspirations as Calcidius, though some, notably Plutarch of Chaeronea and Apuleius of Madaura, were eminent in fields other than philosophy and would not have considered themselves professional expos-itors of Plato so much as amateur symposiasts.

In the early decades of the second century AD, that inveterate after-dinner Platonist, Plutarch, gathered together for the edification of two of his sons his various notes and queries concerning Plato's difficult account of the origin of the World-Soul (*Timaeus* 35a–36b) and published them in the form of a commentary entitled 'On the Generation of the Soul According to Timaeus' (*Moralia* XIII part I). In its final chapters he attempted to reconcile the conflicting theories of world-harmony expressed in the Myth of Er and the Myth of the Craftsman by conceiving the cosmic music heard by Er as the accompaniment, or rather the magical cause, of the cosmic dance en-visioned by Timaeus:

For in the 'Republic' [617b] Plato says that each of the eight spheres carries round upon it a Siren, and that each Siren utters one note in their song, and that from all their notes a single harmony is blended. These Sirens gently and loosely bind together all things in a series, and chant a harmony of eight notes in their sacred revolution and choral dance [tēs hieras periodou kai choreias], for if the unit is counted in each series of proportions the primary terms of double and triple ratios [1:2:4:8 and 1:3:9:27] totalled eight. And our elders handed down to us the tradition that there are nine Muses: eight of them, just as Plato says, to cast a spell over celestial things; and the ninth to keep earthly things from wandering in disorder by settling their differences and dispelling their confusion.

(De animae procreatione 1029c–d)

The two myths are also united by a subtle numerological correspondence Plutarch observed between the eight Sirens singing their eight notes on their eight spheres (Plato in fact referred to 'whorls' rather than 'spheres' in the Myth of Er) and the sum of eight terms in the series of ratios generated by the Craftsman in the construction of the World-Soul.

Absurdly tenuous as this correspondence will seem to anyone who does not assume that a single unified system of thought underlies all of Plato's works, to Plutarch, who did make such an assumption, the mathematical link between the two myths clearly indicated that Plato considered the miraculous unity of the dancers in the celestial chorus to have sprung not from the World-Soul itself or from anything connected with the material world but from principles of numerical order imposed on the original jumble of soul-stuff and body-stuff in the Receptacle by creative forces originating beyond it. If its ties with these divine forces were ever severed, he contended, the celestial chorus would swiftly revert to a state of primordial chaos because of an eternal source of evil lurking within the temporal sphere, an irrational, maleficent, ungenerated World-Soul distinct from and hostile to the rational World-Soul generated by the Craftsman.[7] This menacing psychic presence was restrained by the 'sacred revolution and choral dance' of the stars, but its active influence could still be detected in the errant behaviour of the planets and the frantic or capricious conduct of intemperate men.

Assailed by this enemy of all that was sacred, ceremonious, beautiful, and life-sustaining, of all that was (in Plutarch's understanding of the word) cosmic, the stars needed the supernatural inducement of the Sirens' song to keep their chorus bound 'loosely and gently' together through the unending cycles of time. Conceiving cosmic harmony primarily as an invisible spiritual force (symbolized by the unseen chorus of Sirens) which magically infused order into what would otherwise be confusion and discord, Plutarch applauded the celestial dance from a philosophical and religious standpoint not far removed from that of Philo, who, though his heavens would have resounded with the songs of angels rather than Sirens, had been delighted with the same prospect of a universe enchanted by the laws of perfect music.

Calcidius is charmed by the prospect too, noting in his commentary on *Timaeus* 36d a correspondence between the Sirens and the demiurgic numbers similar to that observed by Plutarch:

We recall from the first description of the psychogony that the World-Soul was composed in such a way that one side of it was ordered according to doubled numbers [1:2:4:8] and the other according to tripled numbers [1:3:9:27], and that each side was divided into three intervals for a total on both sides of seven distinct sections [the number 1 being counted as a section]. Therefore, in the diagram which he used to depict the soul,

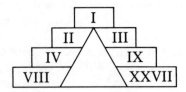

he delineates a schematic image of the universe, fixes the number of planetary circles at seven, and distances the planets one from another according to musical intervals. That is why the rotated stars,

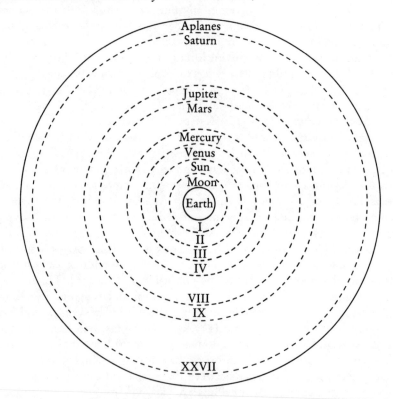

as Pythagoras teaches, move in harmony and produce musical measures in their whirling. Plato teaches the same lesson in the 'Republic' when he says that Sirens are stationed on individual circles, and that when they are rotated with their circles they utter one mellifluous song, and that one concord is produced from eight different sounds.

(*Commentary* xcv; diagrams after those in Waszink)

Turning his attention away from the dynamic visible changes in the 'caelestis chorea' – for that is surely what he is describing here, though the phrase itself does not appear in this passage – Calcidius chooses to concentrate, like Plutarch, on the fullness and sweetness of the musical concord issuing from the macrocosm, the perfect diapason which lay beyond the normal range of imperfect mortal ears but which vibrated in the memories of most Middle Platonists and their Late Antique heirs and would resound in the symphonic spheres of the medieval poetic universe.

As each revolving orb measured its distance from the other macrocosmic choristers in strict accordance with the double and triple ratios of Pythagorean harmonics, it was thought to emit a note unique to itself which blended in with all the other notes in the celestial octave to produce what Calcidius called a 'melliflua cantilena.' (This rather poetic phrase is meant to be taken quite literally: it denotes a melodic flow of notes sung in a certain sequence rather than a discordant drone of all eight notes sounded simultaneously.) Neither Plutarch nor Calcidius claimed to have heard the ravishing concord of this song, but its existence was as much a reality to them as the harmonious motions that first betrayed the mathematical measures of the song to Pythagoras.

In certain respects the correspondences drawn by Calcidius between the concert of the Sirens and the choral dance of the stars differ from those drawn by Plutarch. While Plutarch maintained Plato's original distinction between the heavenly bodies and the goddesses stationed on them, Calcidius appears to have identified the eight Sirens with the fixed stars (counted as one sphere, the Aplanes) plus the seven planetary spheres, and to have regarded the cosmic 'motus' not as the magical effect of supernatural agents of harmony but as the physical or dynamic cause of the cosmic 'cantilena.' Unlike Plutarch, moreover, he evidently arrived at a total of seven demiurgic numbers (instead of eight) by counting the number one at the start of each series of ratios once rather than twice, for from this total he derived the number of planetary spheres corresponding to the seven strips cut by the Craftsman out of the originally undivided band of the Different. This correspondence tends to obscure the numerological connection between Er's Sirens and Timaeus' stars, but since Calcidius explicitly distinguished 'eight different notes' in the celestial song, one can only assume that he implicitly counted eight demiurgic numbers as well.

The Muses whose choral harmony Plato had occasionally compared with the harmony of the cosmos, and whom Plutarch in turn tacitly identified with the celestial Sirens, are not mentioned by Calcidius in xcv or in any of his other references to the Myth of Er. This may simply reflect his close adherence to Theon's exposition of the musical details of the Myth, for Theon too avoided the ticklish problem of fitting nine Muses onto eight Siren-charmed orbs (which Plutarch solved rather mechanically by hoisting eight Muses into the heavens and retaining the ninth here below to guide earth's wayward multitudes into the sacred dance); or it may indicate – if we assume that Calcidius was acquainted with Plutarch's Platonic commentaries – that he deliberately deadened the mythological resonance of celestial music and diminished the pagan religious significance of the cosmic chorus to make the Platonic myths of world-harmony intelligible and acceptable to Christian readers.

Though fine distinctions can certainly be drawn between the world-views of Plutarch and Calcidius, their discussions of the cosmic dance are simply variations on the same Middle Platonic themes – variations which indicate their intellectual kinship within the heterogeneous ranks of Greco-Roman Platonists. These themes are, first, the perfect fusion of 'motus' and 'cantilena' in the immutable spheres above the moon, and second, the divine power of 'caelestis chorea' to sustain the round of the seasons, the conversion of the elements, the circulation of the humours, the ebb and flow of the tides, and every other variety of rhythmical change observable below the moon.

The perpetual synthesis of dynamic and musical harmony in the heavens was a favourite topic of Apuleius of Madaura, who like Plutarch is better known today as a man of letters than as a Middle Platonist. Dull as his omnium-gatherum treatise 'On the Universe' (c 140 AD) seems next to Plutarch's ingenious dialogues on specific Platonic conundra, something of the literary Apuleius, Apuleius the word-flourisher, the poetic enthusiast, comes through in his evocations of the concord reigning among the dancing stars. 'Beyond,' he declared, pointing to the realm beyond the confines of sublunary mutability,

is the home of the gods, which we call the sky. We see that the sky is indeed abounding in divine bodies – the very beautiful and resplendent fires of the sun and moon and other stars. With them it is borne along in its circular courses through the round of days and nights, conducting the choral dances of the stars [agens et choros stellarum] in such a way that they flow perpetually, with no interruption in time to bring them to an end.

(De mundo 1 290)

The prospect of countless celestial gods performing innumerable dances through an endless succession of days and nights is undoubtedly awesome, but if it is contemplated solely from the perspective of the part the intricacy of the choral design may disconcert the very spectators whom it is meant to impress. They might fear that the design is in fact too complex to be intelligible, or that its harmony is merely superficial, or that in the midst of the divine chorus lurks an evil intelligence eager to sow discord and bring back the reign of Chaos and Old Night. To offset such fears Apuleius also considered the celestial dances from the perspective of the whole. 'Despite the diverse movements of the planets,' he insisted, *there is in the world but one rotary movement by which it periodically returns to its point of departure, one concord, and one choral dance of the stars arising from their diverse settings and risings [unus stellarum chorus ex diversis occasibus ortibusque]. The Greek language assigns the very appropriate word 'cosmos' to this necklace-like ornament. For just as in choral dances [ut in choris] when the leader chants the first part of the hymn, the troupe of male and female choristers respond with one resounding harmony by mixing low voices with high, so the Divine Mind, following the model of a single unified concert, resolves the various discords in the world.*

(De mundo XXIX 355)

Plato is not the immediate source for these dogmatic remarks on the relation of the astral chorus to its shadowy conductor, the Divine Mind. Apuleius' treatise 'On the Universe' is a loose translation into Latin of an anonymous Greek work of the same title which was probably written sometime between 40 BC and 140 AD by an eclectic philosopher versed in Platonic cosmology as well as Stoic and Peripatetic physics. 'The centre of the cosmos,' the latter explained,

is unmoved and steadfast, and is occupied by the life-giving earth, the home and mother of living beings of all kinds. The whole region extending everywhere above it to the highest possible limit, the abode of the gods, is called 'heaven.' It is full of divine bodies, which we customarily call 'stars.' Eternally in motion, it dances on high together with all the stars [synanachoreuei pasi toutois] in a single unceasing revolution through all time.

(Peri kosmou II 391b 9–19)

The dry impersonal tone of this unknown pedagogue hardly differs from that of Calcidius, who, though he is not known to have consulted either the Greek or the Latin version of this treatise, evidently derived his theological approach to cosmology and his unitary conception of the cosmic dance from elementary manuals of this sort.

Apuleius and his Greek source would not have distinguished a cosmologist from a theologian, and the same can certainly be said of Calcidius. Doubtless the latter's unshakable conviction that an omnipresent deity directed the harmonious motion and song of the celestial chorus was grounded in theological elaborations of the cosmological topos of choreia such as the following homily on divine providence (thinly disguised as a lesson in astronomy) from Apuleius' source:

For the various movements of all the heavenly bodies arise because of a single revolution of the whole heaven completed in a day and a night, and though all are encompassed by a single sphere some move more swiftly and others more slowly in accordance with their intervals and their individual characters. For the moon completes its circle in a month, waxing and waning and disappearing; the sun and those which run an equal race with it, namely Venus and Mercury, complete their circle in a year; Mars in twice this time; Jupiter in twelve years; and the last planet, Saturn, in two and a half times the orbital period of Jupiter. The single harmony produced by all these as they sing together and dance in chorus throughout the heavens [choreuontōn kata ton ouranon] begins and ends in one and the same spot, truly giving to the whole the name of 'order' and not 'disorder.' In a chorus [en chorōi] when the choral director has given the signal to begin, all the chorus of men and sometimes also of women blend their voices together to produce a single pleasant harmony out of a variety of high and low notes. A similar relation exists between the cosmos and the god who administers it. On high is the keynote sounded by him who might well be called the coryphaeus. Then the stars and all the heavens move forever, and the ever-beaming sun makes his double journey, dividing night from day by his rising and setting, and thereby leading the four seasons of the year as he moves forward to the north and back to the south.

(Peri kosmou VI 399a 2–24)

In the lectures of the Athenian Stranger, Plato employed the image of the chorus to express a pedagogical relation – potentially that of intellectual equality – between man and the stars. Here the relation between educated spectator and educating spectacle is of secondary importance, and the image is used chiefly to express the inferior ontological status of the stars and all they encircle (a potentially disordered multitude of bodies) in relation to God (the dynamic cause of their unity). Assuming the role of coryphaeus or 'head-man in the chorus,' God sounds the keynote by which the celestial choristers ascertain the proper pitch for producing a single pleasing concord out of their diverse voices, and this signal from on high sets the cosmic body whirling, the fixed stars revolving, the planets counterrevolving, and the seasons dancing with the sun.

This version of the image is undoubtedly Stoic in origin and may also be Stoic in significance in this context, especially if the pious author of the treatise conceived the divine coryphaeus as ultimately inseparable from the world-chorus. (He is ambiguous on this point.) Though the Greek original of 'On the Universe' is remote enough from the mainstream of classical Platonism and late Hellenistic Pythagoreanism to have circulated in Antiquity as one of Aristotle's minor works, which in fact it is not, it seems to have been read with particular interest by second-century Platonists caught between the jarring extremes of Aristotelianism and Stoicism. Apuleius' adaptation of it reflects the readiness with which Middle Platonists borrowed terms and distinctions and metaphors from the Hellenistic critics of the old philosophy, and also the dogmatic spirit of the rhetoricians who popularized various theological and ethical themes from Middle Platonism in the wake of the Second Sophistic Movement.

Prominent among these Platonizing rhetoricians was Maximus of Tyre (fl 180–90 AD), in whose orations may be detected distinct echoes of the theological keynote sounded in 'On the Universe.' This is how Maximus, who was in effect a preacher of the old philosophy, urged his audiences to conceive the relation between God and the world-chorus:

Now suppose that this universe is harmonious like a musical instrument, and that God is its craftsman. Its harmony originates in God and then passes through the air, and the earth, and the sea, and all the animals and plants, and afterwards pervades diverse and dissimilar natures and reconciles those that are in conflict. In this way does the supreme harmony burst in upon the many voices sounding in the chorus [eis polyphōnian chorou] and turn their clamour into concord.

(*Oration* XIX.3)

Maximus' God is the dynamic cause of cosmic harmony in three different respects. Like the Platonic Craftsman he is the maker of the 'musical instrument' which comprises the greatest part of the universe, the eight celestial spheres; like the Pythagorean Apollo he is the musician who tunes and plucks the instrument (usually identified in Middle Platonic sources as a lyre) in order to pacify the clamorous crowd of sublunary elements and creatures; and like the Stoic Cosmocrator he is the supreme coryphaeus who transforms the crowd into a chorus by inducing it to sing, move, and live in perpetual concord. Though Calcidius may never have read a word of Maximus, his sympathetic consideration of a Pythagorean poem on the sequence of the planets (moon, Mercury, Venus, sun, Mars, Jupiter, Saturn) which ends with the lines

Likening the arrangement of the planets to the seven intervals
Of a plucked lyre, the Creator joined them into a concordant
group.
(*Commentary* LXXII)

attests to his familiarity with the sort of theology Maximus preached. The poem is followed by a paragraph of philosophical explication which would be read with great interest by the Chartrians and their poetic heirs:

Pythagoras believed that the universe remains constant because it is har-

monically regulated, and that the heavenly bodies emit musical sounds because they are separated from each other by suitable harmonic intervals and impelled by a tremendous thrust and impetus. Following Pythagoras, Eratosthenes agrees that musical sounds are produced by the motion of the stars but proposes a different order for their grouping. He places the sun immediately after the moon in the second sphere after the earth, recalling the famous story of Mercury's ascent through the sky soon after his invention of the lyre. While he was passing through those regions which the motions of the planets cause to resound like a musical instrument, Mercury was amazed to find that this sound was similar to that of the lyre, and that an image of the instrument he had invented should be discovered in the heavens, in the grouping of the heavenly bodies, which is the reason why their concert may be perceived.

(*Commentary* LXXIII)

Since this passage lies only seven paragraphs away from the description of the 'caelestis chorea' in LXVI and may be read as a Pythagorean coda to the exposition of Platonic astronomy in LXVII–LXXI, medieval readers of the commentary naturally tended to associate the visual (if not entirely visible) 'spectaculum' of the celestial dance with the purely mythopoetic 'imago' of the celestial lyre.

This association appears to be Middle Platonic or Neopythagorean in origin. It is not to be found in the works of Plato or in the fragments of the Presocratic Pythagoreans. Like Maximus, Calcidius evidently felt that the Platonic and Pythagorean visions of cosmic order were poetically harmonious and that chorus and lyre belonged together as aspects of a single mythological emblem of universal concord. Neither Maximus nor Calcidius seems to have been in the least disturbed by the clashing philosophical implications of the two visions – the Platonic 'spectaculum' representing an organic cosmos in which a host of rational creatures responded to signals from the World-Soul, the Pythagorean 'imago' a mechanical cosmos in which a neatly calibrated series of concentric spheres emitted notes determined by the immutable laws of harmony. Maximus easily related the two visions by distinguishing the lyre of the heavens from the chorus of sublunary elements and creatures, a distinction which makes considerable theological sense since it implies that the heavens are the material instrument through which the spiritual concord of God is conveyed to the discordant world of Man. But his divided view of the cosmos represents neither a philosophical reconciliation nor a poetic synthesis of the two visions, for it simply eliminates the spectacle of the celestial dance on which depended Plato's theory of knowledge as an extension of vision and Apollo's oracular prospect of the Chorus of Immortal Eros. Calcidius merely juxtaposes the images of the dance and the lyre in his commentary without attempting to unite them philosophically or poetically.

When an image of cosmic unity customarily employed by philosophers as a symbolic emblem of a particular cosmological system or as a metaphoric representation of various parts of a system (like the celestial lyre in the verses cited by Calcidius) takes on a fantastic existence of its own which momentarily eclipses the philosophical reality it is supposed to represent – that is to say, when it becomes the nucleus of a poetic vision which establishes its own universal frame of reference and cannot be abstracted from any system of philosophical dogmas – its spectacular design may excite the sort of wonder which is the opposite of philosophical world-weariness, a primitive world-wonder such as Calcidius recalls in his version of the 'famous story' of Mercury's ascent through the heavens. The implicit subject of this myth is the imaginative discovery of the poetic universe. On his first journey above the moon Mercury is delighted to hear music resounding through regions which to earthly ears seem utterly silent; but his delight soon gives way to amazement when he recognizes in the mathematical arrangement of the seven planetary spheres (visible only from his celestial vantage-point) an image of the musical instrument he has recently invented, the seven-stringed lyre dear to Apollo and the goddesses of poetry. At this moment of discovery the fantasy of a concordant and intelligible cosmos becomes startlingly real to him: the poetic universe is no less a reality for being an invention than is the lyre. Mercury's amazement (which will be shared by the ecstatic pilgrims whom Alanus and Dante send through the choral heavens) does not spring from the discovery of a new planet or a new movement in the celestial chorus but from a new perception of the design of the Whole.

Though the Middle Platonists persistently contemplated the myths of the creation and discovery of the poetic universe and dutifully recorded the ancient Greek images of celestial concord in philosophical poetry as well as prose, their perceptions of the choral cosmos seem on the whole to have been remarkably unimaginative. World-weariness was perhaps closer to their hearts than world-wonder, and Necessity's spindle more on their minds than Mercury's lyre. It was no wonder to them that philosophical contemplation could make the perplexing diversity of movements, sounds, and bodies in the whirl of time fade from the eternal design of the dance: they took it for granted that God or the Divine Mind, or as Calcidius assumed, God and two Divine Minds, caused all celestial movements to flow together into one rotation and all celestial sounds to blend into one concord and all celestial bodies to form one chorus.

Calcidius and his pedagogical predecessors evidently wished their God's-eye view of the world-chorus to represent the educated spectator's ultimate appreciation of cosmic unity, but what it in fact represents is a drastic simplification of the image and a dogmatic narrowing of the universal field of vision. No dazzling poetic image of the unity of life (such as the Plotinian vision of ecstatic initiates dancing around the eternal Kallichoron) rises over the old horizons of their philosophical beliefs to take the place of what those beliefs erase from the world of sensory experience. Cosmic diversity is not transcended in their thought. It is simply reviled or ignored. When a vision of cosmic unity is formed anew out of the chaos of phenomena or wrested anew from the penetralium of mystery by a bold imagistic thinker who refuses to revile or ignore the diversity of the sensory world, and when its novelty can revive in those who perceive it a sense of what Mercury felt at the discovery of the celestial lyre or what the earliest philosophers felt on first looking up to heaven and perceiving the dances of the stars, then it is 'poetic' in a fundamental sense, regardless of the medium in which it is expressed. Calcidius translated the high poetic fantasy of cosmic concord into hard pedagogical facts, and so preserved it, fossil-like, in the sediment of his prose. But something was lost in translation which would not be recovered until the twelfth century: the wonder of the educated spectator.

The Middle Platonists of course acknowledged that the resolution of sub-lunary discord into concord was wondrous to behold, that more amazing still was the uninterrupted concord of the dancing stars, and that most marvellous of all was the god who had set the melodious sky in motion. Ironically, though they were all taught to consider wonder the beginning of wisdom, none of them ever seems to have wondered what the poetic universe would have looked or sounded like from Mercury's celestial vantage-point or to have expressed the world-wonder of the first philoso-phers in high fantastic poetry just as Lucian has expressed the Cynical world-weariness of Icaromenippus in low bathetic prose. If any aspect of the cosmic dance stirred their retrospective imaginations (though not to poetry), it was the daunting antiquity of the Great Chorus rather than the perpetual newness of its concord. 'Because days and nights fill up the spaces of the months,' observed Apuleius wearily,

> months in turn roll up the revolutions of the years. But if those constellations had not begun to shine with their starry light, temporal reckoning could never have started; and the calculation of times would cease to be observed if this ancient chorus [antiquus chorus] should once stand still.

> (De Platone et eius dogmate 1.10, 9–14)

The Apuleian vision of time as an endless series of vacant spaces gradually being filled up by days and months, and as an infinitely long scroll of years gradually being rolled up in tandem with the choral dance of the stars, reflects the typical Middle Platonic conception of temporal order as inseparable from cosmic motion and physical space. This conception owes something perhaps to the Stoic vision of history as the cyclical dance of the Logos, but it is most clearly traceable to the overlapping definitions of 'kosmos' (the spatial image of an eternal model) and 'chronos' (the dynamic image of eternity) in the Myth of the Craftsman.

The Craftsman fashioned the sun as a lamp to light up the motions of the heavenly bodies, declared Plato in *Timaeus* 39b–c, so that man would be provided with 'a visible measure of their relative speeds' by which to learn the science of number and acquire skill in calendar-making. In translating this section of the Myth Calcidius passed on to his medieval readers the Middle Platonic association of the celestial dance with visible measurement of time:

And God, the maker of things, lit that most brilliant light which we call the sun in the region second from the globe of the earth, so that this well-planned variety and rational measurement of motions would be visible and the choral dance of all eight motions would be most clear [omniumque octo motuum perspicua esset chorea].

(*Timaeus a Calcidio translatus* 39b–c)

No Greek clause corresponding to the Latin 'omniumque octo motuum perspicua esset chorea' appears in the original wording of this passage, which simply has the sun illuminating the heavenly bodies as they 'travelled' (poreuointo) rather than 'danced' (choreuointo) along their designated courses. Calcidius may have mistaken a *pi* for a *chi* in his reading of the Greek verb 'to travel' or have based his translation on a manuscript in which this substitution had already occurred. In any event, the result of this misreading was the periphrastic interpolation of a second reference to the cosmic dance into the Latin *Timaeus*, 39b–c, in close proximity to the original reference (translated as 'choreas') in 40d.[8] A translator educated along Middle Platonic lines would not have been disturbed by the echo of 40d in 39b–c, for the interpolated metaphor would have accorded with his conception of time as 'a rational measurement of motions' in the theatre of the celestial chorus.

The image thus gained a new Platonic context in which it was associated not only with the revolutions of the visible gods, as before, but also with the sun's power to illuminate the whole temporal world and with God's plan to make the time-keeping dance 'perspicua' – 'most clear.' These associations were transmitted to Calcidius' medieval readers, who inevitably assumed (because they had no access to the Greek *Timaeus*) that the interpolated metaphor was germane to Plato's mystical definition of time. Alanus will accordingly present a dynamic image of eternity in the perspicuous dance of gems on Natura's crown, and Dante will stage the most visually elaborate performance of the celestial carol in the Heaven of the Sun. Their radiant visions of the choral cosmos are a poetic fulfilment of God's plan – the plan discerned by Calcidius in the revolutions of the 'perspicua chorea' (XCVII) – that 'so great a design of things should not be concealed by any darkness.'

Garlands for the Coryphaeus

One earthly spectator escaped the various kinds of darkness that hid the great design from the unenlightened mass of earthlings, one ancient privileged witness whose vision was never dimmed by dense congealing humours, whose skies were never completely veiled by storm clouds, whose intellect was never blinded by superstitious fears, and whose life was never threatened by the darkness of the grave. That perspicacious creature was the earth herself, the goddess Gaia, whose role as the guardian of night and day was thought by Calcidius to entail the defensive vigilance of a 'custos' ('supervisor' or 'sentinel') and the delighted attention of a 'spectatrix' ('female observer at the theatre or public games'). Since the full spectacle of divine providence was not apparent to his or any other mortal's eyes, Calcidius took comfort in Timaeus' slightest suggestion that the cosmic chorus was protected from chaos by a dependable guardian at the centre of the universal revolution. Gaia deserved to be recognized as such, he assured his more skeptical readers, because she had seen all the rounds of the stars in both celestial hemispheres from the beginning of time and because she kept all the stellar circles focused on a single point by resting secure in her divinely ordained position. Hers was the only naturally static body in all the spinning spheres, he insisted in CXXIII (despite Timaeus' hint in 40c that the earth was always 'winding' about the pole extended through the universe). Beneath the calm drift of his argument at this point may be detected a current of pessimism and uncertainty which runs through the commentary and which seems to spring from the commentator himself rather than from Theon or Numenius or any of his other second-century sources.

Calcidius' insistence that the cosmos needed an ever-vigilant custodian betrays a suspicion on his part that its harmonious design was no more than a temporary concatenation of souls and bodies liable to disintegrate into a chaotic rabble. To reassure himself that the celestial events that Timaeus had pointed to as inciting 'fears and forebodings about the future' in the hearts of ignorant spectators were in fact providentially ordained, Calcidius looked beyond the demiurgic mathematics enshrined in the Myth of the Craftsman to the revelations of the Divine Plan set forth in the Bible – 'a history more holy and venerable,' he avowed, than Homer's tale of the Trojan War (CXXVI). The Gospels in particular seemed to him to confirm Plato's argument that despite all appearances to the contrary the heavens truly declared the glory and rationality of God. Continuing his commentary on *Timaeus* 40d in CXXVI, he noted that three Wise Men had once observed the appearance of a new star (an event which could not possibly have taken place in the immutable Platonic Aplanes) and that this wondrous phenomenon had not disrupted the established order of the celestial dance, as one might have feared, but rather had announced the joyous descent of a god and heralded the triumphant rebirth of the Saved.

In so far as Calcidius' vision of the great design can be distinguished from that of Plato or Theon, it is tinged with a contempt for the human condition and a sense of isolation from the celestial chorus which strongly suggest that he was a Christian Platonist whose knowledge of the Fall had darkened his perception of the Craftsman's cosmos. His scattered allusions to the Bible do not, of course, prove that he was a zealous proponent of the new paideia: similar allusions can be found in the fragments of his thoroughly pagan precursor Numenius. Nevertheless, when his sympathetic references to 'the Hebraic philosophy' (CXXX) are considered together with his unapologetic appeal to the authority of the early-third-century Christian Platonist Origen (CCLXXVI), it seems likely that he was at least nominally a Christian. The most celebrated Latin exponent of Christian Platonism in the fourth century, St Augustine, would praise God for having created a perfect gradation of material things and then condemn man for having corrupted the beauty of the great design by succumbing at the Fall to the sin of carnal concupiscence. While Calcidius' 'ingenium' next to Augustine's seems very 'mediocre' indeed, his consideration of the origins of evil in the long treatise 'On Matter' which ends the second part of his commentary displays a similar mixture of pious respect for the excellence of God's handiwork and utter scorn for man's fallen corporeal nature. He could not bring himself to reject Plato's conclusion that the human soul was a glorious replica of the heavens housed in an ingeniously crafted body, and yet like Origen and Augustine he considered the human race to be 'exceedingly feeble' (CXXXII) in comparison to the unfallen angelic spirits whom God had appointed as the guardians of mankind.

Calcidius' earnest belief that Plato and the Hebrews had both attributed the multitude of evils in the temporal world to the unstable motion of primal matter led him to suppose that the Serpent 'who had ensnared the progenitors of the human race with his evil temptings' (CCC) represented the chaotic instincts latent in man's material nature and in the cosmic body as a whole. The disorderly character of the passive material substrate became, in his view, an active diabolical force. It was 'silva' that opposed the harmonious revolutions of the two Divine Minds, 'silva' that drowned the children of Adam in the bitter tides of this blood-gorged life and prevented them from seeing the true design of the celestial chorus. In the agitated midst of this fallen material world where pagan elements were being transformed by Christian energies, a world whose churning atmosphere seemed to black out the stars and bring tears to the eyes, the architects of the poetic universe (among whom Calcidius figures as prominently as Augustine) rose up against the demons of Chaos.

That Calcidius was active in Christian circles ('flourished' is perhaps too strong a term) during the first half of the fourth century, most likely several decades before the birth of Augustine in 354 AD, may be inferred from a small but noteworthy clue to the commentator's identity: the dedication of his work to a certain Osius, whom he salutes in a brief epistolary prologue as his learned friend and the instigator of the whole project. Osius apparently had the ambition but not the leisure to produce the work himself and so passed the job on to Calcidius. The deferential second-person references to this mysterious friend in sections of the commentary concerned with Christian topics (for example, cxxv and cxxxii) indicate that he was probably a Christian with a detailed knowledge of theology and possibly also an official in some position of authority over the commentator.

Marginal notes in various manuscripts of the commentary dating from the tenth to the fourteenth century state that Osius was none other than Bishop Ossius (or Hosius) of Cordova, one of Constantine's chief ecclesiastical advisors, and that Calcidius was an archdeacon in the Bishop's clergy.[9] This information has yet to be confirmed by any Late Antique source and may be no more than a pious supposition on the part of the monks who preserved the work for the Middle Ages. Still, in the miasma of speculations concerning the identity of Calcidius and 'his Osius,' these scribal glosses shed a clear and welcome light on the commentator's professional status and intellectual milieu – a light not to be shunned as an ignis fatuus simply because it emanates from late medieval sources. If the monks derived their information from trustworthy historical records no longer extant, then the most that can be safely inferred from their testimony is that the translation and commentary were written sometime after the rise of the Spanish Ossius to ecclesiastical prominence in 295 and before his death in the late months of 357 or the early months of 358. If the monks were only guessing, however, then the least that can be said of their speculations is that they are quite reasonable.

The first half of the fourth century would have been a likely period for the undertaking of such a project, for it was during the reign of Constantine that Latin began to eclipse Greek as the standard language of learning in the western provinces of the Empire. That still leaves mysterious the reasons that could have prompted a staunch supporter of Nicene orthodoxy and a busy imperial diplomat like Bishop Ossius to command a lowly archdeacon to translate and comment at great length upon a pagan creation myth. Maybe the Bishop had a purely scholarly interest in Platonic cosmology. Though he has often been portrayed as a man of inestimable faith but little intellectual sophistication, his early education in the old and cultured capital of Baetica probably included a respectable training in Greek literature as well as Latin rhetoric and his later prestige and influence at the court of Constantine could hardly have been attained by a rude provincial upstart with no understanding of the pagan roots of imperial culture. Perhaps his aim in commissioning the translation was polemical rather than pedagogical. Could he have wished his ecclesiastical colleagues in the Latin West to read and comprehend the pagan Genesis as did their counterparts in the Greek East – the better to refute Plato's unhallowed doctrines? Or did he challenge his archdeacon to defend the tenets of Platonic cosmology in the hope that Calcidius might reconcile Plato's vision of providential order with the biblical account of creation and demonstrate once and for all the incapacity of human reason to deduce the principles of world-harmony without divine revelation? Whatever his friend's motives might have been, Calcidius himself evidently preferred to keep his religious beliefs separate fom his philosophical conclusions (except when the former incidentally confirmed the latter) and tacitly refused to take a decisive stand for or against the Christian interpretation of the Divine Plan within the pedagogical bounds of his commentary.

One need not assume that Osius was as deeply interested in the promulgation of Platonic doctrines as Calcidius implies in his dedicatory epistle (such epistles rarely being expressions of the whole truth and nothing but the truth) in order to defend the plausibility of the medieval identification of Osius with Ossius of Cordova. If the ultimate initiative for the project did not come from the Bishop himself, then perhaps it came through him from someone else. And who in the Bishop's professional vicinity might have demanded an annotated Latin *Timaeus*? Someone doubtless with a keen interest in Platonic cosmology whose Greek was considerably weaker than his Latin; someone with a marked Christian bias whose soul was still stirred by pagan myths of cosmic harmony; someone with highly dogmatic notions of education whose approach to cosmology was essentially theological; someone with a stake in promoting the ideal of divinely ordained government whose experiences on the battlefield of the Fallen World had taught him a great deal about the forces of Chaos – someone, one may suspect, very like Ossius' political boss and 'fellow bishop' (as he liked to style himself): Constantine the Great.[10]

According to his biased but informative Christian biographer Eusebius of Caesarea, who was probably familiar with Philo's portrayal of Moses as a Platonic philosopher-king and mystic choragus of the Jewish people, Constantine, the son of a Dalmatian general, was the new Moses whom God had appointed to bring concord to all the peoples of the Empire after the shock of the Great Persecution and the long years of civil war brought on by the breakdown of the Tetrarchy. The new Moses was of course more powerful and more victorious than the old because Christ was with him at all the crucial moments in his miraculous career, particularly before the battle of the Milvian Bridge when he saw in the heavens a sign of the cross imposed on the sun and dreamed that the Saviour appeared to him with the celestial emblem, assuring him that he would defeat his foe Maxentius if his armies bore the sign of victory into battle. They did, he won, and Rome welcomed her first Christian Emperor. Or at least her first Emperor with definite Christian sympathies: whether Constantine was instantly converted to the true faith by his vision of the cross, as Eusebius suggests, or was gradually persuaded by Ossius and his other ecclesiastical advisors to distinguish the Son of God from the Unconquered Sun whom his father Constantius and he as a youth had worshipped, are still disputed questions.

Not to be outdone by the great Jewish biographer, Eusebius also portrays the triumphant Emperor as a philosopher-king – but one whose intellectual mission was to expose the folly of polytheism and to reason with pagan philosophers, in their own terms, so that they too might see the light of Christ shining through the works of the virtuous and the wonders of creation. This portrait of the imperial educator is not altogether fanciful. Though he chose to emphasize the proselytizing zeal of the Emperor, Eusebius also reports that throughout his long reign Constantine admitted pagan philosophers to the inner circle of his court and was accustomed to conduct philosophical seminars at which he trained himself 'in the art of reasoning' (*Vita Constantini* IV.55). He was also in the habit of delivering lengthy orations on theological – and inevitably cosmological – themes which were composed in Latin and then rendered into Greek by special interpreters appointed for this purpose (IV.32), among whom, perhaps, a philosophically competent translator like Calcidius might have gained employment and access to the circle of Ossius.

The Greek version of one such oration, a Good Friday sermon which Constantine preached 'to the assembly of the saints' (that is, in church) perhaps during the second decade of his reign, is preserved in an appendix to Eusebius' biography and praised by the biographer as representative of the Emperor's elevated style and inspired contemplations. Certain passages in it sound suspiciously like a Middle Platonic commentary on the *Timaeus*. For instance:

Now then, can things immortal and unchangeable be the inventions of men? Surely not! These, indeed, and all other things that have been cut off from our senses and can be grasped only by our intellect, receive their existence not from some living being composed of matter, not from a man, but from the intellectual and eternal essence of God. Surely the reason for their orderly arrangement is that providence is at work, ensuring that day is bright because it derives its radiance from the sun, and that night follows day after sunset, and that the succeeding period is saved from total darkness by the choral dance of the stars [dia tēn tōn astrōn choreian]. And what shall we say about the moon, which waxes when it stands away from and opposite to the sun but wanes when the sun comes near it? Do these things not clearly reveal the intelligence and sagacity of God?

(Oration to the Assembly of the Saints vi.6–7)

If members of the Emperor's philosophical seminar had been among the sainted assembly when this passage was declaimed, they would not have been surprised by the speaker's association of the spectacle of the celestial dance with the providential regulation of time. Such an association was typical in recapitulations of the cosmological argument for the existence of God.

But they might have raised their eyebrows – appreciatively, of course – at the Emperor's subsequent exegesis of Matthew 27:45 ('Now from the sixth hour there was darkness over all the land') in terms of the old Hesiodic distinction between chorus and chaos, which the dogmatic philosophers of the pagan Empire had turned into a sharp dichotomy:

The time of his Passion was not without its own miraculous sights, as when the shades of night veiled the light of day and concealed the sun. For then people everywhere were seized by the fear that the end of all things had arrived, and that chaos, such as had been before the organization of the cosmos, would once again prevail. Then, too, they sought to know why that terrible misfortune had occurred and whether some discordant act committed by men had offended the divine realm, until God, who looked down on the arrogance of the ungodly, calmly and generously restored the whole heaven with the choral dance of the cosmos-adorning stars [tēi tōn astrōn katakosmōn choreiai]. And so the sullen face of the cosmos regained its proper appearance of joyous brightness.

(Oration to the Assembly of the Saints xi.16)

One might have expected the imperial champion of the new paideia to emphasize the unnaturalness of the noonday darkness over Calvary, to interpret the dramatic disruption of the unbroken rhythm of day and night as a symbol of the demonic darkness pervading the earth after Adam's fall or as an expression of the sorrow felt by all creation at the death of the Second Adam or as an omen of the total eclipse of the heavens on the Last Day. But he does not treat it as a miracle, though he speaks of it as such.

Just like Calcidius, who regarded the Star of Bethlehem as an unusual but entirely natural (because divinely ordained) sign of the operation of providence in the heavens, a sign which only those who could not calculate the risings of the stars and the times of eclipses would tremble at as a portent of disaster, Constantine shows himself to be an earnest student of the old paideia by calmly considering the noonday darkness from the supracosmic viewpoint of God. As creator of 'the cosmos-adorning stars' God had the power to illuminate or conceal their dance, and as their coryphaeus, to start or stop it. What then could be more natural for him than to exercise that awesome power in accordance with his unvarying plan to punish the ungodly and protect the righteous?

The reappearance of the celestial dance after the Passion provided the Emperor with spectacular evidence not only of God's 'intelligence and sagacity' but also of his generosity: qualities which were all attributed by Timaeus (and Calcidius) to the Craftsman. Towards the end of his oration Constantine cites a prophetic poem warning sinners of that imminent day when God will turn chorus back into chaos and rob the cosmos of its joyous brightness:

> From every direction there will be wailing and gnashing
> of teeth!
> The shining of the sun and the choral dances of the stars
> [astrōn te choreiai] will cease,
> The heavens will roll, the light of the moon will be
> extinguished,
> The valleys will be raised up, and the heights will be
> brought low!
> (Oration to the Assembly of the Saints XVIII.3)

Though this apocalyptic poem (the full text of which contains an acronym spelling out the Greek words for 'Jesus-Christ-Son-of-God-Cross') is evidently a Christian fabrication, Constantine believed it to be the inspired utterance of a famous priestess of Apollo, the Erythraean Sibyl, whose cursed tongue was supposedly moved to proclaim the truth about Doomsday in the distant pagan past. The Sibylline Books were supposed to have supplied Virgil with his prophecy of the birth of Christ in the fourth eclogue, and it is with an extensive analysis of that famous paean to the new god who will turn 'the circling years' into a Golden Age that the Christian Augustus draws his Good Friday sermon to a close. Besides Virgil and the Sibyl, Constantine names in his oration (IX.3) one other pagan author whose works could be read as a glorious prophecy of the Christian Golden Age: 'the gentlest and most consoling of all philosophers, Plato.'[11]

If the strain of Platonism echoed in the Emperor's oration were markedly different from that which can be discerned in Calcidius' commentary – if, for instance, it had a distinctly Plotinian or Porphyrian ring to it – then one might reasonably suppose that Constantine could have had little to do with, and even less interest in, the old-fashioned unmystical exposition of Platonic cosmology produced (perhaps) for his counsellor Ossius. But the Neoplatonic Muses seem to have left him quite alone, unmoved by the One, for his vision of the cosmic dance does not extend beyond the purely spatial and rigidly temporal limits set for it by the Stoics, the Middle Platonists, and the prophets of the Christian Apocalypse. Moreover, his simple distinction in IX.3 (or rather the distinction he believed Plato made) between the God who is the First Cause, the Creator and Ruler of the Universe, and a second deity who descends from the first and carries out the Creator's providential orders certainly recalls Calcidius' Numenian conception of the supracosmic power structure and indicates that Eusebius' philosopher-king was hardly more attuned to the triadic theology of the Neoplatonists than Calcidius. At least one pagan philosopher with Neoplatonic leanings is known to have served as an advisor to Constantine, Sopater of Apamea, and there were no doubt others like him who attended the Emperor's philosophical seminars. Any influence the Neoplatonists may have had on his intellectual or religious life in the early years of his reign must have been rather weak, however, for in 325, the year of his triumph at the Council of Nicaea, the choragus of the Christian Empire ordered the works of the diabolical Porphyry put to the flame.[12]

The old philosophical image of the chorus proved of use to Constantine when he (or his Latin speech-writer and Greek interpreter) came to define his crucial role at Nicaea in an address delivered to the assembly of the bishops at the opening ceremonies of the Council. It was a solemn and impressive occasion. The episcopal audience, representing over two hundred sees, had been summoned by the Emperor to the spacious central room in his palace and arranged according to rank in orderly rows so as to present to the imperial eye a pleasing spectacle of ecclesiastical unity. Ecclesia was not as unified or peaceful as it may have appeared that day, however, and in the months following the first assembly the bishops were to war over the definition of the Son's ontological relation to the Father and to wrangle over the pending excommunication of Eusebius of Caesarea and to worry over the rebellion of the Melitian schismatics in Egypt and to wheedle concessions from the obstinate supporters of Arius before producing the first manifesto of Catholic orthodoxy, the Nicene Creed.

Doctrinal consensus was what Constantine wished from the bishops at Nicaea, regardless of the precise doctrines they might agree to consider orthodox, and as they sat in their orderly rows awaiting his grand entrance many of them no doubt reflected on the slender distinction between an imperial wish and a command. Eusebius, an eyewitness at the Council, presents the scene of the first assembly as the climax of Constantine's victorious career as peacemaker in both the Empire and the Church. In his typically glowing manner he reports that the Emperor appeared before the bishops 'like some heavenly messenger from God' (III. 10) arrayed in a sumptuous purple robe glittering with gold and precious stones. 'My dear friends,' the angelic presence began,

it has been my prayer – my utmost desire – that I might see you assemble as for a choral dance [choreias], and now that I am enjoying that spectacle I shall begin this speech by acknowledging my debt to the Ruler of the Universe. For he has granted me (besides all his other favours) a blessing better than all the others: the opportunity, I say, not only of hearing that you have all assembled together but also of seeing that you are all harmoniously united by a single common purpose.

(*Vita Constantini* III.12)

Though the bishops at this moment all had their eyes on his performance which was carefully staged to highlight his dual role as earth-born guardian of peace and heaven-sent agent of concord, the Emperor tactfully presented himself as a grateful spectator at *their* choral ceremony. That was all he was supposed to be in his official capacity as honorary president of the Council: an august observer (like Calcidius' earth) who stood apart from the measured and harmonious commotion of the bishops and watched over the intricate steps in their procession towards doctrinal unity. From his unique perspective – the perspective of the whole – he could foresee the successful resolution of all their conflicts and perceive an implicit analogy between their single-minded chorus and the Great Chorus over which the Ruler of the Universe presided. Destiny had given them the cue, they must begin the dance of peace, and he would applaud from a respectful distance without seeking to interfere in their proceedings.

They knew otherwise, of course. Since Constantine himself had gathered them together from all over the Empire, chosen the strategic site for their assembly, feasted them at his palace, and led them forth to what was soon to be regarded as the first ecumenical council in the history of the Catholic Church, he was rather more than an honorary president: he was their choragus and coryphaeus combined. Reflecting on the Emperor's creative role at Nicaea (and in a far from impartial light since the Emperor had been personally responsible for securing his vindication), Eusebius marvelled at Constantine's diplomatic skill in selecting the right bishops for his ecumenical chorus and in weaving together so diverse a company into a single crown of glory for the celestial Victor. 'Constantine is the only ruler in history,' he rhapsodized in III.7, 'ever to have tied together a garland such as this with the bond of peace and to have offered it to Christ his Saviour as a token of gratitude befitting a god for the victories obtained over his hated enemies, thus creating in our own times an image of the apostolic choral dance.'

The original 'choreia apostolikē' (as conceived for instance by Clement of Alexandria) was a dramatic response to the cosmos-thrilling music of the Logos and a dynamic symbol of the proselytizing mission of the Apostles, a dance which would outlast the revolutions of the stars to culminate in the eternal participation of the Blessed in the contemplative concord of the angels. Just how fleeting an image of that charismatic movement the Nicene choreia was to prove, and how illusory in the light of Constantine's sub-sequent history, Eusebius was never willing to admit. The circling years would soon see the saintly ruler murder his son Crispus and his wife Fausta; the victorious peacemaker embroil himself in irresolvable disputes between Arian and Orthodox factions; and the hero of the Orthodox bishops in the West turn his back on Rome and side with the Arian prelates in the New Rome established on the banks of the Bosphorus.

Still determined to set an unfading garland of victory on Constantine's troubled brow, Eusebius delivered a lofty panegyric in his honour (and in his presence) at the celebrations marking the end of the third decade of his reign, the Tricennalia, held in the summer of 336. This oration, a virtuoso display of Levantine hyperbole, proves on close inspection to be much more than an exercise in servile flattery. It is a skilful weaving together of classical and Christian versions of the choreia topos designed to justify the Emperor's chief political goals – the securing of doctrinal consensus in the Church and the promotion of religious tolerance in the Empire – in figurative language intelligible to a mixed audience of pagans and Christians.[13] In this prologue the shrewd encomiast assumes the ancient role of mystagogue to welcome his listeners onto the contemplative dancing-ground around the wellspring of piety and prophetic wisdom:

So let those who have stepped into the sanctuary of the holy palace, into the inaccessible innermost chamber, close the gates to profane listeners and de-scribe in detail the Ruler's ineffable mysteries only to those who have been initiated in them. Let those who have purified their ears in the streams of piety and rested their mind on the soaring wing of the soul itself dance in chorus around the Ruler of All [amphi ton pantōn basilea choreuontōn] and perform the divine rites in silence.

(*In laudibus Constantini*, prologue 4)

The setting for these rites of praise was not a church (as one might suppose from the identity of the praiser) but a chamber in the imperial palace at

Constantinople where Stoical Senators imported from Rome consorted with intellectual devotees of the Ineffable One, and unintellectual worshippers of the Unconquered Sun encountered Arian champions of the Subordinate Logos, and Orthodox die-hards tried to restore their straying Emperor to the flock of the Consubstantial Son. It was not a likely setting for the dance of intellectual concord.

Few pagans in the factious chorus would have objected to Eusebius' choice of the word 'sanctuary' to denote the chamber, however, for, the Emperor being in their view a god ex officio or at least a god-in-the-making, any room in which he chose to appear was instantly sanctified by his sun-like presence. The Christians at the Tricennalia would not, of course, have considered the chamber a sanctuary in a literal sense, but they would have been quite prepared to perceive it as a shadowy image of the angelic holy-of-holies in the palace of their Heavenly King. If asked who the 'basileus' (ruler) was around whom their mystic dance revolved, the whole audience would have pointed first heavenwards to the Ruler of All, Helios or the One or God the Father, and then without a moment's hesitation thronewards to the Helios among men, the unitive centre of the Empire, God's invincible general and dutiful servant, Constantine.

Having established this dual reference for the title 'basileus' in his prologue, Eusebius proceeds to alter the imaginative bounds of the sanctuary. The palace chamber dissolves into air and the mystic dance whirls out to encompass all the lights of the firmament and all the revolutions of time, and then expands further, the celestial vault dissolving into intellectual light, to embrace all the spirits in the Empyrean and all the rites of eternity:

Even the resplendent sun in its long journey through the great expanse of the ages acknowledges him alone as Lord, and obedient to his command, never dares to step outside its bounds. And the moon, which retires before the light of the sun, periodically waxes and wanes in obedience to the divine laws. And the stars, the beauties of the heavens, proclaim him the Giver of All Light by glittering in their choral dances [choreias astrōn apostilbonta] and moving in order and harmony and measuring their circles on high. Together all the heavenly luminaries at his command and word join in one melody and complete their long course by revolving through many aeons and competing in ethereal races. The alternating movements of night and day, the changes of hours and seasons, and the rhythms and arrangements of all things honour the highly complex wisdom of his infinitely great power.

To him the unseen powers who soar around the free fields of the air send up their obligatory and fitting tribute of divine praise. The whole cosmos singing together praises him as the Great Ruler. The heavens above and the higher choruses of the heavenly vaults [ouraniōn te apsidōn hyperteroi choroi] honour him. Hosts of angels sing ineffable hymns in his praise. Spirits sprung from intellectual light glorify their divine Father. Ages that were timeless before this firmament and before this cosmos, and besides these other endless ages that existed before the creation of all visible things, recognize him alone as the Great Lord and Absolute Ruler.

He who is above all, before all, and after all, his pre-existing and only-begotten Logos, yes, the great God's great High Priest who is older than all time and all aeons and is dedicated first and foremost to the honour of his Father, intercedes with him for the salvation of everyone. Glorified is he for being the first ruler in the universe, though he is second in command in his Father's kingdom. For he was that very Light beyond the universe which dances around the Father [amphi ton patera choreuon] and mediates between created existence and the eternal and uncreated Form and also divides the one from the other, that Light which gushes forth from on high from the endless and beginningless divinity and proceeds out over the supercelestial realm, shining on everything within the heavens with rays of wisdom brighter than the sun.

(In laudibus Constantini 1.5–6)

Having set the free fields of the air ringing not only with angelic doxologies and the music of the spheres but also with learned allusions to the Platonic myths, the commentaries of Philo, the discourses of the Roman Stoics, the orations of the imperial encomiasts, the apocalyptic passages of the New Testament, the hymnody of the apocryphal Acts, the exhortations of Clement of Alexandria, and the metaphysical apologetics of Origen, Eusebius (who was a pupil of a pupil of Origen) lauds Constantine for offering up his 'fitting tribute of praise' to the heavenly Emperor and them lauds God for presenting his earthly counterpart with an appropriate token of divine favour:

God, who secures our faith by offering tokens of the rewards in store for the righteous, presents to Constantine thirty-year garlands composed of auspicious cycles of time, and now, after three cycles of ten years have completed their revolution, he permits all mankind to celebrate this public – or rather this cosmic – festival. And seeing that those who celebrate on earth are brightly decked with the flowers of divine knowledge, surely we would not be off the mark to suppose that the choruses dancing in the heavens [tas en ouranōi choreias] are attracted by the laws of nature to the earthly celebrants and are united with them in joy, and that the Universal Ruler himself, in the manner of a virtuous father, rejoices to see his virtuous sons worshipping God, and that for this reason he is especially pleased to honour the man who for a long time has been their guide and the instigator of their virtue. And

*far from limiting the latter's reign to three decades, God allots a very long
period to it indeed and extends it even into the far reaches of eternity.*

(*In laudibus Constantini* VI. 1–2)

What this public-turned-cosmic festival celebrated was not primarily the
benevolence or rationality of God but rather 'his infinitely great power' –
the autocratic power which was supposedly passed on from the Great Sov-
ereign to his honoured protégé Constantine. The Logos entered into the
dance only as an intermediate link in the divine chain of command. Eusebius
also referred to him in the oration as 'Saviour' and 'High Priest' (titles which
like 'Logos' belonged to the religious lingua franca of fourth-century paganism and Christianity) but never by any strategically Christian title such
as 'Jesus' or 'Incarnate Son,' evidently preferring, like Calcidius, who spoke
only of a 'new god' in his chapter on the Star of Bethlehem, to communicate
his argument in philosophical and religious language which would be vague
enough to be generally inoffensive and common enough to be generally
intelligible.[14]

The function of an imperial panegyrist was not only to praise the private
virtues of an emperor but also to defend his public policies, to be in essence
an imperial propagandist, and Constantine no doubt expected (perhaps even
commanded) his Tricennial orators to promote his cherished conception of
monarchy as the political corollary of monotheism with all the ingenious
arguments at their disposal. To this political end Eusebius directed his genius
for subtle analogical reasoning and numerological analysis, producing a forceful
current of sophistic propaganda which rivals in sheer cleverness Philo's
Pythagorean encomium of the number seven and Plutarch's symbolic explanation of the demiurgic ratios. 'The triad,' he declared,

*has as many units in it as there are decads in the number thirty. It is also
the constant mathematical limit regulating that luminary which is second to
the sun in brightness: for the revolution of the moon from one conjunction
with the sun to the next completes the cycle of a month, after which, as if
born anew, it makes a fresh start with new light and new days and is adorned
with thirty units, honoured with three decads, and brightened with ten triads.
In the same manner is the reign of our victorious ruler, which resembles that
of the Ruler of the Universe, honoured by the Giver of All Blessings. Now
it begins a new era of good fortune, presently bringing to completion this
thirty-years' festival but afterwards reaching forward to far greater intervals
of time and endeavouring to realize the expectation of future blessings in the
heavenly kingdom. There not one sun but hosts of innumerable lights dance
in chorus around the Ruler of All [amphi ton pantōn basilea choreuousin].*

There every light surpasses the brightness of the sun, glowing and shining with the splendour of the everlasting wellspring of light.

(*In laudibus Constantini* VI. 17–18)

This triumphal march through the platitudes of imperial praise to the heights of theophanic oratory carries us far away – indeed seems to remove us entirely – from the cosmic theatre in which Calcidius admired the dances of the stars. Eusebius ushers us into a cosmic basilica where the stars seem suspended in a glittering apsidal mosaic of the Cosmocrator, whose throne, the golden globe of the Aplanes, is flanked by obedient choruses of angels and apostles in the eternal act of praising the Giver of All Blessings and his only-begotten Logos.

The dance Calcidius strained to see from the viewpoint of a distant apologetic spectator Eusebius celebrates with the breathless enthusiasm of an initiate soaring into mystical outer space. With Calcidius we look back to the second-century heyday of the Roman Empire for philosophical guides to the mathematical design underlying the cosmic spectacle. With Eusebius we seem to look ahead into the long unwinding centuries of the Byzantine Empire for political guides, the glorious successors of Constantine, who will lead the citizens of the New Rome through the garland-like rounds of a ritual dance of peace until the stars at last complete their musical measures and history dissolves into eternity.

6

Living Statues

Now I know that the great Plato and after him a man who though born in less venerable times was by no means inferior to him in nature – I mean Iamblichus of Chalcis, whose philosophical discourses initiated me into these and other doctrines – made use of the hypothetical concept of a generated world and assumed that the creation of the world was in some sense temporal so that the magnitude of the works arising from Helios might be perceived. But it is not for me (wholly inferior as my intellectual ability is to theirs!) to risk making such an assumption. Iamblichus himself, the glorious hero, recognized that it was highly risky to posit a temporal creation for the cosmos even as a bare hypothesis. Risky it is indeed, especially since the god Helios proceeded from an eternal cause or rather led forth all things from eternity by suddenly engendering from invisible things all that is now visible in time by his divine will and with untold swiftness and insurpassable might. For his own abode, Helios chose the middle heavens so that from all sides he might distribute equal blessings among the gods who came forth because of him and with him, and that he might be in charge of the seven celestial spheres and the eighth sphere too, and also, I believe, the ninth creation, namely the sublunary world of generation which revolves forever in a ceaseless cycle of growth and decay. For it is evident that the planets dancing in chorus around him preserve as the measure of their motion an harmonious relation with this god such as may be observed round about their configurations [hoti peri auton choreuontes metron echousi teus kineseos ten pros ton theon tonde toiande peri ta schemata symphonian], and that the firmament by linking itself to him in all its parts is full of gods who proceed from Helios. For this god rules five celestial circles, and when he traverses three of these he begets in them the three Graces. And the remaining circles are the scales of mighty Necessity.

JULIAN THE APOSTATE, *Hymn to King Helios* 146a–d

The Poetic Spectator

In the late fourth and early fifth centuries, the exhausted fields of scholarship raked by humble encyclopaedists like Calcidius sprang to life as the flowery meadows of the Graces in a poetic universe revived by the rays of a Neo-platonic sun. We shall now be guided across the visionary threshold and into the dance of that universe by three Sophists – Julian the Apostate, Martianus Capella, and Synesius of Cyrene – who cannot be firmly placed on either side of the shifting boundary between Hellenism and Christianity. Julian and Synesius moved between the two cultures in opposite directions. While the one abandoned Christianity at an early age to join forces with the pagan revivalists and reactionary humanists opposed to the Church Mil-itant, the other came to Christ late in life fully determined not to give up his philosophical belief in the eternity of the world and the pre-existence of souls. Martianus as far as we know lived and died outside the Church and made no attempt to refute its doctrines or acknowledge its culture in his writings. Conversion seems never to have entered his thoughts. He may be said to have crossed cultures more decisively than either Julian or Synesius, however, for the harmonious curriculum he extolled was destined to affect the education of generations of staunchly Christian schoolmen in the Latin West.

Though none of the three was a typical Sophist socially – Julian ended up an emperor, Synesius a bishop, and Martianus an impoverished old man in a community of uncouth oxherds – they all wrote as 'philarchaioi' and 'philologoi' in the traditional sophistic sense: that is to say, as 'lovers of antiquity' devoutly attached to classical literary culture and 'lovers of learn-ing' eager to display their encyclopaedic knowledge of the liberal arts. Their perverse inclination to be 'philosophoi' also, to be 'lovers of wisdom' in a Neoplatonic sense, set them apart intellectually from the majority of effete literati and anti-philosophical rhetors who kept the satiric spirit of the Second Sophistic alive in the schools of the fourth century.[1] All three were partic-ularly attracted to the solar mysticism and mythopoetic theology of the Syrian Neoplatonist Iamblichus of Chalcis (d c325 AD), who had studied with Porphyry in Rome or Sicily and had founded a school of his own in the vicinity of Apamea. The eccentric path blazed by this 'glorious hero' (as Julian called him) across the frontiers of the occult led them back to the celestial wellsprings of poetry and into a heliotropic universe so grandly and unreservedly poetical, so resonant with Apollonian harmonies, that it refreshed their faith in the reality and inviolable beauty of the cosmic dance.

On first entering their poetic universe we are bound to wonder whether our three guides were capable of distinguishing literature from life in accordance with plain common sense. We shall find that they were quite prepared to disregard the common sense of the illiterate masses and to scorn the worldly-wise pessimism of the Sophists of the schools who tended to reduce all faith to folly. Each in his own way was a man of faith who found the strength to believe in a realm of concord and peace when the world around him seemed close to chaotic absurdity. Each arrived at religious certitude by way of the visual imagination.

The idea of a 'poetic universe,' that is to say a world not only organized like a poem according to principles of rhythm, analogy, strophic repetition, and syntactic coherence but also endowed by its Author with an objective existence that impinges upon our senses in a way no mythical world dreamed up by a human poet and born of what Julian scornfully called 'the incredible and paradoxical frivolities of a poetic Muse' ever can, had certainly occurred to Greek philosophers before Iamblichus. Around 300 BC a dialectician named Alexinus 'proved' the existence of such a universe by means of a syllogism: 'The poetic is better than the non-poetic and the grammatical better than the non-grammatical and the artistic (as defined by the other arts) better than the inartistic; but nothing is better than the universe; therefore the universe is poetic and grammatical.' This and other arguments like it were still being refuted by the Skeptics at the turn of the third century AD and defended in the fourth and fifth by the authors of scholastic treatises on music and prosody.[2]

Symptomatic of this peculiarly literary view of the world was the tendency of Late Antique Platonists to regard ancient poets as beacons of philosophical illumination and ancient philosophers as wellsprings of poetic inspiration, a tendency taken to an extreme by the successors of Plotinus. Porphyry, for instance, found prophetic confirmation of his master's teachings on the procession and return of the soul in Homer's account of the mission of Hermes to fetch Odysseus from the Cave of Calypso (*Odyssey* v. 102–12) – a feat of allegorizing surpassed in pedantic subtlety perhaps only by Iamblichus in his lost commentary on the *Chaldean Oracles*, a collection of Greek hexameters believed to enshrine the theosophical secrets of the Chaldean astronomer-priests.

Iamblichus is not known to have written poetry himself, but he provided his disciples with a model of the philosopher-poet he no doubt aspired to be in his *Peri biou pythagorikou* ('On the Life of Pythagoras' or 'On the Pythagorean Way of Life'), which is extant and appears to have been the introduction to a vast encyclopaedic work on the various Neopythagorean disciplines taught at his school.³ The soul of Pythagoras, he claimed, 'had been sent down among men from the empire of Apollo where it had been either a companion of the god or a relative in some more intimate respect.' (II.8). After ordering a temple to be built in honour of the Muses, the holy teacher was supposed to have introduced his followers to cosmology through the study of music and poetry and to have insisted that they recite verses from Homer and Hesiod whenever their unruly passions needed to be calmed. 'He also made use of dancing,' Iamblichus notes in his enthusiastic account of Pythagoras' Apollonian remedies for mental and physical illness (xxv.111), 'but employed the lyre as his instrument for this purpose because he thought flutes had a wanton, pompous, and by no means free-spirited sound.' Though ancient Pythagorean dance was therapeutic rather than theatrical in function and chaste rather than lascivious in character, it was to be imagined as similar in style to the mimetic 'orchēsis' of the Greco-Roman theatre with its elaborate displays of manual gesticulation or 'cheironomia.' Metrical language, musical tones, and measured motions all served to express the basic Pythagorean doctrine that number was the magic source of order and health and beauty in life.

Those who followed the Pythagorean way of life by striving to bring their bodies as well as their souls into harmony with 'the sublime symphony of the cosmos' (xv.65) could therefore scan their world as if it were a poem, listen to it as if it were a melody, and participate in its unfolding play of figures and fortunes as if it were a pantomime, or conversely, they could perceive the arts of poetry, music, and dance not as disconnected earthly pastimes but as phases in a single, inclusive, numerically systematic art – choreia – the origin and perfection of which lay in the Apollonian design of the heavens, that is to say in 'the eternally unchanging chorus of the Muses' (IX.45). That a cosmos ruled by the Muses and beautified by the Graces, an idyllic province in the empire of Apollo, should have appealed to nostalgic Hellenists caught up in the barbarous and fractured empire of Constantine's heirs is not surprising – though it may come as a surprise that Julian and the other scholars who tried to revive the idyll were not decadent aesthetes seeking an Elysian refuge from the ugliness of their age but earnest ascetics (like Iamblichus' prototypic Pythagoreans) bent on cultural reform through religious education. Their universe was not subjectively poeticized, as one might suppose, but just the reverse: their poetics were objectively universalized. Their visions of the Divine Poet conducting the dance of life with his entrancing lyre reflected a world that was intrinsically and as they saw it inevitably poetic.

It was no accident that the authors who rescued the idea of the poetic universe from the scholastic dialecticians and their Skeptical opponents and created a theatre for the allegorical imagination out of an antiquated Pytha-gorean theory were allied by education and temperament to the Second Sophistic, for as Sophists they had been trained to think in brilliant mytho-poetic images rather than in dreary syllogisms and to compose elaborate 'ecphraseis' or 'word-pictures' which not only described the settings and subjects represented by the visual arts but also brought them to life in the flow of a mythological or satiric narrative. The popularity of exquisitely allusive descriptions of vase paintings, frescoes, statues, and friezes in Late Antiquity is attested by the survival of no less than three collections of sophistic word-pictures: the *Imagines* of Philostratus the Elder, dating from the first half of the third century; the *Imagines* of his grandson Philostratus the Younger, dating from the turn of the fourth century; and the *Descrip-tiones* of Callistratus, written sometime after the latter, probably in the second half of the fourth century. These works testify to a sophistic mode of perception that is unabashedly fantastic, almost hallucinatory, for it dis-penses with the old (and reasonable) philosophical distinction between image and model by endowing art with the creative dynamism of life and life with the formal perfection of art.

Sophistic image-makers were fond of transforming static objets d'art into the living art of the dance because Homer had done so in his celebrated description of the Shield of Achilles and also because the dance had been movingly portrayed by painters and sculptors throughout Antiquity. 'A statue of a Bacchant in Parian marble has been transformed into a real Bacchant,' Callistratus declared, waving an imaginary wand, 'for the stone while retaining its own nature has apparently transcended the law that gov-erns stone. What one saw was in fact an image, but art had carried imitation over into reality. ... You will perceive at once that the image set up to be viewed has not lost its inborn power of movement!' Callistratus claimed to be doing in words what the greatest of mortal craftsmen had done in stone and metal: 'For Dedalus audaciously added movement to his art, the prod-ucts of which had power to transcend their material limitations and to move in a dance [eis choreian kinein].'⁴

The Sophists' Dedalian impulse to bring statues to life, to fuse and confuse the image with the model, deeply affected the style of mythological poetry composed at the end of Late Antiquity. Such poetry abounds in orchestic scenes reminiscent of the imaginary pantomimes in the theatre of the poetic universe. The following scene from an epic on the life and conquests of Dionysus by Nonnos of Panopolis (a fifth-century Egyptian mythographer who appears to have crossed over to Christianity like Synesius after estab-lishing his reputation as a pagan belles-lettrist and to have composed in the same metre as his epic a poetic paraphrase of the Fourth Gospel) may serve as an illustration of rhetorical image-making for its own sake which results in a series of speaking pictures devoid of obvious philosophical significance:

... Dancing with the Immortals [syn athanatois de choreuōn]
And striking up a love-tune with his seven-stringed lyre
Came Ismenian Apollo to the wedding of Harmonia.
The nine Muses too struck up a life-sustaining melody,
And Polymnia, mother of the dance, traced spiral patterns with
her hands
And engraved in the air the mimetic representation of a
soundless voice,
[kai palamas elelize Polymnia, maia choreiēs
mimēlēn d'echaraxen anaudeos eikona phōnēs,]
Speaking with her palms and rolling her eyes to fashion a wise
picture
Silently yet knowingly. With her oft-turning sandal
Victory gave pleasure to Zeus and stood by as bridesmaid
Crying 'Evae!' to Cadmus, the god's champion. Round the
bridal bed
She wove the wedding song with her virginal voice
And spun her footsteps in the lovely circles of a dance
[kai podos ichnos elissen ep' eukykloi de choreiēi]
Fluttering her wings reverently beside the wings of the Loves.
(*Dionysiaca* v 100–12)

From the dancer's silence an articulate image is born, an image of things ordinarily invisible and ineffable but made obvious and eloquent by the extraordinary grace of the 'maia choreiēs.' Polymnia's 'mimetic representation of a soundless voice' clearly symbolizes the highly mannered art of literary imitation and rhetorical delivery (with cheironomic gestures) practised by the Sophists of the fourth and fifth centuries, who occasionally used the word 'orchēsis' to denote a display of public speaking.[5] Beyond that, however, its significance is hard to determine. Nonnos is here so intent on describing the paradoxical process of artistic image-making that he neglects to tell us precisely what it was that Polymnia's expressive hands were describing while her sister Muses were singing to Apollo's lyre. Was the 'wise picture' an image of the poetic universe itself with its victorious dancers circling to the 'life-sustaining melody' of the planetary chorus or a prophetic representation of the tragic consequences of Harmonia's marriage to Cadmus and the birth of Dionysus? Was it meant to warn us of the evanescence of earthly joys and matrimonial concord or to console us with a triumphant Pythagorean demonstration of the permanence of celestial harmony? The meaning of the Muse's 'cheironomia' is no easier to grasp than the exotic air upon which it was expressed.

The hymns of Julian, Martianus, and Synesius to which we shall now turn were composed in a style midway between the two extremes represented by the drily discursive theological prose of Iamblichus and the luxuriantly imagistic poetry of Nonnos. It is a curious style, now muddied with the technical jargon of scholastic Neoplatonism, now gilded with sophistic allusions to poetic mythology, at times ponderous, at times airy. At its best, however, it effectively counteracts the dreary abstruseness of the one extreme by describing vivid pictures of the poetic universe and dispels the vapid frivolity of the other extreme by setting mythological images within a clearly defined philosophical or theological frame of reference and thus charging them with allegorical significance. When Martianus boldly asks his Muse why he must clothe the wisdom of the ages in spangled allegorical garments instead of laying it bare in the expository style of a scholastic encyclopaedist, she responds: 'Why do you not admit that a work such as yours cannot be composed except by means of figurative imagery?'[6] The Muses inspiring Julian and Synesius would have responded no differently. Implicit in her question is an emphatic assertion that their kind of writing, like the dancing of the Muses, is not only didactic but mimetic and not only mimetic but therapeutic, and that some things in heaven and earth (not the least being the mysterious coherence of the cosmos) can be apprehended only by the visual imagination and expressed only by articulate images.

If their elaborate fantasies of order were simply wish-fulfilling dreams induced by the cultural crises of the fourth century, they seem to have been blissfully unaware of it. As poetic spectators of the cosmos – spectators, that is, who created rather than simply contemplated images of the world-chorus – they saw themselves entering into its artistic life in the manner of primitive Pythagoreans and depicting its living art with the skill of ultra-civilized Sophists. Their figurative visions were closer to reality than what met the eye, they suggested, for what inspired them was the radiant memory – if not the actual presence – of all the deities with whom the Graces danced: Helios and the Muses, Aphrodite and the Horae, Hymen and Harmonia, and dawning beyond them in the hymns of Synesius, the Holy Spirit.

Proceeding from Helios

A statue of Constantine crowned with the rays of Apollo Helios dominated the great circular forum at Constantinople in 332 when Julian was born to the second wife of the Emperor's privileged but powerless half-brother Julius in one of the newly erected palaces on the shore of the Sea of Marmora. Under the pagan shadow of his uncle's statue the future Apostate spent the first five years of his Christian boyhood. On 22 May 337, the solar Monarch died of a very earthly fever, and his far-from-Apollonian son Constantius rose to supremacy in the dark political firmament of the Eastern Empire by inciting the imperial troops to murder Constantine's other half-brother

Dalmatius and his sons together with Julian's father and eldest brother. At the age of six Julian was exiled by his wary cousin to the seaside resort of Nicomedia (some sixty miles to the southeast of the capital) where he could be kept under imperial surveillance without being in the public eye.

For the next four or five years the most powerful figure in his life was his tutor Mardonius, a Scythian eunuch. Though probably a Christian for professional reasons, Mardonius seems to have drawn his austere moral precepts from Homer rather than the Bible and to have passed on his quasi-religious reverence for pagan literary culture to the sheltered prince. Decades later, when he was striving as emperor to revive the cult of Apollo in Antioch, Julian would recall his tutor's inspiring lectures on the superiority of the golden world of Homer's gods and heroes to the grey, menacing, and manifestly unheroic world of the fourth century. One such lecture went like this:

Do you long for horse-races? There is one in Homer, very cleverly described. Take the book and study it. Do you hear people talking about the dancers in the pantomime [tous pantomimous akoueis orchēstas]? Put them out of your mind. The youths dance in a far more manly style among the Phaeacians. ... Be assured that you will never see anything more delightful than these!

(*Misopogon* 351d–352a)

In his isolation at Nicomedia, and later at the secluded Cappadocian estate of Macellum where he was forced to languish for much of his adolescence (from 344 to 350), Julian had little choice but to put the pantomime of the everyday world out of his mind. His earliest models of virtue and beauty and cultural harmony having been drawn from poetry, he was bound as an adult to view the universe in a distinctly poetic light and to look down on the mean-spirited acts of his imperial kinsmen and the hypocritical posturings of his Christian subjects from the viewpoint of a Homeric hero, a royal exile returning to the empire of Apollo.[7]

Though his education at Macellum consisted mainly of lessons in rhetoric, Bible readings, and a catechetical course in Christian theology preceding his baptism, Julian had the leisure and opportunity there to acquaint himself with the doctrines of the classical and Hellenistic schools of philosophy. From the extensive library of his friend George, the bishop of nearby Caesarea, he was permitted to borrow works by pagan rhetors and philosophers along with those of Christian authors; from childhood, as he would confess years later in a touching letter requesting the remains of George's library to be sent to him in Antioch, he had been 'penetrated by a fearful longing to acquire books' – a longing born no doubt of his loneliness and insecurity as well as his instinctive love of learning.[8] Plato was probably well represented in George's collection, and we may consider it a certainty that some kind of Platonism dawned on Julian's consciousness during his adolescence if only because the patristic literature he would have read at Macellum (including pedagogical manuals like Eusebius of Caesarea's *Preparation for the Gospel*) abounded in Skeptical arguments against and sympathetic references to Platonic cosmology. Chances are that if he had any help reading Plato at this time it came by way of Middle Platonic rather than Neoplatonic commentaries on the *Timaeus*, for Plotinus had a surprisingly small readership in the Christian East in the fourth century and Porphyry and Iamblichus were effectively blacklisted by the ecclesiastical establishment to which George belonged.

Sometime before his departure from Cappadocia, Julian suffered a severe spiritual crisis which led to his inward break with Christianity, and it is likely that his solitary study of philosophy (regardless of the contents of the books he studied) had something to do with this. Books were apparently not the only cause of his early apostasy. 'I must say in this regard,' he would write in his own defence, casting his adolescent self in the role of a primitive spectator of the cosmic dance, 'that the heavenly light shone all around me then and roused and urged me to contemplate it.'[9]

His contemplative life took a decidedly Neoplatonic turn in 351 when he returned to Nicomedia to pursue his rhetorical studies with the fashionable Sophists Hekebolius and Libanius, the latter a declared pagan whose lectures he was able to read in private but not to attend in public. 'At one time,' Libanius wistfully recalled,

there was the chorus of philosophers from Apamea [ho tōn philosophōn ex Apamea choros] whose coryphaeus, Iamblichus, resembled the gods.

(*Oratio* 51.21)

That chorus was now scattered throughout the Levant, Julian learned, but the intellectual dance initiated by their godlike coryphaeus could still be joined if one had the courage (or at least the money) to join it. When discreet inquiries located in Pergamum a pupil of Iamblichus by the name of Aedesius, the newly liberated prince hastened to his school and showered him with gifts in the hope of being taken on as a pupil. Prudently the aged Aedesius declined the honour, recommending in his stead his disciples Eusebius and Chrysanthius, who turned out to have little interest in the occult side of Neoplatonism – the side that interested Julian most.

His craving for midnight séances and thaumaturgical thrills and chills was satisfied in the next few years by a succession of other philosophers (if such they may be called) who led his willing spirit into the forbidden fields and dank underground chambers of the Greek religious imagination. In Ephesus he was taught the secret meaning of the *Chaldean Oracles* and initiated in the mysteries of Hecate and Mithras by a formidable wizard named Maximus, the enfant terrible of the school of Aedesius. In Athens, where Constantius permitted him to study for a few ecstatic months in 355, he fell under the spell of yet another pupil of Aedesius, a certain Priscus, who escorted him to all the sites dear to nostalgic Hellenists including the gardens of Plato's long-vanished Academy and saw to it that the imperial pilgrim was properly initiated in the Eleusinian Mysteries. To the followers of Iamblichus a proper initiation meant more than the strict observance of fasts and correct performance of ritual acts: it also signified the enlightened perception of the rite as an allegory of the initiate's intellectual assimilation to the gods and subsequent participation in the divine choral dance around the eternal Kallichoron.

The ardour with which fourth-century neophytes in the mysteries of the One surrendered themselves to their guru-like teachers is movingly expressed in the following lines from an anonymous letter addressed to Iamblichus (c 320 AD):

Since you link us together yourself by providing the keynote for our chant and with your words as with the wand of Hermes rouse and stir us from our sleep, let us then be like the followers of Dionysus who run freely to the dance [pros tēn choreian] when the god strikes his thyrsus! Or, like members of a chorus who accompany their director [tōi chorostatēi] by obeying the summons of his rhythm, let us echo you in response to your plectrum.

(Pseudo-Julian, *Letter* 74, 421a–b)

Fanciful as this mythopoetic version of the old philosophical analogy between choreia and paideia may at first seem – we have come a long way from the Athenian Stranger's sternly anti-Dionysian concept of the well-educated chorus – the cultish enthusiasm expressed by this disciple for his divinized master was by no means a fiction in the self-consciously pagan subculture towards which Julian gravitated. After all, was it not a sacred 'fact' of intellectual history (as established by Iamblichus in his life of Pythagoras) that the earliest 'choros philosophōn' had acquired their sublime knowledge of cosmic harmony through action as well as contemplation, through the performance of mimetic dances and the chanting of magical hymns? And had not Iamblichus been a superhuman 'chorostatēs' like Pythagoras? Though Julian could not have written the personal letters to Iamblichus that tradition has ascribed to him, he may well have regarded Priscus or Maximus or any of the other midcentury avatars of 'the glorious hero' as his personal Psychopomp, his Dionysian liberator, his Apollonian coryphaeus.

After Macellum philosophical education became an essentially poetic experience for Julian – poetic in the sense that it was designed to be harmoniously therapeutic and divinely informing. (It could only be *in*forming at this period in his life, for outwardly he was still a Christian and would remain so until the dawn of his unexpected reign.) In 356, while serving as Caesar in Gaul, he attached himself to one other pagan revivalist conversant in Iamblichan theosophy who would have a formative influence on his world-view. This was Salutius Secundus, a high-ranking government official beside whom Maximus and his ilk must have seemed quite unrespectable. To the paternal Salutius Julian would eventually turn for aid in devising a theological handbook for his reformed pagan empire and gratefully dedicate his paean to the poetic universe: the *Hymn to King Helios*.

Before setting the solar crown on Julian's head and reading his apologetic hymn in its light, we should pause to consider the kinds of Late Antique literature that would have given depth and colour to his imaginative vision of the cosmic dance. Since his apostasy did not wipe away from his memory every trace of what he had read or heard as a member of the Church, we should not ignore in this regard the theocentric image of the 'koinē chorostasia' or 'communal dance' of Creation which had been a fixture of Greek patristic literature for as long as there had been Greek Fathers (see chapter 7, pages 363–71); nor, considering the exalted circles in which Julian was brought up, should we underestimate the influence of court panegyrists on his nascent consciousness of the emanation of power from the cosmic choragus to the imperial coryphaeus (see chapter 5, pages 269–72). But in the 350s he was privately defacing the public pictures of world-order imposed on his mind by the political and ecclesiastical establishment supporting his detested uncle. He was a secret iconoclast in search of ancient, indestructible imagery to replace the shattered illusion of Constantius' Christian Monarchy.

The post-Iamblichan Neoplatonists offered him plenty of what he wanted, and in a variety of media. Lost to us for the most part are the sculpted and painted images of dancing gods and the material symbols of their harmonious order that he would have glimpsed by torchlight in the temples of the mysteries; lost, too, for they literally vanished into air, are the eerie lights and ectoplasmic apparitions that danced before the eyes of trembling initiates in the rites of the Great Mother Cybele and her son Helios-Mithras. The imagery of choral order popular with the pagan reactionaries survives mainly in the dense sediment of exegetical prose preserved by the Athenian Neoplatonists of the fifth century and in the fragmentary remains of the corpus of incantatory verses attributed to Orpheus, whom Julian hailed in Iamblichan fashion as 'the most ancient of the divinely inspired philosophers.'[10] With scholarly Neoplatonists like Eusebius and Chrysanthius he may have studied the latest theosophical commentaries on the *Timaeus* – not, of course, the dull, old-fashioned treatises on Platonic cosmology by drudges like

Calcidius (who had no discernible impact on the Greek East) but the provocative avant-garde exegesis of Porphyry and Iamblichus.

Numerous fragments of Porphyry's lost commentary have come to light in Proclus' *In Timaeum*, and we can tell from one of these, an indirect quotation probably close to the wording of its source, that the cosmic dance was not ignored by the teacher of Iamblichus:

The philosopher Porphyry also had a good explanation for the phrase 'a circle turning in a circle' ['Timaeus' 34b]. For he said that it was possible for something that was not circular to move in a circle (for example, a stone made to revolve) and that it was possible for something that was circular not to move in a circle (for example, a rolling wheel moving forward) but that it was a characteristic property of the cosmos, which is spherical, to turn in a circle because of its choral dance around the centre [dia tēn peri to kentron choreian].

(fr LXII, apud Proclum, In Timaeum II 109)

Sensible scholastic annotations like this would not have held Julian's interest for long, however. More to his taste would have been Iamblichus' interpretation of the enigmatic phrase 'a circle turning in a circle' as a mystical revelation of the existence of a purely psychic revolution (centred on the One) which encompasses, initiates, and sustains the corporeal revolutions in the cosmic dance (centred on the earth). The energy of the psychic revolution was transmitted to the sublunary world by an expansive series of supracosmic, zodiacal, planetary, and elemental deities, each associated in a Pythagorean manner with a numerical 'power.'

The little that survives of the five books of Iamblichus' *In Timaeum* indicates that it dealt extensively with the mathematical generation and demiurgic activity of these crucial intermediaries in the chain of command linking the divine Monarch with his distant earthly subjects, and that the commentator was far more interested in the magical powers of healing and harmonizing continually being channelled down this invisible chain of spirits than in the corporeal revolutions of the stars and other visible consequences of the Craftsman's original burst of creativity. Julian's dream was to heal and harmonize his fractured, discordant realm by tapping the gods' inexhaustible supply of creative energy, by drawing it down in a focused beam into his own heroic spirit so that their powers would not be diffused and weakened by the tumultuous atmosphere of the world of generation. According to Proclus, who would have the same dream a century after Julian, the divine Iamblichus stated that

there exists in these powers from the supracosmic gods (whether the powers descend from the twelve Leaders or from certain others) a certain disposition to produce doubles, and that this duplicating order makes its way from the heavenly choruses [apo tōn ouraniōn chorōn] into the world of generation. For from the twenty-one Leaders arise forty-two regiments of creating gods, each allotted to an element, and from the thirty-six Decan-Rulers proceed seventy-two. Other gods arise according to the same principle, their number being double that of the heavenly gods though their power is less.

(Bk IV, fr 79; apud Proclum, *In Timaeum* III 197)

No gibbering shaman could have written this. Arcane and perplexing it may be, but it is also thoroughly scholastic in content and magisterial in tone.

The divine population explosion suffered by the Neoplatonic cosmos in the early fourth century was described by Iamblichus with almost scientific objectivity – as if it were a phenomenon that readily admitted of empirical observation and quantitative analysis (see figure 10). Just as an educated layman may have no way of seeing or comprehending the replication of genes or the binary fission of chromosomes but still have the greatest confidence that professional geneticists can see and comprehend these mysterious processes and actually tamper with them under controlled conditions, so Julian, perplexed as he doubtless was by the proliferation of 'ouranioi choroi' in the Iamblichan cosmos, appears to have accepted the 'facts' of divine genetics as they were presented to him by the professional theologians of his acquaintance whom he assumed to be in the know. But as a layman obsessed with becoming an initiate he wanted something more than the established facts and the assurance that his intellectual superiors knew what they were talking about behind their dense screen of jargon. He wanted a personal god to believe in again, or better yet, the power to conjure up a whole chorus of personal gods with gorgeous Hesiodic names and aristocratic graces.

In Maximus of Ephesus he found a conjuror of Dedalian rank who could bring the statues of the gods to life before his eyes – the astounded eyes of his body – and show him the 'ouranioi choroi' dancing in rainbow-coloured robes through the mansions of the Chaldean Decan-Rulers and around the melodious rotunda in the temple of the cosmic Muses.[12] The particular hymns Maximus chanted for his disciples during his conjuring ceremonies to heighten their sense of participation in the sublime symphony of the cosmos are lost forever, like the symphony itself, but they may have sounded something like this hymn to Helios:

Hear, O Blessed One whose eternal eye sees all!
O gold-gleaming Titan, Hyperion, Heavenly Light
Born of yourself, never resting, sweet to the sight of living
creatures!

On the right you beget Dawn and on the left Night;
You rule the Seasons as you dance to the beat of your horses'
hooves
[Krasin echōn Hōrōn, tetrabamosi possi choreuōn],
O Swift One, Striker-of-Roots, fiery and radiant Charioteer!
You proceed in your endlessly whirling course;
You rage against the ungodly and guide the godly with your
blessings;
With your golden lyre you sustain the harmonious rush of the
cosmos!
O Commander of Good Deeds, nurturing Lord of the Seasons,
World-Ruler, Player of Pan's Pipes, Whirler through a fiery
circle,
Light-Bringer, Displayer of Many Forms, Life-Giver, fruitful
Paian,
Eternal One, undefiled Father of Time, immortal Zeus,
The clear-shining and all-seeing Eye of the Cosmos!
(*Orphic Hymns* VIII 1–14)

Or like this hymn to the Mistress of the Graces:

Heavenly Aphrodite, much-hymned Lover of Laughter,
Sea-born Goddess of Generation, Holy Lover of night-long
festivals,
Nocturnal Coupler, wile-weaving Mother of Necessity,
Everything springs from you who have placed the cosmos under
your yoke!
You control the three realms of fate, giving birth to everything
That exists in the heavens, upon the fruitful earth,
And in the depths of the sea, o Holy Assistant of Bacchus!
You delight in cheerful festivities, o marriage-making Mother
of the Loves,
O Persuasion delighting in the bed of love, clandestine Giver
of Grace ...
Come, whether you are driving your swan-drawn chariot over
the billowing sea,
Rejoicing in the circular dances of whales
[erchomenē chaireis kētōn kykliaisi choreiais],
Or enjoying on land the company of the dark-eyed nymphs
Who leap fleet-footed on the sandy beaches.
(*Orphic Hymns* LV 1–9, 20–3)

The Iamblichan Universe

1. First One: inactive primal unity	}	Realm
2. Second One: creative first principle		of
3. Dyad: Limit and the Unlimited		the One

1. Aion: eternal being	}	Intelligible
2. Zoe: eternal life-force		Realm
3. Nous: eternal intellect		(noētikoi theoi)

1. Chronos: transcendent time	}	Intellectual
2. Psyche: primal soul		Realm
3. Zeus + 11 other Olympians		(noeroi theoi)

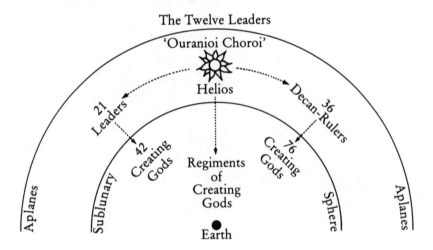

The Twelve Leaders

'Ouranioi Choroi'

Helios

21 Leaders

Decan-Rulers

42 Creating Gods

36

76 Creating Gods

Regiments of Creating Gods

Aplanes

Sublunary

Sphere

Aplanes

Earth

Figure 10

Iamblichus expanded and transformed the Plotinian triad One-Nous-Psyche into three realms or choruses of supracosmic gods. The tension inherent in the old Plotinian One (which had been both absolutely inactive and supremely creative) he tried to eliminate by positing two Ones, the first inactive and the second creative; to these he added the old Pythagorean principles of Limit and the Unlimited ('the Dyad') to compose the first and highest of the supracosmic realms. The second realm embraced the 'noētikoi theoi' or 'intelligible gods,' so called because the two highest principles at this level – Aion and Zoe – did not have to think in order to exist and live but could be thought about by all below them, especially by Nous, with whom thinking itself came into being. The members of the third realm were called 'noeroi theoi' or 'intellectual gods' because they spent their eternal lives actively thinking about and assimilating themselves to their divine superiors. On the peculiar nature and function of Chronos at this level, see chapter 8, pages 434–49. Psyche is recognizable from the old Plotinian triad but has been demoted to the status of an intellectual image of the Primal Life-Force. The Olympian gods fitted into this scheme – rather awkwardly – as hypostasized images of Nous, with Zeus (or Helios-Mithras) corresponding to the Craftsman of the *Timaeus*. They are doubtless the 'Twelve Leaders' mentioned in fr 79 of Iamblichus' *In Timaeum*. Below them in rank, though corresponding to them in power and function, were the highest encosmic gods, the 'ouranioi choroi,' including the fixed stars, the planets, the Decan-Rulers, and the Twenty-one Leaders – all ruled by Helios. Since each Decan-Ruler was thought to preside over ten degrees of the zodiac, there had to be thirty-six of them in all. They were an import from Chaldean theology. As for the Twenty-one Leaders, no one has yet discovered who they were, where they came from, or what they did. Perhaps they represented the conveyors of the influences from the seven planets into the three sublunary spheres of fire, air, and water encircling the earth ($7 \times 3 = 21$). A mysterious, possibly Chaldean process of divine doubling resulted in the pullulating regiments of 'creating gods' below the moon. Their function was to aid the Craftsman in establishing, and Helios in sustaining, the choreia of the Graces and the Seasons in the world of generation.[11]

The vision of the cosmic dance presented in these verses with their shimmering play of Apollonian gold, Cytherean blue, Dionysian purple, and other antique Olympian shades is opalescent in comparison with the opaque conceptions of cosmic and supracosmic order refined in the prose of Neoplatonic exegetes. If the mad Maximus sang hymns even half as enchanting as these in his magical caves, we can hardly blame Julian for rushing to him after prolonged exposure to the tedious theological talk of Aedesius' sane disciples!

The source of these verses is a unique collection of eighty-seven brief incantations now known as *the* Orphic hymns – a rather misleading designation since they were certainly not the only hymns ascribed in Antiquity to the mythical philosopher-poet Orpheus or chanted by cult-societies claiming Orpheus as their founder. The Stoic as well as Hesiodic tinge to the epithets abounding in the collection indicates that these particular Orphic hymns were probably composed by highly literate priests in Greco-Roman times, perhaps a century or two before Julian's birth. That their compositions were not merely literary exercises but were for liturgical use by an actual Orphic sect (resident probably in Asia Minor) can be deduced from the instructions given at the head of each hymn concerning the proper kind of incense to be offered to the god or goddess invoked in it. Like their ancient counterparts, these neo-Orphic bards were enthusiastic worshippers of Dionysus in his various heavenly and earthly guises. Their pantheon also included numerous Hesiodic nature gods, Asiatic fertility spirits, and allegorical deities like Sleep and Death, though these tended to be perceived as manifestations or assistants of Dionysus. The Orphic Helios, for instance, sustains 'the harmonious rush of the cosmos' by strumming Apollo's lyre, but he also blows Pan's-pipes like a bacchic reveller as he whirls through his fiery circle. The Orphic Aphrodite joins him in the revel as the 'holy assistant of Bacchus,' dispensing her graces rather humorously (for she is the laughter-loving goddess) to lumbering whales and fleet-footed nymphs alike and finding sexual partners for every dancer at the wedding of Heaven and Earth.[13]

The pagan revivalists in Julian's secret circle may well have possessed a copy of all or some of the Orphic hymns we possess today, though there is no evidence of the popularity or circulation of this particular cosmic hymnbook in Late Antiquity beyond the mere preservation of the verses themselves. There is also no evidence of its ever having been part of the corpus of Orphic writings piously cited as the authentic theological utterances of Orpheus and dutifully commented upon by the Athenian branch of the Iamblichan movement in the fifth century. Nevertheless, it is just this sort of rhapsodic devotional poetry that would have enchanted a churchless 'philarchaios' seeking a pagan substitute for the Psalms and just this sort of animistic religious vision that would have appealed to an imaginative 'philologos' confused by the regiments of faceless entities thronging the Iamblichan universe.

Iamblichus himself encouraged his followers to seek confirmation of his occult philosophy in the poetry of the Orphic priests by claiming in his biography of Pythagoras (XXVIII.146–7) that the great seer had derived much of the mathematical and cosmological lore enshrined in the oracular verses of his *Hieros logos* – including his central doctrine that number was the golden essence of wisdom – directly from his kindred spirit Orpheus, son of the Muse Calliope. Just as Dionysus and Apollo were thought to have proceeded from a common ancestor in whom their divided natures were eternally merged and magically harmonized, namely Helios, so Orphism with its Dionysian impulse to purify souls and Pythagoreanism with its Apollonian plan to harmonize them were regarded as distinct yet complementary phases of a single religio-philosophical movement initiated by the Light-Bringer himself to preserve the sanity of his followers and to cure the mental illness of their world.

The Graces Reborn

For almost three decades Julian was a relatively insignificant follower in the chorus of the Empire, a contemplative 'choreutēs.' His role changed dramatically in November of 361 when news reached him at Naissus in the Balkans that the ill-fated Constantius, against whom he had been marching at the head of a rebel army for several months, was dead of a fever, and that the armies of the East (knowing a divine omen when they saw one) had already sworn to follow him as their commander-in-chief. Destiny had elevated him to the position of imperial 'chorostatēs.' He wept for joy, sure at last that the old gods were behind him all the way. After making a triumphal entry into Constantinople in December of the same year, he proceeded to rock the city with a series of religious, economic, and administrative reforms designed to narrow the appalling gap between the court of his predecessor, a discordant throng of silken voluptuaries and parasitical influence-pedlars, and the court of his academic dreams, an harmonious circle of free-spirited savants and ultra-conservative counsellors bound by ties of duty and affection to an austere yet approachable philosopher-king.

Though the old gods were given a legal position in society again and worship at their crumbling temples was officially encouraged, their imperial devotee took no steps to persecute his Christian subjects. In fact he issued an edict of toleration permitting all who had been exiled from the capital for religious reasons to return if they desired – a crafty strategem which served to weaken the Christian establishment in the East by exacerbating the tensions between Arian and Orthodox factions. Towards the eunuchs of the imperial household, symbols of the sterile sensuality and endemic corruption that had surrounded Constantius, he was swift to point an accusing finger. They were sent packing along with many of the unscrupulous bureaucrats of the old administration who had fancied themselves above firing. Their replacements were high-minded Sophists like Themistius, pagan visionaries and resistance-leaders like Maximus, and scholarly administrators of proven efficiency like his friend Salutius Secundus, whom he appointed Praetorian Prefect of the East.

It was probably in the early months of his reign while he was caught up in the heady excitement of reform and obsessed with the creative exercise of his new powers that he found the time to write in glistering sophistic prose his *Hymn to King Helios*. Whether he also delivered it as a lecture to the nervous sons and daughters of the audience who had listened to Eusebius of Caesarea's Tricennial Oration we do not know – though it is certain that he treated them to several displays of his rhetorical and dialectical talents before leaving the capital for Antioch in the summer of 362. Emperors were generally expected to pay others to defend their causes and sing their praises on the public podium; but like Constantine, who had spoken on the theme of unity to the bishops at Nicaea and praised the choral order of creation before 'the assembly of the Saints,' Julian was prepared to dispense with protocol in the fond belief that the golden words of a philosopher-king could turn a chaos into a chorus as effectively as the golden numbers of Pythagoras.

Constantinople at the time was rife with professional Cynics who would have read 'Julian' for 'Helios' in the title of the hymn and hailed it as a supreme example of pretentious self-flattery. Here was a fine piece of propaganda indeed, an imperial panegyric that defeated its own purposes by confusing Christians and pagans alike with its outlandish theosophical jargon! The educated urban classes to whom such propaganda was usually directed had sense enough to understand the political rationale behind the cult of dead emperors and to accept (without taking too seriously) the divine mystique in which living emperors, fearful of assassination, were forced to enshroud themselves after the political chaos of the third century. They would not have taken a Cynical view of the respects Julian paid to Constantius at the latter's ceremonial apotheosis or have been at all confused by the new emperor's need to proclaim the divine source of his power. What would have perplexed most of them, however, were the terms in which he issued the proclamation:

Helios creates night and day and manifestly changes the universe by leading the universal revolution. And to which of the other stars does this power belong? Indeed to none. How then, judging from these and other more divine displays of power, can we not now believe that the invisible and divine race of intellectual gods above the heavens are filled with benevolent power by Him whom the whole chorus of the stars obeys [pas men hypeikei choros asterōn] and whom all generated things follow by virtue of his guiding providence? That the planets, dancing around him as their emperor [peri auton hōsper basilea choreuontes], move in a circle with consummate concord and occasionally pause and trace their direct and retrograde courses (as their visible motions are called by experts in the study of the spheres) while the moon increases and diminishes its light in accordance with its distance from the sun, is, I suppose, clear to all. Is it not reasonable for us to suppose then that the older and greater organization of the lives of the intellectual gods is analogous to this order?

(Hymn to King Helios 134d–135c)

It all sounded like old-fashioned Platonic cosmology with a note or two of Stoic piety thrown in for good measure until the part about 'intellectual gods.' Who in heaven's name were they? Where did they fit into the cosmic dance? Why were all the stars suddenly obeying them? And what had they to do with this alarming talk about *changing* the universe with 'divine displays of power'?

Imperial panegyrists in the past had customarily used the images of the solar coryphaeus and the world-chorus to celebrate the status quo as a reflection of the unchanging order of Heaven or the heavens and to praise the emperor for exercising his power in the interests of social stability and religious conservatism. The revolutionary drift of Julian's seemingly traditional argument here could only have been followed by the intellectually adventurous minority who had dipped into Iamblichus' treatise *On the Gods* (now lost) or had studied Salutius' paraphrase of it entitled *On the Gods and the Universe* (extant), which served as the official manifesto and unofficial creed of the Pagan Reformation.

Iamblichus had heroically cut the central snarl in the Gordian knot of Plotinian metaphysics – namely the paradoxical conception of the One as both an utterly transcendent recluse and a supremely creative forefather – by proposing that two Ones were better than one. If a second One could be envisioned as the active First Cause of multiplicity and identified as the archetypal Light-Bringer and Life-Giver from whom the Greek Titan Helios, the Persian sun-god Mithras, and the visible sun all emanated, then the first One, the unattainable stillness towards which all dancers inclined, would be free at last from the taint of incipient duality by abiding – 'existing' was too lowly a term for it – at an even further remove from the material world than the Wellspring at the centre of the Plotinian Circle of Nous. It was one thing to replace Plotinus' vague distinction between the immanent and transcendent aspects of the One with this bold (if not exactly clear) division of hypostatic ranks. It was quite another to believe in the eternal actuality of two first principles as a religious truth.

Given the fragmentary condition of the Iamblichan corpus we cannot be sure that Iamblichus came to regard his idiosyncratic doctrine of the two Ones as a certitude glowing brightly beyond the cloudy realm of hypothesis, but his Platonic commentaries clearly indicate that he was prepared to defend the reasonableness of his doctrine and to explore its theological implications with regard to the Many. The binary fission of the Plotinian One entailed a corresponding division of the Plotinian eternal world into two realms: a so-called 'noetic' realm in which Nous came into existence by receiving eternal being from a god called Aion (the old Platonic Model) and eternal life from his consort Zoe; and its image, a conveniently expansive 'noeric' realm where supracosmic room could be found for the Plotinian Psyche, Helios-Mithras, the Craftsman, and the hypostatized Olympians whose function was to guide and illuminate the chorus of their visible counterparts. The inhabitants of the first realm were called 'intelligible gods' (noētikoi theoi) because they could be thought about by their inferiors but did not have to think in order to be. Those of the second were known as 'intellectual gods' (noeroi theoi) because they existed chiefly for the purpose of thinking high thoughts about their superiors and creating a temporal image of their 'older and greater organization' in the organization of the cosmic chorus.

If the task of reducing Iamblichus' high thoughts and wildly inventive hypotheses into neat gobbets of digestible dogma fell to Salutius, the challenge of persuading an empire full of subtle Galileans and simple Sun-Worshippers – not to mention heckling Cynics and yawning Skeptics – to accept all this as dazzlingly rational and invincibly true was taken up by Julian with the zeal, ironically, of an early Christian apologist. His *Hymn to King Helios* was more than a personal declaration of allegiance to an intensely imagined (and largely imaginary) pagan past. It was the inauguration of an heroic campaign to reform the inner life of the Empire, to bring about its Orphic rebirth and Pythagorean restoration with a divine display of power.

In life Julian strove to realize what he could imagine in rhetoric: the magical animation of Constantine's sun-crowned statue. Whereas Constantine had employed the metaphor of the dance in the manner of Calcidius to sum up and interpret the visual evidence of cosmic order, Julian used the visual evidence of cosmic order to verify the metaphor – to persuade potential converts of the reality of the 'consummate concord' resulting from the essentially intellectual dance of Helios and his chorus. Of course he had a political interest in translating the figurative language of Neoplatonic theology into a proclamation of the facts about his new order. As emperor he wanted none of his subjects to forget that he was a Helios among their restless host, a commander of unconquerable powers, a craftsman of unity, a focus of religious awe, a mystical illuminator, a vital link between the powers that be and the powers that come to be. Just as the heavenly Helios received his power directly from the coryphaeus of the intellectual gods (call him Zeus or Mithras or what you will) so Julian received his from the visible sun once venerated and embodied by Constantine, and it was a power not only to illuminate the world but to regenerate it physically and spiritually by an act of sustained forethought that defied the destructive will of the goddess Necessity.[14]

Political reformers usually dream of thwarting what looks like Necessity to most members of their society, but as Julian saw it only those who dared to harness for virtuous political ends the magical energies that turned winter into spring and engendered living creatures in the warm mud of the Nile – the same energies that had raised the minds of Pythagoras and his followers above the fecund slime of matter – could turn their fantasy into the facts of history. To prove the truth of his vision (or as Cynics would insist, to pull the wool over his converts' eyes by erasing the distinction between his

fantastic image of himself and the actual character of his army-backed leadership) Julian drew upon poetic as well as philosophical and scientific sources
of evidence confirming the sun's eternal ascendency over all temporal things.
Had not Apollo speaking through an Orphic bard hailed Zeus, Hades, and
Helios as three gods in one godhead ages before the Galileans invented their
uncouth Trinity? Had not Hesiod recognized Helios as the son of Hyperion
'who walks above' and Thea 'the most divine of beings'? And had not Homer
called him Hyperion after his transcendent father to show that his nature
was 'superior to all necessity'? As an initiate in the Neoplatonic mysteries
Julian was bound to confess that the divine order revealed to his senses was
but a shadowy image of the supercelestial empire perceived by his intellect.
But as the leading mystagogue of his age, the prophet of the poetic universe,
he was moved by all the spheres in heaven to sing the Old Song instead of
the New and to make the Old Song new to men's ears by teaching the empire
at hand that the poetic vision of Helios and the celestial Muses which most
astronomers mistakenly regarded as a mythological fancy, a mere allegory,
was no less real for being magical than the season 'when earth bursts into
bloom and leaps exultantly, when the crops are all beginning to sprout and
the sea becomes safe for sailing.'[15]

Spring literally sprang from Helios when he traversed three of the five
great celestial circles of the poetic universe and begot in them the three
Graces (see figure 11).[16] Their birth, which Julian closely associated with
the cosmic dance in the fervently Iamblichan section of the Hymn cited at
the head of this chapter, may be regarded as an allegorical enactment in the
cosmic theatre of an event or operation preceding it in the realm of intellectual reality: the procession of numerous 'noeroi theoi' from Helios-Mithras.
But it must also be seen (from Julian's viewpoint) as an actual consequence
of the overflowing of divinity from the Beyond into the 'heavenly choruses'
and as a necessary cause of the proliferation of 'creating gods' in the elemental
spheres below the moon.

Julian's mystical conception of the Graces as spirits of concord who abide
with the sun-god, preside over certain superlunary circles, oversee the vernal
distribution of solar blessings, and rejuvenate the earth with their holy
dance is remote from the fundamentally ethical conception of their role
popularized by the Stoics, but remarkably close to the prephilosophical
vision of their Olympian activities preserved in the corpus of ancient Greek
lyric poetry. As a schoolboy Julian probably studied these famous lines
from the fourteenth Olympian ode of Pindar (518–438 BC):

> O Graces of fertile Orchomenus, guardians of the ancient
>   Minyae,
>   Hear my prayer! For by your aid all things cheerful

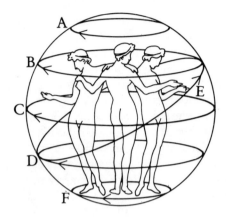

Figure 11

In *Hymn to King Helios* 146d Julian states that the sun rules five celestial circles and begets the Graces in three of them. The five are doubtless the principal circles of the Aplanes: the Celestial Arctic Circle, the Tropic of the Summer Solstice, the Isemerinon or Celestial Equator, the Tropic of the Winter Solstice, and the Celestial Antarctic Circle (A, B, C, D, and F respectively). These were the circles Calcidius identified in sections LXV–LXVII of his commentary as the chief configurations in the 'spectaculum caelestis choreae.' Since the Isemerinon and the two Celestial Tropics are connected by the ecliptic (E), they must be the three circles traversed or touched by Helios when he begets the three Graces. Julian seems to have understood the birth of the Graces to be both a unique celestial event (that is, the procession from Helios of three divine overseers who sustain the harmony of the Isemerinon and the two Celestial Tropics) and a recurrent terrestrial phenomenon (that is, the vernal revival of joy, beauty, and fertility in the lands lying between the Arctic and Antarctic Circles). In *Hymn to King Helios* 148d he notes that 'the Graces imitate a circle in their statues.' But which circle? An ancient sculptural group resting in the Museo dell' Opera della Cattedrale, Siena, and a Pompeian fresco preserved in the Museo Nazionale, Naples, provide us with an outline of the Graces as they might have appeared to Julian. Though they are arranged in a line rather than a ring, their interlinked arms and inclining bodies give a surprising impression of circularity when viewed from the angle chosen by the Pompeian painter. The circular harmony of the group becomes all the more apparent when their outline is set within a diagram of the Aplanes. The two free arms extended on the right seem to rise towards the point of the Summer Solstice, while the free arm extended on the left sinks towards the point of the Winter Solstice. Perhaps a discerning Neoplatonic spectator would have seen the harmonizing ring of the ecliptic in their configuration and their tilted head-bands. To my eye, however, their outline suggests the all-encompassing ring of the Isemerinon.

And sweet are brought about for mortals,
If a man is wise or beautiful or renowned for nobility.
For not even the gods arrange their dances and banquets
Without the aid of the holy Graces.
[oude gar theoi semnan Chariton ater
koiraneoisin chorous oute daitas.]
Why, they are the overseers of all the works in heaven, where
their thrones are set
Beside the Lord of the Golden Bow, Pythian Apollo,
And where they worship the everflowing honour of the
Olympian Father.

O Lady Aglaia,
And dance-loving Euphrosyne, daughters of the mightiest of
the gods,
Listen now! And you too, dance-enamoured Thalia,
After you have looked upon this revel-band stepping nimbly
In honour of the victor's good fortune.
(*Olympian Ode* xiv 4–17)

The cult of these celestial dancers from whom sprang the green of sprouting crops, the sparkle on country brooks, the rose in the cheeks of nymphs, and the joie-de-vivre of a society at peace with itself and nature was among the most ancient in Greece, having been founded at the Boeotian city of Orchomenus by its prehistoric inhabitants the Minyae.

The charm of their youthful universe with its 'radiance' (Aglaia) and 'good cheer' (Euphrosyne) and 'abundant festivities' (Thalia) is hard to resist even now, however joyless and inhospitable we may suspect the heavens really are. Julian found it irresistible. After the trauma of his father's death, the loneliness of his childhood, and the spiritual trials of his adolescence he ought to have been the most cynical of spectators at the dance – an imperial Momus with no gods to rail at save the lifeless statues of his ancestors. Yet in spite of his education in darkness, or perhaps because of it, he was determined to fill the heavens again with 'gods who proceed from Helios' and to make the 'uneducated Cynics' (as he called them) see the light and revel in it as he had done at Ephesus and Athens.[17] His Graces were not lifeless statues decorating a decayed aristocrat's pleasure garden or droll personifications animated by a Sophist's wit or evanescent images painted on the air by a dancer's hands. Like Pindar's goddesses they were powerful overseers reigning in the Aplanes with the mightiest of the gods and worshipping the everflowing honour of their Olympian Father. As the informing and reforming spirits of Julian's new order they were all that sustained the ancient link between the seasonal regeneration of nature and the vitality of civilization. They were his triumphant answer to the Cynics.

Revels of the Horae

To the obdurate Skeptics in his court who might wonder how the Graces managed to dance diaphanously above the moon while displaying their famous bodily charms all over the earth, the philosopher-king (who had lived too long among Christians not to have an answer ready for every theological question) had this to say:

By dividing the three circles with the circle of the Life-Bringer [that is, the zodiac] which communes with each of the three, Helios produces the four arcs of the ecliptic; moreover, by dividing the Life-Bringer into twelve divine powers and then each of these by three, he creates a total of thirty-six gods. Hence, I believe, there descends from the heavens above, that is, from the three circles, a three-fold gift of the Graces; for by dividing them by four this god sends to us the four-fold 'Radiance' of the Horae who control the turnings of the seasons. And indeed on earth the Graces imitate a circle in their statues [Kyklon toi kai hai Charites epi gēs dia tōn agalmatōn mimountai]. In so far as Dionysus is the Giver of the Graces he is said to reign with Helios. Why should I go on to tell you about 'Horus' and of all the other divine names that belong to Helios?

(*Hymn to King Helios* 148c–d)

If that did not answer the Skeptics who questioned the doctrine of the descent of all the encosmic gods from Helios, at least it would muddle and silence them! That the Graces themselves do not dance below the moon but rather convey their gifts of radiant beauty, joyous energy, and festive harmony to spiritual manifestations of themselves dancing in the elemental spheres, namely the Horae or 'Seasons,' and ultimately to material representations of themselves in earthly statuary, namely three or more female figures circling with clasped hands or interlocked arms, is the point that shines most clearly through the fog of Pythagorean computations, Chaldean allusions, and Orphic pronouncements in Julian's bewildering argument. Follow any of the four lines of thought – theological, astrological, etymological, and mythological – that converge like radii in the passage above, and it will lead to this central image of the Graces and their graceful sisters who sustain the cycles of earthly time by imitating the timeless circles of the Aplanes.

The theological line of thought will start to make sense if it is seen as an extension of the argument developed by Iamblichus in the fourth book of his *In Timaeum* (see chapter 6, pages 285–6) concerning the multiplication of sublunary creating gods from the 'ouranioi choroi' who proceed directly from Helios. The Horae are evidently to be placed among the choruses of gods abiding with the forty-two Leaders and the seventy-two Decadarchs who oversee the ceaseless cycle of growth and decay in the 'ninth creation' or the world of generation, though their genesis as Julian describes it has nothing to do with the mysterious doubling process that Iamblichus mentioned in his commentary. By following Julian's astrological line of thought we discover how the Horae paradoxically arose as a sublunary multiplication of the gifts of the Graces through a process of superlunary division. In the course of creating the zodiacal gods (the 'twelve divine powers') and the Chaldean Decan-Rulers (the 'thirty-six gods') Helios divided the ecliptic into four equal arcs by intersecting, or as Julian would say in his mystico-erotic idiom, by 'communing with' each of the three circles associated with the Graces. His primordial communion with the Graces at the points of the vernal equinox, the summer solstice, the autumnal equinox, and the winter solstice produced four divine offspring, the Horae, who have ever afterwards aided him in governing the succession of seasonal phenomena in the world of generation so that its cyclical order miraculously reflects his annual course through the zodiac.

As if all this were not proof enough of the descent of the Horae from Helios and the Graces, Julian further establishes their family connections by punning on their names in a flamboyantly sophistic manner. He chooses the noun 'aglaia' (which happens to be the name of a Grace) to denote the spectacular gift of light that Helios sends down to us from the realm of the Graces and also the splendid pageant of the seasons which his rays not only make visible but also bring to life in the circling chorus of the Horae. What Julian chooses *not* to tell us about 'Horus' – the name of the Egyptian God of Light best known to the Greeks and Romans – is that the name 'Horae' is obviously derived from it and symbolically reflects it as an image reflects its archetype.[18]

From the poetic synthesis of myths and association of mythological names in the passage emerges the vague outline of an argument proving the teleological connection and formal correspondence between the procession of gods from the Sun of the Intellectual Realm and the descent of dance-inspiring rays from the visible sun into the chaos of Primal Matter. A clearer version of the same argument, which basically concerns the origin of the civilizing and revitalizing dance of the poetic universe, appears in the companion-piece to the *Hymn to King Helios*, namely the *Hymn to the Mother of the Gods*, which though written in prose came to Julian 'in the short space of a single night' (178d) like a divinely inspired poem. That productive night fell in 362 during his last spring in Constantinople, probably shortly before 22 March when 'Helios the Corybant' (167d) inaugurated the rites of Attis by completing his ascent to the vernal equinox in the cosmic fertility dance honouring Rhea-Cybele, the Divine Mother. 'According to mythology,' Julian reminded his audience,

Attis was exposed at birth beside the whirling streams of the river Gallus. There he flourished, and when he grew to be beautiful and tall in appearance he was dearly loved by the Mother of the Gods. She entrusted all things to him and crowned him with a starry headdress. Now, if this visible heaven of ours covers the top of the head of Attis, ought we not to interpret the river Gallus as a symbolic image of the Milky Way? For it is there, they say, that the substance that suffers change mixes with the imperturbable changeless revolution of the fifth substance. This was the furthest limit to which the Mother of the Gods permitted Attis, this fair intellectual god who resembles the sun's rays, to leap and dance [skirtan te kai choreuein tōi kalōi toutōi kai tais hēliakais aktisin empherei tōi noerōi theōi, tōi Attidi]. But when he passed beyond these bounds and proceeded all the way to the lowest regions, he was said in the myth to have descended into the cave and to have had intercourse with the nymph. The nymph is to be interpreted as the drenching moistness of matter. The myth does not refer to corporeal matter at this point but rather to the ultimate immaterial cause which subsists before corporeal matter.

(Hymn to the Mother of the Gods 165b–c)

In the conclusion of the myth Attis, tormented by shame, castrates himself, leaves his genitals in the cave, and returns to the forgiving Mother Goddess who soon makes him whole again. The eunuch priests of Attis whom Julian would have seen in action in Asia Minor where they were still called Corybants and in Italy where they were known as Galli re-enacted these barbarous events in a series of clamorous rituals lasting for four days. On the twenty-second of March they felled a sacred pine to commemorate the castration of the fallen god; on the twenty-third they blew trumpets, perhaps to purify the atmosphere or to echo the screams of Attis; on the twenty-fourth, the so-called 'Day of Blood,' the high-priest sprinkled the altar with an offering from his own veins while his clergy, driven wild by the din of shrieking flutes, bellowing horns, and thundering tambours, stabbed themselves with knives or sharp potsherds as they whirled around him in an orgiastic dance; and after all this, on the twenty-fifth, the survivors cheerfully leapt and caroused with the masses in the vernal revels known in Rome as the Hilaria. The cosmic significance of the dance of the Galli had certainly not escaped the notice of philosophical spectators before Julian. Lucretius, for one, had been both fascinated and repelled by the spectacle (see chapter 4, pages 154–5). In contrast to the great Roman Epicurean, who had striven to distance himself intellectually from the raggle-taggle pomp of Cybele's superstitious adorants, Julian boldly broke ranks with the contemptuous intellectuals in the crowd of onlookers and revelled as best he could in the primitive joy and agony of the celebrants of the Day of Blood.[19]

As an initiate in their mysteries he was well aware of the seasonal significance of the myth of Attis. He knew that the dance of Attis down to the shores of the river Gallus represented the movement of the autumnal sun from its equinoctial point to the border of the Milky Way between Scorpio and Sagittarius; that the god's rebellious act of fording the stream and his subsequent disappearance into the cave symbolized the decline in the sun's light and heat during its descent to the point of the winter solstice; that his castration and temporary sterility in the cave corresponded to the sun's agonizing struggle to climb back to the celestial equator and the earth's barrenness in the depths of winter; and that his joyous restoration to Cybele and recuperation in heaven signified the regeneration of the earth in the spring and summer following the sun's return to the northern celestial hemisphere. Such knowledge was enough for the common initiate, of course, but it could not be expected to satisfy a Neoplatonic initiate like Julian who wished to leap like Helios the Corybant beyond the mummery of the seasonal world. And leap he did – with his usual muddling enthusiasm. From his compulsion to find or create a satisfactory substitute for Christ before the Galilean reconquered him and his empire sprang the desperate zeal with which he tried to interpret the savage nightmare of Attis as a serenely rational account of cosmic resurrection and the pathetic earnestness with which he perceived the carnival of the Hilaria as a solemn religious confirmation of the Iamblichan theory of procession and return.

The physical agony of the Galli was notorious for moving crowds of holiday spectators to such a pitch of excitement that not a few among them, their hair streaming, their veins pulsing, flung off their clothes in the streets, screamed their way into the dance, and castrating themselves with a sword kept by the priests for such occasions held up their severed organs before the gasping merry-makers. Though Julian's intellectual agony was in its own way quite as intense as the anguish of these new Corybants, it moved hardly a soul. The harder he struggled to cut himself free of myths and to leap beyond them into a pure field of imageless metaphysical thought, the more enmeshed in their organic strands of imagery he became. Cybele he hailed as the Primal Life-Force, the Creative First Principle, the Wellspring of Intellectual Godhead, the Forethought of Intelligible Godhead, the Supreme Cause of Soul, and so on, but what he embraced in his soul and clung to in this confusing flood of Neoplatonic epithets was a human form rather than a divine formula, an image rather than an idea of universal motherhood.

In her statues he beheld the turret-crowned queen who had set a starry diadem on a rebel's brow, the veiled mourner who had lost her dearest offspring to a seductive nymph, the gentle nurse who had restored a eunuch to virility, and the invincible protectress of Rome who had proved the innocence of a slandered virgin by miraculously impelling a grounded ship some distance up the Tiber – a ship bearing to Italy an image of the goddess which was 'not lifeless clay but something living and possessed of divine powers' (161a). This was the Cybele who came to life in the poetic universe and enlivened it with her presence. As for Attis, what was he in reality but the radiance of Intelligible Beauty which descended into the substrate of Primal Matter, imposed form on what was formless, established the limits of generation with his powers as the cosmic Logos, and inspired all generated things to return to the perfection of Primal Unity? What was his dance by the shores of Gallus but a reminder of the bodiless revelry of the supracosmic gods, an allegorical image of their ontological procession from the Wellspring of Life towards the fluid boundary between spirit and matter? Let the priests of Attis whirl themselves out of mind in the revels of the Horae! Julian was bound for higher revels where he would turn himself *into* mind and escape the shameful darkness of the cave as a ray of pure intellectual light returning to Helios.

Yet such a transformation proved no easier to envision than to effect. Try as he might to see Attis (and himself) as a 'fair intellectual god' – a passionless mind leading a bodiless chorus around a flameless sun – he was unable to abandon the imagery of the priests and the poets or to resist the sophistic tendency to dissolve the philosophical distinctions between image and archetype, formable matter and informing principle. His eyes were all too easily drawn back to the heavenly light that had shone round him as a boy at Macellum, the animating sunbeams of the poetic universe to which he compared the hypostasized Attis. These showed him the living statues he yearned to see and become: the colossal Lord of Life blazing in his circle of fire; the undefiled Father of Time guiding the chorus of the Horae; the Commander of Good Deeds raging against the ungodly.

On his long southeasterly journey over land from Constantinople to Antioch in the summer of 362 Julian paid a special visit to the ancient shrine of Cybele at the foot of Mount Dindymus in the Phrygian heart of Asia Minor. 'O Mother of the Gods, You who delight in Dindymus,' Aeneas had prayed before the start of a decisive battle, ' ... march beside the Phrygian squadrons with your gracious step!'[20] Perhaps the Apostate recalled this prayer as he gazed upon the holy mountain, for he too, a hero in the making, was destined to march into battle for the glory of Rome. First he would rage against the ungodly Galileans of Antioch in the eternal wars of Truth, and then, with the Goddess's special grace, he would triumph over the rapacious Persians in the centuries-old struggle for domination of the Fertile Crescent. As it happened, he was to lose his temper in the first battle and his life in the second.

Eagerly awaiting him at Antioch was a pagan ally of no mean stature, the Sophist Libanius, whose enormous estates in the valley of the Orontes made him a leader of the city's wealthy élite and whose reputation as the Empire's foremost man of letters was by that time undisputed. No longer would Julian have to read the mellifluous Attic prose of this Asiatic nabob in private as he once had to do at his grandmother's palace in Nicomedia. Henceforth his admiration for this public defender of traditional Hellenic culture would be as public as he could make it, come what may. Any aspect or symbol of that culture singled out for attack by Christian preachers was sure to be praised to the skies by Libanius, who, though critical of the newfangled view of the gods promoted by the extremists in the Iamblichan movement, shared with the likes of Maximus and Priscus a deep respect for the ancient mystery cults threatened by the Galilean and a defensive enthusiasm for the mythopoetic world-view revived with them. To the defence of the quintessentially Hellenic and arguably mystical (that is, 'silent' and 'divinely informative') art of 'orchēsis' he would devote an entire oration, declaring that

it would be a wonder if we who agree that time bears witness to the virtue of the other arts were not to praise the cosmic dance which orders and adorns itself [tēn orchēsin autōi toutōi kosmoumenēn]. Indeed the dance should be acclaimed as it was in the olden days by the wisest men because it came into existence along with the universe and sprang from the same great and primordial source as the heavens. And we know this to be true because the march of the stars maintains its set course with a certain harmony and in accordance with divine law.

(*Oratio* LXIV.12)

Thus would the litanist of conservative Hellenism with his deep reverence for divine law in its pre-Christian sense, namely the customary cycle of changes known here below as time but seen from above as an unchanging image of eternity, turn Lucian's preposterous encomium of the pantomime into a serious commendation of the harmony once existing between cosmos and culture in the ancient Greek city-states.

Just as time had testified to the virtue of all the arts cultivated by the Greeks, so would it also bear witness to the enduring validity of their vision of an artistic cosmos. Time which had reduced that vision to absurdity in the second century would hallow it again in the fourth. On 18 July, with Dindymus far behind him, Julian descended from the pass in the Amanus mountains into the valley of the Orontes and beheld for the first time the sun-blessed agricultural domain of Antioch, over which, as Libanius had proudly observed in 360,

the Horae dance in chorus to a graceful melody without destroying the

loveliness of the land [hai Hōrai choreuousin emmelōs ou diaphtheirousai
tēn apo tautēs charin] ...

(Oratio XI.29)

Little did the Sophist suspect at the time he uttered these charming words
that an imperial champion of the old order would one day arrive at his
doorstep with the alarming news that the Horae really did exist, and Cybele
too, and all the other primitive fertility spirits portrayed by highly civilized
'orchēstai.'

The Horae were associated with many other deities besides Cybele in the
cosmic fertility dance depicted by visual artists and celebrated by religious
poets throughout Antiquity (see figure 12). Since the noun 'hōra' commonly
denoted any hour, day, week, month, or season during which a recurrent
event in the natural or social calendar was scheduled to occur, the goddesses
overseeing the agenda of life in the poetic universe were originally indefinite
in number; there were as many of them as were needed to open all the
spring flowers, ripen all the ears of corn, sweeten all the clusters on the
vine, and fashion reeds for all the Pan's-pipes blown in Arcadia. Certainly
more than four Horae figured in the painting, now lost, that Philostratus
the Elder recreates for us in the following exquisite ecphrasis of a rustic
dance:

Let us leave Homer in possession of the special knowledge that the Horae
guard the gates of Heaven ['Iliad' v.749], for he very likely became a close
friend of the Horae when he inherited the skies. A man does not have to be
a genius to understand the easy subject depicted here in this painting. For if
I am not mistaken, the Horae, descending to the earth in their own proper
forms, are dancing with clasped hands as they whirl the year round in its
course [xunaptousai tas cheiras eniauton oimai helittousi], and the wise earth
brings forth for them in abundance all the fruits of the year. Far be it from
me to say to the spring-time Horae: 'Tread not on the hyacinth or the rose!'
For when these flowers are trodden upon they breathe forth a sweeter fra-
grance than that of the Horae themselves. And I shall not say to the Horae
of winter: 'Step not on the soft ploughed fields!' For if the fields are stepped
on by the Horae they will produce the ear of corn. Those yellow-haired
Horae over there are stepping on the hairy stalks of grain, but not so as to
bend or snap them. Why, they are so light and nimble that they do not even
make the field rustle! O grape-vines, how charming of you to wish to grasp
the Horae of autumn! For you doubtless love the Horae because they make
you beautiful and sweet as wine. Now these are what we might call our
harvestings from the painting. As for the Horae themselves, they are ex-
ceedingly pretty – so pretty indeed that they must have been fashioned by

Figure 12

On a silver-gilt plate dating from the late second century AD (found at Parabiago near Milan in 1907) Cybele is depicted as queen of all the cosmic gods who participate in the fertility dance of nature. Enthroned with her on her lion-drawn chariot is Attis with his distinctive Phrygian cap and shepherd's crook. Three whirling Curetes (often identified with Corybants) accompany her chariot as it charges through the world of time. Aion, the god of time, serenely observes the rite from his station within an elliptical zodiac. The serpent-entwined obelisk beside him probably represents the Tree of Life. Below the chariot Winter, a small cloaked figure waving a bough, leads the processional dance of the Horae. Spring follows with a lamb. Summer ought to be next, but the grape-bearing Hora in third place is probably Autumn. Summer (or Autumn?) dances in the rear with a sheaf of grain. Observing their chorus at the bottom of the plate are a water-nymph and a river-god holding a rush; Oceanus and a Naiad with a school of fish; and Mother Earth with her children and cornucopia. From left to right across the top of the plate soar Apollo Helios in his ascending chariot, the Morning-Star Lucifer, Luna in her descending chariot, and the Evening-Star Hesperus. The plate is 39 cm in diameter.

divine art. How they sing! How they whirl in their round-dance [hoia de hē dinē tou kyklou]! See how they all keep their backs turned away from us by appearing to advance towards us. See the arm raised up, the freedom of their loosened hair, the cheek warm from running, and the eyes which dance together [hoi ophthalmoi synchoreuontes]. Perhaps they will allow me to tell a story about the painter: for it seems to me that he came upon the Horae while they were dancing [choreuousais tais Hōrais] and was caught up by them into their art. Perhaps the goddesses are hinting to him that he must paint 'syn hōrai' – 'with grace.'

(*Imagines* II.34.1–3)

Julian imagined and tried to realize on an imperial scale what Philostratus had fancied in miniature: the magical participation of humanity in the artistic life of the gods. In the poetic universe one did not have to be a painter to be drawn through the perishable surface of life as if it were a gauzy veil into a dewy field of everlasting hyacinths and roses. To be caught up in the art of the Horae one had only to gaze upon the loosened hair of the dancers in the rites of spring, to touch their warm cheeks, to inhale the fragrance of the flowers trodden under their feet, to listen for their song in the air.

A sense of the constancy and perfection of the divine forms reflected in their sweet transience came to the Poetic Spectator directly through his senses, and the epiphanic joy resulting from it was sustained in his soul through his physical and intellectual participation in religious festivals like the Apollonian rite celebrated by the Alexandrian poet Callimachus (d c235 BC):

> *Joy, joy! O much-implored Carneius! Your altars*
> *Wear flowers in spring, the many-coloured blooms*
> *That the Horae lead forth when Zephyr breathes dew,*
> *And in winter the sweet crocus. Always burns your immortal*
> fire;
> *Never does the ash feed around the coals of yesterday.*
> *Very joyful was Phoebus that the belted warriors of [the war-*
> goddess] Enyo
> *Danced with the fair-haired Libyan women*
> *When the Horae of the Carneian festival came round. ...*
> *No other dance more divine has Apollo beheld!*
> *[aneres orchēsanto meta xanthēisi Libyssais*
> *tethmiai eute sphin Karneiades ēlython Hōrai. ...*
> *ou keinou choron eide theōteron allon Apollōn!]*
> ('To Apollo,' *Hymn* II 80–7, 93)

Like Antioch, the Libyan city of Cyrene, birthplace of Callimachus, still kept a flame burning on Apollo's altar in Julian's day though its population was by then under Christian control. The cult of Carneius (a Dorian fertility god identified with Apollo in the Archaic period) had flourished there since the colonization of Libya in the seventh century BC by 'belted warriors' from the island of Thera, whose dance at the Carneian festival, observed with great delight by the god himself from his vantage-point on the Cyrenian Hill of Myrtles, doubtless symbolized their cultural domination of the region as well as their fruitful intermarriage with 'the fair-haired Libyan women.' For a thousand summers the Horae had led the Cyrenians into the 'choros theios' of the Carneian festival so that they might behold the splendour of the god in his temple, and the memory of having revelled with these peaceful spirits before his flower-strewn altar and whirled like stars around his immortal flame was not easily extinguished by the Church.

In Athens, where Callimachus had been a student almost six and a half centuries before Julian, the Horae were given individual names like Thallo ('the Flowering One') and Karpo ('the Fruit-bearing One') and worshipped either on their own or in combination with Dionysus, Demeter, Kore, and the other Eleusinian deities. Their participation in the redemptive cosmic dance celebrated by the initiates at Eleusis is recalled in the following verses from the Orphic hymnbook:

> O Horae, daughters of Themis and Lord Zeus,
> Eunomia and Dike and oft-blessed Eirene,
> Chaste nymphs of spring and of meadows full of flowers,
> You are adorned with every colour and scented with every
> flower-sweet breeze!
> O ever-blooming Horae, circling with sweet faces,
> You clad yourselves in dewy robes of flourishing blooms;
> You are the play-fellows of holy Persephone, when the Fates
> And the Graces lead the way up to the light with circling
> choral dances
> [kai Charites kyklioisi chorois pros phōs anagōsi],
> Giving pleasure to Zeus and their fruit-giving Mother.
> ('To the Horae,' Orphic Hymns XLIII 1–9)

Whether the temple dancers at Eleusis portrayed the Horae circling together with the Graces and the Fates in a ritual enactment of Persephone's ascent from Hades the silence of their spectators prevents us from knowing. A dance combining these three choruses, each with three goddesses, would doubtless have been enchanting at the end of an epoptic rite – 'enchanting' in its most potent magical sense – for the numbers three and nine were the great binding powers in the triple world of the mysteries (Hades, Earth, Heaven) and in the nine spheres of the poetic universe (Aplanes, the seven

planets, the world of generation). The Orphic bard derived the three allegorical names of his Horae, their genealogy, and their association with the
Fates and the Graces not from Eleusinian hymnody but from Hesiod's
Theogony (901–9) where they had been transported from their native fields
into the domain of the city-states and endowed with a political significance
foreign to yet compatible with their primitive agrarian character. Bound up
in their dance, or rather bound together by it, were the blessed effects fated
to arise from Themis – the civilizing 'justice' imposed by Zeus on the savage
pre-Olympian universe. And these were the 'good government' of Eunomia,
the 'legal order' of Dike, and the 'peace' of Eirene.

J ulian's Hesiodic conception of Helios-Zeus as a just ruler who governs
the seasonal world by begetting its divine governors and continually revitalizing its peaceful government may have been derived directly from Hesiod
(whom he hailed as 'the most venerable of the poets' after Homer) or indirectly through Orphic and Iamblichan sources.[21] His conception of the
Horae as *four* demiurgic spirits descending from the equinoctial and solstitial
points on the ecliptic is clearly not Hesiodic, however, though it may at
first seem so because of his insistence on their special kinship with the Graces
as peacemakers in the natural world and overseers of human social order.
Their number betrays the Hellenistic origin of his vision. The earliest extant
artistic representations of a solar deity leading a dance of four Horae who
are clearly distinguishable as Spring, Summer, Autumn, and Winter by their
seasonal costumes and botanic emblems are Roman copies of a Hellenistic
relief which probably dated from the third century BC; their thyrsus-bearing
coryphaeus has been confidently identified as Dionysus.[22] Chances are that
Stoic physicists introduced the image of four dancing or processing Horae
into cosmological literature well before the Christian era, for we can find
it in the pseudo-Aristotelian *Peri kosmou* (see chapter 5, pages 253–4) where
the sun is described as a coryphaeus 'leading the four seasons of the year as
he moves forward to the north and back to the south.'

What he led them along was his 'lykabas' or 'path of light' – the circular
path traced by his light as it moved against the daily rotation of the Aplanes
in the course of a year. 'The word "lykabas," noted Julian,

*is used to denote the year not only by Homer [for example, 'Odyssey' XIV.161]
and all the famous authors of Greece, but also by the god himself. For he
says that he brings 'the year, his journey of twelve months, to a close with
a dance' [Orchēthmōi lykabanta duōdekamēna keleutha].*

(Hymn to King Helios 154b)

This oracular pronouncement is of course ambiguous. It may mean that
Helios completes the cycle of the year by dancing for twelve months along

Figure 13

Dionysus with his thyrsus leads a processional dance of tiptoeing Horae in this Roman bas-relief (now in the Louvre) copied from a popular Hellenistic prototype. The Hora with the loosened stole and sheaf of grain (?) is probably Summer.

his path of light or that he ends his journey with a festive dance, namely the 'orchēthmos' performed by his worshippers in late December at the solstitial rites of the Saturnalia which were brought to a triumphant close just before the Roman New Year with the festival of Sol Invictus. Since Julian tells us that he composed his solar hymn in the wake of the latter festival, which he called the Heliaia, and that he fully approved of the old Roman custom of observing the New Year 'in the present season when King Helios is coming back to us again from the distant reaches of the south' (156a–c), we should read it not just as a political manifesto but as a liturgical performance, a sacrifice of words, a display of intellectual dancing to celebrate the god's return.

The 'lykabas' springs to life as a deity distinct from Helios in the world of the four wind-blown Seasons 'painted' by Nonnos in the following iridescent verses:

> And the rosy-cheeked Horae,
> Daughters of restless Lykabas, the storm-footed Year,
> Made their way to the house of Helios.
> One of them sent forth a delicate gleam of clouded light
> Which overshadowed her snowy countenance.
> Her feet were fitted with shoes of chilly hail,
> And her damp tresses were bound tight about her head.
> Across her brow she had fastened a veil of raindrops,
> And on her head placed an evergreen wreath.
> A snow-white sash covered her frosty breast.

Following in Winter's footsteps (but not, praise Helios, in her uncomfortable footwear) is Cytherea's favourite Hora, who literally breezes into the cosmic revels:

> Another blew forth in puffs the fresh air of the swallow's winds
> To gladden the hearts of mortals, and crowned
> The vernal locks of her zephyr-loving head with a dewy band.
> Laughing like a flower and fanning through her gown
> The scent of the opening rose at long-shadowed dawn,
> She wove a merry dance for two – Adonis and Cytherea.
> [diploon epleke kōmon Adōnidi kai Kythereiēi.]

These lovers were the Syrian counterparts of Attis and Cybele, and in their vernal 'kōmos' which corresponded to the Hilaria were celebrated the marriage of the sun and the earth and the annual revival of vegetation. The flower of Cytherea's erotic passion scents the billowing gown of the Hora with promises of bliss, but its perfume is not without a hint of sadness, for the rose that opens in the spring must die like Adonis at the height of summer. (When Julian entered Antioch in mid-July he found few signs of the roseate gaiety and raciness for which the Syrian capital was famed: what assaulted his senses instead were the histrionics of a cosmic funeral and the thrilling lamentations of women mourning the death of Adonis at reaping-time.[23]) In the warm lands where the cult of Adonis flourished, grain was usually harvested in summer rather than autumn, which accounts for the loose costume and energetic movements of the next dancer in the pageant of Lykabas:

> With her sisters came another Hora, offering summer's fruits;
> In her right hand she held high a sheaf of grain with leaves
> Bristling around the top, and the blade of a pointed sickle,
> The harbinger of harvest. The maiden had sheathed
> Her body in white linen veils, and as she whirled in the dance
> The orgiastic secrets of her thighs were revealed through her
> > fine-spun gown.
> [argennais othonēisin, helissomenēs de choreiēi
> phaineto leptaleoio di' eimatos orgia mērōn.]
> As Phaeton grew warmer, the cheeks of her relaxed face
> Grew damp with the dew of perspiration.

As the veils swirl and lift in the torrid air we catch a glimpse of the secret altar in the mysteries of fecundity. The epiphany is utterly, timelessly erotic. Spring may be sweetly seductive, but Summer with her glowing cheeks and perspiring body lives for the moment within the centrifugal vortex of an overpowering sensuality. When the veils of Summer fall and the air grows cool again the storm-footed Year ushers in his fourth daughter:

> Still another came – the leader of the easy dance at ploughing
> > time.
> [allē d' euarotoio proēgēteira choreiēs.]
> She had bound about her bare temples olive-branches
> Wet with the waters of the Nile's seven-streams.
> Sparse and withered was the hair by her temples,
> And dry her body, for she was the autumnal Hora who
> > followed the fruit-harvest
> And sheared the foliage off the trees with her leaf-scattering
> > winds.
> For there were no grapevines yet to trail about
> The nymph's neck with tangled clusters of golden curls;

Not yet had she imbibed the purple Maronian juice
And caroused beside the wine-loving vat;
Not yet had the ivy sprung up with its wild entwining
tendrils.[24]
But then came the fated time when the Horae met
Together and ran to the house of Helios.
(*Dionysiaca* XI.486–521)

By multiplying their fourfold measure by the magic power of three, Chronos, the god of time, supplies Helios with another chorus of Horae – the Hours – to regulate the flow of phenomena springing from his daily revolution:

The four were greeted by the twelve circling Hours,
Daughters of Chronos, who fluttered in a wreathing dance
Around the fiery throne of the tireless Charioteer
[hiptamenai stephanēdon ateiros Hēniochēos];
As the servants of Helios they attend him on his flaming
chariot,
And as the priestesses of Lykabas they take turns in
solemnizing his mysteries.
(*Dionysiaca* XII.15–19)

A hundred stormy years, four hundred whirling seasons, and thousands of flitting hours may separate the floruits of Julian and Nonnos but not the flourishing worlds of their imagination. The historical distance between them is effectively annihilated by their shared perception of time as a festive orchestration of growth and decay, an orchestic mystery solemnized by generations of divine dancers, a chaos of sensory particulars turning constantly into a chorus of universal spirits, and a magical séance with the sun in which we tearful mortals must believe that 'the blessings supplied by the other divine choragi visible to us are perfected by Helios' and that 'certain gods linked to Helios have alighted on our world of generation to guide the fourfold nature of the elements and to inhabit along with the three higher races of angels, daimones, and heroes those souls that are rooted in the elements' (*Helios* 151b–c).

Time in the poetic universe was a synthesis of all the seasonal festivals under the sun – the Saturnalia, the Heliaia, the Dionysia, the Carneian Feast, the Eleusinian Mysteries, and so on – into a perpetual rite of apotheosis in which human souls, rooted in the elements, were led by their visible and invisible choragi into the revels of the gods. So dazzling to Julian was the divine display of power activated by these perdurable festivals that no sign of their cultural obsolescence or historical impermanence – not even the scandalous burning of Apollo's temple in the Antiochene suburb of Daphne in October of 362 which the Emperor predictably blamed on vindictive Galileans – could shake his faith in the timeliness of his mission to reform the inner life of the Empire by housing once again in its collective soul all the time-perfecting gods brought forth by Helios. As a ruler Julian can certainly be criticized for having ignored the pessimistic spirit of the times in which he chose to play out his religious fantasies; but as a poetic philosopher he may be pardoned for this on the grounds that his optimistic conception of time as a preserving and perfecting order compelled him to oppose the eschatological thrust of Christian history.

Eight months after Apollo's immortal flame was extinguished in Daphne a javelin pierced the Apostate's mortal side as he was leading his rear guard against the Persian cavalry near the city of Maranga in the Tigris valley. With his death on 26 June 363 died any hope of victory for those who had supported him on the spiritual or temporal battlefield during his two years in power. How the Church revelled in the hour of his defeat will be described for us in stirring terms by Gregory of Nazianzus in the next chapter (see pages 387–9); for the present let us keep our foothold in the poetic universe, turn our gaze away from the Greek East, and consider how the Horae continued to revel and Helios to shine for educated pagans in the Latin West.

Praesul et Pontifex Solis

The only member of the old Roman aristocracy known to have participated directly and enthusiastically in Julian's Pagan Reformation was Vettius Agorius Praetextatus, the son-in-law of Symmachus the orator and a leader of the pagan faction in the Roman Senate. Before Julian left Constantinople he appointed Praetextatus (who chanced to be in the capital on personal business) to the coveted post of proconsul of Achaea. He outlived Julian by some twenty years. A shadowy figure in the background of late-fourth-century history, he stands out in the foreground of early-fifth-century literature as a monumental character: the last of the great Roman Priests of the Sun.

He owes his literary afterlife to the author of the *Saturnalia*, a compendious philological dialogue distantly related to Plato's *Symposium* and set in Rome in 384 (the year of the historical Praetextatus' death) during the solar festival celebrated two decades earlier by Julian in the *Hymn to King Helios*. We can be certain that the creator of the fictional Praetextatus was named Macrobius, but since no less than three Macrobii have turned up in the generations immediately following Julian's, much uncertainty still surrounds his identity and literary milieu. If he was the Macrobius who served as proconsul of Africa in 410 and belonged to the same generation of educated pagans as Martianus Capella, then he could not have cherished any personal recollections of the era of the Pagan Reformation and may not even have been born at the time the conversations recorded in the *Saturnalia* supposedly took place. His retrospective vision of Praetextatus and the Symmachan circle might have been wistful, nostalgic, even elegiac in spirit – a portrait of pagan gentlemen in attitudes of despair contemplating the bust of Julian. Nostalgic it may be at times, but the character of the work as a whole is triumphantly festive despite the darkness of the year and frequently playful despite the defensiveness of the circle: saturnalian, in a word, rather than saturnine. The fictional Praetextatus commands our attention largely because he is not a ghost summoned from the faded past to bewail the defeat of Julian's cause. He is a reveller in the unfading presence of Sol Invictus, a lively spirit conjured up from the poetic universe in which the orgiastic sensibility of the priests of the once-popular mystery cults merged with the otherworldly spirituality of the Neoplatonic élite.[25]

Macrobius calls him 'sacrorum omnium praesul et pontifex solis': 'leader of all the holy men and priest of the sun' (*Saturnalia* I.xvii.1). The noun 'praesul' literally meant 'he who leaps or dances before' – that is, before the altar of a god or at the head of a procession of priests and initiates. The historical Praetextatus belonged to the Mithraic and Eleusinian priesthood and doubtless led processions as 'praesul' to the shrines of Helios-Mithras, Apollo, Dionysus, Demeter, and Cybele in Italy and Achaea. His ancient title (which the Latin Church was to purge of its pagan connotations and bestow upon its bishops) did not apply to the leader of a dance in the theatre as did the Greek title 'koryphaios.' The fictional Praetextatus draws attention to his role as a purely religious reveller by forbidding the entrance of lewd theatrical artistes into his house, where the Symmachan circle meets on the first day of the festival. The harmony of his companions and his cosmos must not be disrupted by the wanton trill of flutes or mocked by writhing mimes whose cynical representations of the gods are offensive even to barbarian eyes! 'Let no priest enter a theatre or befriend an actor or chariot-driver,' Julian had commanded, 'and let no stage-dancer or mime even approach his door.'[26] None dares approach the door of Praetextatus. Any vulgar intruder into the chamber of this austere yet amiable host would destroy the numerological concord of his party, which, as he points out in I.vii.12–13, forms with its twelve participants (including himself) a convivial image of the cosmic harmony resulting from the union of the nine Muses with the three Graces.

As the theologian of the party he sees fit to begin their round of discussions on a serious note by delivering a lecture on two intertwining themes: the unitive role of the sun in the cosmic chorus and the multiplicity of solar cults in the Roman Empire. A lost treatise on solar theology by Porphyry is thought to lie behind many of his mystical pronouncements and etymological speculations, particularly in 1.xvii–xxii where the 'praesul' provides his Muses and Graces with a Latin hymn to Helios. The historical Praetextatus was undoubtedly familiar with Julian's two theological hymns and their Iamblichan sources, and in view of this we should expect his fictional namesake to echo them now and again in his solar panegyric. Perhaps he does. His derivation of the noun 'horae' (which in Latin as in Greek meant both 'seasons' and 'hours') from the divine name Horus in 1.xxi.12, for instance, recalls Julian's onomastic punning in *Hymn to King Helios* 148d. But echoes are notoriously easy to hear in the resounding chambers of the poetic universe and are often difficult to distinguish from rhetorical commonplaces ringing in the air.

The madness induced by a deafening roar of echoes can be avoided if we focus our attention on the Neoplatonic impulse behind the High Priest's Corybantic argument. Like Porphyry, Iamblichus, and Julian he leaps with exhilarating energy over the broad field of comparative religion in search of answers to the central question in Plotinian metaphysics, namely how the Many sprang from the One. Local beliefs and cult practices furnish him with an abundance of evidence, or what he takes to be evidence, supporting the standard Porphyrian and Iamblichan argument that the many gods worshipped by the Egyptians, Chaldeans, Greeks, and Romans are simply aspects or manifestations of the divinity of the sun, a unique divinity by virtue of its formal relation to the One. 'The Boeotians,' remarks Praetextatus,

speak of Mount Parnassus as sacred to Apollo but consider the Delphic Oracle and the nearby Caves of Bacchus to be holy places consecrated to a single god. Hence Apollo and Bacchus are worshipped on the same mountain – a fact confirmed by Varro and Granius Flaccus. Euripides, too, teaches us this in the following lines [fr 752]:

> Dionysus with his thyrsus and fawn-skins
> Comes dancing [choreuōn] down Parnassus
> With a leap and a bound through the firs.

A bacchic festival is held on Mount Parnassus every other year, at which (they say) many bands of satyrs are seen and their distinctive voices heard. Then too does the din of clashing cymbals often strike men's ears.

(*Saturnalia* 1.xviii.3–5)

The impulse to rise above the din of clashing cymbals and clashing dogmas by perceiving the eternal integration of Apollo and Bacchus in the nature of Helios and by imagining the temporal fusion of their respective dances in the cycle of the pagan calendar was common to the Latin and Greek authors through whose festive consciousness we have entered into the triumphant harmony of the poetic universe. This impulse is sometimes called syncretism, but it did not result in an artificial compounding or a hopeless confusion of deities as this rather pejorative term implies. Apollo and Bacchus retained their distinctive roles in the cosmic dance as long as they were conceived as participants in the procession of life-forces from Helios. When they were imagined from an epistrophic viewpoint as intellectual gods returning to Primal Unity in the natural course of the dance, their earthly discord faded like a satyr's cry in the Caves of Bacchus and their heavenly unison came pouring down from the summit of Parnassus.

The triumph of Helios over the formlessness of Primal Matter and the dissonance of the Many inspired the literary craftsmen of the poetic universe to shape the dense substrate of conflicting facts and fancies provided by their philological education into rhetorical images of the unity of the solar chorus. 'Let us gather from all sources in order to produce one whole work,' soliloquized Macrobius in a Pythagorean vein at the start of the shorter but more influential and in many ways more intellectually ambitious of his two extant works,

just as one number is produced when separate numbers are added together. Let our mind produce this work and show what it has produced, but let it conceal all that has assisted it in the process. ... You see how a chorus is composed of many voices [multorum vocibus chorus constet]: all of those voices nevertheless produce a single unified sound. One voice in it might be high, another low, another of a middle range. Women's voices are added to men's, and then among them sounds the pipe. The voices of individuals are hidden in a chorus while the voices of all are heard, and thus a harmony emerges out of dissonant sounds.

(*In Somnium Scipionis* 1, preface 8–9)

This is not uttered in the apologetic manner of an eclectic encyclopaedist but in the exultant tone of a philosopher-poet who commands the titanic expanses of Late Antique scholarship, imposes concord on the heterogeneous elements of his education, and like the sun hides the sources of his knowledge with a display of his own intellectual brilliance.

The popularity of Macrobius' *Commentary on the Dream of Scipio* throughout the Middle Ages was due in no small measure to the favourable notice it received early on from Boethius, the son-in-law of a great-grandson of Symmachus.[27] But the poetic coherence of the work itself must also have recommended it to posterity, for in the long run it was to attract many more

readers than works containing comparable stores of cosmological information such as Calcidius' commentary and to have a deeper impact on post-
classical literature than the sprawling *Saturnalia*. To a remarkable extent
Macrobius succeeded in doing just what he claimed to do in his preface –
something Calcidius never thought to attempt – which was to turn the chaos
of poetic and philosophical allusions jangling in the minds of Late Antique
philologists into a chorus of sweetly consonant echoes from the classical
past, echoes of the sublime symphony of the cosmos.

These came to him directly from the heavens described by Scipio Africanus
Minor in the sixth book of Cicero's *Republic*, which concludes with a Stoical
retelling of the Myth of Er. Scipio, Er's Roman counterpart, silences his
contentious companions by recounting a dream in which the ghost of his
celebrated grandfather Scipio Africanus Major whisked him up through the
chiming spheres so that he might perceive the contemptible smallness of the
earth from the perspective of the whole and admire the spacious heavenly
abodes where the just leaders of the Roman Republic retired after death.
Whereas Cicero's main purpose in concocting this pseudo-Pythagorean myth
was blatantly political – it served to hallow and advertise his republican
ideals of justice and public duty – Macrobius' purpose in commenting on
it was essentially religious: he sought to restore faith in the reality of cosmic
music by reconciling and verifying the mathematical, astronomical, and
harmonic theories implicit in his source. Scipio's dream was no dream for
the successor of Praetextatus. It was an oracular vision of his soul's epistrophic flight through the poetic spheres once traversed by the soul of
Plotinus ('next to Plato,' he noted in 1.8.5, 'the chief philosopher') in his
ascent to the Chorus of Immortal Eros.

Even as Praetextatus had excluded Cynical poseurs from his charmed
circle, so Macrobius banished Skeptical spectators from the ceremony of
divine praise in the spheres of the Muses. To medieval poets he passed on
his indomitable faith in the validity of Pythagorean poetics, teaching them
in his decorous yet forceful Latin that true poetry – the poetry springing
from what Praetextatus had called 'the secret places of philosophy' (*Saturnalia* 1.xvii.2) – must be a formal imitation of the measures of the celestial
chorus and a therapeutic mode of participation in the mysteries of divine
unity. The first true poets, he explained, were the pagan priests who

*discovered that the heavens sing and consequently made use of musical sounds
in their ceremonies. Some were accustomed to use the lyre or cithara, while
others used pipes or other musical instruments. And in their hymns to the
gods they made use of musical metres for the verses of the strophe and
antistrophe so that the forward motion of the star-bearing sphere might be
represented by the one and the diversified backward motion of the planets*

by the other. From these two motions Nature produced the first hymn in praise of God.

(*In Somnium Scipionis* II.3.4–5)

By recalling the etymological meanings of the prosodic terms 'strophe' and 'antistrophe' the high priest of the poetic universe preserved for the Middle Ages a memory of primitive ritual participation in the cosmic dance. Or should we not say that he tried to recharge these words with the excitement of their dramatic origins – an excitement scarcely felt in his own day when they were used mainly by pedants to denote a series of poetic lines forming a metrical system and the repetition or inversion of that series in an answering sequence of verses? Mere words, of course, could not bring back the turns and counterturns of priests around the sun-god's altar, the cithara touched at daybreak, the pipe haunting the Boeotian dusk, the din of satyrs. But in the poetic universe their echoes carried far and would be heard.

Harmonia's Triumph

The philosopher-poets of the Latin West drew no sharp distinctions between the 'cantus' and 'motus' of their heavens, that is to say between the tonal and dynamic aspects of cosmic harmony. Emphasis on one aspect or the other certainly varied from author to author: while Macrobius and Boethius tended to play up the celestial 'cantus' in their writings, Martianus Capella (who had by far the most active visual imagination of the group) was inclined to highlight the 'motus' of his cosmic pantheon. But like their counterparts in the Greek East they all agreed that the music of the spheres was a weaving of song with motion and the dance of the stars a matching of motion to song. The motion generated the song that regulated the motion that sustained the song that inspired the motion that generated the song. ... And thus their Graces circled. Contemptuous of uneducated Cynics who viewed the dance of life and learning as a vicious circle perpetuating death and ignorance, they championed the belief that according to all the inspired poets and philosophers of remote Antiquity life was preserved and learning perfected by the magically virtuous revolutions of the solar chorus. It was a belief they could have come by in the West even if the Neoplatonic schools in the East had never existed.

Martianus, for one, found a clear expression of it in the Greek textbook on tonal and prosodic theory by Aristides Quintilianus (fl 300 AD?) from which he derived his technical knowledge of the subject he called 'Harmony.' According to Aristides,

divinely inspired poets in their music constantly sing of this same harmonious

motion of the heavens, which they call the dance of the stars [astrōn choron].
Philosophers and pursuers of truth sought to explain this harmony by arguing,
for instance, that when a body moves at a great speed against a uniform
substance which yields and softly billows at impact, it makes a certain sound
like the circles running through water into which a pebble has been dropped.

(*De musica* III.20)

When Martianus himself came to explain the phenomenon of cosmic harmony, as we shall see, he dispensed with arguments drawn from physics
and relied on theological explanations which betray his intellectual sympathy
with the Iamblichan movement of the fourth century. His Pythagorean
vision of the heavens had a distinctly Neoplatonic focus: the inextinguishable
flame of 'extramundane intelligence.'[28]

How he became acquainted with the theology of Iamblichus (whom he
called simply 'the Syrian') is, like almost everything else about him, a complete mystery. Iamblichus attracted few readers in the Latin West even during
Julian's lifetime, and after the Apostate's death those who remained there
to pass on the wisdom of the Syrian must have been something of an endangered species. Not a single Latin translation of a Iamblichan work has
survived from Late Antiquity, if indeed one was ever attempted. The glorious
hero of the pagan revival was much easier to forget than the inglorious
Apostate. If Martianus could be connected historically with the Symmachan
circle or with Macrobius, we should have some grounds for suspecting that
he came across a dusty copy of Iamblichus' *In Timaeum* or Salutius' Greek
paraphrase of *On the Gods* in a private library in Rome. But all attempts
to establish a Roman connection for him have fallen into the abyss of idle
speculation. Martianus refers to Carthage at one point in terms that suggest
it was his native city, and if he was residing there in the early decades of
the fifth century he might have encountered Macrobius during the latter's
supposed term as proconsul in Africa.[29] Though a touching scene might be
imagined in which the proconsul, proud and stiff in the old Roman manner,
introduces the eccentric provincial Sophist to the delights of Iamblichan
theology and leads him into the mystical revels of Helios and the Graces,
it is a scene, alas, that must remain imaginary. Neither mentions the other
by name in his extant writings or even vaguely alludes to the writings of
the other.

We might just as easily imagine Martianus leaving Carthage for a period
of study in Athens where he might have heard of Iamblichus from the aging
disciples of Priscus and Maximus. If anyone led him into the dance of
mystical education and into the pagan dénouement of the drama of Late
Antique intellectual history, it was a mirthful and witty character by the
name of Satire who appeared to him, he tells us, in the winter of his years

while he was living unhappily in rustic retirement, and who taught him during long winter nights by dimming lamplight to hymn the undimming glory of the cosmos and to recite a consoling tale about the end of pagan learning.

Satire in the sense of 'mélange' – a Menippean blend of prose and poetry – is the genre to which he assigned his only known work, the *De nuptiis Philologiae et Mercurii*, which appears to have been written sometime between Alaric's sack of Rome in 410 and the Vandal occupation of Carthage in 439. (Originally the title 'On the Marriage of Philology and Mercury' applied only to the first two books of the satire, but now it commonly designates all nine.) His choice of an aggressively didactic genre like Menippean satire may well have been a response to the threat of aggressive barbarism. The Muses and Graces who presided over the hallowed system of Greco-Roman philological education had endured the skepticism and intolerance of Christian pundits during Constantine's new Golden Age, but could they survive the new Age of Iron heralded by Ginseric's untutored Vandals? As soon as the goddesses dance into the allegorical theatre of the *De nuptiis* they dispel any fears for their survival by heralding the imminent return of Harmonia from her sanctuary in the Aplanes to the Empire's 'ruined academies' (IX.899). Considering the traditional association of Menippean satire with Cynicism, we might expect the aged and socially unhappy author of such a work to take a dim view of intellectual history and to cackle bitterly at the fragility of classical civilization. Yet a less cynical tutor than Martianus would have been hard to find in the era of the barbarian invasions. What he solemnized in his work was the nuptial apotheosis – not the funeral – of Philology. As a Menippean satirist he could satisfy his Neoplatonic urge to fuse the roles of poet and philosopher by combining the magical virtues of metrical language with the illuminating power of philosophical discourse. He could also indulge his Horatian taste for discordant concords by singing of heavenly harmony with high seriousness through the comic mask of a chattering old pedagogue.

The allegorical pageant of the *De nuptiis* begins on one threshold, crosses over a second, and ends on a third. At each we are shown a dance. Before this liminal procession gets under way, Martianus is discovered by his son (also named Martianus) repeating the verses of a prothalamion like a sleepy priest who has risen with the sun to open the gates of his temple:

> *You who sing at weddings, you whom they call*
>   *The offspring of a Muse, the sacred bond of the gods –*
> *You bind the warring seeds with secret fetters,*
>   *And encourage the union of opposites with your sacred clasp;*
> *You link the elements as they change one into another; you*
>   *unify the world*

And breathe Mind into bodies;
You reconcile the sexes and foster fidelity in love
   With the agreeable contract that binds Nature in marriage.
O decorous Hymen! You are most dearly loved by Cyprian
                                      Venus:
   For Cupid, inflamed by Venus, shines on your countenance.
Perhaps because choral dances have pleased you as a son of
                              Father Bacchus
[seu tibi quod Bacchus pater est placuisse choreas]
   Or because you have sung at weddings attended by your
                              mother Venus,
Or because the three Graces have permitted you, their
                              kinsman,
   To adorn prosperous thresholds with vernal garlands –
Calliope, who is arranging the divine marriage,
Is glad to have you begin the ceremonies with a song.
                              (*De nuptiis* I.I)

Like the Orphic Hymn to Aphrodite this is a cosmic wedding-song resonant with Stoic overtones. The Hymen who dances in the poetic universe is a grander figure than the merry youth of Greek folklore whose name became synonymous with happiness in human wedlock; he is a more powerful spirit than the sociable son of Bacchus and Venus whose Olympian role was restricted to arranging the garlands, mastering the ceremonies, and keeping the ambrosia flowing at divine marriages. In the first eight lines of the hymn, which are the first eight lines of the *De nuptiis*, his binding powers are magnificently expanded to match and subsume those of the formative principle in Stoic cosmology.

From his beaming countenance radiates the divine energy that pervades the material substrate, creates the cycle of elemental transmutations, shapes corporeal matter into living forms, infuses these forms with rationality, and unites the sexes in Nature's everlasting fertility dance. His close association with the natural world indicates that he is not an intellectual god in a Iamblichan sense but either a sublunary creating god or one of the many superlunary gods who proceed directly from Helios-Bacchus and abide with the heavenly choruses. (His appearance above the moon in IX.909 suggests the latter.) Though the 'Mind' he is said to breathe into bodies flows into the sphere of Stoic Nature from the Iamblichan 'realm of pure intellection,' as Martianus reveals in II.202, the dance over which Hymen presides at this early stage in the allegory is cheerfully unintellectual in character. It is a bodily 'chorea' like that of the Nonnian Horae, festive, vigorous, instinctively erotic, yet not frenzied or lascivious, for though Bacchus and Venus are always present at wedding-feasts where it is performed their decorous son manages to preserve the ceremonial dignity of his dancers without cooling their blood or diluting their wine.

This hymeneal revel is the dance we discover on crossing the first threshold in the allegory: the 'limen' of Philology's earthly bedchamber. Since the studious young heroine of the tale (as her name declares) embodies all the virtuous characteristics of Late Antique pagan scholars – their dauntless love of learning, their hard-earned erudition, their reverence for classical authorities, their faith in the divine potency of words, and their religious determination to rise above the pedantic controversies of the Hellenistic schools of philosophy into a realm of intellectual concord, serene agreement, boundless certitude – the chamber of her maidenhood must represent the sublunary domain to which novice scholars are normally confined, that is to say, the world of generation, or the bounded range of 'book-learning' mastered by a Corybantic intellect before it has purged itself of earthly interests and ascended to the celestial temple for divine illumination.[30]

After learning in book one that Mercury has fulfilled his destiny as the god of eloquence by selecting her (a mere mortal) for his bride over all eligible nymphs and demi-goddesses, and that her rather dour mother Phronesis, who represents the wisdom of the ages preceding the dawn of scholastic education, has consented to the match with an unwonted display of enthusiasm, Philology retires to her bedchamber for one last wakeful night of study to prepare herself for what she fears will be a rigorous final examination rather than a royal wedding in the court of Jove. A considerable amount of midnight oil is burnt in the first half of book two before she hears 'the chorus of harmonious Muses' (II.117) singing outside her door at dawn above the swelling notes of a water organ and various other sublunary instruments. These fall silent as each Muse approaches the threshold to sing a solo hymn to the bride. Urania prophesies that Philology's knowledge of astronomy will soon be turned into magical power over the 'motus' of the stars – a Iamblichan wish fulfilled. Calliope encourages her to play the lyre of Pindar and to sing forever the 'cantus' of the poetic heavens. Polymnia praises her exquisite sense of rhythm, Melpomene her mastery of the dramatic arts, Clio her talents as an orator, Erato her prophetic knowledge of 'why the circle of the year whirls round to complete the hastening centuries' (II.123), and Terpsichore her unshakable faith in the ancient arts of divination. Thanks to her, chants Euterpe, Plato and Pythagoras perceived the astral origin of their intellectual brilliance. The ninth Muse, Thalia, expresses the eagerness of all the cosmic gods to receive her in heaven:

> O blessed maiden, you who will take
> Your place in the wedding chamber
> Amid such a profusion of dancing stars

[quae siderum choreis
thalamum capis iugalem]
And with the universe so well-disposed –
You will be the daughter-in-law of the Thunderer!
                              (De nuptiis II.126)

Jittery and dispirited after her exhausting lucubrations, Philology responds to these melodious encomia by cowering in her room like a frightened child during a thunderstorm, unable to move, unable even to think of moving. The hymeneal dance cannot begin until the four Stoic Virtues, Prudence, Justice, Temperance, and Fortitude – who may be credited with achieving an early breakthrough in the treatment of hysterical paralysis – have crossed the threshold of her inward-turning psyche and compelled her to face the light of day (II.127). In the therapeutic rites of the poetic universe, the dance must be seen in order to have any effect on the psyche, seen with wide-open eyes: too much studious introspection (represented in II.111 by Philology's maid Periergia, 'Overdoing It') has robbed the educated spectatrix of her primitive Pythagorean vision of the 'siderum choreae,' and worse, has destroyed her will to recover it.

To reverse the tidal current of academic introversion that had swept the fourth-century Neoplatonists into the depths of unintelligibility, to reverse it even for a moment, an imaginary moment, required great strength of will on the part of those who defended the pagan dream of the poetic universe in the early fifth century. And Martianus shows such strength at this psychological turning-point in his allegory – a quietly heroic moment in Western intellectual history – by combining the powers of the noblest pagan virtues to open up the stuffy little room of his academically enervated heroine to the fresh air and pristine radiance of a world that had made its objective order known to Pythagoras and his first disciples through their senses. As soon as Philology summons the strength to look beyond herself, to listen to the music outside her door, to face the dance of phenomena whirling around her, she beholds the divine dancers who have descended to earth to make her one of them. In the wake of the Virtues and their dignified patroness, Lady Philosophy, who will reappear as the coryphaeus of the Muses in the poetic universe of Boethius,

came three radiant girls who were equally fair of face and well-behaved.
They wore delicate wreaths of roses on their heads and clasped each other's
hands as they approached the maiden. The first kissed Philology on the
forehead where the skin is smooth between the eyebrows so that she 'might
breathe joy and honour into her eyes' ['Aeneid' 1.591]; the second kissed her
mouth in order to breathe grace upon her tongue; and the third embraced

*her waist in order to impart gentleness to her spirit. They were called the
Graces, of course, and whatever they touched they made lovely. After they
had filled the maiden with light they mingled with the Muses and performed
in her honour harmonious pantomimic gestures and wedding dances [gesti-
culationes consonas atque hymeneia dedere tripudia]. But lo! With a great
booming of drums and jingling of bells all things everywhere leap up and
fly around in the dance [magno tympani crepitu crotalorumque tinnitu uni-
versa dissultant] with the result that the song of the Muses is to some extent
drowned out by the thunderous din of the drums. Brought in with this noise
is a litter spangled with stars, before which they sang their loud song in the
mystic rite as was the custom when a divine bride was about to participate
in a celestial wedding.*

(*De nuptiis* II.132–3)

With the entrance of the Graces begins an elaborate rite of passage in which
Philology is purged of mortal imperfections, reformed by the divinizing
light of celestial intelligence, and transported from her earthly abode to the
palace of the Thunderer in the distant reaches of the Aplanes. Before Philology can enter into the cosmic revel of Hymen celebrated by Martianus in
his opening hymn, she must be kissed, embraced, and breathed upon by
the Graces. So much is clear.

But who are these Graces? Is their allegorical significance in this scene
wholly determined by their traditional role as leaders of the anagogic seasonal
dance in the mystery religions – the role they danced for instance in the
Orphic Hymn to the Horae? Their descent from the Aplanes, their role as
Philology's illuminators, and their close association in the pageant with Lady
Philosophy (who here represents the venerable harmonizing wisdom of the
ancient Pythagoreans as opposed to the discordant dogmatism of the Hellenistic sects) prompt us to view their dance as a wiser and more complex
movement than the revelry of furrow-stomping, flower-strewing fertility
spirits. Their clasped hands and decorous bearing call to mind the 'Gratiae
decentes' in Horace's fleeting vision of a night in spring when 'Cytherean
Venus leads her choruses with the moon hanging overhead' and 'the comely
Graces joining hands with the Nymphs strike the earth with one foot and
then the other ... ' (*Odes* I.iv.5–7). Martianus' Graces have retained their
old ties with the immortal lover of Adonis. Their rosy wreathes declare it.
But Cytherean Venus is conspicuously absent from their dance at the apotheosis of Philology, which takes place with the sun hanging overhead and of
course does not lead to a melancholy Horatian scene in which pallid Death
strikes the maiden's door with his impartial foot. Death and the maiden will
never meet in the revels to which she is rising, for the light with which the
Graces fill her creates 'the springtime of eternal peace' (II.200) in the blessed
realms where the moon hangs underfoot.

The mingling of the 'three radiant girls' with the nine unmistakably cosmic Muses in 11.132 clearly suggests that Martianus' Graces are the same as Julian's: a Iamblichan triad of superlunary spirits proceeding from Helios and presiding over the three great circles of the Aplanes linked by the ecliptic. Martianus does not have to tell us what they draw in the air with their 'gesticulationes consonae.' Surely it is an articulate image of the unity of 'motus' and 'cantus' in the poetic heavens. Since Philology spent her last night as a mortal 'cramming' the facts of Pythagorean harmonics and astronomy, we may be certain that she recognized in the cheironomic display of the Graces and Muses the celestial archetype of the didactic and therapeutic 'orchēsis' that Pythagoras (according to Iamblichus) had taught his original disciples to perform whenever mental or physical illness threatened their inner harmony. 'Now the number three is certainly perfect,' the precocious maiden reminded herself in 11.105, 'because it may be arranged as a beginning, a middle, and an end in accordance with reason.'

What the Graces and Muses subsequently show her to drive home this lesson and to sustain her faith in the validity of Pythagorean cosmology are perfect dances generated by this concordant number – their 'hymeneia tripudia.' (The noun 'tripudium,' which may be traced to the roots 'ter,' 'thrice,' and 'pes,' 'foot,' denoted in classical Latin a solemn religious dance such as that performed by the Salii or the Galli.)[31] Cured of her cosmic agoraphobia by these preliminary wedding dances, which assure her eyes and ears that the poetic universe is vast indeed, and noisy, but not unimaginably complex or incessantly thunderous, she is able to face the violent dance of sublunary life without falling to pieces.

When the drums boom and the bells jingle and all things leap up and fly around her like the mobs following the clamorous procession of the priests of Cybele, she does not lose her nerve. When the Muses are all but drowned out by the ruckus, she does not forget their song. The epistrophic momentum of divinely illumined reason carries her through the beginning of the mystic rite without a hitch, and up she is borne on the starry litter of the Great Mother with the Graces and Muses flying ahead on the wings of song, up through the swirling thunderclouds, up a full celestial tone to the circle of the moon (11.170) where she sees through the shimmering haze of the lunar mists the lamp of Eleusis burning safely – a lamp extinguished on earth by the graceless troops of Alaric. And beside it, awesomely silent, lie the drums of Cybele.

The wedding party does not stop until it reaches the entrance of Jove's glittering residence in the Galaxy, the second threshold Philology must cross in her rite of passage (11.200–7). Visible at this point is the full array of 'siderum choreae' mentioned by Thalia in her hymn and imitated by all the Muses and Graces in their Pythagorean pantomime. Amazed by the diversity of lights, speeds, configurations, circuits, and intersections in the dance of the stars, but even more astonished by the perfect coordination of so many parts within the compass of a single divinely animated design, the new goddess discovers that she can also see amid the multitude of stars the thirty-six Decan-Rulers and the throng of other astral and planetary spirits 'which a certain Syrian believed to be numberless' (II.172). Physical vision and psychic clairvoyance become indistinguishable at this middle stage of initiation in the dance of the poetic universe.

If Philology were an archetypal Neoplatonic Spectator like the ascendant soul of Plotinus in the Porphyrian oracle, she would now leap with joy into the extrasensory realm of pure understanding and waste little time surveying the Galaxy and its denizens. But she does not abandon the world of her heightened senses. Before a wall with no visible threshold, the mental barrier separating her from the featureless expanses of the Neoplatonic Beyond, she kneels reverently a while and recites a cryptic prayer composed of unintelligible combinations of sounds in honour of the unknown and unknowable entities residing with the Ineffable Monad – presumably the Iamblichan 'noeroi' and 'noētikoi theoi.' Then, quite happily, she turns back to the dancing lights and revelling gods of the Galaxy. The wall of transcendence is left unscaled. The world of living statues is where the bride of Mercury belongs, for Mercury (as Jove observes in I.36) is the wizard-rhetor of her dreams who 'brings life to features sculpted in bronze or marble.'

Thus like Martianus himself Philology proves to be a Poetic Spectator with Neoplatonic eyes but sophistic perceptions, an imagistic thinker who must create speaking pictures or dynamic figures of the cosmos and its overseers in order to approach and comprehend them. Even when her objects of thought are virtually unimaginable she still invents a poetic construct of them to fill the metaphysical void. Unintelligible her glossolalia may be, but it is far from meaningless. As a mimetic act it represents the unfathomable effusion of the Many from the One, and as a symbolic figure the formless First Cause that mysteriously imparts form and logical significance to the otherwise insignificant gestures in the cosmic pantomime.

A refreshing flood of comprehensible sounds spanning the diapason or full octave of the cosmic Muses conveys Philology into the hall of living statues where Mercury in his exaltation awaits her with his bridal gift: seven highly articulate Athenian maidens representing the arts of the Trivium (Grammar, Dialectic, Rhetoric) and the Quadrivium (Geometry, Arithmetic, Astronomy, Harmony).[32] A full understanding of these diverse subjects can be attained only when they are perceived as a unified system in relation to the religious goal of philological education – the divinization of the educated spectator through ritual and intellectual participation in the cosmic dance – for like the seven planetary spheres of the poetic universe they form an ascending scale which the lover of learning climbs with the magic aid of harmonious and illuminating words.

Harmonia, the seventh bridesmaid, binds the arts of her sisters into a choral curriculum by virtue of her numerical association with the rest of the Quadrivium and her prosodic link with the literary subjects of the Trivium. Discordia has not been invited to the nuptials, of course, but since Harmonia delays her entrance into the dance until the very end of the allegory her evil counterpart is able now and then to threaten the unity and married calm of the Thunderer's notoriously stormy court. While Bacchus and his retinue are taking their places in the senate chamber, for instance, she tries to make her unwanted presence felt by inciting a chorus of contentious Greek philosophers to sing off key in the background (II.213). Fortunately their ludicrous chanting, the discordant echo of the Hellenistic sects, is drowned out by the Pythagorean melodies of the Muses – a Iamblichan dream come true.

While their blessed concord prevails, the first six Athenian maidens take the opportunity to deliver a series of encyclopaedic lectures on their respective disciplines, which fill the next six books of the *De nuptiis*. Murmurs of discontent from the hedonistic party in the assembly grow steadily louder during this academic marathon. Though Arithmetic earns 'words of mystical praise' from Plato, who stands by her in VIII.803 expounding the arcane doctrines of the *Timaeus* in the manner of a scholastic Neoplatonist, all she elicits from the drunken Silenus is a belch – a firmament-shaking eructation – which at first frightens the gods but soon has them laughing convulsively.

Discord breaks out again at the end of Astronomy's profoundly tedious lecture when Venus, who has been bored silly but not stiff by the so-called festivities, begins to flirt outrageously with Mars and Bacchus and then casts such seductive glances at Mercury that he seriously considers jilting his bookish bride. The Muses by this time have fallen into glum silence. The Graces have stopped their life-sustaining dance and are sitting forlornly next to an idle and exasperated Flora. Entropic dullness in the world of learning has brought the world itself, the world of poetic concord, to a dismal standstill, and if something momentous (in a literal sense) is not done soon to get the dancers on their feet again and the singers back to their lyres, the cosmic wedding will surely end in chaos just as the Stoics had predicted.

The rebellious Cytherean speaks for many when she begs the Protectress of Brides to end the dance of learning so that the dance of life may begin again:

> *O Juno Pronuba, if you are pleased to listen to these serious*
> *discourses*
> *And are not concerned about the celestial wedding,*
> *Then I shall give in: but accustomed as I am to delightful*
> *choral dances*
> *[ast ego succubui, lepidisque assueta choreis]*

I cannot bear to look upon these sombre Athenian maidens!
(De nuptiis IX.888)

Of course Venus will not give in until the marriage of Philology and Mercury is consummated in a 'lepida chorea' that can communicate the graces of their immortal union to the physical world of pleasure-loving mortals. Her diplomatic plea is in fact an ultimatum. The leaders of the celestial empire must either find a way of reconciling the corporeal and intellectual dancers in the world-chorus or face the cataclysmic consequences, namely the extinction of the pagan cults, the withering of philological culture, and the death of the poetic universe.

The failure of the pagan revivalists to find an earthly leader powerful enough to unite the learned and the lewd had not destroyed their hope that a heavenly power might come to their rescue before all was lost to the Galileans. But did Jove, or the Unconquered Sun whom Philology hailed as 'the exalted power of the Unknown Father' and 'the Ruler of Nature' and 'beautiful Attis' in a hymn chanted on her way to the Galaxy (II.185–93), have the power and inclination to reconcile the few who shrouded the secrets of their thoughts in the impenetrable jargon of the Liberal Arts with the many who exposed the secrets of their thighs in the sweaty revels of the Horae?

The power, perhaps; the inclination, no. So Martianus suggests in the ominous passage immediately following Venus' complaint (IX.890–6): Jove, not to be rushed by his imperious wife or impetuous daughter, for once ignores the demands of Pleasure and decides to lengthen the learned entertainment by commanding seven more lecturers – the Prophetic Arts – to perform at the wedding after the seventh Liberal Art has completed her address to the gods! Only Phoebus and Minerva are pleased at the prospect of another deathly display of erudition. Martianus comes close to defeating his own philological purposes at this point by driving most of his readers over to Venus' side. Clearly his work is failing to reconcile Virtue with Pleasure, to unite the dances of life and learning, to hold the world of the ancient worthies together with harmonious words. Dullness and discord will triumph after all. Chaos will come again. ...

But hark! Fresh music immediately burst forth with sweet flute-like sounds, and its echoing melodies, surpassing the delightfulness of all others, filled the ears of the marvelling gods. For the song was not a simple one produced by the ringings of only one instrument, but a concordant blend of all musical sounds resulting in a plenitude of harmonious pleasure. For some time this song soothed the breasts of those who stood by, including the gods, and the throngs of those who had gone out a little while earlier in anticipation of the maiden's arrival were seen again, walking ahead of a very great retinue. And their return was marked by the sound of a melody that was not without sweetness. For Eratine, a daughter of Cyprian Venus, and Himeros, an attendant of Cupid, and Terpsis, a servant of Dione, were the first to enter, singing together in a most graceful manner; then came the youth [Hymen?] playing on a single pipe; and after him came Persuasion, Pleasure, and the Graces blending their voices to the accompaniment of a lyre and dancing here and there with measured motions [Gratiae admixtis lyrae vocibus atque ipsae harmonicis dissultantes motibus advenire]. At the same time there moved on before to the right and left a number of heroes and long-haired philosophers who were all murmuring in a soft sweet tone: many of them sang hymns in praise of the gods, while some sang musical tones just recently learned.

(*De nuptiis* IX.905–6)

This momentous scene is more than a commemoration of the procession of attendant spirits and heroes and philosophers from the Great Choragus, the wellspring of light and harmony. It is the commencement of a return – the epiphanic return of Harmonia to her ruined academies heralding the epistrophic movement of her corporeal and intellectual dancers to their original state of unity.

Measuring their steps with Harmonia's newly quickened Graces are representatives of the two 'streams' of love in the poetic universe: hedonistic spirits like Eratine and Himeros who sing the sensuous lays of Cupid (the lower, physical Eros); and beside them, deepening but not drowning out their song with religious chanting, heroic souls like Pythagoras and Plato who aspire to rise with Amor (the higher, spiritual Eros). Ushered in by the Muses whose voices swell to the climax of a sublime crescendo is the vibrant soul of the poetic universe:

After them came the even more celebrated chorus of fountain-born maidens [honoratior fontigenarum virginum chorus] who poured forth the nectar of Pegasean song to the accompaniment of the twin pipes of the Phrygian [Olympus] and surpassed all the sweet delights that had gone before. Between Pallas and Phoebus marched the sublime Harmonia, whose head, the source of melodious sounds, was adorned with spangles of glittering gold. Her gown was stiff with thin discs cut out of gold and rustled soothingly with soft little tinklings whenever she moved or stepped, for each of her movements was governed by measure and symmetry [omnibus ad motum gressumque rata congruentia temperatum blandis leniter crepitaculis tinniebat]. Her mother, Paphian Venus, followed her closely: but even though the lovely rose-hued goddess moved with rhythmical and balanced paces she could scarcely imitate the movements of her daughter [numeris ac libratis passibus moveretur, vix tamen poterat imitari]. In her right hand Harmonia bore as usual a shield – or what seemed to be a shield – of a circular design composed of many rings and interwoven with marvellous configurations. The circles encompassing the shield were attuned to each other, and with its circular strings it produced a resounding concord of all the modes. Suspended at equal lengths from the maiden's left hand were several small golden models of musical instruments played in the theatre, but no tortoise-shell lyre or lute or tetrachord appeared on the shield. Why, the concord issuing from that strange rotundity transcended the melodies produced by all musical instruments! As soon as she entered, her concord resounded from the orb. All other musical sounds (which struck the ear as harsh after her sweetness) muted themselves and lapsed into silence. Then Jupiter and the celestial gods, perceiving the grandeur of the superior melody that was pouring forth in honour of a certain arcane fire and inextinguishable flame, revered that most secret and profound song because it issued from the Father. One by one they all rose up to show their respect for extramundane intelligence.

(De nuptiis IX.908–10*)*

All is saved. Luna saves the day by persuading Jove to postpone his sombre examination of the Prophetic Arts, Jove saves the dream of poetic concord by ordering Harmonia's triumphant return to divine and human society, and Harmonia saves the dance by driving away 'the dullness of earthborn stolidity' (IX.899) with her heavenly power to combine 'motus' and 'cantus' in perfectly balanced measures which please and instruct simultaneously.

The measures of her mother's 'lepida chorea' are in themselves merely pleasing, Martianus suggests, but even they become instructive when measured against the standard of 'rata congruentia' or 'exact symmetry' set by Harmonia's ideal performance. Just as Plotinus encouraged us to admire the dance of the Living Being as a splendid display of rhythm and symmetry but also to look down on it as a shambling erotic pantomime in comparison with the mystic dance in the supracosmic temple of Psyche, so Martianus instructs us to form a sanely balanced judgment of Venus and the natural world she embodies as an erotic danseuse. She does her best to mimic her daughter's majestic bearing and supremely rational paces, and for that her supporting performance is to be commended. Indeed, we may even sympathize a little with her for having such a hard act to follow! But for all her efforts she can 'scarcely imitate' the archetypal beauty and order displayed by the sublime Harmonia. The world that gave birth to our vision of the ideal dance cannot compete with the world in which that ideal is vividly realized.

There can be no doubt that Martianus derived his image of the nuptial dance of Venus from the wedding scene at the end of the tale of Cupid and Psyche in Apuleius of Madaura's *Metamorphoses* (VI.24), for he informs us early on in the *De nuptiis* (1.7) that Mercury had intended to marry Psyche before she was snatched up by the uxorious Cupid. When Psyche found her way back to 'the chorus of heavenly stars' after her harrowing adventures in Hades, recounted Apuleius, she was given a standard Olympian reception at which 'the Horae adorned everything with roses and other flowers, and the Graces scattered balsam, and the Muses made their songs ring out, and Apollo sang to his cithara, and Venus outdid herself by dancing beautifully in time with the pleasant music.'[33] Intolerant of rivals, the Apuleian Venus (who proclaimed herself 'the Primordial Mother of all natural things' and 'the Creative Origin of the elements' in IV.30) danced alone at the wedding of Psyche. The Venus whom Philology observes, by contrast, must dance as her daughter's foil and follower.

Harmonia commands all ears and eyes with her great shield, her disciplined gait, and her rustling costume stiff with metallic studs. At first glance she might be taken for a pyrrhic dancer – an incongruously martial figure amid the troops of peaceful philosophers and ceremonious nymphs. But her music tells us with its soothing Cytherean tones that she has nothing to do with battlefields and agonies and never dances to the blare of trumpets and the death roll of tympani. Her shield, a truly 'strange rotundity' reminiscent of the aegis of Pallas Athena and the cithara of Apollo Helios, is composed all of rings like a common armillary sphere. It is a conspicuous symbol of her Athenian wisdom, Apollonian rationality, and cosmic sphere of influence, and that is all it is if we choose to identify it with its bearer. As its bearer, however, Harmonia may also be distinguished from the shield. She dances apart from its rings, moves it forward without being moved by its circulating melodies, and causes it to resound without appearing to touch its strings. Does she carry it then to remind us of the Neoplatonic distinction between the cosmic dancer and the cosmic dance? Does she represent the immanent cause of world-harmony – the aspiring soul of the Living Being – which is independent of the celestial revolutions and their harmonious effects by virtue of its constant intellectual participation in the life of the hypostatic gods?

Certainly she is a mysterious figure, this sacred revenant from the Pythagorean past. If Martianus at first envisioned her only as a living statue of the seventh Liberal Art, he ended up imagining a goddess greater in power and stature than the Harmonia who danced with the Graces in the Homeric Hymn to Apollo (see chapter 1, pages 30–1). The awe she inspires in all who hear the tinkling of her starry gown and learn to imitate the measures of her wisdom transcends aesthetic wonder: it leads to, and is ultimately indistinguishable from, the religious veneration reserved for the hypostatic god whom Harmonia identifies in IX.922 as 'the Primal Form of Intellectual Light' (that is, Nous). Like the contemplative World-Soul she acts as a unitive intermediary between the physical spheres ruled by Phoebus and the world of pure understanding perceived by Pallas. Hence her position between these two deities in the procession. Her 'most secret and profound song' – the otherworldly melody that silences the music of the spheres and all lesser sounds when she makes her appearance – issues from the third threshold in the *De nuptiis*: Harmonia's purely musical access to the temple of the Intellectual Sun. All who follow her final song to its source cross over into the sanctuary where, safe from barbarian intruders, forever ringed round by ecstatic philosopher-poets, burns the arcane fire of extramundane intelligence. It was the gate to this sanctuary that Martianus was opening for his soul (and for many a soul in the Middle Ages) when his son found him chanting the obscure verses of his Hymn to Hymen.

The transcendent thrust and mystical design of his work as a whole can be hard to perceive and easy to forget while the Liberal Arts are rattling off their interminable lectures. But the thrust is there, always upward, and the design, a step-by-step progress from the elemental dance of Hymen to the intellectual dance of Harmonia, is sustained to the last word of the last lecture. After Harmonia's spectacular entrance, her ponderous oration (in the style of Aristides Quintilianus) on modes, intervals, tonal genera, and quantitative metres is bound to strike all but the most enthusiastic musicologist as anticlimactic. What counts in the end is that it perfects the choral unity of Philology's curriculum by drawing the Trivium and Quadrivium together. Since the field of 'music' as defined by Harmonia is universal in a literal sense, it comes as no surprise that she includes cheironomia, pantomimic dancing, rhetorical gesturing, and all other kinds of rhythmical bodily motion, voluntary and involuntary, in her comprehensive discipline. 'Rhythm as a whole,' she teaches in IX.968–9, 'is divisible into three categories because it impinges on the three senses of sight, hearing, and touch: visual rhythms, for example, are those linked together by the motion of the body; aural rhythms are perceptible in the measures of a song or poem; and tactile rhythms are felt when we take our pulse to determine the state of our health. The art of rhythmics is entirely dependent on measures.' And without the immutable foundation of her measures, the theatre of the poetic universe with its glittering choruses and gilded lyres would come crashing down before Philology's eyes.

By providing the allegory with its ninth book Harmonia establishes a mimetic correspondence between the work as a whole and the nine spheres of the choral cosmos ruled by her Muses. Modern commentators on Martianus' articulate image of the poetic universe have tended to draw a sharp distinction between its allegorical and didactic sections, viewing the myth of Philology's apotheosis as a flamboyant frame for the drab encyclopaedia of trivial and quadrivial information provided by her bridesmaids.[34] Harmonia, however, recognizes no such distinction. The allegory reveals to her philological followers the epoptic end of their system of education: a sublimely poetic vision of life from the perspective of the gods. The orations delivered at the wedding are not framed by the allegory. They are justified by it. The information they organize is confirmed by it. However dull the seven pedagogical treatises may be as individual works, collectively they represent the spiritually and physically invigorating flow of wisdom from the intellectual wellsprings in the Empyrean into the spheres of the nine 'fountain-born maidens.' The circulation of that wisdom among the many who revel here below with Hymen (Martianus junior learns from the priest at the threshold) inevitably depends on its concentration in the few who triumph on high with Harmonia.

The Dedalian Chorus

If Porphyry or Iamblichus had composed a Pythagorean hymn for the long-haired philosophers to chant as they measured their rational paces in the procession of Harmonia, it would have sounded something like this:

> *The Wellspring above Being*
> *Is crowned with the beauty of its offspring*
> *Who leap out from the centre*
> *And then flow around it.*
> *Hush, my audacious lyre, hush!*
> *Reveal not to the masses mysteries*
> *Which have no orgiastic initiations.*
> *Go and sing of things here below –*
> *Let silence conceal those above.*
> *And now my mind concerns itself*
> *With intellectual creations of the sort*
> *From which the human spirit has sprung:*
> *The Source of Goodness divided without division;*
> *The Imperishable Mind fallen into matter;*
> *The Small Fragment which despite its size*
> *Produces divine progenitors. And among these,*
> *This one whole Universal Mind,*
> *This whole diffused into the whole,*
> *Spins the hollow sphere of the heavens*
> *And guards the whole cosmos with its presence,*
> *Which has been distributed*

Among many forms.
One part of it guides the revolving stars;
Another enters into the dances of the angels;
[ho d' es angelōn choreias;]
Still another, drawn down by a bond,
Has found an earthly form
And is cut off from its progenitors.

(Hymn 1 67–95)

Like a descending scale of solemn celestial tones, these verses flow earthwards from the threshold of the Neoplatonic Beyond, conveying to us who cannot hear the symphony of the cosmos a sweet echo of its sublime resonance along with a sad reminder of our physical alienation from the dance of the intellectual gods. The hymn itself is all that seems to connect us with their invisible presence. It is a fragile lyrical bond with the mysterious past when all the fragments of the cosmic intellect were united and matter was below us all, inert, sterile, danceless. The joyous clamour of revellers in the pagan mysteries is hushed so that we may concentrate on the dreadful fact of our intellectual fragmentation and on the problem of finding a way back to the eternal Wellspring.

Not a note of Christian jubilation echoes in the hollow sphere of the heavens spun by the Universal Mind, the primordial descent of which into matter is recalled and imitated by the mind of the poet. We might expect to hear such a note from the angels dancing in those heavens, but are they Christian angels? Their subordination to the stars suggests that they are the tutelary 'angeloi' whom pagan Neoplatonists of the fourth century discerned in great numbers on all the celestial spheres and whose role in the cosmic dance was to convey mystical illumination from the astral gods to the planetary daimones and thence to the demiurgic spirits and philosophical souls below the moon.

The hymn was composed in the last decade of the fourth century by an initiate in the Neoplatonic mysteries who would eventually convert (in his own fashion) to Christianity. His name was Synesius of Cyrene.

The poetic world-view of Synesius reflects the uneasy fusion of Hellenism and Christianity in the culture of the four cities that shaped his life. The city of his birth (c 370) was Cyrene in Libya, the myrtle-shaded colony of Theran warriors celebrated of yore by Callimachus in his hymn to Apollo Carneius. Synesius probably knew all of Callimachus by heart in his boyhood, for he received his early education in Greek grammar and rhetoric in his native city and his parents, who were pagan aristocrats, would have insisted that their son be immersed in the lyrical piety of the immortal Cyrenian bard. While completing his rhetorical studies in Alexandria (between 393 and 395), he met his Lady Philosophy in the person of Hypatia, whose hierophantic authority drew him into the chorus of Neoplatonic illuminati. Though Hypatia did not write anti-Christian propaganda, her intellectual allegiance to Porphyry may have incited the wrath of the Christian mob who murdered her on the steps of an Alexandrian basilica in 415.

From Cyrene and the towns in her domain Synesius was sent as an ambassador to the imperial court in Constantinople, and the political experience he gained in the capital between 399 and 402 seems to have taught him the value of allegiance to the state religion, for shortly after his return he was married to a Christian by the Patriarch of Alexandria. His wife and the Patriarch Theophilus doubtless encouraged him to convert at this time, and he may well have done so for the sake of the ceremony. Conversion in a deep sense, however, must have been a slow reflective process for him. His reluctance to embrace the faith as a whole, to cross the ecclesiastical threshold without looking back, is attested by his exclusively allegorical interpretation of the doctrine of the resurrection of the flesh and by his undiminished admiration for Hypatia's philosophical opposition to 'the opinions of the vulgar.'[35] His reputation for justice and fortitude prompted the clergy of the Libyan city of Ptolemais to elect him as bishop of their large diocese in 410. He accepted the position after much soul-searching only when Theophilus assured him that his flock would not be distressed by his private interest in pre-existent souls and eternal creations and intellectual dances around the Imperishable Mind. They were quite content to let him philosophize quietly by himself provided that he stood up for their interests in the Here and Now, which he was to do with admirable energy (though not with boundless enthusiasm) for the last three years of his life. He probably did not live to hear of Hypatia's martyrdom.

His literary remains consist chiefly of orations in the Attic idiom of the Second Sophistic and a group of Doric hymns composed according to the rules of classical prosody. For the fluid measures and allusive depth of his hymns he deserves to be hailed as the Christian Callimachus, though he hailed himself as a disciple of Dio Chrysostom, whose philosophical way of life he considered more civilized and civilizing than the 'other' way, the way of the Christians and their barbarian converts. The dating of his hymns is uncertain. The density of philosophical terms and allusions in the first four suggests that his conversion was far from complete when he wrote them and that parts of them may have been written before Ecclesia had drawn him into her chorus.[36]

Though Synesius recognized but one source of poetic inspiration – the Trinity – his fountain-born verses flow down to us in the wake of a sophistic movement to Hellenize Christian literature which was directly inspired, or incited, by the cultural separatism of Julian the Apostate. None of Julian's measures as a reformer was recalled with greater bitterness by Christian authors in both halves of the Empire than the enforcement of his educational edicts of 362 which made it illegal for grammarians and rhetoricians to expound the pagan classics as Christian allegories. Though this infamous act of repression did not prevent Christian children from going to school or from reading the classics with their tutors, who often happened to be pagan, it did thrust them for a few tense months into the local conflicts between Church and State that Julian towards the end of his reign was striving to escalate into a decisive battle between the forces of Christianity and Hellenism. The decisive battle never took place because the forces were impossible to separate, but the threat of an imminent polarization of the two cultures and the horrifying thought that the State had attempted to gain a monopoly over one of them shocked the Church into an awareness of how dearly it valued the classical legacy its own apologists had often rudely belittled.

In Berytus a Christian grammarian and his son, both named Apollinarius, tried to replace the legacy they feared the Church was losing (or had lost) with a 'superior' corpus of Christian literature based on classical Greek models. With remarkable speed they turned out a Homeric epic in twenty-four books on the Old Testament history of the Hebrews down to the reign of Saul, along with Christian odes in the style of Pindar, Christian tragedies patterned on Euripides, and Christian dialogues in imitation of Plato! (The disappearance of this entire corpus save for a metrical version of the Psalms which is of doubtful authenticity testifies to its literary merits.) Strange as the endeavour of the Apollonarii seems in isolation and in retrospect, it was but an extreme response to a defiant literary impulse felt by many of their class at the time – an impulse powerful enough to stir the genius of Gregory of Nazianzus, for one, decades after Julian's death.

If Julian had reigned as long as Constantine, his educational policy would certainly have retarded the Christianization of the urban upper classes throughout the Empire by forcing into retirement all teachers of literature who could not reconcile their faith with their desire for professional advancement. Among those who were forced to retire because of the edicts was the most celebrated rhetorician and convert in midcentury Rome, Marius Victorinus, whose hymns to the Trinity anticipated those of Synesius in their bold transposition of Neoplatonic terminology into the key of Christian praise. 'Fountain, Stream, Inundation: O Blessed Trinity!' Victorinus had sung to the Latin West, 'Stillness, Procession, Return: O Blessed Trinity!'[37]

Julian's attempt to separate the old paideia from the new had a profound impact on Christian conceptions of choreia in the fifty years following his death. Christian authors who responded defensively to his educational policy tended to polarize ecclesiastical and pagan-philosophical images of the cosmic dance (as we shall see in the next chapter); on the other hand those who responded aggressively to it and refused to be bullied or baptized into accepting one culture or the other tended to create ingenious syntheses of the choral visions characteristic of both. The dance imagery in Synesius' second hymn indicates that he definitely belonged to the latter group:

> Again light, again dawn,
> Again day shines forth
> After the night-roaming darkness:
> With morning-songs, o soul,
> Let me sing of God again,
> Who has given light to the dawn,
> Who has given stars to the night,
> A well-ordered choral dance encircling all.
> [hos edōken astra nukti,
> perikosmian choreian.]
> Ether has veiled the back of turbulent matter,
> Mounting on the fairest fire
> So that the glorious moon may mark off
> The last phase of her curved orbit.
> Above the eighth rotation
> Of the star-bearing spheres
> A starless stream
> Sets in motion the layers of matter
> Hidden within its bosom,
> Driving them onwards in a contrary course.
> It dances around the Great Mind,
> Which bends down with its grey wings
> To the lordly cosmos.
> [megan amphi noun choreuei,
> hos anaktos akra kosmon
> poliois erephe tarsois.]
> A blessed silence covers all
> That lies beyond: the indivisible division
> Of the intellectual and intelligible gods.
> With three lights a form has blazed forth,
> One wellspring, one root.
> For where the profundity of the Father lies,
> There also shines the noble Son,
> Great offspring of his heart,
> And the world-framing wisdom
> And unifying light

Of the Holy Spirit.

(*Hymn* II 1–32)

The god of whom the poet sings again seems for a moment to be Helios the Light-Bringer, the magical coryphaeus who created the living statues of the material world and made them dance to the measures of time around the Great Mind of the cosmos. But then, quite unexpectedly, while the other heavenly bodies are performing their usual strophes and antistrophes, Helios dawns on the poet's consciousness as an image of the Christian Trinity blazing over the horizon of the Empyrean.

Everything beyond the threshold appears in a new light. God the Father emerges from the profound obscurity of the One, the Son and Holy Spirit emanate from him like intelligible gods, the Angels of the Lord spring to mind as intellectual gods, and the descending wisdom of the Spirit brings peace and prophetic understanding to the cosmos on the grey (dove-like?) wings of the Great Mind. As a 'morning song' composed again and again by the poet's soul the second hymn is a mimetic response to the recurrence of light in his dawning universe. If we draw a sharp distinction between his mentally ordered worlds and metrically ordered words, the poem will strike us as nothing more than a sphere-by-sphere survey of the celestial globe and its environs – a strange sort of astronomy lesson! But if we assume that the poetic universe generates and sustains and informs the poem, if we can believe or at least imagine that the two are fused at the Fountainhead, then the poem will unite us to an eternal chorus harmoniously dancing around 'the Centre of all existing things, the Monad of immortal numbers' (II 70–1). It demands participation on our part in an eternal choral rite, or rather induces participation by conveying to us through the artifice of quantitative prosody an impression of the numerical measures governing the dance.

In its closing lines Synesius beseeches God to liberate his soul from sublunary trammels and reminds himself of the ecstatic climax of the epistrophic ascent:

> *Lend a gracious ear*
> *To the hymns of my choruses!*
> *[tanuson choroisin hymnōn!]*
> *Reveal the light of wisdom.*
> *Pour down the glorious bliss,*
> *Pour down the shining grace*
> *Of a tranquil life.*
> *Drive poverty far away,*
> *And disruptive earthly riches.*
> *Drive diseases from my limbs,*

> *Drive passionate impulses*
> *And heart-rending cares from my life,*
> *So that the wings of my soul*
> *Do not fall heavily to earth.*
> *For instead of falling I wish*
> *To raise a free wing and dance*
> *In the rites of your Son,*
> *Rites no words can describe!*
> *[ta panarrēta choreusō!]*
>
> (*Hymn* II 75–91)

The strophe of procession, the joyless descent of mind into matter recollected in the first hymn, is answered in the second with a joyful antistrophe of return. Like a bird on the wing (an image used by Socrates in *Phaedrus* 249c) the poet yearns to defy the graveward pull of gravity by dancing high and free above the torments of the body. The resurrection of Christ in the spirit – and only in the spirit, let the ignorant masses think what they will! – assures the morning-singer that his own spirit can and will rise beyond the fairest fire in the ether.

The hymns of Synesius resemble the incantations of the Orphic priests and Neoplatonic wizards in that they are purely 'performative utterances'[38] which should not be judged true or false like propositions in a philosophical argument but rather effective or ineffective like steps in a therapeutic procedure. To view them from a distance as static monuments of piety is to miss what they are doing for the poet and are supposed to be doing for his lyre-enchanted listeners. They are dynamic acts of praise by which the poet draws himself into the cosmic dance, and if his listeners are to follow him they must enter into the rite, experience the harmony, perform the measures for themselves. So Synesius suggests in his third hymn:

> *A holy act it is to praise you,*
> *Father of Worlds,*
> *Father of Ages,*
> *Creator of Gods!*
> *The intellectual gods sing*
> *Of you, o Lord!*
> *And the cosmic rulers*
> *With their glittering eyes,*
> *The astral intelligences,*
> *Sing hymns to you, Blessed One,*
> *While around them dances*
> *The illustrious body of the cosmos.*

[hous peri kleinon
sōma choreuei.]

(*Hymn* III 265–76)

These incantatory verses sweep us downward from the Father along the processional flow of intellectual gods, cosmic rulers (the star-eyed Decan gods?), and astral intelligences; then whirl us round with the multitudes of corporeal creatures in the dance of the material world; and lastly lift us – or at least our spirits – on the crescendo of divine and human praises streaming back to the Father.

The highest is thus joined with the lowest in an eternal choral round which can be imagined and experienced poetically but cannot be seen as a whole either physically or intellectually. For it is divine law in the poetic universe

> *That the lowest things should not*
> *Strive against the highest*
> *But that all existing things*
> *Should be drawn together into a chorus*
> *So that their order will never perish.*
> *[es choron ontōn*
> *ouket' oleitai.]*
> *One being derives happiness*
> *From another, and all delight*
> *In their reciprocal joy.*
> *An eternal circle,*
> *Formed out of mortal beings*
> *And revived by your breath,*
> *Sets choral dances in motion*
> *For you throughout the universe.*
> *[Soi dia pantōn*
> *histēsi chorous.]*
> *Mother Nature employs*
> *Her Dedalian skill*
> *To embellish the circle*
> *With her own colours and creations,*
> *And out of the diverse sounds*
> *Of living creatures*
> *She creates a single harmony,*
> *Causing all to sing in unison.*
> *All things convey to you*
> *Eternal praise:*
> *The dawn and the night,*

The lightning bolts, the snowfalls,
The firmament, the ether,
The roots in the soil,
The water, the air,
All bodies,
All spirits. ...

                        (*Hymn* III 320–50)

Whereas a strictly Neoplatonic spectator would have looked away from the cosmos in order to contemplate the eternal circle – Plotinus having taught that one could not perceive the perfect form of the intellectual dance without ultimately ignoring the physical poses in the pantomime of the Living Being – Synesius directed his gaze from the eternal circle to the colours, shapes, and motions of the animated sculptures in Nature's Dedalian chorus and audaciously *created* an image in which the circle of Nous and the chorus of Nature can be perceived simultaneously, the latter appearing as a splendid embellishment rather than a contemptible imitation of the former. His imaginative vision of the dance can encompass 'all bodies' and 'all spirits' because it effectively dissolves the old philosophical distinction between the physical image and the spiritual archetype of choral order. It is the vision of an inspired Poetic Spectator.

Helios the Corybant, Hermes the Psychopomp, Attis the Leaper, Apollo the Coryphaeus, Dionysus the Grace-Giver – one spirit takes over all these old roles in the cosmic dance envisioned by Synesius. All hail the Rising Son. All hail the Galilean who conquers in the end. 'I praise you, o Logos!' the Cyrenian chants at dawn, at noon, at dusk, and at midnight in his fourth hymn,

For you abide with the Great Father,
O ineffable Mind. ...
For you an ageless sphere
Turns swiftly round
In its untroubled course.
Under your direction
A group of seven stars
Performs a choral dance
[hebdoma astrōn
antichoreuei]
In opposition to the rapid turning
Of the great concavity.
And the many lights
Of the cosmos adorn

One cloud-enfolded sky
According to your wish,
O illustrious Offspring!
For you run round about
The hollow sphere of the heavens
And hold together
The unbroken course of the ages.
                    (*Hymn* IV 130–2, 152–68)

How clearly Helios shines through these cross-cultural images of Christ directing the antistrophe of the planets, Christ running round the eternal sphere of the Aplanes, Christ uniting the aeons of the cosmic year! The magical rays of the poetic universe are scarcely weakened or diffused as they filter through the clouds of the Fallen World and awaken the Cyrenian's audacious lyre. The role of his strange, unbiblical, heliodynamic Christ is further defined in the sixth hymn:

You lead, o Lord, the angelic choral dances
And rule the phalanxes of daimones;
[su de tas angelikas, Anax, choreias
kai tas daimonias phalanges archeis;]
You also dance around perishable nature,
Distributing indivisible spirit throughout the earth.
[su de kai physin phthitan amphichoreueis
ameriston peri gan pneuma merizeis.]
And by joining again to the Wellspring what it has given forth
You release mortals from the necessity of death.
                    (*Hymn* VI 18–23)

In the processional phase of the dance Christ traces out his unitive and protective circle of grace – his 'lykabas' – around the chorus of mortals trapped in the sublunary cycle of growth and decay, distributing to them in the manner of Dionysus his consoling gifts of health, serenity, and spiritual refreshment. Perishable nature rejoices in his triumph over Necessity. Grace is begotten in the Aplanes where the Graces once sprang to life.

   The immortalizing spirit of the Wellspring (which the Orthodox Church claimed would immortalize its members only) the Synesian Logos scatters over all the earth like the rays of Attis or like the ceaseless rain of astral spiritus descending from the choruses of Iamblichan angels and daimones. There is no place for Ecclesia and her apocalyptic dance in the Cyrenian's vision of eternal cosmic harmony. In his ninth hymn Synesius highlights the purely spiritual character of Christ's epistrophic ascent by presenting it as an amazing scene from a pantomime of living statues, the deferential figures of the classical gods. His lyre reaches new heights of audacity in this bizarre Orphic descant on the Resurrection:

> *The ineffable race of daimones*
> *Soaring throughout the air*
> *Trembled in amazement*
> *At your ascent, o Lord!*
> *Amazed was the ambrosial chorus*
> *Of untainted stars;*
> *[thambēse d' akēratōn*
> *choros ambrotos asterōn;]*
> *Ether, the wise father*
> *Of Harmonia, laughed*
> *And blended notes*
> *From his seven-stringed lyre*
> *Into a song of victory.*
> *The Morning-Star smiled,*
> *The harbinger of day,*
> *As did golden Hesperus,*
> *The star of Cytherea.*
> *Horned Selene waxed bright*
> *In the stream of fire*
> *And led the way as shepherdess*
> *Of the nocturnal gods.*
> *Titan spread out his rays*
> *Under the ineffable footsteps,*
> *Recognizing the Son of God*
> *As the supreme creative Mind*
> *And the Source of his own fire.*
> (Hymn IX 20–43)

Now, while the heights of the poetic universe are glowing in the titanic sunset of Helios and resounding with the blended notes of Hellenism and Christianity, let us close the portals of Harmonia's temple and sink back to the noisy, crowded, insect-trodden surface of the earth for a look at the Dedalian chorus from the viewpoint of Ecclesia.

7

Praise His Name in the Dance

Admire with me if you will the natural intelligence of unintelligent creatures, and try if you can to explain its cause. How does it come about that birds seek out rocks and trees and roofs at nesting-time and make their nests at once safe and beautiful in a manner suited to their nurslings? Whence do bees and spiders derive their love of work and their fondness for ingenious craftsmanship? For bees construct their honeycombs by binding together criss-crossing hexagonal pipes and make them secure with a cross-wall in the middle and by an alternation of interlocking corners and straight lines. And all this they do unseen in their dark hives and moulded cells! As for spiders, they have perfected the art of weaving intricate webs by stretching in many directions exceedingly delicate threads almost as thin as air – threads which seem to come from nowhere! A precious mansion indeed, but at the same time a trap for catching weaker creatures to nourish and regale the master of the house! What Euclid imitated these when he was philosophizing about imaginary lines and racking his brains for proofs? What Palamedes devised the tactical manoeuvres and configurations of cranes (as the saying is) and taught them their orderly motions and complicated flight patterns? What Phidias had the incomparable skill to sculpt such forms? What Zeuxis, Polygnotus, Parrhasius, and Aglaophon knew how to paint things of such exquisite beauty? What Cnossian dance designed by Dedalus for a maiden can compare with the harmony and abundant beauty of their movements [Tis Knōssios Daidalou choros enarmonios, nymphēi eis kallous periousian]? What Cretan labyrinth was ever so hard to traverse and to wind through (as a poet would say) or ever turned back upon itself so many times through the cunning tricks of its construction? I shall not even mention the treasure-

rooms of the ants, or their treasure-keepers, or their store of food meted out in quantities appropriate for each season, or all the other details we know from accounts of their marches and their leaders and the excellent order of their activities.

GREGORY OF NAZIANZUS, *Oratio theologica* II xxv (*Or* 28.25)

The Orthodox Spectator

Midway through his brief archepiscopal career, in the summer or early autumn of 380, Gregory of Nazianzus delivered a series of five Theological Orations on the Nicene doctrine of the Trinity to an enthusiastic crowd in the only Orthodox church within the walls of Constantinople. His was not a lofty church by Byzantine standards, only a makeshift chapel in the house of one of his relatives; but he had given it the grand name of Anastasis (Resurrection) to commemorate the loftiest mystery in the life of Christ and to express his high hope that the city of harlots and heretics would soon witness the revival of Orthodox power in the East and the triumphant return of Ecclesia's holy chorus to the basilicas lost years ago to the Arians.

He was about fifty at the time but looked much older, illness and ascetic mortifications having taken their toll on a constitution which had never been robust. With his balding head and slouching posture, his wizened cheeks and unfashionably plain vestments, he would not have immediately im-pressed his enemies as a force to be reckoned with; he certainly lacked the political experience and commanding presence of his friend Basil of Caesarea, whose championship of Nicene Orthodoxy he would praise to the skies in an oration delivered the following year (*Or* 43).[1] Basil would have been perfect for the role of beleaguered patriarch. No one would have relished it more. But the great hero of the Orthodox cause had died in January of 379, a few days before the new emperor Theodosius had been baptized into their faith, and now the chief hope of Gregory's congregation lay not in Basil but in their advocate on the imperial throne, whom God was bound to protect from barbarians and assassins until he could reach his defiled capital and expel the heretics from the cathedral church of the Apostles.

Nazianzen (as Gregory may be called to distinguish him from the mystical genius of the Cappadocian triad, Basil's younger brother Gregory of Nyssa) was quite content to serve as the interim leader of their church, provided that he had a chance to subdue the jeering ministers of the Devil with his titanic strength as an orator. 'I was not one for making a loud ranting speech merely for the sake of applause, a speech full of stupid tricks and convoluted arguments [lugismata] such as Sophists are pleased to make amongst a crowd of youths,' he would insist in his poetic autobiography, recalling the period in his early thirties when he had just returned from Cappadocia after close to a decade of study in Athens, '… but, as I said, I did dance for the entertainment of my friends [orcheisthai tois philois].'² And now in the Anastasis at the height of his career he was prepared 'to dance' in earnest – that is, to display all his virtuosity as an orator – not just for the entertainment of his friends but for the enlightenment of his flock and the astonishment of his enemies.

'Lugismata' (from the verb 'lugizo,' 'to bend') was a derogatory term the Cappadocian Fathers employed to denote the intricate arguments and truth-bending rhetorical devices of their teachers, the Sophists, and their intellectual adversaries, the Arians and the Neoplatonists. The term was drawn from the theatre, where it signified the contorted postures and sinuous writhings of dancers and also the twists and turns of complicated melodies accompanying displays of 'orchēsis.' Even as the Church looked upon itself as an otherworldly institution officially opposed to the worldliness of the theatre, so the ideal Christian preacher was supposed to be dead against the corrupting sophistications of pagan rhetorical culture.³

So full of 'lugismata' is the passage from Gregory's Second Theological Oration at the head of this chapter, however, that if its source were not known and its author not honoured among Orthodox Saints as 'the Theologian' because of his eloquent defences of the divinity of the Logos, one might suppose it to be the work of a pagan Sophist, a precocious pupil of Libanius or Themistius, say, who for the amusement of his patrician friends (all aesthetes with a taste for Attic salt) was playing the old topoi of the Great Artist and the Dance of Life for all they were worth in a mock-encomium 'On the Birds and the Bees' or 'In Praise of Intelligent Arthropods.' Bees that sculpt with greater finesse than Phidias? Spiders more ingenious than Euclid? Cranes outmanoeuvring Palamedes? These are creatures that could only have been invented by a Dedalus of the Second Sophistic.

Through the labyrinth of the Sophist's paradoxical twists of thought and hyperbolic turns of phrase these admirable creatures dance – instead of flapping, buzzing, wriggling, and scuttling as they do in the dull everyday world of the senses – and not only dance, but instinctively perform a more dazzling series of 'schēmata' than even the famed Cnossian chorus performed long ago on the dance-floor designed by Dedalus for Ariadne. True connoisseurs of Second Sophistic oratory would recall that it was to this same Dedalian marvel that Homer compared the metallic dance-floor and the dance of golden lads and lasses depicted by Hephaestus on the Shield of Achilles (see chapter 1, pages 24–5), and they would doubtless be amused by the bathetic transference of the comparison from the lofty world of Homeric gods and heroes to the lowly realm of ants and spiders.

But turning Homer upside-down, as it were, and twisting the sense of his mythological references to suit incongruous themes were perhaps the easiest tricks of the Sophist's trade. He had to show more inventiveness than that if he was to earn the applause of an urbane fourth-century audience. And show it Gregory did in the Arachnean subtlety of his version of the Argument by Design, the 'exceedingly delicate threads' of which are woven around his Homeric allusion to form an elaborate tissue of rhetorical figures.[4] First figure, oxymoron or paradox: he would have us admire the intelligence of unintelligent creatures (alogōn) and then tell him the reasons for it (tous logous). Second figure, a succession of rhetorical questions: he prods us with a variety of emphatic interrogatives (Pōs? Pothen? Poios? Tinos? Poioi? Tis?) into contemplating the supreme rationality and creativity of God, who though not once mentioned by name in the passage is implicitly hailed as the answer to all mysteries and the end of all scientific investigations. Third figure, a clever combination of ecphrasis (vivid word-painting) and proso-popoeia (personification): bees in the guise of master-architects show us the intricately moulded interiors of their hives, while spiders doubling as master-weavers and crafty landlords welcome us as guests into their airy mansions which serve as traps for 'weaker creatures.' Fourth figure, double entendre: the Greek for 'cunning tricks of construction' (technēs sophismata) refers explicitly to the mind-boggling complexity of the design of the Cretan lab-yrinth but also implicitly to the technical sophistications of the bewilderingly pleonastic prose we must traverse and the seemingly digressive argument we must follow to get to the heart of the orator's meaning. Fifth figure, paraleipsis or the trick of refraining from saying something in order to say it: 'I shall not even mention the treasure-rooms of the ants, or their treasure-keepers, etc.' Need we even mention that the role of the plain-talking, proudly cultureless Christian preacher who depended entirely on the Logos for inspiration was obviously not what Gregory chose to adopt for his Second Theological Oration? Need we suggest that on the cultivated and critical audience of the Anastasis – which must be considered an audience as well as a congregation since it included a number of heterodox and even pagan listeners drawn to the chapel by Nazianzen's renown as an orator – such a rude anti-rhetorical pose, much as it was to be desired, would have fallen disastrously flat?

Gregory was human enough to want applause, having received precious little of it from his Cappadocian brethren in recent years because of his failure to take charge of the miserable little desert outpost of Sasima which Basil had imperiously assigned to him as his see in 371. Humiliated by this rustication and not a little envious of Basil's power to manipulate his clerical allies, he had stubbornly refused to visit his episcopal domain after his ordination or to waste his talents on the boorish congregation of vagrants there. No pride was ever more stubborn than that of a provincial patrician (his family had been wealthy landowners for generations) who had received an expensive cosmopolitan education!

But we should be doing the Saint a grave injustice to imagine him in the

Anastasis with the Devil at his side prompting him to dance pirouettes in the sophistic style merely to show off his Athenian eloquence for the applause of an ultra-refined Byzantine audience. That would be to misunderstand his reasons for raising Christian oratory to pagan heights of refinement, reasons that were not primarily aesthetic but political and pedagogical. On the battlefield of ecclesiastical politics he found himself in command of a demoralized minority who urgently needed a dose of intellectual pride – of the right sort – if they were to withstand the humiliating attacks of Arian extremists like the Eunomians who would split any dialectical hair, twist any syllogism, try any sophistic trick to prove the absolute ontological dissimilarity of the Father and the Son or to make their vulgar doctrine at least sound reasonable. In his Theological Orations Gregory strove to arm his troops with strong conservative arguments for believing Orthodox doctrine to be indeed the 'right belief.' He had to fight fire with fire.

In spite of their political differences he and Basil saw eye to eye on the issue of how much value the Church should attach to the monuments and methods of the old paideia, their humanistic attitudes towards education having been formed during the same decade, the 350s, at the same university, Athens, by the same tutor, the Christian Sophist Prohaeresius. As teachers – hardly distinguishable in their day from defenders – of the faith, the Cappadocians insisted that Christian education could preserve the flower of Greek wisdom without entangling itself in the roots of pagan superstition; that classical literature could furnish the orators of the Church with a rich vocabulary for expressing the human potential for virtue; that while the Bible was all the soul needed to find its way out of the labyrinth of this World, the mystical writings of Plato and the ascetic precepts of the Stoics could strengthen the soul's yearning for release from the perplexities and precariousness of material existence; and that the literary idiom of the Sophists which had evolved in opposition to the philosophical jargon of the Hellenistic schools and yet had absorbed so much of it was not in itself evil (as early Christian apologists had tended to claim) but only became so when employed for evil ends.

In Sasima Gregory had had no mission as a teacher – no mission of his own. In Constantinople he had the chorus of the Empire to conduct with his words. 'To words alone I cling,' he had cried in exultant defiance of the Emperor Julian's edicts forbidding Christians to teach or study the classics, 'and I make no complaint about the arduous journeys by land and sea I had to make to supply myself with them!'[5] And to words like 'choros' and 'kosmos' and 'koryphaios,' ancient Athenian words that still spoke to educated souls of the beauty and order of the All, he clung tenaciously. In the Second Theological Oration they serve as vehicles for his contemplative ascent from creation to Creator which begins at ground level with his meditation on the Cnossian chorus of 'alogoi' swarming over the dance-floor of the living earth.

In addition to his general justification of Christian Sophistic on political and pedagogical grounds he had two special reasons, one polemical and the other thematic, for adopting a highly complicated style of argument and expression – for 'dancing' ostentatiously – in this particular oration. Lest his audience miss the polemical stratagem behind his tour-de-force, he slyly exposes it in mid-performance: 'Now why have I gone into these arguments in a style too subtle perhaps for the ears of the crowd yet conforming to the type of discourse that has got the upper hand at the present time – the type that has no regard for frankness and simplicity and has introduced a crooked and intricate style full of enigmas? So that the tree may be recognized by its fruits! I mean, so that the darkness which is producing these dogmas may be known by the obscurity of its arguments ... ' (*Or* 28.11). No branch of the twisted tree of Arianism cast a darker shadow over the Anastasis than that of the Eunomians, then dominant in the capital, whose arrogant supposition that the nature of God could be completely comprehended by human reason and easily dissected by Aristotelian methods of analysis was intensely offensive to mystical theologians of Nazianzen's Platonic and monastic bent.

It is against this supposition that the argument of the Second Theological Oration, which may be divided into three sections of roughly equal length, is chiefly directed. Section one (1–11) defines the limits of human reason with respect to its ultimate object of contemplation, the transcendent nature of God; section two (12–21) examines the reasons for those limits, for example, God's wish to subdue our intellectual pride and to save the sight of his full majesty as a reward for the Blessed, and considers the causes of pagan error from a Pauline perspective; and section three (22–31), which contains the passage on the Dedalian order of the insects, considers how much – and yet how little – we can discover about the essence of God from the things of this world, which are surveyed, chorus by chorus, from the viewpoint of an ascending soul aglow with the fire of the Holy Spirit and eager to beam the ray of divine wisdom over the vastness of creation.

The argument underlying and uniting the diverse parts of the Oration is essentially epistemological in character rather than cosmological, and (as the Theologian remarks at the start) it is handed down to the faithful from one who has dared to climb to the very summit of the Mount of Truth and to enter into the Cloud of Mystery to converse like Moses with the Divine Presence, but who, unlike Eunomius and his deluded followers, can claim to have seen no more than 'the back parts of God' (2–3). Natural reason may urge us to begin the contemplative ascent, as God intended, but only faith in the illuminative power of the Holy Spirit will keep our eyes focused

on the true upward path out of the maze of transient life and prevent
our minds from being distracted by all the intriguing puzzles along the
way – the military marches of ants, the synchronized flight of cranes, the
retrogradations of Mars – which are worth considering briefly (but
only en passant) as minor miracles confirming the existence of the great
Thaumaturge.

To discredit the Eunomian argument that the essence of God could be
fully deduced from the well-known order of the cosmos Gregory had first
to persuade his listeners that the order of the cosmos was not in fact well
known, that their knowledge of it was merely an accumulation of opinions
and speculations, and that a complete understanding of any one of nature's
innumerable marvels was exceedingly difficult if not impossible to attain
with their imperfect instruments of observation and comprehension. His
attack on Eunomian epistemology is tantamount to a defence of the poetic
or prephilosophical vision of cosmic order as essentially miraculous. If the
display of intelligence in insects is as he pictures it a true miracle, then it
cannot be fully explained in scientific terms and must presuppose a supernatural cause which is more difficult to comprehend than the phenomenon
itself. The failure of the subtlest students of nature to observe, explain, or
conceive all the possible turns and counterturns in the Cnossian dance of
the insects proves the phenomenon a miracle. Therefore, while the existence
of God may be known from the dynamic complexity of the cosmos, God's
essence, the primal simplicity of his uncreated being, may never be, and
only a fool like Eunomius would suppose that the insectile brain of Man –
Fallen Man – could ever penetrate the lofty mysteries of the Father without
the guidance of the Son and the light of the Holy Spirit.

The tortuous style of the Second Theological Oration functions as a general symbol of the awesome complexity of the cosmos as perceived by the
Orthodox Spectator, the sharp-eyed and far-gazing 'I' whom Gregory lifts
from earth to heaven in the third section of his speech. The difficulty of
finding answers to his persistent questions, resolutions for his multiple paradoxes, simple facts in his twisted hyperbolic fancies – finally, of finding
an escape route from theological argument and sophistic discourse – is comparable, he suggests, to the difficulty of finding a direct path to God through
the 'sophismata' of the World. The Eunomians thought they had found such
a path in Aristotle's regression to the First Cause via the multiplicity of
temporal causes and effects, but where had it got them? Peripatetics in an
ironically literal sense, they had merely wandered round and round the
confusing confines of a dubious teleological construct of the universe; they
had lost their theological bearings; they could not even judge the extent of
their error.

The dual theme of complexity and difficulty is highlighted by the symbolic

images of the Cnossian dance and the Cretan labyrinth, which should perhaps be interpreted as a single image since Gregory evidently pictured the
winding of the chorus on the dance-floor of Dedalus as a dynamic extension
of the winding path of the maze. The image appears where it does, at the
commencement of the ascent, as a warning that the contemplative flight
from creation to Creator was a movement away from inconceivable complexity towards inconceivable simplicity (for so the Cappadocian Fathers
experienced it during their periods of monastic seclusion from the bewil-
derments of ecclesiastical politics) and that the Orthodox Spectator must
learn from the start, however fascinated he may be by the intricacy of the
visual field, to clarify, unify, and simplify his field of intellectual vision.
The maze-dance is an arresting image in this context because it invites two
responses to the cosmos which effectively cancel each other out and leave
the contemplative soul momentarily stranded in perplexity.

As we have seen in the orations of Dio Chrysostom and Eusebius of
Caesarea, the customary function of dance imagery in sophistic elaborations
of the Argument by Design was to arouse aesthetic wonder at the choral
order of the macrocosm leading to religious admiration for the all-powerful
coryphaeus directing the spectacle or for the munificent choragus behind
the scenes. Not being a Cynic, Gregory was perfectly content to let the old
topos work its old effects in his microcosmic (one might even say micro-
scopic) vision of the Great Design. However, as a strategic image in his
anti-Eunomian polemic, it also serves to dampen intellectual optimism by
implying the unintelligible complexity of the Design and hence to discourage
the Orthodox Spectator from losing sight of his distant spiritual goals in the
distracting convolutions of his physical environment. By association with
the hazards of the labyrinth, Gregory's choral imagery is darkly admonitory:
it has the force of a Skeptic's warning about the futility of scientific research
and philosophical speculation, though Gregory certainly did not use it to
advocate mental relaxation through Skeptical suspension of judgment. Indeed arrest must give way to energetic ascent, and discouragement to exultation, when we consider the original significance of the Cnossian dance
in relation to Gregory's symbolic conception of Orthodox theology as a
way out – the only intellectual way out – of the deceptive paths and dead
ends of the World.

Theseus was said to have led his chorus of youths and maidens in a sinuous
folk-dance called the Geranos or 'Crane' soon after their departure from
Crete (a mythological detail recalled by Gregory, it seems, for he includes
the complicated flight patterns of cranes among the configurations of Nature's Cnossian dance). The sophistic biographer of Theseus, Plutarch of
Chaeronea, informs us that their reason for dancing the Geranos was not
simply to imitate their anxious migration through the maze but to com-

memorate their release from its toils in a religious ceremony of praise and thanksgiving pleasing to the gods of Greece. It was supposedly first performed on Delos rather than Crete, but because of its association with Theseus' Cnossian victory the Greek Sophists inevitably identified it with the Cnossian dance mentioned by Homer and assumed that Dedalus must have designed its complicated figures to delight the daughter of Minos. The sophistic version of the Theseus myth including the episode of the Delian-Dedalian Geranos appears to have been passed on to the Greek Fathers, whose response to it (as to so many other Greek myths) was probably at first to reject its contents as pagan nonsense and then to interpret its characters and events in a Christian light. Latent in Nazianzen's brief reference to the Cnossian dance is an allegory of salvation in which Christ figures as the New Theseus, Satan as the infernal Minotaur, and the Saved as the apocalyptic successors of the happy band who danced for joy after the terrors of the maze.[6]

Like the late Stoics whose contemptuous attitude to the cosmic dance deeply affected early Christian responses to Platonic cosmology the Greek Fathers tended to restrain their aesthetic enthusiasm for the world-chorus and to reserve their religious awe for 'the Choragus of All Life' (as Origen had hailed the Father).[7] Nazianzen turns this tendency into a compulsion, a mystical drive towards the origin and end of every orderly motion, in the soaring conclusion of the Second Theological Oration. On each of the four levels of existence surveyed during the ascent – earthly, astral, solar, and angelic – the Orthodox Spectator beholds a different dance. The four dances in his comprehensive vision of life are ultimately perceived as interweaving motions in a single continuous rite of divine praise conducted throughout all time and for all eternity in the tabernacle of the universe, but while the ascent is in progress they seem distinct because the choruses performing them vary enormously in appearance, complexity, and intelligence. From the lowly viewpoint of the insects – through compound eyes, as it were – we have seen the dance magnified and multiplied on the first level. Now let us rise to the second:

Who set the heavens circling? Who put the stars in order? No, let us first ask – what are the heavens and the stars? Could you tell me? I mean you who suspend your thoughts in mid-air, you who ignore what lies about your feet and cannot even measure yourself, you who busy yourself in a meddlesome way with things that are above your nature and stand gaping before what cannot be measured. Suppose that you do understand revolutions and periods, and approaches and retreats, and settings and risings, and certain zodiacal divisions and technical fine points – let them be the finest – and everything else that makes you so proud of your marvellous science. Well, so what? You have yet no grasp of the realities themselves. No grasp at all, for what you take to be knowledge is simply the observation of a certain movement which has been confirmed by a great many trained observers. Their many particular observations have been drawn together into one general scheme, and then this, which was supposed to be a reasonable explanation of the heavens, has been given the esteemed name of science. The phases of the moon, for instance, have entered into common knowledge, but that knowledge is derived merely from our sense of sight. Tell me, then, you who are so very knowledgeable in these matters and strive to be justly admired for your scientific expertise, just tell me what caused the order and the movement! How came the sun to give signals like a beacon fire to the whole world, and to appear to all eyes like the coryphaeus in a choral dance [hōsper chorou tinos koryphaios]? Why does the sun conceal all the stars with his brightness more effectively than some of the stars conceal others? It is a proven fact that while they reflect his brilliance or vie with it, he outshines them all, and does not even let it be known that they rose when he did. Fair 'as a bridegroom' is he, and swift and great 'as a giant' [Psalms 19:6]. I cannot restrain myself from extolling him in phrases drawn from my Scriptures, for no other source will do! So great is his power that from one end of the world to the other he envelops all other things with his heat and not a single thing can escape feeling it. He fills every eye with light and every incarnate creature with heat and warms without burning because his temperament is mild and his motion orderly. Presenting himself to all, to all equally he offers his embrace!

(*Oratio theologica* II xxix; Or 28.29)

So long a quotation may seem unnecessary for so brief a reference to the dance of the stars. Indeed, the simple question 'How came the sun ... ?' is all one needs to read of the passage to appreciate the simplicity of Gregory's image of the celestial dance and to grasp his elementary distinction between the astral chorus and the solar coryphaeus, which surely goes back to Stoic versions of the image in Hellenistic physics manuals like the *Peri kosmou* (see chapter 5, page 254). What surrounds the image, however, is a complicated argument designed to undermine the very basis of scientific and philosophical knowledge that supported the Hellenistic vision of cosmic order.

To penetrate this peculiar argument *against* design, that is, against elaborate theoretical paradigms of the universe which supposedly reveal the mathematical and causal structure of reality but which actually cloud the nature of things and distance the spectator from the spectacle, and to catch the Theologian in the daring act of uprooting the image of the dance from the academic context in which it had been embedded for a thousand years, and transferring it, pared down to its essential visual form, to an ecclesiastical universe where it would flourish for another thousand years as a figure of spiritual unity in which the faithful participated rather than a figure of speech by which the educated expressed their distinctive prejudices, one must read the whole quotation through. Only a long stretch of the Oration can reveal how and why the image survived Gregory's epistemological attack on its ancient foundations. Only a long stretch can convey a sense of the tide-turning gravity of his words and the persuasive pull of his faith, the full force of which he here turns on the non-Orthodox spectators scattered among the crowd in the Anastasis: the narrow-minded astronomer who sees no further than his diagrams and calculations; the absent-minded philosopher who loses sight of himself in his vain search for 'one general scheme' to explain the universe; the high-minded Hellenist who looks down on the simple truths of the faith because they are not expressed in the fancy jargon of the schools; and of course the muddle-headed Eunomian who compounds the errors of all the rest with heretical solutions to mysteries that cannot be conceived, let alone solved like puzzles and reduced to common knowledge, by the meddlesome human mind.

To spectators such as these, the educated 'you' whose intellectual pride was definitely of the wrong sort since it alienated them from the ranks of the faithful, the dance of the stars appeared awesomely complex: it tired their eyes, teased their brains, defied their collective expertise with an in-calculable number of revolutions, periods, approaches, retreats, settings, risings, and other 'lugismata.' How ironic that the spectacle so long cele-brated in their schools as the original stimulus for education should still puzzle the educated, and that their educators, their so-called experts, should try to measure the immeasurable without knowing how to measure the value of their own souls! And how Gregory revelled in the irony – even though (or perhaps because) he was as proud of his classical education as anyone in the Anastasis.

To the Orthodox Spectator, who was not one to ignore what lay about his feet or to suspend his thoughts in mid-air except when the Spirit moved him heavenwards, the dance of the stars looked ironically simple after the Cnossian dance at ground level. As everyone could see – and what could not be seen by everyone, regardless of intellectual training, was disregarded by the Orthodox Spectator – the stars turned with a single circular impulse; they followed the directions of a single leader; and when not hidden by his brilliance they, like him, displayed their orderly motions to the educated and uneducated alike. In contrast to Philo and the star-hymning Therapeu-tae, Gregory was not given to rapturous expressions of admiration for the celestial dance, because the sun and stars were of little interest to him in themselves. That their significance for him lay chiefly in their figurative relation to the society of the Heavenly Kingdom may be inferred from the recurrence of choral imagery in the beatific vision at the culmination of the ascent: even as the sun at this preliminary level is seen to outshine the chorus of the stars so the angelic chorus will be seen in the end to eclipse all the lights dancing in the firmament. As both a coryphaeus and a bridegroom, moreover, the sun illuminating the Orthodox Spectator prefigures Christ in his eschatological role as the leader of the Blessed and the spouse of Ecclesia.

Whenever Gregory spoke of the stars as living beings endowed with reason and responsive to the commands of a divine leader it was with the understanding that they were in fact inanimate fires created out of nothing on the Fourth Day to give light and heat to the earth, and since their choral life and vision and consciousness were to him no more than quaint pagan fancies, the stuff of sophistic whimsy, he took care to introduce the image of the astral dance into the Oration with the conditional qualifier 'hōsper' which meant 'like' with the force of 'as it were but not as it really is.' His vision of the heavens was as poetic in its own way as that of the Sophists, however, for he could not look at the sun and stars without recalling phrases from the Psalms which helped to order and define what he saw. Precise without being precious, vivid without being vulgar, the imagery of the Psalms was his rhetorical antidote to the fussy over-extended conceits of the Second Sophistic, and in the passage on the astral chorus we can see him marking his contemplative transition from the earthly to the celestial field of vision with a sudden change of style.

In a dramatic exclamation he declares that he has no choice but to submit to the change: 'I cannot restrain myself from extolling [the sun] in phrases drawn from my Scriptures, for no other source will do!' – by which he means that no other source will do as a stylistic model for a panegyric ostensibly addressed to Helios yet designed to proclaim the greater glory of God. Gregory's 'low' style (befitting lowly subjects like bees and spiders) ironically follows the rules of high-flown pagan oratory, while his 'high' style (befitting lofty subjects like stars and angels) echoes the humble 'koinē' of the Greek Scriptures.

The image of the dance survived this clash and inversion of styles, as it did the clash and inversion of cultures, not because it was deeply implanted in the classical consciousness of the Sophists but because it had roots of its own in the biblical consciousness of the Fathers through which much of its pagan significance could be absorbed without threatening the doctrinal core of Orthodoxy and without stunting or twisting the intellectual growth of the Church. While the ascent section of the Second Theological Oration may certainly be regarded as Gregory's negative reaction to Late Antique elaborations of the choreia topos, and by implication, to sophistic distortions and trivializations of the world-view that sustained the old paideia, it can also be read as his exuberantly positive response to the command in the third verse of the 149th Psalm which had once been addressed only to the Sons of Zion but which the Son of God now directed to all nations and natures: 'ainesatōsan to onoma autou en chorōi' – 'Let them praise His name in the dance!'

Helios was the name most often praised in the dance by the Platonists of Gregory's era, and in so far as Gregory was a Platonist (which was very far from the likes of Julian or Synesius or anyone else who ventured across the forbidden frontiers of Neoplatonic theology) he was inclined to regard the sun as the image of an intelligible archetype and to extol its illuminative and creative virtues in phrases drawn from the lecture of Timaeus. But we should expect him as the harshest of Julian's critics to resist even the slightest inclination to worship Helios as the cosmic incarnation of God. And resist it he does in the third stage of the ascent:

'The sun,' said someone alien to our faith, 'holds the same position in the world of the senses that God holds in the intelligible world.'[8] And what do you make of this if you have noted it? It is a statement worth considering, for the sun gives light to the eye and is the most beautiful of all things seen just as God gives light to the mind and is the most beautiful of all things known. But what imparted motion to the sun in the beginning? What always moves the sun without moving itself or ceasing to abide by its own principle of stability? What is it that turns the truly Unwearying One, the Life-Giver and Life-Sustainer, this planet which poets have celebrated with so many other epithets in their hymns and which never rests in his revolution or in his production of good deeds? How does he come to be the craftsman of day when he is above the earth, and of night when he is below it? Perhaps 'craftsman' is not the right term, but I cannot think of anything else to call him when I look at him! What causes the days and nights to grow longer and shorter and (if I may use a paradoxical expression) to be equal in their inequality? How came the sun to be the maker and divider of the seasons which come and go in a highly regular sequence and interweave themselves as in a choral dance [hōsper en chorōi symplekomenōn allēlais] and stand apart from each other according to the laws of Love and Good Order and merge with each other little by little and steal upon those near them just as night steals upon day so that we are not distressed by their sudden appearance?

(Oratio theologica II xxx; Or 28.30)

What he is attacking with this barrage of questions is not the old Platonic analogy between the sun and the Craftsman (which is worth a moment's consideration as a mere analogy) but the newfangled Iamblichan emphasis on the immanence of the Intellectual Sun in the sun of the senses and the consequent blurring of primary ontological distinctions between the Creator and creation. By meditating on the purely symbolic correspondences between the sun and the transcendent cause of its existence and motion, the Orthodox Spectator removes his thoughts from the multiplicity of the astral chorus, raises his mind from the Dedalian complexity of physical life to a high level of abstraction, and reaches a new vantage-point corresponding to the Stoic perspective of the whole where time is perceived as a divinely ordained pattern of cyclical changes.

At the Great Dividing-Line, the mystical threshold uncrossed and unrecognized by the Stoics, the Platonist in him joyfully shuts his eyes to the shapes and shadows of Becoming and waits for the reverse gravity of Being to lift his soul into eternity. The distance between the second and third stages in his ascent is intellectual then rather than spatial, for it represents a shift in perception from the minute particularities of life to their general cause and from the evanescent moment to the enduring round of the seasons. Gregory's vision of the dance of time is a rather more symbolic prospect of cosmic order – an image further removed from immediate visual experience – than either the Cnossian dance of terrestrial nature or the choral rounds of the stars. Though the effects of the seasonal dance may be clearly observed in nature the dancers themselves are simply temporal units abstracted from the flow of time and momentarily personified in a rhetorical conceit. Coming and going, interweaving and standing apart, approaching and merging, changing places in a predictable sequence – the variety of their motions is reminiscent of the diversified dance of the planets. But what they reveal to the Orthodox Spectator are the laws of Love and Good Order governing an ideally peaceful realm from which the Empedoclean principle of Strife and the Platonic principle of Difference (both associated with the planets) have been eliminated.

Is this realm the poetic universe or the Heavenly Kingdom? For a moment one might suppose it to be the former. Gregory's distinctly mythical view of the sun as the Maker and Divider of the Seasons, the Unwearying One, the Life-Sustainer whom poets have praised 'with so many other epithets in their hymns,' indicates that he was no stranger to the poetic universe envisioned by the mystical philologists and philosopher-poets of his era. He had heard the Sirens singing of it years ago when Basil was summoning him to the priesthood and Julian was falling under the spell of Neoplatonism. 'We suffered no harm from the devotees of the ancient gods,' he said of Basil and himself, recalling their reaction to the pagan revivalists in mid-century Athens (Or 43.21), 'for we had closed up our minds and fortified ourselves against their impious teaching.' Echoes of their hymns, glimmers of their world, still haunted him in his solitary hours when the poet within him – the private self destined to emerge triumphant in the decade after his embattled years as Patriarch – was struggling to invoke the Holy Spirit in the ruins of the Muses' temple. But the Orthodox Spectator, his public self, was not permitted to see or recognize the poetic universe because its heavenly spheres were too animistic and imaginary for a down-to-earth Christian to take seriously.

In the deep pool of his mythological recollections, images of the divine choruses hymned by the poets would occasionally surface, as the image of the Horae does in the passage just cited; but when such images flowed into the current of his theological meditations they invariably encountered resistance from his zealous will to suppress the errors of the polytheistic past. While the Horae sprang to life in the poetic universe as four loose-robed maidens dancing in the rites of Cytherea or by the portals of Helios, in the Orthodox universe they lost their female form, their divine nature, their erotic vivacity, and their tutelary function. Only the memory of their dance remained to enliven the Theologian's 'as-it-were' vision of the love-linked seasons in the Christian year.

The only realm in his universe governed exclusively by the laws of Love and Good Order was the Heavenly Kingdom, and he knew he would not behold its luminous bournes or the eternal dance within it (of which the seasonal round was a faint prefiguration) until the stars fell to earth and the sky vanished like a scroll that is rolled up. The Orthodox Spectator did not leap across the Great Dividing-Line like an impetuous Corybant. He waited patiently on this side of the threshold; humbly thanked God for the prophetic glimpses of Heaven vouchsafed him in the Bible; prayed fervently for illumination to come to his unworthy mind through the grace of the Holy Spirit; and only rarely, when the angels gave him an approving nod, dared to lift the veil of phenomena and peer into the holiest chamber of the universal tabernacle. 'What is that you say?' he whispered at the threshold, putting his hand to his ear to catch the imagined complaint of someone reluctant to take the final step,

Shall we stop at this point in the Oration and discuss nothing further than matter and visible things? Or since your orator knows that the tabernacle of Moses was a figure representing the whole cosmos, I mean the union of things 'visible and invisible' [Colossians 1:16], shall we draw aside the first veil and step beyond the world of the senses and leaning forward direct our gaze towards the holy things – towards the intelligible and supercelestial nature? But not even this nature can we see in an incorporeal way, though it is incorporeal. It is called – or is – fire and spirit. For it is said that God 'maketh his angels spirits' and 'his ministers a flaming fire' [Psalms 103:4], though the word 'maketh' may here mean that God sustains their existence with the Word that called them into being. An angel is said to be a spirit because of his intelligible nature and a fire because of his purifying nature –

though I am aware that fire and spirit are also suitable names for the First Nature. Compared with our nature, at any rate, that of the angels is incorporeal or as close to incorporeal as can be! You see how we are made dizzy by this subject and can go nowhere with it or only as far as this: to know that Angels and Archangels do exist, along with Thrones, Dominions, Princedoms, Virtues, Splendours, Ascensions, Intellectual Powers or Intelligences, and that they are pure unadulterated natures which do not move towards evil or are unmoved by it, and that they are always dancing in chorus around the First Cause [peri to prōton aition aei choreuousas]. Otherwise, how could we sing the praises of those who take their light from the source of purest illumination and shine with different intensities according to their nature and rank? They are so formed and modelled by the Primal Beauty that they have become secondary lights and can illuminate others by flooding them with Primal Light and communicating it to them. As the ministers of God's Will, empowered by their own strength and by that which is imparted to them, they travel throughout the universe and readily present themselves to everyone everywhere in their zeal for the ministry and through the agility of their nature. Some of them are assigned to one part of the earth or another, while others are appointed to various parts of the universe (as is known to Him who orders and disposes all things). They lead all things towards unity in accordance with the approving nod – a single signal given to all – of Him who created the universe. They praise the divine Munificence in their hymns. They contemplate Eternal Glory and do so eternally, not so that God may be glorified – for it is impossible to add anything to the plenitude of the Choragus who bestows his benefits on everyone else [tōi kai tois allois choragōi tōn kalōn] – but that there may never be an end to the blessings bestowed on their natures, which are first after God.

(*Oratio theologica* II xxxi; *Or* 28.31)

We have followed the Orthodox Spectator far enough in his ascent to know that he (like most of us) has no head for theological heights, and so it is not surprising that our down-to-earth spokesman for the unsophisticated man's view of the world should experience a certain dizziness when he tries to see the invisible dance of the angels 'in an incorporeal way' and to push his reluctant intellect and ours 'towards the intelligible and supercelestial nature.' After all, if the most highly educated, intellectually optimistic, and etherealminded of all the spectators in the old cosmic theatre – the Philonic Corybant – was unable to pass beyond the astral chorus without suffering an acute attack of contemplative vertigo, what hope can his unpretentious successor, the God-fearing Christian who sees intellectual pride at the root of intellectual optimism, have of making the same passage with a steady head and an undazzled eye? What can we expect but confusion and uncertainty from him when he takes his first tentative steps into the field of angelology – a field still largely unexplored in the late fourth century and not to be systematically charted until the turn of the sixth?

The expected happens in the passage, and then the unexpected. Instead of succumbing to the dizziness as did the Philonic Corybant when the torrent of supercelestial light blinded his intellectual eye and swept him back into temporal consciousness, the Orthodox Spectator miraculously recovers his mental balance and increases his mystical depth perception and consequently regains his rhetorical fluency and brings his oration to its prophetic conclusion just at the point where he thinks he 'can go nowhere with it or only as far as this.' And the 'this' proves to be quite far indeed. Piercing the heavenly glare with the unblinking eyes of faith, he discerns above the luminous flood not only the presence, ranks, functions, and unadulterated natures of the angels but also their revolutions around a fixed centre, the unique identity of that centre, the motivation for their eternal dance, and its relation to the dances in the Here and Now.

The moment of intellectual transcendence is marked by a change of style as dramatic as that which marked his rise from earth to the stars. Before the 'this' he signalled his confusion and uncertainty with questions addressed to himself and his coreligionists rather than his opponents, with obscure biblical phrases admitting of several interpretations, with hypothetical distinctions weakened by vague terminology, and with concessive clauses qualifying every major statement. After the 'this' comes a flood of unqualified assertions with but one question – 'Otherwise, how could we sing the praises of those who take their light from the source ... ?' – which expresses no new theological query but rather justifies the orator's new-found assertiveness.

The effect of this shift from argument to affirmation is to suggest that the orator is suddenly illuminated by the very spirits he struggles to describe, and that for a few moments before words fail him and his oration abruptly ends he is able to participate directly in the spiritual dance around the Choragus of All Life and to convey his extraordinary perceptions to his flock in the Anastasis. Revealed to them is a series of nine angelic choruses, the number and nomenclature of which anticipate the Celestial Hierarchy of Pseudo-Dionysius.[9] Gregory drew all his angelic names with the exception of 'Ascensions' and 'Intelligences' from the Bible, but if one ignores his scriptural borrowings and considers only the last name in the series ('noas,' a synonym for 'noeras dynameis' or 'Intellectual Powers') one may be tempted to derive his image of the angelic dance from the Iamblichan vision of the chorus of Intellectual Gods encircling the Mystic Wellspring. 'It is impossible to share in the communal arrangements of things in the universe as an isolated individual,' Iamblichus is reported to have argued, 'for participation is possible only if one communes with the divinely harmonious chorus [syn tōi thespesiōi chorōi] of those who with one mind and purpose lead themselves up to the Divine.'¹⁰ Despite their different intensities as sources of illumination, Gregory's angels certainly act with one mind and purpose and like Iamblichan hypostases encircle the First Cause in their efforts to imitate the stability and grasp the unity of its transcendent essence. But there the similarity ends. Whereas the Intellectual Gods concerned themselves primarily with their own return to unity and chose to illuminate only a few élite intellectuals out of the whole human race, the nine angelic choruses as directed by their anti-élitist Creator 'lead all things towards unity' and communicate the 'single signal' of divine approval to every creature in the cosmos.

If Gregory had been open to Neoplatonic influences throughout his career and had not closed his mind to pagan theology at an early age (as he avowed), he would certainly have shuddered at the thought of immersing the Intellectual Powers in the material world and would never have admitted the least degree of corporeality to their nature. His angels shun evil, it is true, but they do not isolate themselves from the choruses whirled round in the abyss of matter. Indeed, as Gregory ventures to speculate, their miraculous ability to enter into the cosmic revolutions may be due to the presence of exceedingly pure and rarefied fire in their nature. Certain angels, moreover, were known to have done what no Iamblichan hypostasis would ever have dreamed of doing. They had broken away from the heavenly dance in open rebellion against God and had moved towards evil by plunging through the river of light into what would eventually be the infernal core of the Fallen World. Though the shock of that first fall could not undermine the eternal foundations of Ecclesia or interrupt the perpetual concord of the angels who remained above, it would unsettle the children of Adam whenever they contemplated God's grandeur in the harmony of nature and realized that hidden in the mazes of the Dedalian dance was a horned monster, the Coryphaeus of the Damned, who was banished forever from the 'choros enarmonios.'

A Triptych of the Blessed Dance

The Second Theological Oration has ushered us into an ecclesiastical universe which to an educated audience in the late fourth century must have seemed rather old-fashioned. Its physical design, which conserves many ancient Platonic and Stoic elements without admitting any newfangled philosophical entities or astronomical systems, hardly differs from that of the harmonious cosmos envisioned by the Alexandrian Fathers of the third century, while its political design, which conspicuously lacks an exalted station between

God and Man reserved for the Christian Monarch, differs considerably from that of the emperor-centred world celebrated by Eusebius of Caesarea during Nazianzen's boyhood. Its spiritual design, however, is what most clearly reveals its anachronistic (or at least conservative) character: it is a world fortified by all the flaming ministers of God against mystical influences from the Neoplatonic Beyond.

Such influences could not be resisted for long by the Orthodox Church. In the Catholic West they had already found an entrance through the translations and theological writings of Marius Victorinus.[11] Soon they would be streaming through the eastern portal of the sun in the hymns of Synesius. Eventually they will pervade the whole angelic realm and penetrate the contemplative life of every participant in Ecclesia's choral rites. But for the present, with Nazianzen as our guide, we must 'fortify' our minds against Neoplatonic spirituality and enter into the choral consciousness of the Greek Fathers who taught the Cappadocians to see the dance in a distinctly Christian light. The Orthodox Spectator has introduced us to his broad and complicated field of vision with the ironic aim of narrowing our intellectual range and simplifying our perceptions so that we may learn to distrust all scientific measurements and philosophical explanations of nature and to accept on faith the validity of certain biblical and poetic images of the cosmic design: the tabernacle, the wedding, the labyrinth, the dance. Strange as it may seem, Gregory's viewpoint in the Second Theological Oration is the closest we shall come in this volume to that of a serious Skeptical Spectator.[12]

From the Fathers before him Gregory inherited three basic images of the dance of divine order: the 'koinē chorostasia' or communal dance of Creation; the 'choreia pneumatikē' or spiritual dance of Ecclesia; and the 'choreia akatalutos' or perpetual dance of Paradise. These sacred movements may be distinguished not only by their respective settings in the ecclesiastical universe but also by the degree of beatitude they impart to their participants, the first being the least exclusive and therefore the least beatific and the third the most exclusive and the most beatific. The first, moreover, was usually associated by the Greek Fathers with the creative and administrative activity of God the Father; the second with the soteriological and pedagogical mission of the Son as Logos, and when the Logos disappeared behind the Orthodox veil of transcendence, with the illuminative and anagogic role of the Holy Spirit; and the third with the mystical union of the Trinity, the Unfallen Angels, the Martyrs, the Virgins, the Elders, and all other ranks of the Blessed in the uninterrupted festival of love celebrated by the Church Triumphant.

If our survey of the dances in the Second Theological Oration (which may be considered phases or submovements of the communal dance of Creation) has shown us anything, however, it is that sharp distinctions cannot be drawn between the spheres of the ecclesiastical universe, that each choral motion in it is either physically involved or figuratively implicated in every other choral motion. The intellectual participation of the angels in a timeless dance around the First Cause does not prevent their fiery forms from flying about the temporal world to sustain the dynamic order of the various choruses to which God has assigned them. The highest creatures are thus intimately involved in the mazy motions of the lowest. Furthermore, even as the labyrinthine dance of nature anticipates the choral service of praise conducted by the Church, so the spiritual dance of Ecclesia foreshadows the triumphant revels of the Saved after their release from the maze of the World. How then can we distinguish three general movements in the blessed dance without distorting Nazianzen's vision of its miraculous unity? Perhaps the simplest way to heed his Skeptical criticism of academic distinctions and still consider the three movements individually is to think of them as images on the separable yet closely fastened panels of a triptych.

Panel One: The Communal Dance of Creation

The image of the 'koinē chorostasia' can be found in its germinal form in the earliest extant Christian work outside the New Testament for which the name, occupation, and floruit of the author are firmly attested.[13] The author is Clement of Rome, St Peter's third successor as Pope (in office from 92 to 101 AD); the work, an epistle to the Corinthians contrasting the discord of their once flourishing church with the abundant concord of Creation:

The heavenly bodies moving to and fro under God's management submit to Him in peace. Day and night complete the periods allotted by Him without hindering each other. Sun and moon and the choruses of the stars [asterōn te choroi] unanimously obey His command and trace out the winding courses [exelissousin] set by Him without digressing from them at all. According to His will the fruitful earth at its proper seasons brings forth food in abundance for men and beasts and all the living things upon it, never disagreeing with Him or changing any of His decrees. The uncharted regions of the abysses and the indescribable realms of the lower world are held together by His ordinances. The sea in its boundless basin is gathered together by His handiwork into its collecting places, and without crossing the shores placed around it does just what He has commanded it to do, for He said: 'Thus far shalt thou come, and thy waves shall be broken within thee' [Job 38:11]. The ocean, impassible to man, and the worlds beyond it, are ruled by the same decrees of the Master. The seasons of spring, summer, autumn, and winter give way to each other in peaceful succession. The winds in their various quarters discharge their public service at the proper time without conflict.

The everlasting wellsprings, created for enjoyment and health, nurse mankind
at their breasts and sustain human life without fail. The tiniest living creatures
meet together to cooperate in harmony and peace.

(*First Epistle* xx. 1–10)

Though it was written about three hundred years before Nazianzen flooded
the Anastasis with his words, this terse account of the evidence of God's
universal rule may be read as a faithful summary of the Argument by Design
(minus the Skeptical argument against design) presented in the Second Theological Oration. After Gregory's lavish periods Clement's prose will certainly seem plain, halting, ingenuously awkward. It does not writhe with
'lugismata.' Still, his description of cosmic order is full of classical echoes
– both poetic and philosophical – which betray his Hellenistic education
and also anticipate the trend towards rhetorical sophistication in Greek
patristic literature that would reach its peak in the late fourth and early fifth
centuries.

Why did Clement choose the rare poetic verb 'exelissousin' to denote the
winding dance of the stars? Perhaps the Euripidean vision of a divinely
ordered realm 'where choruses of Nereids trace out their beautiful winding
courses [exelissousin] with their feet' (*Trojan Women* 1–3) had impressed
itself upon his memory before his conversion.[14] Certainly the Stoic vision
of the cosmic chorus had. Whether we follow Clement's contemplative route
from stars to insects or Gregory's from insects to stars, we end up with the
same panoramic view of temporal order from the Stoic perspective of the
whole.

The old scene of the seasons yielding to each other 'in peaceful succession'
so that all living things might perform their public service at the appointed
time in the chorus of the cosmic state found its way into the 'koinē chorostasia' very early because it implied an all-encompassing order governed
by a succession of peace-loving rulers ordained by God – a paradigmatic
order for the Church throughout the patristic period. 'Consider the works
of God, o Man!' advised Theophilus, the sixth bishop of Antioch, in an
apology for Christianity written around 180 AD,

Consider the timely succession of the seasons and the changes in the atmo-
sphere; the orderly course of the elements; the well-regulated procession of
days and nights and months and years; the diversified beauty of seeds and
plants and fruits; the highly diverse race of quadrupeds and birds and reptiles
and fishes of both fresh and salt water; the instinct inherent in living creatures
to produce and nourish offspring for the benefit of Man rather than them-
selves; the providence displayed by God in preparing nourishment for all
fleshly things; His requirement that all things be subordinate to Man; the

continual flowing of springs and freshwater streams and rivers; the seasonable
supply [epichorēgian] of dew and rains and storms; the highly elaborate
movement of the heavens; the rising of the Morning Star announcing the
approach of the great luminary; the conjunction of the Pleiades and Orion;
Arcturus and the choral dance of the other stars circling around the firmament
[tēn loipōn astrōn choreian genomenēn en tōi kyklōi tou ouranou] to each of
which the highly complex wisdom of God has given a name of its own.

(Epistle to Autolycus 1.6)

There is nothing in this exhortation that would have offended the ears of
Theophilus' Stoic emperor, Marcus Aurelius. Viewed from the Porch or
from the Church the physical world displayed the same harmonious disposition of parts, the same highly elaborate movement reflecting the highly
complex wisdom of God, and the same providential subordination of all
creatures great and small to Man. In the universe of the Fathers, however,
the peacefulness of the old cosmic spectacle was usually offset by scenes of
ecclesiastical dissension and discord – the rebellion of the Corinthian laity
against their presbyters in Clement's era, the controversy over emperor-
worship in Theophilus', the clash between Arian and Orthodox factions in
Gregory's – scenes which spoiled the choral unity of Creation for each new
generation of Christian spectators and effectively shattered the grand Stoic
illusion that natural order was sufficient in itself to pacify the inveterately
sinful and rebellious nature of the human race.

Though the Church in its long struggle to clarify the tenets of Orthodoxy
systematically denounced all sects that held the physical world in total contempt or denied the existence of a rational and benevolent Creator, its
intellectual leaders in the East were sufficiently 'Platonized' by the early
third century to regard the temporal sphere of the ecclesiastical universe as
by no means the best of all possible worlds. Nature had fallen with Adam,
many believed, and now it was the World of the Flesh and the Devil. When
such beliefs were combined with the Platonic doctrine that the cosmos was
a mere image of a supremely beautiful and luminous archetype the resulting
world-view was inevitably tinged with contempt or darkened by guilt. In
homiletic and polemical literature directed to a popular audience, as we shall
see, the Greek Fathers often used the image of the dance to depict a fleshly
and demonic world reeling in opposition to Ecclesia and away from God –
a world almost as vile, certainly as violent, as the dark offspring of the
Gnostic Demiurge. In dogmatic treatises and scholarly commentaries on the
Bible, however, they generally agreed among themselves that Creation remained essentially beautiful and good after the Fall because the Choragus
of All Life continued to shower it with His blessings.

Origen, the most influential Christian Platonist in the early Church, envisioned the heavens as a chorus of rational creatures responsive both to God's will and to Man's in his widely read treatise on prayer dating from the years 233–4:

Just as we have said that God makes use of the free will of every man on earth, purposefully arranging it to fit in with earthly needs, so we may suppose that through the free will of the sun and moon and stars – a will which is united, firm, steady, and wise – He has arranged 'the whole order of the heavens' [Deuteronomy 4:19] and the revolving motion of the stars so that these are harmonious with the universe as a whole. And if I do not pray in vain when my prayers concern the free will of another man, so my prayers will be much more likely to succeed when they depend on the free will of the stars, for the stars are dancing in the heavens for the preservation of the universe [en ouranōi sōtērios tōi panti choreuontōn asterōn].

(*On Prayer* VII)

Though the legislators of Orthodoxy were to reject many of Origen's conspicuous borrowings from Greek philosophy, including his doctrine that the stars were animate free-willed guardians of cosmic order (like the Platonic celestial gods) and his notorious theory that the present cosmos would disappear in a fiery restoration of all things to their original state (as in the Stoic World-Conflagration), the choral consciousness he shared with the Platonists and Stoics and strove to 'Christianize' in his enormous literary output was to endure long after his cosmological theories fell under suspicion.

'How can one believe,' asked Dionysius the Great, Origen's pupil and second successor as head of the catechetical school of Alexandria from 248 to 265,

that the wholly harmonious choral dance of the heavens [tēn panarmonion tōn ouraniōn choreian] is accompanied by music issuing from discordant and untuned instruments?

(apud Eusebium, *Praeparatio evangelica* XIV.25)

It was a question he fired at the Epicurean Atomists, the most deluded of the Greek dogma-mongers in the opinion of Origen and his school. And it was a question the Christian Platonists would fire again – they could sound like fanatic Pythagoreans when provoked – at the Mithraists, the Manichees, and any other sect that spurned their cherished images of world-harmony. The image of the astral dance survived even in apologetical works designed to expose the pernicious errors and destroy the credibility of Pythagoreanism, Platonism, and Stoicism, the three Greek schools of thought that had sustained the vision of the choral cosmos throughout the critical Hellenistic era.

As Eusebius of Caesarea, a pupil of a pupil of Origen, declared in the best known of such works, a pedagogical exposé of heathen doctrines composed sometime after 314 AD for new converts who wished to purge their minds of philosophical prejudices and read the Gospel with open eyes,

By God's word and law the sun itself and the moon and the choral dance of the other stars [tēn tōn loipōn asterōn choreian] fulfil their proper course in this revolving order.

(*Praeparatio evangelica* VII.10)

Eusebian in spirit is the Skepticism promoted by Nazianzen in the Second Theological Oration. It arouses faith rather than suspends judgment; it preserves ancient images of order while rejecting outmoded ideologies; and it results not in an arrogant contempt for all dogmas but in a humble readiness to learn the right beliefs, the beliefs nurtured by Ecclesia.

The Orthodox victory at Nicaea did not stop the stars from dancing in the ecclesiastical universe of the fourth century, but it did incline those Christian Platonists who accepted the transcendence of the Logos and the consubstantiality of the Son and still respected the authority of Origen to perceive the celestial spectacle as the result of a simple and ineluctable conformity rather than a complex psychological response of the stars to 'God's word and law.' The astral dance ceased to be a transfixing vision in itself and became an extension of Ecclesia's choral worship of the Creator. It faded into the conditional realm of 'hōsper.'

As graduates of the school of theology founded by Origen at Caesarea in Palestine after his exile from Egypt, the Cappadocian Fathers were well versed in the Christian Platonism of the Alexandrian school and consequently were more sympathetic to Origenist cosmology than the majority of their Orthodox contemporaries. Though critical of the great Alexandrian's tendency to interpret the Scriptures allegorically in order to justify his adventurous speculations, Basil echoed Origen constantly in his nine homilies on the Six Days of Creation delivered in 370 while he was still a presbyter. Nazianzen in turn echoed the sophistic phrasing of these celebrated commentaries on Genesis 1:1–26 in the Second Theological Oration, the final section of which affirms Basil's view that everything in Creation – even the vilest dragon in the abyss – participates in the virtuous ceremony of praise initiated by the angelic ministers encircling the First Cause. Or as Basil himself expressed it:

For the praise offered to God is completed not only by the water which is

above the firmament (having been raised to its eminent position by the virtues inherent in it) but also by the water which is under the firmament. As the Psalmist says: 'Praise the Lord from the earth, ye dragons, and all deeps' [Psalms 148:7]. Thus the abyss itself, which those who interpret the Scriptures allegorically have scornfully relegated to a mean destiny, has not been judged worthless by the Psalmist, since it has been invited into the communal choral dance instituted for Creation [eis tēn koinēn tēs ktiseōs chorostasian]: even it, according to the rational principles inherent in it, harmoniously completes the hymn to the Creator.

(*Hexaemeron* III.9)

Though the process of creation denoted by the verb 'ktizein' involved a series of divisions – the separation of light from darkness, abyss from firmament, ocean from dry land, male from female – the 'ktisis' or finished product of the Six Days' Labour was a unified institution of worship in which all creatures were stirred by a common impulse to praise the eternal Choragus. Basil probably derived the term 'ktisis' from the Greek New Testament where it signified Creation in the general sense of 'that which God had founded or established' (as in Mark 10:6), and since the divine establishment described in Genesis contained waters above and below the firmament and therefore appeared to extend all the way to the angelic realm – though whether it included the angels themselves as the verse '[God] Who maketh his angels spirits' (Psalms 104:4) seemed to imply remained a disputed question in Cappadocian cosmology[15] – the 'ktisis' encompassed or, its boundaries being fluid, engulfed the material 'kosmos' of the Greek philosophers by uniting the swift current of time with the placid oceanic expanses of eternity. Below the firmament the tides of mutability flowed relentlessly and dragons lurked, remorseless, hideous, yet blessed even in their dark life with traces of the Creator's rationality, as Origen had taught.[16] To deny these creatures a role in the ceremony of divine adoration (which was what the exegetes of Origen's school who preferred subtle allegorical readings of the Bible to the straightforward literal interpretation favoured by Basil were inclined to do because they identified the dragons in the deeps with the demons in Hell) was to ignore the full meaning of 'ktisis' and to slide recklessly towards a Gnostic conception of 'kosmos.'

Hence the emphasis in Basil's phrase 'koinē chorostasia' must fall on the adjective 'koinē.' If the Orthodox were to accept God's own judgment that Creation was good in all its parts and to reject the erroneous Gnostic opinion that only the highest parts of it declared the glory of God, then they had to invite all the works of the Lord into their choral dance so that it might truly be a 'shared' or 'communal' act of worship. A sense of community and common purpose is also implicit in the noun 'chorostasia', which denoted not only the public performance of a choral dance but also the institution of choruses as prescribed by long-established social custom. Basil's God assumed the role of a city-founder who had promoted social and religious unity among his people by calling upon them to serve in a legislative assembly which also functioned as a festive chorus. (The noun 'ecclēsia' originally signified 'an assembly of citizens summoned by a town-crier.') At least part of that which God had founded would stand forever, Basil implied, just as a chorus was left standing at the end of its appointed performances and would continue as a social organization to praise the munificence of its choragus. Perhaps he chose the rare poetic compound 'chorostasia' to emphasize the peculiar character of the 'ktisis' as an ecclesiastical institution – an order simultaneously static and dynamic, spiritual and physical, eternal and temporal – which the common philosophical term 'choreia' could not fully express because of its age-old association with the primarily dynamic, physical, and temporal order of the 'kosmos.'[17]

Whereas Philo had viewed the Mosaic tabernacle as an image of the cosmos, the Cappadocian Fathers reversed image and archetype by perceiving the cosmos as a reflection of the revivifying order of Ecclesia. They recreated Creation, as it were, in the image of their reviving Church. The extent to which their cosmos became an ecclesiastical institution, a vast annex to the sacred assembly instituted by Christ, can be sensed in the opening lines of Nazianzen's celebrated description of the delights of springtime:

See how beautiful is all that meets our eyes! The Queen of Seasons leads her festive procession for the Queen of Days and presents her with the gift of all her most beautiful and delightful possessions! Now is the firmament radiant; now is the sun higher up in the sky and more golden in hue; now is the orb of the moon more luminous and the chorus of the stars more pure [asterōn choros katharōteros]. Now do the billows make peace with the shores, the clouds with the sun, the winds with the air, the earth with the plants, and the plants with our eyes. Now do the wellsprings flow more limpidly; now do the rivers, freed from winter's bonds, flow more abundantly!

(*Or* 44.10)

The Queen of Days to which the Queen of Seasons pays homage is of course Easter, and it was on the Sunday before Easter in April of 383 (almost two years after his stormy departure from Constantinople) that Nazianzen celebrated the renewal of his world and the resurrection of his private self in this jubilant oration – the last he is known to have delivered in public. The old chorus of the stars reappears in this sophistic ode to the newness, the freshness, the pureness of Christian peace; but it is not 'katharōteros' – 'more clear' in a visual sense, 'more open' in a moral sense, 'more pure' in a religious sense – than it was in the days when stars were dancers tricked out like gods in the cosmic theatre of the Platonists or torch-bearers following Zeus along the winding roads of the Stoic world-city. The winter of paganism and persecution is over. With the coming of Easter the stars are transformed into a choir of noble celebrants processing with their royal conductress before the eyes of Ecclesia's peace-loving populace. Pagan onlookers, be not mistaken: the festival of Easter might seem to be simply a Christian version of the vernal fertility rites celebrated in the temple of Demeter or Rhea or Dionysus, but in the eyes of the Orthodox Spectator it was not a celebration of spring. Spring was a celebration of it.

The Cappadocian vision of the communal jubilation of the world-chorus did not fade from the first panel of our triptych when Nazianzen retired from public life into the semi-monastic seclusion of his final years. It was sustained and enlarged in the fifth century for instance by Theodoret of Cyrus (d c 466), who interpreted the canticle 'O all ye works of the Lord, bless ye the Lord!' as the rousing accompaniment to a dance which did not calm the billowing waves and disperse the stormclouds like the mystic procession of the Queen of Days but included even the violent movements of sublunary nature in the vibrant service of adoration conducted by the angels:

'O angels of the Lord,' they say, 'bless ye the Lord: praise Him and magnify Him forever!' And lest I should extend my discourse indefinitely by interpreting each verse, suffice it to say that they call into the choral dance [eis tēn choreian] Heaven and the waters above the firmament and those Powers which circle around the Divine Throne. They also summon the sun and the moon and the other stars, and not only heavenly things but everything that comes to be in the air, thunderstorms, and dew, and winds, and after these, the opposing qualities of freezing coldness and fiery heat. ...

(In visiones Danielis III vs 58–73)

The image of the world-chorus survived the tempests in the intellectual life of the fourth century, as we have noted, because it was deeply rooted in the biblical consciousness of the Fathers. Theodoret here exposes one of its non-classical roots: an apocryphal addition to the Book of Daniel known as 'The Song of the Three Young Men' (composed probably in Hebrew in the second or first century BC) which the early Church assumed to be the hymn sung by Shadrack, Meshach, and Abednego during their imprisonment in the fiery furnace. According to Theodoret, Nebuchadnezzar was enraged to see Daniel's fellow captives 'dancing' – 'choreuontes' – in the midst of the flames while they were singing the hymn.

Though no mention is made of choral dancing in the Greek translation of it cited by Theodoret, this canticle, more than any other shared by the Eastern and the Western Churches, deserves to be considered the official anthem of the 'koinē chorostasia.' Its exultant refrain 'Praise Him and magnify Him forever!' was no doubt echoing in Basil's mind when he alluded in his third hexemeral oration to 'the hymn to the Creator' harmoniously completed by the dragons and all deeps. Its indefinitely extendible series of verses, each directed to a different section of the chorus of Creation, assured Theodoret that the waters above the firmament acted as a medium through which the inexhaustible energy of angelic adoration was transmitted to the elemental world, and that the heavens by transforming this energy into the cyclical processes of nature united the Here and Now with the Beyond and Always, and that the waters below the firmament were therefore swept through the air and sprinkled upon the earth and pushed with the tides in rhythm with the dance of the spiritual powers closest to God.

Like Basil and Nazianzen, Theodoret did not hesitate to mix classical and biblical images of world-harmony in his exhortations to the unconverted. But once a convert had purged his mind of the religious and philosophical errors of the Greeks and was ready to participate in the chorus of true believers, he was warned by the Bishop of Cyrus that a great gulf still separated his soul from the innocent joys of Paradise forfeited by Adam at the Fall. While the song of Shadrack, Meshach, and Abednego might move the whole world to dance before the Divine Throne, it did not restore the original harmony of Heaven and Eden. Man and the angels would not be closely united in what Theodoret called 'hē koinē choreia' – 'the shared choral dance'[18] – until Ecclesia reached the end of her earthly trials and escaped with her undaunted chorus from what the cosmos must ultimately become, a fiery furnace.

Panel Two: The Spiritual Dance of Ecclesia

A description of the spectacular beginning of the Church's 'pneumatikē choreia,' the second movement in the blessed dance, may be found in Ignatius of Antioch's prophetic account of the cosmic and intellectual consequences of the appearance of the Star of Bethlehem:

Hidden from the Ruler of this Age [that is, Satan] were the virginity of Mary, her giving birth, and also the death of the Lord: three mysteries wrought in the silence of God which were proclaimed with a cry. How then was He manifested to the ages? A star shone in heaven before all the stars, and its light was ineffable, and its newness caused amazement, and all the other stars along with the sun and the moon became a chorus for this star [choros egeneto tōi asteri], and it far surpassed them all in its light. And there was

*confusion concerning the origin of this new thing, for it was unlike anything
else in the sky. Hence all magic was abolished and every bond of wickedness
obliterated. Ignorance was overthrown and the old kingdom utterly destroyed, for God revealed Himself as Man to the end that Man should
experience the newness of eternal life. That which God had prepared received
its beginning. Henceforth all things were thrown into a commotion, for the
dissolution of death was being planned.*

(*Epistle to the Ephesians* XIX. 1–3)

Herald of the ecclesiastical order that would eventually replace the old kingdom of Satan and the old empire of Rome, Ignatius wrote his epistle to the
Christian community in Ephesus sometime during the reign of Trajan (98–
117 AD) while he was stopping over in Smyrna on his way from Antioch to
Rome – a journey of triumph and joyous expectation for him for he knew
it would end in the tumult of the arena, the roaring of wild beasts, agony,
martyrdom, and everlasting life. As a witness to the faith he was prepared
to give up his life in the world-shattering 'confusion' and 'commotion'
destined to follow the unexpected birth of the new order; but as a bishop,
the second in Antioch's history, he was determined to resist the political
and moral disorder of his era by encouraging the scattered clergy who would
survive the persecutions to achieve doctrinal agreement among themselves
and to teach their flocks obedience to episcopal authority lest the institution
they were rapidly, urgently building in Christ's name, the assembly they
were forming to save their souls from the ruin of 'this Age,' should fall
apart before it had a chance to restore the harmony between God and Man
lost in the Garden.

The Star of Bethlehem was a cosmic manifestation of the pre-eminence
of Christ among men, a prophetic image of the light of divine wisdom the
Church would shed upon the darkness of human ignorance, and a mystic
symbol of 'the newness of eternal life' promised to all who heard the infant
crying in the silence of God and responded to it first with awe and then
with love. ('Run with the Star!' Nazianzen would cry out in the Anastasis
on Christmas day in 379, ' ... Praise God with the shepherds! Sing hymns
with the angels! Dance with the archangels!'[19]) Before the shepherds and the
rest of mankind could respond to the New Star, Ignatius attested, the sun
and the moon and all the old stars greeted its ineffable light with joyful
amazement and formed a chorus for it or in association with it or belonging
to it – the dative phrase 'tōi asteri' is ambiguous – which effectively brought
the old cosmic dance to an end. The instant the astral chorus was thus
reformed and refocused around its new centre of spiritual concord and
creative energy the old 'magic' of the Age of Satan (by which Ignatius meant
the lore of the Hellenistic astrologers, though possibly also the science of

Timaeus and his successors) was shown to be false or useless because it could not explain the transcendent cause of the miracle or predict its historical consequences.

In the subordination of the greater and lesser heavenly bodies to the New Star Ignatius perceived a dynamic model for the organization of Ecclesia under episcopal rule. The bishop, as Christ's representative, must act as a Star of Bethlehem in the little world of his community; he must be its unifying force and its ceremonial focus. The greater lights within his sphere, his presbyters and deacons, must gather round him in turn and defer to his authority at all times, so that the lesser lights, the congregation at large, may participate in the peaceful order arising from the single-mindedness of their leaders and form an obedient chorus before the altar of the Lord. 'It is therefore fitting,' Ignatius advised the Ephesians,

that you join together in accordance with the will of the bishop, as indeed you do. For your deservedly famous presbytery, worthy of God, is linked together with the bishop like strings fastened to a cithara; consequently in your single-mindedness and harmonious love Jesus Christ is being sung. Now then all of you, become a chorus [choros ginesthai] so that you may be harmonious in your oneness of mind and purpose and catch the tone of God in unity and sing with one voice through Jesus Christ to the Father. Do this so that He might hear you and also recognize you, through your good deeds, as members of His Son. It is therefore advantageous for you to be in blameless unity so that you may always participate in God.

(*Epistle to the Ephesians* IV. 1–2)

To the Christians of Rome he gave the same advice in the form of an entreaty:

Grant me nothing more than that I may be poured out as a libation to God while there is still an altar ready, in order that you may become a chorus in love [en agapēi choros genomenoi] and sing to the Father in Christ Jesus that God has deemed the bishop of Syria worthy to be found where the sun sets [that is, in Rome] after he was fetched from where the sun rises [that is, in Syria]. It is good for me to face God during my sunset from the World, so that I may rise to Him.

(*Epistle to the Romans* II.2)

Ignatius' vision of the ecclesiastical chorus as a manifestation of 'homonoia' or 'oneness of mind and purpose' analogous to that of the astral chorus recalls contemporary Stoic visions of the choral participation of Man in the nature of God or in the God of Nature – it amounted to much the same thing in Stoic terms – which entailed the peaceful submission of a multitude to the will of a single choragus and the performance of good deeds beneficial to the universal 'economy' (cf Epictetus on the chorus of Man, chapter 4, pages 171–2). Few Stoics would have hesitated to argue that the smooth functioning of the world-chorus occasionally depended on heroic acts of self-denial or self-destruction; but none would have believed, as Ignatius fervently did, that the genesis and ultimate significance of choral order within human society was dependent on humble acts of martyrdom such as his own, acts startlingly unimportant and unnecessary in the eyes of the World yet essential to Ecclesia's triumph over the World since they drew attention to Christ's martyrdom, demonstrated the insignificance of earthly life, and strengthened the faith of the whole Christian community.

The association of martyrdom with the formation of a religious chorus in which the order of the cosmos is symbolically implicated can be found in Jewish wisdom literature dating from the first century AD (see chapter 7, pages 394–5). Such literature is as likely a source for the choral imagery in the Ignatian epistles as the ethical discourses of the Stoics; much of it has an overtly Stoic cast, in fact, and can hardly be considered a distinct source in a philosophical sense. If Ignatius knew nothing of it, he was an exception among the Greek Fathers. (Nazianzen, for one, begins an oration in praise of Christian martyrdom by praising the fortitude of the Maccabean martyrs who danced and sang under torture like the youths in the fiery furnace.)[20] Whatever its source may have been, the choral imagery in the Ignatian epistles is distinctively Christian in its emphasis on the self-sacrificing, world-harmonizing love – 'agapē' – as the keynote in the New Song and hence the moving force behind the New Dance.

The primarily spiritual character of the dance of Ecclesia is attested by Hermas in the ninth parable of *The Shepherd*, an apocalyptic work dating from the first half of the second century. Hermas tells us that he was born a slave and sold at Rome to a virtuous woman named Rhoda, who must have played an important role in his conversion to Christianity for her spirit frequently appears in his visions and admonishes him to repent. Most of his visions take the form of allegories concerning the foundation of Ecclesia as an institution at once temporal and eternal in which penitents like Hermas are welcomed, absolved of sin, protected from the Devil, and eventually transformed into blessed spirits like Rhoda. Though *The Shepherd* was regarded as quasi-canonical by many of the ante-Nicene Fathers, including Clement of Alexandria and Origen, it was firmly set outside the Orthodox canon by Athanasius in the fourth century and all but forgotten thereafter.[21] (It was never widely read in the Western Church despite its Roman provenance and the translation of excerpts from it into Latin on two separate occasions.) Like the apocryphal Acts of John, which lies near it in the shadowy field of early Christian literature between the Orthodox mainstream and the hinterlands of darkest heresy, the apocalypse of Hermas is significant in the history of the choral consciousness of the West for the primitive clarity and simplicity of its imagery which foreshadows (without markedly influencing) the visions of the blessed dance elaborated by Ecclesia's greatest preachers and poets.

Hermas is the earliest Christian author known to have envisioned the blessed dance in relation to a tower and a garden. These three images are all rooted in the Old Testament (for example, the Garden of Eden in Genesis 2:8, the tower of the flock in Micah 4:8, and the pastoral dance of maidens in Judges 21:21), but they do not appear there in any symbolic combination. It took a poetic imagination of remarkable force to bring them together for the first time. Scanning the distant horizon, we can see what will happen to Hermas' nexus of symbols in Dante's allegorical vision of the star-maidens dancing in the earthly paradise at the summit of the 'turre' of Purgatory.[22]

In his ninth parable Hermas presents the bare nucleus of this vision without the rhetorical colouration and philosophical background which will deepen its cosmic significance in the homilies of the later patristic period and the allegories of the High Middle Ages. The setting of the parable, a paradisial landscape identified as Arcadia, is revealed to Hermas by the Angel of Repentance who appears to him in the appropriately Arcadian guise of a shepherd. From a mountain vantage-point he surveys a great plain (representing the Roman Empire or the World) in the midst of which a throng of men is busy gathering stones of various colours (the souls of the saintly and the sinful) to place upon a partially completed tower (the Church of Rome or Ecclesia in general). The incompleteness of the tower clearly suggests the imperfection of the Church as a human institution at any time in its history but particularly in the era of the Apostolic Fathers; it may also refer to the incompleteness of the Church in Heaven before the Blessed have risen from the dead and joined the angelic choirs in their dance around the Divine Throne. The ecclesiastical past, present, and future are strangely fused in the vision by the representation of Christ as a great white rock upon which the foundations of the tower were laid, as a powerful lord who owns the tower and periodically visits it to check the progress of its construction, and as a doorway through which the flock of the Blessed will eventually be admitted into the towering stronghold of Heaven.

Before this doorway which marks the Great Dividing-Line in Hermas' universe stand twelve beautiful virgins clothed in linen mantles. They draw Hermas into their liminal company, clothe him in the white vestments of the Saved, declare their love for him, and momentarily embarrass him by requesting that he sleep with them until their lord returns in the morning! Their forthright yet purely innocent gestures of love are the prelude to a dance in which his shame is swiftly, mysteriously overcome:

And she who seemed to be foremost among them began to kiss and embrace me tenderly, while the other virgins when they saw her embrace me began to kiss me also and to lead me in a circle around the tower and to play with me. And like a child I began to play with them. Some of them were circling in chorus [echoreuon], others were dancing solos [orchounto], and still others were chanting [ēidon]. In silence I walked with them round the tower and was joyful in their company.

(The Shepherd, Sim IX.xi.4–5)

The significance of this dance on the threshold and around the base of the tower is not immediately clear. A vaguely cosmic pattern may be discerned in the performance of a choral round by some dancers (representing the fixed stars?) and of solo dances by others (representing the planets?) to the chant of a third group (echoing the music of the spheres?). This Therapeutae-like design may be simply a trick of translation, however, for the visual distinction between the astral chorus and the planetary soloists rests entirely on a semantic differentiation of the verbs 'choreuein' and 'orcheisthai' which is purely hypothetical in this context. They are often synonymous. If the virgins are cosmic dancers in the old sense, why are the heavenly bodies not mentioned at this point in the parable? And why do the virgins direct their movement towards and around the tower – at dusk – when they should be communing with the Ogdoad in the dead of night or leaping up with Helios at the crack of dawn?

To seek an old cosmic pattern in this new dance is perhaps to wander off on the wrong track. We must turn back to the central point of reference in the allegory, the tower, for the meaning of the dance around it is surely bound up with the foundation of Ecclesia and the spiritual identity of the virgins (which Hermas reveals to us in IX.xii.1 and xv.1). The virgins are first said to represent the 'hagia pneumata' or 'holy spirits' of the Saved – the whole company of the faithful – though as a group of twelve they are numerologically related to the 144,000 male virgins who sing 'as it were a new song before the throne' and 'follow the Lamb whithersoever he goeth' (Revelation 14:3–4). In an apocalyptic context, then, their choral activity symbolizes the perfection of the sinless life of virginity – a life in which the shame of carnality is transmuted into the joy of spiritual rejuvenation and the search for erotic pleasure is abandoned in the service of divine adoration. Hermas no sooner observes the dance than he is drawn into it by the virgins. Their movement must therefore also signify the transformation of a pagan (literally 'a man from the countryside') into a believer and an innocent through the ritual purgation of sins, and more generally, the proselytizing mission of Ecclesia which will result in the expansion of Christ's followers from the original twelve disciples into the multitudes mentioned in Revelation.

The virgins are further identified as the 'dynameis' or 'powers' of the Son of God, that is to say the virtues exemplified and activated by Christ during his earthly ministry and now fostered by Ecclesia and sent out into the countryside of the World to lure its inhabitants back to God. Foremost among the Virtues in Hermas' vision – their number, sequence, and names will vary considerably in later patristic and medieval versions of the allegory – is appropriately Faith, the prime mover of converts and penitents; following her are Temperance, Power, Patience, Simplicity, Innocence, Holiness, Cheerfulness, Truth, Sagacity, Concord, and in last place, though the last shall indeed be first as Faith's affectionate gestures indicate, Love. These are not abstract ethical virtues, not passive qualities latent in an ideally dutiful and pious soul. Their embodiment as dancers clearly implies that they are the vital forces of reform and renewal, of constructive order as a religious imperative, mysteriously set in motion by the Lord of the tower and destined to sustain the throng of men who gather new stones for its walls. When Hermas joins the spiritual dance of Ecclesia by calling all the Virtues into play, he does not embrace the faith. Faith embraces him.

His participation in it seems to be a direct response to Christ's warning 'Except ye be converted, and become as little children, ye shall not enter into the kingdom of Heaven' (Matthew 18:3), for he notes how much 'like a child' he felt on first stepping into the holy chorus. The purging of adult anxieties through a return to the blissful security of childhood will remain a distinctively Christian theme in the allegory of the blessed dance. The Greek Fathers generally approve of 'dancing in the spirit' as an expression of the childlike innocence and joy of the faithful and disapprove of 'dancing in the body' as an inducement to lust and debauchery. The fourth-century Church, as we shall see, is unusual for having produced teachers and moralists willing to regard the dance in a classical light as an exercise in self-control and a rational conditioning for maturity. And even they – Basil and Nazianzen – are tentative about it. For the most part the early Church shows little inclination to accept the Athenian Stranger's view of the art of choral dancing as a progressive curtailment of the playful, unrestrained energies of infancy leading to the disciplined actions of responsible adulthood (*Laws* II 653d–c). For Hermas the return to youthful high spirits through the ritualized play of the Church is an essential stage in the procession of the faithful away from the Valley of the Shadow of Death towards the origin of all life and movement in the realm of perpetual spring – the heavenly Arcadia – that is promised only to those who become as little children before the towering might of the Father.

While the twelve dancers in the Gnostic round of Jesus were explicitly associated with the numerological principles governing the order of the zodiac and the Ogdoad, the twelve virgins in Ecclesia's chorus seem to be set apart from the material world even when they set foot in it and to be unaffected by destinal forces originating outside their stronghold. They are what Ignatius of Antioch urged the Romans to become, a chorus 'en agapēi,' and as such they know nothing of the Gnostic fear of darkness and alienation for their movements are inspired solely by the spontaneously unifying love of God for Man. The will of the lawless Serpent and the planetary Archons does not threaten the unity of the holy spirits who dance close to the tower – at least not in the sheltered pastoral world of Hermas.

By the end of the second century the Christian Arcadia was only a memory, its sheltered plain laid waste by conflicting Gnostic sects and intolerant Roman emperors. The vision of its virginal chorus did not fade, however, for as Ecclesia rose in intellectual stature by the addition of stones to its tower from the academic quarries of Athens and Alexandria its first great apologists, authors far more urban in outlook and philosophical in temper than Hermas, expanded the dance of 'ho pneumatikos kai hagios choros' – 'the spiritual and holy chorus' as Clement of Alexandria called the Church[23] – into a revolution encompassing the universe.

The Church's efforts to resist Hellenization while freely borrowing anything it could use from the ruins of classical culture produced no stranger mélange of Greek philosophy and Christian spirituality than the *Symposium* of Methodius of Olympus, an encomiastic treatise on virginity cast in the form of an ironic imitation of Plato's celebrated dialogue on the psychology and mystical consummation of erotic love. Written sometime before 311 (the year of Methodius' martyrdom), it is the only complete work of his to survive in its original Greek, and in it he altered the number of dancing virgins from an apostolic twelve to a Pythagorean ten and removed them from their intimate Arcadia to a spacious garden in a universe of Platonic forms and shadows. They form so harmonious a chorus 'en agapēi' that there is not a dissenting or licentious word spoken among them to remind us, except by severe contrast, of the competitive eloquence of the symposiasts at the house of Agathon. Eschewing dialectic, they calmly assert that their kind of love has replaced Platonic Eros as the dominant spiritual force drawing men and women away from the world of the senses towards the Good and the Beautiful and that the chastity lost by Adam at the Fall has been restored to mankind by the second Adam, Christ, and will be preserved forever by his virgin bride, Ecclesia.

The counterpart of Eryximachus at this exceedingly sober dinner-party is Arete (Virtue), who proposes that each of her companions deliver an enthusiastic speech on some aspect of their chosen life.[24] The sixth speaker, Agatha, proves that she is indeed a 'good woman' by delighting the company with a description of the rewards of virginity awaiting them in Heaven where they will all participate in a mystic dance of love at Ecclesia's wedding — a movement far removed from the 'choroi' led by Eros in Agathon's vision of the concordant society of gods and men (Plato's *Symposium* 197d). The only corcordant society Agatha envisions is the chorus of the Church Triumphant under the leadership of the Logos:

Behold, o beautiful virgins, the sacred rites of our mysteries and the mystic ceremonies of those who have been initiated into virginity! Consider the rewards of those who have striven purely for the sake of chastity! I am wedded to the Logos and accept from the Father a crown, riches, and the eternal gift of incorruptibility. I am crowned with the brilliant and unfading flowers of wisdom and forever take part in a triumphant procession. I dance with Christ the Judge in Heaven [synchoreuō brabeuonti tōi Christōi kat' ouranon] around the Kingdom that has no beginning and cannot be destroyed. Having become a torch-bearer in the innermost sanctuary I sing the New Song with the assembled host of the archangels and announce the new grace of Ecclesia.

(Symposium, Oration VI.V)

The association of crowns with choral dancing in this speech is purely circumstantial: the virgins wear crowns in Heaven because they happen to be brides, victresses, and initiates, and they dance in chorus because wedding feasts, victory celebrations, and initiation rites customarily call for dancing. It is a prophetic association, nevertheless, for the two images will come together again in the writings of the post-Nicene Fathers and be handed on to the Middle Ages as a richly significant emblem of ecclesiastical order. Though no formal relation between them is suggested in Agatha's speech – she does not say, for instance, that the virgins will dance in a crown-formation around the heavenly kingdom or will crown Christ by standing hand-in-hand around him – the symbolic significance of their crowns is hardly different from that of their chorus. Like the crown promised in Revelation 2:10 ('be thou faithful unto death, and I will give thee a crown of life'), Agatha's victory garland symbolizes eternal life, perfect faith, and the wisdom springing from her union with the Logos. Her wedding-dance, too, close as it is in spirit to the excitement of the torchlit processions in the pagan mysteries, represents a distinctively Christian participation in divine knowledge, mystic concord, and eternal life through 'the new grace of Ecclesia' – the grace enjoyed by all who have striven to be chaste in imitation of Christ but especially by those who have initiated themselves into the cult of virginity.

The composite image of the choral crown or coronal chorus (which Dante will draw from the tropes in the chanted portions of the Mass and from the hymns to the Saints and will transform into a comprehensive vision of the new grace of Ecclesia as celebrated by the stellar souls of the Wise in the

Heaven of the Sun) comes into existence during the patristic period, it appears, as a result of two symbolic weddings: first, the union of the crown and the chorus as symbols of Christian beatitude in the apocalyptic writings of the ante-Nicene Greek Fathers; and second, the linking of this double figure of eternal order with its cosmic correlative or temporal counterpart, the crown-chorus of the stars, in the literature of the post-Nicene Greek and Latin Fathers. The association of crowns, choruses, and stars we have seen long ago on the Shield of Achilles with its representation of 'all the constellations crowning heaven,' and beneath these, the chorus of garlanded youths and maidens circling on the Dedalian dance-floor. Perhaps Basil was thinking of the Shield when, commenting on Genesis 1:2 ('And the earth was without form and void') in his homily on the Second Day of Creation, he suggested that

we might also say the firmament too was formless and void, for it had not yet been brought to completion. Nor had it received the beautiful order appropriate to it, since neither the moon nor the sun illuminated it and the choruses of the stars had not yet crowned it [mēde tois chorois tōn astrōn katestemmenos].

(*Hexaemeron* II.1)

Isidore of Seville in the early seventh century will assert that the chorus led by Moses and his sister after the defeat of Pharaoh was formed in the image of a crown (Exodus 15:1–20) and that it was to commemorate their victory that Simon the high priest 'stood by the hearth of the altar with a crown of brothers around him' (Ecclesiasticus 50:12–13). Isidore will also trace the formation of the Christian choir to the Jewish custom of crowning the altar and deduce from this that the word 'chorus' must be derived from the Latin word 'corona' or 'crown' (*De ecclesiasticis officiis* I.iii). But we must leave the Latin Fathers for another volume, noting here only the biblical and Greek patristic roots of Isidore's etymological vision of the chorus of the Church crowning the altar of Christ's sacrifice in concord and charity.

To return to the Christian *Symposium*: though Methodius wrote his dialogue to serve in part as a refutation of Encratism and other third-century Gnostic heresies, his own severely ascetic theology is grounded in a contempt for life in the flesh no less intense or unyielding than that of the Encratites themselves, who were supposed to have abstained from wine, meat, and sex in order to separate their elect souls from the incontinence of the corporeal masses. Not surprisingly, his anti-Gnostic polemic is reminiscent at times of Plotinus' attacks on dualistic cosmology. Methodius may even have read Plotinus or had some acquaintance with the ideas of the early Neoplatonists – uncommon accomplishments for a Greek Father – though his response to their kind of Platonism would undoubtedly have been hostile. From his pen came Ecclesia's first refutation of the fifteen books of Porphyry's *Against the Christians*, which were probably composed after 301.[25] If the Christian *Symposium* was written or revised in the wake of his attack on Porphyry – which is at least chronologically possible – then we would have some grounds for considering his vision of the chorus 'en agapēi' at the wedding of Christ and Ecclesia as Ecclesia's answer to the Porphyrian vision of the Chorus of Immortal Eros at the apotheosis of Plotinus.

The Neoplatonic myth of Eros distinguished a celestial from a supercelestial god of desire but also presupposed a kinship between physical and spiritual love. The ecclesiastical order envisioned by Agatha and her fellow initiates in the sacred rites of virginity had no room for the debased Eros, the love of physical beauty, or for his meretricious mother, the Aphrodite who presided over the reproduction of all forms of life in the natural world. Their wicked impulses were to be suppressed at all cost. Hence, the revolutions of the physical cosmos through which the Neoplatonic Sage had to rise before his soul could join Apollo and the Muses in the Chorus of Immortal Eros did not impinge upon Agatha's vision of her participation with the Logos in the Chorus of Immortal Agape. If her Logos had been the Stoic principle of divine reason permeating the material world or the Philonic intermediary between God and Creation or the New Apollo whom Clement of Alexandria had hailed as the coryphaeus of the heavens – that is, an immanent Logos – then her initiation in his mystic wedding-dance would have united her with the stars, the tides, the thunderstorms, and everything else moving through the shadow-play of time.

It was not to a world of orderly change, however, but to the unchanging order of Heaven that her participation in the rites of virginity led her: even in the flesh she was able to commune through Ecclesia with the transcendent Logos who was with God and was God and shone in the darkness that comprehended him not. Temperance, as Hermas noted before Methodius, was second only to Faith in the virginal chorus of Ecclesia for participation in virginity before death required on the part of the initiate not only complete confidence in the redeeming power of the Logos but also total abstinence from sex in the night before the Lord's return and a zealous suppression of all other fleshly appetites in preparation for the spiritual feast in Heaven.

'Blessed is the one who has fasted all this time,' a prospective bride of Christ was told by her spiritual advisor in a treatise on virginity traditionally (though now no longer confidently) ascribed to St Athanasius,

for he will dwell in the heavenly Jerusalem and dance with the angels [meta angelōn choreusei] and repose with the prophets and apostles. I have written this work for you, beloved sister, dancer with Christ [choreutria Christou], for the edification of your soul.

(*De virginitate* 24–5)

Being a 'dancer with Christ' in the rigorously ascetic, vigorously contemplative, and originally anti-Hellenistic movement that gave rise to monasticism in the fourth-century Church was tantamount to removing oneself from the communal dance of Creation (or at least from that part of it which turned towards the World) in order to enjoy the ultimate repose of the Blessed before death and to participate in the purely spiritual revolutions of the angels without bodily interference. The post-Nicene Fathers never tired of warning the virgins and matrons in their flocks that if they chose to dance with anyone other than Christ in even a remotely worldly way – especially on the feast-days of the Martyrs, which seem to have been favourite occasions for outbursts of drunken revelry – their chances of remaining pure at heart, innocent of the pride of life, and fortified against lust of the eyes were seriously diminished. So too were their expectations of dancing in Heaven after death. The riches of the angelic kingdom, the gift of incorruptibility, the unfading flowers of wisdom – all could be lost for a few fleshly embraces in the heat of the dance.

If Athanasius had not brought the Egyptian monastic movement under episcopal control and defended it as an integral part of the communal life of Ecclesia, and if his spiritual successors, the Cappadocian Fathers, had not striven to reconcile monasticism with the urban Greek culture in which the chorus of Christ had grown demographically and intellectually during its first four centuries, the extreme otherworldliness of the early hermits and coenobites and anchoresses might have blasted the fragile growth of ecclesiastical unity in the Here and Now and exposed the Church to the charge of harbouring or becoming a 'pneumatikos choros' in the old reactionary Gnostic sense: a reclusive society so spiritual in character that it excluded the masses of carnal sinners who groped their way through life in the uncomprehending darkness.[26] What had become of Clement's New Dionysus? Where was the palpable presence of the Logos, the soul-stirring, earth-shaking liberator who had promised grace to all who danced to his pipe?

To offset the remoteness of the transcendent Logos of Orthodox theology (which made the masses, if not the darkness, even more uncomprehending than in Clement's day) and also to support the Orthodox view that every penitent soul in Christ's chorus was to some extent a participant in the spiritual dance experienced and comprehended by the hardy few who devoted themselves to the monastic life, Basil emphasized the immediacy of the impact of the 'Hagion Pneuma,' the Holy Spirit, on the inner life of Christians who have cleared their minds of material concerns and sinful desires through the exercise of ascetic virtues, and the importance of the prophetic and pedagogical role played by the Orthodox 'pneumatikoi' in Ecclesia's historical mission to spread grace to the world at large. In the following incandescent passage from his dogmatic treatise on the Holy Spirit (written around 375) he pictures the reception and diffusion of 'charismata' or 'spiritual gifts' as phases in a continuous process of mystical illumination occurring, appropriately, at the speed of light:

Just as limpid and diaphanous bodies when a ray of light strikes them become very brilliant and radiate from themselves another beam, so those souls who bear the Spirit, who have been illumined by the Spirit, become spiritual themselves and spread grace to others. The foreknowledge of future events, the comprehension of mysteries, the perception of hidden things, the understanding of divine favours, the participation in heavenly order, the choral dance with the angels [hē meta angelōn choreia], the joy without end, the permanent abode in God, the supreme desire of becoming divine – all these follow from this illumination.

(*De spiritu sancto* IX.23.20c)

An Orthodox contemplative grows 'very brilliant' not through his own academic efforts or ascetic practices – though these serve to make his soul 'diaphanous' so that it will be receptive to charismatic illumination – but through the informing and transforming light of the Spirit itself which alone has the power to divinize the chorus of Ecclesia, to draw it up out of the darkness of mortality and to infuse it with the joy of the winged dancers soaring throughout the Empyrean. His understanding of divine favours can never be called his own. It is only his to share. And sharing it was what Gregory of Nazianzus, the most brilliantly unoriginal thinker of his era, was doing when we came upon him in the Anastasis delivering his Second Theological Oration as a dramatic monologue in which a Sophist who begins to scoff at all who strive to perceive hidden things is suddenly struck by the ray of the Spirit and ends up discoursing on the sublimest mysteries of the faith with the glowing confidence of a saint.

Even in retirement, the darkness of the capital behind him, he would strive to share his perception of hidden things through his theological poems. His beam seems never brighter than when he is exhorting his soul to praise the source of its illumination and to join in poetic measures what his mind has divided into theological concepts:

Soul, why do you delay? Sing too about the glory of the Spirit
Lest you sever with words that which nature has not divided!
Let us tremble before the Great Spirit, God's equal, through
                                        whom I know God,
Who is God, rather, and who makes God present in the Here
                                        and Now:

Omnipotent donor of divine gifts, theme of the hymn sung in
the chaste choral dance!
[Pansthenes, aiolodōron, agnēs hymnēma choreiēs!]
(*Carmen theologica* III, 'On the Holy Spirit,' 1–5)

The contemplative experience of the Cappadocian Fathers was quite unlike that of the philosophical Bacchants in Plato's myths of illumination or in Philo's religious versions of those myths. Whereas Plato and Philo had imagined the soul of the ideal sage (Socrates or Moses) flying into the ether and whirling round with the astral chorus in order to gather strength for its independent leap out of temporal consciousness into the light of eternal certitude, Basil and Gregory regarded the Orthodox Seer's comprehension of cosmic order as a consequence – not a cause – of mystical enlightenment and his participation through Ecclesia in the heavenly choreia as a cause – not a consequence – of the divinely ordained advancement of paideia.

By the late fourth century Ecclesia's new paideia was old enough and well enough established (despite the heretics' efforts to undermine it with new-fangled doctrines and terminology) to require no new defence against the attacks of pagan intellectuals on its integrity and distinctiveness. The Cappadocian Fathers belonged to the first generation of conservative Christian teachers who could afford to cultivate a tolerant humanistic attitude towards classical literature without fearing the censure of Bible-thumping proselytizers and bigots within the Church or the repressive measures of Hellenic revivalists and would-be philosopher-kings outside it.[27] If any work in the Cappadocian corpus can be singled out as the birth-announcement and re-trospectively regarded as the manifesto of Christian humanism, it would have to be Basil's *Address to Young Men* – specifically his nephews in Caesarea, who were embarking on a literary education under pagan tutelage in the 370s, but it would still be exhorting young men in the age of Erasmus – *On How They Might Best Profit from the Study of Pagan Letters*. Basil's reconciliation of the old with the new (or once new) paideia is delicately worked out in a series of proportional value judgments based on the ancient Platonic subordination of the body to the soul:

Seeing that it is impossible for you now because of your youth to understand the depth of the meaning of the mysteries indicated in the Scriptures, we offer for the time being a preliminary training to the eye of the soul by means of other analogies – not wholly different from those just used to distinguish the relative values of the soul and the body – which will provide, as it were, shadows and reflections [that is, of the soul's everlasting life in Heaven]. In this we imitate those who practise military tactics by performing drills: after they have gained experience in the sports of hand-gesturing and dancing [en

*cheironomiais kai orchēsesi] they enjoy the advantages derived from these
sports in their contests on the battlefield. And so we too must realize that a
contest lies before us, the greatest of all contests, and that we must do all
that can be done and strive to the best of our ability in preparation for it,
and that we must associate with the poets and prose-writers and rhetoricians
and all other men from whom may be gained any future advantage for the
care of the soul.*

(*Address to Young Men* II.5–8)

How scandalous this declaration of allegiance to the Greek past would have
been to the Christian apologists of Methodius' and even Athanasius' generation
who had striven to dissociate the intellectual life of Ecclesia from the literary
culture of the Hellenistic schools! The mere mention of vulgar theatrical arts
like cheironomia and pantomimic dancing in connection with the mystical goals
of Christian education would have set their teeth on edge. Had such analogies
not appeared in dusty old Stoic treatises on the art of wisdom and the moral
ends of education? And had such arts not appeared on the curriculum of the
ancient Pythagoreans, according to that Syrian occultist of reviled memory,
Iamblichus? A subsequent remark in the same humanistic vein –

*Surely a musician would not be willing to agree that his lyre should not be
in tune, or a coryphaeus that his chorus should not sing with the utmost
harmony [chorou koryphaios mē hoti malista synaidonta ton choron echein]!
Then shall each individual be at odds with himself and display a life not at
all in accord with his words?*

(*Address to Young Men* VI.4–5)

– might even have taken Julian aback, had he been alive to read it, for Basil
has here introduced without the slightest qualm or qualification the Athenian
Stranger's analogy between choreia and paideia into his discussion of how
Ecclesia harmoniously forms the moral character of the young people placed
under her care.

Gregory of Nazianzus goes one step further than Basil by employing
pedagogical analogies of the same sort in arguments intended to *re*form the
mentality of adult Christians who have strayed from the teachings of the
true Church:

*Now suppose that we were to speak to one of them, advancing the following
argument gently and reasonably.*

'*Tell me, admirable sir, do you call dancing and flute-playing [to orcheisthai
to te aulein] something?*'

'*Arts, of course,*' *he would reply.*

'*And wisdom or being wise, which we would define as the knowledge of things divine and human – do you call that something?*'

He would grant that it was.

'*Do you believe that the arts of which I speak are preferable and superior to wisdom, or that wisdom greatly surpasses them?*'

'*Wisdom surpasses all these by far,*' *I know he would say, and up to this point his judgment is sound.*

'*Well now, dancing and flute-playing require systematic training and serious study [orchēseos men kai aulēseos esti didaskalia kai mathēsis]: to master them takes time, and continual effort, and much sweat of the brow, and sometimes the payment of fees, and the procuring of tutors, and long voyages from home, and many other things which must be done or endured in order to gain experience. But as for wisdom, which presides over all things and embraces all that is good and is the name God prefers above all his other titles – for He is called by many names – are we to suppose that it is so trifling an exercise, and so beaten a path, that we need but wish to be wise in order to be so? It would be the height of ignorance to suppose so!*'

But if we – or someone more learned and intelligent – were to say these things to them and try little by little to purge them of their error, it would be like sowing upon rocks and speaking into the ears of the deaf. They are so far from wisdom that they do not even perceive their own ignorance.

(Oratio 2.50)

In the disheartening conclusion of this imaginary dialogue with a heretic Gregory affirms with the voice of experience Basil's point that mastery of the dance of classical education is never an end in itself for a Christian humanist – however mentally and physically arduous and however personally rewarding he might find the training. With Ecclesia's temporal warfare and eternal reward always before his eyes, he must look back on his dance to the ancient music of Hellas as but a limbering of his soul for its lifelong struggle against the errors of the World, the prompting of the Flesh, and the wiliness of the Devil.

Every now and then a major battle was won in Ecclesia's war, praise God, and that was cause for celebration. Troops scattered on the plain would be called back to the tower. An army of sinners would become a chorus of saints before the virgins' doorway. Tired spirits would dance again with the Spirit. Trained as he was to survey the earthly battlefield with the dismissive glance of a Skeptic; inclined as he was to regard the outcome of his bitter contests in the fray (particularly his attacks on Arian ignorance) with Cynical scorn and despondence; driven as he was to give up the fight and retreat into poetic dreams of peace whenever the apparent futility of life in the body overcame his spirit – no sinner struggled with fiercer energy against his pagan training, inclinations, and drives, no saint celebrated Ecclesia's communal victories with wilder joy, than Nazianzen. Listen to his exultant voice calling out as 'from a conspicuous and lofty watch-tower' to the dispersed forces of the Church Militant after the defeat of Julian:

Already my speech leaps and presses forward to the celebration, and rejoices with those who have eyes to see, and summons to the spiritual dance [eis choreian pneumatikēn] all who devoted themselves to fasting and weeping and praying and who begged night and day for deliverance from the troubles that beset them and who found a fitting remedy for their ills in the hope that 'maketh not ashamed' [Romans 5:5]; and all who, having endured great agonies and struggles and having been struck by the many hard blows of this age, have become, as the Apostle says, 'a spectacle to the world, to angels, and to men' [1 Corinthians 4:9].

(*Oratio* 4.7)

The restoration of Christian political power in the East under the emperors Valens and Valentinian meant the return of free speech in educated Christian society, Gregory hoped, and it was the latter glorious possibility quite as much as the former triumphant fact that he chose to celebrate in his two invectives against the Apostate. That his first invective should surge forward with an impulsive spirit as if it had leapt freely from his lips, taken on a life of its own as a reveller, and raced ahead of him at the speed of sound into the 'choreia pneumatikē' would not have seemed strange to anyone who had borne in silence the insult of Julian's educational policy and its repressive consequences. To Gregory's intellectual peers this prosopopoeia would have been much more than a figure of speech. It would have been a free *act* of speech, a logos-leap towards the spiritual freedom of Heaven.

What confidence he here displays in the power of his dancing words to push the Church's disorganized forces forward to the Promised Land after their shattering experiences during the dismally regressive reign of the new Pharaoh! With Mosaic authority he assumes the role of convener and coryphaeus on the far shore of history's red sea. After calling into the dance the loyal Orthodox who have survived the crossing with him, he summons all who have given up paganism without fully accepting the doctrines of the true Church and all who simply stand in dismay and confusion 'around the stage and great theatre of this World' (*Or* 4.9). The odious pantomime of Julian's lascivious and impotent deities is over. The dismayed must regain hope. The confused must come to their senses. Ecclesia must be a united assembly once again and her chorus reformed for the festival. For the sake of ecclesiastical unity he even extends an invitation to a group of rebellious monks at Nazianzus with whom he had quarrelled over some obscure issue of local interest:

Would that our chorus included that company which in days gone by used to chant a hymn to God with us, a company which was neither deceitful nor ignoble but was once deemed worthy of a place at the right hand of God, and which, I trust, will in short time be thought worthy again of that same place! Some misfortune – I do not know exactly what – has caused them to alter their way of life suddenly, and to marshal themselves in opposition to us. And what astonishes me even more is that instead of responding to our common joy by coming out to meet us, they are keeping to themselves and performing a choral dance of their own. And this much, perhaps, they will permit me to say about it – that it is neither well-timed nor harmonious [idian histēsin ouk eurythmon tina tautēn choreian, oude enarmonion]. What sort of dance is this!

(*Oratio* 4.10)

While 'prior love' – 'hē prin agapē' – prompts him to welcome them back to the charitable chorus of Ecclesia, zeal compels him to speak out against their inopportune breach of discipline and to draw their attention to its disruptive effect on the ecclesiastical movement as a whole. Their schismatic choreia represents the sort of minor but exasperating dissension that Ecclesia has had to contend with since the days of the Apostles and will have to suppress on countless occasions before perfect harmony is restored to it on the Last Day. The monks deserve a scolding; but magnanimous faith, Nazianzen goes on to say, checks the harshness of his speech and sustains his hope that they will one day see the disorder in the rival order they have instituted within the Church. The 'pneumatikē choreia' was the one unifying movement within his world before which he could not stand as a Skeptical Spectator.

The same faith, however, cannot tolerate the presence of heretics, apostates, and other perfidious backsliders who bartered away their salvation for mercenary gain, court-favour, or political power during Julian's reign. They are all excluded from the dance 'by proclamation' (*Or* 4.11), though it deeply grieves the orator to pronounce the dread sentence of excommunication. Time and again he has tried to win them over to the company of the Spirit by the force of his words, but they remain insensible to their spiritual peril either because they fail to understand his arguments and prefer to rest in a passive state of ignorance, or worse, because they actively reject the Truth when it is presented to them and fight it by advancing the cause of diabolical sects like the Macedonianists and the Pneumatomachi who dare to deny the full Godhead of the Third Person. Their disordered thoughts pose a far more serious threat to the harmony of the ecclesiastical dance – which the Christian Platonist in Gregory regarded as an essentially intellectual movement, a return of like-minded and love-linked souls to the wellspring of unity – than the disorderly conduct of the schismatics. The proclamation of his first invective thus becomes a purgative as well as a unitive act of faith by anticipating the final exclusion of the heretics and the apostates from the perpetual dance of the Saved.

In his second invective against Julian (written shortly after the first in late 363 or early 364) Gregory further develops the theme of the 'pneumatikē choreia' by exhorting those whom he has not excluded from the triumph to contrast the elements of a pagan and a Christian festival:

Let us raise up hymns instead of drums; let us chant psalms instead of bawdy songs and melodies that twist and turn in a shameful manner (anti tōn aischrōn lugismata]; let us prefer the applause of thanksgiving and the pleasing sound of hands engaged in good works to the applause of the theatre; let us meditate together instead of laughing; let us reason soberly instead of getting drunk; let us behave in a dignified rather than lascivious manner. And if you must dance like a festival-goer and a devotee of revels, then dance [Ei kai orchēsasthai dei se, hōs panēgyristēn kai phileorton, orchēsai men]; but do not perform the dance of the immodest daughter of Herodias which resulted in the death of the Baptist. Rather, perform that which David danced when he stopped with the ark – a dance I take to be a mystical symbol of the many twists and turns in the course of one who moves nimbly and swiftly in a way pleasing to God.

(*Oratio* 5.35)

Thus are the musical and corporeal 'lugismata' of pagan revellers converted by Ecclesia into the smooth unbroken melodic line of psalmody accompanying the charitable acts and serene meditations of the faithful as they step smoothly and gracefully along the 'oft-turning course,' the 'polystrephos poreia,' of the worldly labyrinth. The ecclesiastical dance cannot be wholly spiritual in this world, Gregory ruefully admits, for Christians like anyone else are compelled to lead corruptible bodies along the winding ways of life.

Like Basil, who delivered a stern sermon rebuking certain women in his flock who had celebrated a holy day in a most unholy manner by 'tripping playfully about on their feet' (tois posin ama paizousai) and by 'laughing effusively to the maddening beat of the dance' (gelōti ekkechumenoi pros orchēsin ekmaneisai) and, worst of all, by 'staging choral dances in public in the shrines of the martyrs' (chorous systēsamenai: *In Ebriosos*, PG 31 col 445C), Gregory was reluctant to see any value in unabashedly physical expressions of Christian joy and quick to point out the doom awaiting licentious revellers. Their wanton laughter would change to lamentation on Judgment Day, he warned, for then, as the devils were dragging their souls down into the bottomless pit, they would find out too late what the Preacher had meant in Ecclesiastes 3:4. There was indeed 'a time to weep and a time to laugh, a time to mourn and a time to dance.' but the time for laughing and dancing was not now – not while the Orthodox Spectator could still see his body lurching and twisting and shaking with the palsy of sin and could envision it (as he mortified his flesh) laid low at last in the stiffness of death. Participation in the monastic movement within Ecclesia's spiritual dance had taught him that true revelry, revelry without macabre irony, was only for the soul and only for the Hereafter.

The Scriptures presented him with the image of at least one indisputably physical yet perfectly virtuous and acceptably religious 'orchēsis' which upset his simple opposition of the dances of the body and of the spirit: David's ecstatic performance before the ark. 'And as the ark of the Lord came into the city of David, Michal Saul's daughter looked through a window, and saw king David leaping and dancing before the Lord,' it was written in 2 Samuel 6:16, 'and she despised him in her heart.' Michal's fate – the Lord cursed her with sterility all the days of her life for refusing to participate in the triumphant spirit of the occasion and for publicly rebuking the king when he came to bless his household – was disquieting to the Orthodox Spectator because he too was inclined to look down on the dance as an improper mode of public worship and to despise in his heart anyone who bared his body (David had worn only a linen ephod in his dance) before the symbols of the Divine Presence. Ecclesia was not to be turned into an assembly of Bacchants under any circumstances! And yet, when the time came to celebrate her victories, how could the leaders of her chorus denounce the pre-Christian instinct to leap and dance before the Lord without getting caught at Michal's window?

Any number of purely allegorical interpretations of the episode could be invented to get around this problem, but with their anti-allegorical bias the Cappadocian Fathers were constrained to regard the dance of David as a divinely sanctioned image of the physical order of the Christian life and hence to qualify their puritanical opinion that all bodily dances were erotic preludes to death and damnation like the shameful 'lugismata' of Salome. Still, as exegetes and homilists, they did their best to downplay the physical aspects of David's dance by concentrating on the religious emotions behind it and on the apocalyptic triumph it foreshadowed and by encouraging imitations of it only in the domain of moral action and mystical contemplation. God forbid that Ecclesia's priests and deacons should take to leaping before their altars in the style of David when their congregations were out writing like the Damned before the tombs of the martyrs![28] Gregory of Nyssa, echoing Basil and Nazianzen, insisted that

dancing is simply an outward sign of the stretching or intensification of joy [hē orchēsis sēmainei tēn tēs euphrosynēs epitasin],

and therefore that

David was not behaving in a normal manner when he danced before the ark in triumph [orchēsasthai de ton Dabid teis kibōtou propompeuonta] after it had been recovered from foreigners. For the Scriptures say that as he struck his musical instrument he sang harmonious melodies and moved his feet in time with the rhythm and made public his inward disposition through the rhythmical motion of his body. Indeed, since man is composed of two parts (I mean a soul and a body), there are thus two corresponding sides of life. And this is indicated by the two activities – weeping and laughing – which arise within us. It would be good for those who bewail the life in the body – and many are the occasions for lamentation in this life – to prepare the harmonious dance for the soul [tēi psychēi paraskeuazein tēn enarmonion orchēsin].

(*In Ecclesiasten homilia* vi 709C–D)

Michal had seen only the outward show from her window – that is to say, from her narrow-minded, socially prescribed, rigidly moralistic viewpoint. Such a viewpoint was not that of the Cappadocian Fathers, who, for all their fulminations against the vices incited by dancing in a *pagan* manner, were still Platonic enough in outlook and Greek enough in temper to regard the outward show of certain bodily movements and poses – hands clapping in gratitude, feet stepping nimbly to the New Song, faces raised to Heaven – as signs of the Christian dancer's psychological harmony and intense spiritual joy. Byzantine miniaturists in the wake of the Cappadocians were to depict the 'two corresponding sides' of the living order of Ecclesia as a gracefully flowing, physical 'orchēsis' and a formally static, spiritual 'choros' in illustrations of King David's court (see figure 14). And now, having prepared ourselves by contemplating the harmony of the ecclesiastical chorus, let us make a David's leap into the third movement of the blessed dance.

Panel Three: The Perpetual Dance of Paradise

The association of dancing with happiness in the afterlife was so deeply rooted in the Mediterranean cultures from which the ecclesiastical culture of the Fathers sprang that no single poetic or philosophical or scriptural

Figure 14

Two accounts of David's dance before the ark appear in the Old Testament: 2 Samuel 6:12–15 and 1 Chronicles 15:16–29. The second is based on the first but adds Levites and choruses of singers to the King's entourage and cornets, cymbals, psalteries, and harps to the trumpets accompanying his procession. In the above illustration David is shown enthroned with Solomon by his side. A bust of Samuel appears in a medallion over his head. Flanking him in six wheel-like configurations are the 'choroi' of musicians and singers who entered Jerusalem with the ark, and below him, dressed in short tunics, are two women who commemorate his dance by skipping or leaping energetically and waving veils over their heads. The word 'orchēsis' which appears above the women and directly beneath David's footstool suggests that the two dynamic, unbounded figures represent the art of dancing (in general) or of ecstatic religious dancing (in particular) which is controlled and kept within strict bounds but is not suppressed by the harmony governing David's court. Their physical movements are visually and symbolically the lowest expressions of that harmony, which because of David's ancestral relation to Christ prefigures the harmony of Ecclesia. The miniature is from a ninth-century Constantinopolitan manuscript (*Vat Gr* 699, fol 63v) of the *Christian Topography* of Cosmas Indicopleustes, a work written in Alexandria between 547 and 549 AD. It is presumed to be based on an illustration of the same subject in the original sixth-century manuscript of this work.[29]

passage can be pointed to as the pre-eminent source of the patristic image of the dance of the Angels and the Blessed in Paradise. In the Book of Revelation one finds elders prostrating themselves before the Throne, angels flying through the heavens like shooting stars, celestial armies galloping by on white horses, virgins following the Lamb whithersoever He goeth, and multitudes gathering to thunder out Hallelujahs and to sing the New Song. Such active spirits ought to be dancing for joy, one feels, and the Greek Fathers felt so too. But nowhere in the Apocalypse does St John actually mention dancing or depict the society of the New Jerusalem as a chorus of leaping, skipping, circling, or marching revellers.

Nazianzen and his predecessors found support for their belief that the perpetual psalmody of the Saved must accompany a perpetual dance in certain prophetic remarks of Jesus such as Luke 6:23 ('Rejoice ye in that day, and leap for joy: for, behold, your reward is great in heaven') and in apocalyptic interpretations of such Old Testament verses as Exodus 15:20 ('And Miriam the prophetess, the sister of Aaron, took a timbrel in her hand; and all the women went out after her with timbrels and with dances') and Judges 21:21 ('And see, and behold, if the daughters of Shiloh come out to dance in dances, then come ye out of the vineyards') and Jeremiah 31:13 ('Then shall the virgin rejoice in the dance, both young men and old together'). No doubt Jewish apocryphal and exegetical literature also furnished the Fathers with hints of the apocalyptic dance. The following passage from Philo's treatise on the symbolic significance of the Cherubim guarding the gates of Eden after the Fall (Genesis 3:24) illustrates how visions of a perpetual angelic dance around the Father could have arisen from allegorical extensions of the Platonic image of the astral chorus:

Thus one of the Cherubim becomes the outermost sphere, the final heaven of all, the vault in which the fixed stars perform a truly uniform and divine choral dance [aplaneis theian hōs alēthōs choreian choreuousi] without ever departing from the order which the Father who created them arranged in the heavens; the other Cherub, moreover, is the sphere contained within it which the Father cut into seven circles similar to each other, each fitted with one of the planets.

(On the Cherubim VII.23)

Even to the Christian Platonists like Eusebius of Caesarea who had access to the Philonic corpus and were in sympathy with Philonic mysticism, however, this enigmatic and somewhat arbitrary association of the Cherubim with the heavenly dance would have seemed remote from the Church's prophetic vision of the festival in Paradise. For one thing Philo's visionary perspective here is not eschatological but cosmogonic and post-lapsarian, as it almost always is in his biblical commentaries, and for another his angels, unlike Eusebius' or Nazianzen's, do not actually participate in the divine revolutions so much as preside over them like tutelary genii who establish and maintain and in a vague sense become the eternal boundaries of the 'theia choreia.'

In the mid-first century (probably before 70 AD) an orthodox Jew of a markedly Stoic cast of mind associated choral dancing with the glory of martyrdom and the attainment of immortality in a philosophical treatise on the supremacy of Inspired Reason over the passions which was to be read with great interest by the Greek Fathers and which is certainly closer in spirit to their meditations on the harmony of the afterlife than to Philo's allegorical discussions of cosmic harmony. The treatise is not without flashes of sophistic eloquence. A gruesome inventory of ancient instruments of torture and a harrowing account of the tortures inflicted on seven Jewish youths who went to their deaths chanting and dancing like Shadrack, Meshach, and Abednego lead up to this rapturous panegyric:

O Powers of Reason more kingly than kings and more free than freemen! O Powers governing the harmony of the seven brothers – a harmony that was holy and well-attuned to piety! None of the seven youths proved to be a coward, none shrank at the approach of death, but all hastened to their death under torture as if racing down the road to immortality. For as hands and feet are moved in harmony under the guidance of the soul, so those holy youths, as if guided by the immortal soul of piety, went to death in harmony for the sake of their religion. O all-holy group of seven brothers in harmony! For just as the seven days of the creation of the world dance in a ring around religion, so the youths danced in a ring around their sevenfold union [peri tēn hebdomada choreuontes hoi meirakes ekykloun] and shook off the fear of their tortures.

(4 Maccabees 14:2–8)

Though the seven were martyred in the second century before Christ, their steps towards immortality (as Nazianzen would declare in an oration delivered on their anniversary) were such as any virtuous soul in Ecclesia's chorus should be proud to follow.[30] But what kind of immortality did the Jewish panegyrist have in mind when he envisioned this memorable scene? Personal immortality in a supercelestial realm such as Nazianzen hoped to achieve through spiritual perfection? Probably not, since the 'sevenfold union' created by the brothers in their dance looks back to the creation of the world rather than forward to its dissolution and corresponds to the seven days of the week (and possibly also to the seven planets governing time), which seems to suggest a perpetual order of creatures great and small under Heaven but not an eternal communion of saints and spirits in Heaven. Might the immortality they sought be simply the historical perpetuation of the Jewish nation that Philo perceived in the life-enhancing choral rites of the Therapeutae? Again, probably not: what seems to drive the dancers – besides a Stoic impulse to harmonize the will of the individual with the Will of God and to conquer fear through an exercise of stalwart self-control – is a communal death-wish, a desire to prove to the World and especially to their Nebuchadnezzar, the Syrian tyrant Antiochus the Insane, that even if the Jews are defeated as a nation and extinguished as a race their rational 'piety' or 'religion' (eusebeia) will endure forever. It is inviolable. The order of the cosmos enshrines it, rings it round, protects it from death, for its 'immortal soul' (by which the panegyrist probably meant the moral law handed down to Moses from God) is mystically attuned to the animating and unifying powers of reason in the Divine Mind. For a Christian martyr like Ignatius of Antioch, however, the proof of the immortality of his religion will lie not in this world but in the next and depend more on a divine sacrifice than on any outpouring of human blood upon the altar of the faith.

A distinctly eschatological vision of choral order in Paradise is recorded in the Late Antique collection of rabbinical teachings known as the Babylonian Talmud, where we read of a certain sage named Ulla Bira'ah who declared that 'the Holy One, blessed be He, will hold a chorus for the righteous and He will sit in their midst in the Garden of Eden.'[31] If Ulla's prophecy recalls Jewish apocalyptic traditions antedating Christianity and transmitted for the most part orally, other prophecies like it, lost to us, may have been passed on to the early Church by Jewish converts in the Levant and subsequently modified by the Fathers to suit their New Testament conceptions of beatitude. In contrast to the Talmudic Holy One, the Christian Messiah will lead the chorus of the righteous away from the Garden of Eden towards the enclosed garden prefigured in the Song of Songs, Ecclesia's bridal bower, and across the ever-flourishing meadows of the Lamb, and through the jewelled gates of the heavenly Jerusalem, and into the veiled sanctuary of the angelic tabernacle – paradisial settings for a dance that must exclude forever the Jews who refused to hear his piping in the marketplace.

The classical tradition furnished the Fathers with such prototypic scenes of dancing in the afterlife as the choral revelry of Olympian gods, animate stars, and disembodied human souls in Plato's Myth of the Chariot, and of course the hauntingly sombre and dream-like processions of blessed spirits through the glades of Elysium. Such scenes were already ancient when Virgil had Aeneas drift in a melancholy mood among the scattered groups of shades in the Fortunate Woods and observe there that

Some beat out choral dances with their feet, chanting poems,

[Pars pedibus plaudunt choreas et carmina dicunt]
                                          (Aeneid vi 664)

while Orpheus in a trailing robe answered the rhythm of their footfalls with an exquisite melody, sometimes plucking his lyre with his fingers, sometimes sweeping its strings with an ivory quill.

   The Sophist Themistius, a pagan contemporary of Nazianzen and a defender of Julian's apostasy, described a similar scene in his treatise on ancient Greek theories of the soul (extant only in fragments) but from a rather different viewpoint – one characteristic of the brooding, anxious, acutely introspective intellectuals of Late Antiquity. Whereas Virgil observed the Elysian dance from a dispassionate distance through the eyes of a hero who was still among the living, Themistius enters into it, as it were, by imagining the unheroic fears and ecstatic frissons of a soul emerging from the darkness of a dying body:

The experience of the soul at death resembles word for word and deed for deed the experience of one who is being initiated into great mysteries. At first one wanders through the darkness like someone uninitiated. Then come all the terrors before the end of the ceremony – shivering, quaking, sweating, and astonishment. After this one is struck with a wondrous light, and this is followed by the sight of pure places and meadows filled with voices and choral dances [choreias] and solemn notes of sacred music and majestic visions of holy spirits.

                                          (apud Stobaeum, *Florilegium* iv)

This fragment of what was probably an elaborate ecphrasis detailing the wonders of Hades and the rewards of pagan virtue may record the private experiences of an initiate in the Greater Mysteries of Eleusis, one who had gone beyond the Kallichoron into the secret chambers of Demeter's temple and beheld the loss and recovery of Persephone enacted in solemn pageantry; or it may refer to the typical stages of initiation in any number of cthonic religions revived in Late Antiquity (the cult of Orpheus, for example, or of Rhea, or of Isis) and thus express the immortal longings of all the generations of world-weary pagans who flocked to the telesteria of Greece for 'the sight of pure places' and 'majestic visions of holy spirits.' Taking it to be a collective rather than a personal reverie, we may infer from the Sophist's extended metaphor that many of the emotions associated with the mystic dance of the Blessed in the Christian afterlife – relief after extraordinary terrors, childlike wonder, instinctive joy, an overwhelming sense of security within an enclosed untainted pastoral domain – were deeply rooted in the age-old experience of initiation in the pagan mysteries.

'Better, I well know,' concluded Nazianzen in his funeral oration for his beloved sister Gorgonia who died serenely, a psalm upon her lips, sometime before 369,

and far more valuable than what can be imagined from the things of the visible world are the realities that are present to you now – the song of 'a multitude that kept holyday' [Psalms 42:4], the choral dance of angels [an-gelōn choreia], the orderly arrangement of heavenly ranks, the contemplation of the glory of the other world, and the vision of the radiance of the Supreme Trinity which surpasses all other lights in purity and perfection.

(*Oratio* 8.23)

Better, too, he assumed, and far more valuable than the scenes of ghostly pomp and hollow mirth conjured up by pagan Sophists in their otherworldly fantasies were the holy sights that met his sister's eye – the intellectual eye of an ascetically purified, spiritually perfected Orthodox Spectator. What made those sights 'realities' in the sense conveyed by Nazianzen's term 'paronta' (literally 'present circumstances,' but in theological parlance 'per-manent forms and intellectual activities sustained by God in the eternal present of Heaven') was the unique light in which they were seen and by which they were immortalized: the radiance of the Orthodox Trinity. Unlike Themistius, who would have us believe that when our souls dance out into the Elysian fields all the mysteries of life and death and life after death will be divulged to our reawakened senses, Gregory promises us, if we follow Gorgonia's lead, a far clearer glimpse of 'the orderly arrangement of heavenly ranks' than what we can hope for here below, our bodily eyes being normally blinded by their brilliance, and consequently a deeper knowledge of God than what our sense-bound minds can ever attain through participation in the communal dance of Creation or the spiritual dance of Ecclesia, but not – and here the gulf between Elysium and Paradise widens immeasurably – a complete understanding of the Choragus at the centre of the mystic dance or an end to all the mysteries celebrated by the chorus of immortal initiates. The supreme mystery in Gregory's universe, the Unity of the Three Persons, remains incomprehensible even to Gorgonia.

Ecclesia above, as below, does not wait in suspense for a theatrical 'epop-teia' (a sudden climactic disclosure of the Divine Presence through its ma-terial symbols) like that awaited by the wealthier initiates in the holiday crowd at Eleusis. Gorgonia is rewarded for her ascetic virtues with an ev-erlasting holy-day which delights but does not startle or perturb her soul, and with an immediate (that is, non-symbolic) vision of the Divine Presence which fills her mind to capacity with angelic intuitions without disclosing the fullness of God. The elation experienced by St Paul when he was caught up into Paradise – 'for then,' as Theodoret of Cyrus noted in his commentary on 2 Corinthians (*PG* vol 82, 447D), 'he perceived the beauty of Paradise itself and the choral dances of the Holy Ones within it [tas en ekeinōi tōn hagiōn choreias] and the sound of their most harmonious hymnody' – Gorgonia experiences without interruption, bewilderment, or suspense, for as a Holy One herself she is beyond the reach of the 'messenger of Satan' who buffeted the Apostle lest he 'should be exalted above measure' when he returned to earth and to his earthly senses after his ascent to the third heaven.

Participation in the dance of the Holy Ones removes her from the terrifying suspense of the battle between Satan and Ecclesia described by Nazianzen in his panegyric on the ascetic-martyr Cyprian:

How fearful it is to be taken captive through the eyes, wounded through the tongue, enticed through the ears, burned through boiling rage, brought down through taste, softened through touch! How terrible for the soldiers of salvation to be subject to the soldiers of death! Defended by the shield of faith we should rightly stand firm against the wiliness of the Devil: and having triumphed with Christ and fought in the company of the Martyrs we shall hear that great sound: 'Come hither, o you who have been honoured by my Father! Receive the kingdom promised as your inheritance, the domain of all who joyfully dance the perpetual choral dance [choreuontōn choreian tēn akataluton], the realm echoing with the sound of festival-makers, and with the voice of exultation, and radiant with the perfect and most pure illumination of God which we are able to enjoy at present only through enigmas and shadows.

(*Oratio* 24.19)

Enigmatic and shadowy our vision of the 'choreia akatalutos' must remain until the battle is lost and won, but the main outlines of the image are clear enough now for us to see its connections with the images of the blessed dance on the first two panels of our triptych. The adjective 'akatalutos' literally means 'incapable of being put down, broken up, dissolved, disbanded, or destroyed,' and consequently 'perpetual.' In choosing this resounding word to sum up the characteristics of the dance in Paradise Gregory evidently wished to suggest that the movement of the Church Militant towards salvation was ceaseless and unstoppable and also that the choral order of the Church Triumphant (unlike the choral cosmos envisioned by the Stoics) would be indissoluble because of the perfect intellectual concord and incorruptible nature of its participants. In relation to the 'koinē chorostasia' of Creation the 'choreia akatalutos' may be regarded as a primordial archetype of order in the ecclesiastical universe; in relation to the Church's 'pneumatikē choreia,' however, it must also be seen as an apocalyptic extension of the contemplative lives of 'the soldiers of salvation' and as an eternal reward for active service in the war against 'the soldiers of death.'

If Nazianzen's profound and apparently zealous ignorance of Neoplatonism were not well attested – of the three great Cappadocians he certainly evinces the least knowledge of Plotinus[32] – we might be tempted to see more than a coincidental resemblance between the 'choreia entheos' envisioned by the Neoplatonic Spectator in *Enneads* 6.9.9 (see chapter 4, pages 221–2) and the 'choreia akatalutos' celebrated, though not glimpsed in this life, by the Orthodox Spectator and his spirited militia in the Anastasis. Both dances, after all, symbolize the unthreatened unity of virtuous souls encircling the spiritual centre of life. Both come as a blessed relief after the shame and torment of life in the body. Both are flooded with ineffable light. These similarities would be striking enough to make us ignore for a moment the absence of Christ and the Church in the Plotinian vision and the absence of Nous and Psyche in its Gregorian counterpart if we could also ignore the conspicuous differences between the psychological identity of the dancers in each chorus. Whereas the Plotinian chorus was composed for the most part of undescended intellective souls who did not have to struggle to gain admittance to the dance but only to keep their gaze fixed on the mystic wellspring, the chorus of the Church Triumphant admits from below only those fallen mortals who have fought passionately against their own passions and fortified the gates of their senses against demonic invasion and drawn other souls under the shield of faith. In Plotinus the peace of the eternal dance was discovered in the cosmogonic past and recovered by the soul in the present. In Gregory it is earned by the soul in the present and won in the apocalyptic future.

From their cosmogonic viewpoint the Neoplatonists could admire the erotic play of dancers as an artistic representation of the rampant fertility of nature and appreciate both the image and its model as consequences of the primal burst of creative energy that brought the amorous gods into being and generated the beauty of the heavens. From the apocalyptic viewpoint of the Fathers, however, the shameless writhing of Salome's successors in the theatre and the carnal coupling of male and female revellers beside the tombs of the martyrs could be seen as nothing less than a Satanic mockery of the order of Ecclesia's spiritual chorus and a shocking portent of damnation.

Caught up in the tremendous reversal of what might be called the intellectual sight lines of Late Antiquity – we enter the fourth century looking cheerfully back in the old Platonic direction towards the birth of cosmic order, and we leave it peering anxiously ahead in the new Orthodox direction towards Armageddon and the collapse of the World – was the ancient Greek analogy between the outer dance of the body and the inner dance of the soul. The ruthless zeal with which Nazianzen twisted this once instructive and flexible analogy into a rigid moralistic dichotomy is particularly evident (and arresting) in the following pair of speeches from a verse dialogue to which he gave the sophistic title 'A Comparison of Lives.' The first speaker, a hedonist, soothes our ears with a euphonious advertisement for the pleasures of life in the body:

> For me the sweet odour of perfumes, the delight of song,
> The sound of hands clapping, feet tapping, voices modulating in
> well-timed measures,
> The harmony of musical instruments played together!

His allegorical name is not Body or Matter (as we might expect) but Cosmos, which implies that his music and dance represent not only the corrupting influences of 'the World' in its Pauline sense – the sinful domain of the Flesh and the Devil – but also the seductively harmonious physical order hymned by the poets and hailed by the philosophers of ancient Greece. Quick to reply in the sharply critical tone of an ascetic homilist is his antagonist, Spirit:

> You praise these things, but they are what makes wealth
> Evil to me. They are, as it were, the teacher of sins.
> Better for us than musical instruments is the psalmody
> That harmonizes the soul with the Pure Intelligences.
> More sweet-smelling than all unguents is Christ, the Anointed
> One,
> Who was poured out for us so that he could rid us of the stench
> Of mortal sin, the odour of death that pervades me!
> With my hands I shall clap if my Slayer should fall,
> When he instructs me to say or do anything evil.
> And the only dance for my feet is a strophe inspired by God!
> [Podōn orchēsis, entheos strophē!]

(Synkrisis biōn 99–111)

As a teacher opposed to the World yet operating within it for the preservation of souls, Gregory's Spirit is analogous to but not identical with the Holy Spirit, who of course would not be associated with 'the stench of mortal sin.' What then does this spokesman for the otherworldly life represent – the didactic spirit of Gregory's poetry, the ascetic spirit of Gregory's Christianity, the reviving spirit of the Anastasis, the charitable spirit of Ecclesia's chorus, the angelic spirit protecting every virtuous soul in the battle against the Slayer? Perhaps his identity in the poem (which might be retitled 'A Dissociation of Lives') embraces all of these at once. Of course as a dancer

Gregory's Spirit can have no hands or feet with which to perform an 'orchēsis' in the old cosmic sense, and so the 'strophē entheos' in which he participates must be either the divinely inspired measures of the poem itself which are designed to harmonize the poet's soul (and his reader's) with 'the Pure Intelligences' in the Here and Now, or the ecstatic 'turning' of Ecclesia's chorus away from the scenes of interminable misery and illusory merriment in the theatre of the World towards the reality of the 'choreia akatalutos' on the eternal side of the Great Dividing-Line.

The Greek Fathers' peculiarly fluid conception of that much-disputed boundary underlay and to some extent gave rise to the distinctive fusion of life and afterlife, temporal exertion and eternal repose, physical trial and spiritual triumph in their composite vision of the blessed dance. The Platonists whom they read and the Neoplatonists whom they reviled had conceived the Great Dividing-Line as a kind of shadow screen on which temporal images of an eternal Model were faithfully reproduced so that mankind could form from life's flickering lights and fleeting silhouettes a detailed mental image of what was on the far side of the stars. The screen created a symmetry of parallel correspondences between image and archetype or proportional analogies between the part and the whole. Their mystical adversaries, the Gnostics, and the more pessimistic and anti-philosophical adepts in the art of sophistic oratory tended to conceive the boundary as the cracked or distorted surface of a mirror and the dynamic order governed by the stars as a frightening reflection or ludicrous parody of the dance of free spirits in Heaven. The mirror created a symmetry of inverse correspondences between the actual and the ideal or dualistic contrasts between type and antitype. Genesis 1:7 ('And God made the firmament, and divided the waters which were under the firmament from the waters which were above the firmament ...') suggested to the Fathers that the boundary between Heaven and the heavens was the surface of a luminous river through which the angels could freely pass on their providential missions to the galaxy and above which the Blessed would eventually rise to complete the chorus of the Church Triumphant. The river produced a shifting, fluid sort of symmetry which was sometimes like that of the screen and sometimes like that of the mirror. Through its enigmatic surface Eusebius, Basil, and other Christian Platonists could see – or imagine seeing – multitudes of bright angelic forms encircling the First Cause and meadows glowing with the flowers of wisdom where the Lamb of God would lead his throng of virgins, and from such harmonious visions conclude that the temporal world, being as it were the sunken river-bed beneath the supercelestial current, was a dark but not inherently evil extension of the timeless realm illuminated by the Trinity. Their inclination to see correspondences between the visible order of Creation and the visionary order of Paradise led them to link the two realms with an intermediary order, the chorus of Ecclesia, so that the assembling of the faithful to sing psalms or to celebrate a victory became a symbolic act of participation in the current unity of the angel-guided stars and the imminent unity of the procession of the saints.

Not all the Fathers, however, were inclined to see such parallels all of the time. To the great preachers like Nazianzen and John Chrysostom who tended to look down on the physical world from an apocalyptic vantage-point (when they were not looking *into* it with piercing Skeptical eyes) the order of Heaven often seemed to be mirrored in a bad sense here below, to be inverted and distorted by its reflection in the wide gulf separating Spirit from Cosmos. And the deeper they immersed themselves in the turbulence of their times the wider the gulf between Spirit and Cosmos seemed to grow. Their bitter experience of sectarian conflict, intellectual repression, and political bouleversement taught them to look back on post-Nicene ecclesiastical history as a tragic drama in which they were the unwilling protagonists or as a decadent circus act in which scurrilous clowns burlesqued their priestly dignity. A demonic counterpart to the blessed dance began to take shape in their visual imaginations – a grotesque antistrophe to follow, to rival, to threaten, and to mock their 'strophē entheos.' What they saw on the grand stage of Constantinople and taught their congregations to see in the wicked theatre of the World were the obscene writhings of sinners doomed to dance eternally in an 'orchēsis diabolou.'

The Contortionists of Hell

No strikingly imaginative or allegorically sophisticated vision of the demonic dance appears in Christian literature before the late fourth century. A case could be made that Clement of Alexandria came close to such a vision in his *Exhortation to the Pagans* when he contrasted the demonically possessed Maenads in the old chorus of Dionysus with the divinely inspired virgins in the new chorus of the Logos (see chapter 3, pages 129–30), though we cannot conclude from this antithesis that his universe was divided into two rival orders – one mad and the other sane – since his resounding theme in the *Exhortation* was that the chaos, frenzy, brutality, and licentiousness displayed in the pagan world-theatre had given way to the harmony, peace, rationality, and loving-kindness revived by Christ in the real world, the world of Ecclesia. So bright was the presence of the Logos on Clement's Mount of Truth that it seems to have cast the Devil and his cohorts along with the deserted mystery gods into the shadows of unreality.

Here and there in the exegetical works of the third-century Alexandrian Fathers we can find hints of a demonic antitype of the blessed chorus and vague anticipations of a dualistic allegory of the dance buried amid pious condemnations of the specific incidents of idolatrous or indecent dancing recorded in the Bible. Represented in such scenes as the drunken dance of the Israelites around the Golden Calf (Exodus 32:19) and the notorious performance of Salome before Herod the Tetrarch (Matthew 14:6 and Mark 6:22) were all the evil movements arising from the World, the Flesh, and the Devil – movements that clearly belonged on the shadowy side of the Great Dividing-Line. As Origen tersely remarked,

> the dance of the daughter of Herodias was opposed to the holy dance [hē Hērodiados orchēsis enantia ēn orchēsei hagiai] that was not danced by those who were reproved when they heard these words: 'We have piped unto you, and ye have not danced' [Eulēsamen hymin, kai ouk orchēsasthai].
>
> (In Matthaeum x.22)

And that was that. Whether Origen envisioned the same opposition of an unholy to a holy dance on a universal scale and in an apocalyptic setting we cannot tell from his extant writings. Chances are that he did not, however, for he was willing to consider the possibility that 'infernal creatures' (including Satan himself) would return to 'the ultimate unity and concord' of Heaven in the purgative conflagration at the end of the World.[33]

Why Satan should suddenly find a broad dancing-ground and an eager chorus in the Orthodox universe of the post-Nicene Fathers is not hard to explain: at least three historical circumstances favoured the emergence of the image of the 'orchēsis diabolou' in the homiletic literature of the late fourth and early fifth centuries. One of these (by far the most important) is suggested by Nazianzen in the following gloomy reflection on ecclesiastical history from his otherwise glowing panegyric on St Athanasius:

> At the period when our Church was flourishing and all was going well, the present overly subtle, far-fetched, and artificial treatment of theology had not made its way into our divinity schools. Not at all. In fact, the practice of making and hearing elaborate speeches about God was held at that time in no higher esteem than the game of 'Now you see it, now you don't' which children play with pebbles to trick the eye or the art by which a dancer charms his spectators with the diverse contortions and sexually ambiguous postures of his body [katorcheisthai tōn theatōn pantoiois kai androgynois lugismasi].
>
> (Oratio 21.12)

Though Athanasius had been a luminary of virtue in his time (which spanned the dark middle decades of the fourth century), his time was certainly not the Golden Age of theology to which Gregory looked back in the spring of 379 when this oration was delivered. From the viewpoint of the Cappadocian Fathers the heyday of the Church had been the intellectually progressive era of Origen and his third-century successors – a period sadly interrupted by the Great Persecution, momentarily revived at Nicaea, and brought to a desperate end when Hell unleashed Arius and his fiendish disciples upon Constantine's fragile empire.

Constantine himself had been charmed by the seductive 'lugismata' of the Arians and baptized into their infernal ranks at the very hour when the true Church most needed her imperial coryphaeus. The subsequent establishment of a dominant Arian counter-church in Constantinople had split the East into two opposing 'pneumatikoi choroi' which were still so similar in outward appearance that each could regard the other as its parodic analogue, its demonic shadow. The shock of this great parting of ranks in Ecclesia's chorus was bound to affect perceptions of the order of the ecclesiastical universe as a whole in so far as it was a symbolic extension of the order of the Christian empire, and to be felt no less strongly in the sphere of the visual imagination than in the field of imperial politics and doctrinal warfare. Among the repercussions of the Arian-Orthodox rift at the imaginative level, as we shall see, was the dualistic revision of the image of the dance in the homiletic literature of the post-Nicene period.

A second circumstance favouring such a revision in the fourth century was the sophistic training of the Fathers who were drawn into rhetorical (and sometimes physical) combat with the heretics. The elaboration of 'synkriseis' or 'comparisons' between heavenly and earthly order, heroic and anti-heroic conduct, mythological and historical characters, hedonistic and ascetic ways of life, and so on, was a standard exercise of sophistic wit reflecting a typical mode of sophistic thought. We have seen in Lucian's Cynical comparison of the divine to the human chorus (chapter 4, pages 181–2) how this mode of thought, which had a parodic bent, was inclined to twist classical topoi so that antitheses came to light where analogies had traditionally been perceived. It is surely no coincidence that the cosmic dance should be split into a variety of antithetical movements – a spiritual strophe versus a physical antistrophe, a sacred choral round versus a sacrilegious pantomime, an angelic revel versus a demonic bacchanal – in an era when the Church's leading preachers were mentally predisposed to invent anti-types, to invert established orders, to sharpen distinctions into dichotomies, and to juxtapose the sacred and the profane. In the wake of the Pagan Reformation any dance associated with Julian's orgiastic cosmos (such as the leaping of Attis and the Corybants in honour of Cybele) was bound to appear thoroughly demonic from Ecclesia's defensive viewpoint.

The extreme asceticism of the early monastic movement also tended to polarize patristic conceptions of the dance. The devils whom Clement of

Alexandria had banished from the revels of the New Dionysus were found in droves by St Antony on the barren outskirts of civilization and revived as a terrifyingly palpable presence on the battlefield of the Church Militant. They became as real as angels to the desert ascetics who felt the claws of temptation constantly digging into their flesh. They became as real as Arians to the world-weary bishops who were called out of seclusion to fight the good fight for Orthodoxy. Anyone who was not struggling with the Slayer in the spirit, Gregory contended in his *Synkrisis biōn*, had to be dancing with the devils afoot in the world.[34]

Preserved in the manuscript collections of Gregory's works is a brief oration entitled 'On the Martyrs, and Against the Arians' in which the inverse correspondences between the chorus of Ecclesia and its demonic antitype are so clearly drawn that it might be fittingly subtitled 'A Comparison of Dances' – 'Synkrisis chorōn.' 'Once again,' the orator begins, surveying a scene which belongs on the broad middle panel of our triptych of the blessed dance along with Gregory's watch-tower vision of the revels occasioned by the death of Julian,

honours which have been neglected for a long time before this are here being conferred upon martyrs; once again the priests of God are congregating; once again there are spiritual choral dances and festivities [chorostasiai kai pa-nēgyreis pneumatikai]. The assembly is thronged with people who are eager not to make war but to celebrate a festival. Ah, what a wonder! The weapons have been cast away from hands, the battle-lines have been broken up, and the war has ceased to be a concern. No longer are heard the voices of those who raise the war-cry. In their stead festival-goers and merry-makers and those who celebrate peace are dancing around the whole city [tēn polin pasan perichoreuousi].

(*Oratio* 35.1)

The victory celebrated by these 'choreutai tou hagiou Pneumatos' – these 'choral dancers of the Holy Spirit' as the orator goes on to call them – is not specified in the oration, but it may have been the expulsion of the Arian bishop Demophilus from the capital and the restoration of the churches to the Orthodox following the triumphant arrival of Theodosius the Great in Constantinople in the fall of 380. The long night in which the heretics were in power and the war was raging is over at last, the orator proclaims, and though the recent past has a strange air of unreality about it like a scene in the theatre, a tragic scene of inexpressible horror and despair which quickly fades from view yet haunts the memory of its spectators, he and the faithful warriors on his side who experienced the tragedy not as spectators but as protagonists recall that the demonic forces opposing Ecclesia were all too real. The church of the heretics, or as he prefers to call it, continuing the theatrical metaphor,

their dancing-place [ho choros] was the military headquarters of the Devil! Here he drew up his army and herein established his personal shield-bearers. Here was the army of Falsehood, the warriors of Fraud, the expeditionary force of the demons, the legions of the unclean spirits. And if I may be allowed to utter pagan names – the Furies, that villainous army of devils, thereafter danced and caroused in a riotous revel opposed to Ecclesia [kata tēs Ekklēsias ekōmasen].

(*Oratio* 35.3)

Perhaps 'here' is the Church of the Apostles, the episcopal headquarters vacated by Demophilus, to which Gregory and the congregation of the Anastasis were triumphantly escorted by the troops of Theodosius. Or if we take 'here' to be 'there' (the locative adverb in Greek is ambiguous) the orator may be referring to the cathedral church of the city but speaking in a smaller basilica nearby. In any case, he clearly implies that the scene of Ecclesia's present revels is still redolent of Hell because the whole city has been for a time the Devil's dancing-ground.

Lest his congregation forget how the Devil desecrated their holy rites and filled the streets of their city with unholy clamour, he refreshes their memory with a particularly vivid ecphrasis, a word-painting in the literal sense:

I have seen a painting on a plastered wall. Think of my heart swollen all round with the memory of their evils! Nay, sympathize if you will with the trouble we endured, for it is our suffering – not another's – that we shall narrate in full! What then is that painting to which I compare our troubles? It showed a choral dance of women who were behaving in an unseemly manner [choreia tis ēn gynaikōn aschēmonousa], along with another band of women who were twisting themselves into the highly contorted postures of another dance-figure [allēs kat' alla ti schēma orchēstikon heautēn dias-treblousēs]. The myths call such women Maenads. Their hair is ruffled up by the breezes. Frenzy enters into their expression. Lighted torches are borne in their hands, and flames leap up and curl round with the whirling contortions of their bodies. The wind wreaks havoc with the elegant folds of their robes. They rise on tiptoe and flee. No comely modesty is shown in any of their actions.

(*Oratio* 35.3)

If our triptych of the blessed dance has an imaginary counterpart in the gallery of Hell, it is this Dionysian fresco. Doubtless the various images composing it appeared in actual paintings of the period or recalled well-known classical prototypes, but they are here thoroughly transformed by a sophistic imagination into dynamic figures in a narrative, a sequence of animated scenes, the significance of which is determined by a Christian frame of reference that is both historical and apocalyptic. From a retrospective viewpoint, considering the narrative in relation to ecclesiastical history, we can perceive the dance as a symbol of the havoc-wreaking dynamism of the heretical movement and see the contorted figures in it as Arians performing their theological 'lugismata' before the gullible populace of the city; from a prophetic viewpoint, considering the narrative in relation to the Apocalypse, we can see flames leaping up and curling around Devils instead of Maenads and bodies writhing and twisting in bacchic 'schēmata orchēstika' forever – the bodies of the Damned. Simultaneously a flashback and a foreshadowing, the vision may also be taken as a present warning to all the revellers in the orator's audience (especially the women) not to endanger their immortal souls by flinging off the restraints of Christian modesty. Their spiritual festival must not be allowed to get out of hand lest it degenerate into a pagan orgy.

Unlike Clement's vision of maenadic frenzy on old Cythaeron, which was meant to be replaced by his vision of the dance of the Daughters of God on the Mount of Truth and subsequently forgotten, this 'painting on a plastered wall' – though alien and opposed to everything represented by the chorus of Ecclesia – is clearly intended to be retained in the memory of the Christian revellers. However disquieting its various scenes may be, and however deranged the figures in them, the composition as a whole must be regarded as an artistic order designed to distance the Orthodox Spectator from his recent 'troubles' by externalizing and rendering harmless the evil forces that for a time tormented his soul, and also to clarify his understanding of the disorienting rush of events in the post-Nicene era by sharpening his perception of the universal antagonism between Spirit and Cosmos.

The dominant image in the fresco, the 'choreia aschēmonousa' or 'indecorous dance,' is not a figure of random disorder or chaos pure and simple, for chaos cannot be ritualized. The stylized orchestic postures, frenzied expressions, and choral groupings of the dancers represent on the contrary a highly deliberate order, an impure and sophisticated ritual of evil. Nothing is left out of the ritual that should be there according to the rules of bacchic indecorum: immodest women caper on tiptoe; loosened hair streams over their shoulders; torch-flames lick their bodies; even the wind behaves in a predictably Dionysian manner by shamelessly lifting up their once elegantly folded skirts. Pushing us step by step towards the appropriate climax of the rite, a demonic burlesque of the ceremonial installation of a bishop, the orator notes that *in the midst of the aforementioned choral dance [tēs toioutēs choreias] is the image of a man – a man who is partly female! Ambiguous in nature and effeminate in appearance, he lies on the borderline between the sexes. Loose and abandoned are his gestures like those of a sleepwalker or a reeling drunkard, and as he lies back on his chariot he is drawn by wild beasts through the chorus of Maenads. Around him flows a great stream of strong wine from a basin, and grouped around his sculpted image are a band of chattering hairy-faced monsters [that is, satyrs] who are performing a capering dance on goat-legs about the idol [epi skelōn trageion periskirtōntes to eidōlon]. Such are the events I have to narrate about that night! Women who are a disgrace to their sex – their own kind openly accuses them – are discovered dancing in such a way that they make a mockery of what is customarily considered seemly behaviour in women [tēn nenomismenēn en gynaixin eukosmian exorchēsamenai]. They lead their jeering procession right through the middle of the city, displaying all that is base and shameful in their own nature. Instead of shields they arm themselves with stones. They look forward to a bloody slaughter. Their eyes cast a ruthless glance. Into the sacred precincts they come. Onto the holy throne they have raised up their Corybant!*

(Oratio 35.4)

We have often observed that the central figure in a choral rite projects his divine character or nature onto all the dancers in his circle and not only reveals but actually embodies the mystical significance of the movement he inspires. Much as the Devil likes to defy authority and to dispense with rules, he does appear from the foregoing scene to uphold the ancient principle that whatever a choragus is his chorus becomes; in fact, whenever he captivates the unprincipled mob in the world-city or commands centre stage in the world-theatre, he is liable to turn the custom of choral assimilation to the centre into a rigid, militaristic law. The emasculated Attis-like idol around which his dancers cavort and carouse obviously represents the Dionysian principle of unbridled (and in the orator's view) perverted Eros governing the Fallen World, the dehumanizing love that transforms women into shameless Bacchants and men into 'chattering hairy-faced monsters' and consequently subverts the spiritual order of the chorus 'en agapēi.' Ludicrous and fun-loving and essentially harmless the dancers may at first appear, but like their idol, which at base represents something less obvious yet more awesome than Dionysian eroticism, namely the monstrous duplicity of the Devil, they are shockingly 'ambiguous in nature' and in a trice can be organized into an army of bloodthirsty zealots under the command of a belligerent Corybant.

The enthronement scene at the end of the vision may be closer to history than to fantasy. Gregory was conducting a baptismal service on Holy Saturday in 379 when a violent mob of Arians, including women, stormed the Anastasis and dispersed his congregation. A few months later his false friend Maximus the Cynic, with the covert assistance of several Egyptian bishops, had himself enthroned at night in the Anastasis while Gregory was recovering from an illness. The impostor was promptly driven from the capital by the outraged Orthodox, but the memory of his duplicity darkened Nazianzen's remaining months as their leader and haunted him to the end of his life. Though these scandalous episodes may not have been historically connected in a modern sense, they would certainly have been regarded as such by a persecuted minority who saw the Devil behind all acts of ecclesiastical subversion.

Can we conclude then that the enthronement of the Corybant commemorates one or both of these vicious attacks on Nazianzen's episcopal authority? Does the Corybant represent Demophilus in the Church of the Apostles or Maximus in the Anastasis as well as the Devil on his throne in the City of Man? Are the chattering satyrs the Arian demogogues who reduced theology to a sophistic pantomime or the Arian monks who led the mob into the sacred precincts of the Orthodox? These and many other questions raised by 'On the Martyrs, and Against the Arians' must remain unanswered until the debate over its authorship has been settled. The unusual brevity of the work, the vagueness of its historical references, and the titillating vividness of its imagery have prompted most twentieth-century patrologists and editors of Gregory to reject the traditional view that it is either an excerpt from one of Gregory's extant orations or an authentic fragment from some lost oration, and to assert without the usual display of scholarly trepidation that it is certainly spurious. Their judgment has not gone unchallenged of late.[35] Certainly the Gregory who 'danced' against Julian in two sensational ranting speeches addressed to all the spiritual revellers in Ecclesia's chorus would not have hesitated to depict his defeated Arian foes as diabolical Bacchants.

By the late 380s the 'Comparison of Dances' seems to have established itself as a topos in Greek homiletic literature, for we can find another notable example of a sermon beginning with a commendation of the blessed dance and ending with a satirical depiction of its demonic antitype among the early works of Gregory's successor as the leading rhetor in the Eastern Church, John of Antioch, the Christian Chrysostom. In 387, a year after John became a presbyter, a mob in his native city mutilated the statues of Theodosius and the Imperial Family and dragged what was left of them through the filth on the streets to protest the imposition of a ruinous tax. Their sedition so angered the Emperor that he vowed not only to execute the rioters but to reduce Antioch to rubble, which in turn so terrified its normally peaceful citizens that they sent their aged bishop Flavian to grovel before the imperial throne. Flavian had to grovel for many weeks before Theodosius would grant a complete pardon to the city, and while its pleas for forgiveness were being heard Chrysostom preached twenty-one homilies 'On the Statues' with the aim of casting out the demons of despair that inevitably possessed his fellow citizens during this anxious period and castigating the vices that had provoked the wrath of their heavenly as well as earthly Monarch.

The nineteenth in this celebrated series (the success of which established his reputation both for courage and for eloquence) was delivered shortly after a festival honouring the Martyrs, with whom, needless to say, the Antiochians felt an especially strong bond of spiritual kinship while their fate was being decided by the Emperor. Their orderly conduct and demonstration of fervent piety on this occasion buoyed up the spirits of Flavian, who had returned from Constantinople to prepare for Easter, and prompted their ascetic presbyter to exclaim in their praise:

You have revelled these last few days in the Holy Martyrs! You have taken your fill of the spiritual feast! You have all leapt virtuous leaps [eskirtēsate ta kala skirtēmata]! You have seen the ribs of the Martyrs laid bare and their loins cut to pieces and their blood flowing everywhere – myriad forms of torture! You have seen human nature displaying that which transcends nature, and crowns woven with blood! You have danced a morally beautiful dance throughout the city [echoreusate choreian kalēn pantachou tēs poleōs] with this man leading you on, your noble commander Flavian!

('On the Statues,' *Hom* XIX.1)

Here, as in Philo's panegyric on the Therapeutae, the language of bacchic revelry is employed to highlight the sobriety and moral uprightness of co-religionists who have danced a step or two 'in the body' to test their virtue (and passed the test) but who have mostly leapt 'in the spirit' towards Heaven in anticipation of their final deliverance from evil. But the old oxymoronic image of the sober bacchanal is given a strange new twist in this passage by Chrysostom's quasi-Dionysian exultation in the physical agony of the Martyrs. While the mere thought of ribs laid bare and loins cut to pieces would have dampened the spirits of Philo's contemplative revellers, who, we may recall, had turned away from bodily suffering towards the imperturbable stars and the passionless angels for inspiration in their dance, it was the remembered or imagined sight of bodies subjected to 'myriad forms of torture' – bodies as human as Christ's – that chiefly inspired the dance of the Church Militant by revealing to its soldiers, most of whom were not contemplatives, the divinity latent in human nature.

At the end of his homily Chrysostom wittily contrasts the recreative ease and lightheartedness of those who dance the 'choreia kalē' with the exhausting toil of those who perform the 'orchēsis diabolou':

Let us consider what services the Devil has ordered us to perform and how
wearisome and onerous they are. And yet their difficulty has not hindered
us from carrying out his orders! For what can be more difficult, I ask, than
the activity of a youth who, having handed himself over to experts who
undertake to make his limbs supple, obstinately strives to bend his whole
body into the exact shape of a wheel and to turn over upon the pavement,
and then forces himself to step out of that shape and to assume the likeness
of a woman by a trick of his eyes and a twist of his hands and by other
convolutions? Yet the difficulty of these transformations and the shamefulness
arising from them are not given a moment's thought, are they? Moreover,
what spectator can help being astonished at those who flit across the dance-
floor in the theatre [tous de epi tēs orchēstras palin episyromenous] with their
body trailing behind them and their limbs flapping like wings?

('On the Statues' *Hom* XIX.13)

No doubt the more educated sinners in Antioch were moved to laugh at
themselves for a moment when they heard this demonic version, that is to
say inversion, of the standard humanistic analogy between dancing and
education – the analogy drawn by Nazianzen in his second oration, by Basil
in his treatise on the value of reading the classics, and by generations of
Sophists and Socratic symposiasts before them. (According to Xenophon,
Symposium II.9–13, the sight of a dancing-girl bending her supple body into
the shape of a wheel prompted Socrates to remark, tongue in cheek, that
women can be as easily educated as men!) Chrysostom's golden tongue is
definitely not in his cheek when he suggests that there is a kind of education
that is just like the training of an 'orchēstēs': an education in carnality,
perversion, shamefulness, sin.[36] The sophistic humour in his remarks lies in
his bathetically literal but nonetheless earnestly moralistic interpretation of
the analogy. If education is truly like learning to dance, he implies, then its
goals cannot be the acquisition of wisdom or the perfection of virtue as so
many wise and virtuous souls have taught us to believe. Why, the Devil
himself teaches us (at our expense, of course) to dance for the World's
applause; that is, he commands us to waste all our physical and spiritual
energy in utterly frivolous pastimes, to bend over backward in the pursuit
of wealth and fame, to twist our bodies into every erotic position imaginable,
to trick other people into thinking we are what we are not, in effect to lose
our natural shape, our original uprightness. And so we may be sure that
the World's best-trained sinner after years of stretching his capacity for vice
to the limit will be no closer to wisdom or virtue than the silliest contortionist, the most decadent female impersonator in the theatre of the Damned.

Few 'lugismata' 'danced' by a preacher in the Golden Age of Christian
oratory are more beguiling than the graceful stretch of moralizing at the end
of the nineteenth homily 'On the Statues.' From a Father of Chrysostom's

fiercely ascetic temperament (he spent two years of his youth in a cave denying himself sleep and starving his rebellious stomach into submission) we should expect to hear how difficult it is to dance with the Virtues in this wicked world and how damnably easy to revel in sin. Instead, we find him proclaiming to the repentant sinners of Antioch how blessedly easy it is to leap virtuous leaps and how wearisome to dance with the Devil.

'For where there is dancing,' he later reminded them in a homily on the death of John the Baptist, 'there you will find the Devil.' The admonition could not have been expressed more succinctly: 'Entha gar orchēsis, ekei diabolos.' Drawing their attention to the iniquity of Hell's most accomplished danseuse, the daughter of Herodias, he went on to moralize in his typical sardonic vein:

Surely the reason God gave us feet was not to dance like that woman but to process slowly with an orderly and dignified pace; it was not to make a disgraceful spectacle of ourselves or to leap about like camels – for if you find the sight of dancing camels repulsive, think how much more repulsive, how truly disgusting is the sight of women dancing! – but to dance with the angels [syn angelois choreuōmen]. For if it is shameful for the body to dance in that other way, it is much more so for the soul. That is the way the demons dance [Toiauta orchountai hoi daimones]. That is the way their devilish deacons make fools of us.

(*In Matthaeum homilia* XLVIII.5)

The homily from which this is taken, one of ninety on the First Gospel, was delivered in Antioch around 390. (Buried at Nazianzus in the previous year was the retired Patriarch of Constantinople whose throne Chrysostom was destined to sit upon – he would rise in the World as reluctantly as Gregory – in the winter of 398.) Like Nazianzen Chrysostom felt more than a Stoic's contempt for the performers and spectators of 'orchēsis'; he despised the theatrical dances of his day for reasons transcending aesthetic tastes or social prejudices, reasons far more urgent and compelling than any expressed by the straight-laced Crato in Lucian's dialogue on the dance because they pertained to the salvation of the human race and presupposed a universal war between Good and Evil. To think of them as reasons in the narrow sense of philosophical explanations or rhetorical justifications would be to misunderstand them and their advocate, for they were in essence spiritual forces, divine imperatives. Their persuasive power was that of 'pistis,' 'elpis,' and 'agapē': Ecclesia's faith in the ultimate defeat and destruction of the World by the forces of Heaven; her hope for an eternal holy-day from the war of the Flesh against the Spirit; and her charitable concern for sinners who still had time to escape the Devil and his twisted followers.

It may be Chrysostom's wit that prevents him from sounding like a self-righteous puritan, but it is his courageous devotion to the Virtues that proves he was no sanctimonious prude. If the Virtues had not moved him to speak out against the theatre of his day and the infernal debaucheries it represented, his grimly satirical (and peculiarly Middle Eastern) comparison of writhing female dancers to gambolling camels would have to be read as a distasteful anti-feminist insult – the sort of jeer we should expect from one of Satan's malicious 'deacons.' Indeed the 'synkrisis' is morally effective precisely because it is offensive. It shocks us into seeing just how bestial, undignified, ludicrous, shameful, and graceless the erotic pantomime must appear to the sneering Diabolos – the 'Hurler of Insults' – who stages it for his own perverted amusement. While the Devil's view of the dance turns out to be ironically similar to the preacher's, his view of the dancers is wholly pitiless, wholly possessive, wholly unprejudiced by the love that transmutes the preacher's contempt into compassion.

'And so in ancient times those who were trained in every way to fight for the cause of divine love and concord,' noted Chrysostom in his commentary on the 149th Psalm (v 3), 'were taught to dance in harmony and to sing hymns to God.'[37] As for the present time, he implied, let them praise His name 'en chorōi' provided that their dances are purely spiritual and their choruses simply choirs. While the Neoplatonists were inclined to isolate the dance of life from the war of chaos, the Church Fathers repeatedly combined images of warring and dancing in their visions of Ecclesia's universal order. The 149th Psalm encouraged them to do so:

> Let the high praises of God be in their mouth, and a two-
> edged sword in their hand
> To execute vengeance upon the heathen and punishments upon
> the people. ...
> (vv 6–7)

These verses taken with the third clearly show us, Chrysostom concluded, 'that war must accompany their dance [ton meta choreias polemon] and that if they sing hymns of divine praise like this they will be the survivors.'

8

Chorus and Chronos

It seems to me that the god of time was named Chronos by those who had gained a complete understanding of his nature and wished to speak of a certain 'choronoos' or 'choreuōn nous,' which means 'dancing intellect.' They shortened the name to Chronos perhaps to conceal its meaning or to suggest that the god of time is simultaneously resting and dancing. For a part of him (the half that is 'nous' or 'intellect') remains at rest while another part (the half that is 'choreutikos' or 'related to a choral dance') dances. By thus combining parts of each of these words they fashioned a name to designate the marvellous and craftsman-like nature of this god.

Just as the Craftsman orders the universe by starting from Nous since he is himself an intellectual god, so it seems that Chronos perfects that universal order by starting from Psyche since he is also a supracosmic god. For if Chronos is indeed related to the cosmos as Aion (the god of eternity) is related to Autozoön (the archetypal Living Being on which the cosmos was modelled), then it is clear that Chronos exists not only within the cosmos but also beyond it and that he must have existed long before it. Just as Chronos is an image of Aion, so the cosmos with its intellect and soul is in every respect an image of Autozoön.

If Chronos truly is a dancing intellect, then he dances while remaining at rest [ei d' oun choronoos esti menōn choreuei], and because he remains at rest his choral dances are infinite in number and return to their starting-point [hai choreiai apeiroi kai apokathistantai]. For Chronos was said to be eternal by virtue of his constant identity and intellectual essence when he had completed among the Intellects his first choral dance around the whole of creation. In so far as he is a dancer, however, he leads souls and natures and bodies around in a circle and restores them (in a word) periodically.

While the cosmos moves on its own because it has a soul and moves in an orderly manner because it has an intellect – for, as Plato stated in the 'Laws' [x 897b], 'the soul assisted by a divine intellect teaches what is correct and rational' – it may be said to move in a periodic manner because it passes from the same point to the same point and imitates the repose of Nous in the same way that Chronos imitates Aion. Thus it has increased its resemblance to the utterly stationary Model by returning to one and the same point through its temporal revolution.

From all this you may now understand all the causes of time discerned by Plato. The Craftsman is the efficient cause; Aion is the model (or formal cause); and the periodic revolution of all mobile things back to a single starting-point is the final cause. For that which does not remain fixed in one position tends to turn around a single point, yearning through this motion to reach the One which is identical with the Good.

PROCLUS DIADOCHUS, *In Timaeum* III 28–9

The Theurgic Spectator

Proclus was born about two years after the sack of Old Rome (410 AD) in the New Rome at the centre of the Orthodox Christian Empire – a city and a world in which he was destined to feel profoundly out of place. His father, a wealthy lawyer from the small coastal province of Lycia in southwest Asia Minor, removed him from Constantinople at an early age to be raised in the Lycian city of Xanthos where as a boy he was taught grammar by a local pagan tutor in preparation for the study of rhetoric, Latin, and Roman law in the schools of Alexandria. The Christian majority in Lycia were proud of having sent an Orthodox bishop to the Council of Nicaea, but 'the Lycian' (as Proclus is sometimes called to distinguish him from a Christian contemporary of the same name who became the Patriarch of Constantinople in the middle of the fifth century) did not rejoice in the political triumph of Nicene Orthodoxy since he was born into the even prouder pagan minority and would remain a staunch pagan to his dying day. As an adult Proclus would regard the Christians as 'a race of fearless ungodly men' bent on diverting his Muse-inspired intellect from the dance of contemplation in the temple of Psyche.[1] No doubt the seeds of this alienating prejudice – the fifth-century fruit of Porphyry's contempt for Christianity – were implanted in the last of the great pagan Neoplatonists before his departure from Lycia. Though his early education was probably much like the pagan schooling of the Cappadocian Fathers, he did not develop like them a strong boyhood attachment to his provincial roots. Like the young Plotinus he would spend much of his early academic life searching for an Ammonius to guide him to his proper spiritual haven in the province of the old philosophy.

Alexandria proved to be no haven for him. The decades-old rivalry between the Bishops of Alexandria and the Patriarchs of Constantinople was about to flare up over the Nestorian controversy (which would not be settled for over two centuries) when Proclus arrived in Egypt sometime in the 420s, and though he no doubt admired the finely turned classical phrases of Alexandrian Sophists like his tutor Leonas and drank in the deliciously ancient religious lore of pagan priests like his friend Orion, the dominant intellectual community of the city was excited by issues which could hardly have been of interest to him – for example, whether Cyril of Alexandria was sounding too much like a Monophysite in his condemnations of Nestorius of Constantinople's doctrine that the divine and human natures remained distinct in the Incarnate Christ.

After several years of study he returned to the city of his birth with the intention perhaps of finding behind its Goth-resistant walls an Elysian position in the imperial court or at least a foothold in the bureaucratic underworld of East Roman lawyers where his father probably had hopes of establishing him. Leonas, who had escorted him there, was no doubt surprised – and if he was like most worldly-wise Sophists of his age, horrified – when Proclus suddenly announced that the ascetic life of a philosopher appealed to him much more than the prosperous life of an orator. His future, he realized, lay neither in the lecture halls of Alexandria nor in the courtrooms of Constantinople but in the hallowed precincts of Athens where the Old Academy had first received the revelations of its inspired founder. As he would inform his disciple and biographer Marinus years later, he resolved to become a philosopher at this time because his divine patroness Athena urged him in a vision to give up his legal and rhetorical studies so that he might reside in her city and protect her cult from the pundits and dogmamongers of the Christian Empire. In the run-down little provincial town that Athens had become under the Christian Emperors the Lycian would find – or make – his haven. There his goddess was waiting with the teacher who would open his eyes to the deities governing the order of time and lead his soul into 'the intellectual dance with orders more divine.'[2]

On his return to Alexandria, where he would remain for only a few months, Proclus prepared his uninitiated intellect for its strenuous leap into the Platonic Beyond by mastering two subjects which were to leave their mark on the highly systematic character of his later thought: Aristotelian logic and Euclidean geometry. Of course his subsequent training in Platonic cosmology and Neoplatonic theology would also profoundly affect his interpretation of these 'elementary' subjects. Euclid would doubtless have been surprised to learn that his Fourteenth Definition ('A figure is that which is enclosed by one or more boundaries') was first taught to humanity by the heavenly bodies, which display

in themselves and in their relations to one another a great and wondrous diversity of figures, and present now one, now another shape bearing an image of the Intelligible Forms, and copy in their excellently rhythmic choral dances [tais eurythmois heautōn choreiais] the bodiless and immaterial powers of the figures.

(*In primum Elementorum librum*, Def xiv, p 137)

These mystifying remarks (which would not be out of place in a recondite theological treatise on the reflection of the Intelligible Forms in the design of the Iamblichan heavens) are taken from a discussion of the term 'schēma' in Proclus' pedagogical commentary on the first book of Euclid's *Elements*.

The Lycian's Alexandrian training in rhetoric was also to have a lasting effect on his outlook as a philosopher. When the time came for him to unwind the sacred scrolls of Plato he would admire the eloquence as well as the wisdom of the great speakers in the *Dialogues* and devote much of his immense exegetical energy to the analysis of the subtlest implications of diction, allusion, and etymology. Like Synesius, whose early career as a pagan rhetor was similarly diverted by a calling to the philosophical life, Proclus did not cease to be a lover of words when he became a lover of wisdom. To philological topics such as the etymological significance of divine names and the reflection of cosmic harmony in prosody and syntax his philosophical mind would often turn in the course of his long contemplative life. Different as their holy scriptures and spheres of influence were, the Christian poet and the Neoplatonic exegete approached the study of language with the same religious impulse to tear through the veil of words that simultaneously concealed and revealed the character of the Divine Mind.

Around 431 Proclus reached Athens in accordance with Athena's wishes and enrolled himself in a Platonic Academy located on the south side of the Acropolis close by the Temple of Dionysus. Though this Academy was not historically continuous with Plato's original school, having been founded in the early fifth century AD by a certain Plutarch of Athens, its members considered themselves the rightful heirs of Plato's inexpressible outpouring of wisdom. From Marinus we learn that this Plutarch (not to be confused with the Middle Platonist Plutarch of Chaeronea who flourished around 100 AD) warmly welcomed Proclus into his family circle, placed him with his grandson Archiadas under the tutelage of his colleague Syrianus, and died of old age shortly thereafter.

In Syrianus, who succeeded Plutarch as head of the Academy, Proclus found his Ammonius. Since only one of Syrianus' works (a commentary on Aristotle's *Metaphysics*) has come down to us – our knowledge of the rest being confined to bare titles and to fragments of his commentaries embedded in the Procline corpus – the full extent of his influence on the Lycian is difficult to assess, but it must have been great indeed for Proclus was in the habit of recording Syrianus' comments on their daily readings from Plato and later drew from his seminar notes the raw material for his own Platonic commentaries. Rarely in his commentaries, which as Marinus suggests in his biography (*Vita Procli* XIII) should be read not only as expressions of his evolving personal philosophy but also as edited transcripts of his mentor's oral teachings, does the Lycian pronounce judgment on any controversial point in the old philosophy without appealing to the revered authority of Syrianus. The great Platonists of the past spoke to him through Syrianus like spirits through a medium. That the authority of Plotinus, Porphyry, and especially Iamblichus was revered by the students at the Academy may be inferred from the copious quotations from their works that Proclus as a dutiful doxographer of the Platonic tradition inserted into his volumes of exegesis. Engulfed in the ocean of their words and buffeted by their conflicting doctrines, he must often have thanked his stars that a divinely illumined sage was seeing him calmly through his journey to the bright shores where Apollo welcomed the souls of the wise into the chorus of Immortal Love. No doubt the untimely death of Syrianus in 437 AD deeply affected the new Athenian, who was left a mere neophyte in the Platonic mysteries; but as Athena's protégé he would enshrine the wisdom of 'the most theological of exegetes' (as he called his teacher with Levantine deference) in the metaphysical Parthenon he was constructing around the image of his endangered goddess.[3]

With the completion in 440 AD of his monumental *Commentary on the Timaeus*, which of all his early works most clearly reveals in its fantastic elaboration of the Platonic theory of time and its exuberant synthesis of Asiatic and Hellenic mythologies the peculiarly Iamblichan character of Athenian Neoplatonism, Proclus proved that he could see through the surface meaning of the Pythagorean astronomer's words to the secret theological revelations Plato had conveyed to his original circle of disciples and that like the great Platonic illuminati of the past he could sustain over thousands of Dedalian sentences the most arcane meditations on the psychic life of the stars, the demiurgic activity of the gods, and the ineffable stillness at the centre of the cosmic dance. In old age he would look back on this work with especial fondness because in writing it, as his biographer noted (*Vita Procli* XIII), he 'added knowledge to his moral virtues' and so ceased to be a neophyte in the Platonic mysteries.

One would suppose from the ostensible subject matter of the dialogue that the knowledge he acquired at this time was an amalgam of mathematics, astronomy, music, and astral theology – the usual pedagogical preliminaries for the mystical ascent from the Many to the One. But it was more than that. Syrianus had taught him that the supreme goal of the philosophers at the Academy was not to produce pedantic glosses on Plato but to master the sacred science of theurgy, an occult discipline supposedly derived from the ancient Chaldeans which the unenlightened Christians mistook for sorcery, and it was theurgic wisdom above all that the Lycian sought and found in the Myth of the Craftsman. Adepts in the sacred science regarded it as a branch of learning far superior to magic. Whereas a magician was commonly an illiterate shaman who bound his soul to the material world in order to control the sympathetic energies binding minerals, herbs, and other talismanic substances to elemental spirits, planetary daimones, and astral gods, a theurgist was an academic wizard with exceptional psychic abilities who purged his soul of base material concerns so that he could achieve mystic union with the supersensible Helios and share in the limitless creative powers of the intellectual gods. Literally an art of 'divine works' (theia erga), theurgy was in essence the practical application of Neoplatonic wisdom for philanthropic ends. It was the Iamblichan wizardry that the late lamented Emperor Julian had turned to after losing faith in the efficacy of the Christian sacraments.[4]

Like Julian, who never presumed that a theurgist even of Iamblichus' stature could gain total control over Helios and his legions of demiurgic gods, Proclus hoped simply to persuade the aristocrats of the spirit world to use him as their instrument for healing diseases, averting wars, preventing earthquakes, and mitigating countless other evils within the sublunary sphere. A true theurgist knew that he was exalted above the miserable mass of humanity by his special virtues, the powers that streamed down to him from the undefiled wellspring of the Good and the Beautiful; yet he was humbled by the knowledge that these virtues were bestowed on him by deities more majestic and powerful than the imperious goddess Necessity (whose cruel laws he was often called upon to countermand). Despising both worldly power and sensual pleasure – a Late Antique Doctor Faustus he was not – the Lycian strove to improve the physical and spiritual health of his fellow mortals in the same way that the god Chronos improved the order of the cosmic dance by periodically rejuvenating the body and soul of the dancing cosmos. The Chaldean theurgists, he believed, had discovered the miraculous nature of this god by perceiving time as much more than a measurement of motion or a cycle of changes within the visible world. Convinced that they alone had gained a complete understanding of the intellectual essence of Chronos, he devoted a long and abstruse section of his favourite commentary (*In Timaeum* III 1–52) to the defence of their wildly paradoxical vision of eternal time – his strategy being to make their vision philosophically intelligible or at least respectable by deducing it from Plato's famous metaphysical definition of time as 'a moving image of eternity.'

At first glance even a relatively lucid passage from this section of the commentary such as his discussion of the etymology of the name Chronos (III 28–9) is apt to boggle and discourage an uninitiated reader: it all seems like so much dense theological fog billowing out of nowhere and obscuring the familiar chorus of visible gods in the Platonic world-theatre. The image of the dance seems to be strangely redefined or to lose definition altogether in the vaporous scene-change from the Platonic to the Procline universe. The theurgic vision of the dance of time does make sense after a while, though it requires even of spectators with undimmed Platonic eyes a considerable adjustment of intellectual focus and a willingness to perceive the miraculous in the mundane. The fog will have to remain in the theatre for the present while we consider the perversely antiquarian and profoundly anti-Christian mentality of the Lycian who conjured it up like ectoplasm from a mythical academic past.

No doubt the Chaldean theology of time appealed to Proclus because it was so unlike the prevailing Christian view of the mechanical measurement, imminent cessation, and ultimate insignificance of all things temporal. Defending the Chaldeans was his way of coolly rebelling against the Christians, particularly the Alexandrian school of Christian theologians who had ransacked the Myth of the Craftsman for images and arguments to support their view of history as a Logos-conducted procession from the Creation to the Last Day. He was determined to see the dance from a secret vantage-point as far removed from theirs as could possibly be found in the crumbling tiers of the old cosmic theatre.

Since Iamblichus and his successors had costumed the divine choragi of the cosmos in mythological veils spun from the iridescent language of the *Orphic Hymns* and the *Chaldean Oracles*, no theurgist at the Athenian Academy would have considered his education complete without a thorough study of these two poetic anthologies in harmonious relation to the myths of Plato. Orpheus 'the Theologian' was revered by Syrianus and his circle as an historical personage whose sacred revelations Plato had incorporated into his teachings. The short formulaic hymns addressed to various Greek and Asiatic deities which were ascribed by tradition to the Theologian (but written probably in the second or third century AD) served as models, as we have seen, for the cosmological poems composed by the philological craftsmen of the poetic universe. While no extant Orphic hymn invokes a god by the name of Chronos, several celebrate the seasonal regulation of time by Apollo, Helios, Bacchus, Pan, and the Horae. In the following breathless paean to the 'Inducer of Fantasies,' the Horae seem to rest while their earth-enamoured lord whirls and capers in the cosmic dance:

> *I call upon the mighty Pan and upon the whole cosmos,*
> *The heavens and the sea and the earth who is queen of all,*
> *And the immortal fire: for these are all the melodies of Pan.*

Come o Blessed Leaper, Rushing Whirler, Ruler enthroned
with the Horae,
Goat-limbed Reveller, Lover of Frenzy, Ruler of the Stars!
Out of your playful dance-song you weave the harmony of the
cosmos,
O Inducer of Fantasies, Fearful Inciter of terror in mortal hearts!
You rejoice in gushing springs and herders of goats and oxen,
O Keen-eyed Hunter, Lover of Echo, Dancer with the Nymphs
[synchore nymphōn]. ...
(*Orphic Hymns* 11, 1–12)

From hymns of this sort which confirmed (or seemed to confirm) the late Neoplatonic belief that the cosmic gods were spirits of frenzy and rampant eroticism as well as weavers of harmony, Proclus learned to regard temporal order as an unceasing interplay of destructive and creative forces woven together by a divine dancer. Though he was trained as a philosopher to see the enduring order of 'the Whole' (to pan) by disregarding the transient manifestations of disorder below the moon, as a theurgist he was expected to pay close attention to the tempests, volcanic eruptions, and other sublunary disturbances that sparked fantasies of universal chaos in the souls of Pan's uneducated worshippers and to protect his inferiors from the shocks of time by restoring harmony to their panic-stricken souls and health to their corruptible bodies.

From the *Chaldean Oracles*, a collection of prophetic outpourings and magical incantations put together in the late second century AD by a certain Julian 'the Theurgist' whom the Emperor Julian considered second only to the divine Iamblichus as an expert in the sacred science, Proclus learned that the whirling of Pan (which many philosophers had mistakenly regarded as the cause of time or identified with time itself) was actually the effect of the intellectual activity of a supracosmic god named Aion or 'Eternity.' A few paragraphs before his etymological discussion of Chronos he hailed Aion as 'the Light begotten by the Father' and cited the following verses from an Chaldean oracle to explain the appropriateness of the epithet:

... for having alone plucked the abounding flower
Of Intellect from the Strength of the Father, he [that is, Aion]
has the ability to understand
The Paternal Intellect and to give light to all wellsprings and
principles,
And to whirl round forever and to remain in an unceasing
revolution.
(*In Timaeum* III 14)

While the Orphic Pan whirled on goat's legs through the sphere of time and delighted in the gushing wellsprings of earth's nymph-haunted glades, the Chaldean Aion presided over the purely spiritual 'wellsprings and principles' of a timeless pleroma (which the later Neoplatonists inevitably identified with the domain of the Platonic Forms) where his position was that of intermediary between the numinous entities responsible for creating and sustaining the World-Soul and the divinized faculties of Will, Strength, and Intellect emanating from the Supreme Being or Father.

If Aion had appeared to the theurgists simply as an eternal light-fixture through which the single ray of the Father's Intellect was transmitted to the Empyrean and by which it was divided into the many rays of the empyreal spirits, his nature would probably have been described in the oracle as wholly static; but since he was known to be indistinguishable from the Light begotten by the Father – the current of pure mental energy spiralling around the Forms and encompassing the whole Chaldean pleroma – his conjurors often spoke of him in dynamic terms. In the last verse of the oracle, for instance, the characteristic motion of Aion is denoted by the paradoxical phrase 'dinein aie te menein.' The intransitive verb 'dinein' (to whirl around) specifically denoted the spiral flow of a whirlpool or the fluid twirling and circling of dancers. (Homer established this latter meaning in *Iliad* XVIII.494 and 606, where the verb is used in reference to the dancers depicted by Hephaestus on the Shield of Achilles.) Though no Chaldean text has survived in which Aion's whirling is explicitly called a dance, it was probably conceived as such by the author of the oracle and by the theurgists who according to Proclus (III 20) referred to the god in hymns chanted at their conjuring ceremonies as 'he who winds in a circle.' That this motion was certainly perceived as a dance by Proclus is clear from his meditation on the choreia of Chronos (III 28–9) in which he attempted to resolve the paradox implicit in the oracular collocation of the infinitives 'dinein' and 'menein.' If Aion was forever winding in a circle around the outside of the cosmos, how was it possible for him – as the verb 'menein' implied – 'to remain' in an eternally changeless state or 'to stand still' in an eternally fixed position?

Finding no answer to this question in Julian the Theurgist, who seems to have clouded the issue in further obscurity by treating Aion and Chronos as one and the same god, Proclus tried to shed light on these theurgic mysteries by distinguishing Chronos from Aion in accordance with the Platonic doctrine that time must be inferior to its eternal archetype. As a result, while Aion retained his old Chaldean position high up in the chain of supracosmic entities, Chronos fell in the Procline chain to the status of a peripheral numen existing partly in the cosmos and partly in the domain of the intellectual gods.[5] Proclus might easily have resolved the oracular paradox by associating 'dinein' with Chronos and 'menein' with Aion, which would not only have sharpened the distinction between them but also have dispelled much of the fog obscuring the theurgic vision of the dance. But for some reason, perhaps because this simple way of reconciling Platonic cosmology and Chaldean theology would have toppled Chronos from his lofty station among the Intellects by turning him into a whirling demigod hardly different in character and function from the Orphic Pan, he decided that Chronos would inherit Aion's miraculous ability to wind in a circle while staying still and that Aion would serve as the motionless paradigm of all that was permanent in the unfolding measures of the cosmic dance. Chronos was thus saved from the coils of mutability by his close imitation of Aion, but his nature was still wound up in the paradox of eternal time – time measured outside the body of the temporal world by a timeless and bodiless dancer! Was there no way to make philosophical sense of this bizarre vision? Was there no way to preserve the dignity of Chronos without abandoning the logic of Athena? There *was*, Syrianus had assured him, and it lay as we shall see in the Neoplatonic elaboration of a Neo-pythagorean theory of time which originally had no connection with theurgy.

Though the death of his tutor left him with only a rudimentary knowledge of Orphic and Chaldean theology, Proclus was able nevertheless to master all the fine points of doctrine by studying Syrianus' *Commentary on the Orphic Writings* (now lost) along with Porphyry's *Letter to Anebo* and Iamblichus' pseudonymous reply *On the Mysteries of the Egyptians* (both extant). In his brief epistle Porphyry had expressed a humble yearning for communion with the intellectual gods but had also cast a haughtily Skeptical eye on the hocus-pocus of the theurgists. If his philosophical criticism of their fantastic claims aroused in Proclus any doubts concerning the legitimacy of the sacred science, these would soon have been put to rest by the recondite treatise of Iamblichus, which purports to be a simple description of the goals, rituals, talismans, and divination techniques of an Egyptian initiate in the theurgic mysteries but is actually a sophisticated analysis of Chaldean religious experience from the apologetic viewpoint of a Neoplatonist anxious to translate preaching into practice. In the third chapter of this occult textbook is an eerily objective account of the behaviour of a divinely possessed theurgist as witnessed by the spectators at a conjuring ceremony:

Since there are many ways in which people may be possessed by the gods, there are also many outward signs of divine possession: movement of the whole body or certain parts of the body; complete bodily calm; harmonious arrangements (of limbs) and dances [choreiai] and melodious sounds or the very opposite of these. Sometimes the body is seen to rise or to expand or to be carried high through the air, and at other times phenomena contrary to these are observed. ... But the most important sign is this: the theurgist seeing the spirit descend discerns its size and quality and mysteriously commands and controls it. He who receives the spirit sees it also in a fiery form before it enters into him. Sometimes all the spectators see it very clearly too, either when the god descends or when he withdraws.

(*On the Mysteries* III 5–6)

Did this fiery form (which has been called the ancestor of the luminous ectoplasmic apparitions summoned by modern spiritualists)[6] emanate from Chronos? Iamblichus named no names here, but as Proclus reports in *In Timaeum* III 20 the theurgists were accustomed to bring about the 'auto-phaneia' or 'self-manifestation' of Chronos through the recitation of a certain magical formula which had been passed down the centuries to the teachers at the Athenian Academy. The various external symptoms of divine pos-session listed by Iamblichus are by no means uniquely theurgic in character – dancing, for instance, having been a sign of 'enthusiasm' (in its original sense) since the days of the Corybants. Peculiar to theurgic enthusiasm, however, may be the combination of opposing symptoms on his list. Al-ternating with periods of spectacular physical activity during which the theurgist levitated or flew or danced in ecstasy to unearthly melodies were periods of otherworldly calm in which he sank to the ground in a trance, relaxed all his limbs, and awaited the theophany in silence. If Chronos was indeed the god who entered into him on such occasions, then his extraor-dinary behaviour might be construed as a dramatic imitation of the god's intramundane dance and supramundane repose.

Through theatrical displays of this sort – psychic sound-and-light shows in which the divine actors needed no machines to bring them down from the heavens – the theurgist shared with his inferiors his sublime vision of 'tōn kreittonōn choros,' 'the chorus of the superior powers' (*On the Mys-teries* III 18). In him were combined the roles of producer, performer, and spectator. As producer of the spectacle he was seen to command and control the spirit who answered his summons; as its chief performer he dazzled his spectators with displays of supernatural power; and as the most educated spectator in the cosmic theatre he knew all the names and epithets of the conjured spirit before its arrival and quickly discerned 'its size and quality' during its descent. According to Iamblichus the theurgists preferred to call the gods by their ancient Egyptian or Assyrian names because these were usually not understood by the Greek-speaking spectators at their ceremonies and so served as fitting symbols of the incomprehensible majesty of the gods invoked. 'But as for those names which we may understand through the traditional science of [etymological] analysis,' avowed Iamblichus in *On the Mysteries* VII 4, 'from them we acquire an expert knowledge of the full essence, power, and order of the gods.'

It was in quest of such knowledge that Proclus traced the Greek name of the god of time back to its supposedly archaic form 'choronoos,' a compound of the participle 'choreuōn' ('dancing') and the noun 'nous' ('intellect'). His respelling of the name worked like a charm. In a flash the secret identity of Chronos was revealed to his inward eye as clearly as the Divine Fire had been to the spectators at the conjuring ceremonies. The essence of the god was intellectual, the power of the god was sufficient to set the whole cosmos dancing, and the order of the god was simultaneously static and dynamic. If the respelled name, a hapax legomenon, was not quite as dark and mysterious as the name 'Emeph' given by the ancient Egyptians to their Chronos-like lord of celestial powers – a god 'said to be an Intellect contemplating himself and turning his thoughts back to himself' (*On the Mysteries* VIII 4) – it was at least obscure enough to symbolize the paradox-enshrouded nature of Chronos and to conceal his transcendent activity from all but the masters of the sacred science.

The theurgists of Egypt had passed on to Iamblichus the valuable information that the intellectual gods were eternal arch-conservatives who preferred to be summoned by those names which the wizards of old had received directly from heaven or had ingeniously invented when first opening up their channels of communication with the spirit world. With this in mind Proclus expected to gain not only theological insights from the etymological analysis of divine names but also theurgic power over language, the power to translate words into symbolic talismans which could catch the attention of the gods and lure them into the magic theatre of time. The theurgic spectator did not name the fiery forms dancing above him in order to identify phenomena in the manner of an astronomer or to clarify causal relations in the manner of a natural philosopher. He sought to control what he saw by his poetic act of naming. Proclus never doubted the efficacy of theurgic hymns and invocations because he knew from his early encounter with Athena in Constantinople that the gods truly existed behind their once potent but now sadly time-worn and discredited names.

Marinus proudly reports that Proclus studied Orphic and Chaldean theology for only five years before he attained 'those supreme virtues of the human soul which the divinely inspired Iamblichus in his marvellous way has called theurgic' (*Vita Procli* XXVI). Most aspirants to theurgic perfection spent decades trying to understand Orpheus and the Chaldeans and were greybeards by the time they could summon up Chronos from the Beyond. The Lycian was only about thirty when he reached this pinnacle in his career. His education complete, he decided to stay on in Athens to uphold the Platonic tradition and was duly hailed by his colleagues as the Diadochus or 'Successor' to Plutarch and Syrianus as head of the Athenian Academy.[7]

Dreams of a True Bacchant

The garland of asphodel that Porphyry's Muses set on the ascetic brow of Plotinus when he crossed the threshold of heaven was rewoven by Marinus with lotuses and heliotropes and other theurgic blooms and placed on the saintly head of Proclus while he was still on earth – a 'tear-stained suppliant' as he called himself[8] – leading the dance of the old paideia to its final bacchic pose in defiance of the Christian Empire. Not to be outdone by Porphyry as a pagan hagiographer, Marinus claimed that Proclus was able to surpass rather than merely equal Plotinus in happiness, good fortune, and sanctity because of his devotion to the art of divine works. While Plotinus (if Porphyry is to be believed) was born with certain magical powers which allowed him on at least one occasion to protect himself from the evil spell of a jealous rival, he is not known to have distinguished magic from theurgy or ever to have used the term 'theurgy' in his writings. Philosophers who dabbled in the occult seem to have met with his disapproval. With considerable hauteur he once declined an invitation from his disciple Amelius to attend certain religious rituals at the New Moon (a time associated with magical potency) on the grounds that the sublunary daimones and other cosmic spirits invoked in such rites were to come to him, not he to them![9] Proclus would certainly have agreed with Plotinus that a philosopher should look to the One for spiritual guidance and prefer the exalted company of Psyche and Nous to the lowly rout of elemental spirits. But he would not have turned down an opportunity to commune with Hecate or to summon Dionysus at the New Moon. So eager was he to approach the benevolent gods who kept the ill-tempered and chaotic cacodemons in their chains, gods like Helios and Chronos, that they in turn were always quick to answer his invocations and sometimes came to him without solicitation.

Once he received an unexpected visit in a dream from Apollo's son Asclepius, the divine healer whose sanctuary stood behind the Theatre of Dionysus on the southern slope of the Acropolis, and like an actor in the theatre preparing to deliver a eulogy the god extended his hand towards him and exclaimed: 'The glory of the country!' (*Vita Procli* xxxiii). According to Marinus, the glory of the Diadochus lay not in any one quality of body or soul but in the harmonious combination of all the virtues – physical, moral, political, ascetic, intellectual, and theurgic – which like steps in a celestial ladder permitted him to ascend to a divine state of happiness during his earthly life. Lacking the sixth and culminating virtue in this series, Plotinus had been able to achieve perfect happiness only after his soul had left the shameful chains of the body and risen into the blessed chorus beyond the stars. Marinus had no need to cite an oracle in the manner of Porphyry to prove that his teacher was linked to 'the Golden Chain of philosophers that began with Solon' (*Vita Procli* XXVI). The theurgic virtues crowning the incomparable character of the Diadochus were proof enough that his intellect had circled with the eternal spirits long before his departure from the chorus of time.

Having learned in a dream that he possessed the soul of the celebrated first-century Neopythagorean mathematician and musical theorist Nicomachus (*Vita Procli* XXVIII), Proclus doubtless perceived his succession to the headship of the Academy as much more than a professional promotion sanctioned by his mortal contemporaries. His promotion was but the outward historical reflection of a succession which was in essence psychological: a mysterious concatenation of the intellectual life of the past with the intellectual life of the present ordained by the eternal minds controlling the cycle of reincarnation. Instead of stretching to infinity like a straight line, the Golden Chain of philosophers seemed to coil back upon itself as time went on, forming a circle with a finite number of members whose souls like those of Plato's stars always thought the same thoughts about the same things. As the circle turned, new academic luminaries rose on the horizon of intellectual history to replace those who were setting or had vanished into the past. But the light of the old philosophers was never lost. If Nicomachus had risen again to shine in the life of Proclus, was it not likely that Solon or Orpheus or Pythagoras would return in future Diadochi to rekindle the intellectual brilliance of Athena's city and dispel the Christian darkness that had descended upon it? With Julian's dream of a glorious pagan revival still lingering in their memories the Lycian and his disciples woke up to the sobering realization that they had first to ensure the survival of paganism before they could begin to revive its ancient glory. They had reason to fear that the Academy, their island of philosophical calm in the raging gulf of Eastern Christianity, would be swiftly eroded by the waves of intolerance that periodically threatened its existence as a religious institution; and they half suspected (though the prospect was too appalling to contemplate) that the Golden Chain would be severed in their own generation or the next by the imperial sword of the Church Militant.

Sometime after Proclus became Diadochus, a mob of Athenian Christians boldly removed the statue of Athena from the Parthenon and converted the symbolic centre of Hellenic paganism into a shrine to honour their own virgin patroness of wisdom, Hagia Sophia. With a certain melancholy pride Marinus records that throughout this turbulent period the Diadochus stood firm against the bitter tides of political and religious oppression and contemplated the dramatic impermanence of temporal institutions with Socratic detachment. But deep down he must have seethed with resentment and indignation. What was their Hagia Sophia but a vague allegorical shadow of Athena? What choice had they left him as defender of the Academy but to turn Platonism into a secret mystery cult and theurgy into a locally popular alternative to the Christian sacraments?

During the desecration of the Parthenon he was consoled by a dream in which a beautiful woman commanded him to prepare his house for 'the Lady of Athens' (*Vita Procli* xxx). Her order did not go unheeded. Despite the Church's traumatic incursions onto its home territory, the Academy survived under Proclus' leadership by putting into practice the Athenian Stranger's theory of paideia as a process of conservative indoctrination analogous to the strict regimentation of bodies and souls underlying the harmony of choreia. 'In our city,' boasted the Athenian Stranger,

our virgin goddess, the Lady Athena, is gladdened by the play of the dance [tēi tēs choreias paidiai]. She has judged it unseemly to sport with empty hands and so completes the measures of her dance adorned in a full suit of armour.

(*Laws* VII 796b–c)

It was the intellectual counterpart of this noble dance – at once a warlike display of heroic virtues (pyrrhikē) and a harmonious celebration of traditional cultural values (emmeleia) – that would gladden the unhappy Lady of Athens in the house prepared for her by the Diadochus. Just as the choral dancers of old had submitted to the commands of their instructors, preserved the dances of their ancestors, and learned to move in harmony with their fellow citizens, so Marinus and his peers would follow the intellectual lead of the Diadochus, preserve the wisdom of their philosophical forebears, and work for peace and order within the state.

The spirit of aggressive pagan conservatism displayed at the Academy inevitably brought Proclus into conflict with the Christian authorities in Athens, however, and at least once during his later academic life he was forced to flee the city for a year's exile in Lydia (*Vita Procli* xv). There, in his typically methodical manner, he gathered first-hand information about the vanishing religious customs of the pagan Lydians and had himself initiated into the various mystery cults that were still celebrated in Asia Minor. His hosts also benefited from his enforced sabbatical by learning from their distinguished guest what their Christian oppressors were trying to obliterate from their souls and what the centuries had largely erased from their collective memory: the secret theological significance of their ecstatic rites.

The wealth of unimaginably ancient (and therefore unquestionably authentic) religious lore that Proclus added to his treasury of academic wisdom during his year of mystical field-work in Asia Minor was much admired by the bookish Marinus, who notes in XXII that his teacher on returning to Athens rightly looked down upon 'the many who carry the narthex' because he had become 'one of the true Bacchants.' This allusion to an analogy originally drawn by Socrates in the *Phaedo* (69c–d) was particularly pertinent to the Diadochus during his period of political crisis and exile. Just as the divine Socrates had borne the hostility of the Athenians without fearing death or losing faith in the immortality of his soul, so Proclus endured his exclusion from Athenian society with the calmness and patience of one who knew that his soul was destined for the society of the gods. According to Socrates the narthex-carriers, the uninitiated masses who bore the ivy-tipped wands in processions honouring Dionysus, represented the crowds of Sophists and false philosophers who made a show of being wise but were unable to face death without fear. True philosophers, by contrast, were like the happy few who underwent all the stages of bacchic initiation from ritual drunkenness to ecstatic union with the choragus of the stars. They could face death with the consoling knowledge that though their bodies were destined to be destroyed like sacrificial animals in the maenadic rush of time their souls would leap up to the heavens with the joy of newly released prisoners and enter into the timeless revelry of the gods.

Of course Socrates had not intended his analogy to be construed as a recommendation that philosophers don fawn-skins, leap on the mountain-tops, and abandon the rational pursuit of wisdom for the mystic mania of Dionysian possession. Philosophy, he had implied with characteristic irony, was infinitely preferable to the garbled teachings of the mystagogues as a preparation for death since it alone awakened in its adepts a clear vision of the divine chorus circling in the radiance of the Good and the Beautiful. The militancy of the Christian mystagogues would radically alter the implications of the analogy for Proclus and his school. What he knew as philosophy did not drive him away from the Hellenic and Asiatic mystery religions but rather straight towards them as a tear-stained suppliant. When Marinus identified his teacher as a true Bacchant, then, he was speaking neither ironically nor metaphorically. Not many *true* Bacchants – that is, pagans of the old school who fervently believed in the existence of Dionysus and Demeter and all the other mystery gods – were left to encircle the Kallichoron (lost amid the Goth-pillaged ruins of Eleusis) in those melancholy days of Christian intolerance. And what had become of the many who carried the narthex and clamoured drunkenly after Iacchus along the Panathenaic Way? The only narthex they recognized now (having thrown down their phallic wands long ago before the cross of the Galilean) was the vestibule of their local basilica, and there they were gathered every day like sheep by the sober leaders of the Church's 'koinē chorostasia.' It was indeed 'koinē,' this 'public' government which claimed to have organized the common people into a divine chorus; but as long as there remained even one pagan outside it, one noble pagan who refused to bow his head to the Galilean and worship a common mortal as the universal choragus, it could never be a 'universal' church as its leaders were fond of calling it. It could never be 'katholikē.'

The proximity of the Successor's Academy to the site of the ancient Temple and Theatre of Dionysus (where a marble throne reserved for the priest of Dionysus Eleutherios can still be seen in the front row of the cavea) was a pointed reminder to the Christian Establishment that the old gods of the city were not cast into the shadows when the light of Hagia Sophia streamed forth from the sanctuary of the Parthenon. Their fiery forms were never far from the dreams – and séance chambers – of the great wizard of Athens. A Dionysus without human features, spiritualized, pacified, exalted to a plane of existence far beyond the fire-breathing stars of Euripides, but Dionysus nonetheless, the old god of ecstasy and generation and magic, outshone the sun itself as a living presence in the universal order envisioned by the last of the true Bacchants. Little wonder, then, that Proclus expressed his most magical and dreamlike visions of the cosmic dance in a Dionysian rhetoric almost Euripidean in intensity and that this rhetoric should well up in the driest stretches of his Platonic commentaries and theological treatises without the slightest trace of Socratic irony.

Though the Athenian Stranger had sharply distinguished the rational motions of choral dance from the mad abandon of bacchic revelry and sternly banned the latter from his ideal society except among senior citizens, Proclus seems to have drawn no such distinction and contemplated no such ban with regard to the Academy. Paideia – to modify the Athenian Stranger's dictum – was both a disciplined choreia and an impassioned baccheia for the students of the Diadochus. The choral phase of their education, which trained them to imitate the old philosophers' ascetic way of life and idealistic mode of thought, resulted in the formation of a learned circle of coreligionists bound by ties of intellectual sympathy and personal affection to their divinely illumined headmaster. The bacchic phase began when the chorus of disciples, yearning for something more than academic knowledge, stretched their intellects up towards the One in an agonized search for permanence in the whirl of time; it culminated for a privileged few in a fantastic dissolution of the boundary between the dream world of the senses and the real world of the spirit, that is to say, in their psychic intercourse with the intellectual gods and subsequent acquisition of theurgic powers.

Though distinguishable in theory, the two phases proved in practice to be inherently complementary and historically inseparable. Like the virtues of the Diadochus, the various subjects linked together on his curriculum – Aristotelian logic, Euclidean geometry, Platonic cosmology, Orphic theology, and Chaldean theurgy – reflected the ascending levels of enlightenment through which a pagan intellectual had to pass on the way to theurgic perfection. The more knowledgeable a student became in these subjects the more intense would be his yearning for direct communication with the occult powers governing the order of words, numbers, bodies, souls, and the visible gods; and the more godlike his soul became through ecstatic contact with the occult powers the more brilliant would be his performance as a teacher when the time came for him to lead his own chorus of disciples through the stages of academic initiation.

Clinging to the belief that the gods of the past would protect this age-old cycle of learning and teaching from all that threatened its continuity in the present, the Diadochus assured his students that the future of their school was secure because destiny had allotted him a divine nature like that of his great predecessors. In the preface to his magnum opus, a comprehensive survey of the myriad ranks in 'the chorus of the superior powers' entitled *The Platonic Theology*, he imagined the Golden Chain of philosophers in the dynamic form of a choral procession:

Let me identify the interpreters of the Platonic mysteries, those who have been allotted a divine nature similar to their guide's and have guided us in explaining and revealing the divine principles: first, Plotinus the Egyptian; second, Amelius and Porphyry, who inherited their doctrine from Plotinus; third, we believe, Iamblichus and [his third-century disciple] Theodore of Asinus, who were their followers and whom we might regard as their holy images because they attained a high state of perfection; and certain others, such as there were, who following them in this divine choral dance [tōi theiōi toutōi chorōi] around the doctrine of Plato roused their own thought to bacchic frenzy.

(*Platonic Theology* 1.1, 1 6–7)

Like spirits in a theurgic séance, the illustrious Platonists of Late Antiquity are conjured up in chronological order to circle before the inward eye of the true Bacchant, and what he perceives in their communal revolution around the doctrine of Plato is an ingenious fusion of two old philosophical images dear to his heart: the dance of education and the dance of time. The conclusion of his solemn hierophantic roll call turns his declaration of allegiance to the past into a meditation on the flow of intellectual history into the present. Still referring to himself in the first person plural (though with the implication that his 'we' and 'us' may designate his whole school), Proclus extends the figure of 'this divine choral dance' to include his late tutor Syrianus and inevitably himself:

From their line came one who, after the gods, was our guide in all that was beautiful and good. Having received into the bosom of his soul in a pure manner the most authentic and unclouded light of truth, he caused us to be partakers in all the other philosophy of Plato and made us his companion in those traditions which he received in secret from his predecessors. He indeed it was who revealed to us that we were dancing together [synchoreutas] around the mystic truth of the divine principles.

(*Platonic Theology* 1.1, 1 6–7)

Like the motionless motion of Chronos, the dance of the Platonic Successors seemed to take place in two worlds simultaneously. As the circling years brought new initiates into the dance and led old ones away it appeared to evolve, like all other historical movements, in the world of Becoming. But since the celebrated leaders in the dance (the pagan counterparts of the Orthodox Fathers) based their teachings on a set of doctrines which supposedly remained unchanged through all the years, the dynamic procession of their thoughts could be viewed from the perspective of the whole as a constant and therefore timeless activity – the participation of divine intellects in the order of eternal Being. If Proclus ever stopped to think that his Academy was not in fact historically continuous with the Old Academy or that the Platonic tradition he was preserving from defilement was by the fifth century far from pure, he did not let such trifling considerations blur his grand vision of himself and his disciples as participants in the unbroken and authentic circle of Platonic illuminati.

The course of intellectual history (and for an 'orthodox' Platonist there was but one course to consider) clearly indicated that the school of Plato would go on forever, that no Christian power could stop 'the unclouded light of truth' from streaming into the souls of the Diadochi and perpetuating their cycle of choral instruction and bacchic initiation. Syrianus, moreover, had assured him of the perpetuity of the Succession by revealing that he had been dancing all his life 'around the mystic truth of the divine principles' simply by existing within the endless revolutions of time. But the annals of his school and the assurances of his tutor were not enough to sustain his faith in the continuance of the dance. His intellect demanded a metaphysical proof that his school would survive – a proof not dependent on historical contingencies. His anxious search for that proof may be traced through the labyrinth of hypotheses and deductions he constructed around Plato's metaphysical definition of time. If the dance of education reflected both the dynamism and the stability of the dance of time, as he was certain it did, then the course of intellectual history (that is, the revolution of dancing intellects around the doctrine of Plato) could be viewed as an effect and therefore an image of the archetypal Dancing Intellect, Chronos. And if he could prove from oracular, etymological, and cosmological evidence that the activity and essence of Chronos were eternal, then could he not deduce from this that the cosmos itself would have to stop dancing before the 'theios choros' of the Academy would be brought to a halt? His hopes for the survival of pagan education may thus have rested on his resolution of the paradox of eternal time.

Having spent many laborious years sifting through, sorting out, and setting down the multitudinous opinions of his predecessors, Proclus was well aware that the philosophers in the 'theios choros' had embroiled themselves in doctrinal controversies, bickered over minute points of exegesis, warred over the relative merits of theurgy and philosophy, and failed to reach a consensus on the long-disputed question of whether the Platonic myths should be interpreted literally or figuratively. Might he not then be justly accused of ignoring the obvious historical evidence that ran counter to his harmonious vision of intellectual history? In his own defence, which was tantamount to a defence of the pagan past that was alive in him, the Diadochus simply argued that the discordant opinions of his predecessors had all arisen over Plato's written philosophy. As for 'all the other philosophy of Plato,' the secret wisdom transmitted orally from the original members of the Old Academy down through the centuries to the pupils of Syrianus, there had never been and could never be any disagreement over *it* since those who inherited it invariably accepted their inheritance as a mystical revelation of the Good and the Beautiful and were divinely ordained to keep faith with the other dancers in the Golden Chain.

The esoteric diction and impenetrable technicalities of his Platonic commentaries served to conceal the secret philosophy from readers who were not inclined to believe that logic or philosophical reasoning in general could lift the human intellect to a magic communion with the powers behind the dance of time; but to readers sympathetic to the splendid notion – or at least stimulated by the bare possibility – that academic education might be an initiation into superhuman states of consciousness Proclus still reveals how far a human intellect can stretch itself up towards the Divine Mind before it abandons the dreary abstractions of metaphysics for the consolation of poetic dreams.

The Dancing Intellect

A procession always entails a return, Proclus taught, and so we will pause in our 'pro-odos' through the life of the Diadochus to turn back to the passage at the head of the chapter which we left some time ago enshrouded in transcendental fog.[10] The purpose of our contemplative 'epistrophē' will be, first, to set his vision of the cosmic dance within the allegorical framework of the *In Timaeum* as a whole; second, to uncover the obscure Neopythagorean and Iamblichan sources of his conception of time as an eternal choragus; and third, to unravel the various strands in the complex argument he wove around the etymology of the name 'Chronos.' The fog should begin to lift as our retrospective eyes grow accustomed to the 'unclouded light of truth,' the weird phantasmal light that possessed the soul of the theurgic spectator and glowed in the dilated pupils of his transfixing, far-sighted eyes. Once enough of the fog has lifted to reveal the living form of the Dancing Intellect we will return with Proclus to the passage at the Platonic fountainhead of our history, *Timaeus* 40a–d, and contemplate the dances of the stars from the viewpoint of a theurgic initiate.

The first question all commentators on the *Timaeus* must ask themselves before they attack the minutiae of the dialogue is whether Plato intended the Myth of the Craftsman to be understood literally or figuratively. Those who are inclined to argue that this question is an old and pointless conundrum, that it is wholly unanswerable because Plato's intentions (which must somehow be distinguished from those of his characters) were locked away long ago in the black box of his mind and can never be determined from the deceptive testimony of his words, will be aghast at how little thought was ever given to such theoretical arguments by Late Antique exegetes. Calcidius and Proclus both admitted that the *Timaeus* was an exceptionally obscure work, but they approached it with the decisive attitude that Plato's intentions as a myth-maker were (to them at least) perfectly clear. Calcidius read the dialogue as a work of natural philosophy, a source-book of scientific facts, for he simply took Timaeus' word for it that the Myth of the Craftsman presented a 'likely story' of creation – as likely at least as human reason would ever be able to devise without the aid of divine revelation. Since the Myth focused his attention almost exclusively on the world of the senses, he saw in Plato's image of the cosmic dance little more than the visible revolutions of the heavenly bodies.

Proclus, by contrast, read the Myth as an extended metaphor or allegorical adumbration of the visionary order of the Neoplatonic intelligible world. Since the dialogue was presented to him by Syrianus as a treasury of theological insights rather than scientific facts, he tended to interpret the visible configurations of the astral dance as figures for the purely intellectual activities of his hypostatic gods. Whereas Calcidius paid little attention to the introductory section of the dialogue with its recapitulation of the *Republic* and foreshadowing of the *Critias*, Proclus interpreted every detail in the conversation between Socrates, Critias, and Harpocrates as a divine revelation subsequently confirmed or elaborated by Timaeus in the Myth. For instance, in Critias' deceptively straightforward remark that the empire of Atlantis had extended from somewhere beyond the Pillars of Hercules to Egypt and Tyrrenia (25a) he saw a veiled reference to the metaphysical extension of eternal and temporal reality from the One! Perhaps Old Rome was more on his mind than Atlantis when he observed in *In Timaeum* 1 178 that just as the famous earthly empire had increased in population but decreased in power so had the great chorus of beings expanded into multiplicity and fallen away from the supreme power of the Primal Unity.

Since Proclus rarely missed an opportunity to acknowledge his debt to the Platonists preceding him in the Golden Chain, particularly those who had discovered the theological subtext of Plato's myths, long stretches of his commentary are given over to commendations and modifications and refutations of his predecessors' arguments, and these exercises in academic disputation together with his painstaking analysis of the Atlantis legend swell his commentary to a size far exceeding that of Calcidius' translation and commentary combined. The absence of even a passing reference to Calcidius in the whole of the *In Timaeum* indicates either that Proclus and Syrianus did not consider the Latin commentator sufficiently divine to be a link in their Golden Chain, or, more likely, that they had never heard of Ossius' obscure underling or his mildly pro-Christian opus (which did not circulate widely until the twelfth century and then only in the Latin West). Chances are that even if a rare copy of it had circulated in the Greek East in the fifth century and Proclus had had enough Latin to skim its contents he would have found Calcidius' reading of the Myth naïvely literal and uninformed and his approval of 'the Hebrew philosophy' deeply repulsive.

Among the many disputed questions ignored by Calcidius but treated at great length by Proclus is what Timaeus could have meant by his cryptic remark that the 'was' and the 'will be' were the 'eidē' or 'forms' of time (38d). Did he mean that the past and the future were particular kinds of time (that is, distinctive phases in the orderly process of change initiated by the spinning of the cosmic body) or immutable models of temporal order reflected in the cyclical motions of the cosmos (that is, 'forms' in a technical Platonic sense)? Most Middle Platonists, including Calcidius, understood 'eidē' in a non-technical sense because they tended to conceive time either as a dynamic phenomenon or as a measure of motion within the sphere of Becoming. Most late Neoplatonists, however, opted for the abstruse metaphysical interpretation of the word because it accorded with their theurgic conception of time as an eternal intellect existing primarily and essentially beyond the Great Dividing-Line. Syrianus argued that since the past could always be defined as 'that which has come into existence' and the future as 'that which has yet to exist' they were both in essence immutable, which implied that like the Good and the Beautiful they were ontologically superior to everything caught up in the cycle of the Great Year.

Noting, moreover, that if a cyclical movement were frozen at any moment in its temporal devolution it would invariably divide into a past and a future, part of the cycle belonging to the 'was' and the other part to the 'will be', he concluded that the 'eidē' of time could not be viewed as mere sequences of contingent events but rather as timeless formal aspects or eternally or-dained attributes of a supracosmic god. 'Now,' advised Proclus, summariz-ing his tutor's argument,

if you truly wish to see the 'was' and the 'will be' as forms or unchanging aspects of Chronos, which was how our guide Syrianus seems to have inter-preted these terms, then consider in its entirety a complete revolution and choral dance of Chronos [teleian periodon kai holotelēi tou chronou choreian]. Note that one part of it, the phase that came first, has already come into existence. Another part has yet to occur. The 'was' and the 'will be,' you will see, are thus the unchanging aspects of Chronos. Whenever we hear these words employed with a partial meaning – for they are not always used to convey this full sense – the majestic and complete vision of Chronos is not revealed to us. Then they refer merely to some contingent event that takes place among the things in the mutable world of Becoming.

(*In Timaeum* III 38)

Syrianus evidently trained his pupil to associate the common meanings of words with the incomplete, sense-derived, variable sort of knowledge that Timaeus called 'opinion' or 'belief' and to seek knowledge that was complete, extrasensory, and eternally valid – the wisdom of the true Bacchants – by extending the reference of words beyond the world of change to the im-mutable realm of Being. The masses who employed the forms of the verb 'to be' only with reference to contingent events occurring within the cosmos were not necessarily wrong or careless in what they were saying, but their vision of reality was severely limited and their linguistic usage reflected a vulgar preference for transitory appearances rooted in ignorance of the in-telligible world. By construing the words 'was' and 'will be' as abstract nouns designating archetypal realities unrecognized by the masses, or rather by disclosing what he thought were the mystical meanings inherent in these words since the birth of language, the most theological of exegetes opened his pupil's eyes to 'the majestic and complete vision of Chronos.'

Proclus responded to the hypothesis that a divine choragus of time existed beyond the unending flux of times – and an ingenious hypothesis was all it was originally – like a humble suppliant receiving the word of Apollo at Delphi. The oracle was expressed in enigmas, of course, but these did not discourage the suppliant from discerning the radiance of truth in the darkness of the prophet's inspired utterance or from striving to analyse the majestic vision of Chronos in the language of Platonic cosmology. Following his tutor's lead, Proclus invested almost every cosmological term in the dialogue with metaphysical or theological meanings and effectively turned all its speeches into oracles pertaining not to the Here and Now but to the Beyond and Always. The term 'chronos,' for instance, which Timaeus had used as a common noun, became a divine name with talismanic virtues in the oracular vocabulary of the *In Timaeum*. And raised to transcendental heights by the same mystical updraught that wafted 'chronos' far beyond its usual field of reference, far beyond the cyclical processes of change in the Here and Now, was the noun from which its first syllable was supposedly derived and with which Timaeus had associated the revolutions of the visible gods – 'choreia.'

Though the metaphoric association of dancing with time has Presocratic roots which go deep into the soil of prephilosophical thought, the etymological association of the nouns 'chronos' and 'choreia' may be traced only as far back as Iamblichus. Iamblichus himself claimed that it was an aperçu of his illustrious predecessors:

For some of the older philosophers define time as a kind of choral dance of Psyche around Nous [choreiai tini tēs psychēs peri ton noun] – a definition clearly suggested by the word 'chronos' itself. Others define it as the cycles of Psyche and Nous itself. Still others define it as a choral dance of the physical world around Nous [tēi physikēi peri ton noun choreiai]. Finally there are those who define it as circular revolutions. The Pythagorean school embraces all these doctrines.

(apud Simplicium, *In Categorias* 351.32–352.2)

Of these four definitions only the fourth can be traced back to the cosmology of the Presocratic Pythagoreans (see chapter 1, page 47); the second, which may have originated with the Neopythagoreans of the late Hellenistic era, recalls Philo's vision of the physical world dancing to the laws of perfect music in imitation of the Divine Mind (see chapter 2, page 56); and the first and second, which are barely distinguishable, come straight from Plotinus (see chapter 4, pages 206–7). While the Middle Platonists generally conceived time as an endless series of days, months, and years generated by the revolutions of the heavenly bodies, Plotinus suggested that it might be a continuous process of unification transcending the diversified and ever-changing dances of the visible world – a process resulting *in* rather than from the revolutions of reason in the Platonic World-Soul. He even ventured to identify it with the epistrophic contemplations of the Primal Soul, the perpetual yearning of Psyche for union with Nous and the One that motivated all the undescended intellective souls in their ecstatic dance around the Wellspring of Life.

Iamblichus, in turn, modified these Plotinian hypotheses in his commentary on Aristotle's *Categories* (fragments of which have survived in the Aristotelian commentaries of Simplicius) by associating time with the utterly static circle of Nous rather than with the dynamic revolutions of thought and desire characteristic of Psyche. In sum, while few Platonic cosmologists at any period in Antiquity would have doubted the truth of the proverbial doctrine that the more things change the more they stay the same, the Middle Platonists like the Epicureans perceived the essence of time as change and the Neoplatonists like the Stoics perceived it as constancy.

From what he supposed were ancient doctrines preserved in the writings of the Presocratic Pythagorean Archytas – the actual author of these writings, now identified as Pseudo-Archytas, was a Neopythagorean with Peripatetic leanings whose floruit has been set at various periods between 200 BC and 200 AD – Iamblichus constructed a theory of archetypal or eternal time which was both a synthesis and an extension of the four definitions listed above. Believing that 'the Pythagorean school' had anticipated the Plotinian theory of psychological time by relating temporal order to the constancy of the astral revolutions, he took as his point of departure the following supposedly Pythagorean etymology of the noun 'chronos':

For some of the ancient philosophers defined time as a kind of choral dance of the Now [choreiai tini tou nun], which is clearly suggested by the word itself; others defined it as the revolutions of Psyche; still others as the natural locus of these revolutions. ... The Pythagorean school embraces all these doctrines.

(apud Simplicium, *In Physicorum libros* 786.29–33)

One might suppose that the slurring together of the hypothetical roots 'choreia' and 'nun' would have produced a word like 'chronon' rather than 'chronos.' And so it would have – without undermining the phonological basis of credibility for the etymological definition of time as a 'choral dance of the Now.' The accusative singular of 'chronos' happens to be 'chronon,' and it is this form of the noun that appears before the phrase 'choreiai tini tou nun' in the passage just cited. Thanks to the Greek case system the derivation sounded plausible, but did it make any sense?

For a philosophical justification of the etymology Iamblichus turned to the reflections of Pseudo-Archytas on the paradoxical nature of the present. Time as we experience it in the world of the senses has an air of unreality about it, argued Pseudo-Archytas, because the past no longer exists, the future has never existed, and the present slips away before we have a chance to comprehend its existence. Each 'now,' each instant of the elusive present, seems indivisible and imaginary like a geometrical point; yet somehow, in spite of its evanescent quality, the immediate present feels real to us and has an unchanging identity which is lacking in both the past and the future. Do we not sense that each now is like every other now because the present is invariably the intersection point between the vanished past and the emerging future, and that it retains this formal position regardless of the myriad changes taking place in it? A dancer could reach his final pose or a star could begin its millionth revolution, and still the now would be the point linking the 'was' to the 'will be.' In an effort to resolve the paradox of the transient yet permanent present, Iamblichus distinguished two species of 'to nun': a multitude of transient nows which come into and pass out of existence in the world of the senses and give rise to the longest natural measure of 'sensible time,' the cycle of the Great Year; and a single infinitely extended Now which flows from and resembles the eternal presence of Nous, the first being, and constitutes the 'intelligible time' experienced by the Divine Intellects in their contemplative dance around the One.

Each now we experience here below seems real to us, therefore, because it touches or impinges upon the everlasting present of the Beyond and is indeed the only immutable reality we can perceive before raising our inward eye to the circle of Permanent Being (see figure 15). However unwittingly we participate in the choral dance of the Now our little lives here below begin, progress, and end near the horizon of intelligible time – never more than a moment away from the Great Dividing-Line. We have only to perceive that horizon from the high viewpoint of the ecstatic stars (as Plotinus did before Iamblichus in *Ennead* 4.4.8) or from the higher viewpoint of the intellectual gods (as the Emperor Julian did after Iamblichus in *Hymn to King Helios* 146a–d) to realize without a nagging sense of paradox that intelligible time is effectively timeless because it exists all at once in a fully actualized state like the points in the locus of a completed revolution. And realizing this we may begin to understand the timeless choral consciousness of the great Platonists who though they lived at different times in the Great Year nevertheless seemed to dance together all at the same moment in the fullness of intelligible time.[11]

Proclus' derivation of 'chronos' from 'choreuōn nous' may seem like a 'radical' departure from the theory of the 'choreia tou nun,' but it is in fact a clear sign of his adherence to the supposedly ancient line of thought advanced by Iamblichus. The new root 'nous' would certainly not have

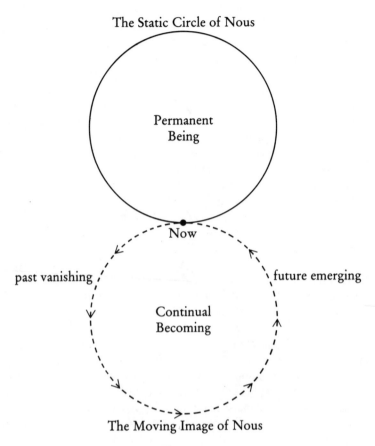

The Static Circle of Nous

Permanent
Being

Now

past vanishing

future emerging

Continual
Becoming

The Moving Image of Nous

Figure 15

Iamblichus conceived temporal order as a 'choreia tina tou nun' (a kind of choral dance of the Now) which he distinguished from the 'periphorai' (revolutions) of the visible world. The latter were related to the former as transient images to an immutable geometrical paradigm. In the diagram above, which represents Iamblichus' adaptation of a linear schema of time described by Pseudo-Archytas, the present moment is shown as the intersection point between the past and the future and also between the worlds of Being and Becoming. It is 'the Now' in actu, the point where we participate in the eternal presence of the Divine Mind; all other points on the broken circle represent the multiplicity of nows in potentia. The choral dance of the Now was simultaneously dynamic and static. Its dynamism sprang from the procession of individual moments into and out of the crucial intersection point, which gave rise to the cyclical pattern of the Great Year. Its stasis reflected the immutable circular form and uninterrupted contemplative repose of the Divine Mind.

appeared in his revised etymology if he had not, like Iamblichus, rejected the Plotinian identification of temporal order with the activity of Psyche and associated intelligible time, or, as he preferred to call it with Neopythagorean abstruseness, 'the Monad of Time,' primarily with the repose of Nous and the intellectual gods. Proclus may have placed more emphasis than Iamblichus on the intermediary position of hypostasized time between the perfect stasis of Nous and the profound dynamism of the Living Being and extolled with greater reverence the divinity of Chronos. He may also have expressed his mathematical and ontological conceptions of time in a more colourful mythological and theological idiom than that employed by Iamblichus in his Aristotelian commentaries. But aside from these subtle changes in emphasis and terminology the theory behind his vision of the Dancing Intellect is substantially the same as the Iamblichan resolution of the paradox of the absent-present Now and can be said to be 'original' only in the sense that it concerns the otherworldly origin of time.

Nevertheless the vision itself *is* novel simply because it is a vision – a theurgic vision of Chronos – rather than a theoretical argument about the cause of temporal order. Proclus writes in *In Timaeum* III 28–9 as one who has seen (or hopes to see) in the Chaldean theatre of wonders what Pseudo-Archytas, Plotinus, and Iamblichus had all groped towards in the tenebrous labyrinth of distinctions and definitions constructed around the old philosophy by the sages of the Hellenistic schools.

The Lycian's principal contribution to the theory of intelligible time can be discerned in the paragraphs of explication following his etymological revelation of the Dancing Intellect: a meticulous analysis of the network of causal, ontological, and mathematical relations linking Chronos to his inferiors (the stars, the cosmos, Psyche), to his fellow intellectual gods (the Craftsman, Athena, Helios), and to his superiors (Autozöon, Aion, Nous, and the One). These relations are typically expressed as metaphysical ratios involving at least four distinct entities or classes of entities. Chronos, we are told in III 28, is an image of Aion in the same sense that the cosmos is an image of the eternally self-sustaining organism, Autozöon, the Craftsman's Model. Chronos measures the movement of the cosmos just as Aion measures the permanence of Autozöon. Chronos creates the periodic order of the cosmic dance just as the Craftsman created the symmetrical structure of the dancing cosmos. Chronos perfects the dance by first regulating the revolutions of Psyche even as the Craftsman generated the dancers by first contemplating the stasis of Nous.

In his valiant attempt to elucidate the vision of the Dancing Intellect, Proclus found himself entangled in a web of Platonic terms which were all defined with respect to each other. The obvious way to extricate his vision from the inevitable circularity of Timaeus' cosmological jargon was to deduce the theory of intelligible time from a variety of Platonic and Neoplatonic myths tangentially related to the Myth of the Craftsman, which is what we see him doing in III 28–9. That was the way of a scholastic philosopher – systematic, logical, impersonal. But he had another approach to the mysterious presence of Chronos which only becomes apparent when we consider his commentary from the perspective of the whole. He broadened his understanding of Aion's 'moving image' by playing freely, intuitively, at times quite artistically with the implications of certain ancient images of order – the dance especially – which recur so frequently in his writings and are elaborated so extensively that his thinking seems in many passages more imagistic than logical. And that was the way of an oracular philosopher-poet, a craftsman of the poetic universe.

Rooted as it is in the metaphors of the Myth of the Craftsman, the Procline conception of temporal order is in certain respects a revision of the imagery of the Myth of the Chariot. In a famous speech from the *Phaedrus* (247a–c) Socrates likened the human soul to a charioteer struggling to control two winged horses, one of which yearned to fly up into the intellectual revels of the gods while the other tried to drag the charioteer down into the mire of sensual pleasures. Periodically the first horse had his way, and the soul succeeded in soaring to the outer reaches of the things perceptible to the senses where it was whirled round with the sphere of the fixed stars. 'Now within the heavens,' declared Socrates,

there are many happy sights and many routes along which the race of the blessed gods turns and returns, each occupied with his own duties; and whoever desires to follow them forever, and has gained the power, can do so, for ill-will is excluded from the divine chorus [exō theiou chorou].

(*Phaedrus* 247a)

Following the god most like it in character and most appropriate to its earthly career, the soul arrived at a liminal vantage-point where it could gaze out beyond the temporal world and perceive the eternal order of the Forms. Here occurred that transport of philosophical madness which Socrates in another dialogue compared half-jestingly to the trance experienced by true Bacchants at the final moment of revelation in the mysteries; here, at the turning-point in the soul's gravity-defying dance, was forgotten for a time the tragic distinction between god and man. After completing a single revolution of the heavens the soul was obliged to return in its chariot to the sublunary world where it normally had to wait ten thousand years before the wings of its better-natured horse were strong enough to bear it again to the stars; however, if it chose to pursue the career of a philosopher during three successive incarnations, its exile from the 'theios choros' was mercifully shortened by Zeus to a mere three thousand years!

Proclus got around these rather arbitrary rules by transferring several motifs from the Myth of the Chariot – the divine leadership of the dance, the periodic cycle of ascent and return, the fusion of choral harmony and bacchic frenzy – to the theurgic vision of Chronos, who, assuming the old role of Zeus, led all things within the cosmos back to their starting-points so that bodies as well as souls (and the mixtures of body and soul Proclus called 'natures') were periodically restored to their original state of blessedness. From his synthesis of the myths of the Craftsman and the Chariot emerges a more optimistic view of temporal change, or rather a more consoling religious prospect of the end of temporal change, than that presented by either Timaeus or Socrates. Instead of exiling human souls from eternity Chronos eternalized all who participated in his dance. Instead of separating the Blessed from the Fallen he miraculously interinanimated them.

Proclus drew upon several other Platonic dialogues besides the *Timaeus* and the *Phaedrus* to compose his vision of the Dancing Intellect in III 28–9. His reference to the Good as the eternal archetype of temporal order is an echo of the *Republic* (VII 540a), and his mention of the One hearkens back to the metaphysical hypotheses of the *Parmenides* (137c). The dense texture of allusions in his commentary also includes a direct quotation from the *Laws* (X 897b), a passage in which the Athenian Stranger distinguished primary psychological motions such as desire and intellection from secondary corporeal motions such as physical growth and locomotion and deduced from his observations of the celestial revolutions the general causal law that a soul aided by wisdom will naturally lead everything in her power towards a happy and virtuous outcome. Proclus refined this theory by further distinguishing the organic complexity and inexorable flow of cosmic motion, which originated in the World-Soul, from its characteristic periodicity and regenerative potency, which he believed were the miraculous effects of the Dancing Intellect.

Moreover, his etymology of the name Chronos is clearly patterned on Plato's punning explanation of the name Kronos:

Now it might seem insolent, at first hearing, to call Zeus the son of Kronos [a proverbially dull-witted god] and reasonable to say that Zeus is the offspring of some great mind. And so he is, for this is the meaning of his father's name: 'child of the pure and undefiled intellect.' This name seems to come from the word 'koros,' which originally signified not 'male child' but rather 'pure intellect' [that is, katharos nous) katharonoos) Kronos; cf choreuōn nous) choronoos) Chronos].

(*Cratylus* 396b)

While Socrates, the ingenious etymologist of the *Cratylus*, jestingly undercut his laborious analysis of the lengthy Hesiodic roll call of divine names with the wry remark that these were probably not the names the gods used among themselves, Proclus, following Iamblichus, regarded such linguistic investigations not as a Socratic jeu d'esprit but as a serious means of discovering the true nature of the gods. The ancients, he earnestly contended, derived from word-origins their first dim understanding that beyond the temporal world was a realm of immutable reality:

Men have commonly supposed that the word 'aiōn' is derived from 'to aie einai,' 'to be forever,' and similarly that the word 'chronos' is from 'choreia,' 'choral dance,' because it is a movement existing essentially in the World of Becoming. It seems to me that both the common people and the wise have understood the nature of time in this way. However, the wise, by gazing steadfastly at the nature that is always moving and at the nature that is always at rest, were the first to acquire knowledge of eternity.

(*In Timaeum* III 9)

Proclus' distinctly philological view of the origin of man's philosophical enlightenment (which accounts for the serious attention he gave to these supposedly primitive etymologies here and in his elaborate commentary on the *Cratylus*) would doubtless have raised the spirit of raillery in Socrates, who, like Timaeus and the Athenian Stranger, assumed that man first acquired his knowledge of temporal order by contemplating the dances of the stars rather than the origins of words. Though Socrates questioned Cratylus' theory that the connections between words and their etymons revealed the interconnectedness of all parts of the natural world, he never doubted the doctrine that the love of wisdom, like Love itself, was begotten in the eyes.

Proclus, however, tended to place as much emphasis on verbal signs of cosmic order as on the visual signs examined by the true Bacchants of the past, because he believed (ironically) that Cratylus' theory had been proved beyond a shadow of a doubt by the inspired word-play of Socrates. That the common people had reached an understanding of time through purely linguistic channels did not in his opinion invalidate the etymological approach to knowledge. Had not the *un*common people, the wise men like Socrates, also gained insights into the Divine Plan through the contemplation of word-origins? And were their insights not deeper than folk-wisdom because they had gazed steadfastly at that which was always in motion and that which was always at rest and discerned the unitive presence of Chronos between these two extremes, and also because they had carried the science of etymology to such dazzling heights of refinement that the eternal character of Chronos and all other gods had been revealed to them? It was a folly of the Christians to object to the time-honoured Platonic doctrine that language was created by the gods to conceal theological truths from the masses while revealing them to the wise. Let the common people conclude from the apparent similarity of the words 'chronos' and 'choreia' that time was no more than a dance. The wise, striving to see the whole truth, did not jump to such hasty conclusions. By perceiving an intellect as well as a dance in the divine name of time Proclus revealed the uncommonness of his own wisdom as well as the uniqueness of his eternal choragus.

While the derivation of 'chronos' from 'choreuōn nous' appears to be the Lycian's own invention – or at least his own ingenious variation of the Socratic pun on 'Kronos' and 'katharos nous' – his notion that 'aiōn' was derived from 'to aie einai' can be traced back to Aristotle's treatise on celestial motion (*De caelo* I 9, 279a 27). Etymological lore was not all he took from the Stagirite. Like all the Neoplatonists he patterned his analysis of disputed questions on Aristotle's method of reviewing the conflicting opinions of earlier philosophers, exposing the confusions in their terminology, proposing subtle new definitions of strategic terms, and finally overriding their arguments with a magisterial determination of the Truth.

His Aristotelian subtlety is clearly displayed in the passage on the Dancing Intellect, which functions as a transition between the third and fourth steps in his long aporetic argument on the 'eidē' of time. Immediately after proposing his new etymological definition he subjects it to a rigorous analysis based on Aristotle's famous classification of the Four Causes (*Metaphysics* IV 1013a ff) in order, first, to ground his strange irrational concept of timeless time in the familiar territory of Greek scientific rationalism; second, to clarify the teleological connections between Chronos and the various gods in the Myth of the Craftsman; and third, to prove the superiority of his definition to Plato's, which, though it seemed to distinguish the genus of time ('image') from its specific differentiae ('moving,' 'of eternity') with admirable clarity, was rightly criticized by Aristotle (*Physics* IV 218b) for clouding the crucial distinction between the cosmic motions measured by time and time itself, and was evidently not a precise description of the essence of time but only an evocation of the paradoxical character of temporal change. The 'efficient cause' of time, that is, the creative agent responsible for bringing into existence both the temporal chorus and its eternal choragus, was easily identified as the Craftsman. The role of 'formal cause' was then assigned to Aion because, according to Plato, eternity was the model of all that was stable and symmetrical in the cycle of changes generated by the cosmic revolutions. Aion was a cause of Chronos only in a passive sense, as the distant intelligible archetype of the god's intellectual identity, and like the formal cause of the cosmos, Autozöon, was in no way affected by the activity of its image. The purpose of that activity was to ensure that all the dancers in the cosmic chorus were moved round together in a cycle of regeneration so that however transient their individual natures might seem in comparison with the hypostatic gods they should nevertheless participate as a group in the eternal beauty and virtue and repose of the highest beings. The perfection of their communal life through imitation of the One and the Good (which were one and the same) was the goal or 'final cause' of Chronos. Though time in its original Platonic sense was a kind of artefact which could conceivably be affected by the raw material in the Craftsman's mixing bowl, Proclus did not carry his Aristotelian analysis of the image of eternity to the point of assigning a 'material cause' to Chronos. In fact the allusive arguments he spun around his vision of the Dancing Intellect were designed to prove, above all, that the god of time was as free from the evil influences of matter as Aion, Autozöon, and the Craftsman.

Plotinus had conceived the dance of time as both an unfolding sequence of potential movements and a perfected artistic whole or fixed pose towards which all physical and psychological movements were tending. By drawing upon Aristotle's distinction between potentiality and actuality he had been able to analyse the difference between the ever-shifting configurations of the cosmic chorus and the permanent configuration of dancing intellects around the Wellspring of Life and at the same time to reveal the close connection between the multiple poses in the pantomime of the Living Being and the single ecstatic pose in the Circle of Nous. The dances which appeared to a detached spectator to be still in progress were simply the potential phases of the Dance; the Dance which suspended the initiated participant in the rapturous peace of eternity was the final actualized state of all the dances.

Like Plotinus, Proclus perceived the cosmic dance from this dual perspective. Even in the lowliest motions of earthly organisms he could recognize an intense and enduring movement of the spirit, a yearning for divine union, which meant not only a turning away from the multiplicity of the material world but also a turning towards the tranquil unity of immortal principles. To describe this universal striving for artistic completion Plotinus had often used the dramatic verb 'ephiesthai,' which literally meant 'to hurl oneself towards' or 'to yearn for something with a passionate desire.' The same verb appears in Proclus' summary of the causes of time in III 29. All mobile things in the chorus of Chronos tended to revolve around a central deity, the earth, because they were 'yearning' (ephiemenon) for the stability of their visionary centre, the One. The impulse behind their dance was a love that transcended carnal desire and defied rational explanation. It was the same craving for spiritual security that had transfixed the intellective soul of Plotinus in the temple of Psyche.

In *The Hieratic Art*, his treatise on theurgy and sympathetic magic, Proclus noted that certain plants such as the sunflower stretch out their blooms towards the eastern horizon and follow the visible Helios in his daily passage across the sky. This tiny detail in the cosmic dance (celebrated thirteen centuries later by William Blake in his lyric beginning 'Ah, sunflower, weary of time, That countest the steps of the sun') was interpreted by the fifth-century theurgist as a sign of the plant's instinctive yearning for spiritual repose in a world of tumultuous and incessant change.[12] Just as Chronos led the whole temporal world in a dance towards eternal perfection, so the sun and other visible gods acted as secondary leaders in the magic round by exerting special influences over sublunary things analogous in one way or another to their celestial identities. The sympathetic link between the sunflower and the sun was revealed not only by the heliotropic motion of the plant but also by the golden hue and circular shape of its blossom.

From biological examples such as this Proclus constructed a general theory of motivation to account for all the physical and psychological motions that made up the cosmic dance. 'All existing things,' he generalized,

stretch out towards the One with an inextinguishable longing, for it is the universal object of desire, unknowable and impossible to grasp. Thus incapable either of knowing or of seizing what they desire, all things dance around it [peri auto panta choreuei] in an agony like the pangs of childbirth. They have a prophetic intuition of its presence and an insatiable and unending desire for it; yet they are deprived of its unknowable and ineffable nature and are powerless to embrace what they desire or to clasp it to their bosom.
(*Platonic Theology* 1.22, I 102)

When the true Bacchant found that the universal object of desire was unknowable except through prophetic intuition, which was at best only a vague understanding of the lives of the hypostatic gods closest to the One, and that even the Primal Intellect was unable to comprehend the plenitude of unity at the Wellspring of Life, he accepted his ordained role in the dance of time and joined with the highest beings – as did the lowly sunflower – in adoring the beauty of what was forever unattainable. Their communal impulse to clasp the One 'to their bosom,' to participate in the generative process that first brought the symmetrical worlds of time and eternity into being, produced in turn the countermovements of physical and spiritual love. Each movement was, in its own way, an agony. The physical world danced with the vital energy of a vast womb endlessly giving birth to new images of the Beautiful, while the spiritual world danced with the ardent abandon of a lover reaching out to embrace his beloved, his vision of the Good, for the first time. And just as the one would never find relief from the pangs of childbirth, so the other would never find release from the paroxysm of insatiable desire.

'Chronos chronou' ('the Time of time') was what wound these two dances, these two agonies, together into a single harmonious whirl. So Proclus learned from the *Chaldean Oracles* (fr 185, cited in *In Timaeum* III 36); and from another work by Julian the Theurgist, a lost treatise on the theology of time and its magical applications entitled *The Seventh Book of the Zones* (cited in *In Timaeum* III 27), he learned that the sublime masters of the art of divine works had worshipped the Time of time not as an insubstantial shadow of eternity but as an eternal god in its own right, an intellectual being with a greater measure of permanence (and therefore of reality) than the visible gods normally associated with the temporal whirl, the stars. The latter work was probably also on his mind in III 32 where he notes that Chronos was the leader of a whole chorus of divinized temporal units including Day, Night, Month, Year, and the Seasons, and again in III 43 where he refers to the theurgic veneration of Chronos as proof that Julian and his followers, unlike the majority of men, had not lost the wings of their souls but had flown up to the threshold of eternity and beheld 'the majestic and complete vision of Time.' Julian had classified the lesser gods and goddesses of time as 'theoi zōnaioi' (deities associated with the five zones of the firmament traversed by Helios during his annual revolution) in order to distinguish them from the supreme deity of temporal order, Chronos, who was said to be 'azōnos' (independent of the celestial zones) and 'pēgaios' (fountain-like) because from his supercelestial presence, as from a magic wellspring, flowed all the times measured by the heavenly bodies in their dance.

The mesh of allusions in Proclus' definition of time reflects not only the wide range of works on the reading list of the Athenian Academy but also the paradoxical mentality of the youthful reader of that list, a mentality at once critical and defensive, methodical and intuitive, retrospective and prophetic, authority-bound and free-thinking. If, as certain historians of philosophy have suggested, the Lycian's preoccupation with theurgy and shamanistic fascination with divine names are signs of the intellectual twilight preceding the utter darkness of the Dark Ages, we should expect to find in any passage culled from the crepuscular shadows of the *In Timaeum* the drily derivative meditations of a Neoplatonic pedant who took greater pleasure in casting spells than in seeking wisdom.[13] Yet the passage we have brought into the light – our demysticized modern light – proves on close examination to be quite unlike anything written in the supposedly golden afternoons of Classical Antiquity preceding the gloom of the fifth century. Even after the Platonic, Aristotelian, Plotinian, Iamblichan, Orphic, and Chaldean strands in his arguments have been unravelled, his theological vision of world-harmony still seems greater than the sum of its sources. It reveals a mind of great vitality – not unlike the intellect of the miraculous and craftsman-like Chronos. The surprising originality of Proclus lies in his almost demiurgic capacity to fuse the disparate elements of his intellectual past into a vision of the magical (and still mysterious) Now.

Retrogradations and Progressions

Proclus was enough of an old-school Platonist to assume that all true images of cosmic order (including those which seemed to arise purely out of verbal association like the chorus of Chronos) were rooted in visual experience, and this assumption predisposed him to accept the theurgic doctrine that Chronos was not a philosophical concept to be defined in words but a divine phenomenon, a luminous apparition with some measure of visual definition. While Athena and Apollo and Asclepius took on human shapes and donned ancient Olympian costumes when they appeared in the dream-theatre of the theurgists, Chronos, being a relatively new god in the intellectual pantheon, had no such familiar earthly guise and so assumed a geometrical form appropriate to his unearthly function and character. That form, surprisingly, was not circular or spherical. Those who had seen Chronos with their own eyes testified that the Dancing Intellect was 'helicoeidēs' – 'spiral-shaped.'

If by a strange twist of fate Iamblichan Neoplatonism had become the orthodoxy of the Eastern Empire in the late fourth century instead of Nicene Christianity, the spiral would doubtless have replaced the circle as the dominant symbolic configuration in the dance of time. The spiral was by no means an arbitrary symbol of Chronos, Proclus argued in III 20–1. As an intermediary form combining the extension of a line with the continuous curve of a circle it seemed to be the natural shape for a god whose dance combined linear and circular motions and whose function was to act as intermediary between the dynamic complexity of the visible world and the static circle of the Primal Intellect. While every circle is geometrically similar to every other circle and every straight line to every other straight line, spirals may be radically dissimilar in appearance. They may be two-dimensional whorls

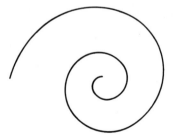 

or three-dimensional coils

or complex vortices

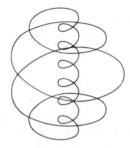

which turn inward upon themselves so that their beginning and ending are coterminous. The innumerable permutations of the form – some of them intricately symmetrical like the pinwheel design in the centre of a sunflower, others perversely asymmetrical like the tendrils of an ivy – aptly symbolized the multiplicity in motion and the multiplicity of motions woven together by the Dancing Intellect.

The spiral of Chronos united revolution with evolution, continuity with variation, progression with return, circumference with centre. It was the paradigm of life-in-motion, the formal cause of all the progressively evolving yet periodically repeated processes in the living cosmos. If Proclus had been divinely blessed with prophetic insight into the realm of chromosomes and amino acids discovered by modern geneticists, he would doubtless have perceived the double helix of the DNA molecule as a microcosmic image of the spiraliform Chronos; unlike the DNA molecule, however, Chronos was not formally defined as any particular type of spiral or combination of spirals since in a causal sense his eternal Form preceded them all. In Chronos all helicoidal designs existed simultaneously. In the cosmos they appeared sequentially as the labyrinthine whorls and interlacings of the Great Chorus. Challenged by Syrianus to break the code of visual phenomena in order to reveal the universal formative principles of life, Proclus revised and perfected a philosophy of time which might best be described as a genetics of the macrocosm. Whereas modern 'microcosmic' geneticists look for these principles in chains of molecules linking the innumerable cells of innumerable mortal creatures, Proclus saw them as chains of gods linking heaven and earth in the magic dance of a single immortal cell.

By interpreting the orbits of the planets not as combinations of perfect circles (which was how Ptolemy and most Late Antique astronomers brought order to the zodiac and 'saved the appearances') but as complex spirals which, though differing from planet to planet, were all alike in that their points of completion were identical with their points of origin, the Lycian was able to relate the helicoidal form of the Dancing Intellect to the visible dances of the celestial gods traditionally associated with the creation and perpetuation of temporal order (see figure 16). In contrast to Theon and Calcidius, who had argued that no deviations from the perfect circularity of the Craftsman's design could possibly occur in the blessed spheres above the moon, Proclus disapproved of the outrageous artificiality and mechanistic implications of the theory of epicycles and boldly returned to what most mathematical astronomers connected with the school of Plato in Greco-Roman times would have considered a rather primitive acceptance of visual evidence. He believed what his eyes told him about all superlunary phenomena save one – the succession of the pole stars in tandem with the precession of the equinoxes – which was so slow a movement (the position of the celestial axis relative to the Aplanes shifting no more than a half a degree per century) that it could hardly be called a 'phenomenon' in the usual sense of the term. The precession had to be an optical illusion, he insisted, because the Craftsman would never have allowed the fixed stars to deviate from the pattern of perfect rationality established for them by the Circle of the Same.[14]

Nowhere did he more clearly express his academically unorthodox view that the retrogradations and other idiosyncratic motions of the planets were compatible with divine reason and therefore not illusory than in his extraordinarily detailed commentary on *Timaeus* 40c–d. 'Plato's statements in this passage must be understood in an astronomical and a philosophical sense,' he explained in III 145, 'for they refer both to the bodily and to the psychic motions of the stars.' In accordance with the Platonic distinction between physical and psychological motions and the Aristotelian distinction between mathematical astronomy and the teleological analysis characteristic of natural philosophy, he divided his explication of the passage into two parts. Part one (III 145–9) surveys the physical movements of the celestial dancers and the geometric order of their visible configurations; part two (III 149–51) complements this astronomical exegesis with a consideration of the illuminative and unitive experiences of the ecstatic stars which inevitably leads to a meditation on the eternal causes of order in the dance of time. Underlying the dual perspective of his commentary is a third distinction drawn from his philosophical past: the Plotinian contrast between outer and inner vision.

An astronomer cannot tell real from apparent motions until he has found a fixed point of reference from which to observe or with which to compare the changing positions of the heavenly bodies. At the start of his astronomical

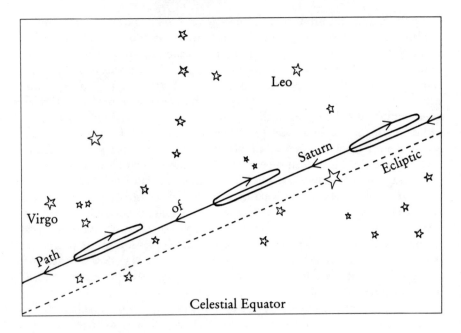

Figure 16

The slowest of the dancers in the ancient planetary chorus, Saturn, took approximately three earth years to complete the complex course through Leo and Virgo pictured above (from plate III, between pages 2 and 3, in Richard A. Proctor's *Saturn and Its System*). In tracing out this path, which would probably be described as 'looping' rather than 'spiralling' today but would have been considered helicoidal (literally 'winding') in Antiquity, the planet appeared to combine linear or direct motion eastward along the ecliptic with curving retrograde motion westward in concert with the fixed stars. Unlike most mathematical astronomers of his era, Proclus was willing to interpret the helicoidal patterns traced out by the planets as their actual rather than merely apparent lines of motion in the cosmic dance. To his intellectual eye such patterns revealed the existence of the archetypal Helix, the god Chronos.

exegesis Proclus swiftly locates such a point at the spatial centre of the celestial chorus:

First, if you wish, let us understand the word 'choreias' in an astronomical sense as a reference to the well-ordered and harmonious revolutions of the heavenly bodies. Plato also added to this word the phrase 'of these same gods,' meaning the stars and planets, and inserted a word about the earth's relation to them. He does not say that the earth is dancing but that it is 'winding' [ou gar tēn gēn choreuein, tēn illomenēn] while the heavenly bodies dance around it. For they dance by moving in a unified and harmonious manner [choreuousi gar hoi mian kinēsin symphōnon] around the same centre.

(*In Timaeum* III 146)

Having already argued in III 138 that the mysterious 'winding' of the earth signified its inborn yearning for divine union, a purely psychological motion incited by its sympathetic affinity with the intellectual gods and reflecting perhaps the helicoidal form of Chronos, he was free here to conclude from visual evidence that the earth remained physically stationary while the heavenly bodies danced in chorus around it. Turning his attention from the harmonious unity of the celestial chorus to the multiplicity of their observable motions, he proceeds to define the astronomical terms in apposition to 'choreias':

Let us understand the term 'juxtapositions' to refer to those occasions when the heavenly bodies arrange themselves along the same longitude (although they differ in latitude and depth) – in other words, when they rise and set together. The terms 'retrogradations' and 'progressions' signify their movements backward and forward. When they progress they approach each other as they return to the same point of departure; and when they retrogress they turn back towards each other.

(*In Timaeum* III 146)

No cobweb-like diagrams such as appeared in Calcidius' commentary accompany Proclus' explanation of the visible irregularities in the celestial spectacle. No attempt is made to catch the wandering stars in a tangle of epicycles and eccentric orbits. When the planets of the theurgic cosmos decided to dance to and fro or up and down or back and forth, they did so without consulting Theon's *Expositio* or Ptolemy's *Almagest* – their only constraint being the law of Chronos that their orbits must eventually end where they began and begin again where they ended. In the periodicity of their juxtapositions, retrogradations, and progressions lay the proof that Saturn and his fellow gods were winding their way through a dance of amazing complexity which was designed to satisfy their Apollonian desire to unify, harmonize, and conform to an imposed mathematical order without repressing their Dionysian impulse to rend, reduce wholes to parts, and loosen the bonds of conformity.

As Proclus explained in II 197, the Craftsman's primordial act of binding together the Same and the Different represented the miraculous integration of the Apollonian and Dionysian movements in the theurgic dance of time. When Apollo led the dance, bodies were linked together in a choral chain or round and harmonized with souls under the spell of musical numbers; when Dionysus took command of the chorus, bodies were torn apart in a frenzied scramble and sundered from souls in the ecstasy of divine posses-sion. However, since both gods sprang from the same divine Father whom Proclus (following the Stoics) sometimes called Zeus and sometimes the Craftsman and sometimes the creative fire of Helios, their respective dances were virtually indistinguishable at their moment of origin and ultimately complemented rather than opposed each other in the cyclical continuum of theurgic time and space. Like a massive wave with its less detectable but nonetheless powerful undertow, the great force of choral harmony in the theurgic cosmos inevitably sucked the lowest parts of life back into the swirling depths of bacchic dissolution and just as inevitably swept them up again, composing their scattered remains into new configurations and joining their souls and bodies into new natures.

In the physical dances of the stars Proclus discerned two signs that these cosmic processes were sustained by the perpetual subordination of Dionysus to Apollo: first, the uniform circling of the Same (which symbolized the Apollonian side of the Craftsman's character) encompassed and directly affected the diversified movements of the planets but was itself unaffected by the defiant counterrevolutions of the Different (which reflected his Dio-nysian aspect); and second, Apollo's visible embodiment, the sun, prevented the other planets from wandering aimlessly across the heavens by restricting their juxtapositions, retrogradations, and progressions to the tilted band of the zodiac. Apollo restrained but could not, and indeed would not, repress Dionysus, for the health of the cosmos depended on their continual inter-action. Without the liberating impetus of the Revel-King, the dance of Apollonian order would have degenerated into a sterile round of passionless conformity or a vicious circle of astral determinism. Conversely, without the providential restraint of the god of harmony, the dance of Dionysian passion would have torn the living world apart and returned its scattered elements to the womb of Chaos.

Like the Craftsman, who was both a cutter and a joiner, Chronos created temporal order according to the Dionysian principle of physical dispersion (figured in the disparate crosscutting lines of planetary motion) and the

Apollonian principle of physical unification (figured in the uniform concentric revolutions of the fixed stars) so that an eternal balance was maintained between linear and circular motion, the one symbolizing the outward progression of all heavenly and earthly bodies from the Wellspring of Time and the other the cyclical return of all indwelling spirits to the pristine condition of their birth. In this light the divine Helix might be regarded as an emblem of the rampantly un-Christian vitalism at the heart of Procline cosmology.

In his long note concerning retrogradation (III 146–9) Proclus conceded that the theory of epicycles served the limited purposes of astronomy well enough: it eliminated spontaneous or apparently random linear motion from the orbital paths of the planets, resolved a confusing multiplicity of spiral motions into a theoretically unified system of revolutions, and thereby made most (though not all) moves in the celestial dance accessible to human understanding. But he also contended on theological grounds that, epicyclical geometry being insufficient to account for the irrepressible Dionysian energies latent in the heavenly bodies, Ptolemaic astronomy inevitably presented a highly distorted picture of celestial activity – an abstract schema rather than a picture – in which only the rationality of Apollo was discernible. The theory of epicycles was first proposed in the Hellenistic era by the astronomers Hipparchus and Apollonius, and though Plato could not possibly have known of it (except by prophetic intuition) most Platonic cosmologists in Late Antiquity assumed that he did because of the peculiar phrase used by Timaeus in 40d to denote retrogradation: 'tas tōn kyklōn pros heautous anakyklēseis,' literally 'the turning-around of the circles back towards themselves,' which to anyone trained in epicyclical astronomy inevitably suggested the systems of circles-upon-circles-within-circles devised by Hipparchus and Apollonius and vastly elaborated by Ptolemy.

Proclus objected to this interpretation of the phrase for three reasons. First, as he complained in III 56, the theory of epicycles made the living heavens seem too much like an earthly theatre where actors playing gods were raised and lowered and spun round on an ingenious system of ropes and pulleys. The old metaphor of the cosmic theatre served to suggest the spectacular order of the visible gods, but it was not to be stretched too far or taken too literally! Second, though a Ptolemaic astronomer could conceivably devise helicoidal orbits for the planets using only the principles of epicyclical geometry (see figure 17), the coiling designs produced in this way did not arise from the combination of circle and line and so did not reflect the demiurgic activity of the spiraliform Chronos. If the planetary gods were truly to imitate the divine Helix by combining in their dance the countermovements of choral integration and bacchic dissolution, they would have to be subject not only to circular motion but also to the linear motions

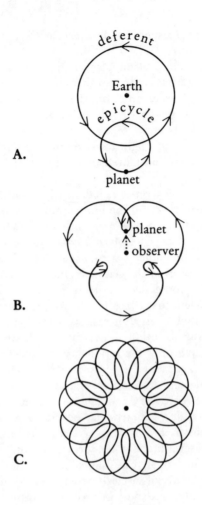

A.

B.

C.

Figure 17

Represented in diagram A is a basic orbital system of one epicycle and one deferent on the plane of the ecliptic. The looping courses resulting from the combination of the two circular motions (diagrams B and C) could be varied 'to save appearances' by positing different speeds for the planetary revolution or for the rotation of the deferent. An observer looking out from earth (arrow in B) at any loop in the planet's helicoidal orbit would see the planet slow down, reverse its course, and then speed up again in its original direction. Proclus contended that diagrams of this sort misrepresented the cosmic choreiai as the motions of an ingenious but lifeless mechanism and reduced the planetary gods to the status of mere 'dei ex machina.' These diagrams are a modification of figure 19 in Thomas S. Kuhn's *The Copernican Revolution* (Cambridge: Harvard University Press 1957), 61.

associated by Timaeus with sublunary mutability. For just as Chronos acted as an intermediary between the static circle of the Primal Intellect and the dynamic thought-processes of the World-Soul, so the planets at their various levels in the Golden Chain served to link the continuous revolutions of the fixed stars with the discontinuous, zigzagging, collision-prone movements of earthly things. And third, the Ptolemaic interpretation of the phrase clashed with what Proclus considered the definitive explanation of planetary motion – that given by Timaeus himself at the end of his discussion of time in 39a–b: 'Now because of the motion of the Same the planets that went round most swiftly appeared to be overtaken by those that moved most slowly, although the swiftest actually overtook the slowest; for they must travel their different courses in two opposing directions simultaneously [that is, daily westward with the fixed stars, annually eastward with the sun] and because of this the motion of the Same, which is swiftest of all, twisted all their circles into spirals. ... '

As a result the planet nearest the Aplanes in distance but moving most slowly against its daily rotation, namely Saturn, appeared to be nearest it in speed. In light of this passage Proclus interpreted the word 'kyklōn' in Timaeus' periphrastic definition of retrogradation as a reference not to circles in a strict sense but to the winding curves of spirals. According to Timaeus these helicoidal paths were traced out along the seven rings of the Different which were measured and cut by the Craftsman after the joining of the Different to the Same (35b–36d). In Procline cosmology these seven unequal rings became seven transparent spheres of diverse sizes which were fastened one inside another and held in place by the celestial pole like the concentric whorls on the spindle of Necessity. While all seven were similarly subject to the diurnal rotation of the cosmos from east to west, each was set whirling at its own speed from west to east. Within the zodiacal limits set by the sun the planetary gods, who were the rulers and visible inhabitants of the planetary spheres, were free to dance in any direction over the surface of their domains just as men could move about on the earth: they could even penetrate the depths of their spheres if they chose to approach the earth on a providential mission or to answer the summons of a theurgist. While the seven 'dei ex machina' wheeled about Ptolemy's geocentric theatre fitted into an exquisitely crafted and perfectly tuned system, unerringly regular in its motions, performing without evolving, safely engineered to exclude the sudden and the spontaneous, the planets dancing in the Lycian's heliotropic heavens – true life-sustaining and life-threatening deities, not theatrical props – belonged to a fantastic organic world with unlimited evolutionary potential, an enchanted island of tempestuous metamorphoses in the calm ocean of Being, a true Bacchant's and a mad poet's dream.

The moment a Procline planet danced away from the ecliptic its line of motion was instantly transformed into a spiral by the rotation of the Same (see figure 18). In the long run its continuous participation in the dance of Chronos produced helicoidal patterns of great complexity, but no matter how complex these became, Chronos always caused the end of the planetary helix to coincide with its point of origin in accordance with the fundamental law of return governing all the physical and psychological motions in the dance. In visualizing eternity the Neoplatonists tended to project the visible configurations of the dance outwards across the Great Dividing-Line onto the causal superstructure of temporal reality. When the circular orbit of a fixed star was expanded to infinity and suspended as a motionless whole around the One it became the Plotinian Circle of Nous; similarly, when the coiling orbit of a planet was magnified to archetypal proportions it (or rather the process of analogical thinking behind its theoretical magnification) generated the Procline Spiral of Chronos. Of course Plotinus and Proclus would both have argued that these formal projections actually operated in reverse: that as the Many flowed out from the One the archetypal forms of the hypostatic gods were brought into Being first and subsequently reflected in the dynamic order of Becoming.

The defence of the theory of homocentric spheres in III 131 is a mark of Proclus' independence from Plotinus, a measure of his boldness as a synthesist, and a testimony to his faith in the ultimate compatibility of Platonic cosmology and Aristotelian physics. Aristotle, who first formulated the theory in the *De caelo* (B 12, 292a 10 ff) after coolly disposing of the Pythagorean concept of moving numbers and the Platonic myth of the joining of the Same and the Different, was also the first to admit that his new and supposedly rational explanation of celestial motion still left many questions unanswered. Why, for instance, did the single sphere of the Aplanes carry a multitude of heavenly bodies around the earth while the multiple spheres of the planets bore only one body apiece?

Proclus' answer to this old conundrum reveals how imaginary, or in Neoplatonic terms, how divinely poetic his vision of the Aristotelian heavens had become under the influence of the most theological of exegetes. The planetary spheres had far more than one inhabitant each, he asserted in III 131. In fact, like 'the earth, our nurse,' they were teeming with living creatures, though their populations consisted not of perishable plants and animals but of apotheosized heroes and daimonic intelligences and angelic spirits under the command of the planetary god appropriate to their innate dispositions and ordained roles in the Great Chorus. The chain-like structure of each planetary society was modelled on the gradation of entities and causal principles in the supracosmic realm. In the society of the seventh sphere, for instance, Saturn reigned as the representative of the One by virtue of his mythical role as divine forefather; below him, corresponding

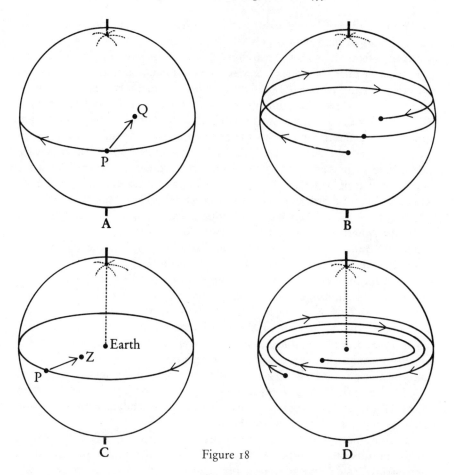

Figure 18

The planetary spheres – the term 'sphere' in Procline cosmology denoting the transparent globes on which the planets danced rather than the luminous bodies of the planets themselves – were thought to be teeming with living creatures. In this respect they resembled the Aplanes with its myriad stars and the earth with its myriad plants and animals, though the choruses of heroes, daimones, and angels who followed the planets in their spiralling dances were invisible to all save the theurgists. Diagram A represents any one of the seven planetary spheres with its ruling planet P on the plane of the ecliptic. If P were to remain still, his body would turn about the earth with the westward rotation of the Aplanes. However, if P were to attempt to journey in a straight line to point Q above the plane of the ecliptic, the combination of his eastward linear motion and his westward revolution would result in the spiral path traced out in diagram B. Diagrams C and D indicate the helicoidal locus of P's motion when the god decides to plunge below the surface of his sphere to point Z.

to the first order of beings to proceed from the One, the intelligible gods, was a chorus of Saturnian angels whose function was to convey prophetic revelations from their slowly marching choragus to the rest of his followers; a host of Saturnian daimones followed them in turn, acting as intermediaries between the angels and the sublunary things sympathetically linked with Saturn (for example, lead, mandrake roots, owls, camels) and reflecting a hypostatic level of Being unique to Athenian Neoplatonism, the Primal Life; and lastly, the Saturnian heroes, the great contemplative mages whose duty was to oversee the rites of purification by which mortals born under the sign of Saturn prepared their souls to return to the stars, formed a chorus mirroring that of Athena, Chronos, Helios, and the other intellectual gods who sustained the order of the cosmos by contemplating the Divine Ideas.

The same triadic arrangement of spirits was repeated on all the other planetary spheres. Accompanying Jupiter were choruses of Jovian angels, daimones, and heroes; accompanying Mars, choruses of Martian angels, daimones, and heroes; and so on down to Luna and her pale attendants, the familiars of many a common sorcerer. In III 162 Proclus identified the ranks in this phantasmagorical populace with the links in the Golden Chain that Homer's Zeus suspended from heaven to earth to prove his supremacy among the gods (*Iliad* VIII.19), and like that other image of the Golden Chain, the chorus of philosophers who roused their thought to bacchic frenzy by dancing around the doctrine of Plato, the procession of planetary spirits was far from static. They spiralled through all the ages in the Great Year, exerting their magical influences on every growing thing in the realm of the Horae and performing an invisible dance in tandem with the visible strophes and antistrophes of the stars.

Invisible, that is, to all save the theurgists: they alone had the power to see the occult dance behind the sparkling veil of phenomena and to induce the transparent dancers to appear on earth through the correct use of talismanic symbols, poetic invocations, numerological spells, libations, and sacrifices. What they saw – a plenitude of souls and spirits dancing through all the apparently empty spaces in the celestial theatre – is unveiled in the second part of Proclus' commentary on *Timaeus* 40c–d. Balancing the downward flow of illumination from Apollo-Helios and his harmony-enchanted stars was a Dionysian exaltation of illuminati, a contemplative leap of human, daimonic, angelic, and astral intellects up the Golden Chain to the transcendent causes of cosmic order. Proclus identified this intellectual ascent with the mystic dances extolled by Socrates in the Myth of the Chariot:

Having explained the astronomical significance of the passage let us consider the philosophical meaning of each of the terms in it. The term 'choreias' interpreted philosophically signifies the bacchic revels of the souls around the

Intelligible [tōn psychōn hai peri to noēton baccheiai] and their intellectual revolutions and reversions to the same point. For as Socrates says in the 'Phaedrus' [250b, 252d], the souls themselves dance while following the more divine of the leaders [synepomenai gar tōi theioterōi tōn hēgemonōn kai autai choreuousin].

(*In Timaeum* III 149)

Within each planetary sphere 'the more divine of the leaders' was the planetary god himself, whose brilliance obscured the whole of his resplendent entourage even as it revealed his eternal presence and temporary positions in the dance observed by the astronomers. The planets in turn followed the sun as their mystagogue, and the sun followed the fixed stars. All followed Chronos, whose dancing intellect spiralled upwards to higher and higher levels of metaphysical abstraction: to the Craftsman-Zeus and his chain of intellectual gods; to Autozöon and Aion; to the Primal Intellect, the Primal Life, and the Primal Being; and beyond the intelligible gods (if one can imagine soaring outside the limits of thought and being) to the first principles of individuality in the universe or to the least degree of multiplicity imaginable before reaching absolute unity, a chorus of gods known to Proclus and his circle as the Henads or 'Units.' The mystic spiral began and ended in the infinite mystery of the One.

Though the 'dancing out' of that mystery through time first revealed to the astronomers the choral unity of the fixed stars and the bacchic disunity of the planets, the Apollonian and Dionysian phases in the dance were ultimately seen in reverse by its inward-looking philosophical spectators.[15] The inner life of a bacchic reveller was always directed towards divine union, a loss of self-consciousness in the erotic embrace of the mystery god; hence, baccheia on a universal scale represented for the true Bacchant the striving of all souls for intellectual assimilation with the One and their consequent turning-away from material concerns in the process of reverting to the purely spiritual unity of their superior causes. The goal of a choral dancer, on the other hand, was to imitate the diverse motions in the world around him and to express through the multiple configurations of his limbs the complex mythological relations between gods and men; hence, choreia on a universal scale represented for the philosophical worshipper of Helios the orderly diversification of all forms of life under the sun and the artistic impulse of the living cosmos to imitate the life and thought and formal perfection of the highest beings on the Golden Chain.

To the inner eye, therefore, the fundamental distinction between the Same and the Different and the opposing movements of choral integration and bacchic dissolution resulting from that distinction were not impressive or even apparent. In their place appeared – or rather came to light, since it was always there and could not be called an appearance – a universal process involving two teleological chain-reactions, the technical Neoplatonic terms for which were 'pro-odos' (the choral 'procession' of multiple effects from a unifying superior cause) and 'epistrophē' (the bacchic 'return' of those effects into the unitary state of their causal progenitor). Despite their abstract metaphysical reference these terms retained something of their original dynamic significance, and so Proclus was able to tie them in quite easily with Timaeus' remarks on the cosmic dance.

In fact, the theoretical distinction between them (and it was only theoretical, since procession and return were virtually inseparable in the Procline continuum of Being and Becoming) may be seen in retrospect to underlie the binary structure of his commentary on 40c–d. While his astronomical section dealt with the multiplicity of complex choral motions proceeding from the simple rotation of the Aplanes, his philosophical exegesis concerns the psychological experiences of the dancing stars during bacchic reversion – their loss of individuality through ecstatic contemplation, their acquisition of sublime telepathic powers, their achievement of an unclouded vision of the eternal causes of temporal order, and their sense of repose after the agonizing labour of generation. 'Their "juxtapositions" are the periods in which the souls gain a deep understanding of each other,' explains the theurgic initiate,

for then everything is clear to them, and they see each other, and no soul is ignorant of the concerns of the others. Moreover, the souls fit their own images to the Intelligible Forms as if relating traces and imprints to their original models. Their 'retrogradations' are the periods in which the souls turn away from the Divine Mind back towards themselves, and their 'progressions' the periods in which they turn away from themselves back towards the Divine Mind [epistrophai]. For they perform both acts throughout eternal time, and when they are away from themselves they understand the Divine Mind, and when they are away from the Divine Mind they understand [that is, are conscious of] themselves.

(*In Timaeum* III 150)

The first stage in the epistrophic movement of the dance is a communal act of introspection resulting in 'gnōseis allēlōn' (literally 'deep mutual understandings') – a phrase with an oddly Christian ring to it despite its reference to the contemplative life of revelling stars rather than repentant sinners or enraptured Seraphim. By retracing in thought the steps in the cosmogonic procession which culminated in their existence as individuals, the leading lights in the temporal chorus raise their souls beyond the fragmented material world and consequently raise the souls of the theurgic élite who follow 'the more divine of the leaders' in order to share their power as well as their vision. Bacchic reversion reaches its climax when the dancing intellects lose all consciousness of themselves as individuals and commune in an ultra-mundane séance with the Primal Intellect.

We know from III 333 that Proclus decided to reject the Plotinian theory that the highest part of every rational soul, its intuitive intellect, never descends into the temporal world but remains above as an eternal participant in the Circle of Nous. The psychological consequences of this decision are evident here in III 150. The souls in his celestial chorus (including his own) could not remain forever in communion with the exalted causes of their thought and life and being, though they were permitted periodic visions of the Divine Mind 'throughout eternal time' – that is, for as long as Chronos led souls and bodies and natures in his regenerative dance and oversaw the cycle of reincarnation. Like the Bacchants of old, they were doomed to lose sight of their divine leader immediately after experiencing his magical immanence and to sink back into the lap of generation with a hideous consciousness of themselves as selves, isolated fugitives from reality, possessing only dim memories of their transcendent choragus.

Ironically, though he set out to free the visible gods from the epicyclical mechanism whirling them through Ptolemy's artificial heavens and to clarify the inner motions of their dance by dispensing with Plotinus' obscure fantasy of the undescended intellective soul, Proclus ended up contemplating a temporal order that was hardly less imaginary in its poetic design than the enchanted plain of everlasting truth and beauty beyond the Circle of the Same. As the ancient boundaries between time and eternity, image and model, motion and stability melted away in the fierce heat of his metaphysical speculations and the pullulating orders of Henads, Ideas, Primal Entities, and Chaldean Principles engulfed the comparatively tiny population of his temporal world, the visible beauty of the old Platonic cosmos all but disappeared into the white radiance of the theurgic Beyond. The Lycian certainly did not forget the orthodox Platonic doctrine that

the visible beauty of the firmament, the order of its revolutions, the measured series of the seasons, the harmony of the elements, and the system of symmetrical correspondences extending to every part of the world are the first things to indicate to those who are not totally blind that the universe is exceedingly beautiful.

But this is one of the very few passages in the enormous expanse of the *In Timaeum* where physical vision is even mentioned as a source of cosmological knowledge. Total blindness would not have been an obstacle to the appreciation of cosmic beauty as he envisioned it. The loveliness of the visible world, he goes on to say, springs from the invisible dynamism of its psychic infrastructure:

An order of invisible forces exists within it, joining its parts together, and the gift of the intellectual essence has been bestowed upon it. Yet these – the visible parts joined together – do not make the cosmos the most beautiful of all creatures brought into existence. 'How so?' one might ask. The reason for this is that there exists within it a harmonious choral dance of souls [psychōn en autōi enarmonios choreia]. ...

And in apposition to this last phrase he adds the following to unfold its occult significance:

... a participation in Nous, an abundant supply of divine life [zōēis theias choregia], an ineffable divinity, a numbering of Henads, thanks to which the whole cosmos has come to be saturated with beauty.

(In Timaeum III 332)

A choreia without a 'choregia' was as hard for an Athenian of the fifth century AD to imagine as it would have been for an Athenian of the fifth century BC: political experience taught that no show in a public theatre would get off the ground until the costs of training a chorus had been defrayed and the dancers had been generously supplied with everything needed for the dance. But in Proclus' day the costumes, masks, wreaths, musical instruments, sumptuous banquets, and so on supplied by the public-minded patrons of the theatre in the age of Euripides were only memories, and the crumbling Theatre of Dionysus a dancing-ground for devils. On the universal stage imagined by the last of the true Bacchants danced a chorus that had no need for expensive material accoutrements – indeed had a positive horror of them – since only the purest pagan souls, those who were thought mad by Christian Athens and were mad in the loftiest Socratic sense, were permitted to participate in the secret revels of the gods. On them was showered an inexhaustible supply of divine blessings.

What Christian saint could boast, even on the Last Day as he was entering the chorus of Heaven, that his soul had shared the vision of the Primal Intellect and the vitality of the Primal Life 'throughout eternal time'? It was not on any hypothetical Last Day but in the perpetual reality of the Now that Proclus saw himself entering into the 'psychōn enarmonios choreia.' Bound as he was to the chain of post-Iamblichan theologians who had turned the dramatic term 'choreia' into a colourless synonym for 'metousia' (signifying 'participation' in its most abstruse teleological sense), the Diadochus was also allied by education and temperament to the Late Antique philologists and philosopher-poets who had revived the mythopoetic vision of the dance of life by leading Lady Philosophy back to the wellspring of the Muses and celebrating in oracular hymns the reasons for their momentous retrogradation.

The Bacchant Awakens

Like Shakespeare's Prospero, the Proclus of Marinus' haunting memoir could have destroyed his mortal enemies with a thunderclap since he had the power to raise tempests with the aid of Hecate, but being a philanthropic wizard who abjured the rough magic of common sorcerers and also an Orphic poet who could pacify the tempestuous world of matter ('the vast wave of loud-roaring generation' as he himself called it) by inducing a chorus of airy spirits to dance out the mysteries of world-harmony in the shadows of the Cave, he strove instead to heal humanity's distempered soul with celestial music. Unlike Prospero, however, Proclus did not think that his revels had to end or that the great globe in which his spirits danced would dissolve and like an insubstantial pageant leave not a rack behind.

The majestic visions he conjured up were of a dance that was 'allēktos kai akamatos' (unceasing and untiring) and of a cosmos eternally harmonized and vivified by the theurgic powers of the sun. The masters of his solar revels were three divine poets – Apollo, Paeon, and Dionysus – who brought concord to the clashing elements, health to earth's demon-plagued masses, and mystic joy to the souls of the just by singing the praises of their royal forefather Helios. And with these resounding apostrophes he joined them in their hymn:

Hear, o Lord of Intellectual Fire, Golden Titan!
Hear, o Distributor of Light, Ruler of Life, King!
You who possess the key of the wellspring and pour forth from
on high
A rich flood of harmony within the material heavens,
Hear! For you are above the ether: you hold the midmost seat
And heart of the cosmos. Having filled the circle of the heavens
With all your intense splendour, may you fill my mind with
your foreknowledge!
Guided by your ever-flourishing flames the planets
Always send life-generating drops to those who dwell on earth
Beneath their unceasing and untiring choral dances
[aien hyp' allēktoisi kai akamatoisi choreiais].
Because you return in your chariot-drive,
Every race is rejuvenated according to the law of the Horae;

The thunderous rumbling of elements colliding with each other
Ceases when you appear, o Offspring of the Ineffable!
To you their chorus has yielded, unshaken by the Fates
Who twist back the thread of ineluctable Necessity
At your will. How powerful you are! How mighty your
                                                    command!
From your chain sprang forth the lord of divinely obedient
                                                    song –
Phoebus who sings to the wondrous lyre and calms
The vast wave of loud-roaring generation.
And from your bacchic revelry, which wards off evil, sprang
                                    the god with the pleasing gifts –
Paeon who fills the cosmos with harmless harmony
And imposes his healthfulness on all the vastness of the
                                                    universe.
Of you they sing, o glorious Father of Dionysus!
Others in the lowest depths of matter praise you
In their songs as Evius Attis and the delicate Adonis.
The cruel-hearted daimones who in their fierce hatred of
                                                    mankind
Prepare evil torments for our unhappy souls
And cause them to suffer under the weight of the body;
They who abide forever in the abyss of loud-thundering life,
Desiring their yokes and yearning to forget the brilliance of
                                    their Father's exalted court –
Even they fear the threat of your agile scourge!
                                                    (*Hymn* I, 1–32)

This is the turning-point in the poem and in the flow of divine harmony it represents, the first movement of which begins in the wellspring of fair dances (the supracosmic intellect of Helios), follows the downward 'pro-odos' of the Many from the One (the procession of Apollo, Paeon, and Dionysus from the Intellectual Sun), and culminates in the dancing of fair wellsprings (the Dionysian revels of the planets resulting in a cascade of 'life-generating drops,' that is, the semen of Attis, into the womb of sublunary matter). Then, in the abysmal realm of colliding elements, malicious daimones, and tormented humanity, the poet awakens to the celestial light and yearns to dance back to God with all the spirits in the heliotropic chorus. Now begins his 'epistrophē':

But, o Blest of Gods, Fire-Crowned One, Blessed One,
Image of the Divine Father of All, You who lead up souls,

Hear, and always purge me of sin!
Welcome the tear-stained suppliant, and deliver me
From destructive faults! May you oversee from afar the
                                    penalties I must pay,
Soothing the sharp eye of all-seeing Justice.

Rising beyond the stage of purgation, the tear-stained suppliant dries his eyes and prays for illumination:

May you always protect me from evil
And give my soul sacred light, rich in blessings,
Dispersing the venomous gloom which is fatal to mortals.

And then for perfection of body and mind, which is tantamount to complete freedom from the coils of Necessity:

May you give strength to my body and the lovely gift of
                                    health,
And bring me to glory by seeing that I respect the laws
Of my forefathers, the gifts of the lovely-braided Muses.
Give me undisturbed happiness through passionate piety,
If such is your will, o Lord! You can perfect all things
With ease, for your strength and power are boundless.
And if misfortune is about to descend upon us through the fatal
                                    influence of the threads,
May you stop it with your great force as it spirals down
From the star-whirling spindles of destiny!

                                    (*Hymn* I, 33–50)

Marinus reports in sections XXII and XXVIII of the *Vita* that Proclus was accustomed to pray to the sun every day at dawn, noon, and dusk, and that at the age of forty he began to compose mystical verses (sometimes in his sleep!) on the flow of Intellectual Light into the cosmos and the fiery ascent of his soul to the empyreal wellspring, the Muses having evidently chosen to inundate him with poetic inspiration after he had demonstrated his philosophical virtuosity as a Platonic commentator and his theurgic virtues as a Chaldean healer and diviner.

Whether his effulgent Hymn to Helios was composed with Alexandrian attention to prosodic and mythological detail during his waking hours or was spontaneously begotten in his dreams his biographer does not say. At first glance it may appear to be such stuff as dreams are made on, a pastiche of world-ordering and wish-fulfilling images; but are these images – the inexhaustible wellspring, the enchanted wave, the whirling spindle, the lyre, the chain, the spiral, the dance – presented to us here as evanescent figments of a melancholy mage's charmingly poetic yet baseless fantasy of universal order like the 'vanities' of Prospero's Art? We may of course choose to regard them that way and to pride ourselves on having awakened from the dream's enticing delusions with far less regret than Caliban, who cried to sleep again. The poet, however, strikes so clear a note of 'passionate piety' in the hymn that we should only be deluding ourselves to suppose that he and his original listeners were fearful of a great nothingness, or worse, an elemental chaos, lurking behind the flimsy veil of images through which the rays of Intellectual Light were supposed to filter.

The same images of order turn up repeatedly in the least poetic (or overtly poetic) passages in his exegetical works, as we have seen, and it was in these works that he conducted his most penetrating philosophical inquiries into the essence of the real, the permanent, the beautiful, the good, the true. His Hymn to Helios may justly be read as a distillation of his entire philosophy because the universe he anatomized as a philosopher and helped to harmonize as a theurgist – the universe evoked in the Hymn – was radically poetic in design. Allusive not elusive, his poetic images were what remained in his consciousness after Helios had cleared away with his purging fire the dense fog of opinions and conjectures and disputed questions enshrouding the truths of the old philosophy. They were his philosophical truths. They were such stuff as his prophetic visions of reality were made on.

What melancholy there is in the Hymn (and there is a burst of it in lines 33–7) is not symptomatic of a desperate idealism on the brink of extinction or of existential angst. It is the tear-stained suppliant's response to the most difficult and disturbing conclusion a Greek rationalist could wrest from his experience 'in the abyss of loud-thundering life': the clear and certain apprehension that without the merciful intercession of a divine thaumaturge, a power mightier than either Justice or Necessity, even the soul of a perfectly virtuous man will welter in the blood-stained tide of history because of humanity's deafness to the music beyond the tempest and perverse obliviousness to the life-lines cast to earth from the high shores of heaven. If the Lycian's cry for deliverance sounds remarkably like the 'de profundis' supplications of Gregory the Theologian, Synesius of Cyrene, and other philosophical Christians who felt the gravity of sin preventing the human spirit from soaring on its own into the heavenly dance, that is only to be expected: behind all their tears, behind their impassioned awareness of man's 'destructive faults,' was the sadness of the Late Stoics who realized that while knowing thyself (which amounted to knowing thine imperfections) made thee a wise spectator of the divine chorus it was not sufficient to make the wisest spectator divine.

The philosophical resonance of Proclus' Hymn to Helios becomes most perceptible when a purely lyrical poem in praise of the sun is set beside it for contrast. Mesomedes, a pagan citharist and manumitted slave from Crete, composed such a poem in the days of Hadrian and Epictetus (c 130 AD):

> Hush! Let all the ether,
> Earth, and winds be still!
> Silence, o mountains, glens of Tempe,
> And birds with clamorous voices!
> For Phoebus with fair locks unshorn
> Is about to approach us.
> Father of snowy-eyed Dawn,
> You who drive a rosy chariot
> With the winged tracks of foals,
> You rejoice in your golden tresses,
> Braiding your oft-turned ray
> About the boundless back of heaven
> And winding your wellspring of light,
> Which sees much, in a spiral about the whole earth.
> The rivers of your immortal fire
> Give birth to charming Day.
> For you the clear-shining chorus of stars
> Dances over Lord Olympus
> [Soi men choros eudios asterōn
> kat' Olympon anakta choreuei],
> Singing always a free untroubled song
> And delighting in Phoebus' lyre.
> Before him goes the Moon with her pale gleam,
> Leading seasonable Time with sweeps of her white branches;
> And his well-disposed mind rejoices
> As he whirls the cosmos with its many robes.
>
> (Hymn to Helios 1–25)

Like the song of the Mesomedean stars, this hymn may be described as free-flowing, relaxed, untroubled, unlaboured – in a word, 'anetos.' There is no tear-stained suppliant crying for deliverance, no chorus of cacodemons clanking their chains and plotting torments for mankind, no elemental thunder, no tempest. The only discordant note in the whole lyrical cosmos seems to arise from the birds in the vale of Tempe, but their clamorous voices echoing off the mountains of Arcady are swiftly hushed so that Phoebus may make his joyous entrance in peace, the peace of a perfect dawn, twirling his golden tresses across the boundless back of heaven and sending the stars before him over Lord Olympus, with pale Selene, who seems to disappear with Time into the radiance of an eternal day.

This exquisite Apollonian paean is so different in tone and mood from Proclus' vehement incantation, which pierces the Aplanes with the mingled strains of Apollo and Dionysus, that one might not at first notice that many of the images of order appearing in the latter (notably the wellspring, the dance, the lyre, and the spiral) also figure in the former. Mesomedes set these images very much in the foreground of his Golden-Age vision, composing them into a familiar emblematic picture of the central figure in the world-chorus or rather into a series of coalescent pictures like the protean 'schēmata' in an imperial pantomime. Now we see Phoebus braiding his unshorn tresses, now floating on a river of light, now surveying heaven and earth with his all-seeing eye, now plucking his lyre to delight the carefree stars, and finally whirling round a draped figure whose many cloaks spread out in the dance to reveal the mysterious character of the cosmos.

Proclus relegates such charming scenes to the background of his vision, the central figure in which turns out to be himself – the poet in prophetic agony – rather than the majestic Offspring of the Ineffable. Instead of inviting us to a public pantomime where we see familiar images of the old gods in human costume delighting in common human activities, he draws us into a private séance where we are blinded by otherworldly displays of prodigious superhuman power. Lyrical serenity is lost amid the dramatic conflicts between the daimones and man, man and the elements, the elements and Helios, Helios and Necessity; or rather it is no longer assumed to arise naturally out of the free and easy life of the stars (and therefore to be easily promoted in their mortal spectators) but is revealed to be a superlunary peace-of-mind imposed on the tormented souls below the moon by the titanic force of Helios, Apollo, Paeon, Dionysus, the Muses, and certain extraordinary mortals whom they charged with demiurgic power – the theurgic poets. Proclus, believing himself to be such a poet, composed the solar images and epithets in his hymn as a theurgist would compose the astrological symbols, numerological pictograms, or Egyptian hieroglyphs in a talisman: to reflect the order and to draw down the power of the beings harmonized in the eternal dance of procession and return. It is this dance, not the temporal dance of the stars, that blazes to the foreground of his 'speaking picture' of the universe and determines the two-movement structure of his poem.

Neither Mesomedes nor the unknown author of the Orphic Hymn to Helios (see chapter 6, pages 286–7) reversed direction in mid-poem, as it were, by commanding the Golden Titan to perfect a specific mortal – an heroic 'I' battling the waves like Odysseus – who yearned to follow the more divine of the leaders back to the Intellectual World in order to dance with him around the ultimate wellspring of light, the Intelligible One. Nor can they be expected to have envisioned the dance in such a light or to have thought of it in such terms, both having written before the dawn of Neoplatonism. 'You proceed in your endlessly whirling course ... ,' sang the Orphic poet, 'With your golden lyre you sustain the harmonious rush of the cosmos!' But no 'I' tried to escape the harmonious rush by wresting the golden lyre from Phoebus' hands and singing his way back to divine tranquillity. It was not until the violent middle decades of the fourth century, when the classical Platonic boundary between poetry and philosophy had been erased by Porphyry and Iamblichus, that a hymn to the sun was written by an intellectual Odysseus who yearned for such tranquillity and who also believed that he was uniquely related to the Ruler of Life by virtue of his imperial destiny. A new strain of personal piety entered the solar paean with the Emperor Julian's humble, tentative, but persistent use of the first person singular in his fourth oration. 'For I am a follower of King Helios,' confessed the Apostate with touching self-consciousness (130c), 'and of this fact I have the clearest proofs, though they are known to me alone; but this much I may say without committing sacrilege, that from my childhood a strangely powerful longing for the rays of the god has penetrated the depths of my soul.' And his soul responded to the divine rays by forsaking the narrow Christian path towards communal salvation in the Hereafter for the ever-widening spiral ascent to theurgic perfection in the Here and Now, the epistrophic course charted for the heroic few by Iamblichus and Salutius and Mithras the Mediator.

While the imperial heliolater turned his hymn almost entirely into a Neoplatonic lecture on the procession of gods from the Intellectual Sun, the theme of the return – the mystical Odyssey from sublunary battleground to supracosmic homeland – surfaced now and then in the flow of his argument as an apologetic reminder of the implicit purpose of the panegyric. Recalling the Myth of the Chariot in 152b–c, Julian praised Helios for raising our souls up 'to the region of those essences that are akin to the god' and for giving us Dionysus and the Muses as 'synchoreutas' – 'fellow dancers' – who lead our thoughts away from earthly toil to the free artistic play of the heavens. And recollecting his own religious aspirations in the final sentence of the hymn, which returns to the private confessional tone of his opening remarks, he implored Helios to grant his soul 'the gentlest of all leave-takings from this life' and to guide it on 'a pathway up and back to him.'

How unlike these meek prayers are the imperious exhortations and exultant commendations of power in Proclus' solar hymn! One would suppose that with their common debt to Iamblichus, their common vision of the intellectual pantheon, their common faith in the ancient mysteries, and their common detestation of Christianity, Julian and Proclus would have sung very similar praises to Helios; but the differences between their hymns – not just in tone but in structure, emphasis, therapeutic function, and what might be called 'Orphic potency' – prove far more striking than the signs of literary and philosophical kinship one would expect to find in two such specimens of Neoplatonic heliolatry. While the Emperor's hymn may be read as a fatalistic apology for his change of religions and as a proclamation to his empire that a new age of pagan enlightenment was dawning, the Lycian's incantation is nothing less than a declaration of independence from Fate: the song of a power-charged wizard who has nothing to apologize for (once he had Helios on his side) and no empire to protect from 'the star-whirling spindles of destiny' (except the empire of his fading gods). The procession of the gods from Helios becomes for Proclus the grand prelude to his own apotheosis; the theme of the return, treated explicitly not in a few stray lines but in the whole second half of his hymn, is anticipated throughout the processional first half in such verses as 'With all your intense splendour, may you fill my mind with your foreknowledge!' and 'Because you return in your chariot-drive Every race is rejuvenated according to the law of the Horae' (lines 7, 11–12). This shift in emphasis from procession to return doubtless reflects the drastic decline of pagan cultural authority and political influence in the hundred years separating Proclus from Julian as well as the sharp contrast in their personalities and self-proclaimed destinies. It betrays a desperate longing in Proclus to draw supreme executive power down from the heavens as a compensation – an over-compensation, more like – for the power lost on earth to the forces of the Church Militant. Whereas Julian wished to cure his soul of its eschatalogical anxieties by celebrating the regenerative order of the poetic universe, Proclus strove to cure the universe of its elemental chaos by celebrating the poetic potency of his bacchic soul. Gone from his hymn are the arguments of the philosopher-king. Gone is the prose of the Platonic commentator. The Bacchant awoke from his deep dreams of the heroic past and like the glorious Father of Dionysus poured forth a flood of healing harmony into the dying inglorious present.

'The awakening of a poet,' he taught his successors, erasing the distinction Socrates had drawn between poetic and prophetic inspiration,

is a stretching of the soul towards the Divine, an activity without distractions or deviations, a process of return in which the poet avoids falling back into the world of Becoming; his bacchic rapture is a divinely inspired movement, an unwearied choral dance around the Divine [hē de baccheia kinēsis entheos kai choreia peri to theion atrutos], a process of perfection for all whom the Muses possess.

(*In Rem Publicam* 1.181.24–30)

For an explicit account of the theory of cosmological poetry or 'cosmo-poetics' implicit in the hymns of Proclus we must plunge again into the deep waters of his Platonic commentaries, where, as in the passage above, the mystical goals of the Late Antique philosopher-poets were lucidly defined and enthusiastically defended. When his thoughts turned to the process of prophetic illumination which awakened the love of wisdom in a philoso-pher's soul and the love of harmony in a poet's soul, loves quite indistin-guishable in the Muse-possessed soul of the poetic universe, the same images of dynamic order and ecstatic energy that had figured in his commentary on *Timaeus* 40d sprang into his mind. Poetics and cosmology merged into a single subject at his Academy: the psychology of inspiration.

'For just as the Muses fill all other creations of the Father both visible and invisible with harmony and rhythmic motions,' he explained in his commentary on the *Republic* (1.180.17–23), 'so also do they produce the art of divinely inspired poetry by making the reflection of divine symmetry shine in the souls possessed by them.' While all human beings according to Plato were images of the divine symmetry observable in the dances of the stars and traceable to the eternal mathematical design of the Model, only a few, the great pagan poets and philosophers, were ever able to recognize the correspondence between their upwardly mobile souls and the bacchic spirits animating the heavenly bodies and to perfect their inherent likeness to the gods. Their divine awakeners were 'the lovely-braided Muses,' and when Proclus sang to the Muses (as in the third of his seven hymns) he was addressing spirits that would not melt into air, into thin air, like the eva-nescent actors in Prospero's revels. Their choral dance was 'atrutos,' 'un-wearied,' and like their plaited locks symbolic of the eternal coherence of the poetic heavens which could not exist but for the Father's providential knowledge of the One. They were the same fountain-born maidens whom Apollo accompanied in the Porphyrian Chorus of Immortal Eros, and whom Philology applauded at her wedding dance in the temple of Harmonia, and whom another allegorical lady – Philosophy – was to call upon in the Latin West, four decades after Proclus' death, to cure the ailing vision of Boethius.

'Kosmopoiia kata logon' (verbal cosmos-making) was what Proclus called the special literary activity inspired by Philosophy's Muses – special because it entailed not only the composition of poems designed to imitate the rhyth-mical sounds and symmetrical movements of the cosmic chorus but also the employment of those poems as theurgic talismans by which health, pros-perity, emotional serenity, unclouded vision, and all the other gifts of the gods could be drawn down from the heavens and distributed to the world-weary prisoners chained by the flesh to the lowest depths of existence. It was the true Bacchant's way of breaking his fleshly chains and freely par-ticipating in 'kosmopoiia kata noun' (intellectual cosmos-making), which was the process initiated by the Craftsman before the birth of time and brought to perfection by Chronos and Helios during time's endlessly unwinding cycles.

The chorus of the stars was the supreme product of intellectual cosmos-making, of course, but what could possibly match it in words? Certainly not the hymns of Proclus, those brief self-centred experiments in the art of cosmopoetics. If the Lycian ever felt the urge to compose a vast hymn to the gods which would recreate in words the strophe of choral procession and the antistrophe of bacchic return, he did not act on it (except perhaps fitfully in his dreams) and the simple reason for this was that in his estimation such a work had already been written by the divine Plato and could not be duplicated. The *Timaeus*, he argued in *In Timaeum* I 9, was that work. In essence an allegorical poem rather than an analytical description of creation, a poem in which each word, metaphor, speech, and speaker mirrored the unified diversity of the temporal world and conveyed to the inner eye consoling images of the diversified unity of the eternal chorus, it presented in the character of its chief speaker an ideal human image of the Craftsman and a model of the Pythagorean philosopher-poet to be emulated by all who seek to link their souls to the Golden Chain. It was fitting, he concluded, that 'Timaeus in his role as the Father of the Words should be analogous to the Father of the Works for "kosmopoiia kata logon" is an image of "kosmopoiia kata noun." '

A total eclipse of the sun in 484 AD warned Marinus and his friends that 'the luminary of philosophy' whose hymns had for so many years drawn their souls into the Muses' unwearied dance was growing weary of his life among the shadows and was soon to vanish from their sight (*Vita Procli* XXXVII). Their reading of the omen proved correct. Weakened by old age and by the rigours of his ascetic life, Proclus died in the following year and was buried beside his beloved Syrianus in the eastern suburbs of Athens near Mount Lycabettus, leaving Marinus as his successor. Though the great luminary was bound to follow Syrianus to the grave as Syrianus had followed all the other sages who had circled around the mystic doctrine of Plato, surely his return to Helios did not portend the final movement in the dance of pagan education. Surely nothing could break the Golden Chain. So the surviving Academicians may have consoled themselves when they read in their almanacs that another eclipse of the sun was due to occur shortly after the first anniversary of Proclus' death. Had they compiled a pagan bible to honour their departed teacher and to ensure the continuity of his fountain-born religion, the *Timaeus* would doubtless have been their Genesis, the *Orphic Hymns* their Psalms, the *Vita Procli* their Gospel, and the *Chaldean Oracles* their Revelation. But by failing in the end to turn the books on their curriculum into a scriptural canon they hastened the impending eclipse of Neoplatonism as a philosophical and religious alternative to Orthodox

Christianity. The Neoplatonists scattered through Greece, Egypt, Asia Minor, and Persia in the early sixth century had no coherent body of doctrine on which to base a creed and no public institution in which to chant it: all they had to offer the prisoners in the Cave (besides the memory of what the Chorus of Immortal Eros had once been) were a dusty heap of commentaries and a few hymns to Helios.

Perhaps the greatest happiness in the life of Proclus was to die before the death of his school. The Golden Chain of philosophers was symbolically (though not actually) broken in 529 when the Emperor Justinian, having issued a general law forbidding pagans to teach, sent a special edict to Athens prohibiting anyone – pagan or Christian – from teaching law or philosophy there. The Academy was not instantly boarded up when the bad news came from Constantinople, as romantic Hellenists have often supposed, for Damascius (the last Diadochus) and his disciples appear to have waited around in Athens for at least two years before voluntarily exiling themselves to the court of King Chosroes in Persia. Since Justinian had not banished them in the first place, he found it fairly easy to be magnanimous a few years later when they wished to come home to civilization after failing to turn Chosroes into a Platonic philosopher-king. Damascius was undoubtedly back in the Levant as early as 538.[16]

Hostile though Justinian was to the ideals of the Academy in 529, his soul was destined to be reconciled with its migrant spirits some eight hundred years later in (of all places) Dante's Paradise. Athena would doubtless have smiled at the ironic prospect of her imperial enemy, the builder of Hagia Sophia, dancing out eternity as a minor hero in the sphere of Mercury at the lower end of the Golden Chain – a sparkling descendant of those lesser planetary spirits who spiralled after 'the more divine of the leaders' through Proclus' unfading poetic heavens.

Following the Leader

Links between the Neoplatonic scholars of the Greek East and the Catholic scholars of the Latin West cannot have been numerous in the early sixth century owing to doctrinal, linguistic, political, and simple geographical barriers preventing intellectual communication between the empire of Justinian and the kingdom of Theodoric. But at least one link can be identified, one link worthy of the Golden Chain, and his long aristocratic Roman name was to be revered by all the philosopher-poets of the Middle Ages: Anicius Manlius Severinus Boethius.

How Boethius, who was about five years old when Proclus died, became acquainted in Gothic Italy with the pagan philosophical culture of Athens and Alexandria can only be guessed at; probably his learned guardian Symmachus (into whose Catholic household he was received after his father's death in the late 480s) played a major role in directing his early literary and religious education and in orienting his mind towards the luminaries of philosophy in the Greek East. A great-grandson of the fourth-century pagan aristocrat of the same name whom Macrobius had portrayed as an urbane philologist in the *Saturnalia*, the Christian Symmachus was praised by his ward for being 'a great expert in both Greek and Latin letters' – a commendation which suggests that fluency in Greek was certainly not taken for granted among the Western senatorial families of his era.[17] That he had a strong interest, one might even call it a strong family interest, in Neoplatonic mysticism of the sort expounded by Macrobius in his *In Somnium Scipionis* may be inferred from his editorial revision of a manuscript of that work which had probably belonged to his family for generations and which Boethius (the first Latin author to cite Macrobius) doubtless studied under his tutelage. There is no record that Boethius ever left Italy, but Symmachus is known to have visited Constantinople at the turn of the sixth century and may there have acquired manuscripts of the theological and exegetical works of the latest masters of the Neoplatonic schools in order to provide his precocious ward with a richer store of academic wisdom than that furnished by Macrobius.

Intent on narrowing the rift between East and West, Symmachus may even have sent Boethius to Athens or Alexandria to complete his philosophical education before launching him on his fateful career in politics. He certainly had the means to do so. As a Catholic scholar Boethius would no doubt have found Alexandria more intellectually congenial than Athens, for the Neoplatonists of the Alexandrian school had learned to suppress their public antagonism towards Christians after the murder of Hypatia and to emphasize uncontroversial subjects such as Aristotelian logic and Ptolemaic astronomy in lieu of those dangerous disciplines around which the anti-Christian Athenian Academy had built its subversive curriculum, Platonic theology and Chaldean theurgy. The intellectual decline of the Athenian Academy after the death of Proclus may also have inclined Boethius (simply as a scholar) towards the Alexandrian school despite its greater distance from his homeland. The leading Neoplatonist in Alexandria at the time when he would most likely have studied there was a certain pupil of Proclus who by chance – or was it by providence? – bore the same name as Plotinus' hallowed teacher Ammonius.[18]

Providence had been Proclus' grand obsession, and it became Boethius'. All his doubts concerning the origin of providence, its relation to fate and evil, its cosmological function, its very existence – topics which Proclus had treated at every turn in his Platonic commentaries and had reserved for special consideration in his theological opuscula *De providentia et fato* and *De decem dubitationibus circa providentiam* – were put to rest in the magnum opus for which 'Boezio' would earn his place in Dante's Chorus of the Wise: the *De consolatione Philosophiae*. Until the Flemish Dominican William of Moerbeke translated Proclus' 'On Providence and Fate' and 'Ten Doubts Concerning Providence' (along with excerpts from the *In Timaeum*) into scholastic Latin in the mid-thirteenth century, the elegant classical Latin of Boethius' 'Consolation of Philosophy' was the only vehicle by which the theodicy of the Diadochus and his school was transmitted without Christian colouration to the philosophers and poets of medieval Europe.[19]

Plato is often cited by name in the pages of Boethius, Proclus never. But it was Proclus' Plato, the Muse-inspired prophet of the poetic universe, who shaped Boethius' conception of providence as a regenerative light emanating from the Divine Mind and overseeing all the operations of fate, and who taught his inner eye to perceive the Now as 'this brief and fleeting moment which because it carries a certain image of the Abiding Presence affects all things to which it is present so that they seem to be' (*De consolatione* v, pr vi, 50). The Boethian moment hung from the great circle of the Abiding Presence that Iamblichus had contemplated in his revision of the mathematical speculations of the Pseudo-Archytas and which Proclus had pictured as the spool of permanence that Chronos steadily unwound in his spiralling dance between Being and Becoming. It was a moment in the history of Western philosophy when the question 'If God exists, whence evil?' was serenely balanced, and effectively answered, by the question 'If God does not exist, whence good?'

The unnamed philosopher to whom Boethius attributes these questions in the first book of the *De consolatione* (pr iv, 150) has been the subject of much speculation since he is referred to as a 'familiar friend,' which seems to rule out all philosophers save those contemporary with the author and close to his circle. But the misleading designation must in fact refer to a philosopher whom Boethius could not have known personally but with whose works he was familiar and with whose thinking he was in deep sympathy – namely Proclus – for the same pair of questions, similarly balanced, have been found in the Lycian's commentary on the *Parmenides* (col 1056, 10–16).[20] On the argument implicit in the second Procline question (that is, 'All good must flow from God since God in truth exists') depended Boethius' faith as a philosopher in the providential governance of the cosmos and his hope as a tempest-tossed mortal in the eventual rescue of his soul.

He voiced an unconditional affirmation of that argument in his celebrated hymn to the Creator 'O qui perpetua,' the central verses of which have rightly been glossed as a masterful précis of the psychogony in the Myth of the Craftsman:

> *Entwining the all-moving Soul through all the harmonious*
> *limbs of the cosmos,*

You have set her free in the midst of threefold nature.
After being cut into rings she has gathered her two motions
                            together within her sphere.
By returning into herself she moves towards and circles round
                            the Highest Mind,
And turns the heavens into an image resembling it.
In the same way you cause the lesser souls and lives
To proceed, and you furnish the lofty ones with swift chariots,
And scatter them over heaven and earth. Then, in accordance
                            with your kind law,
They return to you like flames from a torch blazing back to the
                            sky.

(De consolatione III, m ix, 13–21)

These verses are resonant with echoes not only of *Timaeus* 29c–42d but also of Proclus' 'philosophical' as distinct from 'mathematical' explanation of those sections in the *In Timaeum*. The phrase 'threefold nature,' for instance, recalls the three classes of temporal entities – souls, bodies, and soul-body composites or natures – that Chronos was said to restore in his dance by leading them back to their starting-points in choral imitation of Psyche's revolution around Nous (*In Timaeum* III 28–9). The latter revolution, the eternal paradigm of the harmonious choral dance of souls in the Procline cosmos, is recalled in the movement of the Boethian World-Soul 'into herself' and 'around the Highest Mind.' Her epistrophic yearning for union with God results in the general revolution of 'lesser souls and lives' by which the contrarious motions of quick-leaping fire, ponderous earth, and the other elements are calmed and woven together, and also, as Proclus had noted in his discussion of the astral dances (*In Timaeum* III 149–50), in the special return of the 'lofty' souls scattered at the cosmogony to their original state of union in the presence of God. Boethius is no exception to the rule that the Neoplatonic Spectator pays far less attention to the physical movements of the cosmic chorus than to the cosmogonic scattering and contemplative unification of souls, and his focus on the invisible dynamics of procession and return in lines 18–21 certainly comes as no surprise.

But where is the image of the dance in 'O qui perpetua'? One should be surprised indeed to find no trace of it in a poem so attuned to the philosophy of Proclus and so reminiscent of Neoplatonic hymns to Helios: and yet the word 'chorea' does not appear in the hymn or anywhere else in the work of which it is the poetic and philosophical centrepiece. One must look closely at the poet's Virgilian diction before the dance will come to light around the mystic wellspring, but come to light it does in the following epistrophic verses:

O Father, let my mind ascend to your majestic seat;
Let me encircle and behold the Wellspring of the Good, and
having found the Light,
[Da fontem lustrare boni, da luce reperta]
Let me fix the clear-sighted glances of my soul on you!
(De consolatione III, m ix, 22–4)

The verb Boethius chose to express the intellectual activity of encircling and beholding the mystic wellspring, 'lustrare,' corresponds to the Neoplatonic term 'perichoreuein' which denoted precisely that activity in similar contexts in Proclus' Platonic commentaries and theological treatises.[21] Originally signifying 'to purify by means of a propitiatory offering,' 'lustrare' took on the meaning 'to purify through ritual encirclement' and later 'to encircle for the purpose of close examination' because the priest at a lustral sacrifice was accustomed to process or dance around the person or object to be purified. Virgil associated the verb with choral dancing in the tenth book of the *Aeneid*, line 224: 'adgnoscunt longe regem lustrantque choreis' (They recognized the king from afar and encircled him with dances). Since Boethius composed his hymn to the Creator in the language and metre of the *Aeneid* – paralleling Proclus' composition of hymns in the language and metre of the *Odyssey* – the Virgilian associations of the verb must be considered in interpreting its Boethian significance. Transferring the epic action from earth to the Empyrean, we may picture the aspiring mind of the poet recognizing the King from afar and encircling him with dances: the intellectual dances taught in the Neoplatonic schools.

The remarkable absence of even a passing reference to Christ or the Church in the *De consolatione*, which was written in a prison in Pavia some months before its author was murdered by Theodoric's henchmen (524 AD), has prompted speculation that the world-weary prisoner may have spurned the consolation of Christian theology and denounced his faith in a dramatic eleventh-hour apostasy. Dramatic indeed, but hardly likely: the author of 'O qui perpetua' was not one whose world had fallen apart and whose soul saw nothing but misery and meaningless change in the prison of this life. If his readers wanted the consolation of theology they could certainly find an abundance of it in his Catholic tractates. 'Even things that are put together out of many things, like a heap or a chorus, are still a unity,' he argued in his defence of Chalcedonian Christology (*Contra Eutychen* IV 40), recollecting the old Stoic definition of a chorus as a multitude of easily dispersed individuals exemplifying the least enduring kind of unity. He completed this consoling line of thought by contemplating the highest kind of unity and being, the leader of the Catholic chorus: 'Now we openly and truthfully declare that Christ exists, and we say therefore that Christ is a unity.'

Nothing he wrote in prison about 'the One who holds together that which He has joined' (III, pr xii, 20) would contradict or qualify his declarations of allegiance to the Catholic faith. Imprisonment simply removed him from the courts and basilicas where the mantle of Mother Church was being torn to sectarian shreds like the ancient gown of Lady Philosophy, distanced him from the battleground of Nestorians, Monophysites, and Orthodox in the East, cut him off from effective participation in the power struggle between Arians and Catholics in the West, and freed him, ironically, for epistrophic contemplations of what lay above all temporal discord.

The power of 'musica mundana' – the heavens' perpetual hymn to God – to transform a multitude of dispersed and conflicting things into an harmonious chorus participating in eternal unity was the consoling theme of a treatise on Pythagorean harmonics and quantitative prosody Boethius found time to write in the busy decades before his fall.[22] To this theme he returned in his final work, the form of which, a Menippean satire, announced his dual vocation as a philosophical critic of the ambitious soloists and colliding choruses in the earthly theatre and an oracular poet in tune with the celestial chorus encircling the 'fons boni.' In his philosophical poetry he put to the test Plato's theory that 'words should be akin to the things we speak of' (III, pr xii, 110) and enshrined for the Latin Middle Ages the ancient Greek images of order and unity transcending the division between the Church's disenchanting world and the Academy's enchanted cosmos: images like the Muses' chorus, the Golden Chain, the Orphic lyre, and the Wellspring of Life which could be composed and recomposed into consoling visions of that curious in-between world of the philological imagination, the poetic universe.

Boethius presented himself to his first eminent reader, Symmachus, and to generations of eminent readers in post-classical Europe, as a type of the socially and morally noble man struck down for no good reason by outrageous Fortune, a cosmic force more frightening than any chain-clanking cacodemon and much less easy to blame than the Prince of Darkness. The Stoic Everyman is hard to miss in Boethius; but his literary persona also typifies a rare sort of Neoplatonic soul – the poetic genius whose imprisonment in the body (allegorically represented by the Pavian dungeon) does not and indeed cannot prevent him from experiencing that supreme intellectual 'awakening' which is his peculiar destiny under the kind law of providence, and its rapturous consequences, the liberation of his creative spirit and the perfection of his inner life, which as Proclus had taught came about through 'a process of return in which he avoids falling back into the world of Becoming' and which ensured his participation in that special chorus of souls 'whom the Muses possess' (see chapter 8, pages 472–3). In the first prose section of book one Boethius confessed that his poetry had not always proclaimed the lofty truths of philosophy. For many months after his fall his only companions in misery were a chorus of histrionic Muses – the spirits of his tormented self-consciousness – who helped him express his outrage at the injustice of the world by inspiring a Stygian effusion of elegies, complaints, satires, soliloquies, and curses.

One day his passionate wailing was interrupted by an unexpected vision. Through his tears he perceived a majestic woman who seemed at one moment to touch the heavens with her head and at the next to be of ordinary human stature. By the book and sceptre she held before her, the symbols of her learning and authority, and by her gown embroidered with Greek characters which over the centuries had been torn about the hem by the rival schools of her followers, he recognized the Lady Philosophy. Her mission, she explained, was to cure his blindness, excessive weeping having so weakened his eyesight that he was no longer able to see the stars or willing to perceive the cosmos as the handiwork of a benevolent deity. In classical Platonic allegories of philosophical enlightenment physical blindness normally represented the simple ignorance of the uneducated or the naïveté of the superstitious masses; but here, in a Neoplatonic allegory of poetic awakening, it represents the cynical despair and perverse obliviousness of a highly learned soul whose bodily preoccupations and tempestuous passions have clouded his inborn vision of the Divine. The opposite of that epistrophic process of remembrance Plato called anamnesis, the poet's self-induced amnesia is a far more grievous illness than physical blindness for it robs him of his true self by erasing his knowledge of the source of his existence and transforms a 'tear-stained suppliant' into a maudlin fool who vainly fancies himself a tragic hero.

Philosophy's first salutary act, accordingly, is to rid the hero of his mournful chorus. 'Who has permitted these theatrical harlots,' she sternly inquires, pointing at his dishevelled Muses (1, pr i, 30), 'to gain access to this sick man?' And with that she sends them fleeing from the scene, silent and dejected, before the sick man has a chance to defend their virtue.

Her banishment of 'ille chorus increpitus' ('that chided chorus,' 1, pr i, 42) is certainly meant to recall Plato's banishment of licentious poets from his utopian state. But is it meant to convey a strict Platonic warning that the alluring fictions of poetry can offer the human soul no lasting or worthy consolation in the face of life's bitter realities, and that philosophy must be forever at odds with poetry because the latter only serves to stir up the soul's disorderly passions and to mire it in self-pity and despair instead of soothing and uplifting it with knowledge of divine providence? Philosophy herself gives us the answer – an implicit negative – when she exclaims as the chided chorus is vanishing: 'Leave him to be cared for and cured by *my* Muses!' (1, pr i, 40–1). In accordance with Proclus' doctrine that philosophy is not opposed to poetry provided that it draws its inspiration from the irreproachable chorus of celestial Muses and from their supercelestial choragus, Boethius portrays his nurse as a divinely inspired poetess whose lyre will move the prisoner's drooping soul with Pythagorean harmonies towards a newly heightened awareness of the Divine Plan. Her banishment of the terrestrial Muses is a symbolic act of purgation preceding the illuminative stage in the poet's return (which begins in earnest with Philosophy's discourse on fortune in the fourth prose section of book one) and freeing his mind from the chains of subjectivity so that it can soar into the lustral dance in the unitive stage of the return (as prophesied in the concluding verses of her climactic hymn to the Creator). Like the hymns of Proclus, the metres of Lady Philosophy are theurgic incantations and as such should not be read as versified lessons in ethics and cosmology or as faint evocations of celestial harmony. They are meant to rise above the discordant doctrines of the schools and the vaporous fancies of the Sophists, to blend in with the strophes of the universal hymn chanted by the stars in their choral rounds, and to have a powerful therapeutic effect on all who chant or hear them in good faith in the abyss of loud-thundering life. The source of their miraculous healing power is hailed in the exultant eighth metre of book two as 'the Love that rules the heavens' (29–30), and it is the same Love that will move Dante's soul at the summit of Paradise. By stretching his will up to the light of heaven and circling his intellect about the Primal Mind, the awakened poet responds to Philosophy with the erotic ardour of the Diadochi in the Golden Chain whose souls returned to God like torch-flames blazing back to the sky along the old road to the Kallichoron.

Though he played a major role in the transmission of the Procline theory of 'kosmopoiia kata logon' to the cosmological poets of the Latin West, Boethius is a minor figure in our history of the continuity and variations of the image of the cosmic dance compared with an anonymous contemporary of his in the Greek East who wound together into one spiralling movement the 'noera choreia' of the Athenian Academy and the 'koinē chorostasia' of the Byzantine Church. And for this link in our chain we must reserve a separate chapter.

9

Winding Together

The divine intellects are said to move in a circle because they are united to the beginningless and endless illuminations of the Beautiful and Good; and in a straight line whenever they proceed to the providential consideration of those beneath them and directly accomplish all their ends; and in a spiral because even while they are guiding their needy inferiors they remain perpetually in the same state, ceaselessly dancing [perichoreuontes] around the Beautiful and Good, the cause of their self-identity.

The human soul also has a circular motion: the activity of entering into itself and turning away from the outside world and winding together its intellectual powers into a state of unified concentration. Like a uniform revolution this activity steadies the soul by turning it away from the multiplicity of the outside world so that it is drawn together into itself and united with the perfectly unified powers and finally led on to the Beautiful and Good which is beyond all things, uniquely constant in identity, without beginning or end. The soul moves in a spiral manner when it is enlightened with as much divine knowledge as it can receive and is prompted to argue and speak out its thoughts and to engage in other mixed and variable activities which are distinguishable from the unified process of its introspective thinking. And the soul moves in a straight line whenever it does not enter into itself to be moved by its unified intuition (for this as I have said is the circular motion) but goes forth to the things around it and is led up from the temporal world as if from diverse symbols in an elaborate embroidery to simple and unified contemplations.

Thus these three motions, and their counterparts in the world of the senses, and the individuality, stability, and basis of each divine principle existing before them, are caused and bound together and directed towards a final goal by that which is above all rest and motion, namely the Beautiful and Good, through which, from which, in which, to which, and for the sake of which all rest and motion exist.

PSEUDO-DIONYSIUS THE AREOPAGITE, *The Divine Names* IV.8-10

The Unwinding of Permanence

The winds that wailed through the Telesterion at Eleusis when Demeter was driven from her ancient sanctuary by the Goths wailed again for a time through the empty sanctuary of the Parthenon after Athena's statue was removed by the Christians. But unlike Demeter's temple, the Parthenon was not left to the winds. It stood firm on its old high ground while all its pagan demons were exorcised by the Logos and its timeless structure was lit from within by the candles of Ecclesia. The ecclesiastical authorities who had banished Athena to Proclus' dreams showed their respect for the classical wisdom her temple had once enshrined, and at the same time asserted the supremacy of the new wisdom brought to the Athenians by St Paul, by converting it into a church dedicated to Hagia Sophia. (In 662 AD it would be officially recognized as a centre for the worship of the Virgin Mary as Mother of God.) Like the Parthenon, the imposing edifice of Neoplatonic theology erected by Proclus and his predecessors was purged of its faded gods in the late fifth century and preserved as a monument to the unfading glory (and assimilative genius) of the Church. Thus the successors of St Paul secured their victory over Late Antique paganism both outwardly by maintaining control over the political and religious life of the Roman Empire and inwardly by wresting from the intellectual life of the pagan past all that could nourish faith and sustain hope in the Christian future.

No works produced in this period of victorious assimilation were to have a more profound influence on the development of Christian mysticism in the Greek East – and eventually in the Latin West – than the treatises and epistles known collectively as the Corpus Dionysiacum. The author of the Corpus claimed to be Dionysius the Areopagite, a first-century Athenian magistrate whose conversion to Christianity is recorded in Acts 17:34. A 'pseudo' was firmly affixed to this name by nineteenth-century German scholars who exposed the sainted Areopagite as an impostor – perhaps the most successful impostor in Western intellectual history – after discovering numerous linguistic parallels between his works and those of Proclus.[1] The Corpus Dionysiacum has accordingly been dated to around 500 AD. Like his Latin contemporary Boethius, the Areopagite was destined to be widely read in the Middle Ages as a divinely inspired authority on the providential organization of the universe and is now recognized as a critical link between the pagan scholasticism of the Late Antique Diadochi and the Christian scholasticism of the medieval Doctors of Theology. He also deserves consideration for having grafted the Neoplatonic image of the spiralling dance of time so subtly and unobtrusively onto the orthodox vision of Ecclesia's eternal choral rites that the unwinding stasis and motionless dynamics of Proclus' intellectual bacchanal would strike the great Doctors of the thirteenth century – whose Aristotelian intellects were generally not given to Platonic dancing – as neither pagan nor preposterous.

The almost canonical authority that the works of the Areopagite would acquire in the early Middle Ages and retain for well over a thousand years was in no small measure due to the apostolic aura of his pseudonym, the selection of which (as a glance at Acts 17:16–34 soon reveals) could hardly have been arbitrary. While St Paul was waiting in Athens for his disciples Timothy and Silas, he was met in the marketplace by a jeering crowd of Stoics and Epicureans who accused him of babbling about strange gods. Hoping no doubt to daunt the first Christian philosopher by cross-examining him on the tenets of his new religion in an official place of judgment, the xenophobic philosophers escorted him to the Hill of Ares where the Athenian supreme court (known from its location as the Areopagus) was accustomed to conduct its hearings. Enacted in this symbolic arena was the archetypal scene of confrontation between the old paideia and the new, a scene precipitated by a simple confusion over terms.

When the Athenians first heard Paul discoursing in the marketplace on the glorious 'anastasis' (resurrection) of Jesus, many of them mistakenly construed this term as a divine name like 'Zeus' or 'Logos' and accordingly charged the apostle with vapid obscurantism. Paul countered this charge – and at the same time criticized the general tendency in Greek philosophy to reduce God to an impersonal and unfeeling First Principle – by reminding his opponents that there was a prominent altar in their city bearing an inscription 'To the Unknown God.' Was it not ironic that the wisdom-loving Athenians were still worshipping God in ignorance? Were their subtlest philosophers really any closer to understanding the true nature of God than the intellectually unsophisticated pagans who believed that He dwelt in the temples made by human hands? Though Paul joyfully proclaimed that he was bringing the Athenians a God they could love through the humanity of the Son, a God they could know in a positive sense 'if haply they might feel after him, and find him' (Acts 17:27), the philosophers were predictably unresponsive to the apostle's impassioned rhetoric: they preferred either to ignore his penetrating criticism of their intellectual limitations or to suspend judgment on the esoteric question of the Resurrection.

Among the few Athenians won over to Christ by the sermon on the Areopagus were Dionysius the Areopagite and a woman named Damaris, neither of whom seems to have belonged to the group of Stoics and Epicureans who originally sparked the debate. From the example of Paul's rather unsuccessful incursion among the worshippers of the Unknown God the early proselytizers learned that they had few souls to gain by disputing with pagan philosophers in unphilosophical terms or by rejecting the negative approach to divine knowledge on the naïve grounds that God was not far from anyone who cared to look for him in the pages of the Gospels. The conversion of Athenian (or Athenian-minded) pagans would require a strategy of subtle infiltration rather than direct confrontation. It would have to be an inside operation, and the theologian to accomplish it would have to know the technical language of Greek philosophy so thoroughly that when he faced his pagan opponents once more in the Areopagus they should know precisely what words he venerated as divine names and he should win them over to the known and knowable God by the logic of their own negative theology.

Perhaps the author of the Corpus Dionysiacum adopted the name of the Areopagite to suggest that he was the insider who would bring Paul's mission to the Athenians to its assuredly triumphant conclusion and that his treatises were an authentic revelation of what Paul had seen in his ascent to the third heaven. The strategic name may also have carried with it the suggestion that a revival of the first Christian philosopher's proselytizing spirit was urgently needed in the Athens of Proclus and his disciples, an intellectual milieu where theurgy was challenging the Christian sacraments as a means of inducing angelic concord in the demonic hubbub below the moon. If the Stoics and Epicureans of Paul's day had tolerated the dedication of an altar to the Unknown God, the Neoplatonists of the fifth and sixth centuries were insisting with the enthusiasm of imperilled dogmatists that God was not only unknown to man but also utterly unknowable since even the daimones, angels, and intellectual gods encircling the eternal Kallichoron could not penetrate the mysteries of perfect unity.

Proclus, always sensitive to the psychological strain of trying to worship an isolated abstraction clouded in paradox, attempted in the following passage to draw the One back into some kind of cognitive association with the highest participants in the chorus of the Many:

Is it possible that the Father's Goodness is not known to the daimones who dance in chorus around it [peri auto choreuontes], or to the demiurgic angels who escort the Father in his creative activity, or to the gods who receive the creative powers from the unique First Cause? No doubt, but the gods know him through being at one with him, the angels through their intellectual faculty, and the daimones in a pure and everlasting manner, through their kinship with those preceding them.

(*In Timaeum* 1 369)

Though Proclus could distinguish the various modes of superhuman cognition with relative ease, he was rather hard pressed to explain how man, so low on the Golden Chain, could be expected to participate in the mystic round of the spirits when his kinship with the celestial daimones was far from obvious, his intellectual faculty far from angelic, and his impermanent nature far from being at one with the eternal First Cause. Theurgic initiation seemed to have resolved this problem for him, but it was hardly a satisfying or practical solution for everyone who yearned for insight into the occult powers that turned the heliotrope towards Helios and the human soul towards the Good and the Beautiful. The wizards of the One had to spend long years mastering the abstruse sciences on Iamblichus' Pythagorean curriculum, and even for those who mounted with ease to the heights of Platonic wisdom the winding path from there to theurgic perfection was so steep and hazardous that one false step in conjuring up this demiurgic angel or that intellectual god – the omission of a prescribed epithet in an invocation, say, or the performance of a ritual under inauspicious stars – could spell disaster for all they hoped to benefit and send their hapless souls hurtling down into the dismal cave where Attis, driven from the celestial dance, had embraced the Nymph of Matter.

The Church Fathers were swift to condemn theurgy as a pseudo-philosophical offshoot of black magic and to dismiss as a Satanic delusion the supernatural clarity of vision claimed by its adepts. (St Augustine, for example, flatly declared that theurgic clairvoyance was 'a vision of things that do not truly exist.'[2]) How else but as agents of Satan could these crazed Hellenes who traced their mumbo-jumbo back to the incantations of the ancient Egyptian priests persist in opposing the order of the true Church, the Church that now not only controlled the Empire but *was* the Empire? Who in his right mind could suppose that these hallucinating sorcerers had actually seen the ethereal ranks of the angels ringing the still centre of life, had actually danced in the bright ring itself, when all they could possibly have glimpsed in their odious ceremonies was a chorus of devils in angelic disguise mocking the concordant order of Heaven? For all their vaunted visionary powers the theurgists could see no further into Paradise than the narrow-minded Stoics and Epicureans who had jeered at Paul in the Areopagus.

The author of the Corpus Dionysiacum may have been an Athenian convert to Christianity like his New Testament namesake and perhaps even an associate of members of the Athenian Academy. But he did not have to be either of these to see the glaring weakness of Athenian Neoplatonism as a religion: its desperate encouragement of a desire for divine union which could not be satisfied in this life or the next, through action or contemplation, within or beyond the Cave of the Nymph. If religions (though they may spring like philosophies from fear or love or wonder) can survive only on hope, then the melancholy Athena of Proclus' dreams had more cause for despair than the loss of her temple. The more links her worshippers added to the Golden Chain the fewer connections the unknowable One seemed to have with the procession of the Many, and the more divinely illumined or illuminating spirits they introduced into the mystic dance the less accessible to human understanding their vision of universal order became. By the early sixth century the links in the Golden Chain were losing their distinctness, and the circles in the Great Dance (once the clearest and most tangible image of divine unity in Greek philosophy) were vanishing into a fog of abstractions. Apollonian procession had become virtually indistinguishable from Dionysian reversion; the dynamic cycles of Time had melted into the motionless schema of Eternity; and the participants in Being and Becoming, like the diffused rays of a corona gleaming around the eclipsed sun, were coalescing into a hazy 'radiance of form' around the stillness of the One.

So Damascius, the Head of the Athenian Academy at the time of its dispersion (after 529), conceived the dance – one can hardly say 'imagined it' since as an image it had lost almost all its visual definition – in the following opaque passage from his treatise on time, fragments of which were preserved for the purpose of refutation by his friend Simplicius:

Just as Eternity is the cause of permanence in that type of Being which, though unified in itself, undergoes an intelligible division into parts that are separate from its essential unity, so Time is the cause of the dancing [tou choreuein] of the radiance of form around the intelligible One. This radiance passes thence downwards into the world of the senses and keeps the continuity of the dance [tēs choreias] in order.

(apud Simplicium, *In Physicorum libros* 775, 12–16)

In this purely theoretical context the noun 'choreia,' though used in reference to the world of the senses, has been blanched of all sensory meaning by the dry heat of metaphysical speculation. So too has the verb 'choreuein,' which functions here as a colourless technical term for that vague cosmogonic process by which the 'intelligible' One (as distinct from the 'intellectual' One below it uniting the chorus of the supracosmic Helios and his offspring) manages to generate the first principles of individual unity, the Henads, without itself suffering any change in its essentially indivisible nature, and also for the perplexing and primarily formal relation subsequently existing between the supreme cause of unity and its multiple effects in the united spheres of Chronos and Aion.

In a brave attempt to clarify what Damascius had written about the dance of time, Simplicius only succeeded in losing sight of the image in a further labyrinth of subtle definitions and esoteric hypotheses:

Perhaps permanence does not wholly belong to time, just as Being does not correspond to Becoming. Rather, just as Becoming is a kind of spiralling or unwinding out of Being, so the choral dance around Being [hē peri to on choreia] is an unwinding of the permanence that is in Being. But these words of Damascius do not trouble me so much as those he would often say to me – without persuading me – while he was still alive: namely that all time exists simultaneously in a hypostatic level of reality.

(In Physicorum libros 775, 28–34)

Behind the commentator's apparently dispassionate academic interest in Damascius' elaborations of the bizarre late Neoplatonic theory that each discrete 'now' in the unwinding progress of the temporal dance is an infinitesimally small section of the ring of Being surrounding the One lurks a religious horror of the spectre of Parmenidean non-being, a fear that since past and future seem unreal and the present disappears before its reality can be grasped the World of Becoming might be drifting into a void of unreality where all that a Greek rationalist might consider essential to true being – permanence, unity, limit, form, actuality – would be annihilated. If the present were to serve as an intersection point between Being and Becoming through which the permanent design of the dance conceived by the Divine Mind could be linked to the sequence of movements and pauses performed by the chorus of the Many, no hiatus would disrupt the flow of existence and virtue and knowledge down the Golden Chain of illuminators and illuminati and man would be assured a lifeline to the Unknown God.

Intrigued though he was by the Iamblichan concept of the permanent form of the Now, Simplicius could not be persuaded by Damascius to accept Proclus' theological argument that all the nows generated by the choral round of the stars must spring from, and therefore exist simultaneously in, the perpetual supracosmic presence of the hypostatic god Chronos. In the dancing intellect of Chronos the theurgists claimed to have seen the divine intermediary linking the dances of the stars to the dance of pure form, the god whose special function was to preserve the continuity of the Golden Chain; moreover, as Proclus had demonstrated before Damascius, the existence of a demiurgic spiral-shaped god of time could be logically deduced from Aristotle's doctrines of celestial motion and ultimate causality as well as from Plato's mystical definition of time. Yet Simplicius remained skeptical of the theurgic vision of the divine Helix: he could follow the Aristotelian lines of thought leading up to Proclus' theological conclusion, but when the moment came for him to summon up the deity before his own eyes, his eyes (and his visual imagination) failed him. He was neither a wizard nor a poet. His description of the choral dance around Being as an 'unwinding' (anelixis) of the permanence that originates in the One and sustains the contemplative introversion of the hypostatic gods, an activity which ultimately results in the spiralling of temporal cycles out from the beginningless and endless circle of Nous, is no more than a scholastic definition. The dance itself is not seen or felt or imagined by Simplicius as a living reality. In the fantastic imagery of the theurgic mysteries his dry eyes could discern much that would attract a soul seeking beauty and coherence and security in the illusory flux of life, but little that would make such a poetic vision of the universe philosophically defensible or radiantly true.[3]

If Pseudo-Dionysius had not revised it for Christian eyes by identifying the cosmogonic movements of the Neoplatonic intellectual gods with the apocalyptic processions and contemplative ceremonies of the angels in the Kingdom of Heaven, the theurgic vision of permanence unwinding in a choral dance around God would doubtless have been rejected as a poetic fancy or denounced as a pagan falsehood by the intellectual leaders of the Church. But they were to accept it in the early Middle Ages as a divine revelation and to defend it in the late Middle Ages as a philosophically valid account of supersensible reality. Neither Augustine (when he was reigning over the cloisters) nor Aristotle (when he was reigning over the schools) could override the theological authority of the Areopagite on any point pertaining to angelic contemplations.

In the mid-thirteenth century Thomas Aquinas will open his long commentary on the Areopagite's longest treatise *The Divine Names* with the deferential remark that in spite of his highly elaborate style and outmoded Platonic vocabulary Dionysius 'seems to offer a complete explanation of those things which exist beyond Man.'[4] Dante will make the same observation as an eyewitness in the Heaven of the Fixed Stars (*Paradiso* XXVIII 137–9), pausing before his climactic ascent into the Empyrean to confirm the truth of all that Dionysius had written about the triadic organization and ceaseless choral dancing of the angels. No one, the poet will assert, should be amazed that Dionysius was able to reveal 'tanto secreto ver' – 'so much secret truth' – about the concentric rings of the angelic chorus, for St Paul himself, after his soul had been 'caught up into Paradise' and granted 'visions and revelations of the Lord' (2 Corinthians 12:1–4), must have confided in his Athenian convert all that he had glimpsed on high during his ecstatic trance. The widespread medieval belief that Paul's heavenly visions were accurately recorded and clearly expounded in the writings of the Areopagite was no doubt largely responsible for the exegetical attention lavished on the Corpus Dionysiacum in the era of the great Scholastics. Since only a tiny fraction of Proclus' enormous philosophical oeuvre would reach the schools of Europe in Latin translation before the fifteenth century, Aquinas and Dante can be excused for failing to detect the Areopagite's translation of Neoplatonic commonplaces into Pauline revelations and for accepting the Church's centuries-old view that the pseudo-less Dionysius was just what he professed to be: an ardent disciple and confidant of the first Christian mystic to challenge the authority of the old paideia.

Chorus without Cosmos

The tense bacchic pose struck by the Neoplatonic 'orchēstēs' at the climax of his contemplative dance – head flung back in ecstatic adoration of the stars, eyes rolled inward to focus the scattered rays of Attis, soul stretched out like a heliotrope towards the effulgence of the Beautiful, will convulsed by a desire for union with the Good, intellect strained between the push of cosmogonic procession and the pull of epiphanic return – is serenely but decisively relaxed in the dance of hierarchical communion envisioned by the Areopagite. The angelic and human participants in his theocentric chorus have abandoned the tired Neoplatonic attitudes of learned ignorance, agonized desire, and intellectual Corybantism. They all receive as much divine illumination as their minds can endure without strain; they all enjoy union with the Beautiful and Good through the inexhaustible grace of the Logos; and they all perform their individual roles in the dance as purveyors and recipients of divine knowledge without losing sight of their common unitive centre or sympathy for their inferiors in the hierarchy. Since they perceive God not as an imponderable Eminence totally isolated from the fragmented world of the self and approachable only through a complete transcendence of individual consciousness but rather as 'the cause of their self-identity' (*Divine Names* iv.8), the hierarchical dancers come to know who they truly are and how they should act as individuals by contemplating the unique essence of the triune godhead revealed to them through the communal life of Ecclesia.

The steadiness of their 'simple and unified contemplations' (iv.9) presents a sharp contrast to the vacillations in the contemplative experience of the astral intellects in Proclus' cosmic bacchanal. Since the Procline stars could see the universal forms in the Divine Mind only by losing consciousness of themselves as distinct members of the Great Chorus, they inevitably forfeited their ecstatic clarity of vision as soon as they fell back from the presence of the One to an awareness of their divided natures. 'When they are away from themselves they understand the Divine Mind,' said Proclus of the dancing stars (*In Timaeum* iii 150), 'and when they are away from the Divine Mind they understand themselves.' In the hierarchical Christian universe, however, where the stars have so declined in mystical prominence that they are not even mentioned in the Areopagite's discussion of the configurations and goals of the contemplative dance, the intellects above and below the Great Dividing-Line are always before the Divine Mind because they never leave their assigned places in the chorus. Their individual natures are defined and differentiated only in terms of their relative positions in the hierarchy, which Pseudo-Dionysius defined as 'a sacred order, and knowledge, and activity assimilated as far as possible to the Divine Form and raised up to the imitation of God in proportion to the divine illuminations granted to it.'[5]

Since the Pseudo-Dionysian hierarchy did not include the dancing intellects of stars, planetary daimones, apotheosized heroes, Olympian gods, or
theurgic hypostases such as Chronos, it was a far simpler and narrower
order of beings than the ponderous Golden Chain of the Diadochi; yet in
comparison with what the term 'hierarchy' usually means today, namely a
graded series of objects or categories or a fixed system of ranks within an
earthly power-structure, the 'sacred order' originally denoted by the Greek
roots 'hieros' and 'archē' signified a truly vast chain of heavenly and earthly
beings and was in effect an ontological system, the function of which, as
Pseudo-Dionysius conceived it, was to unite the highest ranks of the angels
with the humblest congregations of the faithful through a shared knowledge
of divinity. Though all who participated in the hierarchy fixed their thoughts
on God and achieved a measure of intellectual repose in the knowledge of
his immutable essence, hierarchical order was not static: it was essentially
an activity, a perpetual service of divine praise and thanksgiving prompted
by the charitable intercession of superior beings in the lives of their inferiors.
Hence the sharing of hierarchical knowledge entailed a series of historical
and sacramental interactions between the angels and man intended to purge
the human soul of sin, illuminate it with prophetic revelations, and lead it
into union with the Beautiful and Good.

The dynamic design of the hierarchy could thus be conceived as a choreia
encompassing the orderly physical movements of ecclesiastical ritual and the
purely contemplative movements of introversion and assimilation of the self
to God – a ceremony of purgation, illumination, and union reminiscent of
the sacred dance witnessed long ago by Philo in the banquet hall of the
Therapeutae. (That Philo's treatise on the Jewish contemplatives was probably known to the Areopagite is indicated by his use of the name 'Therapeutae' to designate the sub-clerical rank in the hierarchy to which he may
well have belonged: the monks.)[6] Like its Philonic prototype, the hierarchical
choreia was an imitative movement gradually leading to ecstatic communion
with God, though even as the setting for the mystic dance had changed from
an isolated hall in a tiny community outside worldly Alexandria to a thousand basilicas in a Christian empire guarded by angels from the Heavenly
Jerusalem so too had its theological significance altered and expanded. It
was no longer simply a victory celebration for the ascetic upholders of the
Old Law: the interlacing circles, lines, and spirals in the hierarchy symbolized the triumphant unification of the whole world under the intellectual
guidance of the teachers of the New Song. Pseudo-Dionysius also used the
term 'hierarchy' to designate each of the two major groups of dancers in his
universe. The angels, whose intellects did not search for God in the elaborate
symbolism of the visible world, circled together in an invisible series of
choruses known as the Celestial Hierarchy. Paralleling their sacred order in

the world below were the bishops, priests, deacons, contemplatives, and general laity whose assembled ranks constituted the Ecclesiastical Hierarchy. By thus restricting his vision of order to these two essential chains of initiators and initiates (see figure 19) the Areopagite vastly reduced the complexity of the late Neoplatonic world-chorus and correspondingly increased the visionary clarity of its symmetrical movements and configurations.[7]

The dynamic design of the heavens which Proclus had contemplated at great length in an effort to demonstrate that choral order (despite all appearances to the contrary) did indeed reign among the wandering stars simply fades from view in the world-picture of the Areopagite. The celestial spectacle so long applauded by Platonic cosmologists and Christian theologians as the surest visible sign of God's creative rationality is certainly not forgotten in the Corpus Dionysiacum, but it is presented either as an obvious sign which can be left behind when the educated spectator enters into the intellectual dance of the hierarchy or as an enigmatic symbol which cannot distract a Pauline Christian who has taken to heart the Apostle's memorable dictum 'For now we see through a glass, darkly' (1 Corinthians 13:12). The Ecclesiastical Hierarchy did not need the stars or the sun or any other part of the visible cosmos to act as a link between the human chorus and the eternal intellects dancing closest to God, for its members derived their vision of universal order from the Scriptures and from the revelations conveyed to them by the angels. Hence the language of light and vision in the Corpus Dionysiacum refers almost exclusively to revealed truth and mystical insight, and the imagery of choral dancing and geometrical figures is almost always symbolic of intellectual activities and supersensible realities.

Though he occasionally paid lip-service to the ancient Platonic doctrine that the internal motions of the human soul had their counterparts in the world of the senses (as in *Divine Names* IV.9), the Areopagite was not compelled like Proclus to deduce his principles of theological order from the visible motions of the stars or to interpret the celestial spectacle as an everlasting reflection of the invisible chorus encircling God. By virtually eliminating the planetary and stellar gods from the dance of divine life in accordance with orthodox Christian teachings concerning the inanimate nature of the heavenly bodies, Pseudo-Dionysius could afford to ignore the tangle of problems involved in reconciling the consistently rational motions of the fixed stars with the confused meanderings of the planets; and by assuming that a direct channel of communication existed between the chorus of bishops at the top of the Ecclesiastical Hierarchy and the angelic messengers who had appeared on earth at key moments in sacred history and were evidently members of the lowest ranks of the Celestial Hierarchy, he could effectively join his two choral chains into a single sacred order and so prevent discontinuities in the series of dancing intellects inspired by the Beautiful and

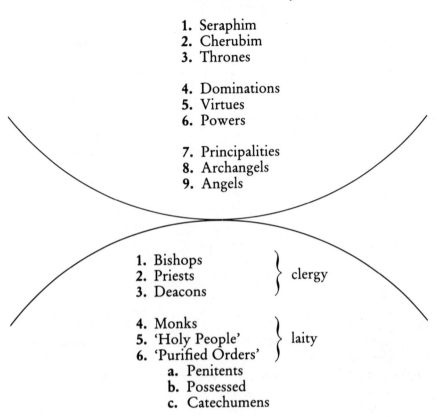

The Celestial Hierarchy

1. Seraphim
2. Cherubim
3. Thrones

4. Dominations
5. Virtues
6. Powers

7. Principalities
8. Archangels
9. Angels

1. Bishops
2. Priests   } clergy
3. Deacons

4. Monks
5. 'Holy People'   } laity
6. 'Purified Orders'
   a. Penitents
   b. Possessed
   c. Catechumens

The Ecclesiastical Hierarchy

Figure 19

The hierarchical choreia began with the introspective circular movement of the angelic intellects around God described in *Divine Names* IV. 8. The three highest angelic choruses, Seraphim, Cherubim, and Thrones, passed their knowledge on to six lower ranks in the Celestial Hierarchy, the last of which, the Angels, illuminated the chorus of bishops at the top of the Ecclesiastical Hierarchy. The bishops in turn taught their priests and deacons (and the clergy their congregations) to participate in the angelic round of theocentric meditations. On the symmetry of the two hierarchies, see note 7.

Good. Had all the stars in his heavens careened from their proper spheres or vanished from the cosmic theatre in a puff of smoke (as they were destined to do when the angels of the Doom blew their hideous trumpets) the two hierarchies would have remained intact – a chorus without a cosmos – free forever to circle about the transcendent source of their motion and stability.

All such simplifications of the late Neoplatonic world-view served to increase the clarity of the Areopagite's mystical symbolism, to make even his philosophical images of intellectual procession and return assume the stark outlines of the prophetic visions recorded in the Old Testament and the Apocalypse of St John. The circular, linear, and helicoidal design of the hierarchical dance may not be as preternaturally vivid or phantasmagorical as the pattern of concentric wheels, flaming vortices, and lightning-quick processions of celestial creatures described in Ezekiel 1:4–16, but it certainly *seems* so next to Damascius' paradoxically formless vision of the dance of pure form and Simplicius' vague notion of time as the unwinding of permanence in a timeless dance around Being. Rather than seeking to justify the triadic schema of hierarchical movements in philosophical terms (as Proclus tried to rationalize the occult spiral of Chronos by fitting it into an abstruse metaphysical argument relating eternal causes to temporal effects), the Areopagite simply presents his vision of the dance as a prophetic glimpse into the sacred order of Heaven and fuses the symbolism of biblical revelation with the imagery of Neoplatonic contemplation in order to draw what St Paul had called 'the invisible things' of God (Romans 1:20) out of the hazy realm of philosophical theory into the intense light of religious certitude.

The Hierarchical Spectator

Pseudo-Dionysius distinguished three ways by which the more contemplative members of the Ecclesiastical Hierarchy could acquire a clear and penetrating (that is, an angelic) insight into the invisible things of God: first, by affirming the uniqueness and constant identity of Father, Son, and Holy Spirit as revealed by divine names and symbols in the Bible; second, by negating any identification of the Creator with his creatures; and third, by combining the first two methods in a verbal or ritual expression of contemplative insight – for example, the composition of a theological treatise or the performance of a sacramental rite – which would affirm the extent of man's positive knowledge of God and at the same time proclaim in negative terms God's transcendent relation to the cosmos and to all who seek knowledge of Him through participation in hierarchical order. These three approaches to divine knowledge correspond in some measure to the three motions of the human soul distinguished in *Divine Names* IV.9. Plato's doctrine that the celestial gods always thought the same thoughts about the same things as they circled in their eternal dance established a long-lasting association between circular motion and introspective meditation which came to the fore in Neoplatonic discussions of contemplative union with the cosmic and supracosmic gods; from the Neoplatonists directly, or from the Cappadocian Fathers who associated circular motion with the intellectual activity of the angels, the Areopagite inherited his definition of the first (in the sense of 'primal' or 'essential') movement of the human soul as a dynamic concentration of its intellectual powers on a fixed body of revealed truths and theological doctrines which united it with the superhuman intellects dancing around the Beautiful and Good.

His association of the soul's linear movement with visual perception and with contemplations of the visible world in relation to its invisible Creator may also be traced back to Plato. An unobstructed ray of ocular fire once it had been emitted from the Platonic eye always travelled in a straight line to meet the light streaming off or reflected from the object of vision, and most visible objects below the moon tended to move in linear patterns up and down, to and fro, back and forth, rather than in circular patterns like the stars. According to Timaeus (39a–b) the natural tendency of the planets was to move in straight lines, but when their linear progressions and retro-gradations were caught up in the diurnal revolution of the heavens the resulting type of motion was neither linear nor circular but a mixture of both: that is, helicoidal. This old theory of planetary motion no doubt lay behind the Areopagite's curious association of spiral motion with 'mixed and variable activities' of the human soul such as the expression of mystical insights in theological language and ecclesiastical ritual. While one may safely conclude from studying the evolution of the Neoplatonic schema of the three motions from its prototypes in Plato and Aristotle (see chart 1) that the Areopagite must have adapted his version of the triad from some Late Antique philosophical source, the conspicuous differences between his ver-sion and its pagan analogues have made the identification of his immediate source a matter of conjecture and dispute.[8] Proclus as usual seems to be the most likely candidate, but he would certainly have been shocked by the Areopagite's extension of the schema from human and angelic contempla-tions to the 'motions' of God.

Taken as a whole, the mixed and variable argument of the Corpus Dio-nysiacum clearly illustrates the third or combined method of attaining divine knowledge, the strategy of the Areopagite being at times to affirm all that a contemplative soul might learn of God through the Scriptures and at other times to contend that man cannot gain a clear understanding of God except through a deliberate loss of physical and intellectual vision. A distinctly affirmative bias, however, is displayed in two of his treatises: *The Divine Names*, a sustained meditation on the proper names, descriptive epithets,

Chart 1: The Evolution of the Triadic Schema
of Cosmic and Contemplative Motions

Circular Motion	Linear Motion	Helicoidal Motion
PLATO		
1 *Timaeus* 34a: intellectual motion of World-Soul reflected in rotation of cosmic body	1 *Timaeus* 40b–c: planetary progressions and retrogradations within the band of the zodiac. (All bodies beneath the stars are subject to linear movements up and down, back and forth, to and fro.)	1 *Timaeus* 39a–b: planetary motion resulting from the combination of the general revolution of the cosmos and the linear motions of the planets
2 *Timaeus* 40a–b: intellectual motion of astral souls reflected in the revolution of the stars		
ARISTOTLE		
1 *Physics* 8.8.261b 28: the first type of physical locomotion defined as rotary, uniform, and continuous	1 *Physics* 8.8.261b 28: the second type of physical locomotion defined as linear, variable, and finite	1 *Physics* 8.8.261b 28: the third type of physical locomotion defined as a combination of rotary and linear, but not explicitly identified as spiral movement
2 *De caelo* 2.3.286a 10–15: the eternal movement of the cosmic body		
PLOTINUS		
1 *Ennead* 4.4.16: the One as the spiritual centre of life; Nous as a fixed circle around it; Psyche as a moving circle concentric with Nous	1 *Ennead* 2.2.1: bodily motion defined as linear, becoming circular only in combination with psychological motion	1 not mentioned
2 *Ennead* 2.2.1: the cosmos moves in a circle in imitation of Nous and Psyche		

Circular Motion	Linear Motion	Helicoidal Motion

PROCLUS

Circular Motion	Linear Motion	Helicoidal Motion
1 *In Timaeum* III 146: physical revolution of the stars	1 *In Timaeum* III 146: physical progressions and retrogradations of the planets	1 *In Timaeum* III 21, 40, and 80: combination of circular and linear motions
2 *In Timaeum* III 149: intellectual revolutions of the stars around the Divine Mind; their permanent spiritual repose in union with the One	2 *In Timaeum* III 149–50: the procession of the Many from the One and the return of the Many to the One	2 *In Timaeum* III 20: eternal archetype of temporal motions identified as the spiral-shaped god Chronos
3 *Platonic Theology* I.1: the intellectual motion of Platonists around the sacred doctrines of Plato	3 *Platonic Theology* I.1: the line of Platonic succession in the choral dance of intellectual history	3 *In Timaeum* III 78–80: affirmation of Plato's theory of the helicoidal motions of the planets

HERMIAS (see n 8)

Circular Motion	Linear Motion	Helicoidal Motion
1 *In Phaedrum* 227b: circular motion symbolic of self-contained contemplation and concentration of thoughts on invisible things	1 *In Phaedrum* 227b: linear motion symbolic of the contemplation of external things, resulting in 'doxa' (opinion)	1 *In Phaedrum* 227b: spiral motion associated with 'dianoia,' the process of contemplating eternal truths

PSEUDO-DIONYSIUS

Circular Motion	Linear Motion	Helicoidal Motion
1 *Divine Names* IV.8–10: angelic and human union with God and contemplation of his goodness and beauty; corresponding circular motion in the visible cosmos	1 *Divine Names* IV.8–10: the providential procession of the angels to their human inferiors; human understanding of the external world; corresponding linear motions in the visible cosmos	1 *Divine Names* IV.8–10: the angelic power to combine introspection with providential procession; the human power to communicate divine understanding in discursive argument and ecclesiastical ritual; corresponding helicoidal motions in the visible cosmos
2 *Divine Names* IX.9: God's eternal sameness, completeness of identity, and power to encompass all his creatures	2 *Divine Names* IX.9: outward flow of God's creative energies and the procession of all things from a common source	2 *Divine Names* IX.9: God's power to create order without suffering any change in identity

and symbolic images of God sanctioned by biblical or patristic usage; and *The Celestial Hierarchy*, a systematic discussion of the names, attributes, and functions of the nine choruses of angels. In the remaining two treatises his approach is just as distinctly negative. His interlocking theories of what the soul experiences during negative contemplation and how it can achieve a totally non-symbolic vision of God are summarized in his briefest and probably most influential work, *The Mystical Theology*. (A fourteenth-century English translation of this treatise has come down to us under the quaintly literal and pleasantly ambiguous title *Hid Divinity*. Whoever translated it probably also wrote *The Cloud of Unknowing*, a famous Middle English manual for contemplatives which derives its eerie title and much of its argument from the Areopagite by way of Latin glosses on the Corpus Dionysiacum.)⁹ In the companion piece to his survey of the angelic orders, a treatise on church offices entitled *The Ecclesiastical Hierarchy*, Pseudo-Dionysius practised what he preached in *The Mystical Theology* by unveiling the spiritual realities behind the symbolic vestments, movements, vessels, and substances involved in the celebration of the sacraments. Instead of bemoaning man's remoteness from the Beautiful and Good, he devised a method of symbolic meditation which employed and controlled the visual imagination so that the spectators of Ecclesia's choral rites might draw near to the divinity hid in the sanctuary of Paradise and confirm Paul's optimistic dictum in Romans 1:20, a fitting epigraph for the Corpus Dionysiacum as a whole: 'For the invisible things of Him are clearly seen, being understood from the things that are made, even his eternal power and Godhead.'

A soul wishing to take the affirmative route to divine knowledge had first to retreat from the distractions of the visible world into the solitude of introspection where it could collect its thoughts, steady its powers of concentration, and begin to meditate upon the sublime attributes of God revealed in the Scriptures. Knowing for instance that David had voiced a desire 'to behold the beauty of the Lord' (Psalms 17:4) and that Christ had declared that 'there is none good but one, that is, God' (Matthew 19:17), the inward-turning soul could assume that beauty and goodness were essential aspects of the divine nature. Perhaps on the authority of such verses as these the Areopagite admitted the Neoplatonic epithet 'the Beautiful and Good' to his list of divine names. Plotinus and Porphyry and Proclus had argued in their turn that God must be both the primary formal cause of all that was beautiful in the cosmic dance and the unique final cause towards which every dancer inclined in his search for unity and stability, and inasmuch as their arguments confirmed the Christian doctrine that all beauty and goodness in creation originated in the Creator their names for God were quite acceptable to the Areopagite. (Their own names, of course, were kept out of the Corpus Dionysiacum in order to keep up first-century appearances.) Turning in the usual direction along the affirmative route, that is, from the general to the particular, the soul would next consider how God's obscure metaphysical names were clarified by metaphorical titles such as 'Father' or 'Ancient of Days' and by symbolic images such as the sun or the burning bush or the pillar of fire, which would open the inward eye to the light of the Divine Presence reflected in every facet of creation. Nature would thus present itself to the student of the divine names not as a glass to be looked through darkly but as a great jewelled book to be read in the positive light of faith, a second Holy Writ revealing the character of its eternal Author in a multitude of symbolic images.

Pseudo-Dionysius was by no means the first theologian in Late Antiquity to trace the steps of the soul along the 'via affirmativa' (as his first approach to divine knowledge would be called by the medieval schoolmen). The 'way' of contemplative introversion and intense concentration on the revealed identity of God had been so clearly defined for him by the pagan Neoplatonists that he had only to substitute the Bible for their collection of oracular books and to purge the egregiously pagan epithets from their list of divine names in order to convert their intellectual dance into an essential hierarchical activity. Plotinus had shown him the way in the ecstatic dance of initiates in the temple of Psyche. With eyes closed to the cosmic pantomime and intellects focused on the perfect beauty, goodness, and rationality issuing from the mystic wellspring, the Plotinian dancers had discovered through introspection the chorus of their unfallen selves united around the One. From this lofty vantage-point, secure in the knowledge of their participation in the Circle of Nous, they had been able to bear the sight of the cosmic dancer and even to applaud his erotic posturings as a symbolic representation of the eternal love binding them to their ineffable object of contemplation.

Proclus, too, had conceived the way of affirmation as a circular dance of ecstatic contemplatives around the theological truths concealed in the old philosophy. All that remained of his favourite image of divine union – the introverted round-dance of the mysteries – once his awesome powers of abstraction had disburdened it of the corruptible bodies, the kinetic sensations, the temporal thoughts and memories, and even the individual souls of the dancers, was the white heat of epistrophic enthusiasm: the ardent desire of the Many to know the One so intimately and so lovingly that their communal act of knowing would somehow annihilate the age-old distinction between chorus (the knowers) and choragus (the purveyor and final object of knowledge). The impossibility of ever satisfying this desire did not dampen the ardour of the Diadochus and his disciples. 'May we join ourselves to the One itself,' he had taught them to pray,

and may we awaken the One within us by warming our souls through this union! May we moor ourselves, so to speak, by standing beyond all that is intelligible within us and by setting aside all our other activity! May our purpose be to keep company only with the One, and by leaving behind all the thoughts of our soul, which revolves around secondary things, may we dance in chorus [perichoreusōmen] around the One!

(*In Parmeniden* VI col 1072)

The prayer of the Diadochus would echo through the cosmic basilica of the Areopagite, but it would be changed from a pedagogical exhortation which only a few learned ears would catch (muffled as it was by the dense exegetical sediment heaped on the Parmenidean hypotheses by generations of Neo-platonic scholars) into a liturgical supplication which all the choristers in the Celestial Hierarchy would stoop to hear, and hearing, raise with their own voices, until God himself, who was rather more receptive to human prayers than the Procline One, would turn their petition for divine union into a hymn of thanksgiving for union achieved, union everlastingly sustained.

As a symbolic image of participation in divine unity, the mystery dance had been associated by Proclus with an intellectual activity of major importance in his affirmative theology: the contemplation of divine names. In his etymological explication of the name Chronos, for instance, he had ingeniously shown that a demiurgic god presided over the cyclical dances of time; and in his fragmentary commentary on the classical source for all speculations concerning the names of the gods, Plato's *Cratylus*, he had turned a discussion of two allegorical names of Athena – Nike (Victory) and Hygieia (Health) – into a revelation of the leading role his divine patroness played in uniting the dances of time and eternity:

And if the universe may be said to be eternal, Athena is the purveyor and director [chorēgos] of its permanent order; and if, as they say, Chronos dances [choreuein] for the benefit of the universe, Athena through her unique rationality and uniform order is the protectress of his leadership of the chorus [chorēgias]. She oversees all the creative work of the Father, and holds it together, and turns it towards him, and conquers all the indefiniteness of matter; on this account she is addressed as Nike and Hygieia, for she employs her intellect to control necessity and the nature of matter, and always takes care to keep the cosmos in a perfected state, undecaying and healthy. Appropriately, therefore, the role of the goddess is to lead up and divide and join the cosmos together through the intellectual dance [dia tēs noeras choreias] with orders more divine. ...

(*In Cratylum* CLXXXV)

Like Athena and Chronos and the other intellectual gods in the Procline pantheon, the dancing intellects in the Celestial Hierarchy oversee all the creative work of the Father, turn the souls of their inferiors towards the source of all wisdom, and lead them up to God through a circling course of meditations on divine beauty and virtue.

In devising his triadic schema of hierarchical motions Pseudo-Dionysius seems to have fused the Plotinian vision of unfallen intellects transfixed in a circle around the mystic wellspring (choreia entheos) with the Procline vision of inferior orders of intellects seeking union 'with orders more divine' (noera choreia); hence, while stillness and motion were usually conceived by the Neoplatonists as opposite or mutually exclusive states in the dance of contemplation, they occur simultaneously in the choral order contemplated by the Areopagite. Human souls would naturally be more aware of the upward mobility of the hierarchical chorus than of its eternal stasis, but through the contemplative life of Ecclesia they would gradually increase their understanding and deepen their experience of angelic repose. Angelic intellects on the other hand would see more stillness than motion in the sacred order. Even while moving to aid the aspiring minds in the Ecclesiastical Hierarchy they would retain their consciousness of divine permanence, and so remain, as Pseudo-Dionysius put it in *Divine Names* IV.8, 'perpetually in the same state, ceaselessly dancing around the Beautiful and Good.'

Their activity of perpetual stasis or state of ceaseless activity is denoted in the Greek by a participial form of the verb 'perichoreuein,' which also appears, as we shall see, in a similar passage on the angelic dance in *Celestial Hierarchy* VII.4. If the cymbal-clashes of Dionysus or the hypnotic piping of the Logos or any other music associated with ecstatic choral dancing still reverberated in the memory of the Areopagite when he wrote this word, which originally meant 'to dance around something' in a physical sense and specifically 'to dance in chorus around an altar, wellspring, hieratic representative or incarnation of a god,' the echoes of its ancient theatrical and religious meanings must have been faint indeed: over the centuries the choragus of the mystic round had grown less and less audible as a source of divine harmony and less and less articulate as a purveyor of divine knowledge. The dying Moses who sang to the spheres in Philo's treatise on the virtues and the phantom Jesus who danced to the hymn of the Aeons in the Acts of John were relatively easy to hear and to understand in comparison with the numinous supracosmic entities – Porphyry's Apollo, Julian's Helios, Proclus' Chronos and Athena – who were to lead 'the intellectual dance with orders more divine' in the pagan evening of Late Antiquity.

Proclus deadened the orgiastic resonance of the verb 'perichoreuein' by using it on several occasions to denote the noiseless, bodiless, timeless processes of mystical intellection. For instance:

Now, since Psyche has not by lot attained thoughts solely rooted in eternity and so yearns to embrace the entire activity of Nous, she stretches herself out to reach the perfection which is in Nous and strains to acquire the formal unity and simplicity of his thought. She turns around him, and dances in a circle [perichoreuei kyklōi], and by her shifting attempts to comprehend his thought divides the indivisible essence of the Forms, seeing separately the Form of the Beautiful in itself, and of the Just in itself, and of all the others, one by one, but not thinking of them all at once.

(*In Parmeniden* III col 808)

And mirroring this on the human plane:

The soul, by withdrawing as it were into her innermost sanctuary, contemplates with closed eyes both the race of gods and the Henads of existing things. Since everything is within us spiritually, we are by nature able to know all things by awakening the powers within us and the images of all that is whole. And this is our most noble activity: in the calmness of our powers to be stretched up towards the Divine itself, to dance around it [perichoreuein ekeino], to gather all the soul's multiplicity towards this unity, and by leaving behind all that comes after the One, to establish ourselves in communion with that which is ineffably beyond all existing things.

(*Platonic Theology* I.3)

Though Pseudo-Dionysius may not have been echoing these particular passages in his summary of angelic and human modes of thought, it was certainly from passages like these – whether in the Procline canon itself or in the lectures and commentaries of Proclus' pupils – that he picked up the term 'perichoreuein' in its specialized theological sense along with many other words denoting the processes and objects of affirmative contemplation.

The 'race of gods' glimpsed by the Neoplatonic Spectator in the sanctuary of his soul continued their intellectual dance in the Celestial Hierarchy as the Seraphim, Cherubim, Thrones, and other angelic races. A Christian afterlife of sorts was also granted to those obscure Procline principles of plurality-in-unity which once acted as intermediaries between the absolute unity of the One and the plurality of Being and Becoming, namely 'the Henads of existing things.' They could not actually be fitted into the Christian Empyrean (spacious as it was) since only God was known to abide beyond the highest chorus of the angels, but their mediating role could be reassigned in some sense to God Himself and a vital link thus preserved between the diversified ranks of immortal spirits and the utterly uniform essence of the nameless Godhead. In *Celestial Hierarchy* VII.4, Pseudo-Dionysius used the term 'Henad' to designate the mysterious union of the individual yet indivisible Persons of the Trinity as distinct from the even more mysterious Primal Unity beyond Being. Perhaps only the Seraphim were able to intuit what the Areopagite meant by this, though he evidently did not mean to imply that God the Father was in essence different from or inferior to the One. For sublunary intellects an analogy might serve to clarify the distinction. If the Henad of the Trinity were conceived as the face God turns towards the chorus of the Many, a face uniting various features which can be discerned and named even by those who gaze upon it from a great distance, then the unique personality suggested by those features – but never revealed in itself – would correspond to the unnameable One.

Instead of closing his eyes to the many faces in the chorus and concentrating all his attention on the reflections of the divine face in the mirror of his soul, the Hierarchical Spectator could also arrive at theological wisdom by deducing from the diversified design of the visible world the unique identity of the Creator. This second approach to God was essentially the same ascending line of thought danced by the Corybantic intellect in Philo's commentary on Genesis; it was the determined search for traces of God beyond the 'temples made with hands' recommended by St Paul in his speech at the Areopagus; and it was the passage from a visual to a visionary perception of cosmic order charted by Proclus in his coldly astronomical, then ardently theological explication of Plato's image of the dance of the stars. The Areopagite conceived this phase in the intellectual dance as a series of probing questions and negative responses which came to be known in the Middle Ages as the 'via negativa.'

A soul wishing to take the negative route to God must begin at ground level, as it were, by considering whether the Creator can be reasonably identified with any earthly object or creature or with the earth itself (which the pagans in their childish ignorance once worshipped as a divine nurse). These possibilities are of course ruled out as soon as the soul goes on to contrast the lowly mutable conditions of terrestrial existence with the unfading beauty and exalted choral order of the stars. But then is God to be identified with any of the heavenly bodies, or with them all, or with an elemental source of creative energy pervading matter, or, as the Stoics argued, with the material cosmos as a whole? Reason soon teaches it to reject all such identifications on the grounds that the Creator must have existed before the creation of matter and the material cosmos if he is to be recognized as their efficient cause. Rising then from visible to invisible things and from temporal effects to eternal causes, the soul will next inquire whether God can be considered a kind of angel, or equated with the Divine Mind, or conceived as the Final Good or Perfect Beauty or Absolute Justice or any other supercelestial principle. Again to all its questions 'no' would be the reasonable reply. The Lord could not possibly be of an angelic nature if he was also the cause of that nature, and so great a cause could not be narrowly defined as the Divine Mind if his perfect unity preceded every intellectual act and transcended the duality of thinker and object of thought. No, if he was truly an inexhaustible fountain of unity, goodness, beauty, truth, justice, rationality, and existence itself, his elusive essence could not be identified with any single eternal Idea or with the sum of all the Ideas in the Divine Mind. Towards the end of the apophatic ascent the soul which has come to perceive the whole universe as an elaborate symbolic artifice designed both to reveal and to conceal its Maker realizes that God must be, properly speaking, nameless, and that even his most abstract titles fall far short of expressing the superabundance of his virtues.

This mode of knowing the One by gradually 'unknowing' the Many was conceived by the Areopagite (and highly esteemed by his medieval expositors) as a safeguard against three psychological reactions to mystical illumination – astonishment, dread, and frustration – which commonly impeded the flow of divine knowledge on the human plane. Philo's philosophical Corybant had suffered the consequences of the first reaction: a sudden dazzling and blinding of the inward eye on first glimpsing the astonishing brilliance of the Divine Presence. The second reaction had prevented Paul (as he confessed in 2 Corinthians 12) from describing his visions of Paradise in vivid persuasive language. He deeply feared that few of his brethren would ever believe what he had to say if he tried to tell them of his transcendent experiences, and worse, that if he did make the attempt some of his hard-won converts would accuse him of self-aggrandizement and abandon the faith. As for the third reaction, a sense of intellectual frustration and weariness which overcame the mystical teacher when his vision receded into a fog of metaphysical abstractions and theological paradoxes, its ill effects were strongly felt by Proclus and his school. Had the Neoplatonic theurgists not dissipated their formidable intellectual energies in constructing a murky labyrinth of hypotheses and deductions around the truths of the old philosophy – truths now eclipsed by the Truth shining forth from the sanctuary of the Christian Parthenon? And was their intellectual dance not doomed to end in spiritual exhaustion and paralysis because, as their patristic opponents never tired of pointing out, they had failed to distinguish theurgic illusion from theological enlightenment?

Perhaps nothing more clearly marks the end of pagan philosophical education as a vital, independent, and continuous movement in Western intellectual history, or more boldly asserts the Late Antique resolution of the debate begun in the Areopagus in favour of Paul's successors, than the Areopagite's daring appropriation of the thoroughly pagan noun 'theourgia' – the very sound of which had once offended Augustine's ears – from the Neoplatonic schools where it had been a polemical byword for about two centuries. His unapologetic introduction of it into discussions of hierarchical contemplation (for example, *Celestial Hierarchy* VII.2–3, immediately preceding his analysis of the contemplative dance of the Seraphim, Cherubim, and Thrones) might be considered a verbal equivalent of the appropriation and reconsecration of the Parthenon. Christianity was thus to have its own science of 'divine operations' to supplant the false science of Athena's discredited mages, but the new theurgy could not be defined as a branch of white magic or as the perfection of an academic intellect. The divine operations in question were now the supremely illuminative and perfective activities of the Trinity, and the chief initiator in the theurgic mysteries was 'the Lord of the Celestial Powers,' Christ, whose chorus of initiates included all the angelic intellects and all the contemplative souls in the Ecclesiastical Hierarchy. To dance around the Logos in a hierarchical sense meant to participate directly in the angelic reception of Christian gnosis, to gain or sustain immortal life through intellectual exposure to what the Areopagite called 'tōn theourgikōn autou phōtōn' (VII.2) – Christ's 'theurgic rays.'

It was the supreme goal of the Hierarchical Spectator to perceive these rays, which were theurgic or 'divinely operative' in the sense that they miraculously actualized the potential in each initiate to become and remain God-like. Their emanation from the Trinity (through Christ) ensured that they were wholly unmixed with the sooty fires of the material world and thus incalculably brighter and clearer than the brightest celestial beam visible to the human eye on the clearest day; but they were also superior in brilliance and clarity to the inner light of reason that the Platonists had for centuries been discovering in the innermost sanctuary of their souls and tracing back to the Forms in the intelligible world. Pseudo-Dionysius had a good reason for insisting that the eye of the understanding was no more able on its own to see the theurgic rays of Christ than the eyes of the body: its unexpected blindness served as a reminder of the utter transcendence of the mystic light-source and also of the special function of the theurgic illuminations. Unaided human reason might light the way to the threshold of eternity; legions of angelic intellects might illuminate the goodness and beauty of God; but only the Logos, glowing with the transforming light of his Father's love, could immortalize and perfect the contemplative soul.

From the viewpoint of a soul nearing the end of the negative ascent (with the final step yet to take) the theurgic illuminations of Christ would seem to shroud the Godhead in what the Areopagite liked to call a 'superluminous darkness.' This was of course quite unlike the darkness that an astronomer might see if he had the power to remove all the stars from the firmament, for it was due not to a perceptible absence of light but to an intensity and abundance of light which the soul temporarily failed to perceive. Far more than a mere process of elimination, the negative ascent was in its ultimate stages the visionary counterpart of that familiar process in visual perception which modern Gestalt psychologists have called 'the reversal of figure and ground.'[10] Certain images become perceptible to a viewer only when he blocks out other images in their vicinity or interprets foreground as background. An arrangement of light shapes on a dark ground can be perceived as an arrangement of dark shapes on a light ground (and vice versa) in a twinkling of an eye. The viewer soon discovers that however hard he may try to see both designs simultaneously only one will appear at a time before his eye, and that by consciously losing sight of one design he can will the other into view.

Similar discoveries seem to have been made by the Areopagite on the lofty plane of mystical psychology, for in his treatise on 'hid divinity' he advised his contemplative readers to avoid a Corybantic loss of inner vision by gazing steadily at the superluminous darkness until a radiant image of the Godhead should emerge out of it. The latent image would appear if only their wills were strong enough to reverse figure and ground, and free enough to choose blindness before sight, at the culmination of the negative ascent. With these words he led them out of the light – the light of Apollo, the light of Athena, the old intellectual light of the pagan theurgists:

We pray that we may enter into this superluminous darkness, and that through blindness and ignorance we may see and know what cannot be seen and known because it exists beyond sight and knowledge. For this blindness is true sight and this ignorance true knowledge. And we pray that by removing all existing things from our thoughts we may celebrate the superexistent Being in hymns befitting his transcendence, just as those who make a lifelike statue remove all the impediments which prevent a clear perception of the latent image and by merely removing these reveal the image itself in its hidden beauty.

(*Mystical Theology* ii)

The negative ascent annihilated sight and knowledge only in the sense that it led the Hierarchical Spectator into a new field of vision, a new plane of truth, on the far side of all the paradoxes and hypotheses blearing the strained eyes of the Neoplatonists. Thus the negative theologian's line of thought ended where the circular thinking of the Scripture-centred affirmative theologian began – in a 'clear perception' of the Divine Presence – though the line remained theoretically distinct from the circle. Long might the sculptor-soul chip away at the massive block of reality before the hidden beauty of God appeared, but the latent image would appear, the Areopagite claimed, it would appear. The artist had only to be persistent with his tools.

Affirmative and negative theology thus led to an understanding of the same Godhead through very different types of revelation. The former started from the public revelation of God's existence and attributes contained in the Scriptures, faith providing both the stimulus and the starting-point for the soul's circular contemplations; the latter, following reason's line of inquiry from temporal effects to eternal causes, ended in a private revelation which (as the Areopagite implied in his references to sculpture and hymnody) was the realization of an artistic or poetic vision – a vision imaginatively conceived and theurgically induced – rather than the mere conclusion of a logical argument. Of course no soul had the power to achieve the beatific vision on its own or to compel God to reveal His hidden beauty. Grace alone could dispel the darkness at the final moment in the ascent. Nevertheless, if the soul did not strive to the end to carve a perfect image of the Divine Countenance or to celebrate the Father in hymns expressing His utter transcendence, if it merely waited in the superluminous darkness for the Initiator's theurgic rays to expose 'what cannot be seen or known,' the beatific vision would elude it.

Negative contemplation in its advanced stages (that is, once reason had removed all that was not God from the mystical field of vision) became a pure act of the visual imagination – resulting in what Dante at the end of his contemplative ascent will call a 'high fantasy.' Until the Hierarchical Spectator had inspected all the divine symbols in church and cosmos, imagined them in amazing new combinations to ravish his inward eye, discarded these to create brighter and more beautiful images of eternal reality, and finally perceived the most brilliant image as no more than a shadowy preface of the Beautiful and Good, he could not hope to achieve that immediate, unobstructed, totally symbol-free vision of God which was the high fantastic goal of the negative theologian.

Since sharing was the essence of hierarchical order and sharing knowledge the essential hierarchical activity, revelations granted at the end of the negative ascent could not remain private for long in the contemplative community of Ecclesia. At the moment of theurgic illumination the negative theologian was moved by the Divine Will – his own will acting in perfect accord with that of the Logos – to make public his personal knowledge of the Beautiful and Good by translating his astonishing visions into symbols familiar to the many who had not yet seen God face to face and to lay aside his old role as spectator in order to carry on the divine operations of the Logos in the dance of grace. And so the end of the ascending line became the start of the expanding spiral: what one Christian soul saw and knew all must in some measure be taught to see and know, the spiral motion of their souls representing the historical dynamism of Christian education.

In contrast to Proclus and Marinus, who regarded theurgic illumination as the highest and last goal of an educated spectator-turned-initiate in the mystic dance of the old philosophy, Pseudo-Dionysius (recalling no doubt that Paul's mystical illumination on the road to Damascus *preceded* his teaching missions to the Gentiles) regarded it as the initial and continual stimulus of the intellectual activity of the Church. But how could Paul's successors discuss 'hid divinity' without sounding offensively self-important? To facilitate the communication of mystical knowledge essential to the charismatic movement of Christian education, the Areopagite developed a distinctive theological vocabulary by adding the Greek prefix 'hyper' – literally 'beyond' and usually translated by its Latin cognate 'super' – to a host of nouns and adjectives traditionally associated with the Godhead. Terms like 'superluminous,' 'superexistent,' and 'supereminent' served not only to express God's transcendence of all known attributes and categories of being but also to emphasize the littleness of all that shed light, enjoyed existence, or attained eminence in the chorus of the Many compared with the solitary grandeur of the One.

The language of negative theology was not really negative at all: it was best suited (as the Areopagite himself suggests) for hymns of exultant religious affirmation which would instruct the chorus of the faithful in the mysteries of hierarchical order and encourage individual souls to confirm their hierarchical knowledge by ascending into the superluminous darkness. For the theurgical illuminati who would seek words to express what Paul had regretfully considered ineffable, the Areopagite provided a psychological and pedagogical justification for the use of symbolic images drawn from the visible world in mystical discourse pertaining to 'the invisible things' of God. They should choose tangible, familiar, visually definable, even preposterously earthly images as divine symbols, he advised in *Celestial Hierarchy* 1.2–3, for the sheer inappropriateness of such symbols would shock the Hierarchical Spectator into a sense of divine transcendence and so induce him to block out all worldly images from his consciousness.

A striking application of this theory of negative symbolism can be observed in the Areopagite's unprecedented projection of the schema of the three motions from its appropriate sphere, the dynamic universe of the two hierarchies, onto the still point marking God's superessential presence (*Divine Names* IX.9) – an imaginative transference quite unintelligible to a pagan Neoplatonist! Its meaning, however, came to the Hierarchical Spectator in a flash: the circular motion of God signified His eternal sameness, the completeness of His identity, and His power to encompass all things within His providential order; His linear motion represented the outward flow of His creative energies and the procession of the Many from the One; and His spiral motion suggested various combinations of the first two activities such as the Father's remaining motionless while creating order and the Son's proceeding into history while concentrating on His eternal origin. But no sooner were these dynamic patterns interpreted as divine symbols than they had to be cast aside in light of God's utter immobility. Thus circle, line, and spiral became negative symbols to the inward eye of the Hierarchical Spectator, and with them the Neoplatonic image of cosmic and intellectual harmony that had combined them all: 'noera choreia.'

Closing the Circle

If an image of order may be said to have its own inner logic consisting of certain rules of symmetry and dynamics which persist through a long series of iconographic variations without being much affected by the rise and fall of schools, sects, and empires, then the inner logic of the theocentric round-dance of the mysteries (or 'gnostic round') might be summed up in two basic rules. First the rule of introversion: initiates dancing in a ring turn their attention inward to a sacred centre occupied by their initiator who represents both the spiritual origin of their choral order and the stable identity of their unfallen or redeemable souls. Then the rule of assimilation: initiates receiving illumination become godlike through imitating the stable identity and formal characteristics of their initiator, the communal character of the chorus becoming in turn a symbolic reflection of the central deity. With its circumference thus related to its centre, the gnostic round can serve as a model for any universal order that preserves a radical distinction between the Many and the One and yet permits some logical (or Logical) connection to exist between them. When the Plotinian One occupied the centre of the dance, the Many tried to fuse themselves into a single motionless circle detached from all physical and intellectual concerns. When King Helios united the round, the planets restricted their movements to the Circle of the Different in order to receive his theurgic illuminations and to imitate the ruler of the intellectual gods. And when Chronos assumed the role of cosmic choragus, his helicoidal form was mirrored visibly in the spiralling orbits of the planets and invisibly in the psychic bacchanalia of the stars.

What the Areopagite perceived at the centre of the round was not simply the One but the Three-in-One, Father, Son, and Holy Spirit, whose selfless love for each other and perfect knowledge of each other were the mysteries in which the two hierarchies participated. With its centre so transformed, the introverted and assimilative chorus underwent a corresponding transformation to demonstrate its participation in divine love and knowledge. It mirrored the Trinity by dividing up (or rather down) into a series of concentric triadic rings, each a miniature hierarchy uniting three classes of angelic or human intellects. Here is how the inner logic of the gnostic round asserted itself in the Celestial Hierarchy:

Participation in divine knowledge, as I may briefly but not unreasonably define it, is a process of purification, illumination, and perfection. For it purifies from ignorance by the knowledge of the more complete initiations granted in due order; it illuminates through the divine knowledge itself by which it also purifies the mind which formerly did not behold what now is revealed to it through the higher illuminations; and it perfects in turn by the light itself, through the knowledge habitually acquired through the most luminous initiations.

In the circle of God and immediately around God is established, as far as I know, the first order of celestial beings. Simply and unceasingly their chorus dances around His eternal gnosis [perichoreuousa tēn aiōnion autou gnōsin] with an eternal motion and with a stability supreme among the angels. In a pure manner they see many blessed visions and are enlightened with simple and boundless illuminations. They are filled moreover with a divine nourishment which is multiplied through the generous abundance of the First-Giver but retains its uniform essence owing to the simple and inclusive unity of the divine banquet. They are judged worthy of much communion and cooperation with God because their order has assimilated itself to God as much as possible in the beauty of its habits and activities.

(*Celestial Hierarchy* VII.3–4)

The harmony of this first circle, the Areopagite goes on to say, could not be contained within 'the simple and inclusive unity of the divine banquet' (by which he meant the angelic prototype of the Christian Eucharist, no doubt, but also the angelic counterpart of the Neoplatonic symposium of ecstatic intellects united in the chorus of Immortal Love). The circle expanding outward and downward from the First-Giver brought order to the world of the senses and moved the Old Testament prophets to translate the glory of God into sensory images:

And thus the Holy Scriptures have transmitted to the inhabitants of earth certain hymns of this hierarchy in which is revealed in a holy manner the supreme illumination allotted to them. Some men, translating this illumination into sensory images, cry out in 'a voice of a great rushing, saying, "Blessed be the glory of the Lord from his place" ' [Ezekiel 3:12]; other men lift up their voices in that most celebrated and revered utterance from the Scriptures: 'Holy, holy, holy is the Lord of hosts: the whole earth is full of his glory' [Isaiah 6:3].

(*Celestial Hierarchy* VII.4)

Like the Philonic Hymn of Moses which brought the Jews into harmony with the chorus of the stars and the angels, or the Apocryphal Hymn of Jesus which set the holy souls of the first Christian chorus in rhythm with

Grace, or the Porphyrian Hymn of Apollo which drew the holy soul of Plotinus into the chorus of Immortal Love, or the Procline Hymn to Helios which channelled the rich flood of harmony streaming down from the intellectual realm into sense-bound human language, the hymns of the Ecclesiastical Hierarchy came to man from spirits more powerful than the stars as an inducement not to sink into the intermittent dances of the body but to soar into the simple and unceasing dance of the spirit.

In the first order of celestial beings danced the fiery Seraphim, the many-eyed Cherubim, and the invincible Thrones; Dominations, Virtues, and Powers followed in the second; and in the third circled Principalities, Archangels, and Angels (the noun 'angelloi' serving both as a general term for all the eternal intellects and as a specific title for the divine messengers who occasionally appeared on earth or in the heavens and were therefore thought to be the lowest-ranking members in the Celestial Hierarchy). While their names can be found here and there in the Old Testament (Ezekiel 1:26, 10:1; Isaiah 6:2) and in the New (Ephesians 1:21; Colossians 1:16), their triadic arrangement has absolutely no basis in Scripture. Its origin – if one ignores Dante's explanation that this must be part of the 'secret truth' conveyed by Paul to his trusted convert and verified by the mystical revelations granted to the Areopagite himself – is manifestly Neoplatonic. It is reminiscent of the threefold sequence of luminary, conveyor of illumination, and illuminati repeated endlessly throughout the Neoplatonic Golden Chain, and specifically of the triadic arrangement of demiurgic gods, angels, and daimones whom Proclus had imagined dancing in chorus around God (*In Timaeum* I 369). Conditioned by a late Neoplatonic education to think in groups of three – a mental reflex which may be traced to Plotinus – the Areopagite evidently associated the triadic formative principle of Procline theology with his vaguely Monophysite concept of the Trinity and subsequently defined the structure of the hierarchical universe as a series of triune triplicities.

Order, knowledge, activity – the three aspects of hierarchy were each multiplied or divided by three in the holy mathematics of the mystic chorus. The order of the Seraphim, Cherubim, and Thrones was repeated in two subordinate angelic orders and extended to the sacerdotal triad of bishops, priests, and deacons; their knowledge of God was acquired through a triple process of purification, illumination, and perfection so that it might be shared through the triple sequence of their circular, linear, and helicoidal motions; and their service of divine praise and thanksgiving was echoed perpetually in the triple chant of the ecclesiastical chorus – 'Holy, holy, holy!'

In light of these correspondences between the two hierarchies, one would expect to find some passage in the Areopagite's treatise on church offices which would complement his description of the angelic dance in *The Celestial Hierarchy* with a vision of human participation in 'the simple and inclusive unity of the divine banquet.' Such a passage can indeed be found, and just where one might expect to find it: in his meditation on the Eucharistic rite described in the third chapter of *The Ecclesiastical Hierarchy*. His occasional use of the term 'Eucharist' in reference to this rite encouraged his medieval expositors to identify it with the Catholic mass, though it was by no means identical with the Western office of Holy Communion. He usually called it the mystery of the Synaxis (literally 'a gathering together') and that is what it will be called here in order to avoid confusion between Eastern and Western liturgical traditions.

Like the initiation rites at Eleusis, the Synaxis had little meaning outside of the architectural setting in which it was meant to be performed – the ornamented interior of a Late Antique Greek or Levantine basilica. While the physical dimensions of this sacred space would not have been impressively large in a typical basilica of the early sixth century, enclosed as it was within thick stone walls and narrowed by dimly lit aisles, its symbolic dimensions (as perceived by the Hierarchical Spectator) were vaster than space and time. What Eusebius of Caesarea did to the throne room of Constantine in his Tricennial Oration Pseudo-Dionysius did to every local basilica in his treatise on church offices: he imaginatively transformed it into a mystical theatre representing both the divine architecture of the temporal cosmos and the archetypal domain of the eternal intellects.

The coryphaeus in this theatre was of course the bishop, who began the Synaxis by positioning himself near the altar and praying. In his 'theōria' or 'contemplative inspection' of the rite (III.3.3) the Areopagite noted that the altar was an appropriate symbol for the One because of its prominence and stability, thereby implying that everything else in the basilica represented the diverse ranks of the Many which the bishop had to transcend intellectually in order to achieve theurgic illumination. In the decorated capitals of the nave and the gleaming mosaics of the vestibule his inward eye would perceive the multitude of divine symbols adorning the physical world, and in the icons displayed on the lattice separating the nave from the sanctuary the multitude of divine beings encircling the Beautiful and Good. The congregation milling about in the nave and gazing at the iconostasis would correspond to what Proclus had called 'all the soul's multiplicity.' Some of them – the penitents, the possessed, and the catechumens – were deemed unworthy of full participation in the rite and would be dismissed from the Synaxis after the reading of the Epistle and Gospel. During its preliminary stages, however, all the sub-episcopal ranks were to be gathered into a unity, purged of unholy thoughts, and mentally prepared for the divine banquet so that the bishop (acting as the highest intellect in their collective soul) could ultimately bring them into communion with the spiritual realities behind the symbols.

Having concluded his prayer – whether it was a private petition for celestial guidance during the rite or a general summons to the congregation to direct their attention towards the altar the Areopagite does not say – the bishop proceeded to lead his flock in a choral chanting of the Psalms after which the deacons read to them from the Scriptures. These preparatory stages in the celebration of the mystery were designed to induce a uniformity of thought among clergy and laity such as the angels were thought to enjoy in their ceaseless choral dance around God. 'Thus does the repetition of holy words in the chant,' observed the Areopagite,

harmoniously prepare the faculties of our souls for the rites presently to be celebrated. And when the chant has placed ourselves and others in harmony with divine realities through the unison of the divine songs as in one single concordant choral dance of holy beings [miai kai homologōi tōn hierōn choreiai], then the more condensed and obscure passages in the holy language of the hymns are expanded in the many lucid images and declarations of the most holy readings from the Scriptures.

(*Ecclesiastical Hierarchy* III.3.5)

The old Constantinian ideal of an ecclesiastical chorus without dissenting members is here revived and affirmed (despite the discordant aftermath of Nicaea and the fierce sectarian controversies of the fifth century) in the Areopagite's vision of the unity established among the chorus of initiates at the commencement of the Synaxis. But where is the emperor in this harmonious scene? Constantine would doubtless have been shocked to find that no special role had been assigned to his successors in the dance of the hierarchical chorus or in the administration of the hierarchical universe. The bishop alone presides over the cosmic basilica and brings concord to the people by fulfilling his role as 'hierarch.' The dream of earthly unity promoted by the apologists of Christian monarchism has faded before the prospect of heavenly unity brought down to earth through the power of Christian theurgy.[11]

If the Areopagite had not twice associated the image of the chorus with movement and vision (*Divine Names* IV.8 and *Celestial Hierarchy* VII.4) one might be tempted to translate the noun 'choreia' in the passage on the Synaxis as 'choir' rather than 'choral dance.' The word is used after all in reference to the unison chanting of the Psalms and the recitation of biblical texts – holy activities which the post-Nicene Fathers often strove to distinguish from the unholy impulses of the bodily dance. In response perhaps to the

Church's deep-seated aversion to the dance as a physical form of worship, a recent clerical commentator on *The Ecclesiastical Hierarchy* has translated the phrase 'miai kai homologōi tōn hierōn choreiai' in III.3.5 as 'only one single homogeneous choir of holy men.'[12] Though not widely off the mark, this translation obscures the broad theological implications of the Areopagite's phrase by restricting the meaning of its key terms. The adjective 'homologos' is hard to render in English since it implies not only a uniformity of language and thought among a group of citizens or coreligionists (hence 'homogeneous'?) but also a willingness on their part to resolve conflicts and to act in accordance with acknowledged principles of conduct. Moreover, the ambiguous genitive 'tōn hierōn' may refer both to the 'holy men' who take part in the Synaxis and to their superiors – the 'holy beings' in the Celestial Hierarchy with whom they are mystically united during the enactment of the rite and from whom they receive the inspiration for their hymns.

By the end of Late Antiquity the image of the mystery dance had lost so much of its ancient erotic glow and physical dynamism through long association with the exalted ranks of the Aeons, Angels, intellectual gods, and other bodiless entities in the Beyond that the Greek Fathers could safely compare the gathering together of the faithful in Holy Communion to a choreia without fear of representing the divine banquet as a theatrical entertainment. 'Remember the venerable congregation,' Basil the Great had urged a lapsed virgin,

Remember the holy chorus of virgins, the assembly of the Lord, the Church of the saints. ... Recall these, and with them the angelic choral dance around God [angelikēs peri ton Theon met' ekeinon choreias] and the spiritual life in the flesh and the heavenly government on earth!

(*Epistola* XLVI)

The Areopagite's meditation on the 'one single concordant choral dance of holy beings' is one of the many passages in the Corpus Dionysiacum that seem to echo the Cappadocian rhetoric of ecclesiastical unity as clearly as the Neoplatonic rhetoric of cosmological unity. Since the concord of the angelic chorus was perceived by him as both a dynamic intellectual order and a musical harmony, the corresponding concord of the participants in the Synaxis should not be identified solely with the unison chanting of the Psalms.

Their music followed a movement – a dramatic physical movement – which the bishop performed before the multitude as a sign that 'the angelic choral dance' was about to encompass them all, that 'the spiritual life in the flesh' did indeed move and quicken the flesh, and that 'the heavenly government on earth' had assuredly arrived to unite and order the lives of ordinary earthly sinners. But for this movement the common people who saw only the symbols in the cosmic basilica might have been excluded from the spiritual fellowship of the Synaxis, or at least have felt excluded, for how could they be expected to participate with alacrity in an intellectual dance out of the light of knowable reality into the superluminous darkness? And if they were left behind by the holy chorus or never taught by outward and visible signs to enter into its introspective revolutions, would the Synaxis (which was also called the Koinonia or 'the shared rite') not cease to be a truly Christian ceremony of communion and become in effect a mystery in the old pagan sense?

Like all hierarchical acts this crucial unifying movement may be divided into three phases. First the bishop paused in the sanctuary after his opening prayer to cense the altar and the veiled symbols of Christ's sacrifice. (The bread and wine would not be exposed to the initiates until the start of the Eucharist proper.) Second, like a spiralling angel whose thoughts remained forever circling on high while his bright form descended to illuminate his needy inferiors, he stepped down from the sanctuary and bore the censer away from the focal point in the mystery through the nave towards the vestibule. A cloud of incense would doubtless have hung in the air behind him, marking his line of motion outwards to the Many and impressing upon their senses his spiritual union with the One. His movement ultimately proved to be circular rather than linear, for its third phase took him around the congregation and up the sanctuary steps past the icons and back again to the foot of the altar. The closing of his circle (see figure 20) was the signal for the clergy and laity to begin the sacred chant.

To a spectator not seeking initiation in the mystery of the Synaxis – a pagan Skeptic, say, who happened to slip into the basilica at the start of the service – the bishop's majestic circumambulation might have seemed little more than an exercise in theatricality, a meaningless dumb show. But to the Hierarchical Spectator whose voice we hear in the mystical exposition of the rite the movement clearly represented all the major processes in theurgic cosmogony and all the main events in Christian history. If we are to see the elaborate significance of this outwardly simple movement, we must attempt to perceive its three phases as a coherent symbolic enactment of the Divine Plan (as the Areopagite advises in iii.3.3) 'in the manner of one who is divinely possessed.'

The stationing of the bishop beside the altar at the beginning and end of his dance 'across the whole range of the divine imagery' (iii.3.3) establishes his primary symbolic role as the Logos who proceeds from yet eternally resides with the Father in the superluminous darkness of the heavenly sanctuary. Hidden in that darkness was the precise ontological relation of the

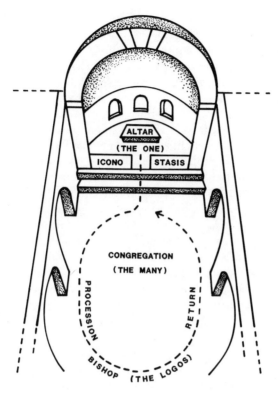

Figure 20

What the outward eye saw in the 'mia kai homologos choreia' preceding the celebration of the Eucharist was so simple that it hardly seemed a dance at all. There
was only one dramatically significant physical movement at the commencement of
the Synaxis (the circling of the bishop around the congregation) followed by only
one choral response (the unison chanting of the Psalms). What the inward eye
perceived, however, was an elaborate symbolic enactment of the chief events in
hierarchical cosmogony and sacred history: the procession of the Many from the
One; Christ's Incarnation and Resurrection; Ecclesia's intellectual movement away
from temporal discord and diversity towards eternal concord and unity. The architectural details of the nave and apse represented above – with the exception of the
schematic altar and iconostasis (position conjectural) – are drawn from a photograph
of the interior of the basilica at Qalb Louzeh in Richard Krautheimer's *Early Christian and Byzantine Architecture*, plate 44b. Qalb Louzeh is located east of Antioch
in northern Syria. The basilica was constructed around the time of the composition
of the Corpus Dionysiacum (c 500 AD). Some thirteen years later the Areopagite
was cited by Severus the Monophysite Patriarch of Antioch, which has led to
much modern speculation concerning the possible Syrian provenance of the Pseudo-
Dionysian writings.

first two Persons of the Trinity, an interminably contested issue at the ecclesiastical councils of the fourth and fifth centuries. Since those who enter into Christological debates almost never experience the peace that passeth human understanding, the Areopagite may perhaps be commended – or at least excused – for having avoided these discordant debates by hiding behind his first-century pseudonym. A muted Monophysitism has been detected in some of his remarks on the divinity of Christ, to be sure, but the tone of the Corpus Dionysiacum as a whole is so unpolemical that only the most sensitive inquisitorial ears might isolate the faint note of heresy in the concord of the holy chorus assembled for the Synaxis.[13] Concord – 'homologia' – was a patristic synonym for orthodoxy, and the orthodoxy of the Areopagite, which was accepted in the Eastern Church by the middle of the seventh century, would not be seriously questioned until recent times.

In his descent from the altar to the people the bishop re-enacted a cosmogonic process, commemorated an historical event, and anticipated a communal act of contemplation. The process was the emanation of the Logos from the Primal Godhead which had resulted in the continuous multiplication of divine goodness and beauty throughout creation and the rational unification of the chorus of the Many. Perhaps only the most learned priests and deacons among the Many would have seen *that* in his procession, but almost everyone might have recognized the historical event it commemorated: the descent of Christ from Heaven to Earth at the Incarnation. The fragrance streaming forth from the bishop's censer represented the divine blessedness that the Incarnate Logos had borne with him during his earthly ministry and which was still being diffused among his attendants at the divine banquet without the slightest diminution of its eternal source. To the monks and other contemplatives in his flock the hierarch's physical journey from the veiled symbols on the altar to the icons, mosaics, reliquaries, and crosses displayed outside the sanctuary would have presented an image of his intellectual journey along the 'via affirmativa,' the procession of his thoughts from the obscure transcendental names of God to the multiplicity of divine images clearly revealed in the Bible. Following his lead, the chorus engaged in a communal act of affirmative contemplation by chanting with one voice 'the more condensed and obscure passages in the holy language of the hymns' and then considering 'the many lucid images and declarations of the most holy readings from the Scriptures.'

By closing his circle the bishop opened up a universe of mystical meanings to the inward eye of the Hierarchical Spectator. The uniformity of divine order as reflected in the astral revolutions, the completeness of divine knowledge as revealed to the circling Seraphim, the all-encompassing range of divine activity as measured by the circular motion of God – to perceive these in the sacred circumference was to follow the bishop's intellect as well as his body in the dance, to participate in his spiritual return to the One as an initiate in the mystical theology of the Areopagite. Though the physical motion of the hierarch necessarily had a beginning and an end, its circularity represented the beginningless and endless existence of the Primal Godhead whose perfections were mirrored in every detail of the cosmic basilica but whose grandeur could not be contained within the temples built by human hands or the circles traced by angelic intellects. In his role as the Son the episcopal coryphaeus enacted the mystery of the Resurrection and the Ascension, his return to the altar signifying the return of the Risen Christ to his exalted position next to the Father. Just as Christ would ultimately complete the temporal phase of the dance of grace by closing the circle of his followers and leading them back to the banquet of the First-Giver, so the bishop in anticipation of that apocalyptic closure drew together the ranks of the ecclesiastical chorus and directed their eyes back to the holy table laden with symbols of their redemption. The third phase of the dance also pertains to the operations of the Holy Spirit. 'Though the multitude has seen only the divine symbols,' remarked the Areopagite in III.2, 'the bishop on account of his godlike purity is always led upwards in a hierarchical way by the Holy Spirit and raised to the holy archetypes of the mysteries in blessed and intellectual visions.' Always yearning to attain such visions himself, the Hierarchical Spectator would see in the bishop's charismatic return to the altar a foreshadowing of his intellectual dance from the Many to the One along the 'via negativa.'

At the conclusion of each Synaxis, then, having achieved 'in a hierarchical way' (through negative contemplation and theurgic illumination) a private vision of the face of God such as Paul had been granted in his ascent to the third heaven, the bishop would emerge from the superluminous darkness to affirm with fresh zeal the inviolable truths of the faith before the symbol-instructed and symbol-distracted multitude. And so, the cycle of affirmative and negative contemplation recommencing, the ranks would be gathered together for a new celebration of the Eucharist. The path from altar to people to altar would be retraced in a fresh cloud of incense. The circle would again be closed. Governing the hierarch's mystical footsteps in the silence preceding the chant – before the note of Christian triumph resounded through the cosmic basilica – was the potent Neoplatonic rhythm of 'monē, pro-odos, epistrophē': the permanence of the ecstatic soul in the presence of the One; the procession of the Many from the Wellspring of Life; and the turning of all holy beings towards the unitive centre of their dance. It was a rhythm which would still be felt in the monasteries and universities of medieval Europe long after the dance of Neoplatonic stars above the pagan Parthenon had faded from Ecclesia's memory.

From Spectator to Dancer

Sixth-century readers of the Corpus Dionysiacum were not all deceived by the first-century disguise of the Hierarchical Spectator. At least one Byzantine theologian, a certain Hypatius mentioned in a report delivered to an ecclesiastical assembly in Constantinople in 533 AD, is known to have questioned the authenticity of the Corpus on the grounds that not one allusion to it or quotation from it could be found in the voluminous writings of Cyril of Alexandria (an early fifth-century theologian celebrated for his erudition) or in the vast range of Christian literature produced before him. Hypatius' sensible conclusion that the Fathers would not have conspired over five centuries to conceal the genuine writings of the Areopagite – if such writings actually existed – seems to have fallen on deaf ears. By 649 AD the reputation of Dionysius the Areopagite as a mystical theologian was well enough established for a delegate at the Council of the Lateran to appeal to his authority in an argument condemning the Monothelete doctrine that the will of Christ was purely divine. Present at this council was the anti-Monothelete theologian to whom the first notable commentary on the Corpus has been attributed, Maximus the Confessor. In order to prevent heretical sects like the Monotheletes from using the theology of the Areopagite to support their own arguments, the subtle commentator strove to demonstrate that the various idiosyncratic and heresy-tinged doctrines enshrined in the Corpus (such as the notion that Christ had two natures but a single divine activity) could be reconciled with the orthodox teachings of the Church.

Soon after the death of Maximus (662 AD), Leontius of Byzantium in the East and Gregory the Great in the West added their voices to the growing chorus of theologians commending the wisdom of the Areopagite. In the eighth century Pope Paul IV sent a copy of the Corpus to King Pepin of France; another copy was sent in 827 AD to Louis the Pious as a gift from the Greek Emperor Michael Balbus. Louis in turn handed the Greek manuscript over to Hilduin, Abbot of St Denys, for translation into Latin. Moved by an ardent desire to enhance the prestige of the Parisian episcopate, a desire which temporarily superseded his regard for honesty in scholarship, Hilduin appended to his thoroughly unreliable translation a biography of the Areopagite in which he claimed that the Dionysius to whom Paul had recounted his mystical visions was none other than the first bishop of Paris and patron saint of his monastery, the martyr beloved by the Franks, St Dionysius or Denys (who died in fact in the third century). Though the Abbot's translation was soon replaced by a slightly more accurate version produced by the Irish-born scholar Johannes Scotus Erigena, who had received his copy of the original from Charles the Bald in 858 AD, the stirring biography of St Denys the Areopagite was destined to attract readers throughout the Middle Ages and to make the Corpus Dionysiacum a subject of local scholarly interest at the University of Paris and religious houses in its vicinity. Thus preserved from oblivion by the apologetic exegesis of a Byzantine monk, the enthusiastic approval of several popes, the pious interest of two French kings, the hagiographic opportunism of a wily Parisian abbot, and the scholarly endorsement of an Irish Christian Platonist, the mystical theology of the Areopagite would be carried down the calm channels of early medieval monastic thought into the turbulent mainstream of scholastic philosophy.[14]

Swept along in the current of Latin translations and annotations of the Corpus produced by the Schoolmen – a current swollen in the eleventh and twelfth centuries by a steady outpouring of hymns, homilies, treatises on church offices, guidebooks to the contemplative life, and other opuscula inspired or influenced by the Areopagite – were two relics of his unique synthesis of Neoplatonic and Christian paideia: his image of the concordant choral dance of holy beings symbolizing hierarchical order; and his triadic schema of angelic and human contemplative motions representing the universal range of hierarchical knowledge and activity. By Dante's time both visions of choreia (the unitary and the triadic) had passed into the collective consciousness of the Catholic Middle Ages and were known not only to the Doctors of the Church but also to the bishops and their clergy and the laity they educated, preached to, chanted before, and guided towards Paradise.

In Dante's Heaven of the Sun a lay pilgrim and his beloved guide will be encircled by a hierarchical image of that consciousness: a dazzling choral dance in three movements performed by the Church's leading intellectual luminaries and modelled on the mystic round of the Seraphim, Cherubim, and Thrones. The sixth dancer of the innermost circle will be introduced to Dante in the following respectful terms by the spokesman for the chorus, Thomas Aquinas:

> At Solomon's side see the light of that candle
> which below in the flesh saw most deeply
> into the angelic nature and its ministry.
> (Paradiso x 115–17)

Who but the New Testament seer with the deepest understanding of the Heavenly Kingdom could hold a candle next to the wisest king in the Old Testament? Aquinas does not need to name him. Dante will know from his exalted position in the chorus of the Wise that the sixth dancer – who was once only a spectator like himself – must be the immortal 'Dionisio.'

Afterword

'All these details,' said the Byzantine historian Procopius of the strange and bewildering architecture of Justinian's Hagia Sophia, 'hang together unexpectedly in mid-air and float away from each other and seem to rest only on the parts nearest them. Yet they fit together in such a way that a single remarkable harmony is produced in this work. They do not permit the spectator to rest his eye fondly on any one spot, at least not for very long, for each detail catches the eye in turn and draws it easily to itself.'[1] The same might be said of the peculiar architecture of this volume, which draws the reader's inward eye here and there and everywhere with a disorienting array of details and leaves a broad and weighty argument hanging – perilously – in the ecclesiastical air of the sixth century. Whether my temporarily suspended work will crack and collapse under its own weight (as the original dome of Hagia Sophia did a few years after its construction) remains to be seen; I trust that time will expose in its ruthless manner any faults in my thinking presently concealed by a gilded overlay of words.

Perhaps there is no better time than now, at this moment of completion when the work stands free of its author at last and seems firm and harmonious, to inspect its foundations and supporting columns; to imagine it stripped of its multitudinous historical details, celestial designs, and sophistic embellishments; to silence the echoing voices of all the Greek and Latin authors who have praised or criticized the Great Chorus down through the centuries; and to uncover the basic lines of thought – the floor-plan, as it were – of the argument I have been building around and above the ancient crowd of spectators as a retrospective participant in their choral consciousness.

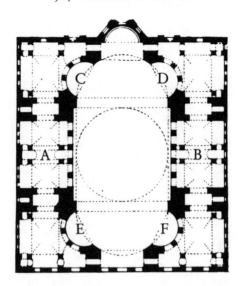

Hagia Sophia, Constantinople. Floor-plan of the cathedral proper, excluding peripheral structures, after Richard Krautheimer, *Early Christian and Byzantine Architecture* (Penguin Books 1965), p 155. Note how the parallel lines of columns along the main aisles (A and B) are interrupted by the semicircular curves of the four colonnaded exedrae or niches (C, D, E, and F).

In the floor-plan of Hagia Sophia, which is much simpler than one might expect from Procopius' description of the complex visual field created by its cylindrical apses and triangular vaults, can be discerned two colonnaded aisles that run the whole length of the church and flank the bulging rectangular area beneath its great floating dome. On their eight massive marble piers rest the weight of the dome and the fame of its designers, Anthemius of Tralles and Isidorus of Miletus. Running the whole length of my historical argument – like these quietly supportive aisles – are two lines of defence for the thesis originally proposed in my foreword, namely that the ancient Greek vision of the cosmic dance never ceased to attract contemplative spectators throughout the Academic Millennium.

Along the first aisle of my argument I have attempted to demonstrate the continuity of the vision empirically by collecting references to it from a wide range of ancient texts and presenting these as evidence of its survival in the form of direct quotations from primary sources. Like the Levantine labourers who hauled columns and capitals from the splendid temple of Diana at Ephesus off to Constantinople for incorporation into Justinian's strange new church, I was a shameless pillager of 'loci classici.' Sometimes, I must admit, I was not sure how to incorporate what I was translating into the emerging design of my argument until the design itself suggested to me that a gap had to be filled here or a support raised there. Doubtless more marble was stolen from the past than was strictly necessary for the construction of the present work. Its basic outlines could have been established with only the primary quotations at the head of each chapter. But I wanted a rich interior for it, and so its fabric of secondary quotations is monumentally heterogeneous.

Along its second aisle I have worked the data of continuity into a causal argument leading to the conclusion that the major philosophical variations of the vision in the Greco-Roman era were critical elaborations of the visual imagery in *Timaeus* 40a–d. By citing this passage at the head of my first chapter I intended to imply that it was not only a springboard for philosophical meditation on the vision for many centuries after Plato's death but also a source, indeed the principal source, of that highly extendible metaphor of world-order which the Sophists stretched to preposterous lengths for comic effects or twisted and inverted to make serious points about world-disorder, and which I referred to from time to time as 'the choreia topos.' Sophistic elaborations of this ever-topical topos confirmed my early suspicion that the popularity and longevity of the circular (or astral) design of the cosmic dance was due in no small measure to the unbroken tradition of Platonic cosmology.

The interior expanses of my argument, the vaulting, arching, circling, and floating parts of it, lead to four other general conclusions – one drawn from my observations of how the vision varied in Antiquity, and three from my considerations of why its principal variations arose. At the risk of sounding like an ancient numerologist I may now present as a fact my hypothesis that at least nine phases can be discerned in the evolution of the vision during the Academic Millennium. I say 'at least' because other spectators may perceive ten or twenty in the evidence I have collected, and because new phases may come to light with the discovery of new evidence. Nine is not a sacred number for me. If the Muses inspired me to produce an ennead of chapters in the style of Porphyry, their influence on my psyche was, alas, subliminal.

I have refrained from using restrictive labels to refer to these fluid phases in my nine chapters, but now that we have transcended their divisions and particularities and can look back on them from the perspective of the whole I think we can distinguish the variations of the dance by name without perceiving them as isolated steps or divinely ordained stages in the progress of Western civilization. Let us say that chapter 1 covers the Demiurgic or Old Platonic phase in the evolution of the vision; chapter 2, the Judaeo-Hellenistic phase; chapter 3, the Gnostic phase; chapter 4, the Early Neoplatonic phase; chapter 5, the Middle Platonic phase; chapter 6, the Cosmopoetic or Heliotropic phase; chapter 7, the Greek Patristic phase; chapter 8, the Theurgic or Late Neoplatonic phase; and chapter 9, the Angelic phase (combining the linear, circular, and spiral motions of the Celestial and Ecclesiastical Hierarchies). While my chapters march forth in strict chronological order according to the floruits of my principal authors, the same cannot be said of the nine phases. They form a much looser and less straightforward sequence than my concatenation of authors and quotations might suggest, for their time-spans overlap a great deal and cannot be measured precisely. They flow out from their Platonic fountainhead in an eddying stream which has a chronological drift, to be sure, but also, with its unexpected undercurrents and meandering tributaries, a tendency to defy the strictures of chronology.

The Early Neoplatonic phase, for instance, spanned the intellectual lifetimes of Plotinus and Porphyry in the third and early fourth centuries AD and carried us several wise steps forward against the irrational tide of Gnosticism. Yet when we tried to see how it varied from the Gnostic phase preceding it (and concurrent with it) the flow of time suddenly seemed to reverse itself, and we were swept back to the era when the Great Chorus came close to losing its Platonic centre and falling apart in a storm of Epicurean atoms, Stoic fire, and Cynical laughter. And there Plotinus kept us, suspended in the Hellenistic past, while he searched for intelligible ways to reunite the idea of cosmic order with the image of choral harmony. Had I been a slave to chronology I would have written ten uniform chapters – one for each century in the Academic Millennium – instead of nine of various sizes and shapes. Like Plato's Demiurge I have deliberately offset the Same and the Uniform with a Dionysian infusion of the Different. My visionary history has its retrogradations and progressions, its pauses and accelerations, its eclipses, sudden gleamings, and reversions to its starting-point, as if it were following the dance along the Lykabas. Its chapters and phases crowd together towards the end of the Academic Millennium like Saturnalian revellers at the end of the solar year. The second century BC is rarely recalled in my study because (so far as I can see) it contributed little of an original or lasting character to the vision. As for the fourth century AD, I found that no less than three full chapters were needed to traverse its tremendous arc.

If I were a levitating theurgist or a mystical theologian, my view of the dynamism of the Great Chorus would doubtless be timeless and phaseless. Instead of an historical sequence of variations my inward eye would behold an eternal continuum. I would rise above chronology entirely – like Chronos himself. Having begun this study as an historian of ideas, however, I was bound to impose a chronological design on my findings and to see an evolution where the ancients had typically seen a revolution. My Great-Chain-of-Being approach to the Great Chorus initially inclined me to regard the variations of the vision as obvious and inevitable consequences of certain critical changes in the metaphysical tastes and dialectical motives of the leading thinkers of the West.[2] This was the strictly ideas-come-first approach championed by Arthur O. Lovejoy, and for the subject of his magnum opus – which was the rise and fall in popularity of various ontological principles attached to the Homeric image of Zeus' Golden Chain rather than the iconological significance of the chain itself – it was perfectly appropriate. Lovejoy dealt with exceedingly durable ideas (such as universal plenitude) in connection with an inherently static and mechanical image of harmony. I found myself dealing with highly mutable ideas (such as nature and culture) in connection with an image remarkable for its protean metamorphoses and harmonious dynamics.

It was often difficult for me to tell whether the cosmological and cultural principles defended by my authors were shaping their perceptions of the dance or vice versa. Plotinus, for one, imagined the cosmos as a dancer shaping the dance that gave life to dancers who shaped images of life as imagined by the cosmos! Was his unitive vision of the cosmos and the dance a consequence of his metaphysical taste for unity? Or was it in some sense a cause? Unable to share Lovejoy's confidence in the causal primacy of abstract principles, I had to abandon his approach early on and search for one more appropriate to my subject. I was puzzling over Plotinus' approach to the One when the elementary thought struck me (or perhaps flowed down to me from Nous) that visions are not the same as ideas. Because of their grounding in the imagistic thought from which much poetry, especially allegorical poetry, springs, visions are at once broader and more personal than most products of pure philosophical reasoning – though considerably less systematic. They seem to be processes rather than products and are often the only ways by which our groping unsystematic souls can reach metaphysical heights without succumbing to mystical vertigo. Plotinus enjoyed a supremely consoling and intimate vision of the One as the Choragus of Life, but neither he nor anyone else in the Chorus of the Many could claim to have formed a clear idea of its unity. Ideas are grasped as bounded objects of thought. Visions are experienced as boundless subjects *for* thought. As an unbounded vision the cosmic dance is forever changing because the idea of the cosmos and the image of the dance which are its heterogeneous elements are variable in themselves and cannot be fused without friction. In the process of forming a stable compound the dance and the cosmos constantly alter their metaphorical relations and adapt their mimetic correspondences to each other with the result that each may deeply affect our perceptions of the other. Understanding the complex interaction of ideas and images through time in relation to the unifying ideals of a culture and in response to the conflicting ideals of rival cultures is the aim, and hence the approach, of an historian of visions.

Specific variations in the membership, leadership, direction, motivation, visibility, geometrical design, musical accompaniment, architectural setting, and intellectual focus of the Great Chorus depended, I found, on a great many historical circumstances including (as one might expect) the character of the particular dances in or out of fashion at a given period. When pantomimic dancing was the rage at the pagan imperial court, the cosmos was duly hailed as the supreme 'orchēstēs.' When its indecency threatened the moral order of Ecclesia and offended the court of Heaven, the world that had given birth to it was roundly condemned as an 'orchēsis diabolou.' Changes in dance styles and social attitudes to the theatre tended to affect only the superfices of the vision in Antiquity, however, and though these were worth noting en passant like the shifting details observed by Procopius in the carved stoa and glittering tesserae of the Great Church they were not the main piers and abutments of my argument.

I cannot draw any final conclusions here about the profound mutability of the vision since my history of it has many centuries left to cover, but I can state with a measure of confidence (and I hope of wisdom) – largely because the great visionaries in my volume are prepared to back me up on this – that the deep changes in the design and significance of the cosmic dance during the Academic Millennium were precipitated by three intellectual and cultural developments unforeseen by the Athenian Stranger: first, the disintegration of faith in the Old Platonic assumption that eyesight gave rise to insight; second, the disruption of faith in the supremacy of classical Greek culture following the rise of Christianity; and third, the displacement of faith in cosmic harmony from philosophical to poetic grounds of belief. I have listed these in chronological order to suggest that they form a causal sequence. If insight had not been radically dissociated from eyesight during the late Hellenistic era, the luminaries of the new paideia would doubtless have found few educated spectators willing to consider and accept the strange revelations of Christ. And if Christianity had not rocked the philosophical foundations of the old paideia with its chorus of evangelical skeptics and eloquent moralists who had miraculously resolved their doubts about the dance through the illumination of the Holy Spirit, the grounds of belief in cosmic harmony might not have shifted back to poetic revelations and allegorical fantasies – back to the old imaginary world of Harmonia – in the fourth and fifth centuries. The deepest change in the vision resulting from the dissociation of seeing from believing was the total spiritualization and transcendent isolation of the divine centre of the dance, which we saw happening in the Judaeo-Hellenistic and Gnostic phases of its evolution. In the Greek Patristic phase we saw the emergence of the Christian counter-culture reflected in the drastic division of the dance into a spiritual or angelic strophe and a corporeal or demonic antistrophe. The philosopher-poets of the Heliotropic phase and the theurgists of the Late Neoplatonic phase reacted to this anti-Hellenic polarization of the vision by heightening its physical beauty and visual impact with the clarifying, unifying, and vivifying rays of their magical sun.

The pendulum-like alternation between classical and Christian viewpoints in the Late Antique chapters of this volume was not part of my original design. It gathered momentum on its own from the rush of polemical texts that assaulted me from the second century on, reaching its antagonistic extremes in the orations of Julian and Gregory of Nazianzus and settling at last upon an equilibrium point in the serenely unpolemical works of the Areopagite.

A disquieting hiatus in my series of spectators may be discerned between chapters seven and eight – that is, between the Greek Fathers and the scholastic Neoplatonists – where one would expect to find some trace of the Latin Fathers, especially Ambrose and Augustine who form a major link between the hostile circles of the 'Monachi' and the 'Academici.' That these two towering figures saw the Great Chorus from an angle all their own and had strong things to say about it one can readily predict. That their voices would sound like sphery music after the dry whispers of Calcidius (which echo only in the aisles of my argument) one can easily imagine. Why then are they missing from the crowd of Late Antique spectators when a chapter on the Latin Patristic phase of the vision is clearly demanded by the chronological design of the volume? All I can offer as an excuse for their scandalous absence is a prophecy: Ambrose and Augustine will appear in due course, as the favourite ecclesiastical authors of Isidore of Seville, in the first chapter of the next volume of this history. The first volume having traced the Greek steps of the Great Chorus across the Academic Millenium, the second will follow the dance westwards into the barbarian kingdoms across what might be called the Catholic Millennium – from the Latin Fathers in the fourth century to Dante in the fourteenth.

It is perhaps no accident that after testing the foundations and measuring the heights of so many kinds of wisdom, worldly and otherworldly, we should end up contemplating the architecture of a church dedicated to Wisdom herself. In the curious design of Hagia Sophia are fused the two architectural settings that figured most often in classical visions of the cosmic dance: the public theatre with its open visual field where the immanence of divine order could be displayed in the choral artistry of educated citizens; and the mystic temple with its enclosed telesterion where the transcendence of divine order could be celebrated in the choral rites of enraptured initiates. We should expect a classically educated Byzantine spectator like Procopius to see at least a faint reflection of the dance of the Great Chorus in the polished marble of the Great Church, and that is in fact what he saw – a very faint reflection. 'The apsidal columns,' he observed,

Figure 21

From a Byzantine spectator's viewpoint the columns in the curved niches of Hagia Sophia – those above are from the northeast exedra – appeared to give place to each other like dancers in a receding chorus.

do not stand in a straight line but retreat inwards, following the pattern of
the semicircular niches as if they were giving place to one another in a choral
dance [hōsper en chorōi allēlois hypexistamenoi]. ...

(*The Buildings* i.i.35)

The dance has literally retreated into the architecture of the Byzantine vision
of celestial permanence and static hierarchical order, and the wise dancers
who once leapt with the choragus of the fire-breathing stars and whirled
with the Horae from birth to death live on as immortal columns in the
monument – if lifeless things can be called immortal.

A Sophist of the third or fourth century would have used his Dedalian
skills to turn marble into flesh and stillness into fantastic motion. Procopius
imagined the metamorphosis in reverse. All the old Greek views of the dance
as a comprehensible representation of cosmic order – optimistic views, for
the most part – seem far removed from the Byzantine Sophist's rather pessimistic and ironical view of the effect of the dancing columns, golden
ceilings, patterned pavements, and other interior decorations of Hagia Sophia
on its contemplative spectators:

And so the vision changes, swiftly, suddenly, constantly, leaving the spectator
utterly unable to choose which detail he should admire more than all the
others. Why, even those who observe it carefully, though they turn their
attention to every side and look upon every detail with knitted brows, are
still unable to understand the craftsmanship that went into it! And so they
exit from it in a state verging on panic, feeling helpless and overwhelmed by
the vision.

(*The Buildings* i.i.48–9)

The same sort of panicky bewilderment was also experienced no doubt by
contemplative spectators who tried to see their way through the confusing
universe of hypostatic causes, invisible luminaries, and abstract correspondences created by Byzantine theologians in the wake of Proclus and Pseudo-
Dionysius. By the mid-sixth century they had expanded the vision of the
Great Chorus as far as the limits of Greek rationalism would allow. Craftsmanship that cannot be understood might as well be chaos. The cosmic
dance ceased to excite their visual imaginations (as did the cosmos) when it
lost its comprehensible form and unifying dynamism and became merely a
chaos of lovely details floating through perilous space. And so the first
millennium of its evolution drew to a close just when the theatres and temples
of the old Greco-Roman world were falling into ruins and supplying Hagia
Sophia with its chorus of columns.

The Great Church has no other chorus to show us. Let us exit from it then with Procopius' bewildered spectators, alarmed perhaps by its magnitude but not panic-stricken. The Great Chorus will spring to life again at the other end of the Mediterranean where a new crowd of spectators is already gathering.

Notes

Foreword

1 George Sylvester Viereck, interviewer, 'What Life Means to Einstein,' *Saturday Evening Post* 202: 17 (26 October 1929), 117

2 *Laws* II 656a–657b. Plato seems to have based his argument entirely on evidence drawn from the highly stylized (and inevitably static) representations of dancers and singers in Egyptian painting and sculpture. Such evidence has recently been considered – in an unphilosophical light – by Irena Lexová, *Ancient Egyptian Dances*, trans K. Haltmar (Praha: Oriental Institute 1935), 36–42.

3 See *The Pyramid Texts* vols 1–4, trans and comm Samuel A.B. Mercer (New York: Longmans, Green and Co 1952); vol 1, 80a, 863a, 884a, 1005a, 1947a, 1974a, 1189a. The two passages of Old Kingdom poetry cited in my discussion of Egyptian mortuary dances are drawn from Mercer's translation. For the sake of clarity I have added to his text a few explanatory notes in square brackets and substituted the name Pepi or Merenrēʿ where Mercer has 'N.' (his abbreviation for the name of the pharaoh). His commentary on Utterances 419 and 466, vol 2, pp 371–5, 450–2, guided my interpretation of these passages.

4 For a detailed discussion of the etymology of this evocative word, see Mercer, *The Pyramid Texts* vol 4, pp 33–6.

5 See Mercer, *The Pyramid Texts* vol 1, 1004b–1005a, p 177, and 2, pp 509–10. See also vol 1, 1508c (star as ferryman); 1216a–c (stars as swallows); and 141a (star as escort and companion).

6 On Nut and Nun, see Mercer, *The Pyramid Texts* vol 4, excursus XIV, pp 60–5.

7 Thorkild Jacobsen, trans, *The Treasures of Darkness: A History of Mesopotamian Religion* (New Haven and London: Yale University Press 1976), 170; see also Alexander Heidel, trans, *The Babylonian Genesis* (Chicago and London: University of Chicago Press 1942; 2nd ed 1951), 19.

8 Werner Jaeger, *Paideia: The Ideals of Greek Culture*, trans Gilbert Highet (New York: Oxford University Press 1939, 1945), vol 1, 248

9 *Laws* 11 654b

10 The civic and artistic aims of the classical Greek chorus have been clearly defined by William Mullen in *Choreia: Pindar and Dance* (Princeton, NJ: Princeton University Press 1982), 46–89. The modern medical senses of the classical noun in Mullen's title (which was suggested to him by Professor R.P. Winnington-Ingram) will not, I am sure, distress the professional classicists for whom his specialized work – a speculative statistical analysis of certain metrical patterns in the triadic odes of Pindar and Bacchylides – was evidently written. For them, no doubt, the ancient term still means what it originally meant.

11 Erich Auerbach, *Mimesis: The Representation of Reality in Western Literature*, trans Willard R. Trask (Princeton: Princeton University Press 1953), 556

1 Chorus and Cosmos

1 Unless otherwise noted, all translations from primary sources in this study are my own.

2 For details concerning the excavations at Eleusis and the ritual significance of the Kallichoron, I have consulted George E. Mylonas, *Eleusis and the Eleusinian Mysteries* (Princeton: Princeton University Press 1961), 97–9; and N.J. Richardson, ed, *The Homeric Hymn to Demeter* (Oxford: Clarendon Press 1974), 326–8.

3 This outline and subsequent descriptions of Greek theatrical dance in this study could not have been written without the following works: Lillian B. Lawler's *The Dance in Ancient Greece* (Seattle and Washington: University of Washington Press 1964; Washington Paperback edition 1967), 74–91, and *The Dance of the Ancient Greek Theatre* (Iowa City: University of Iowa Press 1964), 11–62; Maurice Emmanuel's *Essai sur l'orchestique grecque* (Paris: Hachette 1865), 285 ff; Germaine Prudhommeau's *La danse grecque antique* vol 1 (Paris: Editions du Centre National de la Recherche Scientifique 1965), 285, 330–5; Evanghélos Moutsopoulos' *La musique dans l'oeuvre de Platon* (Paris: Presses Universitaires de France 1959), 123, 134–5; Sir Arthur Pickard-Cambridge's *The Dramatic Festivals of Athens*, 2nd ed revised by John Gould and D.M. Lewis (Oxford: Clarendon Press 1968), 232–57; and William Mullen's *Choreia: Pindar and Dance* (Princeton, NJ: Princeton University Press 1982), 3–89.

4 The anthropological evidence for the astronomical symbolism of the circle

dance among native tribes in Africa, Australia, and South America has been
summarized by Curt Sachs in his *World History of the Dance*, trans Bessie
Schönberg (New York: W.W. Norton 1965; 1st ed 1937), 124–31.

5 Andreas and Joannes Duncan, eds, *Euripidis Opera omnia* vol 1 (London:
Ricardus Priestley 1821), 93–4. My interpretation of this much-debated passage is indebted to Lillian B. Lawler, 'Cosmic Dance and Dithyramb,' *Studies
in Honor of Ullman* (St Louis: *Classical Bulletin*, St Louis University 1960),
12–16. The scholiast's comments concern the woeful strophe, antistrophe, and
epode on 'relentless fate' sung by the chorus of captive Trojan women in
Hecuba 643–7.

6 Since most ancient sources on Pythagoreanism (both as a philosophy and as a
religious movement) were written long after Plato's death, Presocratic Pythagorean cosmology remains a highly conjectural subject. I have followed here
the learned conjectures and conclusions of Walter Burkert, *Lore and Science in
Ancient Pythagoreanism*, trans Edwin L. Minar, Jr (Cambridge, Mass: Harvard University Press 1972), 350–1; W.K.C. Guthrie, *A History of Greek Philosophy* vol 1 (Cambridge: Cambridge University Press 1962), 205–7, 295–301;
G.S. Kirk and J.E. Raven, *The Presocratic Philosophers* (Cambridge: Cambridge University Press 1957), 217–62; and Kathi Meyer-Baer, *Music of the
Spheres and the Dance of Death* (Princeton: Princeton University Press 1970),
70–5.

7 My outline of Petron's world-view is indebted to Kathleen Freeman, *The Pre-
Socratic Philosophers: A Companion to Diels, Fragmente der Vorsokratiker*
(Oxford: Basil Blackwell 1946), 84.

8 Plato's ambiguous participle 'illomenēn' (winding) has puzzled many commen-
tators over the centuries. The simplest interpretation of it is offered by F.M.
Cornford in *Plato's Cosmology* (London: Kegan Paul, Trench, Trübner and
Co 1937), 120–34, and this is what I have followed in the present study. For a
summary of other interpretations, both ancient and modern, see A.E. Taylor,
A Commentary on Plato's Timaeus (Oxford: Clarendon Press 1928), 226–39.

2 The Leap of the Corybant

1 The Myth of the Cave is recounted and explained in the seventh book of Plato's *Republic*, 514a–518b and 532a–c. No 'Creator' or 'Great Ruler' (in a Philonic sense) figures, of course, in the original Platonic version of this myth.

2 Edgar Wind in *Pagan Mysteries in the Renaissance* (London: Faber and Faber
1967), 26–8, has traced the ethical interpretation of the dance of the Graces to
the Greek Stoic Chrysippus (fl 3rd c BC) who, in a treatise now lost but perhaps known to Philo, associated the three goddesses with the triple act of receiving, accepting, and returning favours. This treatise was cited by Philo's
contemporary, the Roman Stoic Seneca, who transmitted Chrysippus' inter-

pretation of 'ille consertis manibus in se redeuntium chorus' – 'that choral dance formed by the interlocking hands of the goddesses as they turn round each other' (*De beneficiis* 1.iii) – to post-classical Europe. Wind does not mention Philo's Mosaic variation of the image.

3 The Corybants of Phrygia were often identified in Antiquity with the Curetes of Crete (the drum-beating guardians of the infant Zeus). The confusion between their originally distinct choruses was due in large part to the early identification of the Phrygian mother-goddess Cybele with Zeus' mother Rhea. For more on the dance of the Corybants and Curetes, see the present volume, chapter 4, pp 153–4, and chapter 6, pp 299–305.

4 A comprehensive study of Philo's bacchic imagery may be found in Hans Lewy's *Sobria ebrietas* (Giessen: Alfred Töpelmann 1929), 43 ff.

5 So W.O.E. Oesterley concluded in *The Sacred Dance: A Study in Comparative Folklore* (Cambridge: Cambridge University Press 1923), 27 and 54. His conclusion pertains both to religious dances mentioned in the Old Testament and to those described in ancient Greek and Latin sources.

3 Chorus and Charis

1 The standard English translation of the Hymn of Jesus is by M.R. James, *The Apocryphal New Testament* (Oxford: Clarendon Press 1924), 253–4. I have followed James in rendering the Hymn into English free verse but have avoided his archaic biblical style and altered his lineation of section 96 from prose to verse (since this seems to be as much a part of the Hymn as sections 94 and 95).

2 *Epistola* CCXXXVII, ed D.A.B. Caillau, in *Sancti Aurelii Augustini Opera omnia* vol 41 (Paris: Parent-Desbarres 1860), 318, 324, 328

3 Joannes Dominicus Mansi, ed, *Sacrorum conciliorum nova et amplissima collectio* vol 13 (Florentiae: Expensis Antonii Zatta 1767), cols 169–74. For various other official condemnations of the Acts of John in Late Antiquity, see Elaine Pagels, *The Gnostic Gospels* (New York: Random House 1979), 75, and 'To the Universe Belongs the Dancer,' *Parabola* 4:2 (1979), 7–9.

4 For a detailed summary of the patristic evidence concerning Valentinian Gnosticism, see Werner Foerster, *Gnosis: A Selection of Gnostic Texts* vol 1, trans R. McL. Wilson (Oxford: Clarendon Press 1972), 121–7. As Elaine Pagels has rightly insisted in *The Gnostic Gospels*, pp xviii–xix, Irenaeus is flagrantly biased against the Valentinians and must be read with extreme caution as a source for their doctrines. With her warning in mind I have only cited passages from Irenaeus in which exposition seems to predominate over exposé.

5 So Jean Doresse concluded in *The Secret Books of the Egyptian Gnostics* (New York: Viking 1958; 2nd ed 1960), 28 n73.

6 *Adumbrationes in epistolam Ioannis* I, cap 1.i, ed Gulielmus Dindorfius, in *Clementis Alexandrini Opera* vol 3 (Oxford: Clarendon Press 1869), 485

7 For the *Apocryphon of John* (not to be confused with the apocryphal Acts of John), see Robert Haardt, *Gnosis: Character and Testimony*, trans J.F. Hendry (Leiden: E.J. Brill 1971), 193; for the *Poimandres*, see Walter Scott, ed, *Hermetica* vol 1 (Oxford: Clarendon Press 1924), Libellus 1.9, p 118.

8 So Max Pulver concluded in 'Jesus' Round Dance and Crucifixion According to the Acts of St. John,' *The Mysteries: Papers from the Eranos Yearbooks*, Bollingen Series XXX.2 (New York: Pantheon Books 1955), 183. Pulver's study is chiefly valuable for drawing attention to the Gnostic significance of several divine names in the Hymn (eg 'Grace,' 'Spirit,' 'Holy One') which may, to a modern reader, seem purely Christian in reference.

9 Clement denounced the 'peculiar dogmas' of the Docetists in *Stromateis* ('Miscellanies') VII xvii, ed Gulielmus Dindorfius, *Clementis Alexandrini Opera* vol 3, p 347.

10 In the second-century *Discourse on the Eighth and Ninth*, trans James Brashler, Peter A. Dirkse, and Douglas M. Parrott, *The Nag Hammadi Library in English* (San Francisco: Harper and Row 1977), 295, an ecstatic disciple of Hermes Trismegistus exclaims: 'Father Trismegistus! What shall I say? We have received this light. And I myself see this same vision in you. And I see the eighth [heaven] and the souls that are in it and the angels singing a hymn to the ninth and its powers. And I see him who has the power of them all, creating those ⟨that are⟩ in the spirit.' His teacher instructs him to participate in the choral hymn of the eternal spirits within his mind, through introspective prayer, but otherwise to keep silent about his divine vision until he has taken leave of his body.

11 Modern interpreters of the Hymn have distorted its meaning by reading it in isolation from the story of John's initiation into Docetism. *In Religious Dances in the Christian Church and in Popular Medicine*, trans E. Classen (London: George Allen and Unwin 1952), 16, E.L. Backman comments that the dancing disciples must consider 'that Jesus wishes to share the sufferings of mankind.' This misses the point of the Hymn entirely. A Docetic Christ cannot share the sufferings of mankind since he never truly becomes a man. As a foreshadowing of his illusory Crucifixion the dance teaches the disciples to consider exactly the opposite, ie, the mysterious fact that their Redeemer will escape the sufferings of mankind. G.R.S. Mead, in 'The Sacred Dance of Jesus,' *The Quest* vol 2 (October 1910), 66, makes a similar error by regarding the dance as 'the earliest Passion-play in Christendom.' Mead fails to consider the Docetic Christ's own commentary on his Hymn, that all his utterances, including his statements about suffering, were uttered in jest. The dance does not enact Christ's Passion but rather his miraculous escape from the ignominy of death.

12 Clement practised what he preached, making ample use of the 'logos protrepōn' in the composition of his *Protreptikos* or 'Exhortation' (c 190–c 211 AD).

13 See for example Hymn 50 ('To Lysios'), line 2, in *Orphica*, ed Eugenius Abel (Lipsiae: G. Freytag 1885), 84.

14 This passage was brought to my attention by Hugo Rahner in 'The Heavenly Dance,' *Man at Play* ch 4, trans Brian Battershaw and Edward Quinn (London: Burns and Oates 1965), 77.

4 Holding the Pose

1 On the 'logos protrepōn,' see *Stromateis* VII.45; Clement's hortatory rhetoric is discussed in the third chapter of the present volume, p 129. English renderings of Plotinus often make his philosophical prose sound like religious exhortation. The standard complete English translation of the *Enneads* is by Stephen Mackenna, revised by B.S. Page (London: Faber and Faber 1956). I have departed from their readings in many passages and have toned down their quasireligious rhetoric for the sake of plainness and clarity.

2 The Valentinians and the Sethians are the two sects usually identified as the 'Gnōstikoi' against whom Plotinus directed his polemical fire. On the evidence supporting both identifications and the difficulties involved in distinguishing Valentinian from Sethian Gnosticism in the third century, see Henri-Charles Puech, 'Plotin et les Gnostiques,' *Les sources de Plotin*, Entretiens Hardt vol 5 (Geneva: Vandoeuvres-Genève 1960), 159–74.

3 The treatise ascribed to Zostrianus has been translated by John H. Siebur, and that ascribed to Allogenes by John D. Turner and Orval S. Wintermute, in *The Nag Hammadi Library in English* (San Francisco: Harper and Row 1977), 369–93 and 444–52. No treatise ascribed to Messos (whom Porphyry also mentions in his list of Gnostic authors in the *Vita Plotini* 16) appears in the Nag Hammadi Library, but the name Messos is given to the son of Allogenes in the *Allogenes*, p 445. Similarly no treatise ascribed to Zoroaster (also mentioned by Porphyry) has come to light at Nag Hammadi, but the name Zoroaster appears at the end of the *Zostrianus*, p 393, and a 'book of Zoroaster' is mentioned in the *Apocryphon of John*, p 109.

4 I have omitted the most dissident of all the groups of dissenting Hellenistic philosophers, the Skeptics, from this list (and from this chapter) for three reasons: first, because the extant fragments of the writings of the early Skeptics yield not a single reference to the cosmic dance; second, because only one brief reference to the 'asterōn eutaktous tinas choreias' appears in the voluminous writings of the last great Skeptic polemicist Sextus Empiricus (*Adversus mathematicos* ix.27, which appears to be a quotation from Aristotle's *De philosophia*, fr 12b); and third, because I shall consider the Skeptical Spectator's vision of the world-chorus – or refusal to believe in that vision – in chapter 7 of this volume.

5 I have been guided through the Garden by A.A. Long, *Hellenistic Philosophy: Stoics, Epicureans, Sceptics* (New York: Scribner 1974); J.M. Rist, *Epicurus: An Introduction* (Cambridge: Cambridge University Press 1972); and Cyril Bailey, *The Greek Atomists and Epicurus* (New York: Russel and Russel 1964). The annotations in Bailey's *Epicurus: The Extant Remains* (Oxford: Clarendon Press 1926), particularly on pp 383–4, have aided my understanding of Vatican Fragment LII.

6 *De rerum natura* II 129, 573–4, and 118. That Plotinus knew Lucretius' poem and echoed it several times in the *Enneads* has been demonstrated by V. Cilento in his 'Mito e poesia nelle Enneadi di Plotino,' *Les sources de Plotin*, Entretiens Hardt vol 5, pp 303–5.

7 The loss of most of the Posidonian corpus has made the precise assessment of Plotinus' debt to Posidonius a matter of ticklish speculation and a question for heated debate. R.E. Witt in 'Plotinus and Posidonius,' *Classical Quarterly* 24 (1930), 200–1, argued that the occurrence of the metaphor of the world-chorus in both authors was evidence of their close intellectual ties, and that Posidonius was the obvious source of 'certain important conceptions' (eg cosmic sympathy) found in the *Enneads*. The shakiness of these conclusions has rightly been pointed out by Andreas Graesner in *Plotinus and the Stoics: A Preliminary Study* (Leiden: E.J. Brill 1972), 78–81.

8 This definition is drawn from Diogenes Laertius' biography of Zeno in *The Lives and Opinions of Eminent Philosophers* (VII.156). My summary of Stoic physics and ethics owes much to the following modern guides to the wisdom of the Porch: A.A. Long, *Hellenistic Philosophy* (New York: Scribner 1974); J.M. Rist, *Stoic Philosophy* (Cambridge: Cambridge University Press 1969) and *Plotinus: The Road to Reality* (Cambridge: Cambridge University Press 1977), particularly chapter 7, pp 84–102, on the difference between the Stoic and Plotinian concepts of logos; R.D. Hicks, *Stoic and Epicurean* (New York: Russell and Russell 1962); and E. Vernon Arnold, *Roman Stoicism* (Cambridge: Cambridge University Press 1911).

9 As Dr R. Ferwerda correctly notes in *La signification des images et des métaphores dans la pensée de Plotin* (Groningen: J.B. Wolters 1965), 185, Plotinus nowhere speaks of the activity of dancing as an end in itself and does not follow Cicero in comparing the self-sufficiency or self-containment of the dance to that of the art of wisdom. Yet Pierre Hadot, in 'Etre, vie, pensée chez Plotin et avant Plotin,' *Les sources de Plotin*, Entretiens Hardt vol 5, pp 138–9, has remarked in reference to *Ennead* 3.2.16: 'La vie ne réalise pas un plan préetabli par une intelligence; loin de copier des idées pré-existantes, c'est elle qui crée les formes intelligibles. Ainsi le danseur: c'est en son activité même que réside sa fin.' Ferwerda is surely correct in criticizing Hadot for imposing too Stoic an interpretation on the Plotinian image of the self-shaping 'orchēstēs.'

10 This classification of unities has been drawn from Sextus Empiricus, *Adversus*

mathematicos IX.78. Willy Theiler, in *Die Vorbereitung des Neuplatonismus* (Berlin: Weidmannsche Buchhandlung 1930), 97–8, has argued that the classification is Posidonian in origin. For a detailed discussion of the objections to this derivation, see Andreas Graesner, *Plotinus and the Stoics*, pp 72–5. Graesner traces the first and third categories of unity back to Chrysippus.

11 *Oeconomicus* VIII.3: 'For a chorus is a collection of human beings. But when each of its members does what he chooses a certain confusion is apparent, and watching it is unpleasant. But when the members act and sing in an orderly fashion, then those same men at once seem worth seeing and worth hearing.'

12 Donald R. Dudley, in *A History of Cynicism* (London: Methuen 1937; rpt New York: Gordon Press 1974), 66, has translated Bion's famous dictum on the drama of life as follows: 'Just as the good actor plays with skill the Prologue, the middle portion, and the dénouement of a play, so should a good man play well the beginning, the middle, and the end of life.' My summary of the historical development of Cynicism is drawn from chapters 1–9 of Dudley's comprehensive study.

13 *Icaromenippus* 27. Drunken dancing 'in imitation of Pans, Sileni, and Satyrs' was sharply distinguished by the Athenian Stranger (*Laws* VII 815c) from the peaceful choreiai which epitomized the education of law-abiding citizens in his ideal state.

14 *Discourses* III xxii.45–50. For a full discussion of this discourse 'On the Calling of a Cynic' in the context of second-century Cynicism and Stoicism, see Donald R. Dudley, *A History of Cynicism*, pp 190–8.

15 Jung claims to have derived his term 'archetype' from Philo and the Hermetic authors (along with St Augustine and Pseudo-Dionysius) in his essay 'Archetypes of the Collective Unconscious,' *The Collected Works of C.G. Jung* vol 9, pt 1, trans R.F.C. Hull (London: Routledge and Kegan Paul 1959), 4–5.

16 Daniel H.H. Ingalls, trans, *An Anthology of Sanskrit Court Poetry: Vidyākara's 'Subhāṣitaratnakoṣa,'* Harvard Oriental Series vol 44 (Cambridge, Mass: Harvard University Press 1965), 79–80

17 For iconographical information on Shiva Nataraja and the temple of Chidambaram, I have relied on C. Sivaramamurti's *Nataraja in Art, Thought, and Literature* (New Delhi: Publications Division, Ministry of Information and Broadcasting, Government of India 1974), 383–5, and on J.M. Somasundaram Pillai's *Śiva Nataraja: the Cosmic Dancer in Chid-Ambaram* (Annamalainagar: J.M. Somasundaram 1970), particularly 'The Dance of Shiva' by A.K. Coomaraswamy, pp 30–41.

18 Manomohan Ghosh, trans, *Bharata Muni: The Nātyaśāstra* vol 1, ch IX 4–210 (Calcutta: Granthalaya Private Limited 1967), 172–93. In ch IV 253–64, Bharata states that Shiva revealed his divine dance to Tandu, an unidentified and perhaps mythical sage, in whose honour the dance is known as the 'tandava'; see Ghosh, vol 1, pp 66–7.

19 I have drawn the notion of collective consciousness (or the 'collective conscious') from the following wry comment on the popularization of Jungian psychology in Owen Barfield's *Saving the Appearances* (New York: Harcourt Brace Jovanovich 1965), 135: 'I believe it will seem very strange to the historian of the future, that a literal-minded generation began to accept the actuality of a 'collective unconscious' before it could even admit the possibility of a 'collective conscious' – in the shape of the phenomenal world.'

20 On the shamanistic significance of the choral round, see Curt Sachs, *World History of the Dance*, trans Bessie Schönberg (New York: W.W. Norton 1937), 144–51.

21 Before his exile Dio had been the critic and later the disciple of a Roman Stoic by the name of Musonius. That his years as a Cynic did little to undermine his youthful faith in the precepts of the Porch is attested by the recurrence of Stoic themes and metaphors in all the philosophical orations he composed after his return from exile. As Louis François noted in his *Essai sur Dion Chrysostome* (Paris: Librairie Delagrave 1921), 202–4, Dio's synthesis of Stoic theology, Cynic ethics, and Socratic dialectic is reminiscent of the eclectic philosophy of Epictetus (who was also a pupil of Musonius).

22 In his essay 'Concerning Mandala Symbolism,' Jung remarked: 'The goal of contemplating the processes depicted in the mandala is that the yogi shall become inwardly aware of the deity. Through contemplation, he recognizes himself as God again, and thus returns from the illusion of individual existence into the universal totality of the divine state. As I have said, mandala means "circle." '; Hull, trans, *The Collected Works of C.G. Jung* vol 2, pt 1, p 357.

23 M.M. Kashinath Vasudev Abhyankar and Jayadev Mohanlal Shukla, trans, *Patañjali's Vyākaraṇa-Mahābhāṣya-(Navāhnikī) (Poona: Cultural Research and Publications Department of Sanskrit Vidya Parisaṁsthā 1969)*, 125–6. For the legend of Shiva's revelation of grammatical rules to Panini, see Somadeva's *Kathā-Sarit-Sāgara* (written in the eleventh century AD), translated and annotated by C.H. Tawney and N.M. Penzer in *The Ocean of Story* vol 1 (Delhi: Motilal Banarsidass 1924), 31–2. On the philosophical significance of Shiva as Lord of the Dance and Lord of Speech, see Alain Daniélou, *Hindu Polytheism* (London: Routledge and Kegan Paul 1964), 119–20.

5 Chorus in Chaos

1 I have translated the verses from Hesiod from the Greek rather than from Calcidius' Latin version of them, which reads: 'Prima quidem haec caligo, dehinc post terra creata est / Spirantium sedes firmissima pectore vasto.' (Indeed, the misty darkness was created first, and immediately thereafter the broadbreasted earth, the very secure seat of living creatures.) Calcidius' rendering captures the general sense of the original but noticeably reduces the theological

significance of the lines. Chaos becomes an atmospheric condition; Gaia a planet; and the immortal inhabitants of Gaia simply 'creatures who live and breathe.' This adaptation of the lines is in keeping with the commentator's subsequent appeal to Hesiod's authority as a physicist and astronomer.

2 See *Bernardus Silvestris: Cosmographia*, ed Peter Dronke (Leiden: E.J. Brill 1978), *Megacosmus* I, lines 1, 8 etc, p 7 ff; *Magistri Alani Enchiridion de planctu Nature*, ed Nikolaus M. Häring, *Studi Medievali* III (Spoleto: Centro Italiano di Studi sull' Alto Medioevo 1978), II.96–7, p 812; *Dante Alighieri: Paradiso, The Divine Comedy* vol III, trans Charles S. Singleton, Bollingen Series LXXX (Princeton: Princeton University Press 1975), canto IV, line 49.

3 The image of the dance in *Timaeus* 40d is noticed but not explicated by A.E. Taylor in *A Commentary on Plato's Timaeus* (Oxford: Clarendon Press 1928), 240; it is virtually ignored by F.M. Cornford in *Plato's Cosmology* (New York: Harcourt, Brace and Co 1937), 185. Late Antique commentators on the *Timaeus* did not assume (as do Taylor and Cornford) that the philosophical implications of Plato's vision of the cosmic dance are self-evident.

4 Theon's discussion of the principal celestial circles (which is probably the basis for Calcidius' astronomical interpretation of the image of the 'caelestis chorea' in LXV–LXVI and CXXIV) may be found in *Theonis smyrnaei philosophi platonici Expositio rerum mathematicarum ad legendum Platonem utilium*, ed Eduardus Hiller (Lipsiae: B.G. Teubner 1878), 129–31. Though Theon has much to say about the music of the spheres (see pp 10–25), he does not use the word 'choreia' or any of its relatives to denote cosmic harmony. His apparent indifference to the vision of the cosmic dance may reflect a similar attitude on the part of Adrastus of Aphrodisias, the Peripatetic commentator from whom he derived most of the information in his chapters on mathematics and harmony.

5 The impressive array of evidence Waszink has marshalled in support of his controversial thesis (none of it conclusive) is set forth on pp lxviii–lxxxii of the introduction to his monumental edition *Timaeus a Calcidio translatus commentarioque instructus* (London and Leiden: Warburg Institute and E.J. Brill 1962; 2nd ed 1975).

6 For a detailed summary of the objections to Waszink's thesis that Calcidius wrote in the late fourth century under Porphyrian influence, see John Dillon, *The Middle Platonists* (Ithaca, NY: Cornell University Press 1977), 401–4. For support of Dillon's views on Calcidius, see John M. Rist, 'Basil's "Neoplatonism": Its Background and Nature,' in volume 1 of *Basil of Caesarea: Christian, Humanist, Ascetic*, ed Paul Jonathan Fedwick (Toronto: Pontifical Institute of Mediaeval Studies 1981), 151–4. I am indebted to Rist (p 157) for the suggestion that Calcidian Platonism is reflected in Constantine's *Oration to the Assembly of the Saints*.

7 The roots of Plutarch's dualistic cosmology have been traced by John Dillon in *The Middle Platonists*, pp 202–3, to Plato's postulation of the existence of

an irrational World-Soul (*Laws* x 896d ff) and to Zoroastrian theology (which Plutarch praises in his treatise *De Iside et Osiride* 396e).

8 Cicero, the first known translator of the *Timaeus* into Latin, effectively eliminated the image of the dance from his version of the dialogue by rendering the phrase 'choreias de toutōn autōn' (40d) as 'lusiones autem deorum'; see *M. Tulli Ciceronis Timaeus*, ed Franciscus Pini (Milan: Mondadori 1965), section 37, p 50. The noun 'lusio' (from the verb 'ludere,' 'to play') generally meant 'game' or 'sport' and specifically 'ball-game.' Dancing was no doubt included in the range of amusements covered by these two words, but they were not even vaguely synonymous with the Greek words 'choreia' and 'choreuein' unless modified by some such phrase as 'in numerum' (rhythmically). In his efforts to demonstrate that Latin could be as subtle and copious a medium for philosophical discourse as Greek, Cicero may have been inclined to choose 'lusio' because it was a native Latin word and to reject 'chorea' because it was a poetic loan word from Greek. Then again, being a sage and serious Roman moralist and consequently no great aficionado of the dance, Cicero may have found the notion of dancing gods offensive or the image of dancing stars ridiculous.

9 For instance, in the *Codex Riccardianus* 139 (eleventh or twelfth century) appears the following marginal ascription: 'Osio episcopo hispaniae conflator huius operis archidiaconus.' (The author of this work was an archdeacon of Bishop Osius of Spain.) For a complete list of manuscripts identifying Calcidius' Osius with the Spanish bishop, see J.H. Waszink, ed, *Timaeus a Calcidio translatus*, p x. All medieval scribal evidence linking Calcidius with Ossius of Cordova is of course dismissed by Waszink as too late to be of any value.

10 I am indebted throughout this section to Victor C. De Clercq, whose magisterial biography *Ossius of Cordova* (Washington DC: Catholic University of America Press 1954) sheds considerable light on the Bishop's intellectual training, diplomatic career, and complex association with Constantine. De Clercq presents a spirited defence of the medieval scribal testimony linking Calcidius with Ossius of Cordova (pp 69–75) and accepts the plausibility of the hypothesis that the increase of Latin translations in the first decades of the fourth century was due in some measure to Constantine's interest in Greek literature and Platonic philosophy (pp 62–3). This hypothesis was advanced by Hans von Schönebeck in *Beiträge zur Religionspolitik des Maxentius und Constantin* (Leipzig: Dieterich 1939), 83.

11 See A. Kurfess, 'Platos Timaeus in Kaiser Konstantins Rede an die Heilige Versammlung,' *Zeitschrift für die neutestamentliche Wissenschaft und die Kunde der älteren Kirche* 19 (1919–20), 72–81.

12 This edict is recorded by the Byzantine historian Socrates Scholasticus (d 450 AD) in his *Historia ecclesiastica* I.ix.31, ed W. Reading (1720), repr J.P. Migne, *Patrologia Graeca* vol 67 (Paris: Migne 1859), col 87.

13 H.A. Drake's *In Praise of Constantine: A Historical Study and New Translation of Eusebius' Tricennial Orations* (Berkeley and Los Angeles: University of
California Press 1976) has been my model both for translation and for interpretation of the passages pertaining to the cosmic dance in Eusebius' *In laudibus Constantini*. Particularly instructive are Drake's remarks on the ambiguity
of religious vocabulary in the fourth century (pp 52–3) and his discussion of
Constantine's role as mediator between Christians and pagans (pp 61–79).

14 I owe the notion of a 'shared vocabulary' of theological terms, divine epithets,
and mystical idioms comprehensible to both pagans and Christians, ie, a 'lingua franca' of religious phraseology and symbolism, to H.A. Drake, *In Praise
of Constantine*, p 54. Drake derived the concept from E.R. Goodenough,
Jewish Symbols in the Greco-Roman Period (Princeton, NJ: Princeton University Press 1954), vol 4, p 37. The choreia topos certainly belonged to this lingua franca.

6 Living Statues

1 I have borrowed the term 'philarchaios' from the title of a treatise by Longinus mentioned by Porphyry in *Vita Plotini* 14. When this treatise was read to
Plotinus he remarked rather haughtily: 'Longinus is a lover of learning [philol-
ogos] but he is certainly not a lover of wisdom [philosophos].' The treatise has
not survived.

2 I have based my translation of passages from Julian on the text provided by
Wilmer Cave Wright in *The Works of the Emperor Julian* vols 1–3 (London:
Wm Heinemann 1913 and 1923). When he referred disdainfully to the 'poetic
Muse' in *Hymn to King Helios* 136d, *Works* vol 1, p 370, Julian did not imply
that the philosophical Muses worshipped by the Iamblichan theologians differed in nature or function from the Muses of Homer and Hesiod. He simply
wished to contrast their divine sources of inspiration with the purely fictitious
spirits invoked by frivolous love-poets and Sophists. Alexinus' syllogism is
cited by Sextus Empiricus in his Skeptical polemic *Adversus dogmaticos* iii.108
(= *Adversus mathematicos* ix.108), *Sextus Empiricus* vol III, ed and trans R.G.
Bury (London: Wm Heinemann 1960), 60. The concept of the poetic universe
is defended by Aristides Quintilianus in his *De musica* III.20, ed R.P. Winnington-Ingram (Lipsiae: B.G. Teubner 1963). The phrase 'carmen universita-
tis,' 'poem of the universe,' is used by Augustine in his *De musica* VI.29, ed
J.-P. Migne, *PL* vol 32 (Paris: Migne 1845), col 1179.

3 I have based my translation of excerpts from this work on *Iamblichi De vita
pythagorica*, ed Augustus Nauck (St Petersburg 1884; rpt Amsterdam: Hak-
kert 1965). Porphyry also wrote a biography of Pythagoras, and like Iamblichus included orchestic dancing among the therapeutic arts taught by the
divine sage to his original disciples; see *Vita Pythagorae* 32, in *Porphyrii philo-*

sophi platonici Opuscula selecta, ed Augustus Nauck (Lipsiae: B.G. Teubner 1886), 34. In *De antro nympharum* 8, *Opuscula selecta,* p 61, Porphyry claimed that the Pythagoreans were the first to perceive Calypso's cave as an allegorical image of the cosmos.

4 *Descriptiones* 2.2, 2.5, and 9.3, ed and trans Arthur Fairbanks, *Philostratus: Imagines; Callistratus: Descriptiones* (London: Wm Heinemann 1960), 380, 384, and 408. The translations from Callistratus are my own. Dedalus' ability to animate statues is also mentioned by Euripides in *Hecuba* 383, ed and trans Arthur S. Way, *Euripides* vol 1 (London: Wm Heinemann 1959), 312; and by Lucian in *Philopseudes* 19, ed and trans A.M. Harmon, *Lucian* vol 3 (London: Wm Heinemann 1960), 351.

5 See chapter 7 of this volume, pp 346, 403–4; cf the metaphorical usage of the noun 'lugisma,' chapter 7, n 3, pp 549–50.

6 *De nuptiis Philologiae et Mercurii* III.222. I have based my translation of this and all subsequent passages from the *De nuptiis* on the text edited by Adolfus Dick in *Martianus Capella* (Lipsiae: B.G. Teubner 1925). The complex significance of the terms 'schēma' and 'figura' has been discussed by Erich Auerbach in 'Figura,' the first essay in his *Scenes from the Drama of European Literature* (New York: Meridian Books 1959), 11–76. 'But since in the learned Greek terminology ... ,' notes Auerbach, p 15, *'schēma* was widely used in the sense of "outward shape," *figura* was always used for this purpose in Latin. Thus side by side with the original plastic signification and overshadowing it, there appeared a far more general concept of grammatical, rhetorical, logical, mathematical – and later even of musical and choreographic – form.'

7 My biographical sketch of Julian is based on Robert Browning's *The Emperor Julian* (Berkeley and Los Angeles: University of California Press 1976) and G.W. Bowersock's *Julian the Apostate* (London: Duckworth 1978). I have followed their lead in ascribing the Neoplatonic treatise *On the Gods and the Universe* to Salutius Secundus rather than Flavius Sallustius. On the authorship of the treatise, see Bowersock, appendix 3, p 125.

8 *Epistle* 23 ('To Ecdicius, Prefect of Egypt'), *Works* vol 3, pp 72–4. This letter was written from Constantinople in January of 362.

9 *Hymn to King Helios* 131a, *Works* vol 1, p 354.

10 *Hymn to King Helios* 137b, *Works* vol 1, p 371.

11 I have based my schematic outline of the Iamblichan universe on the second chapter of the introduction to John M. Dillon's *Iamblichi Chalcidensis In Platonis dialogos commentariorum fragmenta* (Leiden: E.J. Brill 1973), 26–53, and on his lucid discussion of *In Timaeum* IV, fr 79, pp 368–70. I have not ventured to alter Dillon's ingenious explanation of the Twenty-one Leaders.

12 The following anecdote attesting to Maximus' Dedalian powers as an animator of statues is told by his colleague Eusebius in Eunapius' *Lives of the Philosophers* 475, ed and trans Wilmer Cave Wright (London: Wm Heinemann 1952),

432–3: 'Not long since he [Maximus] invited us [Eusebius and Chrysanthius] to the temple of Hecate and summoned many witnesses to his folly. When we had arrived there and had saluted the goddess: "Be seated," said he, "my well-beloved friends, and observe what shall come to pass, and how greatly I surpass the common herd." When he had said this, and we had all sat down, he burned a grain of incense and recited to himself the whole of some hymn or other, and was so highly successful in his demonstration that the image of the goddess first began to smile, then even seemed to laugh aloud. We were all much disturbed by this sight, but he said: "Let none of you be terrified by these things, for presently even the torches which the goddess holds in her hands shall kindle into flame." And before he could finish speaking the torches burst into a blaze of light. Now for the moment we came away amazed by that theatrical miracle-worker.' It was this anecdote that prompted Julian to seek Maximus in Ephesus.

13 For an extensive discussion of the social and theological background of the Orphic Hymns, see W.K.C. Guthrie, *Orpheus and Greek Religion* (London: Methuen and Co 1935; 2nd ed 1952), 257 ff. Philostratus the Athenian (b c170 AD) noted that when the great wizard Apollonius of Tyana observed the Athenians 'writhing lasciviously in a dance to the notes of a flute and posing as Horae and nymphs and Bacchants during the recitation of the poetry and hymns of Orpheus, he stood up and rebuked their behaviour ... ': *The Life of Apollonius of Tyana* vol 1, ed F.C. Conybeare (London: Wm Heinemann 1960), IV.xxi, p 392

14 In *Hymn to King Helios* 146d Julian refers rather cryptically to the two circles not crossed by Helios as 'the scales of mighty Necessity.' These are doubtless the Celestial Arctic and Antarctic Circles, which lie beyond the sun's annual path. What is not touched by the enlivening sun, Julian suggests, must fall under the deathly influence of the mother of Atropos. But why does he associate Necessity with scales? 'Necessity played an important part in the cult of Mithras and was sometimes identified with the constellation Virgo who holds the scales of Justice,' observed Wilmer Cave Wright in *The Works of the Emperor Julian*, vol 1, n 3, p 401. I am reluctant to identify the scales of Necessity with the constellations Virgo and Libra because these lie well within the sun's immediate circle of influence and have nothing to do (so far as I know) with the Celestial Arctic and Antarctic Circles. Nevertheless I can come up with no better explanation of Julian's enigmatic vision of Necessity than that suggested by Wright.

15 *Hymn to King Helios* 136c, 155c, *Works* vol 1, pp 370, 426

16 On the depiction of the dancing Graces in ancient painting and sculpture, see Edgar Wind, *Pagan Mysteries in the Renaissance* (New Haven: Yale University Press 1958), 31–8, pl 9.

17 For Julian's oration *To the Uneducated Cynics*, see *Works* vol 2, pp 5–65.

18 In fact there is no etymological connection between the names 'Horus' (from ancient Egyptian 'Hōr') and 'Horae' (from ancient Greek 'hōra').

19 Two comprehensive studies of the myth and cult of Cybele have guided me in interpreting Julian's *Hymn to the Mother of the Gods:* Sir James George Frazer's *Adonis, Attis, Osiris,* pt 4, vol 1 of *The Golden Bough* (London: Macmillan and Co 1963), 263–87; and Maarten J. Vermaseren's *Cybele and Attis,* trans A.M.H. Lemmers (London: Thames and Hudson 1977), esp pp 71–125.

20 *Aeneid* x.252–5, *Virgil* vol 2, ed and trans H. Rushton Fairclough (London: Wm Heinemann 1960), 188. The translation of these lines is my own.

21 *Hymn to King Helios* 136d, *Works* vol 2, p 370. Iamblichus refers to Hesiod in similar terms in *De vita pythagorica* xxv.111, ed Nauck, p 81.

22 George M.A. Haufmann, *The Seasons Sarcophagus in Dumbarton Oaks* (Cambridge: Harvard University Press 1951), 113. For other illustrations of the marble relief of Dionysus and the four dancing Horae, see Ed. Schmidt, *Archaistische Kunst in Griechenland und Rom* (Munich: B. Heller 1922), 26, 40, 92, pl 18.

23 So the Antiochene historian Ammianus Marcellinus reports in his *Rerum gestarum libri* xxi.9.15, *Ammianus Marcellinus* vol 2, ed and trans John C. Rolfe (London: Wm Heinemann 1956), 250.

24 The procession of the Nonnian Horae takes place before the 'fated time' when Dionysus invents wine-making and crowns Autumn's sparse locks with ivy.

25 As Alan Cameron has observed in 'Paganism and Literature in Late Fourth Century Rome,' *Christianisme et formes littéraires de l'antiquité tardive en occident* Entretiens Hardt vol 22 (Genève: Vandoeuvres-Genève 1977), 22–3, Macrobius 'writes a dialogue to which he assigns the dramatic date 384 with, as interlocutors, the last generation of committed pagan aristocrats – and then gives them nothing in particular to say, certainly nothing that is even positively much less polemically anti-Christian. 384, of course, was the very year in which Praetextatus and Symmachus made their joint bid to get the altar of Victory restored. Of this not a word.' Cameron goes on to argue on p 24 that the literary paganism of Macrobius (who may have been a Christian for economic or political reasons) reflects the religious complacency and philosophical nostalgia of Roman literati of the 430s. A rather more polemical and pagan Macrobius emerges from J. Flamant's *Macrobe et le néo-platonisme latin, à la fin du IVe siècle* (Leiden: E.J. Brill 1977). I am inclined to accept Cameron's view of Macrobius' elusive character.

26 *Fragment of a Letter to a Priest* 304c, *Works* vol 2, p 334: 'mēde orchēstēs mēde mimos autou tei thurai prositō'.

27 *Boethii In Isagogen Porphyrii commenta,* ed Samuel Brandt (Vindobonae: F. Tempsky; Lipsiae: G. Freytag 1906) *CSEL* vol 48, pp 31–2. Boethius explicitly alludes to the first book of the *In somnium Scipionis* and aptly describes its author as 'a most learned man' (doctissimus vir).

28 *De nuptiis* IX.910. The Iamblichan character of Martianus' theology (particularly his demonology) has been convincingly demonstrated by Robert Turcan in 'Martianus Capella et Jamblique,' *Revue des études latines* 36 (1958), 235–54.

29 *De nuptiis* IX.999: 'beata alumnum urbs Elissae quem vidit.' For a critical survey of the scanty internal evidence and masses of speculation concerning the life of Martianus, see William Harris Stahl, Richard Johnson, and E.L. Burge, *Martianus Capella and the Seven Liberal Arts* vol 1 (New York and London: Columbia University Press 1971), 9–20. My reading of the *De nuptiis* has been guided at almost every turn by their pioneering study, though I do not share Johnson's and Burge's low opinion of Martianus' talents as an allegorist.

30 Philology (before her apotheosis) certainly also represents many of the faults of Late Antique pagan scholars: eg their excessive bookishness, their verbosity, their intellectual timidity, their moroseness, and their unwillingness to reconcile virtue with pleasure.

31 The twelve Salii, according to Livy, 'paraded through the City, chanting their hymns to the triple beat of their solemn dance [cum tripudiis solemnique saltatu]': *Ab urbe condita* I.xx.4, *Livy* vol 1, ed and trans B.O. Foster (London: Wm Heinemann 1961), 70

32 Martianus appears to have been the first Latin author to allegorize the arts of the Trivium and Quadrivium, though he did not devise the curriculum itself. On the Stoic and sophistic roots of the Trivium and the Pythagorean and Platonic roots of the Quadrivium, see Stahl, Johnson, and Burge, *Martianus Capella and the Seven Liberal Arts* vol 1, pp 90–8. The terms 'Trivium' and 'Quadrivium' are of medieval origin.

33 *Metamorphoses* VI.19 (ad istum caelestium siderum redies chorum) and VI.24 (Venus suavi musicae superingressa formosa saltavit). I have based my translation on this edition: *Apulei Metamorphoseon Libri XI*, ed Caesar Giarratano and Paulus Frassinetti (Torino: Paravia 1960), 169–74. Martianus' vision of the celestial chorus may also have been influenced by Apuleius' Middle Platonic treatises; see chapter 5 of this volume, pp 252–3.

34 In *Martianus Capella and the Seven Liberal Arts*, pp 21 and 26, Johnson and Burge describe the *De nuptiis* as 'a fairly compact treatise [on the liberal arts] dressed in fantasy and allegory' and 'encyclopedic learning capsulated with a sweet coating.'

35 *Epistola* CV ('To Theophilus'), in *Synesii Opera quae exstant omnia*, ed J.P. Migne, *PG* vol 66 (Paris: Migne 1864), col 1488A. The hymns of Synesius are to be found in the same volume, cols 1588–1616, and in *Synésios de Cyrène* vol 1 (*Hymnes*) ed and trans Christian Lacombrade (Paris: Les Belles Lettres 1978). On the life of Synesius, see Johannes Quasten, *Patrology* vol 3 (Westminster, Maryland: Newman Press 1960), 106–8; Christian Lacombrade, *Synésios de Cyrène, hellène et chrétien* (Paris: Les Belles Lettres 1951); and Jay

Bregman, *Synesius of Cyrene: Philosopher-Bishop* (Berkeley, Los Angeles, London: University of California Press 1982).

36 See Synesius' panegyric *Dio vel de ipsius vitae instituto* (Dio or His Way of Life) in *Opera*, ed Migne, *PG* vol 66, cols 1112–1164. According to Lacombrade, *Synésios de Cyrène, hellène et chrétien*, pp 170–98, and Bregman, *Synesius of Cyrene*, pp 78–9, Hymn I was probably written in the 390s while all the others were composed between 402 and 408.

37 Hymn III, 30–3 and 71–4, ed Pierre Hadot in *Marius Victorinus* (Paris: Etudes Augustiniennes 1971)

38 J.L. Austin coined this useful phrase in *How to Do Things with Words*, ed J.O. Urmson (New York: Oxford University Press 1962), 6.

7 Praise His Name in the Dance

1 The forty-third oration was delivered some months after his retirement from Constantinople (probably in August or September of 381) in Nazianzus, though parts of it may well have been composed during his years in the capital. Sections 15–24 paint a vivid picture of the student days of Basil and Gregory in mid-century Athens.

2 *Carmen de vita sua* XI.267–74, ed J.-P. Migne, *PG* vol 37 (Paris: Migne 1862), col 1048. This long poem – amounting to 1949 iambic trimeters – is our chief source of information concerning the first five decades of Gregory's life, ie from the year of his birth (probably 330) to the year of his retirement from Constantinople (381). In *Carmen de vita sua* XVI.83, col 1260, he speaks of the 'chorostasiai erateinai' (the lovely choruses) formed by the congregation of the Anastasis under his leadership. For other biographical details, including the chronology of his works, I have consulted: Eugène Fleury, *Hellénisme et christianisme: Saint Grégoire de Nazianze et son temps* (Paris: G. Beauchesne 1930); and Paul Gallay, *La Vie de Saint Grégoire de Nazianze* (Lyon: E. Vitte 1943), esp pp 252–3.

3 In Hellenistic Greek (and possibly in classical Greek also) the neuter noun 'lugisma' signified 'something twisted' in the human body, ie a sprain. It seems to have been an exclusively medical term until the fourth century AD. The masculine form 'lugismos' was used by Aristophanes in *The Frogs* 775 (405 BC) to designate the twists and turns in the sophistic speeches that Euripides supposedly delivered in Hades to the mob when he was attempting to wrest the tragic chair from Aeschylus. In Aristophanes' *The Wasps* 1487 (422 BC) the verb 'lugizo' is used to designate a characteristic movement in the Dionysian dance – the twisting and bending of the dancer's torso. Nazianzen appears to have transferred the Aristophanic senses of 'lugismos' and 'lugizo' to 'lugisma.' As a musical term 'lugisma' suggested to him the soft, sinuous, and fatal melodies of the Sirens. In his *Tetrastichae sententiae (Poemata mor-*

alia I.ii.xxxiii.66–7; *PG* vol 37, 933A) he gave the following advice to the war-weary Christian returning like Odysseus to his homeland: 'Stop up your ears with wax when you hear wicked speeches / And the dissolute twisting melodies [ekmelē lugismata] of songs that delight the senses.'

4 The pioneering study of the influence of Second Sophistic oratory on the style and thought of the Theologian is Marcel Guignet's *Saint Grégoire de Nazianze et la rhétorique* (Paris: A. Picard 1911). Rosemary Radford Ruether in *Gregory of Nazianzus: Rhetor and Philosopher* (Oxford: Clarendon Press 1969) sees the main cultural crises of the fourth century reflected in Gregory's complex response to his rhetorical training and virtuosity. Their complementary studies have alerted me to much that I otherwise would have missed in Gregory's sophistic elaborations of the choreia topos.

5 *Oratio* 4.100 ('First Invective against Julian'), ed J.-P. Migne, *PG* vol 35 (Paris: Garnier 1886), col 636A

6 See *Theseus* XXI, in *Plutarch's Lives* vol 1, ed and trans Bernadotte Perrin (London: Wm Heinemann 1948), 44. Plutarch defines the choreia of Theseus and his youths as a 'mimēma tōn en tōi Labyrinthōi periodōn kai diexodōn' – 'an imitation of their windings and escape routes in the Labyrinth.' Consonant with this are the accounts of the maze-dance given by the pagan Sophists after Plutarch: eg Pollux (late second century AD) in the *Onomasticon* IV.101, ed Ericus Bethe (Lipsiae: B.G. Teubner 1900), 230–1; Lucian (second century AD) in *Peri orchēseōs* 34, *Lucian* vol 5, ed and trans A.M. Harmon (London: Wm Heinemann 1962), 244; and Philostratus the Younger (fl c 300 AD), in *Imagines* 10.18–22, ed and trans Arthur Fairbanks (London: Wm Heinemann 1960), 340. In her rambling but informative article 'The Geranos Dance – a New Interpretation,' *Transactions of the American Philological Association* 77 (1946), 112–30, Lillian B. Lawler speculates that the name of Theseus' dance goes back to an Indo-European root '*ger-,' meaning 'to wind,' and is not related (except as a homonym) to the noun 'geranos' meaning 'crane.' The dance itself, she argues, may have originated in ritual imitations of the winding motion of snakes rather than in Theseus' imitation of the winding path of the Cnossian maze. A detailed study of the symbolic significance of the Labyrinth and the Cnossian dance in Western literature has yet to be written. Digressive steps towards such a study were taken by W.F. Jackson Knight in *Vergil: Epic and Anthropology*, ed John D. Christie (New York: Barnes and Noble 1967), 109, 208–10, 248–50. In a Latin grammatical treatise attributed to the fourth-century Christian Sophist Marius Victorinus, Theseus is said to have invented the strophe-antistrophe-epode structure of Greek choral poetry 'by imitating the twisted and crooked path of the labyrinth with the youths and maidens'; see *Ars grammatica* bk 1, ch 15, in *Scriptores artis metricae* ed Henricius Keilius (Lipsiae: B.G. Teubner 1874), 60. A cosmic interpretation of the three movements of the choral ode is also offered in the same passage.

7 The phrase 'tōi pasēs zōēs chorēgōi' appears in Origen's *Contra Celsum* VIII.19, *Origenes Werke* vol 2, ed Paul Koetschau (Leipzig: J.C. Hinrichs'sche Buchhandlung 1899), 236. Henry Chadwick has translated it as 'to the author of all life' in *Origen: Contra Celsum* (Cambridge: Cambridge University Press 1953), 465. His translation preserves the theological sense of the phrase but loses its metaphorical implications. The phrase 'zōēs chorēgos' is used by Basil in reference to the Son (v.7.7d) and the Holy Spirit (IX.22.19c) in *De spiritu sancto*, ed Benoit Pruche in *Basile de Césarée: Traité du Saint Esprit* (Paris: Editions du Cerf 1947; Sources Chrétiennes no 17), 120, 146. Basil was probably echoing Origen rather than Plotinus (*Ennead* 6.9.9).

8 Glaucon said something like this in *Republic* VI 508c: ie 'As the Good in the intelligible world is related to reason and the objects of reason, so is this [the sun] in the visible world related to vision and the objects of vision.' The person 'alien to our faith' has replaced the Platonic term 'tagathon' (the Good) with the noun 'Theos' (God), thereby suggesting that the sun as craftsman of temporal order corresponds to the supracosmic Craftsman of the *Timaeus* and functions as a divine intermediary between Man and the First Cause. The Emperor Julian interpreted Glaucon's remark in this way in his *Hymn to King Helios* 133a–c, though he retained the term 'tagathon' for the First Cause and conceived Mithra-Helios as the 'Theos' to whom the visible sun most clearly corresponds. Gregory may have had Julian in mind at this point in the Second Theological Oration, though his subsequent questions in section 30 are directed against Platonic cosmologists and heliolaters in general.

9 See chapter 9 of this volume, pp 510–12. Assuming that Gregory's 'noeras dynameis' are the same as the 'noas' mentioned immediately after them and that these correspond to the 'dynameis' in the Celestial Hierarchy of the Areopagite, we can find a total of seven names shared by the two groups of nine angelic ranks. Missing from Gregory's group are the Cherubim and Seraphim of the Celestial Hierarchy, and from the Areopagite's group the Splendours and Ascensions of the Cappadocian Empyrean. Conspicuously absent from the latter, moreover, is the triadic arrangement of spiritual ranks that Pseudo-Dionysius imported from Athenian Neoplatonism. On the comparison of the two angelic orders, see Paul Gallay, ed, *Grégoire de Nazianze: Discours* 27–31 (Paris: Editions du Cerf 1978; Sources Chrétiennes no 250), 172–3, n 5; and J. Rousse, 'Les anges et leur ministère selon S. Grégoire de Nazianze,' *Mélanges de Science Religieuse* 22 (1961), 134–52.

10 *In Philebum* fr 6, in *Iamblichi Chalcidensis in Platonis dialogos commentariorum fragmenta*, ed and trans John M. Dillon (Leiden: Brill 1973). The translation is mine, though it has been checked against Dillon's.

11 See Pierre Hadot, *Marius Victorinus* (Paris: Etudes Augustiniennes 1971), 204. According to Augustine, *Confessions* 7.13, Victorinus translated certain 'libri platonicorum' into Latin. It has often been assumed but never proved that

among these lost 'books of the Platonists' were translations of works by Porphyry and Plotinus. Traces of Porphyrian influence have been found in Victorinus' theological writings against the Arians, which were probably written a few years after the translations (ie between 357 and 363).

12 Around 200 AD Sextus Empiricus, the last major pagan proponent of Skepticism, mentioned 'the well-ordered choral dances of the stars' (asterōn de eutaktous tinas choreias) in his treatise *Against the Physicists* 1.27 (= *Adversus dogmaticos* III.27), ed and trans R.G. Bury, *Sextus Empiricus* vol 3 (London: Wm Heinemann 1960), 14. His reason for doing so, however, was to point out the falseness of all poetic images of world-order and to undermine all versions of the Argument by Design based upon such images. 'That the cosmos is ordered according to harmony is shown to be false by a variety of proofs,' he asserted in *Against the Musicians* 37 (= *Adversus mathematicos* VI.37), *Sextus Empiricus* vol 4, pp 388–90. We should not be too surprised that Sextus and his school produced no distinctively Skeptical vision of the cosmic dance, for they not only rejected all philosophical concepts of world-harmony but also ridiculed the basic notion of a vision of world-harmony. They refused to be spectators in any sense of the term. Their 'vision' of the dance was simply a blank. The Orthodox Spectator, by contrast, strove to clear his mind of philosophical concepts of cosmic order in order to concentrate on purely figurative visions of the miraculous order of Creation.

13 Without the three lucidly organized volumes of Johannes Quasten's *Patrology* (Utrecht-Antwerp: Spectrum 1962–4) I should have been a trembling and dispirited wanderer in the maze of Greek patristic literature. Unless otherwise noted, all dates and biographical details pertaining to the Greek Fathers have been drawn from Quasten. On Clement of Rome, see *Patrology* vol 1, pp 42–53.

14 This parallel was drawn to my attention by J.B. Lightwood in his edition of Clement of Rome in *The Apostolic Fathers* pt 1, vol 2 (London and New York: Macmillan 1890), 71.

15 The closest Nazianzen ever came to setting forth his cosmological ideas in a systematic way was in his Christmas oration (*Or* 38.8 ff; *PG* vol 36, 320A ff). The incoherence of his cosmology, particularly at the angelic level, is clearly exposed and generously excused on semantic grounds by Rosemary Radford Ruether in *Gregory of Nazianzus: Rhetor and Philosopher*, pp 130–4.

16 *De principiis* II.1.2 and 8.1, in *Origène: Traité des principes* ed and trans Henri Crouzel and Manlio Simonetti (Paris: Editions du Cerf 1978; Sources Chrétiennes no 252), 236–8 and 336–8. However, in *De principiis* I.5.5, p 193, Origen does not hesitate to identify the dragon mentioned in Job 40:20 with the Devil.

17 Athena is associated with 'chorostasiai' by the Alexandrian poet Callimachus (d c240 BC) in his fifth hymn, 'On the Bath of Pallas,' line 66; see *Callima-*

chus: Hymns and Epigrams ed and trans A.W. Mair (London: Wm Heinemann 1960), 116. Gregory of Nazianzus appears to have been the first poet to
use the noun 'chorostasia' in reference to the spiritual order of the ecclesiastical universe; eg in *Carmen de vita sua*, lines 292–3, *PG* vol 37, col 992A (eu-
sebeōn te / Psychōn pamphanoōsa chorostasiē te kleos te: the splendid and
renowned chorus of pious souls).

18 J.-P. Migne, ed, *Theodoreti Sermones et homiliae*, in *Auctarium ad tomum* IV,
 PG vol 84 (Paris: Migne 1864), col 53C. The phrase appears in a fragment of
 Theodoret's panegyric on John Chrysostom.

19 *Oratio* 38.17 ('On the Theophany'), ed J.-P. Migne, *PG* vol 36 (Paris: Garnier
 1885), col 332A

20 *Oratio* 15.1 ('In Praise of the Maccabees'), ed J.-P. Migne, *PG* vol 35 (Paris:
 Garnier 1886), col 912A. See my discussion of Maccabees 14:6–8 in relation to
 the Christian image of the dance in Paradise, chapter 7 of this volume,
 pp 394–5; and W.H.C. Frend's discussion of the political and eschatological
 significance of the martyrdom of the Maccabean youths in *Martyrdom and
 Persecution in the Early Church: A Study of a Conflict from the Maccabees
 to Donatus* (Oxford: Blackwell 1965), 63 and 85.

21 *Epistola* XXXIX, in *S.P.N. Athanasii Opera omnia quae exstant*, ed J.-P. Migne,
 PG vol 26 (Paris: Garnier 1887), col 1437C. On the Latin translations of Her-
 mas, see Robert Joly, ed and trans, *Hermas: Le Pasteur* (Paris: Editions du
 Cerf 1958; Sources Chrétiennes no 53), 63–4.

22 See *Purgatorio* V 13–15, XXVIII 22–42, and XXIX 120–32 in *The Divine Comedy*
 vol 2, trans Charles S. Singleton (Princeton: Princeton University Press 1973).

23 *Stromateis* VII.xiv.87, in *Clemens Alexandrinus* vol 3, ed Otto Stählin and
 Ludwig Früchtel (Berlin: Akademie-Verlag 1970), 62

24 In so far as Arete is the hostess of the banquet (which takes place in her garden) she may also be considered the counterpart of Plato's Agathon. Her allegorical identity as the daughter of Philosophia links her, moreover, with the
 priestess Diotima whom Socrates praises as an authority on the mysteries of
 divine love.

25 On the dating of this controversial work, see T.D. Barnes, 'Porphyry *Against
 the Christians*: Date and Attribution of the Fragments,' *Journal of Theological
 Studies* 24 (1973), 424–42; and in support of Barnes, John M. Rist, 'Basil's
 "Neoplatonism": Its Background and Nature,' in volume 1 of *Basil of Caesarea: Christian, Humanist, Ascetic*, ed Paul Jonathan Fedwick (Toronto: Pontifical Institute of Mediaeval Studies 1981), 142–7.

26 On the distinction in Valentinian Gnosticism between three races of men –
 'pneumatikon,' 'psychikon,' and 'choikon' ('spiritual,' 'psychic,' and 'earthly')
 – see Irenaeus, *Adversus haereses* 1,7,5, ed Adelin Rousseau and Louis Dou-
 treleau (Paris: Editions du Cerf 1979; Sources Chrétiennes no 264), 110.

27 I do not mean to imply here that Basil and the two Gregories escaped or were

never exposed to such censure in their highly intolerant era. They met with it in one form or another all their lives – particularly during the reign of Julian (who ironically took the Christians' word for it that they did not need pagan literature to raise their minds into the heavenly dance). Nazianzen's diatribes against Julian indicate that the early Christian humanists certainly suffered with the rest of the Church 'the many hard blows of this age' (*Or* 4.7) but did not fear their adversaries or permit them to establish impassible, artificial boundaries between Hellenic and Christian culture.

28 In *The Early Church* (Harmondsworth, Middlesex: Penguin Books 1967), 275, Henry Chadwick noted that 'in orthodox eyes dancing did not succeed in becoming a natural and approved vehicle of religious expression, except in Ethiopia.' The origin of the dance of priests during the Ethiopian Eucharist is obscure. Perhaps the custom grew out of ancient pagan tribal ceremonies which were gradually absorbed into Christian worship following the evangelization of Ethiopia by St Frumentius in the fourth century; perhaps at some point in the long history of the Ethiopian Church its priests decided to imitate or commemorate David's dance before the ark. The 'tabot' (altar-box) in the cathedral of Aksum is venerated by Ethiopian Christians as the original ark, which the Queen of Sheba or her son by King Solomon was supposed to have brought to Africa from Jerusalem; the presence of this holy object may have led the Ethiopian clergy to preserve or develop the ritual of sacred dancing at a time when most other Christian communities were rejecting it. In *The Church of Abyssinia* (London: Luzac and Co 1928), 199, Harry Middleton Hyatt reports that the priests sing in a nasal manner during their dance and rhythmically brandish long staffs which serve as crutch-like misericords during the recitation of prayers. In *The Christian Churches of the East* vol 2 (Milwaukee: Bruce Publishing Co 1947–8), 221, Donald Attwater claims that ritual dancing was one of the 'surprising modifications' of the Coptic rite introduced into Ethiopia in Late Antiquity. Precisely when the modification was made he does not say. The ceremony of the 'Seises,' a dance of choir-boys in the Cathedral of Seville, has been pointed to as a survival of early Christian ritual dancing by E.L. Backman in *Religious Dances in the Christian Church and in Popular Medicine*, trans E. Classen (London: Allen and Unwin 1952), 82–4. Like the religious dance in Ethiopia, however, this isolated Spanish ritual (which dates from at least the fifteenth century) is an exception to the general rule that dancing 'in the body' was discouraged as a mode of worship in the Church.

29 For a discussion of the names associated with the six 'choroi' in this illustration, see *Cosmas Indicopleustès: Topographie Chrétienne* vol 2, ed and trans Wanda Wolska-Conus (Paris: Editions du Cerf 1970; Sources Chrétiennes no 159), v, 122, n 122¹, pp 180–3. On all the illustrations in *Vat Gr* 699, see Cosimo Stornajolo, *Le miniature della Topografia cristiana di Cosma Indicopleuste: codice vaticano greco 699* (Milano: U. Hoepli 1908).

30 'Priests, mothers, children – let us imitate them!' urged Nazianzen in *Oratio* 15.12 (*PG* vol 35, 932C) after a long paraphrase of 4 Maccabees in which he portrayed the mother of the seven martyrs as a prototype of the Mater Dolorosa. The sufferings of her sons, as Gregory has the mother declare in *Oratio* 15.9 (928C), 'are now acclaimed by the survivors as a delight, a glory, a reason for instituting dances [chorostasiai] and joyous celebrations.' In contrast to the Jewish author, Gregory clearly relates the choral ceremonies performed and inspired by the seven martyrs to the triumph of the Blessed in Paradise. The enthusiastic response of the Greek and Latin Fathers to 4 Maccabees is discussed in detail by R.B. Townshend in the introduction to his translation of the work in volume 2 of *The Apocrypha and Pseudepigrapha of the Old Testament*, ed R.H. Charles (Oxford: Clarendon Press 1913), 658–62: and by W.H.C. Frend in *Martyrdom and Persecution*, p 63 ff.

31 *The Babylonian Talmud* vol 4, pt 2, ed and trans Rabbi Dr I. Epstein (London: Soncino Press 1961), 164–5. The translation is by Dr Epstein.

32 Plotinus is not mentioned by name or directly cited in any of Nazianzen's extant works. According to P. Henry and H.R. Schwyzer, *Plotini opera* vol 2, Gregory echoes *Ennead* 5.2.1 in one of his dogmatic poems (1.xxix.12, *PG* vol 37, 508A) and *Ennead* 5.2.8–9 in his Third Theological Oration (*Or* 29.2, *PG* vol 36, 76C). The faintness of these echoes (particularly the first) and their inconclusiveness as evidence of a Neoplatonic strain in Gregory's thought have been pointed out by John M. Rist in his sobering article 'Basil's "Neoplatonism," ' *Basil of Caesarea: Christian, Humanist, Ascetic* pt 1, ed Paul Jonathan Fedwick (Toronto: Pontifical Institute of Mediaeval Studies 1981), 215–16. Rist has heroically declared war on 'false parallels' which have been used to support the oft-repeated claim that the theology of the Cappadocians was deeply imbued with Neoplatonism. He has shown how difficult it is to find precise verbal connections between the works of the Neoplatonists and the Cappadocians, and how easily 'errors of interpretation' can be generated from 'errors of fact' (p 138). Rist's skeptical spirit has frequently guided me away from both sorts of error in this chapter and in this volume as a whole.

33 In *De principiis* 1.6.1, ed Crouzel and Simonetti, p 195, Origen advises his readers to regard his statements about the Apocatastasis as tentative suggestions rather than dogmatic assertions. That he was willing to consider the possibility of a universal return 'to Goodness,' ie an Apocatastasis in which all three orders of beings (celestial, terrestrial, infernal) were reunited with God, is clear from *De principiis* 1.6.3, p 203, though here he encourages his readers to decide for themselves whether it was likely that Satan and his devils would be cut off forever from 'the ultimate unity and concord.' Quasten is certainly in error when he states in *Patrology* vol 2, p 87, that Origen believed that 'even the demons and Satan himself will be purified by the Logos'; for a summary of the evidence indicating that he eventually rejected the controversial doctrine of the salvation of Satan, see Henri Crouzel and Manlio Simonetti,

eds, *Origène: Traité des principes* vol 2 (Paris: Editions du Cerf 1978; Sources Chrétiennes no 253), 91 n 7, 99 n 25; and Henri Crouzel, 'L'Hadès et la Géhenne selon Origène,' *Gregorianum* 59 (1978) 291–331.

34 See *Vita Antonii* 8–9, in *S.P.N. Athanasii Opera omnia quae exstant*, ed J.-P. Migne, *PG* vol 26 (Paris: Garnier 1887), cols 853C–857C. 'But the demons have no power,' the hagiographer (probably St Athanasius) wrote in *Vita Antonii* 28, col 888A, 'and so they act like players on the stage who change their shape and frighten children with the appearance of their riotous mobs and with their pompous posturings.' Opposed to the discord and histrionics of these diabolical 'orchēstai' are the harmonious psalmody and peaceful inward-turning lives of the 'holy choruses' of ascetics ('theiōn chorōn'; 44, 908A) who were inspired by Antony's preaching to turn the desert into 'a land filled with piety and justice.'

35 See Rosemary Radford Ruether, *Gregory of Nazianzus: Rhetor and Philosopher*, pp 101–2. Jean Bernardi has called the thirty-fifth oration 'un discours supplémentaire, apocryphe' in the textual notes to his edition of *Discours 1–3* (Paris: Editions du Cerf 1978; Sources Chrétiennes no 247), 55. On the same page, n 1, he mentions a thesis presented at Lille in 1973 on the subject of Gregory's mythological allusions and references to pagan religion (still, so far as I can tell, unpublished) by Marie-Paule Masson-Vincourt who has defended – or as Bernardi says, 'a essayé de défendre' – the authenticity of the thirty-fifth oration. I have not read this thesis but am in sympathy with Masson-Vincourt's view that Gregory may well have been the author of 'On the Martyrs, and against the Arians.'

36 Cf Tatian's *Oratio ad Graecos* 22, ed Ioann. Carol. Theod. Otto (Wiesbaden: Sändig 1969; rpt of 1851 ed), 94–8. Tatian, a second-century Christian apologist and virulent anti-Hellenist, regarded the performance of a pantomimic actor-dancer as a travesty of Christian education. By 'a bend and twist of the hand' (touto de tō cheire lugizomenon) and with a wink of the eye the gesticulating dancer, he argued, played the role of a diabolical Sophist who 'gives lessons in adultery on the stage' (moicheuein epi tēs skēnēs sophisteuontas). See also Chrysostom's homily *Contra ludos et theatra* (Against the Games and the Theatres) in *S.P.N. Joannis Chrysostomi Opera omnia quae exstant*, ed J.-P. Migne, *PG* vol 56 (Paris: Migne 1862), cols 262–70.

37 *Expositio in Psalmum CXLIX*, in *S.P.N. Joannis Chrysostomi Opera omnia quae exstant*, ed J.-P. Migne, *PG* vol 55 (Paris: Migne 1862), cols 494–5. We have no evidence that Chrysostom's 'Explanations' of 58 Psalms (which probably date from the mid 390s) were ever delivered as homilies.

8   Chorus and Chronos

1 'adeisithōn genos andrōn': *Hymn to the Muses* line 12, ed A. Ludwich, in *Carminum graecorum reliquiae* (Lipsiae: B.G. Teubner 1897), 144. Proclus is known to have written only one explicitly anti-Christian work – *Eighteen Arguments for the Eternity of the World against the Christians* – fragments of which survive in John Philoponus' *De aeternitate mundi contra Proclum*, ed H. Rabe (Lipsiae: B.G. Teubner 1899).

2 This phrase (tēs noeras choreias synaptein tois theioterois) appears in an etymological discussion of the names Athena and Chronos in Proclus' *In Platonis Cratylum commentarii*, ed G. Pasquali (Lipsiae: B.G. Teubner 1908) CLXXXV, p 113. For my translation of this passage, see chapter 9, pp 501–2.

3 *In Timaeum* III 14. I have relied on K. Praechter's extensive article on Syrianus in Pauly-Wissowa's *Realencyclopädie der Classischen Altertumswissenschaft* 2nd series, vol 4 (Stuttgart: J.B. Metzlersche Verlagsbuchhandlung 1929) cols 1728–1775.

4 The standard study of the complex and enigmatic mélange of theurgic beliefs inherited by Iamblichus and his school remains Hans Lewy's *Chaldean Oracles and Theurgy: Mysticism Magic and Platonism in the Later Roman Empire*, ed Michel Tardieu (Paris: Etudes Augustiniennes 1978).

5 Lewy suggests in *Chaldean Oracles and Theurgy*, pp 104–5, that Proclus substituted the name Chronos for Aion in order to reconcile the *Timaeus* with the *Oracles*. As E.R. Dodds has rightly pointed out in 'New Light on the "Chaldean Oracles," ' *Harvard Theological Review* 54 (1961), 266, the name Chronos could not have been introduced by Proclus into the Chaldean system since it can be found in several fragments of the *Oracles* (including one cited by Proclus in *In Timaeum* III 36). The original relation between Chronos and Aion in the Chaldean system remains murky, but I think Proclus can at least be credited with sharpening the distinction between the two gods (if such a distinction originally existed) by defining their relation in Platonic terms.

6 E.R. Dodds, *The Greeks and the Irrational* (Berkeley and Los Angeles: University of California Press 1964) 299

7 Between Syrianus and Proclus the position of Diadochus was briefly held by the mathematician Domninus of Larissa; according to Marinus, however, Syrianus himself had looked to Proclus as the only true heir of his 'divine doctrines' (*Vita Procli* XII). On the life and works of Domninus, see F. Hultsch's article in Pauly-Wissowa's *Realencyclopädie der Classischen Altertumswissenschaft* vol 5 (1903), cols 1521–1525.

8 'hikesiēn polydakryon': *Hymn to Helios*, line 36. See within, pp 465–7, for my translation of this hymn. The adjective 'polydakryos' appears several times in Homer (eg *Iliad* 3.132, 165; 17.544).

9 *Vita Plotini* 10. Porphyry admits that he and his fellow disciples did not un-

derstand their teacher's curious remark to Amelius and did not dare to ask what it meant. I have followed the second of A.H. Armstrong's interpretations of the incident in *Plotinus* vol 1 (Cambridge, Mass: Harvard University Press 1966) n 1, pp 34–5. Armstrong has also suggested that Plotinus may have made the remark simply to stop Amelius, who had become obsessed with religious rituals, from bothering him.

10 *Elements of Theology*, prop 31: 'Everything that proceeds from a certain principle returns, according to its essence, to that from which it proceeds.' Without E.R. Dodds' lucid notes on propositions 25–39 in his critical edition of *The Elements of Theology* (Oxford: Clarendon Press 1933; 2nd ed 1963), 212–23, I would not have survived the gruelling technicalities of Proclus' theory of procession and return. The 211 propositions in this systematic summary of the main tenets of the theology of the Athenian Academy yield not a single reference to the cosmic choreia, though the term 'chorēgein' and its close relatives appear fairly often in the work (eg twice in prop 18) and faintly imply the image of the dance. The *Elements* is entirely concerned with first principles and metaphysical processes, and in it we look at the world-chorus from the highly abstract viewpoint of the entities that 'bestow' (chorēgein) life, beauty, perpetuity, being, and unity on the temporal participants in the dance.

11 I am indebted to S. Sambursky and S. Pines for drawing my attention to, and guiding my understanding of, the difficult passages concerning time in the commentaries of Pseudo-Archytas and Iamblichus in their pioneering study *The Concept of Time in Late Neoplatonism* (Jerusalem: Israel Academy of Sciences and Humanities 1971), 12–17. For a comprehensive and scholarly discussion of ancient and early medieval concepts of time, see Richard Sorabji, *Time, Creation, and the Continuum: Theories in Antiquity and the Early Middle Ages* (Ithaca, NY: Cornell University Press 1983). The temporal mysticism of the Late Antique Neoplatonists has been weirdly synthesized with Darwinian evolutionary theory, and ardently defended on modern psychological and anthropological grounds, by Leonard Charles Feldstein in *The Dance of Being: Man's Labyrinthine Rhythms: The Natural Ground of the Human* (New York: Fordham University Press 1979). 'All creatures,' he observes ecstatically on p 38, 'similarly execute their own "dances of being". Each etches for itself the broader contours of its dance; the entire community composes the choreography. Yet modification and adjustment are always needed. Ideals are envisaged, entertained, sought, denied, attained, but always with the perception, dim but haunting, of limits which each creature imperceptibly imposes upon the remainder. A community's destiny consists in a synchronized movement, step by step, all integrated into an elaborate balancing of the separately executed movements of the solitary creatures – towards a most inclusive ideal: that ideal which ever potentiates novel possibilities for attainment by the individual ... The dance of being!' The spirit of Proclus is clearly not dead.

12 *Peri tēs hieratikēs technēs*, ed and trans J. Bidez, in *Catalogue des manuscrits alchimiques grecs* vol 6 (Brussels: Maurice Lamertin 1928), 148. For Blake's poem, see *Songs of Experience* in *The Complete Writings of William Blake*, ed Geoffrey Keynes (London: Oxford University Press 1966), 215.

13 The theory of intellectual decadence is implicit for example in the subtitle of Laurence Jay Rosán's *The Philosophy of Proclus: The Final Phase of Ancient Thought* (New York: Cosmos 1949) and explicit in the title of Paul Bastid's *Proclus et le crepuscule de la pensée grecque* (Paris: J. Vrin 1969).

14 *In Timaeum* III 124–6. On the discovery of the precession of the equinoxes by Hipparchus, see Sir Thomas L. Heath's *Greek Astronomy* (New York: J.M. Dent and Sons 1932), 143. For a concise explanation of the phenomenon, see D.R. Dicks' *Early Greek Astronomy to Aristotle* (London: Thames and Hudson 1970), 15–16.

15 'Those who divulge the mysteries,' noted Lucian in *Peri orchēseōs* 15, 'are said "to dance them out" [exorcheisthai].'

16 I am indebted here to Alan Cameron's refreshingly unromantic account of the impact of Justinian's edict on Damascius and his school in 'The Last Days of the Academy at Athens,' *Proceedings of the Cambridge Philological Society* no 195, new series no 15 (1969), 7–29. 'Such precarious life as the Academy continued to enjoy [after the return of Damascius and his colleagues from Persia] will have been extinguished for a second time,' Cameron concludes on p 25, 'in the terrible sack of Athens by the Slavs in 579.'

17 'utrarum peritissimus litterarum': *De institutione arithmetica, praefatio*. Boethius received from Symmachus not only an education in the two classical tongues but also the hand of his daughter Rusticiana in marriage.

18 The impact of Alexandrian and Athenian Neoplatonism on the thought of Boethius has been exhaustively treated by Pierre Courcelle in *Les lettres grecques en occident* (Paris: Boccard 1948), 257–300; and by Henry Chadwick in *Boethius: The Consolations of Music, Logic, Theology, and Philosophy* (Oxford: Clarendon Press 1981), 16–22.

19 In *Procli Opuscula*, ed H. Boese (Berlin: W. de Gruyter et Socios 1960), 144, 192, and 196, may be found three scattered references to the world-chorus in two minor treatises of Proclus translated by William of Moerbeke: *De providentia* 34.33 ('psychōn hyper heimarmenēn choreuousōn' rendered as 'animarum supra fatum excédentium,' 'of souls proceeding beyond fate'); *De malorum subsistentia* 12.7 ('chorus virtutum,' 'the chorus of powers'); and *De malorum subsistentia* 16.2 ('angelicum chorum,' 'the angelic chorus'). These are not significant elaborations of the image. In the first, William's unmetaphorical translation entirely obscures the image of the dance, while in the second and third the word 'chorus' may simply denote 'group' or 'class.' What survives of William's translation of Proclus' *In Timaeum* has been edited by Gérard Verbeke in 'Guillaume de Moerbeke, traducteur de Proclus,' *Revue*

philosophique de Louvain 51 (1953), 349–73. The translation (a patchwork of passages between *In Timaeum* II 219 and II 253) yields no reference to the cosmic dance.

20 I am indebted to Henry Chadwick, *Boethius*, p 129, for drawing my attention to this verbatim quotation from Proclus in the *De consolatione*. On the echoes of Proclus' *In Timaeum* in 'O qui perpetua,' see Fritz Klingner, *De Boethii Consolatione philosophiae* (Berlin: Weidmann 1921), 38–67.

21 The verb 'perichoreuein' (or the idiom 'peri ... choreuein') may be found, for example, in Proclus' *In Timaeum* I 369, *In Parmeniden* III col 808 and VI col 1072, and *Platonic Theology* I 3. For a discussion of its significance, see chapter 9 of this volume, pp 502–3.

22 *De musica libri quinque*, ed J.-P. Migne, in *Patrologia latina* vol 63 (Paris: Garnier 1882), cols 1167C–1300B. On the Pythagorean theory of 'musica mundana' or 'world music,' see bk 1, ch 1.

9 Winding Together

1 The extensive influence of Athenian Neoplatonism on the theology of Pseudo-Dionysius was demonstrated by J. Stiglmayr in 'Der Neuplatoniker Proklus als Vorlage des sog. Dionysius Areopagita in der Lehre vom Uebel,' *Historisches Jahrbuch im Auftrage der Görres-Gesellschaft* 16 (1895), 253–73 and 721–48; and by Hugo Koch in *Pseudo-Dionysius Areopagita in seinen Beziehungen zum Neuplatonismus und Mysterienwesen* (Mainz: Franz Kircsheim 1900). I have made use of Koch's list of passages from Proclus (p 171) which parallel the Areopagite's discussion of the mystic dance in *Divine Names* IV.8–10. Since the Areopagite mentions the dance only in his treatises, the ten epistles attributed to him will not be discussed in this study.

2 *De civitate dei* x.ix. Porphyry's two lost works on theurgy, *On the Ascent of the Soul* and *Letter to Anebo*, shaped Augustine's conception of the art of divine works. Porphyry was by no means convinced by all that the theurgists were claiming they could see and do. His great error, according to Augustine, was to consider their diabolical rites worthy of objective philosophical investigation.

3 I am indebted to S. Sambursky and S. Pines for their lucid explanation of Damascius' theory of time and Simplicius' criticism of it in *The Concept of Time in Late Neoplatonism* (Jerusalem: Israel Academy of Sciences and Humanities 1971), 18–20.

4 *In librum Beati Dionysii De divinis nominibus expositio* i.i.1–3, ed Ceslas Pera (Turin, Rome: Marietti 1950), 6.

5 *Celestial Hierarchy* III.1. For a detailed analysis of this complex definition, see René Roques, *L'univers dionysien: structure hiérarchique du monde selon le Pseudo-Denys* (Paris: Aubier 1954), 35–91.

6 *Ecclesiastical Hierarchy* VI.1.3. The noun 'therapeutai' (lit 'devotees') appears in the works of at least two Christian authors before the Areopagite. In *Stromateis* 7.7 Clement of Alexandria used it in a general sense to designate all the worshippers and servants of the Christian God. Eusebius of Caesarea refined Clement's usage in *Vita Constantini* 2.2 by associating the term with Christians who express their devotion to God by leading an ascetic life. In his *Ecclesiastical History* 6.1.3 he recalled the ascetism of the Egyptian Therapeutae praised by Philo in his treatise *On the Contemplative Life*. The Areopagite may thus have picked up the term either directly from Philo or indirectly from Christian authors who had read Philo. No author before him, however, is known to have used it as a synonym for 'monachoi' (monks) or as the title for an ecclesiastical rank.

7 As René Roques observed in *L'univers dionysien*, p 196: 'Il faut donc reconnaître que l'ordonnance de la hiérarchie ecclésiastique ne présente pas la rigoreuse symétrie de la hiérarchie céleste.' The symmetrical design of the hierarchical universe would seem to demand nine ecclesiastical ranks to mirror the divisions of the celestial hierarchy; yet the Areopagite distinguishes only *six* and divides the lowest rank of the laity into a triad (which further obscures the symmetry). Dom Denys Rutledge, in *Cosmic Theology: The Ecclesiastical Hierarchy of Pseudo-Denys* (London: Routledge and Kegan Paul 1964), 26–8, has attempted to balance the two hierarchies by counting the three principal sacraments – Baptism, Unction, and Holy Communion – as Ecclesia's missing triad. He places this sacramental triad between the clergy and the angels because (as he argues on p 26) the offices of the Church were perceived by the Areopagite as man's 'direct link with the invisible world.' Ingenious as Rutledge's hypothesis is, it strikes me as untenable for two reasons: first, because it fails to fit the other sacraments recognized by the Areopagite (eg Ordination, Final Unction) into the triadic symmetry of Ecclesia; and second, because it violates the ontological order underlying the unity of the two hierarchies. The sacraments may be considered the means by which man participates in eternal Being, but they are not 'beings' like bishops and archangels and do not belong in the hierarchical chain of initiators and initiates.

8 Hugo Koch suggested in *Pseudo-Dionysius Areopagita*, p 153, that the Areopagite may have derived his triadic schema of contemplative motions from a fifth-century Alexandrian Neoplatonist by the name of Hermias who was a friend of Proclus and the author of a commentary on Plato's *Phaedrus*. For Hermias' version of the triad, see *In Platonis Phaedrum scholia*, ed P. Couvreur (Paris: Emile Bouillon 1901), 227b, pp 20–1. Placid Spearritt has dismissed Koch's suggestion in *A Philosophical Enquiry into Dionysian Mysticism* (unpublished thesis, University of Fribourg, Switzerland 1968), 102, on the grounds that Hermias' association of linear and helicoidal motion with 'doxa' and 'dianoia' respectively (implying an opposition between mere opinion de-

rived from sense-knowledge and mystical understanding of supersensible realities) is radically different from the interpretation of those motions in the
Corpus Dionysiacum (with its emphasis on the perfect harmony of all contemplative activities within the hierarchical universe). In contrast to the Areopagite, moreover, Hermias did not extend the triad to the realm of
superhuman cognition or compare the circling of ecstatic intellects to a mystery dance. Spearritt has concluded – I believe, correctly – that *In Phaedrum*
227b must be considered simply an analogue of *Divine Names* IV.8–10 rather
than its immediate source. The same conclusion was reached by Ceslas Pera in
his editorial notes to Aquinas' *In librum Beati Dionysii De divinis nominibus
expositio*, p 124; but according to Pera, pp 126–7, Pseudo-Dionysius did not
derive his triad from Proclus or any other late Neoplatonic source but rather
from Clement of Alexandria and Basil the Great, his predecessors in the
Christian mystical tradition. This last hypothesis strikes me as untenable for
two reasons: first, because Clement and Basil never mention helicoidal motion
in their many references to the angelic dance; and second, because Proclus
(probably following Syrianus) is the only author before the Areopagite known
to have ascribed spiral motion to divine intellects and to have associated it
with the image of the mystery dance.

9 In *Mystical Theology* II the Areopagite refers to the 'darkness' of ignorance
preceding theurgic illumination, an image invariably expressed by the Latin
noun 'caligo' (signifying either 'darkness' or 'fog') in medieval translations of
the passage. Recalling this image in *Benjamin Major* IV.22 and V.2 the twelfth-
century scholastic commentator Richard of St Victor speaks of the 'nubes ig-
norantiae' (cloud of ignorance) and the 'nebula oblivionis' (fog of forgetful-
ness). The Middle English phrase 'cloud of unknowing' may sound like an
inspired poetic coinage, but it is probably only a translation from the Latin of
Richard of St Victor. So Phyllis Hodgson argues in her introduction to *The
Cloud of Unknowing and The Book of Privy Counselling*, Early English Text
Society, old series no 128 (London: Oxford University Press 1944), lxii.

10 For a technical discussion of figure and ground and a convenient summary of
Gestalt theories concerning visual ambiguity, see Lloyd Kaufman, *Sight and
Mind: An Introduction to Visual Perception* (London, Toronto, New York:
Oxford University Press 1974). 473–81.

11 A determined attempt was made by the Emperor Justinian (ruled 527–65 AD)
to restore confidence in Constantine's vision of a dogmatically unified Empire.
The Orthodox still call Justinian 'the Great' in recognition of his success –
brief though it was – in making the dream of Christian monarchism a reality.
To his persecuted opponents, the Monophysites of Egypt and Syria, his political success seemed only to have turned that dream into the nightmare of
Caesaropapism. Justinian and his immediate predecessors may have regarded
themselves as members of the priesthood ex officio; on their assumption of

such titles as 'Hierus' and 'Archierus,' 'Priest' and 'High Priest,' see Wilhelm Ensslin, 'The Emperor and the Imperial Administration,' in *Byzantium: An Introduction to East Roman Civilization*, ed Norman H. Baynes and H. St L.B. Moss (Oxford: Clarendon Press 1948), 275. The interest shown by Severus of Antioch and other Monophysites in the Corpus Dionysiacum may have been due in part to the Areopagite's implicit exclusion of the emperor from the episcopal administration of the Ecclesiastical Hierarchy.

12 Dom Denys Rutledge, *Cosmic Theology*, p 98

13 The hypothesis that Severus the Monophysite Patriarch of Antioch (d 538) or a Syrian monk under the influence of Severus wrote the Corpus Dionysiacum was first proposed and defended on theological grounds by J. Stiglmayr in 'Der sog. Dionysius und Severus von Antiochen,' *Scholastik* 3 (1928), 1–27 and 161–89. R. Devresse in 'Denys l'Aréopagite et Sévère d'Antioche,' *Archives d'histoire doctrinale et littéraire du Moyen Age* 4 (1929), 159–67, enthusiastically endorsed Stiglmayr's hypothesis on the grounds that numerous parallels could be observed between the actual career of Severus and the fictional career of the Areopagite (as deduced from the epistles). Their arguments have been refuted by René Roques in *L'univers dionysien*, pp 313–15.

14 A detailed history of the transmission and translations of the Corpus Dionysiacum has yet to be written. I have relied here on the historical notes provided by Rev Thomas L. Campbell in *Dionysius the Pseudo-Areopagite: The Ecclesiastical Hierarchy*, Catholic University of America Studies in Sacred Theology, second series no 83 (Washington DC: Catholic University of America Press 1955), xiv–xv.

Afterword

1 *The Buildings* 1.i.47, in *Procopius* vol 7, ed and trans H.B. Dewing and Glanville Downey (London: Wm Heinemann 1965), 20.

2 See Arthur O. Lovejoy, *The Great Chain of Being: A Study of the History of an Idea* (Cambridge, Mass: Harvard University Press 1943). I have taken the phrase 'dialectical motives' from Lovejoy, p 10.

Index

526, 561–2; ecclesiastical 510, 512, 561
triangle 46, 51, 524
– of chorus-cosmos-culture 15–16
Tricennalia 269–73
Tricennial Oration. See Eusebius of
Caesarea
Trinity 295, 345, 362, 383, 389, 397, 401,
491, 495, 503–4, 506, 512, 518
– Neoplatonic hymns to 335–8, 362
– centre of cosmic dance 337–8, 362, 510–
12
triptych 361, 370, 398, 405–6
tripudium. *See* dance
Trivium (*see also* grammar, dialectic, *and*
rhetoric) 326–7, 332–3, 548
Troy 24, 260, 535
trumpet 149, 300
– of Doom 149, 495
truth 79, 97, 99, 109–10, 119, 123, 127,
130, 151, 183, 202, 224, 235, 237, 238,
241–2, 263, 266, 293–4, 319, 339, 346,
354, 402, 407, 432, 434, 437, 444–5, 463,
468, 481, 490, 493, 496, 498, 500, 505,
507, 512, 519
– Valentinian deity 112–13, 125
– wars or dramas of 129–31, 302, 388
tuitio. *See* vision
tumbler 25, 40
Turcan, R. 548
Turkey 75
turning (*see also* antistrophe *and*
strophe) 44, 96, 102, 105, 123, 139, 163,
165, 196, 201, 221–2, 226, 231, 234, 285,
298, 318, 341, 346, 354, 356, 382, 389,
401, 425, 427, 442, 446, 450, 453, 461–2,
469, 478, 483, 487, 499, 501–4, 519, 536,
556
Twelfth Discourse. See Dio Chrysostom
twilight (dusk) 191, 318, 341, 376, 448, 467
twirling. *See* whirling
typos. *See* image
Tyrrenia 435

ugliness 186
Ulla Bira'ah 395
unbinding. *See* releasing *and* breaking
Unchangeableness of God. See Philo
underworld
– Egyptian (D3.t) 6, 7, 533
– Greco-Roman 22, 34, 38, 135, 307, 331,
363, 395–6
– Christian, *see* Hell
– and dance 307, 395–6
union (*see also* binding, harmony, love, *and*
sympathy)
– of 'archē' and 'telos' 221–2, 225–6, 253,
453, 461, 478, 483

– of cause and effect 205, 221–2, 462, 488,
501
– of beholder and beheld 210–15, 217–22,
226
– of diverse choruses 78–9, 86, 120, 253–4,
316, 321, 340, 349, 352, 362–3, 370–1,
380, 431, 443, 453, 455, 461–2, 483, 486,
488, 493–4, 501–2, 514
– of highest (invisible) with lowest
(visible) 340–1, 358, 363–4, 368, 447,
454, 461, 478, 483, 486, 488, 492–4, 501
– of 'motus' and 'cantilena' 248–52, 324–5,
340, 518
– of nature and nation 72–3, 103, 394–5
– of thinker and object of thought 218–22,
226, 461, 483, 501, 518–19
– of time and eternity 368, 370–1, 394–5,
401, 431–3, 443, 447–8, 461, 483, 488,
501
– of worldly and otherworldly things, *see*
next six subheadings
– (i) bodies with bodies 72, 125, 136, 144,
153, 159, 174, 188, 212–13, 218, 238, 249,
253–4, 257, 270–1 320–1, 326, 340, 370–1,
376, 381, 446, 453–5, 478
– (ii) bodies with souls 144, 218, 260, 381,
401, 443, 454, 478
– (iii) souls with souls 220–2, 230, 373,
394–5, 431–2, 478, 514
– (iv) souls with gods or divine
intellects 65, 72–3, 120, 125, 128, 130,
220–4, 230, 323, 338, 361–2, 370, 395,
419, 423, 425–6, 430–2, 443, 483, 491–3,
502, 514–15, 518
– (v) gods with gods 112, 115–16, 125,
221–2, 249, 253–4, 298–300, 314, 321,
324–5, 328, 337–8, 453, 454, 496, 501,
503
– (vi) souls or intellects with God or Divine
Mind 74, 76–80, 103, 124, 128, 131, 138,
148, 195, 215, 218, 220–2, 224, 226, 231,
243, 253, 271, 321, 334, 337, 370–1, 373,
376, 379, 381, 394, 399, 401, 431–3, 446,
453, 460–3, 478, 483, 486–8, 491–3, 496,
498, 500–3, 510–11, 514, 516, 518, 541,
555, 558
unity (*see also* Henads *and* One) 12
– Pythagorean 47–8
– Platonic 125
– Cynic 182
– Stoic (hēnōmena, synaptomena,
synkeimena) 166, 169–70, 479, 539–40
– Jewish or Philonic 72–3, 125, 200, 242,
394
– Gnostic 112, 121, 131
– Middle Platonic 89–90, 248–50, 253–4,
257